For the Common Defense

A Military History of the United States from 1607 to 2012

Third Edition

Allan R. Millett
Peter Maslowski
William B. Feis

FREE PRESS
New York London Toronto Sydney New Delhi

FREE PRESS
A Division of Simon & Schuster, Inc.
1230 Avenue of the Americas
New York, NY 10020

This Free Press trade paperback edition September 2012

FREE PRESS and colophon are trademarks of Simon & Schuster, Inc.

For information about special discounts for bulk purchases,
please contact Simon & Schuster Special Sales at 1-866-506-1949
or business@simonandschuster.com.

The Simon & Schuster Speakers Bureau can bring authors to your live event.
For more information or to book an event, contact the Simon & Schuster Speakers Bureau
at 1-866-248-3049 or visit our website at www.simonspeakers.com.

Manufactured in the United States of America

12   13   14   15   16   17   18   19   20

Library of Congress Cataloging-in-Publication Data

Millett, Allan Reed.
For the common defense : a military history of the United States from 1607 to 2012 /
Allan R. Millett and Peter Maslowski.—Rev. and expanded.
p. cm.
Includes bibliographical references and index.
1. United States—History, Military. 2. United States—Armed Forces—
History. I. Maslowski, Peter. II. Title.
E181.M6986 1994
973—dc20
94-5199
CIP

ISBN 978-1-4516-2353-6
ISBN 978-1-4391-1827-6 (ebook)

Acknowledgments

Writing the acknowledgments for a book that is thirty years old and now takes new life in a third edition is more challenging than writing the book. It does not become easier when the book has three authors. As the senior author, I have usurped the role of writing these acknowledgments in order to avoid pronoun confusion. Peter Maslowski and William B. Feis are blameless for any oversights or insensitivities our readers may spy.

This book had its start in my first exposure to a class in American military history taught by my adviser, the late Harry L. Coles, at The Ohio State University. Harry assigned us Walter Millis's *Arms and Men* (1956). Given the choices in 1963, the book was the right one for a course that stressed civil-military relations and the political and social influences on strategy. Having just finished three years as a Marine infantry officer, I didn't want to read a textbook written for ROTC cadets about leadership and patriotism, the general focus of the other potential texts. On the other hand, Millis had little feel for how military organizations work (or don't), and his grasp of operational problems lacked expertise. Harry agreed— and said I should try to do better some day. That day came sooner than he and I anticipated.

I had the good fortune to return to The Ohio State University in 1969 after teaching at the University of Missouri-Columbia for three years. Harry Coles had become department chair, and I inherited his one-quarter (ten-week) course on American military history, from Jamestown to the nuclear age. I had used Millis at Missouri and did not like it for a semester course. I liked it even less on the quarter system. On the other hand, I also inherited a stellar group of graduate students, among them Calvin Christman, Robert Daugherty, J. Frederick Shiner, and Peter Maslowski. Peter and I shared several interests, among them bird-watching and basketball. Peter finished his dissertation despite my mentoring, went to the University of Nebraska-Lincoln, taught American military history, and agreed with me that the book choices still left much to be desired. By now we had a new candidate, Russell F. Weigley's *The American Way of War* (1973); but Russ, I thought, worked too hard to make military history (often just army history) fit his criticism of American strategy in Vietnam. Through the 1970s, as Peter and I taught and wrote other books, we talked about writing our own text. Peter took the initiative in opening negotiations with the Free Press, and soon we had a contract and a chance to write, not just gripe.

No general history of American military policy could exist without the contributions of the two generations of scholars whose books, essays, and articles provide the foundation for this book. Our debt to them, acknowledged in the online chapter and general bibliographies (http://www.bvu.edu/faculty/feis/ftcd/FTCD_Bib.html and the Free Press author pages at http://www.SimonandSchuster.com) is complete. We hope they recognize their contributions among our breezy assertions and breathtaking generalizations. We are indebted to our colleagues who volunteered their considerable talent and precious time to critique our individual chapters. Peter, the author of Chapters 1 through 9 for the first two editions, appreciated the advice of Dr. Douglas E. Leach, Dr. Don Higginbotham, Dr. Charles Royster, Dr. Richard H. Kohn, Dr. Craig L. Symonds, Dr. Francis Paul Prucha, Dr. K. Jack Bauer, Dr. Archer Jones, Dr. Frank E. Vandiver, Dr. James A. Rawley, Dr. John Y. Simon, Dr. James M. McPherson, Dr. Robert M. Utley, Dr. Benjamin Franklin Cooling III, Dr. Graham A. Cosmas, and Dr. David F. Trask, all experts on the American military experience from the colonial period to the twentieth century. Dr. Patrice M. Berger of the University of Nebraska-Lincoln history department, Lawrence J. Baack (a former history professor), and Ms. Barbara Rader also provided Peter with evaluations from perspectives professional but unspecialized in U.S. history. Peter asked his mother, Edna H. Maslowski, to read portions of several chapters to check his literary English in the first edition.

I wrote Chapters 10 through 17 of the first edition with the sound advice of a distinguished platoon of specialists in twentieth-century American military history: Dr. Timothy K. Nenninger, Dr. Dean C. Allard, Dr. Daniel R. Beaver, Dr. Donald Smythe, Dr. Forrest C. Pogue, Colonel J. F. Shiner, USAF, Dr. Gerald E. Wheeler, Dr. Williamson Murray, Mr. Kenneth H. Watman, Mr. Charles MacDonald, Dr. Ronald H. Spector, Dr. John L. Gaddis, Colonel Roy K. Flint, USA, Lieutenant Colonel Harry

Borowski, USAF, Brigadier General Douglas Kinnard, USA (Ret.), Dr. David Alan Rosenberg, Brigadier General Edwin H. Simmons, USMC (Ret.), Dr. George C. Herring, Dr. David S. Sorenson, and Dr. Joseph J. Kruzel. We also want to thank those members of the history departments of the U.S. Military Academy and the U.S. Air Force Academy who reviewed parts of the original manuscript.

From its inception, this study enjoyed the support of the Mershon Center for Education and Research in National Security at The Ohio State University, directed successively by Dr. Richard K. Snyder and Dr. Charles F. Hermann, when this book was first written. In addition, the University of Nebraska-Lincoln provided Peter with a Faculty Development Fellowship and Maude Hammond Fling Summer Fellowship in order to work on this book.

Mrs. Yvonne Holsinger and the staff of the graphic arts division of The Ohio State University's Teaching Aids Laboratory drew the maps that have graced this book for almost thirty years. In addition, Joyce Seltzer and Robert Harrington of the Free Press offered valuable suggestions on the original manuscript.

After ten years, Peter and I agreed that *For the Common Defense* needed a fresh coat of learning and updating. We had suggestions for improvement from reviewers, from other historians who used the book in their classes, and from our students, never shy in commenting about their readings. Since our readers had not found whole sections of the book wrongheaded, we agreed that peer review of every word in every chapter need not slow our revision process. The only original addition was Chapter 18 and the Epilogue, which started with the end of the Vietnam War and carried the narrative through the Gulf War, which I wrote. Even though Peter did not have to rewrite Chapters 1 through 9, he sent these chapters or portions of them to Dr. Ira D. Gruber, Dr. Robert Wooster, Dr. Donald R. Hickey, and Dr. Brian Linn for review. As I recall, they liked the chapters very much. Since I had one new chapter that needed close review, I asked my colleague Dr. Williamson Murray to read it, and we turned to an uncommon graduate student, Jay Young, whose government service in the 1980s made him especially expert on the defense policy of the Reagan era. For the Gulf War, I relied upon Brigadier General Edwin H. Simmons, USMC (Ret.), director of the Marine Corps History and Museums Division and my former commanding officer when I headed the fighting historians of MTU DC-4. After my retirement from the USMCR in 1990, the dedicated reserves of DC-4 covered the Gulf War on the ground, and I saw their early drafts, as well as some operational summaries. To finish the review process, we asked Dr. Stephen E. Ambrose to read the whole manuscript and participate in a panel discussion of the book at the March 1993 meeting of the Southwestern Social Sciences Association in New Orleans. Steve read the entire manuscript with the highest standards of professional attentiveness and made recommendations I accepted without regret.

The last and most important participant in the second review process was a graduate student from Lincoln, Nebraska, named William B. Feis. Bill had taken large doses of *For the Common Defense* as an undergraduate history major and an MA graduate student, administered by his adviser, Professor Peter Maslowski. As my advisee and Civil War reenactor "pard," Bill was unlucky enough to become a research assistant and copy editor on the second edition. He escaped the editorial trap only by completing his dissertation in 1997, fleeing to a faculty appointment at Buena Vista University in Iowa. Peter and I tracked his escape route and agreed that we would find more work for him someday.

When we persuaded the Free Press that a book in continued use in American classrooms should be revised again, Peter and I turned for help to Dr. Calvin Christman, another Ohio State graduate who had just retired from a distinguished teaching career at Cedar Valley Community College in Dallas, Texas, with graduate teaching experience at North Texas University. We asked Cal to work on the bibliographies and read any new material we wrote. His work had just begun when Cal learned he had cancer, which killed him on August 24, 2011. Fortunately, Bill Feis responded to our mild coercion and joined us as a full partner, happy with the opportunity to exact red-pencil revenge on his former advisers. Bill became the essential editor in making the third edition possible against tight deadlines. With the aid of his academic assistant Zoey Reisdorf, he also assembled the online bibliographies. We know we tried his legendary patience and that of his talented wife, Dr. Dixee Bartholomew-Feis, an accomplished teacher and published historian of the World War II Vietnamese-OSS collaboration. Bill took over assembling the final manuscript under demanding time and distance conditions that would have staggered anyone. In the fall of 2011, Bill lost his father and grandfather, but pressed on.

In addition to using Bill's wide knowledge as the foundation for the review of the third edition, we continued to seek student reaction to the book. I had a class of graduate students at the University of New Orleans critique the whole second revision in 2009, and they found several errors and gaps. The next summer I had a class at the University of Hawaii-Manoa do a chapter-by-chapter review as part of a class on American military history. One of this group, Manuel Ortega, proved especially careful in his analysis.

As I coped with two new chapters that dealt with the complex interventions in Somalia, Haiti, Bosnia, Kosovo, Afghanistan, and Iraq, I sought the advice of former students who had seen these distant wars at close range: Peter Mansoor, Mark Jacobson, Jay Young, and David Gray. I sought information on Iraqi missiles and their nemesis, the Patriot antimissile missile, from Bryon Greenwald, a career air-defense officer. Wick Murray provided me with the publications of the Iraqi Perspectives Project. Dr. Richard W. Stewart, chief historian of the U.S. Army Center of Military History, graciously provided the high-quality maps and sound advice.

Peter, Bill, and I are indebted to all those who contributed to this book, and we thank them for their role in its publication. Any errors or omissions are our burden and not theirs.

There are those whose influence deserves special mention. Peter and I were fortunate to have role models for perfection and perseverance in two World War II veterans, Technical Sergeant Karl H. Maslowski and Colonel John D. Millett, who remained interested in our writing until they died.

We are especially indebted to our wives. Peter's wife, Linda Maslowski, has always been a source of patience and wise counsel. In my case, I had the good sense to marry Martha E. Farley, whom I met at Ohio State and married in 1980 before publication of the first edition. As a historian and teacher, Martha brought special insight to writing a book designed principally for university undergraduates. Her contribution as researcher, editor, and typist for the third edition was essential to the book's completion. She also has been a full partner in our association with our colleagues in the International Commission of Military History, who have used this book abroad with their students and arranged to have it translated into Spanish, Japanese, and Chinese.

The challenge of defending the United States of America will not disappear, and all of us should try to understand the nation's peculiar exercise of military power for the common good. As I write this, the nation is beginning celebrations (for lack of a better word) of the bicentennial of the War of 1812, the sesquicentennial of the War of the Rebellion (known in some areas as the War Between the States), the seventieth anniversary of American participation in World War II, and the sixtieth anniversary of the end of the Korean War. Will we celebrate the commitment of ground troops to Vietnam in 2015, the fiftieth anniversary of that perilous fight? I suspect so. One hopes that American students will think long and hard about this nation's wars and that this book will help them deal with a past that will not go away.

Allan R. Millett
New Orleans, 2012

Contents

The Chapter Bibliographies and General Bibliography can be accessed online at the Free Press author pages: http://www.SimonandSchuster .com, and Professor Feis's webpage at Buena Vista University: http://web .bvu.edu/faculty/feis/ftcd/FTCD_Bib.html

Introduction

Although we are pleased that the original 1984 edition and 1994 revised edition of *For the Common Defense* have stood the test of time so well, the ongoing important national defense issues of the last eighteen years and the superb scholarship in military history since 1994 warrant this third edition. We have been encouraged in our efforts by teachers who have continued to use the second edition, even though American military history took on new directions in the Balkans and Muslim world since its publication.

We have reviewed all of the text for currency and accuracy. Where we found errors of fact and printing, we have corrected them. We have made the most changes in areas where our own research interests have taken us in the last eighteen years. I rewrote the account of the Korean War to reflect fifteen years of research. The Vietnam War is now divided into two chapters written by Peter, a subject of his recent research. There are now two chapters on the end of the Cold War and the new wars in Iraq and Afghanistan, 2001–2011, the decade characterized by the George W. Bush administration as the "Global War on Terrorism."

Readers will search in vain in this book for dramatic new interpretations or radical departures in intellectual approach. We are aware that others may take issue with our reluctance to add novel twists and unexpected turns to our narrative. We have not taken the easy road of alternative or counter-factual history. We have tried to maintain the distinction between "what if" and "what was," although "so what" remains a matter of reasonable debate. We hope we have provided the right balance of fact and interpretation to make any discussion of American military history meaningful, whether the debate involves contemporary defense policy or some aspect of American history, such as race relations, in which military history provides relevant testimony.

Our bibliographic suggestions (http://web.bvu.edu/faculty/feis/ftcd/FTCD_Bib.html and the Free Press author pages at http://www.SimonandSchuster.com) require some explanation. Except in special cases, we have omitted journal articles, for several reasons. Many articles become books. Others are superseded by other books. The availability of journal contents on the internet makes finding an article by subject relatively easy. By stressing books, we have chosen works that are current, reliable, tested, and probably available at public and university libraries. We have leaned toward books that are in print. We have chosen to make selections on the principles of "If you were to read one book on . . . ," although we know two or three books might be useful. We apologize to those authors who feel ignored or aggrieved, but modern technology has saved the works of the just and the unjust, so everyone now has electronic immortality, or at least their books do.

Writing military history is an ancient craft, but since classical times military historians have focused almost exclusively on battles and the conduct of war. After World War II, however, American historians began to treat military history in broad political, economic, social, and institutional terms. Although retaining some elements of the "old" military history, this book falls more clearly into the "new" military history genre of the post–World War II era. Battle connoisseurs will sniff a hint of gunpowder throughout the book, since it discusses the major campaigns in all of America's wars. The details of military operations and the problems of combat leadership and tactics are limited to those developments and events that demonstrate the capabilities and limitations of the armed forces as they implement national policy. The primary purposes of this book are to analyze the development of military policy and to examine the characteristics of military policy as influenced by America's international relations and domestic development.

Six major themes place United States military history within the broad context of American history. First, rational military considerations alone have rarely shaped military policies and programs. The political system and societal values have imposed constraints on defense affairs. A preoccupation with private gain, a reluctance to pay taxes, a distaste for military service, and a fear of large standing forces have at various times imposed severe limitations on the availability of monetary and manpower resources.

Second, American defense policy has traditionally been built upon pluralistic military institutions, most noticeably a mixed force of professionals and citizen-soldiers. These pluralistic institutions reflect the diverse

attitudes of professional soldiers, citizen-soldiers, and antimilitary and pac-
ifistic citizens about the role of state-sponsored force in the nation's life.

Third, despite the popular belief that the United States has generally
been unprepared for war, policymakers have done remarkably well in preserving the nation's security. For most of American history, especially from
the nineteenth century onward, policymakers realized that geographic distance from dangerous adversaries, the European balance of power, and
growing material and manpower mobilization potential were powerful
assets. When gauging America's strength against potential enemies, policymakers realized that the nation could devote its energies and financial
resources to internal development rather than to maintaining a large and
expensive peacetime military establishment. However, mobilizing simultaneously with a war's outbreak has extracted high costs in terms of speed
and ease with each new mobilization.

Fourth, the nation's firm commitment to civilian control of military
policy requires careful attention to civil-military relations. The commitment to civilian control makes military policy a paramount function of
the federal government, where the executive branch and Congress share
the power to shape policy. The Constitution makes the president commander in chief (Article II, Section 2) and gives Congress the responsibility of organizing and funding the armed forces it creates, as well as passing
laws about what forces do and how they are managed (Article I, Section
8). The Congress has the power to declare war, and it can influence any
military activity through the legislative and appropriations process, should
it choose to do so. The two branches are supposed to work in concert for
"the common defense."

Although the influence of the federal system on military policy faded by
the end of the twentieth century, national-state-local relations have defined
much of defense policy for the preceding three centuries. While the Constitution defines what the national government can do, the Bill of Rights (the
first ten amendments) tells the national government what it cannot do, and
one prohibition is that the national government cannot monopolize military
power. The Second Amendment permits other levels of government, like a
state or county, to form military forces to meet local emergencies. In 1789
these crises might have included an invasion from Canada or Florida, piracy,
Native American raids, slave revolts, urban or rural uprisings, political protests and election disruption, and ethnic and family feuds. It was an era in
which civilian policing was notoriously ineffective in the hands of county
sheriffs and urban constables. Depending on the threat and the powers of
"calling forth" authority, citizens were supposed to arm themselves and be
available for emergency service as an obligation of citizenship. There are, of
course, other more novel interpretations of the Second Amendment.

Fifth, the armed forces have become progressively more nationalized and professionalized. Beginning with the American Revolution, the services have increasingly been raised and supported by the federal government and used for purposes defined by the federal government. Although civilians ultimately control military policy, the professionalization of officership, a trend that has progressed rapidly since the early nineteenth century, has had important consequences for the conduct of military affairs, since career officers in the national service (as opposed to officers appointed only in wartime) have progressively monopolized high command positions and advisory positions.

Finally, beginning in the mid-nineteenth century, but especially during the twentieth century, industrialization has shaped the way the nation has fought. In particular, the United States has used increasingly sophisticated technology to overcome logistical limitations, primarily in transportation, and to match enemy numbers with firepower. This dependence upon industry and technology in executing military policy has placed enormous burdens on career military officers and the defense industry, and it is very costly.

Military history requires some attention to definitions. *Policy* is the sum of the assumptions, plans, programs, and actions taken by the citizens of the United States, principally through governmental action, to ensure the physical security of their lives, property, and way of life from external military attack and domestic insurrection. Although military force has been used in both domestic and foreign crises that did not involve national survival, the definition of policy remains rooted to the prevention or termination of a military threat faced collectively by the American people. *War* is a less elusive concept, since it enjoys centuries of political and judicial definition. It is the application of state violence in the name of policy. It involves killing and wounding people and destroying property until the survivors abandon their military resistance or the belligerents come to a negotiated agreement. *War aims* are the purposes for which wars are fought. *Strategy,* the general concepts for the use of military force, is derived from war aims. In wartime, strategy is normally expressed in terms of missions, geographic areas of operations, the timing of operations, and the allocation of forces.

Each element of the armed forces has an *operational doctrine*, which is an institutional concept for planning and conducting operations. Taking into account such factors as their mission, the enemy situation, the terrain, and the combat and logistical capabilities of the available forces, service leaders develop their organizations' capabilities. For example, the U.S. Army Air Forces of World War II expressed a strategic theory when arguing that Nazi Germany could be bombed into submission. But when the USAAF chose to conduct the bombing with massed bomber formations in daylight raids against industrial targets, it defined an operational doctrine. *Tactics* is the actual conduct of battle, the application of fire and maneuver by fighting units in order to destroy the physical ability and will of the enemy's armed forces. To continue the example of the bombing campaign against Germany, the USAAF bombers grouped themselves in combat "boxes" to create overlapping arcs of machine-gun fire against German fighters; their fighter escorts—when they had them—attacked the German fighters before they reached the bomber formations. In addition, the bombers varied their altitude and direction to confuse antiaircraft artillery fire. They also dropped tons of metallic chaff to foil enemy radar. These techniques were tactical, since their goal was the immediate destruction or demoralization of a specific enemy force.

Americans have had a peculiar ambivalence toward war. They have traditionally and sincerely viewed themselves as a peaceful, unmilitaristic people, and yet they have hardly been unwarlike. Statistics alone testify to the pervasive presence of war in the nation's history, for tens of millions of Americans have served in wartime and more than a million have died in uniform. Understanding both this paradoxical love-hate attitude toward war and the relationship among military institutions, war, and society is essential in comprehending America's past, its present, and its future.

Of the authors of *The Federalist Papers,* James Madison could claim the least familiarity with military affairs, for unlike Alexander Hamilton and John Jay, he had known neither the sting of battle nor the tension of international diplomacy during the American Revolution. In contrast to Hamilton, who had conducted an inquiry on post-Revolution defense policy, or Jay, who had directed the perilous diplomacy of the new nation under the Articles of Confederation, Madison had made his postwar reputation as a cerebral congressional surrogate for his famous Virginia colleague Thomas Jefferson. During the Constitutional Convention, however, Madison emerged as one of the architects of the Constitution with which its framers hoped to reorganize the newly independent states. Thus when the fight for ratification came to the crucial state of New York, Madison was a natural choice to be one of the three authors of *"Publius"* essays, advocating a stronger central government. Surprisingly, Madison contributed an essay on Article I, Section 8 of the Constitution, applying his analytical skill to No. 41 of *The Federalist Papers*. The issue was empowering the government to conduct the nation's defense.

To Madison, the Constitution's provisions for the central control of military policy seemed self-evident. "Security against foreign danger is one of the primitive objects of civil society. It is an avowed and essential object of the American Union. The powers requisite for attaining it must be effectually confided to the federal councils." It was unthinkable to him that defense would not be the domain of the national government.

"Is the power of raising armies and equipping fleets necessary?" Madison could imagine no constitutional limits upon the government because there would be no limits upon the nation's potential enemies. "How could the readiness for war in time of peace be safely prohibited, unless we could prohibit in like manner the preparations and establishments of every hostile nation?" Perhaps he remembered George Washington's quip that the Constitution would not limit the size of other nations' armies even if it set a ceiling on America's standing forces. "The means of security can only be regulated by the means and danger of attack. They will, in fact, be ever determined by these rules and no other. It is in vain to oppose constitutional barriers to the impulse of self-preservation. It is worse than in vain. . . . If one nation maintains constantly a disciplined army, ready for service of ambition or revenge, it obliges the most pacific nations who may be within the reach of its enterprises to take corresponding precautions."

Many seasons have passed and years have rolled by since Madison argued that the Constitution provided the best hope for the common defense, but his rationale stands intact. Although he could have foreseen neither the global reach of American interests nor the intricacies of dividing the responsibility for the common defense between the executive and legislative branches, Madison would not have been surprised to see the contentiousness with which the nation makes its decisions to spend the lives and treasure of its citizens. Thus it has been since the first shots on Lexington Green and at Concord Bridge. Madison understood that the cost of defense would always compete with the individual and collective "pursuit of happiness." He could only hope that the innate wisdom of the American citizenry would correctly evaluate the degree of shared danger, the measure of ever-present risk, and allocate resources accordingly.

The dominant leaders of Madison's generation understood that moral suasion alone could not guard the Republic. The question of national survival is no less compelling now than it was in the nation's infant years. Whether or not the United States will rightly judge the delicate balance between its internal development and its influence upon world affairs, still shaped by the exercise of military power, remains a question that history can only partially answer. Yet the history of American military policy suggests that the dangers will not disappear. Neither will the political responsibility to face them, for they will not evaporate with wishful thinking. When the olive branches wilt, the arrows must be sturdy. Only another history can answer whether the people of the United States in the twenty-first century understand that constant vigilance is the price of liberty.

Allan R. Millett
New Orleans, 2012

Chapter Bibliographies and General Bibliography
for the Third Edition
can be accessed online at
the Free Press author pages:
http://www.SimonandSchuster.com
and
Professor Feis's webpage at Buena Vista University:
http://web.bvu.edu/faculty/feis/ftcd/FTCD_Bib.html

ONE

A Dangerous New World,
1607–1689

C rossing the Atlantic during the seventeenth century was a perilous voyage, entailing weeks or months of cramped quarters, inadequate food, and unsanitary conditions. Yet in the late 1500s Englishmen had begun to hazard the venture, and in 1607 they planted their first permanent settlement on the North American continent at Jamestown. By the early 1730s, thirteen separate colonies hugged the seaboard. Although great diversity prevailed among the colonies, most colonists shared a common English heritage and clung to it tenaciously. Their religious attitudes, economic views, political thoughts, and military ideals and institutions were all grounded in English history. In no aspect of colonial life was this heritage more important than in regard to military matters. The colonists' most revered military institution (the militia) and their most cherished military tradition (fear of a standing army) both came from England.

The English Inheritance

The earliest English settlers arrived in a dangerous New World. The initial colonies represented little more than amphibious landings on a hostile coastline followed by the consolidation of small, insecure beachheads. The settlers did not take possession of an uninhabited land, but settled in regions controlled by various Native American tribes. Fortunately for the colonists, they unwittingly landed in areas that had recently experienced precipitous population losses among the Indians. Europeans made

1

periodic contact with the natives long before they established permanent colonies. These transient visitors left a devastating legacy of smallpox, measles, and other European diseases, for which the natives had no built-in immunities. But the colonists soon learned that the Indians, even in their weakened state, were a formidable adversary. Nor were Indians the only military threat. The English settled in lands also claimed by their European rivals, and the memory of the raids conducted by the Spanish, French, and English against each other's outposts in the Caribbean and along the Florida coast undoubtedly haunted many colonists. The fear of pillaging buccaneers and pirates who infested coastal waterways compounded the potential problem posed by European enemies.

Colonists faced these threats alone. Although the English monarch authorized their expeditions and granted extensive lands for settlement, the Crown expected the colonists to defend themselves. With few illusions about their precarious position, colonists came to the New World armed and, anticipating conflict, gave prompt attention to defense. Professional soldiers accompanied the expeditions to Jamestown, Plymouth, and succeeding colonies. Indeed, the first heroes in American history were far from ordinary settlers. The profit-seeking Virginia Company hired Captain John Smith, a veteran of Europe's religious wars, to teach military skills to the settlers at Jamestown in 1607. Other experienced soldiers, such as Lord De La Warr, Sir Thomas Gates, and Sir Thomas Dale, soon followed him. The pious Pilgrims wisely did not rely on God's favor alone for protection, but employed Captain Myles Standish, a veteran of the Dutch wars for independence, to ensure Plymouth's success. Although Smith and Standish are the most famous of the soldier-settlers, practically all the other colonies had similar veterans who provided military leadership during the founding period. The importance placed on military preparations could be seen in the attention given to fortifications. Less than a month after their arrival, the settlers at Jamestown had constructed a primitive, triangular fort, and by 1622 the Pilgrims had erected a 2,700-foot-long defensive perimeter guarding their fledgling plantation.

The most important response to the dangerous military realities was the creation of a militia system in each colony. The British military heritage, the all-pervasive sense of military insecurity, and the inability of the economically poor colonies to maintain an expensive professional army all combined to guarantee that the Elizabethan militia would be transplanted to the North American wilderness. No colonial institution was more complex than the militia. In many respects it was static and homogenous, varying little from colony to colony and from generation to generation. Yet the militia was also evolutionary and heterogeneous, as diverse as the thirteen colonies and ever changing within individual colonies.

At the heart of the militia was the principle of universal military obligation for all able-bodied males. Colonial laws regularly declared that all able-bodied men between certain ages automatically belonged to the militia. Yet within the context of this immutable principle, variations abounded. While the normal age limits were from sixteen to sixty, this was not universal practice. Connecticut, for example, began with an upper age limit of sixty but gradually reduced it to forty-five. Sometimes the lower age limit was eighteen or even twenty-one. Each colony also established occupational exemptions from militia training. Invariably the exemption list began small but grew to become a seemingly endless list that reduced the militia's theoretical strength.

If a man was in the militia, he participated in periodic musters, or training days, with the other members of his unit. Attendance at musters was compulsory; militia laws levied fines for nonattendance. During the initial years of settlement, when dangers seemed particularly acute, musters were frequent. However, as the Indian threat receded, the trend was toward fewer muster days, and by the early 1700s most colonies had decided that four peacetime musters per year were sufficient. Whether few or many, muster days helped forge a link between religious duty and military service, particularly in New England. An integral part of each training day (and of all military expeditions) was a sermon, which invariably fostered an aggressive militancy by emphasizing that the Bible sanctioned martial activity and that warfare was a true Christian's sacred duty. "Hence it is no wayes unbecoming a Christian to learn to be a Souldier," Chaplain Samuel Nowell preached to Massachusetts militiamen in 1678, because being a soldier was "a Credit, a praise and a glory." When the colonists unsheathed their swords, they did so in God's name, serene in the belief that the Lord was on their side against their heathen and Papist enemies and that whatever happened was God's will.

Militiamen had to provide and maintain their own weapons. Militia laws detailed the required weaponry, which underwent a rapid evolution in the New World. Initially a militiaman was armed much like a European soldier, laden with armor, equipped with either a pike or matchlock musket, and carrying a sword. But Indian warfare was not European warfare, and most of this weaponry proved of limited value. By the mid-1670s colonial armaments had been revolutionized. Armor, which made it difficult to traverse rugged terrain and pursue Indians, had disappeared. Pikes were equally cumbersome and of little use against Indians, who neither stood their ground when assaulted nor made massed charges. At times the matchlock was superior to Indian bows and arrows, but its disadvantages were many. It took two minutes to load, and it misfired approximately three times in every ten shots. The weapon discharged when a slow-burning match* came in contact with the priming powder, but keeping the match lit on rainy or windy days was difficult, and the combination of a burning match and gunpowder in close proximity often resulted in serious accidents. By the midseventeenth century, the matchlock had given way to the flintlock musket. Depending on flint scraping against steel for discharge, flintlocks could be loaded in thirty seconds and misfired less often. Swords remained common weapons, but colonists increasingly preferred hatchets for close-quarter combat. Although both weapons were valuable in a melee, hatchets were also useful for a variety of domestic purposes.

Militia laws emphasized the importance of a well-armed citizenry in numerous ways. To ensure that each man had the requisite weapons and accoutrements, colonies instituted a review of arms, imposing the duty of conducting it on militia officers, muster masters, or other specially appointed officials. Each colony's law detailed how destitute citizens could be armed at public expense, and legislatures provided for public arsenals to supplement individually owned armaments. Colonies also required that even men exempted from attending musters should be completely armed and equipped. Although the basic tactical unit in all the colonies was the company, or trainband, regional variations and changes over time were as important as the superficial uniformity. No standardized company size existed, some companies containing as few as sixty-five men and others as many as two hundred. Some trainbands elected their officers, but in others the governors appointed them. Southern colonies, with widely dispersed populations, often organized companies on a countywide basis; while in New England, with its towns and villages, individual communities contained their own trainbands. As populations increased and the number of trainbands grew, colonies organized companies into regiments to preserve efficient management. As one last example of the variety and change within militia units, the initial all-infantry composition evolved into a mixture of infantry and mounted units, the latter providing increased maneuverability and speed, which were valuable assets in Indian warfare.

Militia officers, like colonial politicians, overwhelmingly came from the upper classes, and men moved with ease from important political positions into high military offices and vice versa. The practice of plural officeholding, whereby a man simultaneously held political and military office, epitomized the integration of political and military leadership. For example, in Salem, Massachusetts, between 1765 and 1774, twelve of the twenty-nine active militia officers also held important positions in the municipal government. Similar instances could be cited for other colonies.

---

* A match was a length of stringlike material that had been soaked in saltpeter (or a similar substance) so that it would burn slowly and steadily.

The militia was, above all else, a local institution, and officers rarely ordered their men to serve far from home. Each colony organized its militia for its own defense, a principle frequently embodied in legislation prohibiting the militia's use outside a colony's boundaries. Every colony faced Indian attacks, worried about rival Europeans, and experienced financial stringencies. How could Virginia help South Carolina without rendering itself less secure, or New York assist Pennsylvania without subjecting itself to increased danger? It could not—or at least it believed that it could not.

Within a colony civil authority controlled military matters, establishing America's revered tradition of civilian control over the military. However, a shift occurred in the governmental branch exercising predominant influence over the militia. Initially the governors dominated, often receiving their power directly from the King, who gave them wide latitude in appointing officers and waging war. But people considered the governor analogous to the King, the colonial assemblies analogous to Parliament. In England the King and Parliament, and in the colonies governors and assemblies, battled for supremacy. The legislative branch emerged triumphant in both Britain and America. By the mideighteenth century a governor's military authority lacked substance without the cooperation of the legislature, which had gained almost exclusive control over expenditures, including military appropriations. Using the power of the purse as a lever, legislatures gradually assumed control of the militia. By the Revolution, civilian authority over the military meant *legislative* control.

As the frontier advanced, the militia decayed. The rot appeared first in the more densely settled seaboard regions, where the Indian threat had diminished by the waning years of the seventeenth century and spread into the interior. Militia service became more of a social or ceremonial function than a military function. The fewer muster days witnessed little serious training and instead became occasions for picnics for the privates and elegant dinners for the officers. Men clamored for more restricted age limitations and an expanded exemption list and complained about the burden of maintaining weapons and equipment. Increasingly men sought militia officership not from a sense of duty but because, as one critic wrote, they had "an amazing infatuation" with military titles as symbols of social prominence. Authorities everywhere laxly enforced the militia laws.

As the common militia based on universal and obligatory service deteriorated, a new phenomenon emerged, partially filling the military void. In George Washington's words, some men always had "a natural fondness for Military parade," enjoyed soldiering, and willingly devoted time and money to it. Thus "volunteer militia" companies arose, distinct from the common militia, with their own uniforms, equipment, organization, and esprit de corps. Like so much of the American military heritage, independent volunteer militia units traced their roots to England, especially to London's Honorable Artillery Company, chartered in 1537. The first similar New World organization was the Ancient and Honorable Artillery Company of Boston, founded in 1638. Exclusive little societies of fifty to one hundred enthusiastic and relatively affluent men, the volunteer organizations kept the martial spirit alive in regions more and more remote from immediate danger.

The Diversity of Colonial Military Forces

Paradoxically, trainbands and regiments were not combat units, rarely functioning in warfare as colonial assemblies organized them on paper. In fact, legislatures did not design the common militia as a fighting force except, perhaps, for extreme local emergencies. Instead it served primarily as an induction center, a training school, and a reservoir of partially trained manpower. Upon reaching the requisite age, a man automatically joined his local trainband; then he underwent periodic training for the next thirty years or so and acquired at least a rudimentary knowledge of military practice. In wartime, authorities formed expeditions by tapping this manpower pool, drawing men out of the trainbands on an individual basis and organizing them into fighting units.

In theory the militia could provide local defense during an emergency, such as an Indian or rival European assault on an exposed settlement. During such crises settlers had little hope of assistance from the colonial government. The unexpected nature of an attack and the poor communications precluded an appeal to the government for timely aid. And the nature of the resulting warfare—usually little more than guerrilla skirmishes amidst the enveloping wilderness—placed a premium on local self-reliance. Knowing they might be unable to exert much influence over events in isolated areas, colonial officials delegated a great deal of power to local officials, but this decentralization of authority was of questionable value. Suppose an Indian war party suddenly descended upon a frontier outpost. Even if word of the attack reached local militia officers, travel was so slow that a complete trainband could not be mobilized and dispatched in time to save the settlement. Nor would it have been wise to send the trainband out: If all the able-bodied men in an area rushed to one beleaguered location, the entire vicinity would be left unprotected against further enemy depredations. Even for local defense the militia, as organized on paper, was of limited effectiveness.

As a practical solution for the problem of local defense, pioneers adopted a stronghold concept. Garrison houses, blockhouses, and stockades dotted the frontier. When danger threatened, inhabitants crowded into these fortified structures. The men at the loopholes were militiamen, but, few in number, they acted as individuals rather than members of a militia unit. The stronghold concept had disadvantages. Maintaining a large number of people created logistical problems, not only for arms and ammunition but also for food and water. Abandoning homes and farms for the security of a garrison house or stockade left other property vulnerable to destruction. The colonists, in effect, allowed themselves to be surrounded, leaving no avenue for retreat. Fortunately for them, Indians rarely conducted siege operations, and strongholds could often survive. Strongholds may have preserved settlers' lives, but the smoky plumes from burning homes, the steady stream of refugees, and the long roll call of abandoned settlements all attested to the militia's inability to provide defense when and where colonists most desperately needed it. The militia failed to perform its theoretical local defense function, and in a war's early stages the frontier invariably retracted toward the more heavily populated seaboard.

The militia was more effective as a local police force or as a standby posse comitatus. It preserved the domestic peace, protected propertied and privileged colonists from the disadvantaged elements within society, and quelled movements against the established political order. Militiamen frequently performed riot control duty. In the south, colonies merged their slave patrols with the militia and converted it into an internal police force to recover fugitive slaves and suppress slave insurrections. New Englanders in essence converted their militia into a civil police by mating it with the night watch. As a final example, when the Regulators of western North Carolina demanded substantial local governmental reforms and defied colonial authority during the late 1760s and early 1770s, the governor mobilized a thousand militiamen, who routed the Regulators at the Battle of Alamance in May 1771. Thus a sharp distinction arose between the militia as a domestic police and a colony's expeditionary military forces.

When authorities launched a military expedition, they did not "call out the militia" per se. Instead they commissioned officers specifically to command the expedition and established manpower quotas for militia districts. Sometimes the commanding officers appointed for an expeditionary force were regular militia officers, but oftentimes they were not. Based upon a formula related to population, the quotas demanded a certain number of men from each affected trainband. Sound reasons supported the quota system. A community needed most of its able-bodied men to defend it from an enemy that often seemed to appear magically where least expected. Settlements also required men at home to plant, tend, and harvest the crops. What good would be accomplished by creating a large army only to have the soldiers in the field and their dependents at home face the grim specter of starvation?

Militia districts filled their quotas by a combination of volunteers, draftees, substitutes, and hirelings, with volunteering being the preferred method. To spur volunteering from among the men in the trainbands, governments usually offered volunteers a bounty. Even lucrative bounties rarely enticed sufficient volunteers, in which case militia officials drafted men out of their trainbands. However, a draftee could avoid service by obtaining a discharge from the governor or a high-ranking militia officer, by providing a substitute, or by paying a commutation fine. Authorities used the money collected from fines to hire additional men or to buy arms and ammunition for destitute soldiers or the community arsenal. A draftee unable to obtain a discharge or a substitute and too poor to pay the fine had one last option to avoid soldiering: He could flee. Movement of men from town to town evading wartime service was a common problem.

The men serving in expeditions increasingly came from society's lower classes. Individuals of wealth and status were often exempt and unlikely to volunteer, and they could easily secure a discharge, find a substitute, or pay the commutation fine. In fact, colonies sometimes consciously excluded more prosperous citizens from active duty. For example, in the mid-1750s Virginia sought to raise 1,270 men for service. Local justices of the peace, field officers, and militia captains were to hold a court of inquiry, examining the occupations of men between the ages of eighteen and fifty on the muster rolls and making a list of all able-bodied men "as shall be found loitering and neglecting to labor for reasonable wages; all who run from their habitations, leaving wives or children without suitable means for subsistence, and all other idle, vagrant, or dissolute persons, wandering abroad without betaking themselves to some lawful employment." The court was also to list "such able-bodied men, not being freeholders or housekeepers qualified to vote at an election of burgesses, as they shall think proper. . . ." A second court would meet the quota by drafting men from among those on the list, which automatically omitted the colony's best citizens.

Yet, as always, colonial military affairs were not subject to easy generalizations, and an acute threat could result in an expeditionary force that more nearly represented a colony's social composition. For example, at a time when Virginia was raising its army almost exclusively from among the poorest elements of its population, Massachusetts was acting quite differently. Far more immediately threatened by the French in Canada than was Virginia, Massachusetts fielded military forces during the 1750s that were not heavily weighted toward the permanently poor and vagrants but instead reflected the colony's overall social composition.

From whatever social class they came, once enlisted for an expedition the men who filled the ranks believed they had a legal contract with the provincial government that could not be breached without the mutual consent of both parties. Their military ethos contained little of the emphasis on loyalty, subordination, and discipline that characterized European armies. When a colony failed to fulfill its legal obligations by not providing sufficient rum and food, by forcing men to serve beyond the expiration of their term of service, or by demanding additional duties not covered in the initial contract, colonial soldiers felt that their contract was void. Once authorities broke the contract, the troops felt no compunction against staging a mutiny or deserting in mass, even in the midst of a campaign. To the colonial soldiers these actions were legal and sensible, but to British regulars serving alongside the provincials during the colonial wars, such violations of military discipline were intolerable. No wonder British Major General James Abercromby, who observed colonial troops during the French and Indian War, complained that they were "the rif-raf of the continent." All too often they were! Not only were they primarily indigents and down-and-outers, but they did not behave as European professional soldiers thought they should behave.

Expeditions composed of militiamen drawn from the common militia's manpower reservoir represented only one type of military activity. Sometimes authorities sanctioned the formation of ad hoc volunteer companies bearing no official relationship to the militia. Two famous examples occurred in New England during King Philip's War. One company, commanded by Captain Samuel Moseley, was a conglomeration of apprentices, servants, seamen, and even a few convicted pirates who had in fact been captured by Moseley and gained their release from prison by agreeing to serve. Captain Benjamin Church, one of the most remarkable Indian fighters in American history, led the other. In July 1676, the governor of Plymouth Colony authorized Church to raise a volunteer company of about 200 men, consisting of not more than 60 whites augmented by approximately 140 friendly Indians. Volunteers, who often came from the lowest social strata, were normally outside the formal militia structure, which excluded Indians, criminals, servants, and men on the move, such as seamen. Bold and aggressive, these men served in anticipation of a rich reward of captured Indian booty and prisoners, who could be sold as slaves.

Some colonies also periodically tried to develop a static defensive line by building forts along the frontier. Virginia, for example, built four forts in 1645–1646 and undertook similar projects throughout the colonial era. Garrisons raised from the militia manned the strategically situated forts. In contrast to typical militia expeditions, garrison troops served for extended periods of time (up to a year in some cases) and in that respect resembled temporary standing armies. Forts often created more problems than they solved: The wooden structures decayed, they were expensive to build and maintain, garrison troops inevitably suffered from low morale, and, perhaps most important, Indians easily infiltrated between the forts. To ameliorate this last problem, Virginia also created "scout" or "ranger" units that patrolled the frontier between and beyond the forts on long-range reconnaissance missions, hoping to expose or disrupt attacks before they descended in full force upon settled areas. Thus colonial military forces were extremely diverse. Supplementing the peacetime common militia, from which authorities organized wartime expeditions through a quota system, were volunteer militia units, garrison troops and rangers, and volunteer companies completely outside the militia framework.

During the first seventy years of settlement a series of Indian wars severely tested colonial military institutions. The natives' overall initial reaction to the pale-skinned arrivals was cautious hospitality, but within two decades the whites' land greed, plus a general cultural incompatibility, created open hostility. Before considering the resulting wars, it is necessary to understand Indian methods of warfare, the problems Indian tactics posed for the whites, and the ways in which the Europeans overcame these difficulties.

Before the white man's arrival tribes living along the east coast engaged in endemic warfare, but the fighting was seldom costly in lives or property. To the first explorers and settlers, Indian warfare seemed almost playful or sporting. Roger Williams observed that Indian warfare was less bloody than European warfare, and many whites reacted contemptuously to the mild manner in which Indians fought. For instance, John Underhill affirmed that "they might fight seven years and not kill seven men. They came not near to one another, but shot, remote, and not point-blank, as we often do with our bullets, but at rovers, and then they gaze up in the sky to see where the arrow falls, and not until it is fallen do they shoot again. The fight is more for past-time, than to conquer and subdue enemies." That is, whites initially encountered Indians who did not wage total war, rarely striking at noncombatants or engaging in the systematic destruction of food supplies and property.

These original observations were not universally applicable. As with conflicts among whites, the scope, intensity, and magnitude of Indian warfare differed depending on prevailing conditions and ideas and hence varied across time and geography. While some Indian "wars" consisted of little more than persistent low-intensity raids to inflict revenge, acquire plunder, or take captives, others were wars to the death, designed to destroy an enemy, capture prime land, or at least establish hegemony over other tribes. These wars had nothing sporting about them. Instead they featured prolonged campaigns, strict military discipline, pitched battles, fortified positions, sieges, and the unmerciful slaying of women and children.

Native Americans were shrewd strategists, clever tacticians, and resilient warriors. Since they had no written languages, Indian strategic debates cannot be reconstructed from records housed in some repository but must be inferred from their actions. As for their tactics, the eastern woodland Indians generally fought in small war parties that kept on the move, acted in isolation, and repeatedly conducted sophisticated ambushes and raids. Warriors would move stealthily, spread out over a considerable distance to avoid being ambushed themselves, and rapidly concentrate for a whirling attack—often at night, during storms, or in dense fog so as to catch their adversaries off guard and confuse them. Then the Indians would vanish into the wilderness. Rarely would they stand and fight if hard pressed; their warrior ethic lacked the European concept of holding a piece of land no matter what the cost in casualties. These hit-and-run tactics baffled and angered the English, who did not lack "courage or resolution, but could not discern or find an enemy to fight with, yet were galled by the enemy."

Indian hit-and-run tactics were dangerous enough when executed with bows and arrows but became even more deadly when mated with flintlock muskets. Ironically, the Indians were more proficient than the colonists at using flintlocks. Having been taught hunting skills and the use of aimed fire with bows and arrows since childhood, the Indians readily adapted flintlocks to their guerrilla warfare. Colonial legislatures passed laws banning the firearms trade with the natives, at times even imposing the death penalty for violators, but Indians managed to acquire European weapons, often through illegal trade. And at least in New England, they learned how to cast bullets, replace worn flints, restock muskets, and make a variety of other repairs. Only one technical capability continued to elude the Indians: They never mastered gunpowder production and therefore experienced frequent powder shortages.

In contrast to the Indians, few whites had been hunters in the Old World or knew how to shoot well. Moreover, the colonists were steeped in formal battlefield tactics, which included firing unaimed mass volleys rather than aiming at individual targets. These may have worked well on Europe's open plains but were virtually useless in the dense North American forests against an enemy that neither launched nor endured frontal assaults. Yet most colonists made little effort to adjust to Indian-style warfare. On muster days militiamen practiced the complicated motions and maneuvers prescribed by European drill manuals. One commonly used drill book described fifty-six steps for loading and firing a musket. In battle many militiamen never lived to crucial Step 43: "Give fire breast high." And despite blundering into ambush after ambush, colonists persisted in marching in close order, so that, as one Indian said, "It was as easy to hit them as to hit a house." The settlers' reluctance to adjust to New World conditions was partly psychological. They considered Indian warfare barbaric; if Europeans fought in the same way, would they not also be barbarians?

The English compensated for the militia system's weaknesses by employing Indian allies, by waging ruthless warfare against the foundations of Indian society, and at least in a few cases by adopting Native American methods. Colonists learned—often the hard way—that Indians were the only match for Indians. Whites were so inept at forest warfare that launching an expedition without Indian allies invited disaster. The English especially needed natives as scouts to keep from blundering into an ambush, but native allies were also invaluable as spies, guides, and sometimes fighters. Fortunately for the whites, Native Americans were not united but consisted of tribes, subtribes, and quasi-independent bands. Virtually every tribe considered itself "the People"—not "a People" but "*the* People"—and various tribes and subtribes held such deep-seated suspicions and hatreds toward one another that they constantly struggled over territorial rights, power, and the loyalty of potential allies. This intertribal enmity allowed the whites to divide and conquer, for they invariably found Indians who wanted access to European goods and welcomed Euro-American assistance in fighting traditional foes. When Europeans paid their Indian allies, gave them weapons, and fought alongside them, the recipients considered themselves fortunate. European largess, firepower, and reinforcements allowed one tribe to strike more effectively at another tribe with which it was *already* at war.

Rarely did whites fight Indians; instead, Indians killed Indians, or whites and some Indians fought other Indians, or some whites and some Indians battled other whites and Indians. Determining exactly who was exploiting whom in these conflicts was difficult. Europeans, of course, realized that intertribal tensions could be exploited. But many tribes perceived that they could exploit animosities among white people and cleverly manipulated the British, French, Spanish, and (eventually) Americans against one another and against their native enemies for their own purposes.

Even when augmented by friendly Indians, colonists had a difficult time bringing the quick-moving warriors to decisive battle, and the real objective of colonial strategy became enemy villages, food supplies, clothing, and noncombatants. In a trend that continued for nearly three hundred years, white settlers waged war against Native Americans with remorseless, extravagant violence. Gratuitous devastation and killing was not unique to North America; the English perpetrated similar atrocities in Ireland, and the Thirty Years War (1618–1648) at times seemed to be little more than a long roll call of atrocities. Nor were the Indians always on the side of the angels; ferocity, savagery, and barbarous behavior were common to both sides. Shepherded by Indian scouts, often guided by Indian informers, and invariably accompanied by Indian warriors, colonial forces struck at Indian villages, killing old men, women, and children, scalping and raping, burning homes, and destroying crops and food caches. Men who believed they were fighting to protect their own homes and families from savage heathens eagerly torched Indian dwellings and slaughtered noncombatants. They pursued survivors ruthlessly, executing or enslaving captives, and many fugitives died of starvation and exposure.

Along with Indian allies and their terror tactics, the settlers had another advantage, one that nobody at the time understood: Disease. Europeans spread Old World diseases such as typhus, cholera, tuberculosis, measles, and smallpox. Because Native Americans had no immunity against these unseen killers, a tribe was often reduced by 50 to 90 percent, leaving survivors demoralized, and sometimes even suicidal, as they watched loved ones die painful, rotting deaths and their communities, tightly woven together with bonds of kinship and clan, disintegrate. As just one example, in 1633–1634 a smallpox epidemic reduced the once-powerful Pequot tribe from 13,000 to 3,000, rendering them vulnerable to retribution from Indian foes and conquest by the Puritans.

Waging war against society rather than against warriors was new and shocking to the Indians. Captain Underhill, who was so condescending toward the gentleness of Indian warfare, recorded the reaction of native allies who watched the English destroy an enemy Indian community. The Indians expressed astonishment at the way the English fought, crying out that it was wicked "because it is too furious, and slays too many men."

Nevertheless, when Indian and European military cultures collided, an acculturation process took place as the adversaries adjusted to each other's technology and methods. By the late 1600s the colonists had shed such cumbersome accoutrements as armor, pikes, and swords. And while formal militia training had not changed, some expeditionary forces began to employ Indian guerrilla techniques, including the use of cover and concealment and aimed fire. Meanwhile the Indians embraced certain aspects of European technology, including the flintlock, and quickly accepted the colonists' "war to the death" mentality. Although Indians had fought with each other long before whites arrived in the New World, the newcomers taught them how to wage war more ruthlessly.

Fighting for Survival

At dawn on Good Friday, March 22, 1622, Virginia was at peace. Just a few months before, Opechancanough, the chief of the Indian confederation in the Tidewater area, had assured the whites that "he held the peace so firme, the sky should fall [before] he dissolved it. . . ." Relations between

Indians and settlers seemed amiable. Suddenly the Indians fell upon the unsuspecting whites and, as one contemporary put it, "basely and barbarously" murdered them, "not sparing eyther age or sex, man, woman, or childe." This surprise attack was an excellent example of Native American strategic thinking, as Opechancanough orchestrated simultaneous assaults against farms and villages scattered for eighty miles across the landscape, certainly no easy task in an era without modern communications. Within hours the Indians had killed 25 percent of Virginia's population. Terrified survivors abandoned outlying plantations and huddled together in fewer settlements, where they planned a counterattack despite their meager resources. Fewer than two hundred men remained for active service, and arms and ammunition were in short supply.

The colonists enlisted the Potomack Indians' aid against Opechancanough's warriors, appealed to the King for weapons, and through a mighty effort launched military expeditions. For ten years the First Tidewater War ravaged eastern Virginia. Throughout the hot, humid summers and the cool, dreary winters the colonists, guided by Indian allies and defectors from Opechancanough's forces, struck at enemy villages, cornfields, and fishing weirs. Although it inflicted severe punishment on the Indians, this continual effort imposed tremendous strains on colonial society. By the early 1630s both sides approached exhaustion, and in 1632 the governor signed a peace treaty with the major tribes in the enemy confederation.

The peace was short-lived. In 1644 Opechancanough, now nearly a hundred years old, directed another surprise attack reminiscent of 1622. His warriors killed nearly five hundred colonists during the first morning, more than had fallen on Good Friday in 1622, but the effect was not as devastating. Instead of striking a feeble outpost as they had two decades before, the Indians now attacked a rapidly maturing society of some eight thousand settlers with a much greater ability to defend itself. In the Second Tidewater War, which lasted only two years, the Indians suffered a decisive defeat, as colonists pursued their previous strategy of destroying the foundations of Indian society. Colonists captured Opechancanough; after he spent a short period in captivity, a soldier shot him. His death symbolized the demise of any future resistance to white expansion in the Tidewater area.

The importance of the Tidewater Wars transcended the fact of ultimate Indian defeat. Equally significant was the resultant attitude toward the natives. When Englishmen settled in America, they had a dual image of Indians. Viewing the natives as noble savages, some settlers felt a sense of mission to convert them to Christianity and bring them the blessings of "civilization." But other settlers considered the Indians ignoble savages, brutal heathens prone to treachery and violence. Although some people continued to advocate moderate treatment of the Indians, the 1622 attack, seemingly without provocation, confirmed the ignoble savage image in the minds of most settlers, ensuring that the predominant attitude toward Indians would be hatred, mingled with fear and contempt. It also released white inhibitions in waging war. Facing what they perceived as an inhuman enemy, Englishmen responded with extreme measures. Many spoke of exterminating the natives. For example, the Virginia Company urged "a sharp revenge upon the bloody miscreantes, even to the measure that they intended against us, the rooting them out from being longer a people uppon the face of the Earth." At the least, settlers wanted to subjugate the Indians completely, since, as the Virginia assembly repeatedly declared during the war, relations between whites and Indians were irreconcilable and the natives were perpetual enemies.

After 1622, then, whites responded ruthlessly to any Indian provocation. The colonists punished the offending tribe (or tribes) severely and, just as important, terrified other tribes into submission by setting a frightful example of what happened to natives who aroused colonial wrath. A perfect illustration of this occurred in New England in 1637. In the early 1630s, before being devastated by new diseases, the Pequots were the most powerful tribe in New England. They had a well-deserved reputation for ferocity, gaining the enmity of both their white and Indian neighbors. When a complex series of events led to war between the Pequots and the English, practically all other natives in the area joined with the whites.

The major "battle" of the Pequot War took place at a palisaded Pequot fort along the Mystic River. Colonial troops commanded by Captain John Mason of Connecticut and Captain Underhill of Massachusetts Bay, accompanied by several hundred friendly Indians, attacked at dawn. Barking dogs alerted the Pequots, many of them women and children, who briefly put up a stout defense until Mason and Underhill personally set fire to the wigwams inside the fort. Within half an hour all but a handful of the Pequots had been put to the sword or had burned to death, fouling the air with a sickly scent and, as Mason put it, "dunging the Ground with their flesh." Accounts differ as to how many Indians perished, but the number probably approached four or five hundred. The attackers lost only two dead and twenty wounded.

The slaughter at the Mystic River fort broke the back of Pequot resistance, and survivors sought asylum with neighboring tribes or fled northward toward the homeland of the Mohawk Indians. But mere victory did not satisfy the colonists. Having learned from Virginia's misfortune in 1622, they thirsted for annihilation. Aided by Indian allies, New Englanders systematically hunted down the fugitives. The Mohawks were especially helpful, capturing the Pequot chief, Sassacus, and forty of his warriors. The war reduced the once fearsome Pequot tribe to impotence, and other tribes warily pondered the totality of the colonists' victory that, ironically, they had helped achieve.

Following the Pequots' destruction, New England experienced nearly forty years of uneasy peace before King Philip's War erupted in 1675. The war took its name from the chief of the Wampanoag Indians, Metacomet, upon whom the English had conferred the classical name of Philip as a symbol of esteem and friendship. They treated Philip with respect because he was the son of Massasoit, who had signed a peace treaty with the English in 1621 and faithfully adhered to it until his death four decades later. But Philip was not Massasoit. Seeing his people increasingly subjected to English domination, he became restive, and gradually Wampanoag hospitality turned into hostility. Some evidence indicates that Philip tried to form an Indian confederation to launch a coordinated attack against the whites, but whatever his intentions, the war began before any widespread conspiracy had matured. Philip fought as one of several important chieftains, not as the leader of an intertribal confederation.

The war began in a small way in a limited area but eventually engulfed New England, bringing suffering to nearly all its English and native inhabitants. In June 1675, a few Wampanoags looted and burned several abandoned buildings in a frontier community. The destruction was more an act of vandalism than a military attack, but as so often in the relations between whites and Indians, seemingly inconsequential events had momentous consequences. Plymouth colonists mobilized to retaliate, the Wampanoags prepared to defend themselves, and before long a war was in progress. Almost immediately the conflict took an adverse turn for the English when the Nipmuck tribe joined Philip's warriors. Fearful colonists wondered how many other tribes would join the Wampanoags and especially worried about the Narragansetts, the most powerful tribe in the area and the Wampanoags' traditional enemies. In 1637 the Narragansetts had helped eliminate the Pequots, but in the intervening years they became truculent as whites encroached upon their Rhode Island homeland. Now English efforts to elicit a firm pledge of friendship from them gained only an equivocal response.

Rather than abide fickle friends, the colonists delivered a preemptive strike against the Narragansetts, resulting in the war's most famous battle, the Great Swamp Fight of December 19, 1675. Many Narragansett families had taken up winter residence in a secret fortified village in Rhode Island's Great Swamp. During the morning and early afternoon of the 19th, a day memorable for its bitter cold and the tremendous snowfall shrouding the land, an intercolonial army trudged the last few miles to the Indian fort. The governor of Plymouth Colony, Josiah Winslow, commanded the 1,100-man force, composed of soldiers from Plymouth, Massachusetts, and Connecticut and a substantial contingent of Indian allies, including a Narragansett defector who led the army to the concealed encampment. The Narragansetts resisted with valor, but the English gained the upper hand by resorting to fire, as they had previously done along the Mystic River. The immediate Indian losses numbered in the hundreds, but of equal importance was the destruction of the Indians' clothing, housing, and winter food supply. Those Narragansetts fleeing into the swamp carried practically nothing with them and faced the grim prospect of freezing or starving to death.

The Narragansetts had suffered a stunning defeat, but the colonial victory was not cause for unmitigated joy. Colonial casualties were about 20 percent of the army. Furthermore, the Narragansetts still had considerable fighting power, and the preemptive attack pushed the enraged tribe into the enemy camp. Still, though tainted by the casualty list and the prospect of additional enemies, the victory bolstered sagging morale. Until the Great Swamp Fight the colonial effort had been inept. One explanation for the initial blunders was the failure to use Indian allies. Despite many contemptible actions by whites toward even friendly Indians, approximately half the natives of New England refused to join the Wampanoags. However, when the war began, the settlers viewed practically all Indians with suspicion, fearing they might be plotting to repeat Good Friday of 1622 on a grander scale, and were reluctant to employ them. By the spring of 1676 necessity overrode prejudice and suspicion, and with Indian assistance the strategy of waging total war against Indian society became more successful.

Two of New England's most famous soldiers were William Turner and Benjamin Church. Leading 150 volunteers, in May 1676 Turner attacked a huge Indian base camp on the Connecticut River, killing hundreds of women and children and destroying a large cache of ammunition and two forges that the Indians used to repair firearms. Just as the colonists completed their destruction, Indian warriors counterattacked and inflicted severe losses on Turner's command, but irreparable damage to the Indians' cause had already been done. Church, who used Indian auxiliaries and imitated Indian methods, was New England's foremost war hero. He had participated in the Great Swamp Fight and then retired from the war until the summer of 1676, when he offered to form a volunteer company of Indians and whites and fight Indians by fighting *like* Indians, emulating their stealthy guerrilla tactics. Church personally persuaded the small Sakonnet tribe to abandon Philip and then enlisted the Sakonnet warriors into his own company. His men captured Philip's wife and nine-year-old son and, guided by one of Philip's own men turned traitor, also killed the

Wampanoag sachem on August 12, 1676. Church ordered Philip's head and hands cut off and had the body quartered; then each quarter was hung from a separate tree.

Although the roundup of stragglers went on for several months, Philip's death marked the end of concerted Indian resistance. For the English the war's cost was grievous: expenses of £100,000 and debts larger than the colony's property value, three thousand fresh graves out of a white population of only 52,000, hundreds of homes burned, thousands of cattle killed. But white society recovered. The Indians did not. King Philip's War was analogous to the Second Tidewater War, as it settled the question of whether Indians or whites would dominate the region. The conflict reduced the once-proud Wampanoags, Nipmucks, and Narragansetts to insignificance. Even tribes allied with the English suffered acute degradation as the natives rapidly declined in the war's aftermath. A visitor to New England in 1687 noted: "There is Nothing to fear from the Savages, for they are few in Number. The last Wars they had with the English . . . have reduced them to a small number, and consequently they are incapable of defending themselves."

Simultaneously with this New England war, Virginia endured a curious affair known as Bacon's Rebellion, which was part Indian war, part civil insurrection. The chain of events precipitating the rebellion would make good comic opera, had the results not been so lethal. In 1675 whites murdered some members of the friendly Susquehannock Indians, forcing the tribe onto the warpath. When the Susquehannocks retaliated, Virginians divided on how to respond. Governor William Berkeley represented one viewpoint. For reasons of humanity and policy, he believed colonists should differentiate between friendly and hostile Indians, protecting the former and waging war only against the latter. The governor knew of the recent upheaval in New England and wanted to preserve the loyalty of neighboring Indians, whose help would be essential if war broke out in Virginia too. To protect the frontier, Berkeley proposed a series of forts manned by militiamen; to reassure Virginians of the inability of subjugated Indians in their midst to do any harm, he disarmed the natives. Nathaniel Bacon, Berkeley's cousin by marriage, symbolized the other perspective. Bacon believed all Indians were enemies and launched a crusade to kill them without distinguishing between hostile and loyal tribes. Bacon's attitude represented the majority of frontiersmen who, resenting the expense of maintaining Berkeley's forts, wanted to raise volunteer companies and slaughter Indians indiscriminately. When Berkeley opposed the formation of volunteer units, Bacon defied him, becoming an unofficial, uncommissioned "General of Volunteers." Thus a dispute over Indian policy bred civil revolt.

Under Bacon's leadership the volunteer frontiersmen did not kill a single enemy Indian, contenting themselves with persecuting and slaughtering innocents. Meantime, Bacon also waged civil war against Governor Berkeley's loyal forces. The whole sorry incident ended when Bacon died of the "Bloody Flux" (dysentery) in October 1676. The rebellion against constituted authority soon sputtered to a conclusion, and in the spring authorities reached a peace agreement with the terrified friendly tribes, whom Bacon's volunteers had driven from their homes.

In the hundred years prior to the American Revolution, colonists fought other wars strictly against Indians. For example, in 1711 the Tuscarora Indians in North Carolina launched a surprise attack that began the Tuscarora War (1711–1713). And in 1715 the Yamassee Indians staged an attack in South Carolina, beginning the Yamassee War, which intermittently sputtered on until 1728, with the Indians, as usual, being defeated. But purely Indian wars were relatively unimportant following King Philip's War. After 1689 English colonists fought a series of wars against rival European colonies in which both sides made liberal use of Indian allies. By then the colonists had developed attitudes toward military institutions and war that set them apart from the European experience. First, unlike European nations, the colonies did not develop professional armies, instead relying on a militia system. During the Indian wars from 1622 to 1676, colonists gained confidence in this system and romanticized it, believing that citizen-soldiers defending their homes were far superior to an army of mercenaries. From their perspective they were at least partially correct. The militia had its deficiencies, but it proved adequate, since the Indians were the vanquished, not the whites. Second, the colonists did not enjoy an "Age of Limited Warfare" like that which prevailed in Europe from the midseventeenth to the mideighteenth century. To the colonists (and to the Indians), war was a matter of survival. Consequently, at the very time European nations strove to restrain war's destructiveness, the colonists waged it with ruthless ferocity, purposefully striking at noncombatants and enemy property. The colonial wars fought between 1689 and 1763 perpetuated the attitudes fostered by the military experience between 1607 and 1676. Colonists remained disdainful, even fearful, of professional soldiers and augmented their quest for the Indians' subjugation with an equally intense desire for the complete removal of French influence from North America.

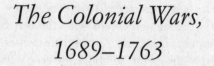

TWO

The Colonial Wars,
1689–1763

By the time Benjamin Church left King Philip's butchered body hanging from four trees, North America had become a divided continent, as three imperial powers struggled for dominance. The English had established a thin band of civilization along the eastern seaboard and also claimed the shores of Hudson Bay. An even sparser line of French settlement thrust along the St. Lawrence River into the Great Lakes region. The Spanish claimed much of the Gulf coast, with its eastern anchor in Florida, where they founded St. Augustine in 1565. However, Spanish power was waning, leaving England and France as the primary competitors for an enormously rich prize, the interior of North America drained by the Mississippi River and its tributaries. Geography favored the French, since the St. Lawrence gave them relatively easy access into the heart of the continent. By contrast, with the Appalachian Mountains blocking their westward advance, English colonists seemed doomed to occupy a coastal ribbon. Only two major gaps breached the northern half of the Appalachians: In central New York the Mohawk River pierced the mountains; farther north a corridor, consisting of the Hudson River, Lakes George and Champlain, and the Richelieu River, linked New France and the British colonies. Along with the St. Lawrence itself, these gaps were practically the only avenues over which the enemies could strike at each other.

Although nature had blessed New France, the British had two compensating advantages, manpower and sea power. Throughout the colonial wars, British colonists outnumbered French colonists by about fifteen to one. Several factors somewhat reduced this disproportion in manpower. Only New York and New England, containing about half the English North American population, consistently fought in the wars, while France drew on all of Canada for support. The French colony also contained a higher proportion of males. One government capable of imposing unity of command ruled Canada, while the English, fighting under their individual colonial governments, lacked overall coordination. But would a single unified command be enough to overcome the British numerical advantage on both land and sea?

Beginning in the late seventeenth century, the British navy increasingly controlled the Atlantic Ocean. Reinforcing the Royal Navy were privateers, which were merchant ships that their owners converted into warships for the express purpose of raiding the enemy's seaborne commerce. Because a privateer's owners and crew shared the proceeds from any captured ships (called prizes), the prospect of substantial prize money attracted thousands of colonial businessmen and mariners to the enterprise, especially from the port cities of Newport, New York, and Philadelphia. Since New France remained dependent on imports from the mother country, it could be likened to a sapling striving to reach maturity in a harsh environment. The sea lanes to France represented the roots, the St. Lawrence was analogous to the trunk, and the Great Lakes were the branches. Anything impeding the flow of supplies along the root system stunted the growth of the trunk and foliage. In wartime the Royal Navy, supplemented by numerous privateers, periodically severed these roots, allowing British land forces to attack a foe suffering from malnutrition.

Euro-Indian Alliances and Early Conflicts

The colonial wars cannot be understood without recognizing the complex relationship among Europeans, Indians, and the fur trade. Colonial competition for mastery of the continent inevitably affected the native tribes. Realizing that Indian alliances might ultimately determine which nation prevailed, perceptive white men sought Indian allies as warriors and as agents in the economically important fur trade. In the quest for Indian allies the French had two advantages, the British one. Less race-conscious than Englishmen, Frenchmen embraced Indian culture in ways alien to the British, and the natives recognized the difference. Nor were the French as greedy for Indian land as the British. Many French colonists were single males (fur traders, priests, and soldiers) and required only a few acres for their trading posts, missions, forts, and garden plots. But the rapidly multiplying English came primarily in family units to farm. Their thirst for

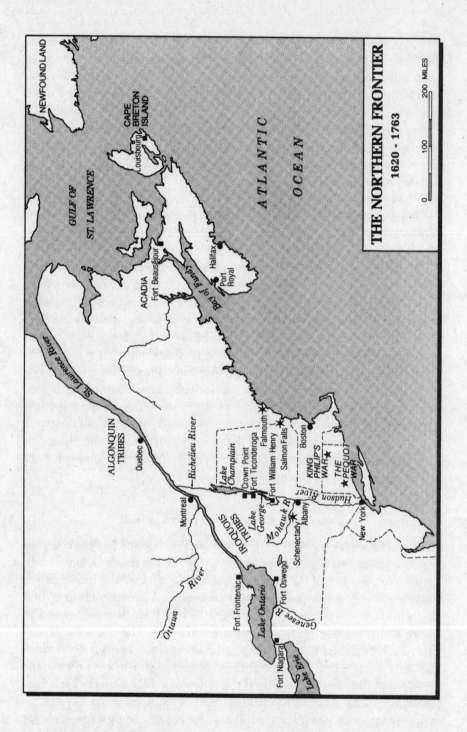

THE NORTHERN FRONTIER
1620 - 1763

0   100   200 MILES

NEWFOUNDLAND

CAPE
BRETON
ISLAND
Louisbourg

GULF OF
ST. LAWRENCE

ATLANTIC
OCEAN

ACADIA
Fort Beauséjour

Bay of Fundy

Halifax

Port
Royal

St. Lawrence River

ALGONQUIN
TRIBES

Quebec

Richelieu River

Lake
Champlain

Crown Point
Fort Ticonderoga

Falmouth

Fort William Henry

Salmon Falls

Boston

Montreal

Lake
George

Fort
Edward

Mohawk R.

Schenectady

Albany

Hudson River

KING
PHILIP'S
WAR

THE
PEQUOT
WAR

New York

IROQUOIS
TRIBES

Ottawa
River

Fort Frontenac

Fort Oswego

Genesee R.

Lake Ontario

Fort Niagara

Lake Erie

land seemed unquenchable, and they frequently resorted to unscrupulous methods to obtain it.

The British advantage was in the fur trade, which bound whites and Indians in an interdependent relationship and brought the European rivals into more direct competition. Colonists profited from the trade, while the Indians, who exchanged pelts for manufactured goods, gradually abandoned their self-sufficient existence as they became dependent on these wares. Since English manufactured goods were better and cheaper than French goods, Indians preferred to trade with the British. Under intense pressure to procure pelts, Indians killed off the nearby supply of fur-bearing animals and had to trap in more remote areas. White traders followed them, pushing the frontiers of New France and the English colonies closer together.

The crucial European-Indian alliances in the northeast emerged early in the colonial era. Two major Indian cultures existed in the region, the Iroquoian and the Algonquin. Not only were these groups hostile to each other, but internal conflict among tribes belonging to the same group also occurred. Various Algonquin tribes—such as the Abnakis, Montagnais, and Ottawas—living in areas the French explored, welcomed the newcomers as allies against their traditional enemies, the Five Nations of the Iroquois confederacy (the Onondaga, Oneida, Cayuga, Seneca, and Mohawk tribes). The Five Nations occupied the territory from the Hudson River and Lake Champlain westward to the Genesee River.* Living in the Great Lakes region were the Hurons, Neutrals, and Eries, all akin to the Iroquois but, like the Algonquin tribes, periodically at war with the confederacy. South of the Five Nations were the Susquehannocks, an Iroquoian tribe also in conflict with the confederacy.

When the French allied themselves with the Algonquins and Hurons to ensure the safety of their settlements and to gain access to rich fur sources, they automatically gained the enmity of the confederacy. Although the Five Nations could never count on more than three thousand warriors, they were aggressive fighters. The confederacy's geographic position also allowed it to control the economic and military balance of power between Canada and the English colonies. Inhabiting the Mohawk and Hudson River gaps, it sat astride the northern frontier's most vital crossroads of communications and trade. The Five Nations served like a belt of armor that the French had to penetrate before striking the English. The Iroquois were also in an ideal position to divert the flow of pelts from the St. Lawrence to the Hudson River.

* The Tuscarora Indians, an Iroquoian tribe in the Carolinas, moved northward after their defeat by the whites and were admitted to the confederacy in the early 1720s. Thereafter the Five Nations became the Six Nations.

The Dutch settled the Hudson Valley, building Fort Orange (Albany) nine miles below the mouth of the Mohawk River. The Iroquois, anxious to acquire firearms to counter the French-Indian threat to their north, and the Dutch, eager to profit from the fur trade, established cordial relations. Seeking new access to furs, the Five Nations waged a series of expansionist wars during the midseventeenth century. They defeated the Hurons, Neutrals, and Eries and then turned against the Susquehannocks. The Iroquois intrusion into the Great Lakes region disrupted New France's fur trade, threatening the colony with economic disaster. In 1664 the English conquered New Netherland, renaming it New York. Realizing that friendship with the Five Nations was important for their economic and military security, the conquerors preserved the Dutch relationship with the Iroquois. Thus when the colonial wars began, the battle lines were well formed. New France, the Algonquins, and remnants of the Iroquoian tribes that had recently been defeated by the Five Nations opposed the English colonists and the Iroquois. Although the northern frontier ultimately would be decisive during the colonial wars, the clashing interests of Spain, France, and England along the southern frontier helped mold the final outcome. After the founding of Charleston in 1670 and the subsequent growth of the Carolinas, a parallel search for Indian trade and alliances developed in the south, where the Appalachians tapered off in central Georgia. Settling in territory claimed by Spain, the Carolinians struggled with the Spanish and their Indian supporters. Forming alliances with various Indian tribes, the English drove the Spanish frontier southward to the Florida peninsula. With the Spanish barrier eliminated, Carolina traders penetrated into the interior, where they established trading relations with the most important tribes of the old southwest. In eastern Tennessee and western Carolina they encountered the Cherokees. Further westward, in the Yazoo River valley and along the upper reaches of the Tombigbee River, were the Chickasaws. The Creeks inhabited western Georgia and eastern Alabama, and the Choctaws lived west of the Tombigbee. Like the northern tribes, these four powerful tribes frequently warred with each other.

The Anglo-French frontiers collided in Louisiana, as they had already in the Great Lakes region. Both sides sought the allegiance of the four primary tribes living between the Appalachians and the Mississippi. The French had the advantage of easy water routes, while the Carolinians had to rely on difficult overland trails. The French were also much less abusive toward the Indians and did not traffic in Indian slaves, a practice the English avidly pursued. However, the Carolina traders, like their northern counterparts, sold better-quality goods more cheaply. The Indian alliance system remained fluid during the early 1700s. The Choctaws were generally in the French camp, while the Cherokees, Creeks, and Chickasaws favored the Carolinians. However, diplomatic maneuvering, trading opportunities, and strategic considerations made alliances undependable. The only certainty was that Indian assistance in the south, as in the north, would be vital in the wars for continental domination.

The colonial wars take their formal dates from simultaneous wars in Europe, but the fighting between English and French colonists, and their Indian proxies, often preceded the declarations of war and continued after the signing of Old World peace treaties. Colonists had their own reasons for fighting, reasons divorced from European diplomacy. Conflicts over fishing rights, religious differences, and the desire for revenge reinforced the struggle to dominate the fur trade and the western areas. The colonial wars merely gave intermittent official sanction to the nearly constant warfare that plagued North America between 1689 and 1763.

Although neither side was prepared for conflict in 1689, when King William's War began, the French reacted more quickly. Count Frontenac, who became Canada's governor in October of that year, understood the importance of the Iroquois–New York alliance and brought from France a plan for the conquest of New York, which would isolate the Five Nations militarily, weaken the English colonies by cleaving them in two, and safeguard the fur trade. However, the plan was too ambitious for Canada to implement, and Frontenac settled for a loosely coordinated three-pronged attack against the New England-New York frontier. In the first half of 1690, combined forces of French and Indians inflicted massacres on Schenectady, Salmon Falls, and Falmouth.

Even as Frontenac's grisly offensive unfolded, Massachusetts was preparing the first British colonial attack of the war, aimed at thinly populated French Acadia. Leading the venture was Sir William Phips. In May 1690, his 700-man force captured Port Royal, the principal outpost in Acadia, subdued the remainder of the area, and returned to Boston in triumph. Phips's exploits were strategically insignificant, since the French soon reoccupied Port Royal, but they bolstered morale throughout New England.

Meanwhile, the northern colonies girded for a major effort. In late April an intercolonial conference met in New York City, attended by representatives from New York, Connecticut, Plymouth, and Massachusetts. This conference demonstrated that some colonists realized the problem posed by Canada was beyond the resources of any single colony and required intercolonial cooperation. The delegates adopted a sound plan that became a virtual blueprint for almost all subsequent efforts against New France. The plan envisioned a dual thrust to sever the vital artery of the St. Lawrence River. Moving overland from Albany, an army would strike Montreal while a seaborne force ascended the St. Lawrence and attacked Quebec. If the forces could converge on their targets simultane-

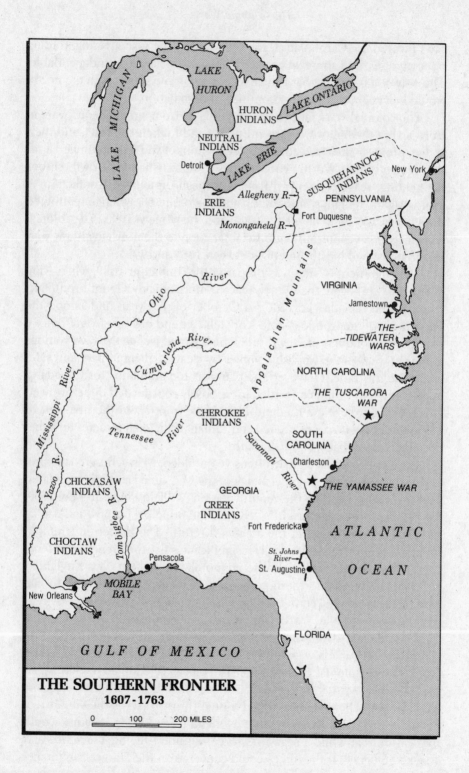

LAKE MICHIGAN

LAKE HURON

LAKE ONTARIO

LAKE ERIE

HURON INDIANS

NEUTRAL INDIANS

Detroit

ERIE INDIANS

Allegheny R.

SUSQUEHANNOCK INDIANS

New York

PENNSYLVANIA

Fort Duquesne

Monongahela R.

Ohio River

Appalachian Mountains

VIRGINIA

Jamestown

THE TIDEWATER WARS

Cumberland River

NORTH CAROLINA

THE TUSCARORA WAR

CHEROKEE INDIANS

Tennessee River

Mississippi River

SOUTH CAROLINA

Savannah River

Charleston

THE YAMASSEE WAR

Yazoo R.

CHICKASAW INDIANS

GEORGIA

CREEK INDIANS

ATLANTIC

Tombigbee R.

Fort Fredericka

CHOCTAW INDIANS

Pensacola

St. Johns River

OCEAN

St. Augustine

New Orleans

MOBILE BAY

FLORIDA

GULF OF MEXICO

THE SOUTHERN FRONTIER
1607-1763

0   100   200 MILES

ously, Canada's sparse manpower would be divided trying to defend both cities. Either Montreal or Quebec would capitulate, making the other city easy prey once the attackers united their forces. With the trunk severed, the colony's roots and branches would wither and die.

The proposal was good in theory but poorly executed. The colonies raised fewer militiamen for the Montreal army than had been promised at New York, and instead of the expected hundreds of Iroquois warriors, only a few dozen met the militia at Wood Creek near Lake Champlain. A smallpox epidemic swept the ranks, provisions were scarce, and too few boats existed to transport the army down Lake Champlain. In late summer the commander canceled the expedition. Meanwhile the Quebec force, some 2,000 strong and commanded by Phips, departed late and made slow progress, not arriving at its objective until early October, when the nip of winter was already in the air. The city occupied a strong defensive position atop steep cliffs, and with the threat to Montreal evaporated, Frontenac had reinforced the garrison so that it now out-numbered the attackers. Phips put a substantial force ashore, but it made little headway against the French and suffered from inadequate supplies and the bitter cold. Discouraged, Phips and his army headed home.

Exhausted in spirit and heavily in debt, the colonies made no effort similar to the 1690 campaign during the remainder of the war. The conflict became "a Tedious war" of frontier raids for the next seven years. Canadian raiding parties, composed of a few *coureurs de bois* (woodsmen) and militiamen and numerous Indians and perhaps commanded by a French regular officer, struck outlying homesteads and settlements. These war parties of "Half Indianized French and Half Frenchified Indians" appeared suddenly, destroyed livestock and property, killed or captured settlers, and then disappeared into the wilderness. The high success rate of these assaults demonstrated—as had the previous Indian wars—the militia's inability to provide frontier protection. Relief columns usually arrived only in time to bury the mutilated corpses. Unable to prevent these calamities, the English retaliated with similar expeditions against the Canadians. Both sides also urged their Indian allies on to the warpath; acting independently, they added to the mayhem.

By 1697 the combatants in North America and in Europe had battered each other into exhaustion without either side achieving an appreciable advantage, and in September the European powers signed the Treaty of Ryswick. Under its terms the situation on both continents essentially reverted to the prewar condition. It did not take prophetic genius to foresee that the conflict would soon be renewed. "For the present the Indians have Done Murdering," wrote a Puritan minister, adding "they'll Do so no more till next Time."

In 1701 a new war erupted in Europe and spread to the colonies, where it became known as Queen Anne's War. During the brief interval after the Treaty of Ryswick, New France had been able to view the future with optimism. Emerging unbeaten from a decade of warfare against a more numerous enemy, it built an outpost at Detroit and established settlements in Louisiana. Most important, in 1701 the French achieved a stunning diplomatic success. The Iroquois, who had suffered grievously in King William's War, resented the inability of the English to unite among themselves and with the Iroquois confederacy in a concerted effort to destroy New France, and in 1701 they signed a neutrality treaty with Canada. British colonists feared encirclement by a French empire stretching from Acadia up the St. Lawrence to the Great Lakes and down the Mississippi to the Gulf.

Fighting occurred in three regions in North America during Queen Anne's War. Since France and Spain were now allied, military operations took place along the southern frontier. In the fall of 1702 South Carolina's governor, James Moore, conducted a campaign against St. Augustine. He easily occupied the city, but when Spanish reinforcements arrived, his army retreated to Charleston. The next year Moore, although no longer governor, partially avenged his failure when his army devastated the Apalachee region between Pensacola and St. Augustine. Encouraged by Moore's success, others undertook similar, though smaller, expeditions into Spanish territory. The English also sent their Indian allies, notably the Creeks, to attack the Choctaws and other French-aligned natives. The only significant enemy effort came in 1706 when a Spanish-French force unsuccessfully attacked Charleston. Indian allies of Spain and France, bearing the brunt of English offensives and seeing the feebleness of Spanish and French defenses, increasingly came under British influence. By 1712 the English had, as one Carolinian asserted, "firm possession . . . from Charles Town to Mobile Bay, excepting St. Augustine."

While the southern frontier was a new arena of strife, New York, which had been in the maelstrom of the previous conflict, did not become involved in Queen Anne's War until 1709. When the war began, Canada and the Five Nations adhered to their neutrality treaty. Concerned for the safety of its citizens and eager to profit from an uninterrupted fur trade, New York's government took no action that endangered the peace along its border.

The entire war in the north fell upon the third region, New England. As in King William's War, New Englanders primarily fought "a barbarous war with cruel and perfidious savages" rather than with Frenchmen. But colonists realized that "the root of all our woe" was Canada, which supplied the Indians with the necessities of war. New Englanders agreed they could never live in safety as long as New France survived, but, remembering Phips's disaster, they believed the mother country must assist them. England had viewed the war in North America as a sideshow to the greater struggle in Europe, but in early 1709 the Queen approved a plan reminiscent of the 1690 campaign. She pledged ships and men to a dual thrust aimed at conquering Canada, one army moving through the Champlain trough toward Montreal and another sailing up the St. Lawrence to Quebec.

New Englanders believed these expeditions would be no repetition of 1690, since they would be well supplied and steeled by professionals. Furthermore, New York could not refuse to participate in a campaign sanctioned by the Queen. Forced to go to war, New Yorkers persuaded the Iroquois to discard their neutrality pact with Canada. The colonies responded to the opportunity to destroy Canada with unparalleled cooperation and enthusiasm. By July, after great exertion and expense, two forces stood poised to assault the archenemy. One army of more than 1,500 men, composed of militiamen from four colonies and several hundred Iroquois, assembled at Wood Creek under the command of Colonel Francis Nicholson. The other army, composed of more than 1,200 New England militiamen, gathered at Boston, ready to sail up the St. Lawrence with the promised British armada when it arrived. But in early summer England canceled its part of the bargain. Although the government immediately dispatched a message informing the colonies, it did not arrive until October. Militiamen had endured months of deprivation for nothing, and the vast expenditures had been for naught.

Her Majesty partially redeemed herself in 1710 when British warships and a regiment of marines aided a militia force in capturing Port Royal and made Acadia a British province. Encouraged that the home government had not forsaken them, colonists implored London to resurrect the 1709 plan. In 1711 England again agreed to attempt the pincer movement against New France. In late June a British fleet commanded by Sir Hovenden Walker arrived at Boston, accompanied by seven regular regiments and a marine battalion. Walker was in overall command of the Quebec pincer, and Brigadier General John Hill commanded the regulars, who were reinforced by thousands of militiamen. Colonel Nicholson again commanded the western pincer of more than 2,000 militiamen and Indians.

When the armada departed for the St. Lawrence, the northern colonies exuded confidence. But Walker lacked the courage and determination that allows great commanders to overcome adversity. He knew that fog, storms, and uncertain currents and tides made the St. Lawrence difficult to navigate, and he worried that his force might be trapped by ice and forced to winter in Quebec, where resupply would be impossible. He became obsessed with these problems. On the night of August 23, as his fleet inched upriver in dense fog, it strayed against the north shore of the river, several ships foundered, and almost a thousand men drowned. A hastily convened council of war agreed to abandon the attempt on Quebec. Walker believed the armada should attack a lesser target, perhaps Placentia, but Hill disagreed. A second war council concurred with Hill, and eventually the fleet returned to England without striking a single blow against New France. Nicholson's army, toiling through the northern forests, was recalled far short of Montreal. Canada rejoiced, the disillusioned Iroquois hastily renewed their neutrality treaty with the French, and New England and New York brooded.

The fiascos of 1709 and 1711 had a significance beyond the simple fact of failure. Both years witnessed extensive efforts at intercolonial cooperation from Pennsylvania northward. The question of security had a nationalizing influence, forging mutual military efforts on the stern anvil of survival. As the colonies gained confidence in each other, the nonarrival of one British fleet and the precipitous withdrawal of the other sowed a sense of disgust with England and its professional military men. The Walker expedition's appearance in Boston especially strained relations between professional soldiers and New Englanders. The colonists argued that despite the imperious behavior of Her Majesty's officers, they themselves had done as much as possible to aid Walker, whom they blamed for the expedition's failure. Walker and his fellow officers responded that citizens had provided insufficient provisions and inflated the price of what they supplied, they sheltered deserters, and pilots knowledgeable about the treacherous St. Lawrence refused to accompany the fleet. In their opinion, the colonists had begged the Queen for help, she had responded generously, and now the recipients of her kindness were ungrateful. The British found such behavior incomprehensible and reprehensible. Echoing his comrades, a colonel wrote that until England placed the colonists under more stringent control "they will grow every day more stiff and disobedient, more burthensome than advantageous to Great Britain." Lexington and Concord were years in the future, but the events of 1709 and 1711 planted a seed of distrust in the imperial relationship.

When the European combatants signed the Treaty of Utrecht in 1713, New France, except for Acadia, remained unconquered. But at the negotiating table France surrendered much of what its colony had preserved by force of arms. The mother country, defeated in other areas of the globe and economically exhausted, ceded to England the shores of Hudson Bay, Acadia, and Newfoundland. The situation in the south returned to the status quo antebellum, disappointing the Carolinians, who had hoped to eliminate French control in Louisiana and Spanish sovereignty in Florida.

England's territorial gains shifted the North American balance of power in its favor, but New France, though wounded, was far from moribund.

Struggling for Control of North America

The Treaty of Utrecht ushered in twenty-five years of uneasy peace between England and the Bourbon powers (France and Spain). In North America, however, relations among the colonists continued in turmoil. One cause was the continuing quest for Indian allegiance. Indian diplomacy heightened colonial anxieties. The apparently fickle natives, squeezed by technologically and numerically superior white cultures and striving to maintain their independence, played the Europeans off against each other with consummate skill. A second, related, cause was the colonists' construction of outposts in strategic locations to improve security and to exert influence on nearby natives. Located in the unoccupied zones between expanding colonial frontiers, these forts created new tensions.

Along the northern frontier, New France tried to bring the Iroquois into its orbit. To upset French designs, the English established Fort Oswego on the Great Lakes, but the French countered with a fort at Crown Point, which was in territory claimed by New York and gave the French access to the Mohawks. The French also worried about their eastern flank, now vulnerable with Newfoundland and Acadia in British hands. Fortunately for Canada, Cape Breton Island had not been ceded to England, and here the French built Louisbourg, a formidable fortress that guarded the mouth of the St. Lawrence.

In the south, the Carolinians suffered hard times after Utrecht. Their desire to eliminate the Bourbon powers had been forestalled, and in 1711–1712 the French scored a diplomatic triumph akin to the Iroquois treaty of 1701 when they made peace with Carolina's foremost Indian allies, the Creeks. Then in 1715 the Yamassee War stunned the English. The origins of the war, which was a widespread revolt led by the Creeks and other erstwhile friends, the Yamassees, involved callous actions by Carolina traders, white land greed, and Spanish and French intrigue. To the English the war was a classic example of the omnipresent danger they faced as long as the Bourbons maintained a foothold in the region, and of the Indians' untrustworthy behavior. Carolina escaped a potentially disastrous situation when the Cherokees refused to join the uprising and instead aided the whites. Although Carolina won the war, its situation was grim. As one man wrote, "We are just now the poorest Colony in all America and have . . . very distracting appearances of ruine."

Recognizing that the recent Indian war had weakened its North American southern flank and worried that the prospect of French encirclement was no idle nightmare, especially after the French strengthened their hold on the lower Mississippi by founding New Orleans, the British government responded vigorously. The English established several new forts and in 1732 founded the colony of Georgia, which was in part intended as a military buffer zone. Under James Oglethorpe's assertive leadership, Georgians constructed a series of fortified outposts stretching southward into territory claimed by Spain and coveted by France. When Oglethorpe built Fort St. George on the St. Johns River, the gateway to Florida's interior and the backdoor to St. Augustine, passions flared and thick war clouds gathered.

Storms had also been brewing in Europe, and in 1739 the clouds burst into a British-Spanish conflict known as the War of Jenkins' Ear. What began as a drizzle became a deluge when this war merged into the War of the Austrian Succession, embroiling one European power after another until 1744, when Britain and France declared war on each other. The war in America—lasting from 1744 to 1748 and pitting English colonists against those of France and Spain—was known as King George's War, but the entire conflict, first against Spain and then against the combined Bourbon powers, can be labeled the War of the 1740s. From 1739 to 1744 the North American struggle centered around Spanish possessions; after 1744 the focus shifted to the north.

When Oglethorpe learned of the war with Spain, he tried to fulfill Moore's dream of capturing St. Augustine. Descending on Florida with a force of Georgia and Carolina militiamen, Creek and Cherokee warriors, a newly raised regular regiment, and a small British squadron, he hoped to surprise St. Augustine and take it by storm. But the Spanish were alert, and although Oglethorpe had proclaimed he would succeed or die trying, he did neither, retreating ignominiously with his bedraggled army.

The next year Americans participated in the assault on Cartagena, the most important port on the Spanish Main. In 1739 Admiral Edward Vernon had captured Porto Bello, and the elated British government reinforced his command so that he could make further conquests. A large fleet and army left England to rendezvous with Vernon in Jamaica, while for the first and only time the government asked the colonies to provide troops for a campaign beyond the mainland. In early 1740 the call went out for volunteers. To expedite volunteering, colonial governments offered bounties and promised the troops a fair share of captured booty. Eleven colonies provided thirty-six companies of a hundred men each, organized into an "American Regiment" commanded by Virginia Governor William Gooch. The regiment sailed to Jamaica, meeting Vernon's fleet and the British army under Brigadier General Thomas Wentworth. The expedition then moved against Cartagena and met with a disastrous repulse. Like

Walker's expedition thirty years earlier, Vernon's failure had long-term significance, spreading discord between Englishmen living on opposite sides of the Atlantic. The soldiers in the American Regiment fared badly at the hands of the British military establishment. They ate "putrid beef, rusty pork, and bread swimming with maggots," did an inordinate amount of fatigue duty, were forced to serve on British warships, and for their efforts received little but contempt. Thus Cartagena further reduced British military prestige in America and reinforced the emergent antagonism Americans felt toward regulars.

With the colonies weakened by their exertions at St. Augustine and Cartagena, Spain struck back, attacking Frederica, Georgia, in 1742. Although outnumbered more than four to one, Oglethorpe displayed military capabilities conducting a defense that he had not exhibited while on the offensive at St. Augustine and forced the Spanish to withdraw. The war along the southern frontier then became little more than a series of minor clashes.

As major campaigning petered out in the south, it commenced in the north. In mid-January 1745 the Massachusetts general court met in secret session to hear an extraordinary proposal from Governor William Shirley: Massachusetts should mount an expedition to capture Louisbourg! Since Louisbourg commanded navigation up the St. Lawrence, its capture would ultimately mean the downfall of all of New France. If the prospect was tempting, the dangers were great. From outward appearances the city was impregnable. The channel into the harbor was narrow and guarded by two supplemental fortifications, the Grand Battery and the Island Battery, both bristling with cannons. On the land side, stout walls and a wide trench protected the fortress. However, from exchanged prisoners who had been held captive in Louisbourg, Shirley had learned that the powder supply was low, the garrison was undermanned and mutinous, the fortifications (especially the Grand Battery) were in disrepair, and excellent landing sites existed along Gabarus Bay just west of the city.

The general court approved the expedition by only a single vote and on the condition that other colonies participated. No doubt many people feared this might be another Cartagena, but New England ministers roused the populace, portraying the venture as a crusade against the "stronghold of Satan." William Pepperrell commanded the expedition, which by any rational calculation should have failed. The badly trained and poorly disciplined 4,000-man militia army was, as one professional soldier wrote, led by "People totally Ignorant" of the military skills "necessary in such an undertaking." Yet after a siege of about seven weeks, the fortress capitulated. The French had conducted an inept defense, failing to contest the initial landing and then abandoning the Grand Battery without a fight.

The volunteers fought surprisingly well, and a British naval squadron had blockaded the fortress, preventing outside succor from relieving the city.

Louisbourg's capture was the most brilliant military achievement by the American colonies in the pre-Revolutionary era and had far-reaching implications. Most New Englanders saw "the Finger of God" in their success and believed more firmly than ever that they were His chosen people, destined for some great purpose on earth. The capture also gave colonists confidence in their martial abilities, particularly when they contrasted their performance with the Cartagena affair. Citizen-soldiers doing God's will seemed infinitely superior to British regulars serving an earthly sovereign.

After Louisbourg the fighting took on a pattern similar to previous colonial wars. Hoping to capitalize on the victory by attacking Canada in 1746, Governor Shirley proposed the familiar two-pronged plan to the British government. When the government tentatively approved, the colonies raised an army and eagerly awaited the promised English force. However, various delays and European commitments caused Britain to abandon the campaign. Remembering the mother country's failure in 1709, colonists pondered anew England's solicitude for their well-being. The colonists also tried to derail the Iroquois from their neutrality but failed. Lacking support from both England and the Iroquois, colonists launched no more major offensives. Meanwhile, the French perpetrated a few massacres but mostly dispensed death in small doses.

By 1748 the war was a stalemate. France dominated the European continent, but Britain controlled the seas and, having conquered Louisbourg, held the advantage in North America. The Treaty of Aix-la-Chapelle angered English colonists. The guiding principle was restoration of the status quo antebellum, which meant that Britain returned Louisbourg to France. In return, as a concession to England's interests, France withdrew from Flanders, but this did little to diminish colonial anguish. Colonists believed the mother country had callously disregarded their sacrifices and had sacrificed their security on the altar of England's own selfish interests.

The Great War for Empire

In June 1758 an army of more than 12,000 British regulars and colonial troops commanded by the British commander in chief in North America, James Abercromby, labored along Lake Champlain toward Fort Ticonderoga, a French stronghold near the northern tip of Lake George. He planned to smash Ticonderoga and Crown Point and move into the St. Lawrence Valley. The French commander, the Marquis de Montcalm, had fewer than 4,000 troops at Ticonderoga, but they had constructed a log breastwork and covered the ground in front of it with sharpened branches pointing outward. On July 8 Abercromby hurled his force against this position in an ill-conceived frontal attack. Almost 400 Iroquois, who in their own form of warfare always tried to avoid excessive casualties, had joined the British that morning and watched incredulously as the white troops advanced into the bristling abatis and French guns. For four hours the intrepid soldiers repeatedly attacked, recoiled, reformed, and attacked again, reddening the battlefield with their scarlet coats and their blood. Finally, mercifully, having lost more than 1,600 regulars and 300 provincials, Abercromby halted the assault. Although he still possessed numerical superiority, the unnerved British commander ordered a retreat.

For the English, Abercromby's disaster was another loss in a series of defeats in the renewed war between France and Britain. The war began in 1754 over control of the Ohio Valley. During the 1740s the English had gained de facto sovereignty in the Ohio country, but their hold was tenuous, and between 1749 and 1753 New France acquired superiority in the area, thereby strengthening the link between Canada and Louisiana. In 1754 a French expedition ousted a Virginia volunteer unit from the most strategic position in the west, the forks of the Ohio, and began building Fort Duquesne. Meanwhile, a second Virginia force, commanded by a young George Washington, marched toward the forks with orders to expel all Frenchmen from the area. But the French outnumbered Washington's men and forced the Virginians to surrender. By exerting superior military power, New France possessed the Ohio Valley.

Although France and England remained officially at peace until 1756, the last colonial war had begun. The sparks struck in the Ohio wilderness ignited a conflagration that became the first true world war. Unlike the previous wars that began in Europe and embroiled the colonies, the Great War for Empire—also known as the French and Indian War—commenced in the colonies and engulfed reluctant parent countries. Both belligerents had been anxious to avoid another struggle while still recuperating from the previous wars' debilitating effects.

Even before England was formally at war with France, the British ministry had ordered a series of preemptive strikes to drive back Canada's ever-advancing military frontier. The ministry hoped to present France with such an overwhelming fait accompli that it would accept the situation rather than risk an international confrontation. The positions selected for elimination were Fort Duquesne, Niagara, Crown Point, and Fort Beausejour. Success on all fronts would oust New France from the Ohio country, sever communications between Quebec and the Great Lakes (and hence Louisiana), force the Canadians back to the St. Lawrence, and safeguard Nova Scotia.

The British government might have relied on colonists and their Indian allies to carry the military burden of this far-flung campaign, but this prospect inspired little optimism. The disunited colonies seemed incapable of concerted action, either for defense or in Indian affairs. In the summer of 1754, seven colonies sent representatives to Albany to discuss defense problems and to entice the Six Nations out of their neutrality. Although the Albany Conference proposed a Plan of Union calling for united action in defense matters and Indian relations, no colonial assembly approved the plan; and the Iroquois, far from being receptive, inclined dangerously toward France. Thus the British ministry was forced to commit regular troops to the enterprise and centralize Indian affairs under imperial control.

Early in 1755 Major General Edward Braddock arrived in Virginia with two understrength regular regiments that were to be recruited to full strength in the colonies. The commander in chief also had authority to raise two new regiments in America and to appoint qualified men to superintend Indian affairs. The British government expected Braddock's four regiments, along with Nova Scotia's permanent garrison, to conduct the campaign with only minimal assistance from provincial troops. However, since the colonies had begun raising men for attacks on Crown Point and Fort Beausejour, Braddock integrated these forces into his planning. A British regular officer commanded colonial troops in the Fort Beausejour area, but the commander at Crown Point was New Yorker William Johnson, whom Braddock also appointed as superintendent for northern Indians. Leading the Niagara expedition was Governor Shirley, Braddock's second in command. The commander in chief personally headed the Fort Duquesne prong of England's fourfold advance against Canada's outer bastions.

The 1755 campaign resulted in one success, one semi-success, and two failures. A combined force of regulars and militiamen easily captured Fort Beausejour. Johnson's army crawled northward and in early September defeated a French army at the Battle of Lake George. Colonists naturally lauded the victory, but Johnson failed to exploit his success and abandoned the projected Crown Point attack. Ominously, with the pressure relaxed, the French began building Fort Ticonderoga twelve miles south of Crown Point. Meanwhile Shirley's expedition got as far as Oswego but did not advance farther before the campaigning season ended.* Braddock suffered a greater calamity. Hacking his way through a hundred miles of uninhabited wilderness, Braddock achieved a logistical masterpiece in get-

---

* Prior to the twentieth century most campaigning occurred between May and October. A winter expedition in northern climates was rare because of the increased logistical problems.

ting his army to within a day's march of Fort Duquesne. But on July 9 near the Monongahela River, the British advance party unexpectedly collided with an enemy army that was hurrying from the fort to lay an ambush farther down the trail. The initial encounter surprised both sides, but the French force recovered quickly, fanned out along the flanks of Braddock's column, and gained possession of a hill dominating the British position. The English regulars in the vanguard fell back on the main force advancing to the scene. Chaos and panic ensued as the British fought an invisible enemy hidden in the dense foliage on either side of the road. Before being fatally wounded, Braddock valiantly tried to rally his men, but the remnants of his shattered army fled from the battlefield.

The failure to take Crown Point, the abortive Niagara venture, and Braddock's defeat established the pattern for Britain's war effort during the next two years. Ambitious plans produced meager results, while New France seemed to succeed in every endeavor. The operations proposed by Shirley for 1756 were almost a replica of 1755, but these grandiose plans did not produce a single victory. Instead, the colonies endured a crippling setback when Montcalm demolished Oswego, severing British access to the Great Lakes. The next year was equally bad for the British. Montcalm captured Fort William Henry, and, as he had at Oswego the previous year, the French commander razed the fort and withdrew. Almost simultaneously Lord Loudoun, the new British North American commander in chief, canceled his major offensive, an assault on Louisbourg, when he learned that a French naval squadron had reinforced the harbor. British General John Forbes gloomily summarized the situation at the end of 1757, writing that "the French have these severall years by past, outwitted us with our Indian Neighbors, have Baffled all our projects of Compelling them to do us justice, nay have almost every where had the advantage over us, both in political and military Genius, to our great loss, and I may say reproach."

Despite the succession of losses, Britain had established the preconditions for victory in North America. Beginning in midsummer 1758, its prospects brightened. Fundamental to this transformation was William Pitt's ascent to power within the British ministry. In June 1757 he assumed control over the war effort, and by the next summer his strategic concepts prevailed. Since the late 1730s a debate had raged over which should dominate, a continental or a maritime and colonial strategy. Continental advocates argued for a large-scale military commitment in Europe. Devotees of a maritime and colonial strategy, including Pitt, asserted that the Royal Navy should sweep enemy commerce from the seas; then, using its seaborne freedom of movement to hurl superior forces into the imperial domain, England should make its primary effort against enemy colonies.

In particular, Pitt believed that America was the main prize. Under his leadership the war's foremost objective was to obtain security for the thirteen colonies. Realizing that this meant the conquest of Canada, Pitt was prepared to commit vast resources to the task.

Under Pitt's guidance the British navy asserted its superiority in numbers and spirit, blockading French ports to prevent the departure of squadrons, reinforcements, and supplies. Since Canada depended on constant transfusions from the mother country, the French position in America became increasingly anemic. Starvation stalked the land, the economy collapsed, and when Montcalm pleaded for more troops, he received only token forces. France could not risk losing large numbers of transports to British ships patrolling the North Atlantic. By 1758 Canada's resources were so limited that it adopted a defensive strategy, and the initiative passed to the Anglo-Americans.

In late December 1757, Pitt wrote to the colonial governors assuring them that England had "nothing more at Heart, than to repair the Losses and Disappointments of the last inactive, and unhappy Campaign." To ensure future success Pitt dispatched massive reinforcements of regulars, and to inspire the colonists to greater efforts he promised to repay most of their expenses. His objectives for 1758 included Ticonderoga and Crown Point, Louisbourg, Fort Duquesne, and, if conditions permitted, Quebec.

Abercromby failed at Ticonderoga, but other British endeavors met with success. The Louisbourg expedition, commanded by Jeffery Amherst, succeeded. In early June he sent his men toward shore against stout defensive positions at Gabarus Bay. Brigadier General James Wolfe, leading four companies of regulars, made a lodgment and audaciously ordered his outnumbered men to attack, surprising the French and establishing a small beachhead. The defenders scurried into Louisbourg and the siege began, ending with the stronghold's capitulation in late July. Since it was late in the campaign season, Amherst decided against attacking Quebec. Meanwhile Abercromby, following his defeat by Montcalm in July, destroyed Fort Frontenac in late August. Several months later General Forbes approached Fort Duquesne, haunted by the memory of Braddock's defeat, hindered by transportation problems, and handicapped by difficulties with Indian allies. But when he arrived at the fort, he found it abandoned.

Although the central approach to Canada remained blocked, England had penetrated its perimeter defenses in the east and west. British targets for the next year were obvious: Niagara, to remove the last French bastion in the west; Ticonderoga and Crown Point, to open the way to Montreal; and Quebec, to rip the heart out of Canada.

British arms won victories on all fronts in 1759. The Niagara expedition captured the French position in late July, and Amherst succeeded where Abercromby had failed. With an 11,000-man army he approached Ticonderoga and Crown Point. Since the French commander in the area had only 3,000 men, Montcalm ordered him to delay the British but to retreat northward rather than lose his army in a futile defense. By early August both strongholds were in British hands. Amherst entrusted the crucial Quebec operation to Wolfe, who had performed so nobly at Louisbourg. Learning of the expedition in advance, Montcalm concentrated most of Canada's manpower there. With an army 8,500 strong, supported by about one-fourth of the British navy, Wolfe arrived at Quebec in late June. Once he was there his real problems began. The city's natural strength and large garrison confronted him with "such a Choice of Difficultys, that I own myself at a Loss how to [proceed]." By early September, after several unsuccessful attempts to breach Montcalm's defenses, Wolfe was pessimistic. Deciding on a last desperate gamble, in the early-morning hours of September 13 he landed an elite force at the base of steep cliffs barely two miles from the city. In the darkness the infantry struggled hand over hand up the precipitous slope and overwhelmed a French outpost. Within hours 4,500 redcoats had assembled on the Plains of Abraham just west of Quebec, while Montcalm hastened his regulars to the scene. In a brief midmorning battle, fought in accordance with accepted European standards, the British routed the French army. Four days later the citadel surrendered, although the French army's escape to Montreal prevented the victory from being decisive.

The once expansive Canadian domain now consisted only of Montreal, and the stricken colony's only chance for survival was the recapture of Quebec. In the spring of 1760 a French force made a gallant effort to reclaim the city but failed. The pitiful remnants of Canada's army then huddled in Montreal as powerful British forces converged on it from Quebec, Lake Ontario, and Crown Point. When all three armies arrived simultaneously in early September, the Canadian governor had to surrender.

Montreal's capitulation ended the war in North America, but it continued on the seas, in Europe, in the West Indies, and in Asia until February 1763, when the combatants signed the Peace of Paris. British arms were victorious everywhere. Even Spain's entry into the war against England in January 1762 could not save France from a humiliating defeat. Territory around the globe changed hands, but the treaty's most momentous provisions concerned America, where France lost all its territory except for two small islands off the Newfoundland coast. To England it ceded Canada, Cape Breton Island, and all its land claims east of the Mississippi except for New Orleans. France ceded this city and all its territorial claims west of the Mississippi to Spain, which in turn gave Florida to Britain. From St.

Augustine to Hudson Bay, from the Atlantic to the Mississippi, England reigned supreme.

British Regulars and Colonial Militias at War

Colonial troops and, to a lesser extent, Indians contributed to Canada's defeat, but British regulars bore the brunt of the fighting. The relationships among redcoats, colonials, and Indians were strained, but the developing rift between British officers and colonial civilians was even more ominous. Regular officers believed colonial troops had no merits. They were, wrote one of Braddock's subordinates, "totally ignorant of Military Affairs." They were ill disciplined and lazy and, lacking even elementary knowledge of camp sanitation, suffered an appalling rate of sickness. Colonies never fielded as many men as the legislatures voted, officers failed to report accurately their unit's strength, and men deserted in droves, so the number of colonial troops was always uncertain. The large enlistment bounties that were needed also made colonial recruits exorbitantly expensive.

This catalog of shortcomings was true in many respects, and understanding why is important. The Great War for Empire was a war of conquest, requiring extended offensives far from the homes of most militiamen. But the militia was a system for local defense. Large numbers of militiamen could not be absent long without leaving their colonies vulnerable to enemy raids and without dislocating the local economy. Militiamen were *part-time* citizen-soldiers who had to run businesses, tend crops, and conduct the fishing and fur trades. Consequently, authorities hesitated to impose militia drafts and instead relied on volunteers, who came primarily from the lowest social strata. In the few cases when a colony resorted to a draft, the sending of substitutes and paying of commutation fines ensured that few middle- or upper-class citizens served. But of all the high-ranking British officers serving in North America, Lord Loudoun alone seemed to realize that colonists marching with English regulars against some distant fort were different from the men enrolled on militia musters. "The Militia," he wrote, "are the real Inhabitants; Stout able Men, and for a brush, much better than their Provincial Troops, whom they hire whenever they can get them, and at any price." Almost all other British officers confused the expeditionary forces with the actual militia, thus misjudging the militia's military potential in defense of its own terrain.

Holding such a low opinion of colonial soldiers, British officers relegated them to auxiliary functions. They built roads, served as wagoners and boatmen, and repaired and constructed forts. With their aristocratic ties and long years of experience, English officers were reluctant to treat American officers, who were usually young and newly commissioned, as equals. While provincial officers had traditionally relied on exhortation and admonishment to maintain discipline, English officers inflicted ferocious punishment upon enlisted men, including liberal use of the lash and, for serious offenses, execution by hanging or firing squad. To colonial soldiers, whippings and executions were horrific and unnecessary. And because the redcoats engaged in swearing, excessive drinking, and whoring, the colonists also condemned them as profane, irreligious, and immoral—pollutants in a pure land. And initial British defeats mingled with earlier memories, making a lasting impression. The Walker expedition, Cartagena, Braddock, Loudoun at Louisbourg—what right did professionals have to claim superiority? All in all, serving with British regulars graphically reminded colonists of a standing army's threat to free people living in a free society, and persuaded them that their own military institutions were morally and militarily superior.

British officers also considered Indians questionable allies. Amherst described them as "a pack of lazy, rum-drinking people, and little good," and Forbes accused them of being "more infamous cowards than any other race of mankind" and having a "natural fickle disposition." These impressions flowed in part from cultural ethnocentrism, but also from the natives' difficult position in the white rivalry swirling around them. Between 1748 and 1760 England and France negotiated constantly with the Indians and tried to buy their allegiance through lavish gift giving. While the natives listened to, and took presents from, both French and English ambassadors, they were naturally anxious to be on the winning side. Inactivity, duplicity, and hesitancy to go on the warpath were stratagems to buy time until a clear-cut winner emerged. But these traits exasperated British professionals, who demanded unwavering commitment.

Initially, with English arms suffering reverses, Indians tended to support the French, and the British maintained the neutrality of important tribes, such as the Creeks and Iroquois, only through astute diplomacy coupled with large expenditures for gifts. The turning point in Indian relations, as in the war itself, came in 1758 when a reversal of battlefield fortunes occurred and the naval blockade prevented French goods from reaching Canada. Addicted to European products through the fur trade and white gift giving, French-aligned natives suffered. The tide of allegiance shifted to England.

Although the British found that friendly Indians were useful, in the final analysis they were not essential. To combat American conditions and the enemy's guerrilla methods, the British recruited white frontiersmen and organized them into ranger companies to perform duties traditionally done by natives. Regulars also made certain tactical adaptations. They formed light infantry companies composed of agile, lightly armed men who received training in irregular warfare tactics. Some units learned to deliver aimed fire rather than volleys, to maneuver by companies instead of battalions, and to march single file to lessen the impact of an ambush. These modifications, however, were not widespread, and the British army's success depended on standard European practices. The regulars' discipline and organized persistence counterbalanced the virtues of Indian-style warfare.

Relations between British regulars and colonial civilians were a reenactment of the Walker expedition performed on a continent-wide stage. Conflicts over recruitment, quarters, transportation, and provisions fueled mutual resentment. To fill understrength regiments and raise new ones, the British hoped to tap the colonial manpower reservoir. In 1755 and 1756 they met considerable success, enlisting some 7,500 colonists, but thereafter the number of recruits dwindled. One reason was that men had a choice: long-term service in the regulars with low pay and harsh discipline, or short-term service in a provincial unit with an enlistment bounty, higher pay, and lax discipline. Another reason was the often violent opposition to the unscrupulous methods British recruiters used. For example, they recruited heavily among indentured servants, a practice that colonists considered "an unconstitutional and arbitrary Invasion of our Rights and Properties" that cast suspicion on all recruiting. By 1757 mobs regularly harassed recruiters and "rescued" men whom they assumed had been illegally recruited. The inability to find men outraged professionals and forced Pitt to rely on full-strength regiments from the home islands.

Redcoats needed quarters, especially during winter, but America had few public buildings that could serve as barracks. The only option was to quarter them in private houses, but citizens argued that soldiers could not be quartered in a private home without the owner's consent. Civilians had the law on their side, but Loudoun insisted that "Whilst the War lasts, Necessity, will Justify exceeding" normal quartering procedures. He told the Albany city government "that if they did not give Quarters, I would take them" by force. Albany officials maintained that Loudoun "assumed a Power over us Very inconsistent with the Liberties of a free and Loyal People. . . ." Civilians and soldiers invariably reached an accommodation over quarters, but only at a high cost in mutual trust.

The British government also counted on colonial assemblies to provide adequate provisions and timely transportation, but the colonies proved stingy and dilatory—at least in the opinion of regular officers. Every British officer complained about the reluctance of assemblies to comply "with the just and equitable demands of their King and Country," but legislators acted at their own deliberate pace. They were so slow in fulfilling requests that the British frequently impressed or seized what they needed, which was an unjustified exercise of arbitrary power from the colonial perspective.

British officers thought they perceived sinister motives in the colonials, who seemed "bent upon our ruin, and destruction," working tirelessly "to disappoint every Plan of the Government." Professional soldiers simply misunderstood colonial institutions and political philosophies. England's appointment of a commander in chief for North America imposed centralized military control on a decentralized political system. Each colony considered itself sovereign and was anxious to maintain its freedom of action in military affairs. Allowing the Crown's representative, who was also a high-ranking officer in a suspect standing army, to direct the war effort would reduce every colony's independence. Furthermore, many colonists accepted radical Whig ideology, which preached a dichotomy between power and liberty. Every accretion of power reduced freedom's sphere. When the British army recruited fraudulently, quartered men illegally, impressed property, and tried to bully assemblies, colonists feared that growing military power threatened their liberty. Colonial legislatures believed they were fighting two wars of equal importance, one *against* France and one *for* liberty.

Several important themes emerged from the colonial wars. First, most Americans gained a high opinion of their martial abilities and a low opinion of British professionals. Colonists typically emphasized British defeats and insufficiently praised the triumphs of Amherst, Forbes, and Wolfe. Such attitudes were a tribute to the colonists' selective military memory and help explain colonial confidence in 1775. Second, the wars had a nationalizing impact. In 1763 each colony still jealously protected its sovereignty, yet during the wars against New France important experiments in cooperation had occurred. The Albany Plan, though rejected, was an evolutionary step leading to the First Continental Congress. During the colonial wars English colonists became *Americans*. Finally, a growing estrangement between England and the colonies emerged. Many Englishmen agreed with Loudoun that the colonies assumed "to themselves, what they call Rights and Privileges, Totally unknown in the Mother Country." Many colonists concurred with the Albany city council, which stated that "Upon the Whole we conceive that his Majesties Paternal Cares to Release us [from the threat of France] have in a Great Measure been Made use of to oppress us." The Peace of Paris, which should have pleased Englishmen everywhere, left a bitter heritage.

THREE

The American Revolution, 1763–1783

Britain's triumph in the Great War for Empire contained the seeds of the American Revolution. England emerged from the war with an expanded empire and a staggering national debt, much of it resulting from the struggle in North America. Britain wanted to administer its new empire with maximum efficiency, which in part meant enforcing the Navigation Acts, a series of laws designed to regulate colonial trade for the mother country's benefit. Americans had consistently violated laws through smuggling and bribery. Strict enforcement would help alleviate England's financial distress but would crimp the colonial economy.

The North American interior also concerned Britain. It had fought the war primarily to ensure colonial security; the interior had been wrested from France for that purpose. But even as the Canadian menace waned, it became apparent that the colonies were still not secure. During the war settlers and speculators continued to push westward, threatening to oust the Indians from their hunting grounds. In the spring of 1763 an Ottawa chief named Pontiac led a coalition of tribes against whites in the Old Northwest. Pontiac represented a new type of Indian leader who emerged from the colonial wars. By the 1740s some sachems had concluded that all Indians were a single people, united by their "color" or race, with a mutual interest in halting British-American expansion. These "nativists" attempted to overcome traditional Indian localism and ethnic rivalries and advocated unified action against the advancing whites. Although efforts to forge a pan-Indian movement persisted into the early nineteenth century, neither Pontiac nor his nativist successors could overcome Indian faction-alism or the influence of "accommodationist" leaders who believed that the whites were too strong to be resisted effectively.

Under Pontiac's direction, Indians attacked frontier posts from Penn-sylvania to Virginia, captured or forced the abandonment of almost a dozen forts, and besieged Fort Pitt and Detroit. However, neither siege was successful, and the Indians' campaign perceptibly slowed. In 1764 General Thomas Gage, Amherst's successor, launched an offensive that pacified many of the tribes that had supported Pontiac. As more and more of his followers submitted to the British, Pontiac's cause became hopeless, and in July 1765 he agreed to preliminary peace terms. A year later the Ottawa chief signed a final agreement, formally ending the war.

Pontiac's rebellion demonstrated the need for a British policy that would keep peace on the frontier. England responded by adopting three interrelated measures. It established the Proclamation Line of October 1763 that temporarily closed the area beyond the Appalachians to white settlement, thus removing Indian fears of illegal land purchases and encroachments. Britain also decided to garrison the west with regulars to enforce the Proclamation Line and regulate the fur trade equitably, thereby eliminating abuses that fueled Indian resentment. Finally, England began taxing the colonies to help pay for the army in America. From the British government's perspective, these actions represented a tidy package that would protect the colonists, prevent the outbreak of costly Indian wars, and help meet the expenses of administering the empire. And, a few offi-cials noted, if the colonists misbehaved, the army would be conveniently located to compel obedience to imperial rule.

Every element in England's postwar policy rankled the colonists. Efforts to enforce the Navigation Acts threatened the colonial desire for economic growth. With France's removal from the continent, land speculators, fur traders, and frontiersmen anticipated an unhindered westward surge. It seemed inexplicable that England should prevent them from exploiting the resources of the west. And why was a standing army needed *now*? Colonists had always defended themselves against Indians, and they could continue to do so. Some people suspected that the army was intended to coerce the colonies into obeying unpopular Parliamentary laws. As if to confirm the suspicion, in 1765 England passed two laws—the Stamp and Quartering Acts—that Americans considered illegal because they taxed the colonies. Colonists asserted that only their own legislatures could tax them, that Parliament had *no* right to levy *any* direct taxes on the colonies.

The imperial program sparked colonial resistance. In the west, Ameri-cans refused to conform to the Proclamation Line or obey the trade regu-lations. But on the seaboard resistance was more ominous, as colonists defiantly challenged Parliament's authority to impose taxes, especially the Stamp Act. An intercolonial Stamp Act Congress met in New York and issued protests. People adopted nonimportation agreements, uniting most Americans in an attempt to put economic pressure on England to repeal the act. Most important, colonists responded with violence. Groups calling themselves "Sons of Liberty" enforced the nonimportation agreements, forced stamp agents to resign, and mobilized mobs to ransack the homes of unpopular Crown officials. The Connecticut and New York Sons of Liberty even signed a treaty pledging mutual aid if British troops tried to enforce the Stamp Act. In the face of this opposition, Parliament repealed the act but passed a Declaratory Act proclaiming Parliament's right "to bind" the colonies "in all cases whatsoever."

The series of events that led the colonies from resistance to Parliamentary sovereignty in 1765 to outright rebellion in 1775 cannot be recapitulated here. But two points need to be made. First, the crisis represented a clash between a mature colonial society and a mother country anxious to assert parental authority. Britain had previously never exercised much direct control over the colonies. Prospering under this "salutary neglect," the colonies enjoyed de facto independence and developed a remarkable degree of self-reliance. Colonial aspirations thus collided with England's desire to enforce subordination and diminish colonial autonomy.

Second, the Revolution began in 1765, not 1775. The events of 1765–1775 marked the first phase in a colonial war of national liberation. Only a handful of colonists advocated outright independence in 1765, but they vigorously championed their cause and slowly gained adherents over the next decade. During this initial stage colonial leaders organized themselves politically while subverting the established government's authority through terrorism and propaganda. The Stamp Act Congress, followed by the two Continental Congresses, reflected the emergence of a national political organization. At the local level the Sons of Liberty evolved into a network of committees of correspondence and of safety. These extralegal bodies coordinated the opposition against Parliament, prevented the Revolutionary movement from degenerating into anarchy, and intimidated individuals who supported England. Radical leaders also organized riots against important symbols of British rule. Mob actions were not spontaneous but instead represented purposeful violence by what were, in essence, urban volunteer militia units. Supplementing the violence was a propaganda campaign portraying every English action in the darkest hues.

The violence and nonviolent protests had the cumulative effect of undermining confidence in the British government. Frightened Loyalists found the government unable to protect them, while other colonists were persuaded that the ministry and Parliament *were* despotic. Either way, Americans lost faith in England. Mistrust bred contempt, creating a political vacuum that was filled by radical political agencies. John Adams correctly observed that "the Revolution was in the minds and hearts of the people, and in the union of the colonies; both of which were substantially effected before hostilities commenced." By 1775 many colonists were convinced, as one town meeting stated, that the British government had "a design to take away our liberties and properties and enslave us forever." Rather than submit to what they perceived to be an iniquitous government, the colonies united through the Continental Congress to defend themselves against England's alleged schemes.

As resistance broadened, England's attitude toward the colonies hardened. In late 1774 King George III stated that the New England colonies, which were at the center of colonial turmoil, were in rebellion and that "blows must decide whether they are to be subject to this country or independent." Both sides were determined to fight rather than retreat over the issue of Parliament's authority. The stage was set for Lexington and Concord, which did not begin the Revolution, but only escalated the war to a higher level of violence.

The Strategic Balance

By the spring of 1775 colonial leaders and the British commander in chief, General Gage, were expecting a fight. In September 1774, Congress recommended that the colonies begin military preparations, and many of them stockpiled supplies and undertook militia training with a long-absent seriousness. Activity was particularly feverish in New England, where the British army was concentrated. After the Stamp Act crisis, the turbulence in the seaboard cities had replaced the frontier as the primary concern of the ministry, which had ordered Gage to redeploy most of the army eastward. Gage had a large garrison in Boston, where he fortified the city's approaches, trained his troops rigorously, and gathered intelligence from spies, including Dr. Benjamin Church, a trusted member of the Revolutionary inner circle. Church informed Gage of the buildup of military supplies in Concord. When Gage received secret instructions to restore royal rule in Massachusetts through force, Concord was the logical target.

On April 18, 1775, Gage dispatched Lieutenant Colonel Francis Smith to destroy the Concord supplies. In the early-morning hours of the 19th, as Smith's men tramped down the road, rebels alerted the countryside. Irritated by the slow advance and worried by the prospect of resistance, Smith sent Major John Pitcairn ahead with six light companies and asked Gage for reinforcements. Pitcairn arrived at Lexington as the rising sun revealed about seventy militiamen in martial array. No one knows who fired first, but in a brief confrontation eight Americans died and another ten were wounded. The British pushed on to Concord, where a skirmish with several hundred militiamen occurred, resulting in casualties on both sides.

The fighting at Lexington and Concord did not last five minutes, but as the British withdrew from Concord a real battle began. Responding in a massive popular uprising, thousands of irate militiamen hemmed in the redcoats and fired at them from concealed positions. By the time Smith reached Lexington, his men were panicked, and only the arrival of reinforcements saved them. The reinforced column fought its way back to Boston, but about 20 percent of the 1,500 regulars engaged were casualties. Worse yet, 20,000 New England militiamen soon besieged Gage. For the first time, the British had experienced the damage that an armed and angry populace employing irregular tactics could inflict on a conventional military organization.

It looked as if the colonies were embarked upon an unequal war. A population of two and a half million (20 percent of whom were slaves), without an army, navy, or adequate financial resources, confronted a nation of eight million with a professional army, large navy, and vast wealth. Yet many colonists were confident and determined. They believed in the "natural courage" of Americans and in God's divine protection. Congress admitted that colonial soldiers lacked experience and discipline but insisted that "facts have shown, that native Courage warmed with Patriotism is sufficient to counterbalance these Advantages." And a British captain wrote that Americans "are just now worked up to such a degree of enthusiasm and madness that they are easily persuaded the Lord is to assist them in whatever they undertake, and that they must be invincible." Colonists were determined because they struggled for high stakes, summed up by George Washington: "Remember, officers and soldiers, that you are freemen, fighting for the blessings of liberty; that slavery will be your portion and that of your posterity if you do not acquit yourselves like men." The Revolution was no European dynastic squabble, but a war involving an ideological question that affected the population far more than did the kingly quarrels of the age of limited warfare. Large numbers of colonists ardently believed freedom was *the* issue, not only for themselves but for generations yet unborn.

While Americans claimed natural courage, God, freedom, and posterity as invisible allies, Britain encountered difficulties that negated its advantages in men, ships, and money. England had underestimated the militia's military potential and rebel numerical strength. Officials, remembering the pathetic provincial soldiers of the last war and ignorant of the distinction between the wartime units and the actual militia, believed sustained resistance was impossible. Compounding this misunderstanding was England's belief that the rebels were a small minority. British hopes for Loyalist support were high, but Loyalist strength was an illusion: Tories represented less than 20 percent of all white Americans.

Britain also misunderstood the difficulties of conquering a localized, thinly populated society. Colonial decentralization meant the colonies had no strategic heart. To win the war, England had to occupy vast expanses of territory, a task beyond its military resources because of logistical problems and manpower shortages. The British never solved the difficulties involved in waging war across three thousand miles of ocean in a relatively primitive country. Part of the problem was England's cumbersome administrative machinery, staffed with incompetent patronage appointees, and the lack of coordination among departments. Uncertain communications across the Atlantic and over crude North American roads hindered every military operation. During the Great War for Empire, America had for the most part fed the British army, but now rations had to come primarily from the mother country. They often arrived moldy, sour, rancid, or maggoty; even worse, many ships fell victim to storms or hostile craft. No matter how many supplies came from England, the army still foraged in America for hay, firewood, and some fresh food. But foraging often became indiscriminate plundering, which alienated colonials and drove many of them into the rebel camp. The rebels also tried to deny the enemy access to supplies by conducting guerrilla operations against foraging parties.

The British populace at home was not united behind the war because some people doubted its wisdom and justness. One result of the antiwar sentiment was difficulty in recruiting troops, a difficulty aggravated by George III's reluctance to incur the huge expenses necessary to expand the army. To fill the ranks, England hired German soldiers, collectively known as Hessians, and sent almost 30,000 of them to America. But Hessians alone were insufficient, and England also enlisted slaves, mobilized Indians, and depended on Loyalist soldiers. England still suffered manpower shortages, and these expedients were also partially counterproductive. Hiring mercenaries, using slaves, inciting "savages," and fomenting a civil war within a civil war heightened colonial disaffection.

Perhaps England's fundamental error was its inability to implement an unambiguous strategy early in the war. Although most authorities believed the rebellion could be crushed by brute force, some questioned the expediency of ramming Parliamentary supremacy down the colonists' throats. Unable to form a consensus on this question, England wavered between coercion and conciliation, vacillating between a punitive war to impose peace and an attempt to negotiate a settlement through appeasement. Unclear about its objectives, Britain inspired neither fear nor affection in the colonies.

Finally, England had no William Pitt to rally the population and direct the war effort. The two men most responsible for conducting the war were Prime Minister Sir Frederick North and Lord George Germain, the secretary of state for the American colonies. Neither possessed a charismatic personality or an abundance of wisdom. As for the generals, no one would mistake any of them for another Frederick the Great or, for that matter, George Washington. A series of cautious and weak commanders plagued British strategy. The odds against the colonists were not as great as they appeared. Britain's difficulties in projecting military power into the colonies offset America's obvious deficiencies. The war began as a balance of military weakness, ensuring a long conflict despite optimistic expectations by both sides that the war would be short.

The "Dual Army"

The Revolution created a "dual army" tradition that combined a citizen-soldier reserve (the militia), which supplied large numbers of partially trained soldiers, with a small professional force that provided military expertise and staying power. As much as Americans mistrusted a standing army, Congress realized one was necessary and created the Continental Army. By establishing this national regular army, Congress implicitly accepted the ideology of English moderate Whigs, who had argued that a regular force under firm legislative control was not only consistent with constitutional freedoms but also essential to preserve those liberties. Throughout the war the Continental Army complemented rather than supplanted the state militias, and at practically every critical juncture these disparate forces acted in concert.

Even before Lexington and Concord, the colonial assemblies had revitalized the militia system by increasing the number of training days, stiffening punishment for missing musters, tightening exemption lists, stockpiling powder and shot, and, in some colonies, creating a distinction between militiamen and minutemen. The latter were generally younger men who received special training and took the field on short notice. Rebels also purified the militia by purging Tory officers, ensuring that only "the inflexible friends to the rights of the people" held commissions. The militia's renaissance had a profound impact. With every colony's military establishment under rebel control, British armies encountered an unfriendly reception wherever they went. Loyalists were immediately on the defensive and never gained the initiative, as rebel militias beat down counterrevolutionary uprisings. For example, Lord Dunmore, Virginia's royal governor, tried to mobilize Loyalists and appealed to runaway slaves, but in December 1775 the Virginia militia, reinforced by 200 Continentals, defeated Dunmore at the Battle of Great Bridge. Two months later a similar fate befell Josiah Martin, the royal governor of North Carolina, when the North Carolina militia defeated his Loyalist forces at the Battle of Moore's Creek Bridge. In both states the militia had extinguished Loyalist power and expelled royal authority. Greeting enemy forces with small-scale warfare and maintaining internal security were only two of the militia's functions. Militiamen patrolled against slave insurrections, fought Indians, repelled seaborne raiding parties, garrisoned forts, guarded prisoners of war, collected intelligence, rallied the war-weary, transported supplies, and battled British foragers.

One thing the militia usually could not do was stand *alone* against large numbers of enemy regulars. But in most battles militiamen did fight alongside Continental troops. The militia had a mixed battlefield record. Sometimes it behaved shamefully, sometimes valiantly. The militia's performance often depended on the commanding officer; one who understood its limitations against disciplined regulars could utilize militiamen with surprising effectiveness. A British general, while barely suppressing his distaste for such undisciplined irregulars, perhaps best assessed the militia's battlefield contribution. "I will not say much in praise of the militia of the Southern Colonies," Lord Cornwallis wrote, "but the list of British officers and soldiers killed and wounded by them . . . proves but too fatally they are not wholly contemptible."

Although many men shirked militia duty by paying commutation fees, hiring substitutes, or running away, a large percentage of adult males did some service because few localities escaped mobilizing their militias. Units formed quickly, executed their short-term tasks, and vanished. British commanders never understood how these militia forces proliferated. Steeped in the traditions of limited warfare, they did not perceive that the Revolutionary War was one in which military service was being democratized and nationalized. Military authority no longer resided in a sovereign, but in the people and their chosen representatives. War aims were not tangible and limited but abstract and not easily compromised—the colonies could not be half independent—and the politically alert population cared about the outcome.

Since the militia generally adhered to its parochial traditions, Congress realized it needed a national army that could be kept in the field and sent to fight beyond the boundaries of any particular colony. It was for this purpose that it organized the Continental Army, which initially consisted of the New England militiamen penning Gage's force inside Boston. In mid-June 1775, Congress adopted the besieging throng and then voted to raise ten companies of riflemen from Virginia, Maryland, and Pennsylvania to give the army a more "continental" flavor. Having formed an army, Congress selected George Washington to command it. Washington had been with Braddock and with Forbes's expedition to Fort Duquesne, and in between service with the regulars he had commanded the Virginia militia. As the crisis with England worsened, Washington played an active role in Virginia's evolution from resistance to revolution, and he attended both the First and Second Continental Congresses. He was the only delegate attending the deliberations in Philadelphia attired in a military uniform, perhaps symbolizing his readiness to fight for American rights. Washington was a reasonably experienced soldier, a firm advocate of American liberties, impressive in looks, and articulate without being flamboyant. Equally important, he was a Virginian whose appointment, like the rifle companies, gave the army a continental appearance.

"I declare with the utmost sincerity," Washington wrote the president of Congress, "I do not think myself equal to the Command I am honoured with." He probably meant it, since his frontier service had given him no opportunity to become acquainted with cavalry tactics, massed artillery, or the deployment of large forces. Yet Washington eventually embodied the Revolution, with the cause and the commander so intertwined in rebel eyes that they became synonymous.

During the war with France, Washington had developed an aversion to militiamen and an appreciation for British professionals. He had experienced nothing but problems with the Virginia militia. They never turned out in sufficient numbers, and those who did he considered insolent and prone to panic and desertion. His opinion did not change during the Revolution, and most Continental officers shared his conviction that "to place any dependence upon Militia, is, assuredly, resting upon a broken staff." Paradoxically, Washington repeatedly depended on the militia to buttress the Continental Army during innumerable crises. If the militia dismayed Washington, British regulars impressed him, and he strove to mold the Continental Army into a mirror image of Britain's army. He insisted it should be "a respectable Army," not only well organized and disciplined but also officered by "Gentlemen, and Men of Character." He believed the prospect of such an army endangering civilian supremacy was remote; the slight risk was necessary because the consequence of fighting without a regular army was "certain, and inevitable Ruin."

Although Washington intended to fight the British as they had fought the French, employing a regular army commanded by long-serving officers and using citizen-soldiers only as auxiliaries, he never quite succeeded. The reasons were a dearth of competent officers and too few Continentals. America had no reservoir of men experienced in conventional warfare, and it took long years and hard trials to develop effective battlefield leadership. The consistent shortage of Continental soldiers forced militiamen to fill gaps in the fighting line. Ironically, the militia's existence was one reason regulars were so few. Given the choice between a militia unit or a Continental regiment, most men chose the former. Militia duty carried no stigma, being patriotic, necessary, and often dangerous. But brief militia service entailed little of the long-term misery Continentals experienced. The high wages paid laborers and the possibility of profit from privateering also retarded recruiting. Despite land and monetary bounties, despite the resort to state militia drafts to fill manpower quotas set by Congress, and despite varied enlistment terms—from one year to the duration of the war—the army never approached its authorized strength. For example, in the fall of 1775 Congress voted for an army of 28 regiments (20,000 men), and a year later it increased this to 88 regiments (75,000 men), but the army's *actual* size was invariably less than half, and frequently less than a third, of its paper strength.

In terms of social composition the rank and file approximated that of the British army. The ranks contained some farmers, tradesmen, and mechanics, but they included many more recent immigrants, enemy deserters and prisoners of war, Loyalists and criminals (both of whom sometimes had the option of joining or hanging), vagrants, indentured servants, apprentices, free black men, and slaves. The soldiers thus overwhelmingly came from the bottom strata of society. Although the social origins of many Continentals resembled those of British regulars, the similarity fades when one asks *why* men served. Obviously, some Continentals, like their British counterparts, had little choice. But most American recruits served willingly. The methods of avoiding service were so numerous that few people became regulars against their will. Poor and propertyless men may have found substitute payments, bounties, and army pay attractive, but less dangerous ways to make money and acquire land abounded in American society. Financial benefits simply reinforced the primary motivation to serve, which was probably ideological. Appeals to freedom and liberty—and the vision of a better future these abstractions conveyed—could strike an especially intense chord in men of humble means and origins. One soldiers' song emphasized this ideological motivation:

No Foreign Slaves shall give us Laws, No Brittish Tyrant Reign
Tis Independence made us Free and Freedom We'll Maintain.

Proof of the Continentals' willing service was the way so many of them endured continuous hardships with a fortitude that made foreign observers marvel. Baron von Closen of the French army exclaimed: "I admire the American troops tremendously! It is incredible that soldiers composed of men of every age, even children of fifteen, of whites and blacks, almost naked, unpaid, and rather poorly fed, can march so well and withstand fire so steadfastly." And a Hessian captain asked in wonderment:

With what soldiers in the world could one do what was done by these men, who go about nearly naked and in the greatest privation? Deny the best-disciplined soldiers of Europe what is due them and they will run away in droves, and the general will soon be alone. But from this one can perceive what an enthusiasm—which these poor fellows call "Liberty"—can do!

Money could not buy, and discipline could not instill, the Continentals' type of loyalty; an ideological motivation that promised a better life for themselves and their posterity held them in the ranks. Of course, not every Continental could tolerate prolonged deprivation, and many deserted. But the desertion rate declined as the war progressed, and the army became the heart of resistance.

Shouldering arms freely and believing freedom was the issue, Continentals never became regulars in the European sense. They became good soldiers, but they remained citizens who refused to surrender their individuality. They asserted their personal independence by wearing jaunty hats and long hair despite (or perhaps to spite) their officers' insistence upon conformity in dress and appearance. Furthermore, they were only temporary regulars. Unlike European professionals, they understood the war's goals and would fight until they were achieved, but then they intended to return to civilian life.

Congress was mindful of the irony in creating a standing army. Americans had consistently inveighed against regulars, their threat to liberty, and the taxes necessary to maintain them. Now Congress, having established its own regular army, shouldered two onerous burdens. First, as Samuel Adams said, since a "Standing Army, however necessary it may be at some times, is always dangerous to the Liberties of the People," it had to "be watched with a jealous Eye." Congress was careful to keep the army subservient to civil authority. It enjoined Washington to "observe and follow" all orders from Congress and to report regularly to the legislature, and appointed all subordinate generals, who would look to Congress, not Washington, for preferment. It also determined the war's objectives, controlled the army's size and composition, provided money and resources for its maintenance, established disciplinary regulations, and conducted foreign affairs. At times Congress even directly guided strategy.

Considering the hypersensitive fear of military ascendancy, Congress's selection of Washington was fortuitous. He repeatedly stated his belief in civil supremacy, remaining deferential to Congress even when its inefficiency threatened the army's survival. Having served in the Virginia assembly and in Congress, he understood the often maddeningly slow political process in representative governments and the nation's inadequate administrative machinery for conducting a large-scale war. By reporting to Congress on all matters great or trivial, by religiously adhering to congressional dictates, and through his immense patience in the face of nearly unbearable frustrations, Washington alleviated concern that he would capitalize on his growing military reputation to become a dictator. Although revolutions have frequently given birth to permanent presidents, kings, and emperors, Washington had no desire to become an American Cromwell. Like the men he commanded, he never forgot that he was a citizen first and only second a soldier.

The second congressional burden was furnishing logistical support for the army. The fundamental difficulties were insufficient financial resources, inadequate administrative organization, and primitive transportation facilities. War is never cheap: As General Jedediah Huntington observed, "Money is the Sinews of war." But the colonists, having rebelled against English taxation, refused to give Congress the power to tax. To finance the war, Congress resorted to the printing press, emitting $200 million worth of paper money by the fall of 1779, when it ceased printing money. Since Congress had no source of revenue from taxation, the value of Continental bills depreciated rapidly, reducing their purchasing power. With the states also issuing paper money and many counterfeit bills in circulation, the nation wallowed in worthless paper. As the currency depreciated, inflation soared, further fueled by war-induced dislocations in agriculture and commerce and by shortages of manufactured goods. Only foreign loans, primarily from France, allowed Congress to muddle through.

To administer the army, Congress initially relied on ad hoc committees to deal with problems as they arose. Not until June 1776 did it form a five-member Board of War and Ordnance to give continuity to army administration. But board members devoted only a fraction of their time to army matters, since congressmen serving on the board usually sat on several other committees and also attended to their regular congressional duties. Congressional membership also changed rapidly, and few delegates remained long enough to comprehend the army's needs. Thus in October 1777 Congress reconstituted the board to include military officers. Congress also created rudimentary staff departments such as a commissary general of stores and provisions and a quartermaster general. Neither the board nor the supply departments were efficient. They never attained institutional stability because of frequent reorganizations and changes in both civilian and military personnel as Congress strove to find a combination that would produce results. Finding good men was not easy. The United States had few men experienced in large-scale logistical management. Like battlefield officers, staff officers had to be nurtured, and they made mistakes as they matured. Many appointees proved to be incompetent or corrupt; others were simply overwhelmed by the magnitude of

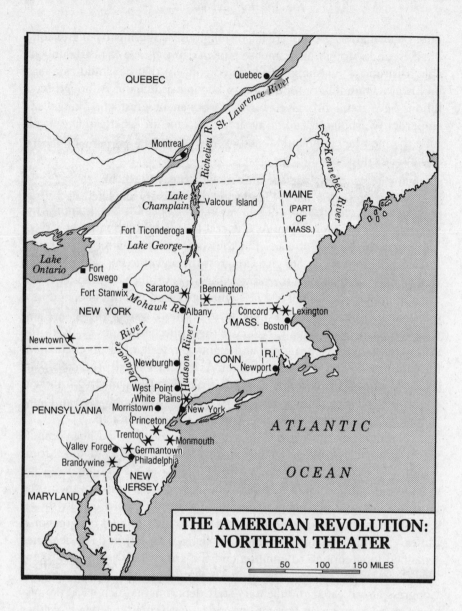

QUEBEC

Quebec ●

St. Lawrence River

Richelieu R.

Montreal ●

Kennebec River

Lake Champlain — Valcour Island

MAINE
(PART
OF
MASS.)

Fort Ticonderoga ■

Lake George

Lake Ontario

■ Fort Oswego

Fort Stanwix ■

Saratoga ✶ ✶ Bennington

Mohawk R.

NEW YORK

●Albany Concord ✶✶ Lexington

MASS. Boston ●

Delaware River

Newtown ✶

Hudson River

Newburgh ● CONN. R.I.

Newport ●

West Point ●

White Plains ✶

PENNSYLVANIA Morristown ●

New York

Princeton ✶

Trenton ✶ ✶Monmouth

ATLANTIC

Valley Forge ● ✶Germantown
Brandywine ✶ ●Philadelphia

OCEAN

NEW
JERSEY

MARYLAND

DEL.

THE AMERICAN REVOLUTION:
NORTHERN THEATER

0   50   100   150 MILES

their responsibilities contrasted with the meager resources at their disposal. Persuading talented officers to forsake field command for a desk job was especially difficult. Soldiers knew that their way to glory and historical immortality lay with the sword, not the pen. Another problem was the feeble coordination among the staff departments, which often competed with each other—and with state logistical agencies and civilians—for scarce goods, driving prices up. Worst of all, the perpetual financial crisis made supplying the army virtually impossible. Supply officers had too many items to buy and too little money to pay for them.

By the winter of 1779–1780, with the treasury depleted and army storehouses empty, Congress abdicated much of its responsibility for the army to the states. It asked each state to pay its own troops in the Continental Army and adopted a system of requisitioning the states for "specific supplies." Under this plan Congress apportioned quotas of food, clothing, fodder, and other necessities among the states according to their special resources. Unfortunately for the starving Continentals, the situation did not improve. States did not have adequate administrative machinery and were reluctant to commandeer supplies from their citizens. Almost every state argued that its quota was unfairly high and refused to cooperate until Congress made adjustments—which never quite met all the objections. The requisition system's failure compelled Congress to reassert its own authority, and in 1781 it centralized the management of financial and military matters in executive departments. But by then active hostilities were drawing to a close.

Even if Congress had enjoyed unlimited funds and an efficient logistical organization, the army's supply situation would have remained precarious because of the nation's underdeveloped transportation network. The British blockade hampered coastal trade, forcing reliance on land transportation. But roads were few and all but impassible during inclement weather, wagons were in short supply, and horses and oxen were scarce. At times the army nearly perished in the midst of plenty when supplies could not be moved from wharves and warehouses to the famished troops. Unpaid, unfed, unclothed, and unsheltered, many Continentals became stoical, viewing themselves as martyrs to the "glorious cause." As one colonel wrote, "We have this consolation, however, that it cannot be said that we are bought or bribed into the service."

The militia and the Continental Army were two sides of a double-edged sword. Neither blade was keenly honed, and even in combination they usually did not make a lethal weapon. Washington's task was never easy, but without either army it would have been impossible.

The Militia's War, 1775–1776

The majority of men who took up arms during the "popular uprising" phase of the war in 1775–1776 were not fighting for independence, but for their rights as Englishmen within the empire. Although a growing number believed independence inevitable, most maintained allegiance to George III, who, they assumed, was being misled by corrupt ministers conspiring to enslave the colonies. Congress insisted that the colonies were only protecting themselves from these conspirators, that reconciliation would occur as soon as the King restrained his advisers.

Although colonists issued proclamations portraying the English as aggressors and themselves as aggrieved defenders, rebel forces quickly assumed the offensive. On May 10, 1775, frontiersmen under Ethan Allen and Benedict Arnold overwhelmed the British garrison at Ticonderoga, and two days later another rebel force captured Crown Point. Meanwhile, the New Englanders around Boston were organized into a makeshift army, with the men enlisted until the end of the year. British General Gage considered their entrenched positions strong and pleaded for more men. Instead of reinforcements, the government sent Major Generals William Howe, Henry Clinton, and John Burgoyne to act as advisers. They demanded that Gage take the offensive. In mid-June, when colonists ordered to entrench on Bunker Hill mistakenly dug in on Breed's Hill, he consented to let Howe oust them. When Howe's effort to outflank the colonial position failed, he believed that he had no choice but to make a frontal assault. Three times the redcoats advanced, and twice the colonists hurled them off the hill. On the third try, with the colonists weary and short of ammunition, the British swarmed over the parapet and the Americans fled.

British success at the misnamed Battle of Bunker Hill was costly; more than 1,000 of the 2,500 regulars engaged were casualties. If the immediate price of victory was exorbitant, even more disturbing for British prospects was the fighting spirit Americans displayed. Gage recognized that opinions formed during the French and Indian War were wrong, and he advised the ministry to "proceed in earnest or give the business up." The government, realizing that it faced a genuine war requiring a regular campaign, replaced Gage with Howe and began to plan for 1776.

When Washington took command of the Continental Army on July 2, he was eager to pursue an aggressive strategy. But he could do little immediately. A severe shortage of weapons and powder prevented him from attacking the British army, and his own army appalled him. The New Englanders struck him as "exceedingly dirty and nasty people" characterized by "an unaccountable kind of stupidity" and a lack of discipline. Knowing the eyes of the continent were upon him and expecting some momentous event, Washington found the inactivity around Boston galling, so in late summer 1775 he ordered Arnold to advance through the Maine wilderness to capture Quebec. Unknown to Washington, Congress had meanwhile ordered General Philip Schuyler to attack Montreal. Americans hoped the invasion would incite a Canadian revolt against Britain and convert the region into the fourteenth colony. Washington also struggled to discipline the army, but before he could achieve much success, that army almost disappeared. When enlistments expired at year's end, most men refused to reenlist. Washington had to discharge one army and recruit another while the enemy was only a musket shot away. He did it by calling on militiamen to fill the gaps until new Continental recruits arrived.

In November 1775 the novice commander sent Henry Knox, a self-taught soldier, to Ticonderoga to fetch the artillery captured there. Knox dragged the ordnance across three hundred miles of ice and snow, arriving back at Boston in January 1776, and Washington shrewdly placed it behind hastily constructed entrenchments atop Dorchester Heights outside Boston. American artillery now dominated the British position, and Howe, unwilling to fight another Bunker Hill to dislodge the guns, had to evacuate the city. On March 17, 1776, the enemy army sailed for Halifax, leaving no British force anywhere on American soil.

Grim news from Canada offset the good news from Boston. Schuyler had relinquished command to General Richard Montgomery, who had occupied Montreal in mid-November. Arnold's men, reduced to walking skeletons by their arduous trek, reached the St. Lawrence simultaneously, and Montgomery hastened downriver to unite forces. The commanders audaciously stormed Quebec in late December during a raging blizzard, but when Montgomery fell dead and Arnold was wounded, the attack fizzled. Arnold doggedly directed a siege from his hospital cot, but when British reinforcements arrived in May, the demoralized Americans retreated in disorder to Ticonderoga.

Even as the invasion force retreated, sentiment for independence advanced. On balance, the first year of fighting went to the Americans. The British retreat from Concord, the capture of Ticonderoga and Crown Point, the militia successes at Great Bridge and Moore's Creek Bridge, and the evacuation of Boston all augured well for American success. But although doing tolerably well on their own, Americans believed they needed assistance to win. However, neither France nor Spain was likely to aid them openly unless independence, rather than reconciliation, was the American goal. English actions also alienated Americans. Both King and Parliament rejected conciliatory appeals for redress of grievances and instead showed a determination to conquer the colonies. Employing mercenaries, instigating Indians, and appealing to slaves to join royal armies angered men who previously favored reconciliation, as did the senseless destruction of Falmouth, Maine, in October 1775, and Norfolk, Virginia, four months later.

When Thomas Paine's *Common Sense* excoriated monarchy in principle and George III in person and declared that "the weeping voice of nature cries, *'Tis time to part,*" it found a receptive audience. Jefferson's famous document severed the last strand of colonial allegiance. Americans had already rejected Parliamentary sovereignty, and now the Declaration renounced fealty to the King. Americans were aware, as John Adams said, "of the toil and blood and treasure" entailed in maintaining independence. "Yet," Adams continued, "through all the gloom I can see the rays of ravishing light and glory."

From Disaster to Victory, 1776–1781

By July 1776 the war's "uprising" phase had ended and the last stage of the war of liberation had begun. In this phase rebels fielded their own regular army, which represented a new government claiming sovereign status. Although conventional operations never fully replaced guerrilla activity, the roles of opposing regular forces became increasingly important. The conventional war consisted of a northern period that climaxed at Saratoga in 1777 and a southern period that culminated at Yorktown in 1781.

Both the Continental Army and America's very claim to sovereignty received a severe test in 1776 when the ministry made its largest effort of the war, hurling 32,000 troops and almost half the Royal Navy against New York City. Howe commanded the land forces; his brother, Richard, Lord Howe, commanded the naval component. Down from Canada came Sir Guy Carleton with 13,500 men, following the Richelieu River–Lake Champlain route. England aimed these formidable forces against the Hudson River for strategic reasons. New York was a superb harbor from which the navy could conduct operations. Control of the Hudson would link British forces in Canada and those in the colonies and split America's resources and population by isolating New England. The middle colonies reportedly teemed with Loyalists, who would provide manpower and logistical support.

Washington brought the army from Boston to defend New York, splitting his forces between Manhattan Island and Long Island. To the latter's defense he committed about half his 20,000 fit soldiers (mostly raw Continentals and even rawer militia), under the command of General Israel Putnam. The Americans entrenched on Brooklyn Heights, hoping Howe would attempt a frontal assault, but Putnam also deployed about 4,000 men in forward positions. On August 27 the British general, who had landed more than 20,000 British and Hessian troops on Long Island, moved around the left flank of the advanced units and routed them. But Howe failed to smash the rebels by assailing Brooklyn Heights and instead began a formal siege of the American position. His caution allowed the Americans to escape to Manhattan, uniting the two wings of Washington's army.

The American situation was still desperate. Thousands of dejected militiamen deserted, and the army's position in New York City could be outflanked by a British amphibious landing anywhere farther north on Manhattan. On September 15 the enemy landed at Kip's Bay, threatening to trap the American army. But Howe moved across the island lethargically, and Washington escaped. The Americans took up a prepared defensive position at Harlem Heights near the northern tip of Manhattan Island, leaving New York City to the British, who made it their headquarters for the remainder of the war. Howe sent a probing party against Washington's defenses, but in the Battle of Harlem Heights that followed the Americans repulsed the enemy and the campaign settled into another prolonged lull.

Washington's new position was no safer than Brooklyn or New York. As long as the British could ferry men up the Hudson or East Rivers, they could outflank the Americans. A month after Kip's Bay, Howe did just that with disembarkations at Throg's Neck and then Pell's Point. Had the British made a rapid thrust inland, they could have cut off Washington's retreat from Manhattan Island. But Howe again acted with caution, allowing the Americans to escape and assume another strong defensive position at White Plains, where Washington again hoped Howe would make a frontal attack. At the Battle of White Plains, Howe refused to accept the bait and instead executed a flanking movement, forcing the Americans to retreat and presenting the British with still another opportunity to annihilate Washington. But Howe again dallied, and Washington withdrew five miles to North Plains.

Throughout the entire New York campaign, Howe never utilized his maneuverability—which command of the waterways in the area gave him—to trap and destroy the Continental Army. He has been criticized for his failure to do so, but he faced at least two constraints. Howe fought according to the precepts of eighteenth-century warfare, which emphasized avoiding battles and deemphasized ruthless exploitation of success. Furthermore, as members of a peace commission that accompanied the military forces, the Howe brothers had a dual role as soldiers and diplomats. Sympathetic to America, they hoped to end the rebellion with a minimum of bloodshed by a judicious combination of the sword and the olive branch. Their peacemaking faltered because the United States had declared independence, which the Howes could not concede. Their warmaking failed because they allowed Washington to escape when he should have been crushed.

The British had nevertheless jostled Washington's army from Manhattan. As the Americans withdrew northward, Washington left garrisons at Forts Washington and Lee, on opposite banks of the Hudson. Rather than pursue Washington to North Plains, Howe suddenly turned southward, captured Fort Washington and its garrison, and forced the evacuation of Fort Lee. Howe then dispatched Clinton to capture Newport, Rhode Island, while the remainder of his army fanned out into New Jersey. Washington fled across the Delaware River, trying to stay between the advancing enemy and the rebel capital at Philadelphia.

With Washington's army numbering fewer than 3,000 men, the Revolution seemed about to expire. However, one bit of success pierced the gloom: The British advance from the north had failed. Arnold, recovered from his wound sustained at Quebec, built a flotilla of small ships on Lake Champlain, and Carleton paused to construct his own fleet. At the Battle of Valcour Island, Arnold's outgunned fleet fought a stout delaying action that unnerved Carleton, who retired northward. Washington saw other possibilities for successful operations. Howe's army was scattered throughout New Jersey in winter quarters. Perhaps one or more of these encampments could be surprised. Washington knew it would be a daring enterprise, but something had to be attempted "or we must give up the cause." With an unorthodoxy born of desperation, he began a winter campaign. On Christmas night his men crossed the Delaware and assaulted the Hessian outpost at Trenton, capturing or killing almost 1,000 men. He retreated back behind the Delaware, called up militia reinforcements, recrossed the river, and occupied Trenton. When Cornwallis approached with 6,000 troops, Washington sidestepped them and attacked Princeton, inflicting another 400 casualties. The Americans then took refuge near Morristown. Trenton and Princeton revived the Revolutionary cause, and Howe, twice stung, withdrew his garrisons from almost all New Jersey. The 1776 campaign ended with the Continental Army small but intact and with the British in control of only New York City and Newport, which were minimal gains for England's maximum effort.

The British had learned a sobering lesson. Washington was a clever commander whose army could fight well, even though the men were so ill-shod that they left bloody footprints in the snow. Henceforth the American commander would be an even more formidable adversary, for Washington had gained great insights from the 1776 campaign. He knew he was fortunate to have survived his eagerness to fight around New York. And he realized that the Revolution would continue as long as the Continental Army, the backbone of the Revolution, existed. Since his army was inferior to the enemy's, it should not be risked except in an emergency. No city, except perhaps Philadelphia, could warrant hazarding the army because, said Washington, "it is our arms, not defenceless towns, they have to sub-due." After 1776 Washington assumed the strategic defensive and became determined to win the war by not losing the Continental Army in bat-tle, fighting only when conditions were extraordinarily advantageous. He would frustrate the British by raids, continual skirmishing, and removing supplies from their vicinity, always staying just beyond the enemy's poten-tially lethal grasp. This strategy entailed risks. Americans might interpret it as cowardice or weakness, and since defensive war meant protracted war, they might lose heart. But Washington believed he could be active enough to prevent excessive war-weariness. Prolonged resistance would also fuel opposition to the conflict in England, as well as strengthen America's hand in European diplomacy.

England made its second greatest effort in 1777, but the campaign demonstrated the government's inability to provide coherent strategic guidance. When operations began, the men who played major roles in the planning—Germain, Howe, and Burgoyne—were unsure of each other's precise orders and intentions, resulting in two uncoordinated expeditions. Burgoyne followed the Champlain route southward while a secondary force under Lieutenant Colonel Barry St. Leger moved eastward along the Mohawk River. These forces were to unite on the Hudson and capture Albany, where, Burgoyne assumed, they would cooperate with Howe. But Howe left a garrison in New York and took 13,000 troops to capture Phil-adelphia. Instead of marching overland, he went by sea, which ensured that he and Burgoyne would be incapable of mutual assistance. The move-ment baffled Washington, who mistakenly believed British plans would be logical. Britain's flawed strategy allowed Washington to plan wisely. He accurately estimated Burgoyne's strength and calculated that the Continen-tals in upstate New York, reinforced by militia, would stop him. He also guessed Howe's destination and wheeled his army toward Philadelphia.

For political and psychological reasons Washington had to defend the capital. He took up a position behind Brandywine Creek, but Howe out-flanked him and defeated, but once again did not destroy, the army. Howe garrisoned Philadelphia, but he quartered part of his army at nearby Ger-mantown and used another detachment to reconnoiter Forts Mercer and Mifflin on the Delaware, which had to be cleared so the army could be supplied. Noting the dispersed deployments, Washington attacked Ger-mantown. His army again fought hard but lost, and by mid-November Howe had also captured the Delaware River forts. Washington's twin defeats and the capital's loss were troublesome but not disheartening. The army had performed well and rapidly replaced its losses, and word from the north was joyous.

Burgoyne had started his campaign successfully by capturing Ticonderoga. From there he inched forward, burdened by an enormous artillery and baggage train. The troops under Philip Schuyler, commander of the American forces in upstate New York, hampered the advance by felling trees into a tangled labyrinth and hastening crops and cattle out of Burgoyne's reach. In mid-August, Burgoyne sent a detachment to Bennington, Vermont, to raid a rebel supply depot. Angered by atrocities committed by Burgoyne's Indian allies and elated that Horatio Gates had replaced the hated Schuyler, militiamen annihilated the column. At almost the same time St. Leger turned back after an unsuccessful siege of Fort Stanwix. The arrival of Continental reinforcements, especially a corps of riflemen, made Burgoyne's situation worse. The riflemen drove his scouts inside their own lines, leaving the British blind in a swelling sea of militiamen. "Wherever the King's forces point," moaned Burgoyne, "militia, to the amount of three or four thousand assemble in twenty-four hours." Reinforced by the militia, Gates's regulars fortified a position on Bemis Heights, on the west bank of the Hudson, barring the route south. At the Battles of Freeman's Farm and Bemis Heights the English failed to penetrate this barrier and Burgoyne retreated to Saratoga, where militiamen and Continentals hovered about his dying army like vultures. On October 17 he surrendered.

After two mighty exertions England was no closer to victory than it had been at Lexington and Concord, and support for the war plummeted. British forces held enclaves at New York, Newport, and Philadelphia, but the Continental Army and rebel militias controlled the countryside. As the rival armies entered winter quarters, their mutual weakness remained in equilibrium.

The winter at Valley Forge was one of discontent and privation. Rumors about a plot to replace Washington with Gates, although without foundation, kept the commander in ill humor. The troops' plight did not improve his disposition. Without adequate shelter, food, or clothing, they huddled around their campfires exercising a soldier's inalienable right to complain. In particular the forlorn men cursed Congress, which they blamed for their distress. In truth, Congress was doing the best it could. The soldiers' condition was caused by soaring inflation, currency depreciation, the scarcity of goods, primitive transportation, and a rudimentary administrative organization. These were beyond the control of Congress, which was a weak central government that could neither tax nor enforce its requests to the states for resources.

But Valley Forge was not entirely bleak, and the army emerged a better fighting force and with high morale. Friedrich Wilhelm von Steuben, a former captain in the Prussian army, introduced a training system emphasizing simplicity and standardization in drill and musketry, and the men, who had experienced enough confusion under the old system, responded readily. In February, Nathanael Greene, one of Washington's best subordinates, became quartermaster general and miraculously improved the logistical system. The soldiers, tempered in the fires of adversity, developed a common pride in their military proficiency and ability to survive.

Best of all, in February 1778, France, convinced by Saratoga that America could win the war, signed a treaty of alliance. France had been providing covert aid, but America could now anticipate far greater assistance. In 1779 Spain also declared war on England, and in 1780 so did the Dutch. Thus a colonial rebellion had expanded into a world war, a development that was essential to the American cause. After 1778 England's European enemies diverted British resources from North America, disrupted British operations there, and provided loans and equipment that helped sustain the rebels during some of the war's darkest periods. Equally important, a French army and fleet eventually deployed in North America, providing direct support to Washington's army. After the French alliance the scales of weakness became unbalanced in America's favor, although it would be three years before the tilt brought conclusive results.

After 1778 England considered America a secondary theater and consequently reevaluated its strategy there, resulting in a shift in strategic focus to the south. It would be necessary to coordinate operations on the mainland and in the Caribbean, where the French threat was acute. Some officials believed southerners would not be as intransigent as New Englanders because "their numerous slaves in the bowells of their country, and the Indians at their backs will always keep them quiet." But the most compelling factor was the belief in widespread Loyalism in the region. The ministry pinned its hopes on the existence of southern Loyalists, who would have to carry the burden of the fighting, since Parliament refused to send many reinforcements.

As a prelude to southern operations Clinton, who replaced Howe as commander in chief, abandoned Philadelphia and consolidated his forces at New York. As he marched north with 10,000 men, the New Jersey militia mobilized to resist the advance, so that, as a Hessian officer succinctly phrased it, "Each step cost human blood." Washington also attacked the rear of the extended British column near Monmouth Courthouse. He entrusted the initial assault to General Charles Lee, a retired British major who had settled in America and adopted the rebel cause, but Lee's half-hearted assault soon fell back in disorder. Riding to the sound of the guns, Washington rallied the men, and in weather so hot that soldiers died from heatstroke, the armies exchanged volleys and bayonet charges in European fashion. The Continentals, displaying the benefits of von Steuben's training, more than matched the British for five hours until darkness ended the battle. Washington resolved to renew the assault in the morning, but

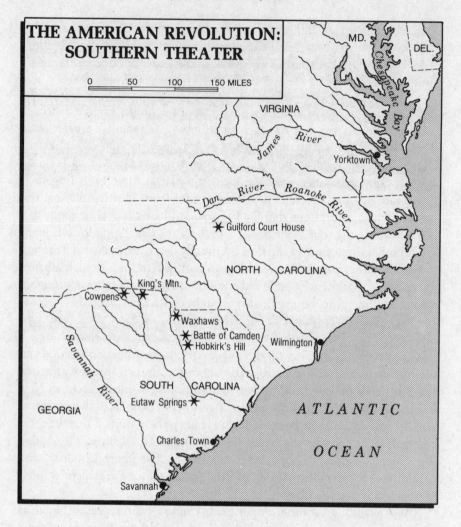

THE AMERICAN REVOLUTION: SOUTHERN THEATER

0   50   100   150 MILES

MD.

DEL.

VIRGINIA

James River

Yorktown

Dan River   *Roanoke River*

★ Guilford Court House

NORTH CAROLINA

King's Mtn. ★

Cowpens ★

★ Waxhaws
★ Battle of Camden
★ Hobkirk's Hill

Wilmington

SOUTH CAROLINA

Eutaw Springs ★

GEORGIA

Savannah River

Charles Town

ATLANTIC

OCEAN

Savannah

Clinton escaped during the night. Monmouth Courthouse was the last major battle in the north. For the next three years the British remained in New York City and Washington's army kept watch on them from an arc of defensive positions in the Hudson Highlands above the city. The armies skirmished and raided constantly, but they engaged in no battles. At least Washington had the satisfaction of knowing that after two years of maneuvers and battles in the north, "both Armies are brought back to the very point they set out from."

England's southern strategy began in November 1778 when Clinton embarked 3,500 men under Lieutenant Colonel Archibald Campbell to attack Savannah, which was easily captured. A full year elapsed before

Clinton followed up the initial success by investing Charleston from its landward side. In May 1780 the city surrendered, including the entire American army in the south. Two weeks later Lieutenant Colonel Banastre Tarleton, commanding the Loyalist British Legion, defeated South Carolina's last organized rebel force at the Waxhaws, killing those soldiers who surrendered. The British quickly established posts throughout the state. In June Clinton departed, leaving Cornwallis to consolidate British gains by protecting and encouraging Loyalists. Hundreds of men renewed their allegiance to the Crown, and Major Patrick Ferguson organized a potent Loyalist militia force. Rebel resistance in South Carolina and Georgia had apparently collapsed.

The Charleston and Waxhaws disasters capped a very bad winter and spring for the Americans. The army, which had its 1779–1780 winter quarters at Morristown, had endured a more miserable experience than it had at Valley Forge, since the weather was colder with more snow, and most of the causes of privation at Valley Forge had grown worse. On three occasions between January and June, Continental units mutinied. The men were incapable of suffering further misery and believed that the populace had betrayed the foremost defenders of the Revolution by failing to support them. The wonder is that no mutinies occurred sooner. Because the soldiers wanted to continue to serve the Revolutionary cause and mutinied only as a means of self-preservation, officers quickly quelled the outbreaks. But the mutinies were an ominous sign that the Revolution had reached its lowest point since Washington's flight across New Jersey in 1776.

The rebel situation deteriorated further when Congress, against Washington's wishes, appointed Gates to command a new southern army formed around 1,400 Continentals, reinforced by militiamen. In August Gates marched into South Carolina, met Cornwallis's advancing army at Camden, and deployed his regulars on his right wing while entrusting his left to militiamen alone. When Cornwallis attacked, the militiamen threw down their weapons and fled. The outnumbered Continentals fought valiantly but were overwhelmed. In just three months, two American armies had disappeared.

Compounding the agony was the treason of Benedict Arnold, who conspired to sell the plans of West Point—the crucial fortress in Washington's Hudson Highlands defense system—to the British. While some Americans believed the conspiracy's failure afforded, as Greene said, "the most convincing proofs that the liberties of America are the object of divine protection," others wondered whether the cause would survive. If Arnold, who served so nobly at Quebec, at Valcour Island, and during the Saratoga campaign, had lost all sense of honor and patriotism, how many others might follow his treasonous path?

Despite Morristown, the southern calamities, and Arnold's defection, three factors furthered the American cause in 1780. First, in July a 5,000-man French expeditionary force commanded by the Comte de Rochambeau and accompanied by a small fleet arrived at Newport, which the British had evacuated. Second, the Revolutionary spirit revived in the south. British troops and Loyalists plundered and raped, and they angered the neutral Scotch-Irish by persecuting the Presbyterian Church. The British decreed that anyone who failed to take an oath of allegiance would be considered in rebellion. Men who had adopted a passive stance had to choose collaboration or resistance, and many chose the latter. The dying embers of the Revolution ignited in guerrilla warfare under men like Thomas Sumter, Francis Marion, and Andrew Pickens. Convincing proof of resurgent resistance came at King's Mountain, where five backcountry partisan bands coalesced against Ferguson's Loyalist militia and annihilated it. Finally, bowing to Washington's request, Congress appointed Greene to replace Gates. Greene found the difficulties of his command "infinitely exceed what I apprehended." His minuscule army was in wretched condition, and the bonds of society had disintegrated as rebels and Tories committed "dreadful, wanton Mischiefs, Murders, and Violences of every kind, unheard of before." But Greene skillfully coordinated rebel maraudings with the activities of his army, which slowly grew larger and stronger. Greene was especially heartened by the arrival of Daniel Morgan, who had commanded the rifle corps that had fought so well against Burgoyne.

Greene was an unorthodox strategist who took grave risks that yielded great dividends. He assumed command in December 1780 and divided his outnumbered army between himself and Morgan, inviting defeat in detail. Somewhat mystified, Cornwallis split his own army, sending Tarleton directly after Morgan while he took a circuitous route to cut off Morgan's retreat. Morgan stopped retreating at Cowpens. Shrewdly deploying his mixed force of Continentals, cavalry, and militiamen, he inflicted a crushing defeat on the British, and 90 percent of Tarleton's 1,100 men became casualties or prisoners.

After Cowpens, Morgan hastened to join Greene. Anxious to refurbish British prestige, Cornwallis gave chase. A game of hounds and hare ensued, with Greene playing the rabbit's role willingly. By luring Cornwallis away from South Carolina, the partisans could harass enemy outposts with relative impunity. Still, the race was desperate. Frequently the American rear guard skirmished with the British van, but Greene always eluded the main body and finally crossed the Dan River into Virginia. His men exhausted, Cornwallis reversed course to Hillsborough to refit his army, but Greene decided the time to fight had arrived and recrossed the

Dan. The armies met at Guilford Courthouse in a furious battle in which the British won a Pyrrhic victory. Cornwallis's losses were so severe that he moved to Wilmington, where he could recuperate and be resupplied by sea. Soon he marched into Virginia, which he believed was the Revolution's southern center. The move betrayed southern Loyalists, who had offered support and in return expected protection.

When Cornwallis entered the Old Dominion, Greene marched southward to reclaim the Carolinas and Georgia, where 8,000 enemy troops under Francis Lord Rawdon remained in scattered garrisons. At Hobkirk's Hill, Greene fought Rawdon, who won another hollow British victory. While the American main army kept Rawdon occupied, guerrillas picked off isolated British posts. In early September, Greene tangled with Rawdon's successor, Alexander Stewart, at Eutaw Springs in a three-hour slugfest. If the militia failed at Camden, it now redeemed itself by fighting splendidly. As at Guilford Courthouse and Hobkirk's Hill, the British won the battlefield but suffered irreplaceable losses. Eutaw Springs was Greene's last battle. He could not claim a single victory—Morgan deserves credit for Cowpens—but he and the partisans had reconquered all the south except Savannah and Charleston. Greene's operations rank with Washington's performance at Trenton and Princeton as the war's most brilliant campaigns.

As Greene's activities diminished, the war's final drama unfolded in Virginia. In December 1780, Clinton sent Benedict Arnold—now a British general after his treason—to Virginia with 1,200 men, and Washington countered by dispatching the Marquis de Lafayette's division. Like a magnet Virginia attracted reinforcements on both sides, and when Cornwallis arrived in the spring of 1781, he assumed command of the British forces there. As Lafayette's army expanded, Cornwallis fortified Yorktown in order to have access to the sea should he need to receive reinforcements—or escape.

Far to the north the French expeditionary force finally left Newport and united with the Continental Army in July 1781. Washington and Rochambeau knew that a powerful fleet commanded by the Comte de Grasse had departed France under orders to cooperate with them. Washington hoped de Grasse would come to New York and seal it off so that the Franco-American army could capture Clinton, but on August 14 Washington received a message from de Grasse saying he was sailing for Chesapeake Bay. Bagging Clinton was thus impossible, but perhaps Cornwallis could be cornered. Washington ordered the army southward and directed the French naval squadron still at Newport to bring siege artillery and provisions.

The movement of land and naval forces to Yorktown was unique in the war because nothing went wrong. Lafayette kept Cornwallis from flee-

ing to the Carolinas; de Grasse fended off a British fleet at the Battle of
the Virginia Capes, preventing seaborne succor from reaching the garrison
at Yorktown; the Newport fleet arrived unscathed; and the army rapidly
reached Virginia. The concentration of two naval squadrons and 5,700
Continentals, 3,100 militiamen, and 7,000 French troops at Yorktown was
a tour de force that trapped Cornwallis, whose situation was hopeless. On
the fourth anniversary of Burgoyne's capitulation, surrender negotiations
began, and two days later 8,000 British troops marched out of Yorktown
and stacked arms. The southern phase of the war ended with a British
disaster comparable to Saratoga.

Fighting on the Frontier and at Sea

Like the colonial wars, the American Revolution involved the Indians,
although they played a minor role compared to the main armies. Resenting the aggressive expansionism of Americans and desiring English trade
goods, Native Americans generally supported the British. Frontier warfare took place in three distinct theaters: a central front in the Ohio Valley
and Kentucky, a southern front in the Carolina and Georgia backcountry,
and a northern front in western New York and northern Pennsylvania.
Indian wars in the Ohio country actually began in 1774 when the Shawnees
resisted the land encroachments of Virginia settlers. In order to force the
Indians to cede their lands, Lord Dunmore, the governor of Virginia, organized an expedition into Shawnee territory. Lord Dunmore's War involved
only one battle, when 1,000 Indians attacked an equal number of militiamen at Point Pleasant on the Ohio. The assault failed to prevent Dunmore's column from penetrating to the Shawnee villages, which compelled
the Indians to give up extensive land claims. An uneasy peace prevailed
until 1777, when the British commander at Detroit, Henry Hamilton, dispatched raiding parties to Kentucky to divert American attention from
Burgoyne, forcing the Kentucky pioneers to huddle together in Harrodsburg, Boonesborough, and other strongholds. The Indian raids continued
into 1778, making life on the Kentucky frontier dangerous and miserable.

George Rogers Clark proposed to end the Indian menace by first attacking British-controlled settlements in the Illinois country, then assaulting
Detroit. Virginia, the parent state of Kentucky, authorized the expedition,
and in 1778 Clark captured Kaskaskia, Cahokia, and Vincennes. With a
small force that included Indians allied to the British, Hamilton marched
from Detroit and recaptured Vincennes in December. Clark immediately
left Kaskaskia to retake the town. To discourage Hamilton's Indian allies,
Clark had six captured Indians tomahawked to death in sight of the British defenses. "It had," he said, "the effect that I expected." Vincennes

surrendered, but it was Clark's last important triumph. He never received enough reinforcements to attack Detroit, and Kentucky was on the defensive after 1779, as intermittent Indian raids scourged the Ohio Valley.

In the south, the Cherokees rose against white settlers in May 1776, but the uprising was ill-timed. With no British forces in the region, Georgia and the two Carolinas could concentrate on subduing the Indians. The three states committed 4,500 militiamen to a three-pronged campaign that inflicted severe devastation on the Cherokees, forcing them to sue for peace. The display of American might dampened the warlike ardor of other southern tribes, and for the next two years England received much sympathy but little military aid from them. With the capture of Savannah and the subsequent British conquests in the south, England persuaded a few Creeks, Cherokees, Choctaws, and Chickasaws to assist them. The rebels responded in late 1780 with a punitive expedition against the Cherokees, who again endured the loss of villages and crops. This second chastisement of the Cherokees, combined with England's deteriorating position in the south throughout 1781, ended Indian participation in the southern war.

In the New York–Pennsylvania region the war shattered the Iroquois Confederacy, as the Oneidas and Tuscaroras supported the United States and the other four tribes assisted the British. Joseph Brant, a well-educated Mohawk chief, led the pro-British Iroquois and worked closely with Loyalist leaders. In 1778 Tory-Indian raiding parties operating out of Niagara terrorized the frontier, destroying the communities of Wyoming Valley, German Flats, and Cherry Valley. Pleas for protection resulted in General John Sullivan's 1779 expedition. Washington told Sullivan he wanted Iroquois country not "merely *overrun,* but *destroyed.*" Aside from punishing the Indians, Washington had a second motive: He did not want the United States confined to the seaboard, and Sullivan's activities, like Clark's, might allow America to acquire the west during peace negotiations. Sullivan's force was powerful, consisting of some of the best Continentals and commanded by excellent officers. Unprepared for such a massive invasion, Brant and the Loyalists made only one effort to stop Sullivan. At the Battle of Newton they fought briefly before fleeing, leaving Iroquois territory open to the invaders. Although Sullivan inflicted extensive damage, the campaign was not decisive. As one participant observed, "The nests are destroyed, but the birds are still on the wing." They roosted that winter at Niagara, more dependent than ever on British aid, and in the spring they returned to the frontier bent on revenge. Northern wilderness warfare pitting rebels against Loyalists and Indians continued until the war's end, although it never again matched the scope of 1778–1779.

If frontier warfare saw the repetition of a familiar—and frightening— theme, Americans also fought on a new frontier, the sea. During the colonial wars Americans helped man the Royal Navy and served as privateers, but they never tried to maintain a separate navy. As soon as the Revolution began, some men contemplated confronting Britain on the ocean as well as on land. No one advocated building a fleet to challenge British supremacy, since in 1775 the British navy included 270 ships of the line, frigates, and sloops (the three largest categories of warships), while America did not have a single warship. Although the Royal Navy could not be directly challenged, an American naval effort could still hurt England by attacking its lucrative seaborne commerce and disrupting its military lines of supply and communication. Drawing upon its extensive shipbuilding experience, vast timber supplies, large seafaring population, substantial merchant and fishing fleets, and strong maritime tradition, the United States floated not just one navy, but four distinct types.

Washington created a private navy during the siege of Boston. His army was destitute, while the besieged enemy received ample supplies via the sea. Capturing supply ships would reduce American distress and increase enemy logistical problems. In September 1775 Washington chartered the schooner *Hannah,* put a few cannons and a volunteer crew aboard, and sent it into Massachusetts Bay. During the next few months he chartered another half-dozen small ships. Before the enemy evacuated Boston, Washington's ships had captured fifty-five prizes, providing valuable cargoes of muskets, gunpowder, flints, and artillery to the rebel army.

All the colonies except for New Jersey and Delaware organized state navies, primarily for coastal defense. The state navies generally consisted of shallow-draft barges, galleys, and gunboats, but a few states, such as Massachusetts and Pennsylvania, also commissioned small deep-water vessels that could prey upon British merchantmen. Often the navies acted as maritime militia, fending off British naval raids to gather provisions and preventing Loyalists from supplying ships lying offshore. Occasionally a state navy saw more dangerous action. Pennsylvania's navy, for instance, participated in the defense of Forts Mercer and Mifflin during Howe's Philadelphia campaign in 1777.

A third type of navy consisted of privateers, which were privately owned armed ships sailing under a commission or letter of marque authorizing the vessel to attack enemy merchantmen. Privateering was licensed piracy, and it had great appeal. The proceeds from the sale of captured ships and cargoes went to the privateer's owner, officers, and crew, so the capture of a few merchantmen could make everyone rich. Before the war ended, an estimated 2,000 privateers had sailed under commissions from Congress, state governments, and diplomats abroad. They harmed Britain more than any other facet of the American naval war. England's losses exceeded $65 million; maritime insurance rates skyrocketed; and to protect merchantmen, England resorted to convoys, which siphoned warships from other vital tasks. The privateers also disrupted communications between England and its forces in America.

The fourth navy was the Continental Navy, established by Congress in the autumn of 1775, when it created a Naval Committee and authorized the acquisition of armed ships. The first were eight converted merchantmen commanded by Esek Hopkins, who had limited qualifications but was the brother of a member of the Naval Committee. Nepotism played a role in the selection of commanding officers for all the vessels. Symptomatic of the officers' questionable competence was the infant fleet's first voyage, which, as it turned out, was the only fleet operation by the Continental Navy during the war. Hopkins disobeyed orders to cruise in Chesapeake Bay and instead raided Nassau in the Bahamas. On the return voyage the fleet encountered HMS *Glasgow,* which, though outnumbered and outgunned, outfought the Americans.

Congress was not content to rely on converted merchantmen. In December 1775 it voted to build thirteen frigates and eventually authorized construction of approximately thirty more vessels. But shipyards, hindered by shortages of cannons, iron, canvas, and seasoned timber, never completed the authorized vessels, and the fate of most ships that slid down the ways was dismal. For example, of the thirteen frigates, the Americans burned three to keep them out of enemy hands, the British burned two and captured seven, and one sank in battle.

The Continental Navy's worst handicap was a shortage of trained seamen. Privateering was more attractive than naval service because crews received a greater share of prize money, discipline was lax, and it was relatively danger-free, since privateers avoided enemy warships. Continental ships often sat in port for lack of crewmen, and squadron operations became difficult. Thus ships usually sailed alone and, like privateers, concentrated on commerce raiding. Several captains carried the commerce war to European waters with spectacular success. Lambert Wickes and Gustavus Conyngham captured dozens of ships at England's doorstep, and John Paul Jones won his renowned victory over *Serapis* while trying to plunder a convoy off Britain's coast.

One aspect of the naval war deserves special mention. In 1772 David Bushnell, a brilliant mathematics student at Yale, proved that gunpowder would explode underwater, and by 1774 he had developed a submarine mine. He then designed and built the *Turtle,* the world's first submarine. This one-man craft could be used to deliver a mine to an enemy warship's hull. When Howe's force appeared at New York in 1776, Washington consented to let Bushnell try the *Turtle* against *Eagle,* Lord Howe's flagship. Although Ezra Lee, who operated *Turtle,* positioned the submarine under

Eagle, he was unable to attach the mine to the hull. Two subsequent efforts against other ships also failed. Despite the *Turtle*'s failure, Bushnell's efforts foretold the future. Not only did submarines eventually become potent weapons, but Bushnell had also mated engineering science to war.

Approximately fifty ships saw service in the Continental Navy, most of them small and of limited usefulness. By 1780, with only five warships in commission, the navy had practically disappeared and America was relying totally on privateers and the French navy. Indicative of the navy's negligible role was Yorktown, where de Grasse had forty ships of the line and the United States did not have a single ship. Had there been no national navy, its absence would not have affected the war's outcome. John Adams, one of the navy's earliest proponents, provided its epitaph when he wrote that, looking back "over the long list of vessels belonging to the United States taken and destroyed, and recollecting the whole history of the rise and progress of our navy, it is very difficult to avoid tears."

After Yorktown

Although no one was thinking about the navy, few dry eyes could be seen in Fraunces Tavern in New York during the afternoon of December 4, 1783. Washington had assembled a small group of officers to bid farewell before departing for Congress to submit his resignation. The commander offered a brief toast to his subordinates, thanking them and wishing them well. Then, one by one, the battle-hardened veterans filed by to embrace Washington in an emotional scene suffused with that special affection that develops among soldiers who have triumphed against seemingly impossible odds. Washington did not greatly exaggerate the sense of wonderment at their own success that many of the revolutionaries felt when he wrote to Nathanael Greene:

> If Historiographers should be hardy enough to fill the page of History with the advantages that have been gained with unequal numbers (on the part of America) in the course of this contest, and attempt to relate the distressing circumstances under which they have been obtained, it is more than probable that Posterity will bestow on their labors the epithet and marks of fiction: for it will not be believed that such a force as Great Britain has employed for eight years in this Country could be baffled in their plan of Subjugating it by numbers infinitely less, composed of Men sometimes half starved; always in Rags, without pay, and experiencing, at times, every species of distress which human nature is capable of undergoing.

The fighting had ended unexpectedly. No one, least of all Washington, believed Yorktown would be the war's last campaign. The British had already lost one army at Saratoga and the Americans two armies in the south, yet both sides were able to persist. England still held Charleston, Savannah, and New York with more than 20,000 troops, which was more men than Washington had. He expected that the spring of 1782 would see new campaigns, but none took place in America. The war was going badly for England around the globe. In the Caribbean, the French captured several important islands and threatened Jamaica. Minorca in the Mediterranean fell to the French, Gibraltar was under siege, Spain conquered West Florida, and in India the British precariously held on in the face of intense French pressure. Yorktown broke Parliament's will to continue the American war, thereby reducing a drain on England's resources that could be used to preserve the rest of its empire. Carleton, who replaced Clinton, received orders to remain on the defensive. Peace negotiations, which began in 1780, intensified, and on September 3, 1783, the combatants signed the Peace of Paris. The liberal terms England granted the United States astounded Europeans and Americans alike. The former colonies achieved not only independence but also the right of navigation on the Mississippi, access to the Newfoundland fisheries, and enormous territorial acquisitions in the west.

It had been a long and costly war, resulting in at least 25,000 American war-related deaths, which represented almost 1 percent of the entire population. Except for the Civil War, which killed 2 percent of the population, no other United States war took such a frightful toll.* Like most revolutionaries, Americans improvised with extraordinary ingenuity. Starting from scratch they organized a government, a navy, and an army, and they conducted diplomacy with an astuteness that achieved the indispensable French alliance and an incredibly favorable peace. Even though England confronted great difficulties fighting in its distant colonies, especially after 1778, the American performance was still remarkable.

Equally remarkable was the Revolution's impact on political and military affairs. Politically, it sparked the feeling in Europe that a new era was dawning. News of American events and institutions filtered into Europe through the press, the efforts of American propagandists, discussions in literary clubs, and reports of returning soldiers. The Enlightenment's liberal philosophical ideas lost their abstractness as Americans seemingly put them into practice, thereby intensifying the revolutionary and democratic spirit in Europe. In France the new spirit mingled with rising discontent fomented by a soaring cost of living and a bankrupt treasury, both of which resulted primarily from France's support of the United States. Six years

---

* By contrast, Mexican War deaths were only 0.06 percent of the population, World War I deaths 0.12 percent, and World War II deaths 0.28 percent.

after the Treaty of Paris, France exploded in its own revolution, plunging Europe into a generation of nearly ceaseless violence.

War after 1789 was radically different from what it had been during the age of limited warfare. Restraints on warfare began eroding during the American Revolution, and the French Revolution completely washed them away. Americans reintroduced ideology into warfare, fought for the unlimited goal of independence, and mobilized citizen-soldiers rather than professionals. In the spring of 1783, Washington summarized the drastic implications of these changes. "It may be laid down as a primary position, and the basis of our system," he wrote, "that every Citizen who enjoys the protection of a free Government, owes not only a proportion of his property, but even of his personal service to the defense of it." To protect the nation, "the Total strength of the Country might be called forth." Mass citizen-soldier armies would be motivated by patriotic zeal as they fought for freedom, equality, and other abstract ideological virtues.

The French followed Washington's prescription for national defense when the government issued a *levee en masse* in 1793, theoretically conscripting the entire population. France's national mobilization portended a new, more destructive type of warfare that would culminate in the twentieth century. Huge armies required large-scale production to equip, feed, and transport them, which in turn necessitated economic regimentation. The line between soldiers and civilians, both indispensable to the war effort, became blurred. To sustain the patriotic ardor of troops and workers, governments resorted to mass indoctrination. And since national survival seemed at stake, nations fought with grim determination, surrendering only when battered into abject helplessness. The American and French Revolutions, politically and militarily, transformed Western civilization.

FOUR

Preserving the New Republic's Independence, 1783–1815

The post-Revolutionary era, which was one of serious peril for the infant republic, necessitated the development of a military policy that reconciled ideological concerns for liberty with military effectiveness. Complicating the task of devising an appropriate policy were three events during 1783 that reawakened traditional fears of a standing army and poisoned civil-military relations. The first episode leading to this crisis in civil-military relations was the Newburgh Conspiracy. Early in the war Continental Army officers began demanding half pay for life as a postwar pension, a tradition in European armies. Despite opposition to the creation of a favored class, in 1780 the Continental Congress promised the officers half pay for life. But by the winter of 1782–1783, when the army was at Newburgh, New York, nothing had been done to implement the promise. Officers feared their service was going to go uncompensated and that the new Confederation Congress, which assumed authority after the ratification of the Articles of Confederation in 1781, would repudiate that pledge as it disbanded the army.

The officers drew up a petition offering to have half pay for life commuted into a lump-sum payment, and a committee, headed by General Alexander McDougall, carried it to Congress. The army delegation played into the hands of those congressmen, known as nationalists, who desired a stronger central government. They especially wanted the government to have the power to tax, a function that public creditors also favored. The nationalists tried to combine the army's discontent with the civilian creditors' clamor to secure a permanent taxing power for Congress and thereby strengthen the government. McDougall and the nationalists implied that if the officers' demands were not met, the army might defy congressional control over the military. Despite the threat of a mutiny, Congress refused to capitulate to the commutation proposal and the nationalists' demands.

To intensify pressure on recalcitrant congressmen, the nationalists fomented further demonstrations among the officers at Newburgh. Whether or not some officers actually contemplated a coup d'état remains unclear, but two anonymous documents, known as the Newburgh Addresses, circulated in camp. One called for a meeting to discuss means for obtaining redress; since Washington had not been consulted, such a meeting was against regulations. The other denounced Congress and threatened its supremacy over the military.

These documents shocked Washington, though perhaps they did not surprise him. He shared the officers' belief that their valorous service had been rewarded by ingratitude and injustice, and he received hints that nationalists were using the army as a lobby group. Washington adhered religiously to civilian rule, believing that "the Army was a dangerous Engine to Work with." He acted quickly to stop the growing protest by calling his own meeting, at which he warned the men against impassioned actions and argued that an attempted coup would tarnish the army's reputation and "open the flood Gates of Civil discord." With a touch of theatrics, he recalled his own sacrifices, noting he had grown gray and nearly blind in the service. Pledging to do everything he could in their behalf, he implored the officers to continue their "unexampled patriotism and patient virtue." Washington's virtuoso performance undermined whatever scheme was afoot. When he departed, the officers adopted a memorial affirming their "unshaken confidence" in Congress and deploring the Newburgh Addresses. Meanwhile, under the pressure of the threats and unaware of the dramatic reversal at Newburgh, Congress enacted a plan commutating half pay for life into full pay for five years. The crisis was over, but many people considered the episode a frightening example of a standing army's potentially subversive nature.

As winter yielded to spring, another cloud drifted out of Newburgh to cast a shadow on the army. In mid-May, Henry Knox formed the Society of the Cincinnati to unite army officers in a fraternal and charitable organization. But outsiders saw sinister designs in the Cincinnati's constitution. Membership was hereditary: Was this a step toward an American nobility? The society also permitted honorary memberships: Would it become a powerful pressure group by adding important politicians to its ranks?

Each officer contributed to a charitable fund: Could this be a war chest to finance diabolical plots? Auxiliary state societies were to correspond through circular letters discussing, among other things, "the general union of the states": Did this imply a political purpose, perhaps to overthrow the Confederation? Washington's acceptance of the Cincinnati's presidency indicated that the organization had none of these corrupt motives, but the public furor against the society was nonetheless intense.

As critics pilloried the Cincinnati, another thunderbolt was brewing. On April 11, 1783, Congress proclaimed an end to hostilities, even though no definitive peace treaty had been signed. Men wanted to be discharged and paid immediately, but Congress was reluctant to do the former until final peace was achieved, and it lacked the money to do the latter. Troops became riotous, and in mid-June some of the Pennsylvania troops in the Continental Army mutinied. The men marched on the Pennsylvania State House, where both Congress and the state government were meeting, and sent in a message threatening "to let loose an enraged soldiery on them" if their demands were not met. The legislators refused to comply and courageously left the building to a flurry of insults; but Congress moved to Princeton as a precaution.

These ominous events overshadowed the Confederation's efforts to devise an effective postwar military policy. In April 1783, Congress appointed a committee to study future policy. Alexander Hamilton, one of Washington's former aides and an ardent nationalist, chaired the committee and sought advice from the commander in chief, who responded with his "Sentiments on a Peace Establishment." The general mentioned the need for a navy and seacoast fortification but emphasized four necessities. First, the country should have a regular army to garrison the west, "awe the Indians," and guard against attacks from Spanish Florida or British Canada. Considering the nation's poverty, its distance from Europe, and the widespread prejudice against professional military forces, Washington proposed a small regular army—specifically, 2,631 officers and men. Second, with the army so tiny, the nation required a "respectable and well established Militia." Contrary to the colonial system, Washington insisted the militia should be nationalized, with the central government imposing uniformity in arms, organization, and training. In particular, within each state he wanted "a kind of Continental Militia," modeled after the war's minutemen, under stringent national control. Thus Washington proposed a three-tiered land force: A regular army, a ready reserve similar to the volunteer militia, and an improved common militia. Third, he suggested arsenals and manufactories to support these armies. Fourth, he wanted military academies to foster the study of military science.

Washington later wrote that his "Sentiments" conveyed what he thought would be politically acceptable, not what he "conceived *ought* to be a proper peace Establishment." Considering his distaste for the militia, he undoubtedly preferred to minimize its role and depend on regulars. But he was aware of the resurgence of the pre-Revolutionary fear of a permanent army and knew a large army would be unacceptable. Paradoxically, although militia and regulars complemented one another in the Revolution, proponents of each now viewed them as rival defense systems. Regular army advocates stressed militia debacles, while militia enthusiasts eulogized Concord and Bunker Hill and emphasized the compatibility of radical Whig ideology and the militia system.

Hamilton's committee report followed most of Washington's recommendations, although it put less emphasis on the militia and stressed a greater reliance on a standing army. But antinationalists rejected as unnecessary the arguments in favor of peacetime preparedness at the national level. After all, the colonies had had virtually no organized military strength in 1775, yet they had prevailed against the British. So why was more strength necessary now? Moreover, the antinationalists believed that a strong central government and a regular army went hand in glove, and they wanted neither, preferring a decentralized system of sovereign states each exercising complete control over its own militia. Because antinationalists were in the ascendancy in Congress, the legislature rejected Hamilton's report and on June 2, 1784, disbanded all but eighty men and a few officers of the Continental Army.

Having discarded Hamilton's plan, Congress had to do *something* to meet the urgent military problems in the west. The British refused to evacuate their western posts, from which they controlled the fur trade, subverted the Indians, and threatened to contain American expansion. In the southwest, Spain exerted similar influences, though not as strongly. The nation had to preserve peace with the Indians, if for no other reason than Congress lacked the funds to fight a war. Somebody had to protect envoys to the Indians, evict squatters on Indian lands, and defend surveyors and settlers. Since the states had ceded their land claims in the Northwest Territory to the Confederation, these problems were beyond the scope of any individual state militia. They were also beyond the capacity of eighty soldiers.

Congress recognized its military challenges, and the day after disbanding the Continental Army it created the 1st American Regiment—the first national peacetime force in American history—by calling on four states to raise 700 militiamen for one year. The regiment was a hybrid, neither strictly militia nor regular. Its formation depended on the states' goodwill to provide men, but Congress organized, paid, and disciplined the regiment, and the commander, Josiah Harmar of Pennsylvania, reported to both Congress and the Pennsylvania state government. When enlistments expired in 1785, Congress continued the regiment but made it a regular force by calling for three-year recruits and omitting all reference to the militia. When the end of this enlistment period approached, Congress again authorized the same number of men for three years. Thus the Confederation created a very small standing force. Like the prewar British garrison, the regiment failed to police the west effectively. Harmar never received enough men to "awe" the Indians, with whom relations continued to deteriorate, or the white squatters, who encroached on Indian territory with impunity. And least of all did Harmar's troops awe the British. To nationalists, the regiment's ineffectiveness symbolized the Confederation's weakness.

Events in Massachusetts in 1786 dismayed nationalists even more than the precarious frontier situation. Burdened by debts and taxes, farmers led by Daniel Shays rebelled against the government. Publicly hiding behind the subterfuge of preparing for frontier defense, Congress voted to expand the army to 2,040 men but could raise only two artillery companies and was powerless to intervene. Eventually Massachusetts volunteers quelled the rebellion, but this did not lessen the nationalists' sense of humiliation and fear. In their minds Shays' Rebellion proved the impotence of the Confederation Congress and seemed to be the first stumble toward anarchy.

The Confederation's military weakness on the frontier and in Massachusetts was one of the primary reasons for the Constitutional Convention. Nationalists believed that unless the government was strengthened, the United States would remain weak at home and contemptible abroad. Since they had a vision of a great nation that would protect life, liberty, and property and be respected in foreign councils, the situation was intolerable.

The Constitution, the "Dual Army," and the Navy

The delegates to the Constitutional Convention generally agreed that the government needed enhanced coercive powers. "But the kind of coercion you may ask?" Washington wrote to James Madison. "This indeed will require thought." And indeed it did, since military force is the essential concomitant of governmental authority. The extent of the government's military power had profound ramifications, affecting not only the distribution of power between the states and the central government but also perceptions of the relationship between security and liberty. Was it possible to invest sufficient power in the government to defend against foreign and domestic enemies without transforming it into an oppressive instrument? The Constitution tried to create a delicate balance in which the central government received enough power to "provide for the common defense" and "insure domestic tranquility," without extinguishing state sovereignty and individual liberty. The document divided military power between the federal government and the states, giving paramount power to the former while guarding against excessive centralized authority by sharing national power between Congress and the president.

Congress could "provide and maintain a navy" and "raise and support armies"; to ensure money for these purposes, it could levy and collect taxes and borrow funds. However, since the Constitution limited Army appropriations to two years, a permanent standing army was possible only with Congress's continuing consent. Congress was to provide for calling forth the militia "to execute the laws of the Union, suppress insurrections, and repel invasions," as well as establish regulations "for organizing, arming, and disciplining the militia" and for governing the militia when in national service. Congress also had the power to declare war. Congressional tyranny was unlikely, since the president was not only the commander in chief of the Army and Navy, but the militia "when called into the actual service of the United States." He also appointed military officers, with the advice and consent of the Senate. The Constitution thus gave national military forces two masters, neither of which could attain a despotic preeminence.

As for the states, the Constitution guaranteed them a republican form of government and promised them protection from invasion or domestic violence. The states could not form alliances, authorize privateers, keep nonmilitia troops or warships in peacetime without Congress's consent, or engage in war "unless actually invaded, or in such imminent danger as will not admit of delay." But they retained their own militias. The right to do so was not explicitly stated in the Constitution proper, but it was implicit in the states' authority to appoint militia officers and train the militia "according to the discipline prescribed by Congress." The Second Amendment made the states' militia authority explicit.

The Constitution institutionalized the dual-army tradition. The historic militias remained, and the new government had ample authority to establish a regular Army. Since one of the nationalists' primary goals had been to permit the central government to maintain a peacetime army, they had achieved an impressive victory. Nationalists also wanted a nationalized militia, but in this they were only potentially successful and were dependent on the laws that Congress would pass implementing its authority over the militia. Despite the careful restraints on military power, many antinationalists inveighed against the proposed government's despotic potential. Unlike nationalists, they were less concerned with military effectiveness than they were with maintaining a proper constitutional balance between the states and the federal government. They disliked the new government's concurrent power over the militia, a dramatic departure from past practice that might diminish state autonomy and undermine the militia's local nature. Fearing "the natural propensity of rulers to oppress the people," they were also alarmed by the prospect of a standing army. But with painstaking thoroughness the nationalists parried every antinationalistic thrust, and the Constitution took effect on June 21, 1788, after the ninth state had ratified it.

When the new government assembled in 1789, it had to translate the Constitution's military provisions into actual policy. Action was necessary in three areas: The government needed an agency to administer military affairs, implement its militia responsibilities, and decide whether to create an army and, if so, how large it should be. The legislature acted upon the first issue expeditiously. Under the Confederation, a War Department headed by a "secretary *at* war" (Henry Knox since 1785) administered military matters. In August 1789 Congress maintained continuity by creating a Department of War, and in September it confirmed Washington's nomination of Knox as the first secretary *of* war.

In regard to the militia, Congress foiled nationalist aspirations. Washington and Knox urged Congress to reorganize the militia into an effective force under national control, but militia legislation was a touchy political question. It struck at the root of state versus federal power and had a direct impact on every citizen. Congress delayed acting until the spring of 1792, when it passed the Calling Forth Act and the Uniform Militia Act. The former implemented the constitutional provision allowing Congress to call forth the militia by delegating that authority to the president. In case of invasion, Congress gave the executive a relatively free hand, since both nationalists and antinationalists feared foreign invasion. However, antinationalist fears of a despotic central government hedged the president's authority to summon the militia to execute the laws or suppress insurrections. Before he could do so, a federal judge had to certify that civil authority was powerless to meet the crisis, and then the president formally had to order the insurgents to disperse and give them an opportunity to disband. In no case could a militiaman be mobilized for more than three months in any one year.

The Uniform Militia Act, which remained the basic militia law until the twentieth century, enshrined the concept of universal military service, requiring the enrollment of all able-bodied white men between the ages of eighteen and forty-five. It contained an exemption list (to which the states could add), required men to arm and equip themselves, and outlined a tactical organization that states were to adopt only if "convenient." From a nationalist perspective, the law had severe shortcomings. It did not provide for a select corps in each state or for federal control over officership and training, and it imposed no penalties on either the states or individuals for noncompliance, thus representing little more than a recommendation

THE MILITARY FRONTIER IN THE OLD NORTHWEST 1778-1817

to the states. The government virtually abdicated responsibility over the militia; the states were free to respond to the law according to their diverse impulses—which they did. The Uniform Militia Act killed the nationalized militia concept by failing to establish uniform, interchangeable units, a prerequisite for a national reserve force. What little vitality the militia retained reposed in volunteer units forming a de facto elite corps; this was far from what Washington visualized, because the units were neither standardized nor nationalized.

The failure to forge reliable state militias made a standing army imperative, and Congress slowly moved toward that goal. In September 1789 it adopted the 1st American Regiment and the artillery battalion raised during Shays' Rebellion. Six months later Congress added four companies to the regiment, bringing the total authorized force to 1,216 men, but this minuscule Army proved inadequate to the challenge of an Indian war. In Indian relations the administration preferred diplomacy over war. The government secured a precarious formal peace south of the Ohio

River through the Treaty of New York (1790), and Secretary of War Knox worked diligently to restrain Tennessee frontiersmen who opposed the peace policy. Although Tennesseans occasionally ignored his pleas and conducted unauthorized campaigns, the intermittent fighting between settlers and Indians fortunately never escalated into genuine war. Neither militarily nor monetarily could the nation afford confrontations on two fronts, and north of the Ohio the situation had reached a crisis.

In the Northwest the Indians, determined to make the Ohio the boundary between the races, tried to form a confederacy to stop white migration across the river. In these efforts they received British support. By 1790 the violence between settlers and Native Americans assumed near-war proportions, and westerners cried for federal assistance. In June 1790 Knox ordered Harmar and Arthur St. Clair, the governor of the Northwest Territory, to organize an expedition into hostile territory along the Wabash and Maumee Rivers. The two-pronged campaign was a disaster. One wing departed Fort Knox and headed for the upper Wabash but turned back far short of its objective. The other, led by Harmar and consisting of 320 regulars and 1,133 militiamen, managed to reach its objective. Harmar's force destroyed a few villages along the Maumee, but the Indians ambushed two substantial detachments, and the column retreated in disorder. The regulars fought well, but the militiamen acted disgracefully. Most of them were substitutes who were at best disobedient, at worst mutinous, and in battle they followed the principle of fleeing before fighting.

Having failed to chastise the Indians with one understrength expedition, the government organized another—with even worse results. Congress added another regiment to the Army, authorized the president to call out militiamen, and allowed him to enlist 2,000 "levies" for six months. The levies were an innovation, a method of manpower mobilization halfway between regulars and militia. They were federal volunteers raised and officered by the national government, but like militia, they served only a short term. In the nineteenth century federal volunteers became the normal method of utilizing citizen-soldiers.

Washington appointed St. Clair to command the mixed force of militia and levies that assembled near Fort Washington (now Cincinnati, Ohio) during the summer. The militia again consisted mostly of substitutes, and the levies were little better. Neither type of citizen-soldier got along with the regulars. The composite "army" was little more than a rabble, and St. Clair had no time to train it properly because Washington had urged him by "every principle that is sacred" to march as soon as possible. When the horde moved northward, one veteran prayed that "the Enemy may not be disposed to give us battle," but his prayers were not answered. On November 3 the army camped along the Wabash. As the 1,400 men began their morning routine on the 4th, 1,000 Indians attacked and inflicted over 900 casualties—the worst defeat ever suffered by an American Army against Native Americans.

In response to this new calamity, the administration followed a dual policy. It reopened Indian negotiations to appease easterners, who believed aggressive frontiersmen caused the violence, and to save the country from bankruptcy. But the government also began building a capable Army. Congress authorized three more regiments, and Knox reorganized the expanded Army into the Legion of the United States, composed of 5,280 officers and men divided into four equal sublegions. The president pondered over a commander, finally selecting Anthony Wayne, who had a reputation for being courageous and offensive-minded. For two years, while negotiations continued, Wayne drilled the Legion, molding it into a disciplined force. In September 1793, after the diplomatic effort failed to dissuade the Indians from their insistence on the Ohio River boundary, Knox ordered Wayne to use the Legion "to make those audacious savages feel our superiority in Arms."

Wayne's campaign was an enormous success. He built Fort Greenville, where most of his Army overwintered, and Fort Recovery, which was on the site of St. Clair's defeat. In response to Wayne's presence the British established Fort Miami at the Maumee rapids, and by June 1794 some 2,000 Indians gathered nearby, confidently expecting British aid. On June 30 and July 1 the Indians, reinforced by some Canadians, attacked Fort Recovery, but the defenders (outnumbered ten to one) repulsed them. Meanwhile, deploring the government's inability to recruit the Legion to full strength, Wayne called on Kentucky for mounted volunteers. When 1,500 of them arrived in late July, the reinforced Legion moved out. Wayne expected to meet "a Heterogeneous Army composed of British troops the Militia of Detroit & all the Hostile Indians N W of the Ohio," but at the Battle of Fallen Timbers he fought a mere 500 Indians. The Legion routed the Indians, who fled toward Fort Miami, where, to their chagrin, the British refused to help them. Indian losses in the battle were small, but the psychological shock of England's broken promises was great. Defeated and dismayed, the Indians had no hope of maintaining the Ohio boundary, and in the Treaty of Greenville they ceded most of Ohio and a sliver of Indiana. The victory also lessened British influence in the Northwest and convinced the English to relinquish the posts they had garrisoned since 1783. Finally, the Legion had demonstrated the government's ability to maintain an Army that could "provide for the common defense," at least to the extent of waging a successful Indian campaign.

Simultaneously with the Indians' defeat, the government also proved it could "insure domestic tranquility." The Whiskey Rebellion erupted in western Pennsylvania as a protest against an excise tax on distilled spirits. Discontent also flared in western Maryland, Kentucky, Georgia, and the Carolinas. Washington initially acted cautiously. He feared the use of force without an effort at conciliation might precipitate rebellion throughout the west, and with the Legion committed against the Indians, he would have to rely on the militia, which might not mobilize to suppress the tumults. But when negotiations with the whiskey rebels broke down and they defied a presidential proclamation to disperse, the administration believed that "the crisis was arrived when it must be determined whether the Government can maintain itself." Washington sent orders to the governors of New Jersey, Pennsylvania, Maryland, and Virginia for 12,500 militiamen, and to his gratification the states' forces assembled. Never before had the militia functioned as a national, rather than a local, institution. Rebel leaders swore they would resist, but as the massive posse comitatus crossed the mountains, the rebellion evaporated.

By applying two kinds of force—regulars and militia—in two different situations—against Indians and domestic insurrection—Federalists (formerly "nationalists) believed the government had demonstrated it deserved respect. However, the Federalist utilization of force showed how thoroughly military policy had been politicized. The coercive power that comforted Federalists frightened Republicans, the newly emerged opposition political party. While Federalists applauded the Whiskey Rebellion's demise, Republicans viewed the episode as an example of a strong government's armed tyranny. Republicans also cast an anxious eye toward the Legion, believing it should be drastically reduced. The Treaty of Greenville and England's promise to evacuate the western forts, they argued, made such a substantial Army unnecessary. An armed populace could provide frontier defense more cheaply than regulars and with less danger to liberty. Republicans especially feared that Federalists might use the Legion for despotic domestic purposes. Administration spokesmen asserted that any reduction was inadvisable. The nation needed the regular Army to garrison western posts, deter aggression, and preserve "a model and school for an army, and experienced officers to form it, in case of war." Furthermore, the militia's deplorable condition made the Legion doubly necessary.

In 1796 Republicans apparently won the argument when Congress abolished the Legion and reorganized the Army into a reduced force of two light dragoon companies and four infantry regiments. Yet, in a sense, Federalists had also won. A peacetime standing Army *did survive,* and ever since Washington presented his "Sentiments" to Hamilton's committee, this had been a major objective of Federalist military policy. The 1796 legislation irrevocably committed the nation to the maintenance of a frontier constabulary that spearheaded western expansion for the next century.

Federalists not only established an American Army, but a Navy as well. The Confederation sold the Continental Navy's last ship in 1785, and the nation had no Navy when trouble at sea loomed on two fronts in 1793. The French Revolution exploded into a world war when France declared war on England, Spain, and Holland. The belligerents, especially England, began interfering with American neutral commerce, which also suffered from Algerine corsairs. The Barbary States—Algiers, Morocco, Tunis, and Tripoli—traditionally engaged in piracy, but the European powers bottled up their activities within the Mediterranean Sea. After 1793, with the Europeans preoccupied, corsairs from Algiers, the most powerful of the petty North African nations, entered the Atlantic and preyed upon American shipping.

Washington's administration thus confronted a major crisis with a formidable enemy and a minor crisis with a weak adversary. It responded to England's challenge by passive defensive measures and negotiations. In 1794 Congress voted to create four arsenals, to build coastal fortifications protecting important seaports, and to form a Corps of Artillerists and Engineers to garrison the seaboard forts. Americans assumed the forts would prevent an enemy *coup de main,* giving land forces time to assemble to repel an invasion at a nonvital location. The president also dispatched John Jay to London to resolve Anglo-American differences, resulting in Jay's Treaty, which temporarily restored amicable relations. To combat the Algerians, Congress passed the Naval Act of 1794, authorizing the construction of six frigates but providing that the act would be suspended if Algiers agreed to peace. In 1796, before completion of any of the frigates, the United States negotiated a treaty with Algiers. Rather than stop construction, Washington asked Congress for further guidance, and it agreed to continue building three of the ships.

Like the Army, the Navy became entangled in partisan politics. Support for a navy came from the commerce-oriented North Atlantic seaboard and parts of the tidewater south, the strongholds of Federalism, while opposition came from agrarian areas and the interior states, the bastions of Republicanism. Believing that preparedness deterred war, Federalists wanted a standing Navy to match the standing Army. A Navy was necessary to protect maritime commerce, the whaling and fishing fleets, and the territorial waters. It would also be a unifying force benefiting the whole country, drawing timber and naval stores from the south, iron from the middle Atlantic states, and shipbuilders and seamen from the north. Even a small fleet, said Hamilton, would allow the United States to "become the arbiter of Europe in America, and be able to incline the balance of European competitions in this part of the world as our interests may dictate." A squadron capable of decisive intervention in the West Indies would guarantee American neutrality during a European war; no nation would risk its New World interests by alienating the United States. Finally, Federalists envisioned the country as a future world power and were concerned about prestige and diplomatic leverage. A Navy, they asserted, symbolized national strength, ensuring European respect.

Republicans argued that instead of deterring war, a navy might provoke it. The prospect of a growing navy might so alarm a European power that, said one Republican, it "would crush us in our infancy." A navy might be an invitation to imperialism and adventurism abroad. No European nation would attack the United States, unless provoked by a naval challenge, because of the predatory European balance of power and the difficulty of bridging the Atlantic moat. Far from benefiting all sections of the country, the Navy would primarily aid New England merchants and shippers. Yet a fleet would be expensive, imposing an oppressive tax burden on the entire country and increasing the national debt. Republicans did not relish a role in European affairs, preferring to direct national energies toward developing the west. Thus while Federalists hoped to parlay the small Army and the tiny kernel of a Navy into military greatness, Republicans wanted to limit future armed forces expansion. The debate over military policy soon reached a furious crescendo.

Federalists and Republicans in Peace and at War

When France and England went to war in 1793, the American political elite fractured along party lines. Federalists were pro-British, emphasizing a common heritage and the commercial connections between England and America. Republicans sided with France, stressing the 1778 treaty that bound the two nations in "perpetual friendship and alliance" and the French Revolution's antimonarchical aspect. Washington decreed, and Congress sanctioned, a neutrality policy, but perfect neutrality in an imperfect warring world was impossible. Jay's Treaty, which prevented war with England, outraged the French, who viewed it as establishing an Anglo-American alliance. In retaliation, France increased its depredations against American shipping and refused to receive a new American minister. In 1797 President John Adams sent a special commission to avert war, but France rebuffed it in the notorious "XYZ affair," in which the French foreign minister demanded a huge bribe before he would even open negotiations with the commission. The result was the Quasi-War with France.

In the spring of 1798 war hysteria engulfed the nation, especially Federalists, who believed the nation faced both a foreign threat and a domestic menace. They feared French agents were subverting the country from within and that Republicans were eager to foment civil war if the United

States and France went to war. Viewing themselves as defenders of constitutional liberty, Federalists considered Republicans disloyal, domestic Jacobins conspiring to convert the country into a French province. To deal with the dual danger of French invasion and French-inspired insurrection, Federalists enacted a preparedness program that Republicans opposed, providing, said Federalists, further proof of their treason.

Congress passed the Alien and Sedition Acts to suppress internal opposition; to enforce the laws and meet the anticipated invasion, it enacted a welter of Army legislation. It created a 10,000-man Provisional Army to be raised in the event of war and empowered the president to accept volunteer companies into national service. Four months later it authorized the president to raise immediately a New Army of twelve infantry regiments and six troops of dragoons. Congress also provided for a massive Eventual Army that, like the Provisional Army, the president could mobilize only in an actual emergency. Legally the United States had five distinct armies: the "old" Army on the frontier, the Provisional Army, the volunteer corps, the New Army, and the Eventual Army.

The government organized only the New Army for the crisis. The old Army remained in the west, and the War Department practically ignored the Provisional, volunteer, and Eventual Armies. Washington agreed to command the combined old and New armies, but he would not take the field until war commenced. Hamilton, who was his ranking subordinate, really commanded the New Army. President Adams disliked and distrusted the New Yorker, but he appointed him second in command upon Washington's insistence. Hamilton craved military glory and devoted his considerable skill to mobilizing the New Army, believing he could use it to quell Republican rebellion, repel French invasion, and—so he dreamed— conquer the Floridas, Louisiana, and perhaps all South America. Naturally, Hamilton excluded Republicans from the officer corps, making this the only wholly political army in American history.

The New Army never matched Hamilton's grandiose expectations. War fever ebbed before serious recruiting began, supplies were inadequate, and, most important, Adams undermined Hamilton's efforts, believing he was a truly dangerous man. The only opportunity to utilize the Army came in 1799, when farmers in eastern Pennsylvania, led by John Fries, resisted the taxes levied to pay for the new military establishment. Adams proclaimed the area in rebellion and ordered 500 New Army regulars and several volunteer militia companies to restore peace. Hamilton applauded the action, but when the Army arrived on the scene, all was quiet. Federalists thought they had nipped a budding revolution, while Republicans asserted that the massive response to Fries' Rebellion was another example of Federalist military despotism.

The Federalists also pursued a naval expansion program. Congress appropriated money to send the three nearly completed frigates to sea, to build the other three authorized in 1794, and to acquire another twenty-four warships. The Marine Corps, which functioned during the Revolution but expired in the postwar demobilization, was revived to provide ships' guards, who could also be ordered to serve on shore. As a maritime reinforcement, Congress permitted merchant vessels to arm themselves and attack armed French ships. The burgeoning land and naval forces imposed an onerous burden on Secretary of War James McHenry, and in April 1798 Congress cleaved his workload in half by creating the Department of the Navy. As the first secretary of the navy, Adams selected Benjamin Stoddert, who requested a building program of twelve 74-gun ships of the line, an equal number of frigates, and twenty or thirty smaller warships, all supported by a system of shipyards and dry docks. Not even the Federalist-dominated legislature could swallow that many masts without choking, but in 1799 it authorized construction of six 74-gun ships and two dry docks, and the purchase of timber lands for naval use.

The first clash in the Quasi-War occurred in July 1798, when the converted merchantman *Delaware* captured *Croyable;* the last encounter took place in October 1800 when the frigate *Boston* defeated *LeBerceau.* In between these two engagements the Navy escorted merchant convoys in the West Indies, hunted enemy privateers infesting the area, and occasionally fought the few warships France sent to the Caribbean. More than a thousand armed merchantmen augmented the fifty-four warships Stoddert assembled, and they had hundreds of encounters with French privateers. Throughout the conflict the Americans enjoyed considerable success, due in large part to British assistance. The Royal Navy aided in convoy duty, freeing American ships for other tasks, and controlled the Atlantic, preventing substantial French forces from sailing to the New World. American ships used British guns, supplies, and Caribbean bases.

The Quasi-War remained limited and undeclared. When Adams received French assurances that a new peace mission would be properly received, he dispatched another commission, which negotiated the Convention of 1800 ending the Quasi-War. Congress soon dismantled the wartime military establishment, disbanding the New Army and authorizing the president to sell all the ships except for thirteen frigates, only six of which would remain in active service. The convention also aided Jefferson's election in 1800. The Hamiltonian wing of the Federalist Party refused to support Adams's reelection bid, having never forgiven him for choosing peace over war and robbing it of an opportunity to crush the Republicans, defeat the French, and conquer a vast American empire. The sudden end to the crisis also gave Republicans an armory of political ammunition by making Federalist preparedness measures appear despotic.

As the Federalist era ended, the party of Washington and Hamilton had not infused as much military strength into the republic as they desired. Yet military policy as it evolved during the 1790s basically remained intact for a century. The nation would keep a small professional Army, augmented by militia and federal volunteers during wartime. The embryonic system of arsenals, shipyards, dry docks, and coastal fortifications would be expanded. The nation would rely on a small navy to show the flag in peacetime and to protect American shipping while plundering enemy commerce during wartime. In essence, a passive defense policy emerged that theoretically would preserve the country during a crisis until its latent strength could be mobilized.

The survival of the Federalist-established military institutions initially depended on their acceptance by the new president. Jefferson had a defensive conception of United States military power and advocated non-involvement in foreign affairs, governmental economy, and reduction of the national debt. In his mind none of these goals accorded with a substantial peacetime establishment. But he also believed the international arena was predatory and that military weakness invited aggression, and he had no intention of completely dismantling the Federalist military apparatus. Although Jefferson viewed the militia as the first line of defense, its purpose was to buy "time for raising regular forces after the necessity of them shall become certain." He urged Congress to reform the militia, making it an effective immediate defense force so that the regulars could be safely reduced, but not abolished.

The Republican-controlled Congress refused to tamper with the Uniform Militia Act, but on March 16, 1802, it passed the Military Peace Establishment Act, which demonstrated Jefferson's commitment to a regular Army, but one that was "Republicanized." The administration inherited a Federalist-dominated Army, and Jefferson believed he needed to ensure that it would respond to Republican direction. The 1802 act provided the mechanisms for breaking Federalist control and creating a source of Republican officers. Under the guise of an economy measure, the act "reduced" and reorganized the Army. The reduction was cosmetic. The Army had never attained its authorized strength under the Federalists, and the Republicans simply cut the Army's authorized size to approximately its actual strength. The reorganization eliminated eighty-eight officers' positions, allowing Jefferson to remove officers who had been Federalist partisans, but also added about twenty ensigns. The president appointed Republicans to these new positions.

The 1802 act also established the Military Academy at West Point, creating a Corps of Engineers distinct from the artillery and stating that "the said corps . . . shall constitute a military academy." The president received exceptional powers over the Corps of Engineers and the Military Academy, permitting him to select the officers who would establish the academy and teach there, and the cadets who would attend it. Ironically, since the early 1780s Federalists had supported such an institution, while Jefferson had always opposed this idea. He reversed his position for two reasons. First, the president had wanted a national school that would emphasize the sciences and produce graduates useful to society. Officers trained as scientists and engineers would, for example, benefit the nation as explorers and road-builders. Equally important, West Point would be a Republican avenue into the officer corps. In selecting faculty and cadets, Jefferson searched for eligible Republicans and avoided Federalists, furthering the process of "Republicanizing" the Army that would continue throughout his years in office.

Naval retrenchment under Jefferson initially bordered on liquidation, but when war with Tripoli appeared likely, the administration lifted its budgetary ax from the Navy's neck. At first Republicans discontinued work on the 74s, the dry docks, and the navy yards, discharged officers and men, and sold ships as rapidly as possible. However, the pasha of Tripoli threatened to unleash his pirates if he did not receive increased tribute, which the United States had been paying since the 1780s. The president detested Barbary corsairs more than an expensive Navy, and in June 1801 he dispatched a small squadron under Commodore Richard Dale with orders to "protect our commerce and chastise their insolence" if Tripoli declared war. Dale learned that the pasha had done so, but neither he nor Commodore Richard Morris, who arrived with a replacement squadron in 1802, was very aggressive, and they accomplished little. In 1803 Jefferson sent a third squadron under Commodore Edward Preble, who clamped a tight blockade on the city of Tripoli and subjected it to naval assaults that damaged the town, its fortifications, and enemy ships in the harbor. A fourth squadron under Commodore Samuel Barron followed up Preble's work with a combined land-naval expedition that forced the pasha to sign a peace treaty in June 1805.

The Tripolitan War spurred Jefferson's fascination with gunboats, which had been useful in the shallow North African waters. Congress authorized construction of fifteen gunboats in 1803, and eight of them crossed the Atlantic to serve in the Mediterranean. In the postwar period the president embraced them as the heart of his naval policy, and by 1807 Congress had authorized another 263 of them. The gunboats were cheap to build, were so simple to operate that maritime militiamen could man them—which coincided with Jefferson's preference for citizen-soldiers over professionals—and were incontrovertibly defensive. Combined with stationary batteries at strategic coastal locations, mobile land batteries, and floating batteries, he believed gunboats would protect the country from invasion by even the strongest maritime power.

What the gunboats could not do was protect seaborne commerce, which badly needed protection. In 1803, after the brief Peace of Amiens, Napoleon declared war on England, reigniting the contest for European supremacy. Both combatants struck at American neutral trade, trying to strangle each other economically. Having gained command of the sea at the Battle of Trafalgar, Britain was the worst offender. The Royal Navy seized more than 500 American vessels between 1803 and 1807, hovered off the coast imposing a virtual blockade, and impressed American seamen. The ultimate indignity came in June 1807, when the British frigate *Leopard* fired on the *Chesapeake,* killing and wounding twenty-one men and impressing four alleged deserters.

Jefferson's administration responded to these provocations in several ways. It launched an intensive diplomatic effort and supported it with several defensive measures: Increasing the Army's authorized strength to 10,000 men; appropriating money to complete, repair, and build coastal fortifications; and authorizing $200,000 annually for arming the militia. Diplomacy failed to budge England on the crucial questions of neutral rights and impressment, but rather than go to war, Jefferson undertook an experiment in economic coercion. In December 1807 Congress passed an Embargo Act that prohibited all exports. Jefferson hoped that by depriving the belligerents of American products, he could wring concessions from them regarding neutral rights, but he was wrong. The embargo had little effect on the European antagonists, and British impressment and neutral rights infringements continued unabated.

Although the embargo did not deter the Europeans, it brought the United States to the verge of civil war. Federalist New England mercantile interests saw their local economy ruined, as ships rotted at their wharves and seaborne commerce languished. The Francophobe Federalists also believed the embargo hurt England far more than France. They so strenuously opposed the law that Jefferson had to use both regulars and militia to enforce it, employing military force domestically at least as readily as Federalists had done during the Whiskey and Fries Rebellions. Now it was Jeffersonians who spoke glowingly about the necessity of preserving orderly government and Federalists who screamed about tyranny. Thus the embargo sapped internal unity without alleviating the war-provoking problems with England.

Western concerns as well as maritime grievances pushed the United States toward war. Farmers believed British commercial restrictions depressed grain prices, and some westerners squinted at Canada and Florida with expansionist greed. Most important, although the English had withdrawn across the Canadian border, they continued to aid the Indians, especially Tecumseh, a Shawnee chief who tried to revitalize the Indian confederacy quashed at Fallen Timbers. In 1811 the governor of the Indiana Territory, William Henry Harrison, defeated the Indians at the Battle of Tippecanoe; when British-supplied equipment was found nearby, frontiersmen seethed with anger at British treachery.

By 1812 many Americans believed the country's options were either to fight or surrender national honor and sovereignty. A group of young congressmen, known as the War Hawks, voiced the public's frustration over relations with England. Led by Henry Clay and John C. Calhoun, the War Hawks, tired of wordy diplomacy and spineless economic sanctions, waxed belligerent in their advocacy of strong war measures. Even Jefferson admitted that "every hope from time, patience, and love of peace are exhausted and war or abject submission are the only alternatives left to us." His successor as president, James Madison, submitted a war message to Congress on June 1 and, after favorable votes of only 79–49 in the House and 19–13 in the Senate, signed it on June 18.

The War of 1812

Rarely have nations gone to war so reluctantly. At war with Napoleonic France, the British did not want a North American conflict. Despite the War Hawks' verbal bellicosity and a decade of acute tension, the United States had made few warlike preparations, so the declaration of war and preparations for war came almost simultaneously. Legislation enacted early in 1812 increased the Army to 35,000 and provided for 50,000 volunteers and 100,000 militia. While these numbers were awesome on paper, when war began the regulars numbered only 12,000 and the volunteers and militia remained unorganized. The Navy consisted of only sixteen ships, seven of them frigates inherited from the Federalists, including three superb heavy frigates.* By contrast, the Royal Navy had about 1,000 warships.

Aside from its tardy preparations, the country had four other handicaps. Madison was a weak commander in chief. A poor judge of men, he filled many positions with incompetents. For example, his general officers were Revolutionary veterans, now averaging sixty years of age. Although they had been good soldiers in their youth, time had sapped their vigor and ability. Also, Madison claimed to govern by Republican principles, including minimal government cheaply run, a distaste for standing forces, and opposition to a national debt. The war made all three principles impossi-

---

* The seven frigates were the *United States,* 44 guns; *Constitution,* 44; *President,* 44; *Constellation,* 38; *Congress,* 38; *Chesapeake,* 38; and *Essex,* 32.

ble to follow, but the Madison administration never quite adjusted to this reality and, for instance, failed to formulate an adequate taxation system. Therefore the nation went to war on a financial shoestring, resulting in inadequate logistical support for the armed forces.

A third difficulty was the factionalism that pervaded all aspects of waging the war. In the field, generals rarely cooperated with one another, and Navy and Army officers paid little attention to each other's concerns. No government agency existed to plan, much less impose, intra- and interservice coordination. Personal and political rivalries rent Madison's cabinet, reflecting the deep divisions even among Republicans as to the war's wisdom and the most effective measures for waging it; meanwhile the Federalists opposed the war almost unanimously.

Finally, conflict between national and regional strategic concerns also hampered the war effort. From the administration's perspective, the crucial strategic task was to conquer Canada in the hope that Britain would make concessions on the maritime issues to regain it. Though a Canadian offensive was Madison's primary goal, American coastal localities were more concerned about naval raids, the southwest considered the Creek Indians a primary threat, and the northwest believed Tecumseh's confederacy to be the foremost security problem. The government's weakness and the slow, primitive means of transportation and communication resulted in the war becoming so regionally oriented that national strategy was often irrelevant. Imposing the administration's will on the war effort was impossible; local leaders simply ignored its injunctions. But regionalism could be a strength as well as a weakness. Local strategists understood regional realities and could adopt appropriate measures; and because they were so autonomous, defeats in other theaters did not shatter their morale.

Factionalism and regionalism united in Federalist-dominated New England, where the war's unpopularity not only hamstrung the war effort but threatened national unity. Every Federalist in Congress voted against the declaration of war. Traditionally pro-British, the Federalists believed that the United States should help, not hinder, Britain against France. In the fall of 1814 the Federalist governor of Massachusetts sent an agent to Halifax to probe for prospects of a separate peace; the Federalists' collective disaffection culminated in December at the Hartford Convention, a conclave that seemed so ominous the Madison administration prepared to use force to crush any secessionist movement that might burst from behind the meeting's closed doors. Although the convention only proposed certain defensive measures and a series of constitutional amendments that would strengthen New England's position in national affairs, it implied that if the demands were not met New England might secede from the Union.

Deleterious consequences flowed from Federalist opposition. New England Federalists (and even some Republicans) carried on illicit trade with England, providing supplies to enemy armies in Canada, and withheld financial assistance for "Mr. Madison's war." Since Republicans failed to impose sufficient taxes, they resorted to loans and borrowed $40 million, of which less than $3 million came from New England, the nation's richest section. Federalist governors also refused to mobilize their militias when Madison called for them. Under the Constitution the militia could be called into national service only for specific purposes. The governors insisted that they, not the president, had the right to determine when these exigencies existed, and they denied their existence.* They also argued that militia could not be used outside the country for a Canadian invasion. Since New England's militia system was the country's best, the obvious invasion route via Lake Champlain bordered New England, and the small Army needed militia reinforcements to conduct an invasion, the governors' refusal to cooperate was near crippling.

In broad terms, fighting occurred in four theaters. The northeast encompassed the Canadian border from the Niagara River and Lake Ontario to the Richelieu River and Lake Champlain, while the northwest stretched from Lake Erie to the northern reaches of Lake Huron. A southern theater included the Gulf coast from New Orleans to Pensacola and jutted inland along the Alabama River and its tributaries. The fourth theater was the eastern seaboard and the Atlantic Ocean.

Neither England nor America had thought about the strategy they would employ, but the initiative belonged to the United States. England could devote few resources to the New World and assumed the defensive in Canada, where 7,000 regulars garrisoned the border. The commander in chief for Canada, Lieutenant General Sir George Prevost, could also call on the militia, but this was scant comfort. He described it as "a mere posse, ill arm'd and without discipline," and he worried about its loyalty because of the numerous former French citizens and American immigrants in the population. Aid might come from the Indians—if American control in the Northwest could be neutralized.

Correctly assuming that Canada was vulnerable, the administration prepared to attack it. The obvious strategy was to capture Montreal. Madison preferred a powerful thrust along the traditional invasion route, but New England's lethargy made such a movement difficult. On the other hand, war fervor in the west beckoned for offensives in the Great Lakes

---

* In 1827 the Supreme Court ruled that the president had the authority to determine when an emergency existed in which he had the constitutional right to call forth the militia.

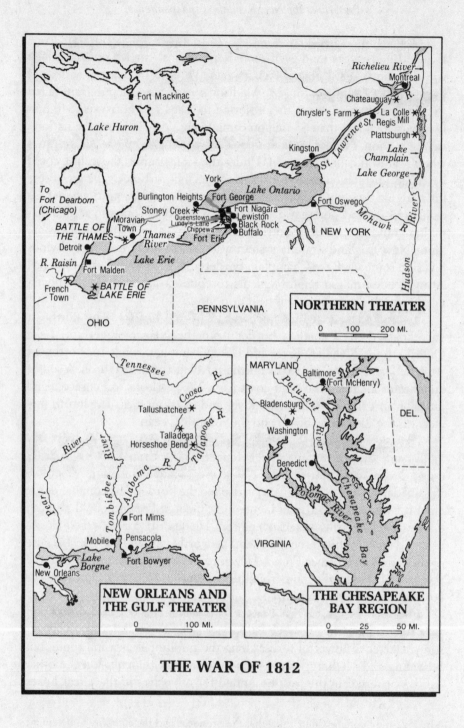

Northern Theater

Fort Mackinac
Richelieu River
Montreal
Chrysler's Farm
Chateauguay
La Colle Mill
St. Regis
Plattsburgh
Lake Champlain
Lake George
Kingston
Lake Huron
York
Lake Ontario
Burlington Heights
Fort George
Fort Oswego
Stoney Creek
Fort Niagara
Lewiston
To Fort Dearborn (Chicago)
Queenstown
Black Rock
Moravian Town
Lundy's Lane
Buffalo
Mohawk R.
NEW YORK
BATTLE OF THE THAMES
Thames River
Chippewa
Fort Erie
Detroit
Lake Erie
Hudson R.
R. Raisin
Fort Malden
French Town
BATTLE OF LAKE ERIE
PENNSYLVANIA
NORTHERN THEATER
OHIO
0 100 200 MI.

New Orleans and the Gulf Theater

Tennessee
Coosa R.
Tallushatchee
Talladega
Tallapoosa R.
Horseshoe Bend
River
Tombigbee River
Alabama R.
Pearl River
Fort Mims
Mobile
Pensacola
Lake Borgne
Fort Bowyer
New Orleans
NEW ORLEANS AND THE GULF THEATER
0 100 MI.

The Chesapeake Bay Region

MARYLAND
Baltimore (Fort McHenry)
Patuxent River
Bladensburg
DEL.
Washington
Benedict
Chesapeake Bay
Potomac River
VIRGINIA
THE CHESAPEAKE BAY REGION
0 25 50 MI.

THE WAR OF 1812

region. From these considerations emerged a three-pronged offensive, one prong moving from Detroit, another attacking along the Niagara River, and a third marching toward Montreal. Attacks on three fronts should have stretched British resources to the snapping point, but failure to coordinate the advances allowed the English to meet each one in turn.

Begun with confident expectations, the campaign yielded dismal results. General William Hull entered Canada from Detroit in mid-July intent on capturing Fort Malden, but he encountered logistical difficulties. The enemy controlled Lakes Erie and Ontario, preventing easy supply by water, and Indian ambushes cut his overland supply line. Then came word that the British had captured Fort Michilimackinac. Fearing that thousands of Indians would descend on him from the north, Hull timidly pulled back to Detroit, where he surrendered in mid-August to a British force of regulars, militia, and Tecumseh's Indians. The previous day the Fort Dearborn garrison evacuated its post on Hull's orders, only to be slaughtered by Indians. Hull's successor, William Henry Harrison, tried to redeem the situation with a winter campaign to recapture Detroit, but the British surprised an advance detachment at Frenchtown and annihilated it. The debacle in the northwestern theater was complete.

On the Niagara front General Stephen Van Rensselaer, a political appointee with no military experience, commanded an army of regulars and militia. In mid-October he attacked Queenston, achieving initial success. But when militia reinforcements refused to cross the Niagara River into a foreign country, the British counterattacked and won the Battle of Queenston Heights. Van Rensselaer was replaced by General Alexander Smyth, who excelled at issuing bombastic proclamations to "plant the American standard in Canada." Unfortunately his words spoke louder than his actions, and the American standard remained in America. Despite the Detroit and Niagara failures, if General Henry Dearborn's offensive could capture Montreal the United States would still gain a decisive advantage. He moved slowly northward to the Canadian border where, as on the Niagara front, the militiamen would go no further. So Dearborn returned to winter quarters and all Canada was safe—at least until spring.

While the effort on land was a demoralizing tale of poor strategy and weak leadership, the opening sea campaign was as refreshing as a cool ocean breeze. Americans had several advantages. The Federalist heavy frigates were the finest ships of their class in the world. Unlike the Army commanders, who had earned their reputations in the Revolution, ranking naval officers were generally young and had developed professional skills and attitudes during the Quasi- and Tripolitan Wars. Moreover, the British navy could commit only a fraction of its strength to American waters.

The administration contemplated deploying the Navy in a single fleet, but this proved impractical. However, a squadron commanded by John Rodgers did get to sea, while other ships cruised alone to prey on British commerce or fight enemy warships. The result was a series of spectacular single-ship victories, with *Constitution* destroying the frigate *Guerriere* and then later defeating the frigate *Java,* and *United States* capturing the frigate *Macedonian.* In all these actions the American ship was larger and more heavily gunned, but knowledge of this did not detract from the celebrations following the news of each victory.

These encounters persuaded Congress to authorize new ships: four 74s and six 44-gun frigates in January 1813, and six sloops in March. But the Navy's glory days were over. Stung by the defeats, the British Admiralty ordered its frigates to avoid single-ship engagements and sent more ships to blockade the coast, trapping the American frigates in port. The few American warships that got to sea after 1812 could not repeat earlier successes because the British no longer underestimated them. When, for example, the frigate *Shannon* disobeyed orders and fought USS *Chesapeake,* the British vessel prevailed. However, the *Chesapeake's* captain, James Lawrence, exemplified the Navy's fighting tradition. When he was mortally wounded he told his subordinates, "Don't give up the ship. Fight her till she sinks." Although the ship did not sink, the English captured it only after boarding it and engaging in savage hand-to-hand combat.

Meanwhile, the blockade became a noose, choking American commerce. By 1814 merchant trade was about 17 percent of what it had been in 1811. Beginning in 1813 the Royal Navy also made punitive coastal raids, and Jefferson's gunboats, designed to prevent such excursions, proved ineffectual. Although the blockade penned up the frigates and crushed seaborne and coastal trade, it could not prevent privateers and small warships from slipping out of port. What success Americans enjoyed on the ocean after 1812 came from privateers and the sloops authorized in 1813. Five hundred privateers received commissions and took 1,300 prizes, and the sloops captured numerous merchantmen and a few small warships. But neither the 1812 frigate victories nor the depredations by privateers and sloops significantly altered the war's course.

Despite the setbacks on land in 1812 the United States remained on the offensive in 1813. Since the failures had been more the consequence of American ineptitude than British skill, optimism still prevailed. But the United States again dissipated its strength in several disjointed assaults on Canada. The Americans had limited success on the Detroit front when Oliver H. Perry's ships destroyed a British squadron on Lake Erie on September 10. Perry scribbled a hasty report to Harrison on the back of an old letter: "Dear Gen'l:—We have met the enemy and they are ours; two ships, two brigs, one schooner, and one sloop. Yours with great respect and esteem. O. H. Perry." His communique was a model—perhaps unique—battle report, being both accurate and brief!

The Battle of Lake Erie forced both British General Henry Proctor and Harrison into action. With his supply line across the lake cut, Proctor retreated eastward along the Thames River and Harrison pursued. Proctor confronted his pursuers two miles west of Moraviantown with about 1,000 regulars and Native-American allies. Harrison had thrice that many men, including 1,000 mounted riflemen from Kentucky, whom Colonel Richard M. Johnson had trained more rigorously than was usual for citizen-soldiers. In the Battle of the Thames the Americans won a smashing victory, killing Tecumseh and capturing most of Proctor's army. With Tecumseh's death the Indian confederacy collapsed, fulfilling a vital northwestern war objective. But, although satisfying a regional war aim, the campaign did little to advance the national war effort, since Harrison's front was subsidiary to the more important front further east.

Secretary of War John Armstrong, who believed that the Lake Champlain force was too weak to attack Montreal directly, instead proposed thrusts against Kingston, York, and Forts George and Erie. Triple success would make all British positions west of Kingston untenable. The campaign began well. In late April General Zebulon Pike—of Pikes Peak fame—raided York against minimal resistance. A month later General Henry Dearborn attacked Fort George and the British commander, General John Vincent, retreated, taking the Chippewa and Fort Erie garrisons with him. So far so good, but the tide of war soon flowed against the Americans when Vincent routed a pursuing force at Stoney Creek and compelled the Americans to abandon Chippewa and Fort Erie. The American commander at Fort George tried to strike one of Vincent's advanced posts, but the enemy captured the entire column at the Battle of the Beaver Dams, a defeat that left the Americans precariously isolated in Fort George.

At this point Secretary Armstrong replaced Dearborn with General James Wilkinson, who had become the Army's ranking officer when Wayne died in 1796. Wilkinson proposed that Kingston be bypassed and that he and General Wade Hampton, commanding at Plattsburgh, attack Montreal, with each army approaching the city from a different direction. Command disputes foiled the plan. Unfortunately, despite Wilkinson's call for a coordinated dual advance, he and Hampton so detested one another that bickering rather than cooperation was the hallmark of the campaign. Armstrong came to the front to placate his feuding generals, but his presence only muddled an already tangled problem when he tried to exercise direct field command. British forces turned back Hampton at the Battle of Chateauguay and Wilkinson at the Battle of Chrysler's Farm. In mid-

December the Americans evacuated Fort George, unleashing a British offensive that captured or burned Fort Niagara, Lewiston, Black Rock, and Buffalo. These enemy successes canceled out the earlier American victories, leaving the Niagara front in British hands.

After two campaigning seasons the United States was no closer to victory than it had been when the war began. It had frittered away precious opportunities to invade Canada while England fought for survival against Napoleon. Now news from Europe indicated that it would be an entirely new war in 1814, with the United States on the defensive. France collapsed in the winter of 1813–1814, Napoleon abdicated in April, and a victorious England could send reinforcements to America, transforming its war there from a desperate defensive to a punishing offensive. The British planned offensives from Canada, in Chesapeake Bay, and at New Orleans, and they were as confident as the Americans had been two years earlier. Yet the same obstacles that England had encountered in fighting the Revolution remained, especially America's sponge-like nature. As the Duke of Wellington said, he could perceive no operation that would so badly injure America that it would be forced to sue for peace. Furthermore, by 1814 aggressive younger men had replaced the Army's original commanders. Coming to the fore were Jacob Brown, Edmund R Gaines, Alexander Macomb, Winfield Scott, and Andrew Jackson. These men would direct the nation's military fortunes for decades to come.

Before British reinforcements could cross the Atlantic the United States launched two offensives. Wilkinson moved northward from Lake Champlain to La Colle Creek, where a stone mill occupied by fewer than 200 British soldiers blocked the advance. An artillery bombardment consumed all the American ammunition without damaging the mill, and Wilkinson retreated. On the Niagara front, Jacob Brown commanded an army of two regular brigades and one militia brigade. After capturing Fort Erie he moved northward, while General Phineas Riall, the enemy commander at Fort George, marched south. The armies collided at Chippewa, where they engaged in a classic eighteenth-century battle featuring close-range volleys and bayonet charges. The British broke the militia but then ran into a regular brigade under Winfield Scott, which fought back fiercely. At one point, as Scott's brigade deployed into a battle line, Riall exclaimed, "Those are regulars, by God!" Technically he was correct, but Scott's "regulars" were mostly recent recruits whom he had converted into disciplined troops in just a few months. An avid student of the history and theory of war, Scott had established a training camp where he drilled recruits intensely, proving that under competent officers citizen-soldiers could become quality troops without years of rigorous instruction.

After Chippewa, General Gordon Drummond assumed command of

the British force shortly before the armies clashed at the Battle of Lundy's Lane, which was more fierce than Chippewa, with opposing lines firing volleys almost muzzle to muzzle. The battle was a tactical standoff, but with both Brown and Scott wounded the Americans withdrew to Fort Erie, which they soon blew up just before returning to American soil. As usual, the Montreal and Niagara fronts were indecisive.

As the rival armies battered each other along the Niagara, the British offensives began elsewhere. General Prevost advanced down the Richelieu, arriving at Plattsburgh in early September with 10,000 men and a flotilla under George Downie to guard his left flank and maintain his supply line along the lake. Opposing him were Alexander Macomb with 3,400 men and Thomas Macdonough's squadron anchored in Plattsburgh Bay. Prevost decided to attack simultaneously on land and water. On September 11 Downie's ships sailed into the bay, and a furious naval battle resulted. When the lake breezes wafted away the acrid smoke, the British flotilla was in ruins. Meanwhile Prevost's land assault had developed slowly, and when he realized Downie was beaten he ordered a halt. His magnificent army was still intact, but he believed that loss of control on the lake made his logistical situation hopeless. The next day he retreated.

The British Chesapeake Bay offensive began in August with Vice Admiral Alexander Cochrane commanding the naval element and General Robert Ross the land forces. The ministry had authorized them to undertake punitive raids against seaboard cities to divert American attention from Prevost's offensive. As Cochrane sailed up the bay Joshua Barney's gunboat flotilla fled up the Patuxent River. The British anchored at Benedict, disembarked 4,500 men to march along the river banks, and sent some small craft upstream. Trapped, Barney destroyed his gunboats.

Ross now marched toward Washington, which Armstrong had never fortified, considering it strategically insignificant. The administration hastily organized a predominantly militia force under General William H. Winder, but he neglected even obvious delaying tactics such as destroying bridges and sniping at the redcoats as they traversed dense forests. Winder established a three-line defensive position at Bladensburg, but the first two lines quickly collapsed, the soldiers departing at sprint speed. Barney's 500 sailors, footsore from the unaccustomed marching, stood in the third line. Here hard fighting occurred, as Barney's men fended off attacks and, crying "Board 'em, board 'em!" counterattacked. When the British outflanked their position the seamen finally retreated, ending the Battle of Bladensburg and opening the way to the capital. There the British burned the public buildings, including the White House and the Capitol.

The next target, Baltimore, disappointed British hopes of another easy victory. The American commander, Samuel Smith, was a determined fighter, and militiamen rallied to his standard. In a testimonial to aching muscles and blistered hands, the city's citizens fortified defensive positions. Guarding the harbor was Fort McHenry, one of the fortifications authorized in 1794. As Ross's army marched from North Point, militia blocked the route about halfway to Baltimore. Although the British punched through the force, a sniper killed Ross. His replacement, Colonel Arthur Brooke, pushed on but halted before the city's entrenchments. At dawn on September 13, Cochrane began a twenty-four-hour bombardment of Fort McHenry. A Washington lawyer, Francis Scott Key, watched the rockets' red glare and the bombs bursting in air, saw the flag flying proudly over the fort in the dawn's early light, and was mightily inspired. He jotted down some verses, later revised, that became "The Star-Spangled Banner." But what was inspirational to Key was disheartening to Cochrane and Brooke, who withdrew on September 14. The second of Britain's three offensives had now been blunted.

The United States not only repulsed but shattered the New Orleans offensive, primarily because of Andrew Jackson's cyclonic energy and iron-willed determination. Jackson became a hero after he won the Creek War of 1813–1814, a conflict in which he was virtually an independent warlord, often acting on his own authority and sometimes contrary to the secretary of war's orders. In 1813 a large portion of the Creek nation, seizing the opportunity presented by the Americans' war with England, went on the warpath and killed more than 200 whites at Fort Mims, Alabama. With concentrated loathing the entire southwest struck back. When word of Fort Mims reached Tennessee, Jackson, a state militia general even though he had never led troops in battle, was recuperating from a wound suffered in a frontier brawl. With a bullet lodged close to his heart and his arm in a sling, he struggled from bed, summoned volunteers, and won the Battles of Tallushatchee and Talladega. Other columns from east Tennessee, Georgia, and Mississippi Territory also defeated the Creeks in isolated engagements. Lacking centralized direction, the campaign failed to end the Creek War, but the Creeks had lost at least 20 percent of their warriors.

As the year ended Jackson's army disintegrated when the volunteers' enlistments expired and the men returned home. But reinforcements arrived in early 1814, and Jackson invaded Creek territory a second time. With incredible tenacity considering their reduced manpower, the Indians attacked three times, forcing Jackson to retreat. However, when he learned that more than 1,000 Creeks had fortified a bend in the Tallapoosa River, the Tennessean invaded a third time. At the peninsula's neck the Creeks had a log breastwork, and at the far end they had canoes to flee in if hard pressed. Jackson sent his Cherokee allies and mounted volunteers to seal the escape hatch and stormed the barricade, pushing the Indians back in savage combat. Even Jackson admitted "the *carnage was dreadfull*" as the Creek nation's fighting strength expired in a hundred acres of gullied terrain. The Battle of Horseshoe Bend ended the Creek War.

In May, Jackson became a regular Army major general commanding the 7th Military District, which included Louisiana. His responsibility was to stop Britain's New Orleans venture, a responsibility he shouldered alone, since time and distance prevented the national government from affording him timely assistance.

Admiral Cochrane, who had gone to Jamaica after his exploits on Chesapeake Bay, planned to capture New Orleans by taking Mobile, marching an army from there to the Mississippi, and then moving downriver to the Crescent City. While a roundabout approach, it was the easiest route, since New Orleans was a hundred miles up the Mississippi, situated amid a maze of bayous, swamps, and flesh-rending reeds. It could be attacked directly, said a British officer, only if troops were "assisted by the aerial flight of the bird of prey, or astride the alligator's scaly back." The ministry appointed Sir Edward Pakenham to command the army, but he did not reach Jamaica before the armada departed and General John Keane became acting commander.

Jackson suspected that the British might use an overland route, and when they attacked Fort Bowyer, Mobile's main defensive work, his alert men repelled them. Three weeks later he counterattacked, capturing Pensacola. His vigilance foreclosed Cochrane's preferred route and doomed British hopes of recruiting legions of Indians and Spaniards to assist them. Having blocked the land route to the city, Jackson hastened to New Orleans. He was not well, but those who glimpsed his fierce, hawklike eyes sensed that the emaciated exterior belied his inner strength. Jackson ordered the likely approaches to the city guarded, and to defend it he assembled a large amount of artillery and a cosmopolitan force that included sailors, a few marines, several regular regiments, Tennessee and Kentucky militia and volunteers, the Louisiana militia, two brigades of New Orleans free black men, some Choctaw Indians, and Jean Lafitte's 800 pirates.

"By the Eternal, they shall not sleep on our soil!" thundered Jackson on December 23 when he learned that British troops were only nine miles from the city. They had arrived undetected by coming across Lake Borgne and using an unaccountably unguarded bayou leading inland. The Americans made a night attack on Keane's position; it became a melee pitting British bayonets against American hatchets and knives. After this First Battle of New Orleans, Jackson withdrew two miles, assuming a defensive position behind the wide but dry Rodriguez Canal. On the right was the Mississippi and on the left a cypress swamp, making enemy flank attacks difficult. In front was a plain dominated by Jackson's parapet.

Pakenham, who arrived on Christmas Day, probed the American defenses on December 28 and on New Year's Day—the Second and Third Battles of New Orleans. The Fourth (and main) Battle came on January 8. Although Pakenham probed Jackson's flanks, sending a West Indian black regiment through the swamp and dispatching another force across the Mississippi to assail the American forces there, his major assault was on the broad plain toward Jackson's main position. The British general planned to attack at night, but the advance was delayed until morning. It appeared that fortune might shine on the British as fog shrouded the plain, but the fog suddenly lifted and the slaughter began. By eight-thirty the battle was over, with 500 prisoners in American hands and another 1,500 British dead and wounded littering the plain, most of them victims of Jackson's artillery. American casualties numbered about 70.

Ironically the victory had no influence on the Treaty of Ghent, which had been signed on Christmas Eve, 1814. Efforts at negotiations had begun almost as soon as the war commenced. Allied with England in the war against Napoleon, Russia offered to mediate the dispute. Having bungled the 1812 campaign, the United States accepted Russia's offer, but England did not. The British, however, suggested direct negotiations and Madison agreed. By the time the negotiators met, England was in no hurry to conclude a peace, believing its 1814 offensives would improve its bargaining position. Still, Britain was not prepared to fight a prolonged war for New World territory or for the benefit of its Indian allies. Not only was England's population war-weary after two decades of continuous strife but, with the French population seething with discontent and Britain squabbling with its allies, England feared a renewed European war.

After Prevost's retreat and Cochrane's repulse at Baltimore, Wellington in essence advised the British government to settle the war. These defeats indicated that England could not project power into North America any more effectively in 1814 than during the Revolution—a fact confirmed by New Orleans. As in that earlier war, both combatants were militarily weak in America, with the United States being just barely strong enough to stave off defeat.

Britain agreed to terms based on the status quo ante bellum. The treaty was a cessation of hostilities that mentioned none of the war's causes. Of course, with the European war over, British violations of neutral rights ceased and they were no longer an urgent issue. Although the United States did not acquire Canada and annexed only part of Florida, it escaped territorial losses. For the west and south the defeat of Tecumseh's confederation and the Creeks signified clear-cut gains. Perhaps New England "lost" the war, since its influence in national affairs waned rapidly after 1815. And from a national perspective even a stalemate against Napoleon's conquerors was no embarrassment. By fighting England a second time and surviving intact, the United States had preserved its independence and gained new respect in the international arena.

In early February 1815, three messages converged on Washington from separate locations. News of Jackson's victory came from New Orleans, quickly followed by the treaty from Ghent. The two announcements set off national rejoicing, erasing grim memories of earlier defeats. Amidst this euphoria the third communication arrived, borne by a committee from the Hartford Convention. The Federalists' veiled threat of New England secession tainted the party with treason, and they never recovered from the stigma—a sad end for the party that a quarter-century earlier had laid the foundations for the republic's future growth.

The nearly simultaneous arrival of the glad tidings from Louisiana and Ghent made it appear as if the United States had defeated Britain again, a myth Americans willingly embraced. New Orleans had a further importance: It enshrined the western hunter-soldiers who had supposedly mowed down England's veterans (artillery inflicted most of the casualties) and glorified the militia at a time when the militia system was virtually dead. The Treaty of Ghent was also significant in that it marked the end of an epoch in American history. For more than a century, the large wars wracking the Old World had become the New World's wars as well. But for a century afterward no general conflict afflicted Europe, and the United States avoided the Continent's numerous smaller wars. Hence the nation turned inward, devoting its energies to domestic development and territorial expansion. America's armed forces played vital roles in both activities.

FIVE

The Armed Forces and National Expansion, 1815–1860

During the War of 1812 the Republican Party converted to Federalist military policy. In the war's aftermath, amid fervid nationalism and with full Republican support, the armed forces prospered. But by the 1820s the magnified nationalism waned, and the Army and Navy entered an era of neglect. Yet these poorly financed and undermanned forces participated in three significant developments. First, the Industrial Revolution's technological advances transformed the conduct of war. Second, the postwar decades witnessed the beginnings of military professionalization. Finally, the armed forces aided the nation's territorial expansion and economic development. The Army explored the wilderness, built transportation networks, guarded settlers, and fought wars against Indians who resisted President Andrew Jackson's removal policy and against Mexico, which contested America's claim to a "Manifest Destiny." The Navy, too, advanced national interests by protecting foreign trade and conducting diplomatic-commercial missions abroad.

Postwar Nationalism and Military Policy

In early 1815, in words that Alexander Hamilton might have written, President James Madison told Congress that experience "demonstrates that a certain degree of preparation for war is not only indispensable to avert disasters in the onset, but affords also the best security for the continuance of peace." The president asked Congress to maintain a defense establishment similar to the one Federalists had long advocated: a strong Navy to protect commerce, fortifications to defend the coast, and a substantial regular Army and a reformed militia to guard the frontiers and repel invaders. Although Congress had no desire to tamper with the militia, it responded favorably to the other items.

In 1816, for the first time, the United States established a peacetime long-range naval building program. Congress voted $1 million annually for eight years to build nine 74-gun ships of the line, twelve 44-gun frigates, and three coastal defense steam batteries—a larger building program than ever before. But by 1820 a movement toward naval retrenchment, spurred by the Panic of 1819, was underway, and in 1821 Congress cut the appropriation in half, although it extended this reduced annual outlay for three years beyond the original 1824 termination date. In 1827 and in 1833 Congress continued the $500,000 expenditure for six more years. Slowly, most of the ships authorized in 1816 were completed, but the Navy Department took many of them out of active service ("laid them up in ordinary," in the terminology of the time) and depended to a great extent on smaller warships periodically authorized by Congress.

The reliance on small ships was not ill-founded. The Navy's primary responsibility was to protect America's expanding commerce. No great nation threatened this trade, but pirates and irregular privateers employing small, fast ships did. Trying to catch these buccaneers with ships of the line and frigates was futile. Thus instead of forming a battlefleet, the Navy Department divided its ships into squadrons that sailed in geographic areas called stations. A squadron normally consisted of one or two frigates or ships of the line and a larger number of smaller but swifter vessels. The first squadron established was in the Mediterranean, where in 1812 Algiers had renewed its depredations. Shortly after Congress ratified the Treaty of Ghent, it declared war on Algiers. After the Navy had subdued the petty state, a squadron remained on station in the Mediterranean, and the department periodically established other squadrons in trouble spots around the globe. By 1843 six squadrons existed.*

Between 1815 and 1842 a Board of Navy Commissioners helped the secretary of the navy administer the squadrons. Since the Navy Department's founding, a civilian secretary, aided by a few clerks, had directed all naval activities. Some experts had urged formation of a professional board

---

* The six squadrons were the Mediterranean; the Pacific (1818); the Brazil, or South Atlantic (1826); the East India (1835); the Home (1841), which absorbed the West Indies Squadron that had been established in the early 1820s; and the African (1843).

to help the secretary, and the War of 1812 demonstrated the navy's poor administration. Consisting of three captains, the board had authority in such specialized duties as the procurement of naval stores and materials, and the building, repairing, and equipping of ships. The board provided the secretary with technical assistance without impinging on civilian control, since the secretary retained control of policy.

The board had two defects. Its collective nature was, as one secretary said, "extremely unfavorable to that individual responsibility, which it is so necessary to impose upon every public officer." The board was also extremely conservative and opposed maritime technological innovations. Aware of these problems, Congress abolished the board in 1842, replacing it with five bureaus: Yards and Docks; Construction, Equipment, and Repair; Medicine and Surgery; Provisions and Clothing; and Ordnance and Hydrography. The bureaus inaugurated an era of specialized management, with each bureau chief acting independently and reporting to the secretary. Congress also established a Corps of Engineers to service the Navy's few steam warships, thereby acknowledging the growing importance of the new motive power, which the Board of Navy Commissioners had been slow to accept.

The bureaus and the Corps of Engineers, while reformist in intent, created problems that bedeviled the Navy for decades. The bureaus carried individual responsibility too far. Without any compulsion to cooperate, they rarely coordinated their activities, resulting in fragmented management. Conflict arose between line and staff officers. Line officers viewed staff officers, such as paymasters, surgeons, and engineers, as socially and professionally inferior and not entitled to equal rank and the privileges and esteem that went with it. Staff officers disliked the line officers' assumed superiority. Engineers, for example, designed, directed the manufacture of, installed, and operated steam machinery on warships. These were taxing and dangerous tasks, and the men who performed them demanded equal rank and pay.

The Republicans were as favorably inclined toward coastal fortifications—few could forget Fort McHenry—as they were toward the Navy. The new ships would be the nation's sword, new fortifications its shield. During war scares in 1794 and 1807 the country began fortifications systems, but most of the structures rapidly decayed. In 1816 Congress appropriated more than $800,000 for a fortifications program. Begun *after* the crisis had passed, the new system, like the new Navy, was to proceed methodically during peacetime and be permanent. Madison appointed a Board of Engineers for Fortifications to deal with seacoast defense. Its first report (February 1821), combined with a supplemental report five years later, outlined a theory of defense that remained in vogue until the 1880s.

The board declared that the first line of defense was the Navy, but since it was likely to remain small, it must be supported by seacoast fortifications, an interior communications network, a regular Army, and a well-organized militia. The 1821 report suggested 50 sites for defensive works, and by 1850 the board had recommended nearly 150 more. Long before then, however, congressional enthusiasm for the program had diminished, and the gap between fortifications projected and those completed became a chasm.

The Army also benefited from the postwar nationalism. Not only was its peacetime strength increased, but the army's bureaucracy underwent an important reorganization. In March 1815 Congress established an Army of 12,000, dwarfing any army the United States had maintained except in wartime or acute crisis. Bureaucratic reforms consisted of the creation of a General Staff and the position of commanding general of the Army. The United States had been no better prepared for war in 1812 than it had been in 1775, and the Revolution's logistical deficiencies had soon reappeared. Part of the problem stemmed from Republican unwillingness to use the taxing power, but much of the difficulty lay within the War Department, which had developed no support service administrative machinery. An overburdened secretary, aided by a handful of clerks, usually acted as quartermaster general and commissary general, along with all his other duties. At best the department exercised loose supervision over logistical matters, and what services existed were small and decentralized. The casual administration of logistics, troubling in peace, was intolerable in war. In 1812 Congress revived several staff offices that had sporadically existed since the Revolution, such as a quartermaster general and a commissary general of purchases. However, confusion reigned due to overlapping responsibilities. In 1813 the legislature tried to bring order from chaos by creating a General Staff, which was a group of autonomous bureau chiefs, such as an adjutant and inspector general and quartermaster general, with each chief reporting to the secretary of war.*

The General Staff was unable to improve logistical support appreciably during the conflict. But two postwar secretaries—William H. Crawford (1815–1816) and John C. Calhoun (1817–1825)—realized that a peacetime staff organization was essential preparation for war. Two acts, one in 1816 and the other in 1818, expanded and improved the staff and ensured the staff's permanence; it remained essentially intact until the twentieth century.

* The American General Staff was quite different from the Prussian General Staff created between 1803 and 1809. The Prussian staff had the responsibility of planning for war in peacetime, which involved systematic intelligence gathering, intensive study of military history, and critiques of tactics and strategy employed in peacetime maneuvers.

Operational command had been as dismal as logistical support throughout the War of 1812. No single officer commanded the entire Army. The War Department divided the Army into districts and departments, with each commander acting independently, coordinated only by the secretary of war. A commanding officer such as Andrew Jackson often failed to cooperate with other commanders and invariably resented the secretary's "interference" in military matters. In 1821, when Congress reduced the Army's high command to one major general and two brigadier generals, Calhoun seized the opportunity to create a centralized command system, which might prevent the emergence of a Jacksonian-style warlord in any future war. He ordered the sole major general, Jacob Brown, to Washington and designated him the commanding general.

Most officials considered the Army's new institutions important reforms. In theory the War Department now had a balanced organization. For technical advice the secretary called on the General Staff, while he directed military operations through the commanding general. In practice three problems arose. First, the commanding general's responsibilities were unclear. Could he really *command* the Army? If he did, he would usurp the secretary of war's constitutional duty as the president's appointed deputy; but if he did not, his position was meaningless. A strained relationship between the commanding general and the secretary resulted. Second, a line-staff rivalry developed. Line officers wanted preferential treatment because they believed they endured privation while staff officers lived a soft life. Line officers also insisted on the right to command staff personnel in their district, but bureau chiefs asserted that staff officers in the field were responsible only to their superiors in Washington. Finally, Army bureau chiefs did not cooperate among themselves, and even the secretary was often unable to control them. Secretaries rarely stayed in office more than a few years, so power gravitated to the bureau chiefs, who held commissions for life. Chiefs became consummate bureaucrats and extremely knowledgeable about their specialized functions, but they often confused their own bureau's well-being with the Army's welfare.

Congressional goodwill toward the Army evaporated during the Panic of 1819. In 1820 the House told Calhoun to prepare a plan for reducing the Army to 6,000, and in response he submitted one of the most important military papers in American history. Declaring that reliance on militia was foolhardy and that the nation must depend on regulars, Calhoun proposed a peacetime "expansible" Army that could readily expand in war without diluting its capabilities. His fundamental principle was that when war came, "there should be nothing either to new model or to create." In peacetime the Army should maintain a complete organization of companies and regiments and full complements of both line and staff officers but a reduced number of privates. In wartime *preexisting* units would be augmented by recruiting privates, who would be trained by experienced officers. The transition from peace to war, wrote Calhoun, could "be made without confusion or disorder; and the weakness and danger, which otherwise would be inevitable, be avoided." Calhoun suggested an Army of 6,316, expansible to 11,558 without adding a single officer or company. With only 288 additional officers the Army could expand to more than 19,000. Calhoun's proposal made no headway against congressmen such as Charles Fisher, who said he "always thought, that one of the best features of our Government is its unfitness for war." In March 1821 Congress rejected Calhoun's expansible Army concept, slashing the Army's strength to 6,183 by eliminating regiments and reducing the number of officers. Yet the idea lived on, advocated by those who believed regulars should be the foundation for war planning.

Several postwar trends were clear. The armed forces enjoyed a few years of unprecedented peacetime support before economic ills and fading memories of the war led to cutbacks. Both services experienced bureaucratic growth in an effort to give civilian secretaries ready access to professional advice; to ensure long-term institutional stability in technical and logistical functions; and, in the Army, to impose centralized command on a previously decentralized system that had been a breeding ground for disaster. Although the bureau system represented an important administrative development, it ushered in new problems. Extreme specialization within the bureaus and lack of cooperation among them often hamstrung effective management, staff-line squabbles afflicted both services, and the commanding general's ambiguous position created turmoil in the War Department.

Technology and War

"What hath God wrought?" asked Samuel F.B. Morse in May 1844 in the first message transmitted over the telegraph, a device he had invented. Whether the invention was God's creation or man's was debatable, but what had been wrought was a communications miracle that diminished time and distance in the transmission of information. Military communications—for centuries tied to a messenger's uncertain speed—became almost instantaneous. Dramatic as it was, Morse's telegraph was only one of the technological innovations that so profoundly influenced warfare as to constitute a military revolution, inducing acute anxiety among strategists needing to discern the impact of a bewildering range of developments. Not the least of the policymakers' problems was the tremendous expense involved in keeping pace with new technologies. So rapidly did innovations appear, wrote one secretary of war, that a mere decade marked "an epoch in the onward progress of modern invention and improvement.

Even five years may modify, materially, plans of defense now reputed wisest and most indispensable."

During the first half of the nineteenth century armies harnessed the Industrial Revolution's technology, resulting in dramatic increases in mobility and firepower. Enhanced mobility came from the steamship and the railroad. In 1789 John Fitch built the first successful steamboat, in 1807 Robert Fulton's *Clermont* began commercial operations, and by the 1830s hundreds of steamers plied inland waters. Steamboats could defy currents and wind, but low water or ice brought them to a halt, and they had to go where rivers went. Neither drought nor winter stopped the railroads, which had the additional advantage of going anywhere people chose to lay tracks. A group of New Yorkers organized the first railroad company in 1826, and by 1860 there were 30,000 miles of track traversing the United States. Although developed for commercial purposes, steamboats and railroads had benefits equally important for commerce and war: Travel was faster and cheaper.

Increased firepower came from innovations that made infantry weapons dramatically more lethal. The flintlock mechanism gave way to percussion caps, cylindro-conoidal bullets replaced spherical lead balls, rifles superseded smoothbores, and breechloaders and repeaters competed with single-shot muzzleloaders. The development of fulminates in the 1790s led to a replacement system for the notoriously unreliable flintlock mechanism. By 1820 Joshua Shaw of Philadelphia had perfected a copper percussion cap containing mercuric fulminate. An infantryman placed a percussion cap on a hollow cone connected to the breech; when the hammer struck the cap, the fulminate exploded, sending flame through the cone to the main charge. The percussion cap, being simpler and more reliable than the flintlock, meant infantrymen fired at a faster rate than ever before.

Rifles had greater range and accuracy than smoothbores. Yet in 1815 no army had more than a few elite rifle units because rifles were slower to load than smoothbores. In a smoothbore the ball did not have to fit tightly in the barrel, but for a rifle to work, the bullet had to "grip" the rifling inside the barrel. The only way to achieve this "grip" in muzzle-loading weapons firing round lead bullets was to force the projectile down the barrel—sometimes by pounding a steel ramrod with a mallet—so that it fit snugly against the rifling. The perfection of the elongated cylindro-conoidal bullet by a French army captain, Claude E. Minie, made it feasible to load rifles quickly. The so-called "Minie ball" slipped easily down the barrel but had a hollow base that expanded under the impact of the powder charge's explosion, causing the projectile to grip the rifling. In the mid-1850s the Army adopted as its standard weapon a .58-caliber, percussion-cap, muzzleloading rifle firing cylindro-conoidal bullets. Smoothbores were accurate to only about fifty yards, but the new weapon could be deadly at ten times that distance.

By 1861 arms makers had developed breechloaders and repeaters. In 1811 John H. Hall patented a breechloading rifle, and in 1819 he signed a contract to produce his guns at the Harpers Ferry Armory. In manufacturing these rifles, Hall attained the goal Eli Whitney popularized but never achieved: Mass production using precision machine tools that resulted in interchangeable parts. Hall's production system rapidly spread, spurring America's economic growth, but his rifle had a fundamental problem. Gas and flame leaked from the breech, which detracted from the bullet's velocity and endangered the soldier. The self-contained metallic cartridge, developed during the 1850s, solved the difficulty. The thin metal shell casing possessed the property of obturation (when the powder detonated, the casing expanded, sealing the breech). The new cartridge made possible effective breechloaders and repeating rifles. Prior to the Civil War, Samuel Colt, Christopher M. Spencer, and others had patented repeaters; and in 1862 Richard Gatling produced the first machine gun.

Railroads, steamboats, and rapid-fire rifles transformed land warfare. Strategically, armies could be transported long distances with unprecedented speed and be supported logistically with relative ease at a reasonable cost. They could also be controlled from afar by telegraph. At the same time the tactical system utilized by Napoleon lost its ability to achieve decisive battlefield results. Napoleon generally concentrated his artillery close to the enemy lines and, following a furious barrage, sent his massed infantry and cavalry forward in frontal assaults. By 1860 these tactics were suicidal. The longer range, better accuracy, and increased rate of fire of infantry weapons made it difficult to bring artillery near the enemy lines, potentially converting mass attacks into mass butchery.

Changes in naval warfare were no less startling, as steam and iron began to replace sails and wood. Indeed, naval technology seemed to be changing so swiftly that one congressional committee even suggested building a throw-away Navy. Instead of expensive iron construction, the Navy should rely on cheaply built vessels of white oak, sell them when they decayed, and build new ships "so as to keep the Navy up with all the improvements of the day, and in a condition to introduce, without sacrifice, any new invention."

Robert Fulton built the world's first steam warship, *Fulton,* completed in 1814 to defend New York harbor. Although entrepreneurs quickly adopted steam for commercial purposes, the Navy did not rush to embrace it. During the reign of the Board of Navy Commissioners the Navy built only four steamships. In the mid-1830s Secretary of the Navy Mahlon Dickerson partially implemented the 1816 congressional authorization for three steam batteries when he ordered construction of one steamer, a new *Fulton,* completed in 1837. Two years later Congress authorized three additional steam warships. One of these never performed well, but the other two, *Mississippi* and *Missouri* (both completed in 1842), were seagoing paddlewheelers representing a high state of technical proficiency.

Why was the Navy so reluctant to convert to steam? Part of the answer was naval conservatism regarding innovations. Many officers viewed the noisy, dirty steamships as ungainly sea monsters. Practical problems also delayed the acceptance of steam. Engines were bulky, weak, and unreliable. It took about one ton of machinery to generate one horsepower, and engines consumed coal voraciously, limiting a vessel's range. The exposed paddlewheels made the vessel vulnerable, since a single shot into them would be crippling. The paddlewheels and the cumbersome steam machinery also left little room for broadside guns, reducing a ship's own firepower.

Experimentation gradually produced more efficient engines, and the introduction of the screw propeller to replace the paddlewheels solved the problems of vulnerability and firepower. Placed underwater at the stern, the propeller was secure from enemy fire, allowed the ship's vital machinery to be placed below the waterline, and freed the broadside for guns. The first screw-propeller warship was *Princeton,* launched in 1843. Its design made steamships equal to sailing vessels in fighting power, with the additional advantage of machine propulsion, and in the fifteen years preceding the Civil War the Navy increasingly converted to steam.

The steam warships built before the Civil War were actually obsolete. They had unprotected wooden hulls that could absorb a terrific pounding from solid shot, but explosive shells splintered the hulls and set wooden ships afire. Shells had long been used in land artillery because howitzers and mortars, fired at relatively high angles, required low projectile velocities. But naval guns required a flat trajectory to hull enemy ships and hence high velocity and breech pressures. In 1823 a French artillery officer, Henri-Joseph Paixhans, solved the technical difficulties in firing shells from naval guns. In the late 1830s France and England adopted the shell gun, as did the United States.

The answer to incendiary shell guns was iron. Two related innovations occurred simultaneously: iron construction and the use of iron plates as armor. The first armed vessel built of iron was *Michigan,* launched on the Great Lakes in 1843. The previous year Congress authorized Robert L. Stevens to build a "shot and shell proof" ironclad screw-propelled warship, the first modern ironclad* authorized for any navy. Initially the ves-

---

* The term "ironclad" referred to either a wooden or iron-hulled ship protected by iron plates.

sel was to have 4 to 6 inches of armor, but inventors soon built guns that could penetrate it. Designers planned to install thicker armor, but even more powerful ordnance was soon available. The metallurgical advances permitting thicker, more resistant armor could also be used to build stronger guns capable of hurling larger projectiles at greater velocity. Stevens never filled his contract, and France launched the first seagoing ironclad, *La Gloire,* in 1859. The British countered the next year with *Warrior,* the first seagoing iron-hulled ironclad. Both ships were theoretically obsolete, since they carried only four and a half inches of armor. The fate of Stevens's ship and the instant obsolescence of *La Gloire* and *Warrior* were indicative of the "race" between guns and armor—between penetration and protection—that lasted into the post–Civil War era.

The ascendancy of steam over sail and iron over wood had *not* been achieved by 1860. Steam warships carried full sail rigging, and most naval officers considered steam auxiliary to sails. The American Navy boasted no large iron-hulled ships or ironclads. Yet the implications of iron and steam were discernible. Steam completely altered maritime strategy and tactics. Ships could travel in direct lines rather than in sweeping deviations necessitated by prevailing winds and currents. Steam increased travel speed, allowed for a precise calculation of how long a voyage would take, and made in-shore maneuvering easier. However, steam also acted as a tether, binding warships to their coal bases. Previously the wind had been all-important in battle, but now its influence was negligible and speed became a more significant factor. The effects of iron construction were equally profound. It made possible ships that were larger, stronger, and more variable in design than wooden-hulled ships, providing more stable gun platforms capable of carrying enormous weapons. Iron hulls were more durable than wood and could be divided into watertight compartments that contained damage. In terms of initial cost and economy in repairs, iron was also cheaper than wood.

Schools of War

On September 16, 1871, an elderly man committed suicide by leaping into the paddlewheel of a Hudson River steamer. Melancholy for some time, Dennis Hart Mahan became morbid when the Military Academy's Board of Visitors recommended his mandatory retirement from the West Point faculty. For Mahan, life without the Academy was not worth living. He had arrived at West Point in 1820 as a cadet, graduated first in the class of 1824, and served as an instructor there for two years. Then Superintendent Sylvanus Thayer sent him to France to study military engineering and fortifications. He resumed teaching duties at the Academy in 1830—and left again only in death. During his more than four decades at West Point, no one was more influential than Mahan in the transition of officership from a craft into a profession.

All professions exhibit three characteristics: specialized expertise attained by prolonged education and experience; a responsibility to perform functions beneficial to society; and a sense of corporateness, a collective self-consciousness that sets professionals apart from the rest of society. A professional officer's expertise is the management of violence, and his responsibility is to provide national security. A sense of corporateness flows from the educational process, the customs and traditions that develop within the profession, and the unique expertise and responsibility shared by group members.

No nation had a professional officer corps in 1800, but all the European powers and the United States did by 1900. The impetus for professionalization came from changes in warfare foreshadowed by the American Revolution but made more obvious by the French Revolution and the Napoleonic Wars. Fundamentally, as armies became larger, they created new administrative, operational, and tactical problems and possibilities. To deal with these, an ever-larger number of more highly skilled officers was necessary. Thus the magnitude and complexity of Napoleonic warfare gave birth to two elements essential for training such professional officer-specialists: military schools and a literature on warfare to guide officers in their studies. These developments appeared first in Prussia, crushed by Napoleon in 1806–1807. Lacking a genius like Frederick the Great to counter the French genius Napoleon, Prussian leaders established a school system—culminating in the *Kriegsakademie*—to forge the nation's officers into collective competence. From the *Kriegsakademie* and lesser schools came studies dealing with the theory and principles of war. The most important was Karl von Clausewitz's abstract commentary on the Napoleonic Wars, *On War* (1831). Although the most profound treatise on war ever written, Clausewitz's book remained unknown to Americans until translated into English in 1873.

France emulated the Prussian schools, since military genius appeared so erratically that France could not depend on the timely arrival of another Napoleon. But the French and Prussian institutions had important differences. Prussian officers studied strategy and its relationship to policy, while the French emphasized military engineering, fortifications, and tactics. The Prussians wrestled with Clausewitz's metaphysical discourse, while the French studied Baron Antoine Henri de Jomini's *The Art of War* (1838). Clausewitz and Jomini, the two major commentators on Napoleonic warfare, tried to discover universal elements in war. They examined the same campaigns but presented different interpretations. Clausewitz understood the bloody, violent, and often chaotic style of war unleashed by the French Revolution and Napoleon. Jomini, however, found unrestrained war repellent and stressed decisive geographic points, speed, movement, and lines of supply and communication. These concerns missed the central point of Napoleonic warfare: the quest for decisive battle.

West Point followed the French example. The most obvious deficiencies during the War of 1812 had been well-trained officers and basic strategy. The two were not unrelated, since able officers could devise appropriate strategy, which required competent officers to implement. Thus postwar Republicans supported improvements at the Military Academy, which was near extinction in 1815. The revival began in July 1817, when President James Monroe ordered Captain Sylvanus Thayer, who had studied French military schools and fortifications, to become superintendent. During his superintendency (1817–1833), Thayer sought to transplant French professional standards to the banks of the Hudson, using Mahan as his conveyor. Mahan was professor of civil and military engineering and—as he insisted on adding to his title—of "the Art of War." Textbooks were not available for either the engineering or the warfare course, so Mahan wrote his own. Known as *Outpost* (1847),* his military text was a pioneering American study of war that relied on Napoleon (as interpreted by Jomini) to convey its lessons. In 1846 Mahan's former student Henry W. Halleck had written *Elements of Military Art and Science,* a more original discussion of military theory than his mentor's book, although still dependent on Jomini's (and Mahan's) portrayal of Napoleon. Mahan and Halleck initiated American strategic studies and consciously promoted professionalism, arguing that military science was a specialized body of knowledge understandable only through intense study, especially of military history.

Devoting only a fraction of the curriculum to military theory and history, West Point could instill only a limited professionalism in officers. A complete professional education required higher military schools. West Point would introduce cadets to military art and science, but graduate schools would give special preparation for service in the three line branches (infantry, cavalry, artillery) and in staff positions. In 1824 Calhoun established the Army's first postgraduate school, the Artillery School of Practice at Fortress Monroe, and three years later his successor founded an Infantry School of Practice at Jefferson Barracks. But the movement was abortive. The Artillery School closed in 1835, and the Infantry School existed in name only. A permanent postgraduate system emerged only after the Civil War.

* The complete title was *An Elementary Treatise on Advanced-Guard, Out-Post, and Detachment Service of Troops, and the Manner of Posting and Handling Them in the Presence of an Enemy. With a Historical Sketch of the Rise and Progress of Tactics, etc. etc.*

The Navy had no West Point equivalent until 1845, when Secretary of the Navy George Bancroft, temporarily also serving as secretary of war, transferred Fort Severn, Annapolis, from the Army to the Navy. Bancroft then ordered midshipmen returning from sea, as well as a small instructional and administrative staff, to report there. The new school began to nurture naval professionalization and in 1850 was named the Naval Academy. However, the Navy also lacked postgraduate schools to hone its officer corps' expertise, responsibility, and corporateness.

Despite savage criticism of West Point (and later the Naval Academy), professionalization continued during the age of Jackson, an era known for its emphasis upon egalitarianism and amateurism. Critics deemed the Academy unnecessary and extolled the natural martial ability of citizen-soldiers—a trait personified by Jackson himself. They denounced the Academy as un-American, claiming it established a military aristocracy that monopolized the officer corps and degraded enlisted men. Critics also charged that West Point was expensive and produced more officers than the Army needed.

The clamor against West Point had little effect, as the proportion of West Point graduates in the officer corps grew from less than 15 percent in 1817 to more than 76 percent in 1860. And because of accelerating professionalization, the officer corps in 1860 was far different from what it had been a generation earlier. Between the 1st American Regiment's formation in 1784 and the end of the War of 1812, the officer corps had been characterized by administrative instability, amateurism, high turnover (because men considered military service little more than a brief interruption in their civil careers), and internal dissension. Indeed, few armies had ever been led by such an unruly, contentious group of officers; as one general wrote in 1797, the Army was an "Augean stable of anarchy and confusion."

But after 1815 a distinct military subculture emerged, aided by the comparative political harmony that prevailed immediately after the War of 1812. Military careers became dramatically longer as men increasingly viewed officership as a lifelong commitment; in 1797 the median career length for all officers was only ten years but by 1830 it had extended to twenty-two years. The expanded, permanent General Staff developed formal regulations and methodical procedures that brought stability to military administration, a structure later emulated by private corporations. The nascent educational system socialized aspiring officers into their craft and instilled values that united men from different regions and social classes. Professional officers believed that the Army should avoid strident political partisanship and instead be a neutral instrument of government policy. Perceiving themselves as distinct from the civilian world, they developed a near-unanimous contempt for citizen-soldiers and collectively wallowed in self-pity, convinced that the public showed little appreciation (but much apathy) for the Army's difficult and dangerous task of policing the Indian frontier.

After the War of 1812 military planners realized that no matter how often politicians glorified citizen-soldiers or how severely Congress cut the Army, regulars would provide the first line of land defense. They also knew that reliance on the common militia to reinforce the regular Army was chimerical. In 1808 Congressman Jabez Upham had argued that the notion of prosecuting a war with militia "will do very well on paper; it sounds well in the war speeches on this floor. To talk about every soldier being a citizen, and every citizen being a soldier, and to declaim that the militia of our country is the bulwark of our liberty is very captivating. All this will figure to advantage in history. But it will not do at all in practice." The War of 1812 proved Upham a prophet. Aside from Baltimore and New Orleans, the militia performed badly, and after the war it lived on only in Fourth of July oratory. Presidents stopped urging, and Congress ceased debating, militia reform, and the number of states submitting militia returns to the War Department declined precipitously.

Volunteer militia units partially filled the void left by the common militia's demise. To preserve the Ancient and Honorable Artillery Company and other traditional volunteer units, a section of the Uniform Militia Act permitted states to incorporate volunteer companies. Under this clause a volunteer militia movement swept the country after 1815, providing an outlet for men who still took citizen-soldiering seriously. Despite the myth of a "militant south," the volunteer phenomenon was particularly strong in the north, with earnest amateurs in New York, Massachusetts, and Connecticut representing a substantial military force.

In his second annual message President Franklin Pierce praised "the valuable services constantly rendered by the Army and its inestimable importance as the nucleus around which the volunteer force of the nation can promptly gather in the hour of danger." Perhaps unknowingly the president acknowledged that a crucial change in military policy had occurred since the War of 1812. Militia no longer figured in the commander in chief's calculations, an admission no president would have made just a generation earlier. Professionalized regulars reinforced by enthusiastic volunteers had replaced the common militia as the foundation for national defense.

Military Forces and National Development

The hallmarks of the age were territorial expansion and the westward movement. Florida, Texas, Oregon, the Mexican Cession, and the Gadsden Purchase increased the national domain, and settlement reached the Pacific. In this surge of national development, the Army served as an advance agent of a continental empire. Soldiers explored the west and built, improved, and protected transportation networks. Communities arose in the vicinity of forts where bluecoats provided security and consumed goods and services. The Army was also a law enforcement agency, especially in Indian affairs. West Point graduates were well suited for developmental activities. Under Thayer's guidance the Academy not only produced officers with professional ideals but also became the nation's finest scientific and engineering school, and graduates readily utilized their scientific and engineering skills for national development.

Army explorations began before the War of 1812, halted during the war, and then scoured the west after 1815. Captain Meriwether Lewis and Lieutenant William Clark led the most noteworthy prewar expedition, which departed St. Louis in 1804, crossed the continent to the Pacific, and returned in 1806. The expedition was the first direct federal aid in developing the west, setting a precedent for the future. Perhaps the most famous postwar army explorer was Lieutenant John C. Fremont, whose three long reconnaissances, between 1842 and 1845, won him the nickname "the Pathfinder." But Fremont was only one of dozens of officers who helped unlock the region's geographic mysteries. The Army also cooperated with civilians. Scientists, scholars, and artists normally traveled with Army expeditions, and civilian-led parties depended upon Army assistance. Although the trans-Mississippi west was unknown to Americans in 1800, sixty years later people understood its geography and knew much about its geology, flora and fauna, and native peoples. Pioneers did not blindly enter the wilderness.

Army personnel made the west increasingly accessible by assisting with internal improvements. Distinguishing the military from the commercial significance of roads, improved rivers, canals, and railroads was impossible, and in the General Survey Act of 1824 Congress authorized the use of military engineers for transportation improvements of commercial or military importance. Under this act Army engineers worked on state and private projects as well as federally sponsored improvements. The War of 1812 had demonstrated the handicaps imposed by inadequate transportation, and Army efforts to remedy the situation began immediately after the war. Soldiers began work where the war had shown the greatest need, building, for example, "Jackson's Military Road" from Tennessee to New Orleans. As the nation expanded, the soldier-roadbuilders followed the moving frontier. In many cases troops did the construction, but in other instances military engineers supervised civilian crews working under War Department contracts. Army engineers improved rivers and harbors and assisted in the construction of canals, such as the Chesapeake and Ohio. They worked with railroad companies, beginning in 1827, when the Baltimore and Ohio Railroad Company asked for and received government engineering aid. By the mid-1830s, between ten and twenty companies were receiving Army engineering assistance every year.

Army posts offered economic opportunity, often making the difference between a stagnant local economy and a prosperous one. Although soldiers spent much of their time farming, building barracks, doing maintenance work, and cutting firewood, few forts achieved self-sufficiency. They depended on the local community for building materials, corn, beef, hay, and firewood. Garrisons employed civilians as clerks, teamsters, and skilled laborers, and soldiers primed the economy by spending their pay in the immediate vicinity.

Troops made the west reasonably safe. Since colonial times forts had been built to control the fur trade, impress the Indians, deter potential foreign enemies, and protect settlers. The fur trade remained profitable and the Indians belligerent, Britain retained Canada, Spain held the southwest, and settlers wanted to keep their hair. Thus the War Department built new forts at strategic locations as the frontier swept westward. In 1817 a loose cordon of forts ran from Fort Mackinac at Lake Michigan's eastern tip, to Fort Howard on Green Bay, to Forts Crawford, Armstrong, and Edwards on the Mississippi, and to a post at Natchitoches in central Louisiana. By the early 1850s the military frontier ran along the Columbia River, the California coast, and the Rio Grande. Army posts dotted the west, leaving only a handful of troops east of the 1817 perimeter.

One of the Army's most onerous duties was enforcing the trade and intercourse laws in Indian country. Beginning in 1790 Congress passed a series of acts, codified in 1834, to regulate trade with the Indians and preserve peace by eliminating Indian grievances. The laws forbade settlement on Indian lands, licensed the Indian trade, and prohibited liquor in Indian Territory. Upholding the law's majesty made the Army unpopular with avaricious settlers, traders, and whiskey vendors. Troops were too few, lawbreakers too numerous, and the frontier too vast for bluecoats to be effective policemen. Violators could not be tried by courts-martial but had to be remanded to civil courts, which rarely convicted alleged offenders. When the Army expelled intruders and seized liquor, aggrieved parties frequently filed civil suits against commanding officers, and the prospect of court actions deterred rigorous enforcement.

The Navy played a vital role in national development by laying the foundations for America's overseas commercial and territorial empire. Antebellum naval missions presaged a post–Civil War global commitment, especially to the Pacific. Between 1838 and 1861 maritime expeditions combining scientific objectives with commercial and diplomatic purposes explored the Amazon River and the Rio de la Plata, searched the Isthmus of Darien for an interoceanic canal site, reconnoitered the River Jordan and the Dead Sea, sailed the Arctic seas, charted Africa's west coast, and ranged over the Pacific.

The most spectacular examples of the Navy's commercial-diplomatic role concerned China and Japan. Although the United States remained neutral during the Opium War in China (1839–1842), a naval squadron commanded by Lawrence Kearny was posted to protect American merchants. Kearny's astute diplomacy paved the way for the Treaty of Wanghia (1844), which opened five ports to American merchants on a most-favored-nation basis. The treaty placed American economic relations with China under diplomatic protection for the first time and heralded an American entrance into Far Eastern international politics. Equally significant was Matthew C. Perry's expedition to Japan in 1853–1854. Perry purchased land for a coaling station at Port Lloyd in the Bonin Islands and negotiated the Treaty of Kanagawa (1854), which opened two Japanese ports to American commerce, promised humane treatment to shipwrecked sailors, and permitted an American consul to reside at Shimoda. This treaty was Japan's first step in a meteoric ascent from feudal isolation to great power status.

The Navy also participated in numerous punitive expeditions to protect American lives and property, suppress piracy, uphold national honor, and enforce treaties. During the antebellum era dozens of landing parties composed of sailors and marines supported American interests in Asia, in the Caribbean and Mediterranean Seas, along both coasts of South America, and along the East African coast. Most of the expeditions were brief and bloodless, but occasionally fighting did occur. For example, the first official American armed intervention in Asia took place in February 1832 at Quallah Battoo, Sumatra, to avenge an attack on a merchant vessel. President Jackson, who feared the incident might presage other attacks on America's growing Asian commerce, ordered John Downes, commanding the frigate *Potomac,* to the scene. After a cursory investigation, Downes sent sailors and marines ashore, where they destroyed the town and several forts and probably killed at least 100 Sumatrans.

The unofficial alliance between the Navy and American commercial interests produced astounding results. Between 1790 and 1860 total exports (including reexports) increased from $20 million to $334 million; this helped to transform the United States into one of the world's foremost economic powers by the end of the nineteenth century. So stupendous was this antebellum maritime commercial expansion that one astute foreign observer, contemplating "the ardor with which the Anglo-Americans prosecute commerce," predicted that America would "one day become the foremost maritime power of the globe."

The armed forces played indispensable roles in national development despite acute manpower problems. Conditions in both services were often deplorable, featuring low pay, coarse and monotonous rations, primitive medical facilities, and near-sadistic discipline. Army recruits were predominantly northern laborers or immigrants, many of the latter unable to speak or understand English. In 1840, for example, only four recruits came from the Deep South but 1,444 came from New York alone, and between 1850 and 1859 two-thirds of the enlisted men were foreign born. Economic factors were often foremost in a man's decision to enlist. Laborers who lost their jobs during economic depressions sometimes turned to the Army in desperation, while immigrants were frequently destitute when they arrived at a seaport. Isolated in small frontier posts, many with fewer than 100 officers and men, soldiers had few opportunities for martial glory and none for becoming officers. Instead, they performed manual labor, building and maintaining forts and roads, farming, caring for livestock, and cutting wood. Since they had enlisted to be soldiers rather than laborers, they found these conditions onerous, often resorting to the bottle and to desertion to escape them. Deserting sometimes reached absurd proportions: In 1830 1,251 out of 5,231 men fled the Army!

Conditions in the Navy were no better. Like soldiers, sailors were isolated, floating on distant stations in tiny, cramped warships where the work was hard, life was boring, and an atmosphere of brutality prevailed. Common punishments included confinement in irons, informal floggings with the end of a rope, and formal lashings with a cat-o'-nine-tails that could leave the flesh "fairly hanging in strips" on a man's back. Such conditions attracted few high-quality American citizens, and by 1860 the Navy's foreign-born component approached 50 percent. Those Americans who did enlist, said one naval officer, came from "the most worthless class of our native population." As in the Army, drunkenness and desertion were frequent occurrences; charges relating to these crimes composed 25 percent of all charges at Navy courts-martial between 1799 and 1861.

Reform movements tried to ameliorate conditions, especially in the Navy. Humanitarians, who often unfavorably compared sailors to slaves, focused on the abolition of flogging and the grog ration. The Army abolished flogging in 1812, though it was reinstated as punishment for desertion in 1833, and ended the daily liquor ration in 1830. The Navy clung to both. Most naval officers and their conservative congressional allies argued against "hyperphilanthropy," maintaining that the lash held crews in line and the grog ration was healthful. Although reformers eventually achieved success against flogging in 1850 and against liquor in 1862, overall conditions aboard ship improved only slightly.

Officers had to deal with truculent men and endured the same general milieu, but they also had a special problem. Guided only by seniority, promotion was slow. It often took twenty or thirty years for an Army officer to become a major, and fifty-year-old naval lieutenants were commonplace. Shut away in frontier posts or distant ships, scanning the news for deaths or resignations among more senior officers, men became quarrelsome and inordinately sensitive about personal honor. To escape the boredom, low pay, lack of esteem, and pettiness, many officers resigned, especially from the Army, because they could exploit their West Point education in civilian pursuits. Yet some good officers remained, proud of their profession and their role in national development.

The Army and Indian Removal

In the west, President Jackson told the Indians, "Your white brothers will not trouble you; they will have no claim to the land, and you can live upon it, you and all your children, as long as the grass grows or the water runs, in peace and plenty. It will be yours forever." The president's promise of a permanent Indian Territory was important in Indian removal, which meant trading land in the Louisiana Purchase to Indians living east of the Mississippi in exchange for their traditional homelands. After the War of 1812 the government informally pursued a removal policy until 1830, when Congress finally authorized the president to negotiate land-exchange treaties. Four years later Congress defined Indian country as land west of the Mississippi except for Louisiana, Missouri, and Arkansas. The government adopted removal as official policy for several reasons. Increased trans-Appalachian settlement made eastern territory more desirable, while humanitarians, motivated by an arrogant paternalism, argued that removal would save the Indians from extinction, the inevitable fate for people who resisted "superior" white civilization.

The Army had several duties under the removal policy. Initially civilian contractors organized Indian traveling parties, but they were so corrupt that in 1832 the secretary of war assigned these tasks to the Army. Army personnel helped the emigrants settle in their new lands and protected them from the Plains Indians. Operating from forts along the border of Indian country, the bluecoats tried to preserve peace between whites and Indians. Most important, when Indians resisted removal, the Army went to war. Removal was supposedly voluntary and a few tribes went west without opposition, but most preferred to remain. To persuade them to emigrate, Jackson employed wholesale fraud and deception, and when chicanery failed, he used force. In 1836 three Creek bands went on the warpath, but more than 11,000 regulars, citizen-soldiers, and friendly Creeks quickly ended the resistance. When most Cherokees also opposed removal, force again compelled submission.

Although the Creek and Cherokee troubles were hardly wars, removal did provoke two genuine conflicts, the Black Hawk War and the Second Seminole War. The Sac and Fox tribes occupied prime Illinois real estate, and in 1827 the state petitioned the War Department for the Indians' removal. When nothing had been done by 1831, Governor John Reynolds mobilized volunteers and forced Black Hawk, an aged Sac chief, to sign an agreement to stay west of the Mississippi. But during the winter Black Hawk received false assurances of assistance from Canada and from other tribes. In April 1832 he and his followers, including women and children, recrossed the river. The resulting war was a deadly farce, "a tissue of blunders," as one colonel called it. Learning that he would receive no British or Indian support, Black Hawk tried to surrender three times, but on each occasion the whites rejected the peace overture. The Black Hawk War ended in early August at the so-called "Battle of Bad Axe," where the whites slaughtered men, women, and children.

Seminole removal was more difficult. The United States first tangled with the Seminoles in 1817–1818 when Jackson, under War Department orders, invaded Florida. The motives behind the invasion were complex. Seminoles were raiding the Georgia frontier and escaping to safety under the Spanish flag, and Spanish authorities appeared powerless to restrain them. Florida was also a sanctuary for escaped slaves, who participated in the Indian forays. The hope of extending United States territory and removing a proximate foreign influence reinforced the desire to eliminate the sanctuary and recapture the slaves. With typical zeal, Jackson destroyed Indian villages, captured Spanish towns, and deposed the Spanish governor. Although Jackson eventually withdrew from Florida, Spain realized it would ultimately lose the territory and decided to negotiate. The Adams-Onis Treaty, ratified in 1821, ceded Florida to the United States. The Seminoles also negotiated, signing a treaty in 1823 calling for them to concentrate on a reservation in central Florida. Few had done so by the early 1830s, and Jackson's administration negotiated new treaties, which it claimed obligated the Seminoles to emigrate. The Indians maintained the treaties were invalid.

When the Second Seminole War began in December 1835, defeating the Seminoles seemed relatively easy. Fewer than 5,000 Indians lived in Florida, and the 1,200 warriors often fought with bows and arrows. Several factors made the task difficult, and the war became the Army's longest, most costly Indian conflict. The terrain and climate proved formidable, and the black fugitives stiffened Seminole resistance. Removal for the Indians meant a new western home, but blacks feared they would be returned to slavery. The Seminoles and their black allies were adept guerrillas. A frustrated War Department even authorized the use of bloodhounds to track the elusive Indians, prompting an antiwar congressman to ask for a report on the "natural, political, and martial history of bloodhounds, showing the peculiar fitness of that class of warriors to be associates of the gallant army of the United States."

Eight commanders tried to remove the Seminoles. Although their cumulative effect was to sap Seminole strength, by the time the eighth commander, Colonel William J. Worth, took charge in April 1841 the war seemed interminable. Determined to end the conflict, Worth conducted the war ruthlessly. With more than 5,000 regulars under his command, he launched the war's first summer campaign, preventing the Seminoles from raising and harvesting their crops. The regulars suffered a high incidence of disease, but striking at the Indians' villages and means of subsistence reduced the Seminole population to about 250 by the next spring. President John Tyler sent Congress a special message saying "further pursuit of these miserable beings by a large military force seems to be as injudicious as it is unavailing." He authorized Worth to proclaim the war ended, which the colonel did in August 1842. The original goal of complete removal had not been achieved despite great manpower and monetary costs. Approximately 10,000 regulars and 30,000 citizen-soldiers served, at a cost of more than 1,500 deaths and $20 million. Yet enough Seminoles remained to wage a comparatively minor Third Seminole War during the 1850s.

By the mid-1840s Indian removal was nearly completed. In 1820 an estimated 125,000 Indians were living east of the Mississippi; twenty-five years later fewer than 30,000 remained. But removal of the eastern Indians did not end Indian-white conflicts. After the Mexican War white settlement reached the Great Plains and leaped across the Rocky Mountains to the Pacific coast, igniting new confrontations. Between 1850 and 1861 the Army clashed with the Sioux, Cheyennes, Kiowas, and Comanches on the Plains; with the Apaches, Navajos, and Utes in the deserts and mountains of the southwest; and with the Yakimas, Rogues, Walla Wallas, and other small tribes in the Pacific northwest. Despite Jackson's promise, no Indian territory was permanent. Most whites believed they needed the entire west in order to fulfill the nation's Manifest Destiny.

The Mexican War, 1846–1848

The "re-occupation of Oregon and the re-annexation of Texas at the earliest practicable period," read the 1844 Democratic Party platform, "are great American measures." This shrewdly contrived plank appealed to both southern and northern expansionists and averted charges of imperialism by implying that the United States had once occupied Oregon and owned Texas, neither of which was true. Despite the political opportunism and historical fabrication, the plank captured the spirit of Manifest Destiny sweeping the nation and expressed the avid expansionism of the Democratic presidential candidate, James K. Polk. Polk interpreted his narrow election victory as a mandate to acquire Oregon and Texas, as well as California and New Mexico. Pursuit of these territorial ambitions almost provoked a two-front war. Britain, whose claim to Oregon was as good as America's, resented Polk's assertion that the United States had a "clear and unquestionable" right to all Oregon. It seemed that a third Anglo-American war might explode over Oregon, but a powerful England could accept a compromise without loss of dignity and, despite some vociferous Democratic sentiment for all Oregon, so could Polk. In June 1846 the two nations split Oregon by extending the 49th Parallel to the Pacific.

The settlement with England was fortunate because the United States had gone to war with Mexico the previous month. Many issues soured United States-Mexican relations, but the war began over Texas, which had gained independence in a brief but bitter war in 1835–1836. The United States and other nations recognized the new country, but Mexico refused to accept the results of the Texas revolution and warned the United States that it would consider annexation an act of war. When the United States annexed Texas in 1845, Mexico broke diplomatic relations and threatened reprisals against Texas. A final diplomatic effort by Polk delayed hostilities, but war was inevitable after annexation. Mexico believed it could not accept territorial dismemberment and maintain national honor. Determined to have Texas and the Mexican provinces of New Mexico and California, Polk was willing to fight for them.

The question of Texas's southern boundary aggravated the annexation issue. Texas claimed the Rio Grande, but Mexico insisted the Nueces River was the border. Accepting the Texans' interpretation, Polk ordered Brigadier General Zachary Taylor to assume a position "on or near" the Rio Grande. Taylor stopped at Corpus Christi at the mouth of the Nueces, which was neither on nor very near the Rio Grande, but Polk acquiesced. However, on January 12, 1846, Polk learned his special envoy had failed to persuade Mexico to accept the Rio Grande boundary and to sell New Mexico and California. The next day he ordered Taylor to the Rio Grande. By late March the general's Army of Occupation had concentrated opposite Matamoros. From Polk's perspective Taylor had assumed a forward defensive position; the Mexicans considered Taylor's advance an invasion.

In late April the Mexican commander, Major General Mariano Arista, sent his cavalry across the Rio Grande, and some of his horsemen ambushed two dragoon squadrons. Unbeknownst to either Arista or Taylor, Mexico's president had already declared a "defensive war," and even before Polk learned of the incident, he had also decided on war. On May 9

Polk told his cabinet that he wanted to send Congress a war message. Taylor's report of the ambush arrived that evening, and with unanimous cabinet approval Polk delivered his message on May 11. Mexico, he said, "has passed the boundary of the United States, has invaded our territory, and shed American blood on American soil." War, Polk insisted, "exists by the act of Mexico herself." Although these assertions were half-truths, the United States declared war on May 13.

Two major battles had already occurred. On the last day of April Arista's army crossed the Rio Grande, and on May 8 it confronted Taylor at Palo Alto. Taylor told his men "that their main dependence must be in the bayonet," but American artillery bore the brunt of the battle and forced the Mexicans to withdraw. Just south of Palo Alto the open prairie gave way to dense chaparral sliced by ancient river beds known as resacas. At Resaca de la Palma, Arista's army assumed a strong defensive position. The tangled growth made it difficult for American artillery to deploy, and the resaca formed a natural breastwork. The battle was a melee as the chaparral shattered unit cohesion. The Mexicans again lost and were sent fleeing across the Rio Grande. In two battles Taylor's smaller army had inflicted 800 casualties and sustained fewer than 200.

The battles stunned Mexico, which believed it would win the war. Many leading Mexicans judged the United States politically and militarily weak. Slavery and the tariff were such divisive issues that some Mexicans thought that northern states would not aid the south in a war against Mexico. Two fifth-column elements would make a war difficult for the gringos: Slaves would rebel, and Indians would seek revenge for removal. The U.S. regular Army was small, and Mexican officials considered citizen-soldiers worthless. Even if Americans mounted an offensive, logistical support would be impossible across Mexico's arid expanses. An amphibious invasion would confront tempestuous waters, bad roads leading inland, and Mexico's staunch lowland ally, yellow fever. By contrast, Mexico seemed powerful. European observers considered its armed forces superb, an opinion shared by most Mexicans. Privateers would swarm to sea, feasting upon American commerce. Mexico also believed it would receive European aid, especially from England, since an Anglo-American war over Oregon seemed imminent. "We have more than enough strength to make war," exhorted the editors of *La Vox del Pueblo*. "Let us make it, then, and victory will perch upon our banners."

The only accurate aspect of Mexico's assessment was its belief that the war would divide American society. Antiwar movements—Loyalists during the Revolution, Republicans in the Quasi-War, and Federalists in 1812—had become traditional, and the Mexican War was no exception. Four major groups criticized the conflict. Abolitionists believed the war was a southern plot to extend slavery. Pacifists argued that war violated every Christian principle and that "false and pernicious principles," such as *"our country, right or wrong,"* had subverted the people's moral character. Whig politicians believed Polk had provoked Mexico in order to launch an imperialistic invasion. A small group of "Conscience" Whigs voted against military appropriations, but the larger number of "Cotton" Whigs, though critical of the war, affirmed their loyalty by praising American soldiers, eulogizing their commanders, and voting for the men and money Polk requested. By denouncing "Mr. Polk's War" while loyally supporting it, the Whig Party avoided political suicide. Democratic followers of expresident Martin Van Buren and of John C. Calhoun, now a South Carolina senator, joined their Whig opponents in castigating the war. Van Burenites disliked Polk and opposed the expansion of slavery. Calhoun hoped his stand would lead to the presidency in 1848 but feared the impact of slavery's expansion on the nation's political stability. He also thought the seemingly unrestrained war power Polk exercised was unconstitutional, presaging a dangerous consolidation of power in the executive branch.

The antiwar movement had little impact. Diverse critics never united, and no civil rights issue allowed militant dissenters to become martyrs. Since military service was voluntary and government loans rather than direct federal taxes financed the war, activists could not resist a draft or refuse to pay taxes. Nor could they decry government censorship: Polk never suppressed critics despite their vicious attacks on him. However, the president questioned his critics' loyalty. He referred to the Whigs as "Federalists" and claimed the antiwar agitation encouraged the enemy, thus protracting the war.

Although Polk had no military experience, he acted as not only commander in chief but also as coordinator in chief for the war effort. In the country's first example of *prewar* strategic planning, after consulting with his cabinet Polk had contingency war plans drafted more than six months before Arista's cavalry attacked Taylor's dragoons north of the Rio Grande. Once the war began he exercised tight control over every aspect of it, setting precedents that subsequent presidents built upon to make the White House, not the Capitol, the center of wartime authority. No problem perplexed Polk as much as the senior Army commanders, Scott and Taylor, who were as different as their nicknames implied. "Old Rough and Ready" Taylor rarely wore a uniform and had limited strategic and tactical abilities. His interest in military intelligence and planning for campaigns was so deficient that Scott assigned Captain William W. S. Bliss as his chief staff officer. Considered the Army's brightest intellect, "Perfect" Bliss would compensate for Taylor's own conception of warfare, which rarely went

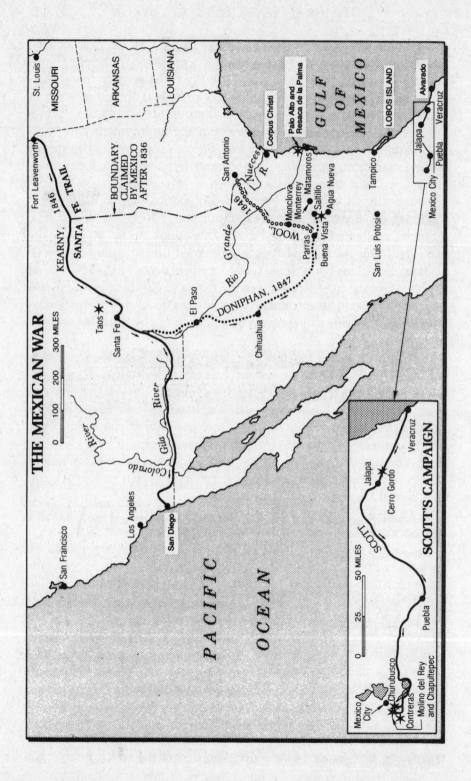

THE MEXICAN WAR

MISSOURI

St. Louis

ARKANSAS

LOUISIANA

Fort Leavenworth

SANTA FE TRAIL

KEARNY, 1846

BOUNDARY
CLAIMED
BY MEXICO
AFTER 1836

San Antonio

Nueces R.

Corpus Christi

Palo Alto and
Resaca de la Palma

GULF
OF
MEXICO

LOBOS ISLAND

Alvarado

Veracruz

Jalapa

Puebla

Mexico City

Tampico

1846

WOOL,

Monclova

Monterrey

Matamoros

Saltillo

Agua Nueva

Parras

Buena Vista

San Luis Potosi

Rio Grande

El Paso

DONIPHAN, 1847

Chihuahua

Taos

Santa Fe

Gila River

Colorado River

River

0 100 200 300 MILES

Los Angeles

San Diego

San Francisco

PACIFIC
OCEAN

SCOTT'S CAMPAIGN

Veracruz

Jalapa

Cerro Gordo

SCOTT

Puebla

Mexico City

Churubusco

Contreras

Molino del Rey
and Chapultepec

0 25 50 MILES

beyond marching, firing, and charging. Taylor's strength was his battlefield imperturbability. Sitting atop Old Whitey, one leg crossed over the pommel and chewing on a straw, he never panicked. "Old Fuss and Feathers" Scott, who became the commanding general in 1841, loved fancy uniforms and had considerable strategic and tactical abilities. Although not a West Pointer, he had a keen interest in military affairs, read widely on the subject, and wrote tactical manuals. A meticulous planner, he insisted upon a thorough military reconnaissance before maneuvering or fighting.

Taylor and Scott were both Whigs with presidential ambitions. Since Polk had no desire to win the war with a Whig general who might capitalize on his military reputation to become president, he tried to circumvent them. He proposed creating the position of lieutenant general, last held by Washington, and intended to nominate an ardent Democrat for the post. But Congress refused to establish the lieutenant generalcy, and so Polk waged war with commanding officers whom he distrusted. The generals feared a conspiracy to deprive them of success and felt, as Scott put it, doubly endangered by *"a fire upon my rear, from Washington, and the fire, in front, from the Mexicans."*

Polk oversaw many details of manpower mobilization. Three options were available, one being to call out the common militia. When the war began, Taylor, with War Department authorization, called out 1,390 three-month militia; and General Edmund P. Gaines, without authority, mobilized 11,211 more for six months. Also, on May 13, 1846, Congress extended the militia's term of service from three to six months and authorized the president to call militiamen into service, although no one believed the nation could rely on common militia. Even a six-month term was too brief for a distant conflict, and the constitutional question about foreign service remained. Most of the militiamen mobilized by Taylor and Gaines were demobilized before they did any fighting.

Another possibility was to increase the regular Army. In the War of 1812 Congress created many new regiments, forming an impressive paper army. However, the understrength units composed of raw men and officers usually lacked proficiency. The government avoided repeating this mistake because after the Seminole War the Army had been reduced to 8,600 men along expansible lines, eliminating privates but not regiments. In May 1846 Congress authorized Polk to increase the number of privates, doubling the Army's authorized strength. New recruits, placed among veteran soldiers and under experienced officers, soon marched and fought like veterans themselves. Only in February 1847 did Congress vote for ten additional regiments.

The final option was to mobilize the volunteer militia, and on May 13, 1846, Congress called for 50,000 volunteers to serve for twelve months or the duration of the war at the president's discretion. The War Department understood that it was to enlist volunteer militia units under the call for 50,000 volunteers. The president erred when he delegated to the states, or even to the units, the decision of whether the newly raised troops would serve for a year or the duration; states and volunteer units almost unanimously chose the former. The mass infusion of volunteers led to traditional problems associated with citizen-soldiers. Ill-disciplined, they murdered, robbed, rioted, and raped with such abandon that Mexicans considered them "Vandals vomited from Hell." Regulars and volunteers viewed each other with contempt. A regular described Louisiana volunteers as "lawless drunken rabble" who emulated "each other in making beasts of themselves." In turn, a volunteer complained that even if he captured the entire enemy army single-handedly, "it would not be deemed a deed worthy of remark, being done as it would be, by a man not a graduate of West Point." Volunteer regiments drained recruits from the regulars. Finally, volunteers were expensive since, invariably, land and monetary bounties had to be offered in order to entice them to enlist.

It became harder to fill the ranks as the war progressed. Antiwar criticism dissuaded some potential recruits, but increased knowledge of conditions in Mexico did more to dampen enthusiasm. Said one young man:

> No sir-ee! As long as I can work, beg, or go to the poor house, I won't go to Mexico, to be lodged on the damp ground, half starved, half roasted, bitten by mosquetoes and centipedes, stung by scorpions and tarantulas— marched, drilled, and flogged, and then stuck up to be shot at, for eight dollars a month and putrid rations.

Compensating for the lack of quantity was the troops' fighting quality, which resulted primarily from competent officers, especially West Pointers. Academy graduates did not dominate the regular Army high command but served brilliantly in the junior ranks as skillful troop instructors, combat leaders, and military engineers. Professionally educated officers also served with the volunteers. Many West Point graduates who had resigned received volunteer commissions, as did men who had attended the Academy but never graduated. Mexican War volunteers occasionally performed badly, but normally they fought as tenaciously as regulars, demonstrating anew what Scott had proved at Chippewa and Lundy's Lane: that good leaders could quickly transform ordinary citizens into excellent soldiers.

No matter how brave and well led, troops need logistical support to fight effectively. Three staff departments shared logistics responsibility. The Ordnance Department provided weapons, the Subsistence Department rations, and the Quartermaster Department clothing, equipment, and transportation. No one (except staff officers) thought the supply bureaus worked efficiently. Polk believed staff officers had become too accustomed to easy living, displayed little energy but great extravagance, and were "Federalists." He held numerous conferences with staff officers, maintaining that he and Secretary of War William L. Marcy had to "look after them, even in the performance of the ordinary routine details in their offices." Taylor and Scott agreed with Polk about the staff's incompetence. Both generals complained about inadequate logistical support, as did nearly every private. Suppliers joined in the critical chorus because staff officers sliced profit margins too thin.

Most of the complainants hindered rather than helped the supply bureaus. Polk, who wanted to conquer an enormous empire at small cost, followed a parsimonious policy that crippled procurement and transportation. Taylor was usually tardy in submitting requisitions, and Scott demanded more of everything no matter how much he already had. Wastefulness characterized the troops, and contractors engaged in unscrupulous price gouging, made doubly criminal by the shoddy goods they often supplied. In truth, logistical support excelled that of any previous war. Steamships and railroads helped make the logistical effort reasonably successful. Wherever possible the railroads moved supplies and troops to ports, and steamboats ferried them to Mexico. Although room for improvement existed, the bureaus performed creditably considering the vast distances and difficult geographic and climatic conditions.

Initial strategy, which Polk discussed with his cabinet and Scott, was obvious: blockade Mexico's east coast and seize the provinces west and south of Texas, including Nuevo Leon, Coahuila, Chihuahua, New Mexico, and California. Economic pressure and conquest, Polk hoped, would force Mexico to yield to his territorial demands. The Home Squadron, commanded by David Conner and his successor, Matthew C. Perry, conducted the blockade. From a strictly military viewpoint blockade duty was not dangerous, since the United States enjoyed unchallenged naval superiority. Not a single enemy warship entered the Gulf, and the privateering threat never materialized. Yet the duty was not easy. Men and ships were in short supply, scurvy struck many sailors, vicious northerly gales appeared between October and April, and yellow fever raged from April to October. Boredom reigned most of the time, except during infrequent moments when lookouts spotted a strange sail or when naval forces attacked enemy ports in an effort to make the blockade more effective. The Navy unsuccessfully assaulted Alvarado twice but captured Frontera and Tampico.

Taylor's army invaded Nuevo Leon after occupying Matamoros without a fight. Old Rough and Ready's objective was the capital of Monterrey, but he advanced slowly, not arriving there until September 19. Monterrey stood on high ground on the north bank of the Rio Santa Catarina, which effectively guarded its rear. To the west were two fortified hills. The citadel, an uncompleted cathedral surrounded by bastioned walls, protected the city from the north, and two smaller fortifications anchored the defenses on the east. The stone houses were loopholed, the streets barricaded, and General Pedro de Ampudia, who had replaced Arista, had 7,500 men and forty-two artillery pieces to defend the city.

Monterrey's defenses would have given pause to a less resolute commander than Taylor, who had only 6,200 men and lacked proper siege guns. But Taylor, displaying serene confidence, ordered a daring double envelopment. He sent Colonel William J. Worth's division around the city to the west; the army's other two divisions would batter into Monterrey from the east. Aside from the problem of coordinating the two wings, Taylor's plan invited defeat in detail. But the Mexican commander failed to grasp the opportunity, and between September 21 and 24 Taylor's forces fought their way into the city. Ampudia and Taylor then signed an eight-week armistice, allowing the Mexican army to withdraw intact and giving the Americans Monterrey without further bloodshed.

When Polk learned of the armistice, he was irate. Had Taylor persevered, captured Ampudia's army, and pushed farther into the country, "it would have probably ended the war with Mexico." He obviously did not understand Taylor's critical situation. The enemy army could not be captured without vicious street fighting and heavy casualties. Taylor's army had already suffered more than 500 casualties and was tired and demoralized, barely capable of further combat. Ammunition was in short supply, and Taylor had no plans for restocking. In any event, convinced of Taylor's ineptitude, Polk ordered the armistice abrogated. Old Rough and Ready wondered whether Polk was trying to discredit him for political reasons, but he followed the order and marched to Saltillo, the capital of Coahuila. Taylor had no desire to advance farther, since San Luis Potosí, the next potential target, was 300 miles to the south across rugged terrain.

In both New Mexico and California the pattern was one of conquest, revolt, and reconquest. Commanding the Army of the West, Stephen W. Kearny departed Fort Leavenworth in June, marched 850 miles in less than two months, and took Santa Fe without firing a shot. Kearny then continued westward with 300 men to aid in California's conquest. En route he met Kit Carson, who reported that California was already in American hands. The conquest involved American settlers engaged in the Bear Flag Revolt, the navy's Pacific Squadron, and John C. Fremont's "exploring" party of sixty-two heavily armed men. Kearny sent most of his command back to Santa Fe and marched westward with a mere hundred men. Unbeknownst to Carson or Kearny, Californians loyal to Mexico revolted against the American conquerors in late September, as did loyal New Mexicans in mid-December. Kearny's weary troopers arrived in California just in time to help Fremont and the Pacific Squadron quell the rebellion in late December and early January. Colonel Sterling Price, Kearny's successor at Santa Fe, defeated the New Mexicans at Taos in early February 1847, ending their uprising. In neither province was American authority challenged again.

Meanwhile, two columns advanced on Chihuahua, the capital of Chihuahua Province. Commanding three volunteer regiments and a few regulars, John E . Wool departed San Antonio in late September, and Alexander W Doniphan's 850-man 1st Missouri Mounted Volunteers left Valverde, New Mexico, in mid-December. Wool occupied Monclova, where he received reports that Chihuahua's garrison had fled. Since he believed it made little sense to continue toward Chihuahua, Wool asked for and received permission to advance farther south. When Wool's men eventually joined Old Rough and Ready in late December 1846, they had marched 900 miles and not fired a shot. Doniphan's horsemen traveled more than twice as far and won two battles: El Brazito, just north of El Paso; and Rio Sacramento, fifteen miles from Chihuahua. Upon entering the city they found themselves isolated in a hostile community. Doniphan wrote Wool asking for instructions and received orders to join the main army. The Missourians reached Taylor in mid-May; thus they had missed the Battle of Buena Vista. Wool's men had not been so lucky.

Buena Vista resulted from Polk's new strategic approach. During the summer and fall of 1846 he received good news from the war zones. The blockade grew tighter, Taylor was deep into enemy territory, and initially New Mexico and California easily succumbed. Yet Mexico rebuffed peace initiatives. Successful on the battlefield, the initial strategy failed because it did not bring Mexico to terms. Polk and his advisers rethought their strategy and in October 1846 decided to capture Veracruz and send an expedition from there to Mexico City.

Designed to force Mexico to the negotiating table, the new strategy raised two difficult questions: Who should command the expedition, and where could the troops be found? The invasion of the enemy heartland would make the commander a war hero and a presidential prospect. Polk considered five men for the position. Congress prevented Democratic Senator Thomas H. Benton from being named the commander when it refused to establish the rank of lieutenant general. Major Generals Robert Patterson and William O. Butler were Democrats and thus potentially excellent choices; but Patterson was ineligible for the presidency because of foreign birth, and Polk did not know Butler very well. Taylor was a winning general, but the cabinet agreed with Polk "that he was unfit for the chief command, that he had not mind enough for the station, that he was a bitter political partisan and had no sympathies with the administration." By process of elimination the command devolved on Scott, who at least would keep all the glory from Taylor.

Scott was an excellent choice. Since the war began he had argued that only a repetition of Cortes's march to the Valley of Mexico would end the war. When the administration first contemplated the expedition, Scott wrote the planning papers detailing the military requirements and establishing the operation's feasibility. He estimated that 4,000 regulars and 10,000 volunteers would be needed and insisted that the Veracruz assault had to take place before the yellow fever season began. Since little time remained to raise new regiments, Scott took more than half Taylor's men, including almost all his regulars, and prudently ordered Old Rough and Ready to remain on the defensive. The expedition was a double blow to Taylor. Denied the opportunity to command it, he also lost most of his army. Polk and Scott, he fumed, had conspired to cut short his military career and deprive him of the 1848 Whig nomination.

A copy of Scott's order listing the troops withdrawn from Taylor fell into enemy hands. Santa Anna, the new Mexican commander, decided to attack the weakened army at Saltillo; he massed an army at San Luis Potosí and trekked across the desert wastelands. Taylor did not believe Santa Anna would attempt such an arduous march, and to demonstrate his confidence he advanced to Agua Nueva, disobeying Scott's defensive orders. By February 20 Santa Anna's 15,000-man army reached Encarnacion, thirty-five miles from Taylor's army. Major Ben McCulloch of the Texas Rangers infiltrated the Mexican encampment, accurately estimated enemy numbers, and hastened to Taylor with the bad news. Taylor immediately retreated from Agua Nueva to a strong defensive site just south of Buena Vista. He had only 4,500 men, almost 90 percent of them volunteers who had never been in battle.

On February 22 Santa Anna sent Taylor a message inviting him to surrender, since he could "not in any human probability avoid suffering a rout, and being cut to pieces." When Taylor declined, the Mexicans attacked late in the afternoon and some inconclusive skirmishing resulted. Santa Anna renewed the attack early the next morning, and by nine o'clock the American situation was critical. Taylor assumed a conspicuous position near the center of the battlefield, while Bliss reconnoitered the deteriorating American lines. The battle, Bliss reported, was lost. "I know it," replied Taylor, "but the volunteers don't know it. Let them alone, we'll see what they do." What they did was fight like veteran regulars. Everywhere the Mexicans outflanked or staved in the defenses, but the volunteers repeatedly rallied, oftentimes behind regular artillery batteries that heroically supported the citizen-soldiers throughout the day. By nightfall Taylor's army had not been routed, but it had been cut to pieces. About 14 percent of his men were dead, wounded, or missing. Although Mexican losses had been severe and Santa Anna retreated, Old Rough and Ready took little joy in the victory. "The great loss on both sides," he wrote, "has deprived me of everything like pleasure."

The day before Buena Vista began, Old Fuss and Feathers arrived at Lobos Island, staging area for the Veracruz assault. By early March enough troops, transports, and naval vessels had reached the island, and the expedition commenced. On March 9 Scott made the first major amphibious landing in American history, the troops going ashore in surfboats specially requested by Scott. The Mexicans did not contest the landing, and 10,000 troops came ashore without loss of life. In less than a week siege lines spanned the city's landward side, while the Home Squadron maintained a sea blockade. Isolated and defended by only 4,500 men, Veracruz capitulated on March 29. The surrender was not a day too soon, as Scott expected the dreaded *vomito* (yellow fever) to strike soon. He had the bulk of his men heading inland on the national highway during early April.

Fifty miles from the coast the highway ran through a rocky defile at Cerro Gordo. Here Santa Anna, who had traveled a thousand miles and raised a new army since Buena Vista, established defenses manned by 12,000 soldiers. If he stopped the advance, the Yankees would have to remain in the *vomito*-ridden lowlands. For the Americans to attack the fortifications head-on would be bloody business. Captain Robert E. Lee found a path skirting the Mexican left flank, and on April 18 the Americans attacked it. After three hours of tough fighting the Mexicans fled, and the next day the Americans entered picturesque Jalapa above the yellow fever zone.

At Jalapa the enlistment of 3,700 twelve-month volunteers expired. Apparently without a qualm about leaving a depleted army deep inside enemy territory, they refused to reenlist and marched back to the transports at Veracruz. Scott now had only 7,100 men left, but he continued to Puebla, where he paused to await reinforcements. By early August he had 10,700 effectives, and the advance toward Mexico City began. Resolving "to render my little army a *self-sustaining machine*," Scott abandoned his supply and communication lines, a sensible though risky solution to a difficult situation. Guerrillas infested the region between Veracruz and Puebla, and Scott did not have spare manpower to guard the road. Following the war from afar, the Duke of Wellington said that "Scott is lost. . . . He can't take the city, and he can't fall back upon his base."

The indefatigable Santa Anna raised 30,000 men to defend the capital and built strong fortifications facing eastward, assuming Scott would attack along the road from Puebla. Scott reconnoitered the city's various approaches and, as at Cerro Gordo, executed a flanking maneuver that promised success without an all-out battle. He avoided Santa Anna's prepared defenses by assaulting Mexico City from the south. The Mexican commander rushed troops into new positions, resulting in the Battles of Contreras and Churubusco. The Mexicans lost 10,000 men; Scott's casualties were a tenth that many.

Having twice battered the enemy, Scott agreed to an armistice, believing Mexico would negotiate a favorable peace rather than allow the invaders into the capital. But Santa Anna used the cessation of hostilities to revitalize his shattered army. Realizing he had been duped, Scott renewed his offensive in September, defeating the Mexicans at Molino del Rey and Chapultepec. Molino del Rey was particularly costly for Scott, who had received reports that it contained a cannon foundry. Contrary to his normal flanking tactics, he ordered a headlong assault by Worth's division. Two hours and 781 casualties later, Worth captured Molino del Rey only to learn that Scott's intelligence about a cannon foundry was erroneous. Chapultepec fell after an artillery bombardment on September 12 and a well-planned hour-long attack on the 13th. Seeing the American flag flying over Chapultepec, Santa Anna exclaimed that "if we were to plant our batteries in Hell the damned Yankees would take them from us." Meanwhile, American troops rushed down two narrow causeways toward Mexico City and captured the Belen and San Cosme Garitas (gates), thereby gaining access to the city. The next day Scott's army, numbering fewer than 7,000 effectives, occupied the Mexican capital.

When Wellington learned of Scott's victory, he declared that the American commander was "the greatest living soldier" and urged young English officers to study the Veracruz–Mexico City campaign, which he considered "unsurpassed in military annals." Old Fuss and Feathers deserved the praise, having brilliantly conducted an audacious campaign. Yet, like Taylor's victories, Scott's expedition did not result in immediate peace. Mexican national pride made it difficult to accept defeat, and political turmoil frustrated the government's decision-making process. The growing American antiwar movement also indicated that continued resistance might secure more favorable terms. Intense guerrilla warfare, the traditional recourse for a nation with limited conventional military power, involved the occupation forces in constant patrolling and numerous clashes.

With its armies defeated in every battle, its northern provinces conquered, and its capital occupied, Mexico's refusal to negotiate frustrated Polk and his supporters. As the war's toll in blood and treasure had increased, Polk believed the United States should take as an indemnity more territory than he originally demanded. Some Democrats even demanded "All Mexico." In April 1847 Polk had dispatched the State Department's chief clerk, Nicholas E Trist, to accompany Scott's army with an offer to the Mexican government to negotiate. Trist's instructions embodied Polk's original territorial goals. By October 1847 the president not only wanted more land but also believed Trist had performed badly and, even worse, had become Scott's political ally. Polk recalled Trist, but the diplomat refused to obey. On February 2, 1848, Trist signed the Treaty of Guadalupe Hidalgo, which he negotiated on the basis of his original instructions. Under the treaty's provisions the United States would pay Mexico $15 million and assume the damage claims of its own citizens against Mexico totaling $3.25 million. In return Mexico would recognize the Rio Grande boundary and cede New Mexico and California.

Few people liked the treaty. Polk was appalled that Trist had ignored his recall, avid expansionists believed the United States would gain too little territory, and war opponents thought the country had taken too much land. Yet on March 10 the Senate ratified the treaty. "The desire for peace, and not the approbation of its terms," wrote Calhoun, "induces the Senate to yield its consent." Direct war costs amounted to $58 million, plus the money paid under the treaty's terms. The human price was also high: American deaths were approximately 14,700. As usual, disease and accidents, not bullets and bayonets, were the big killers: Only 1,733 men were killed in action or died of wounds.

Like most wars, the conflict with Mexico yielded glaring ironies. Polk, the staunch Democratic partisan, waged war both militarily and politically. In military terms he was spectacularly successful against Mexico, but he lost the political battle against popular Whig generals. In 1848 the Whigs nominated for the presidency Old Rough and Ready, who led them to victory. More fundamentally, the vast territorial expansion of America's western empire precipitated the Civil War. Although historians do not agree on all the war's fundamental causes, few deny that the immediate question of whether the newly acquired land would be slave or free played a significant role in shattering the nation. Manifest Destiny had made disunity manifest.

SIX

The Civil War, 1861–1862

At 4:30 A.M. on April 12, 1861, a lightning-like flash and thunderous roar shattered the predawn stillness at Charleston, South Carolina. A mortar shell arced across the sky, its burning fuse etching a parabolic path toward Fort Sumter. Moments after the shell exploded, guns ringing the harbor began battering the fort as if "an army of devils were swooping around it." For thirty-four hours artillery commanded by General Pierre Gustave Toutant Beauregard fired at Sumter, setting numerous fires and knocking huge masonry flakes in all directions. Miraculously, the seemingly murderous barrage killed none of the fort's soldiers or workmen. But the commanding officer, Major Robert Anderson, who had been Beauregard's artillery instructor at West Point, knew the good luck could not continue. Having satisfied the demands of duty and honor, he ordered the Stars and Stripes lowered and the white flag raised. The Civil War had begun.

Decades of sectional disagreements over the expansion of slavery into the territories and, for a small minority of northerners, the moral implications of the institution, fueled sharp differences over states' rights versus national authority and propelled the divided nation toward that fateful moment in Charleston Harbor. Once war became a reality, many people on both sides offered predictions regarding its probable duration and who would triumph. Few, however, foresaw exactly what the war would be like. Most people optimistically predicted a brief conflict waged with the romantic heroism of a Sir Walter Scott novel. Instead, the outlines of modern total warfare emerged during a four-year ordeal. Since both sides fought for unlimited objectives—the North for reunion and (eventually) emancipation, the South for independence and slavery's preservation—a compromise solution was impossible. No short, restrained war would convince either side to yield; only a prolonged and brutal struggle would resolve the issue.

As the North and South pursued their objectives, sheer numbers of men and industrial capacity became extremely significant. One Confederate general wrote that the war became one "in which the whole population and whole production of a country (the soldiers and the subsistence of armies) are to be put on a war footing, where every institution is to be made auxiliary to war, where every citizen and every industry is to have for the time but the one attribute—that of contributing to the public defense." Neither belligerent could depend upon improvised measures to equip, feed, and transport its huge armies. Men with administrative skills working behind the lines were equal in importance to men at the front. Furthermore, the coordination of logistical and strategic matters on a vast scale could not be left to individual states. Massive mobilization required an unprecedented degree of centralized national control over military policy.

Mobilizing for War

The North's warmaking resources were much greater than the Confederacy's. Roughly speaking, in 1861 the Union could draw upon a white population of 20 million, the South upon 6 million. Two other demographic factors influenced the numerical balance. First, the South contained nearly 4 million slaves who were initially a military asset, laboring in fields and factories and thereby releasing a high percentage of white males for military service. However, after 1862–1863, when the North began enlisting black troops, the slaves progressively became a northern asset. Second, between 1861 and 1865 more than 800,000 immigrants arrived in the North, including a high proportion of males liable for military service. Approximately 20 to 25 percent of the Union Army's men were foreign-born. Ultimately more than 2 million men served in the Union Army, which reached its peak strength of about 1 million late in the war. Perhaps 750,000 men fought in the Confederate Army, which had a maximum strength of 464,500 in late 1863.* This nearly total mobilization of southern white males created a dilemma: Fattening the thin gray ranks limited the number of workers in agriculture, mines, foundries, and supply bureaus, risking such reduced output that the soldiers could not be fed and supplied.

* Not all of the men on either side were "present for duty." For example, out of the 464,500 Confederates, only 233,500 were "present for duty."

The Confederacy did not have the financial structure to wage a long war. It had few banking experts and institutions, had very little specie at its disposal, and had its wealth invested primarily in land and slaves, which were hard to convert into liquid capital. For income the South traditionally sold cotton to the North and to Europe, but the war interrupted this trade. These financial weaknesses undermined the South's ability to pay for the war by fiscally responsible means. Taxation produced less than 5 percent of the Confederacy's income. The Confederate constitution prohibited protective tariffs, and although the congress enacted a variety of tax measures, they produced little revenue. The South also tried to borrow money at home and abroad, but few southerners had money to invest, and foreigners had doubts about the new nation's survival. In all, bonds produced less than 33 percent of government income. By necessity rather than choice, Secretary of the Treasury Christopher Memminger turned to the printing press, churning out more than $1.5 billion in paper money, which represented approximately two-thirds of Confederate wartime revenue. As in the Revolution, overabundant paper money combined with severe commodity shortages to create rampant inflation.

Compared to the South, inflation was not so severe in the North, which also financed the war through taxation, loans, and paper money. However, drawing upon its superior fiscal strength, the Union relied primarily upon taxes and borrowing, the former yielding approximately 21 percent of government income, the latter 63 percent. Beginning in 1862 Congress also authorized the Treasury Department to print paper money, called "greenbacks." During the war it issued $450 million in greenbacks, but this represented only one-sixth of government expenditures.

The North's industrial superiority was also impressive. In 1860 the northern states had 110,000 manufacturing establishments, while the southern states had only 18,000. The total value of manufactured goods in Virginia, Alabama, Louisiana, and Mississippi was less than $85 million, but New York's alone was almost $380 million. However, these numbers do not completely reveal the South's industrial weakness. Southern states relied on northern technological know-how and skilled labor, and many skilled laborers went back north. The Confederacy's raw-materials base could not support needed industrial expansion. For instance, during the year ending June 1, 1860, the states forming the Confederacy produced 36,790 tons of pig iron, while the figure for Pennsylvania alone was 580,049 tons. Furthermore, Confederate mines and factories, clustered in the upper south and in coastal cities, were vulnerable to enemy assault.

Railroads were the indispensable element in Civil War transportation, but the South contained only 9,000 of the 30,000 miles of track in 1860. Again, these figures do not fully expose the disparity. Most southern lines were short and single track. The numerous and competitive railroad companies used different track gauges, and when rival lines entered a city, they invariably remained unconnected. Gaps existed in seemingly continuous lines, tracks and bridges were often poorly constructed, and repair facilities were negligible. Locomotives, rolling stock, and rails were scarce, and the South could not produce them during the war. The government's reluctance to supervise the railroads compounded all these problems. In May 1863 the Confederate congress granted the government broad authority over the railroads, but President Jefferson Davis hesitated to wield the power. Not until early 1865, far too late, did the Confederacy finally take control of the railroads.

The South did not have a railroad network that tied its scant industrial base together or readily permitted long-distance strategic movements. Only one genuine trunk line, running from Memphis through Corinth, Chattanooga, and Lynchburg to Richmond, linked the Mississippi Valley with Virginia. A second trunk line from Vicksburg to Atlanta, where it branched to Wilmington, Charleston, and Savannah, remained unfinished. Four lateral lines crossed those two "main" railroads. One ran from Memphis to Jackson to New Orleans; another stretched from Columbus, Kentucky, through Corinth to Mobile; a third connected Louisville, Nashville, Chattanooga, and Atlanta; the fourth hopscotched along the seaboard from Savannah to Charleston to Wilmington, then ran north to Petersburg and Richmond. Should the North sever any of these fragile arteries, the result would be disastrous.

Northern railroads formed a much better network and suffered less than their southern counterparts from different gauges, poor terminal facilities, gaps, shoddy workmanship, and shortages. The North's industrial facilities allowed it to produce ample rolling stock and rails. Equally important, President Abraham Lincoln did not share Davis's sensitivity about government interference with railroads. In January 1862 Congress authorized Lincoln to take possession of any railroads whenever public safety warranted it and place them under military control. The next month Lincoln appointed Daniel C. McCallum director of the United States Military Railroads, and in May the president took formal possession of all railroads. However, he intimated that provided a company sustained the war effort, he would not actually seize the railroad and direct its internal affairs. The president also saw to it that cooperative lines received government aid. He secured such a high degree of cooperation that McCallum's organization, with but a few exceptions, operated only railroads captured or built in Confederate territory.

Northern water and wagon transportation was also better. Yankee sea power restricted Confederate coastal traffic, and Union gunboats soon

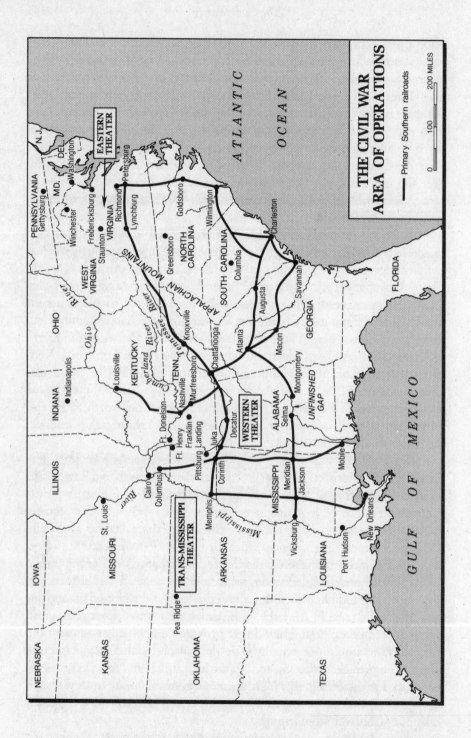

THE CIVIL WAR
AREA OF OPERATIONS

— Primary Southern railroads

0   100   200 MILES

plied most of the great western rivers. The South had few barges and steamboats and could not build very many; the North's situation was the opposite. While railroads and steamboats were vitally important, armies straying from the railhead and wharf depended upon horse- and mule-drawn wagons. When Confederate wagons fell into disrepair, shortages of iron tires and leather goods delayed or prevented repair or replacement. When Union wagons broke down, quartermasters simply requisitioned new ones.

Divisiveness within southern society exacerbated its manpower and resource problems. Southern Unionists were especially numerous in the Appalachian highlands, where, vowed a Knoxville newspaper editor, they would "fight secession leaders till Hell froze over, and then fight them on the ice." This was no idle boast. Viewing the mountain Unionists as a traitorous wedge thrusting into the Confederacy's heartland, the South conducted military operations into the region but could not eradicate the loyalists. Two mounted regiments escaped from North Carolina to fight for the Union, thousands of east Tennesseans joined bluecoated units, and northern Alabama Unionists formed the Federal 1st Alabama Cavalry. In all, more than 100,000 southern Unionists fought for the North, with every Confederate state except South Carolina providing at least a battalion of white soldiers for the Union Army. Given the South's limited manpower and the North's seemingly insatiable need for soldiers, this "missing" southern army that turned up in the enemy's ranks was a crucial element in the ultimate Confederate defeat.

States' rights enthusiasts also disrupted southern harmony. The Confederate constitution guaranteed state sovereignty. Unwilling to surrender much state power, prominent politicians such as Vice President Alexander H. Stephens and Governors Joseph E. Brown of Georgia and Zebulon B. Vance of North Carolina resisted the centralization of authority necessary for efficient warmaking.

Although facing long odds, the Confederate cause was far from hopeless. Many imponderables made northern advantages less imposing than they seemed. One of the greatest uncertainties was the fate of four border slave states that had not seceded. Delaware's resources were minimal, but Maryland, Kentucky, and Missouri contained 2.5 million whites and extensive agriculture and industrial resources. Should these states join the Confederacy, the manpower and resources imbalance would be partially addressed. Another unknown was the war's duration. The North required considerable time to convert its warmaking potential into actual military power. A short war would render the North's manpower and industrial superiority superfluous. Foreign intervention was also possible; the South expected English and perhaps French assistance. Because it supplied four-fifths of the cotton used in European mills, the South felt confident that the English and French economies would falter without its raw material. When war began, the Confederacy, by popular consensus rather than government decree, imposed a cotton embargo, anticipating European recognition and aid in return for renewed cotton shipments.

High-level leadership could also make a difference, and a comparison of the commanders in chief seemingly favored the South. An 1828 West Point graduate, Jefferson Davis performed gallant Mexican War service and served in both houses of Congress before becoming President Franklin Pierce's secretary of war, a position he administered with considerable skill. Lincoln served four terms in the Illinois legislature and one term in the House of Representatives and was best remembered for his humorous yarns and great strength. He was ignorant of the theory and history of war, and his own military experience was a fifty-day militia stint during the Black Hawk War, when, he said only half-jokingly, he led charges against wild onion beds and lost blood battling mosquitoes. By training and experience Davis seemed ideally qualified to lead a nation at war; Lincoln appeared equally unqualified.

And, finally, what of morale? Statistics and accounting ledgers do not win wars, but courage and tenacity at home and at the front are often decisive. The South's determination seemed more certain than the North's. Men on both sides viewed the situation through the past's prism, and history apparently favored the Confederacy. Southerners considered themselves akin to their Revolutionary forefathers, fighting for lofty principles against a tyrannical government and in defense of home and hearth. On the other hand, cast in the conqueror's role, the North had a task similar to Britain's during the Revolution. How long would northerners sustain a war to force southern states back into a Union they hated, especially if the cost in blood and treasure became high? From the first some northerners, especially Peace Democrats, urged the Lincoln administration to let the South go.

The widespread sentiment that southerners were more militarily inclined than Yankees reinforced the South's sense of invincibility. Whether Confederates were more militant is debatable, but large numbers of people on both sides of the Mason-Dixon Line thought they were. Many antebellum Americans believed that northeastern commercialism sapped manly virtues, while plantation life accustomed young men to live outdoors, to ride and shoot, and to enjoy violence. Thus in the eastern theater where Union armies came from the northeast, southerners may have had a psychological edge. When a Confederate boasted that he could whip ten Yankees, many Yankees believed him.

War Aims and Strategies

As telegraph lines spread the news of Fort Sumter across the sundered nation, the Lincoln and Davis administrations pondered their strategic options. Strategy flows from an amalgam of factors. National policy is of primary importance, but strategists must also consider geography, local political pressure, military theory and training, resources and logistics, foreign opinion, and enemy intentions. The North's initial policy objective was to reunite the Union by conquest and subjugation if necessary, which required offensive operations and complete military victory. For the South, which only needed to defend itself, a stalemated war that eroded northern determination and brought foreign assistance would suffice. Thus the strategic equation was simply stated: Could the North conquer the Confederacy before the South convinced the northern populace and the British government that it was unconquerable?

As the combatants surveyed the battleline, stretching from the Atlantic Ocean to the Kansas prairies and more than 3,500 miles along the coast, four main theaters were evident. Compressed between Chesapeake Bay and the Appalachians, the eastern theater consisted of two subtheaters: The Shenandoah Valley, and the remainder of Virginia east of the mountains. The Shenandoah was a bountiful southern granary and an excellent invasion route into the North, allowing Confederate forces to threaten Washington and other cities, as well as two vital northern transportation systems, the Baltimore and Ohio Railroad and the Chesapeake and Ohio Canal. By contrast, the Valley was a strategic dead end for northern forces, channeling them deeper into the mountains. In eastern Virginia, four large rivers (the James, York, Rappahannock, and Potomac) and several lesser streams flowed west to east, dividing the region between Washington and Richmond. These waterways made superb defensive positions against an army coming overland but provided penetration routes deep into the interior if northern invaders came by sea. Thus while each combatant had inviting possibilities for conducting end runs around the enemy's right flank, a direct approach toward Richmond or Washington would involve desperate fighting. With both capitals located in the eastern theater, events there exerted an especially strong pull on national emotions and strategy.

Lying between the Appalachians and the Mississippi River, the expansive western theater also had two subtheaters: Middle and east Tennessee, and the Mississippi River line. Here geography favored the Union, since no natural barriers—unless Kentucky seceded—barred an advance. The Cumberland, Tennessee, and Mississippi Rivers ran north and south, puncturing any defensive line. The third theater was the trans-Mississippi region, equally vast but not as important, and events in the eastern and western theaters determined its fate. The last theater was the sea, controlled by the North. What happened on the oceans and along the Confederate seaboard greatly influenced the war in the two critical land theaters.

Union strategy evolved gradually, ultimately combining a strategy of exhaustion with one of annihilation. In the broadest terms, the North's high command emphasized an exhaustion strategy in the western theater, where the rivers provided penetration routes into the South's most important resource areas, and emphasized annihilation in the constricted eastern theater, where Robert E. Lee's Army of Northern Virginia blocked any southward advance. The strategies interacted in a cycle that, for the South, was vicious. West of the Appalachians the Union exhausted the South's warmaking capacity by conquering territory, crippling its railroad system, and capturing cities possessing logistical and political significance. The North thereby deprived Confederate armies of logistical resources and cut them off from their manpower pool, while sapping the southern populace's will to continue resistance. In the process the North also practically annihilated the enemy's main field armies both in the west and in Virginia. As the Union battered the weakening gray armies in battle and Confederate morale cracked, the South was less able to defend its remaining resources and communications networks. By late 1864 the South's capacity for defense had been so reduced that the Union could send massive raids into the enemy's shrinking domain with virtual impunity.

Commanding General Winfield Scott made the first coherent strategic proposal, the so-called Anaconda Plan, named after the South American snake that slowly crushes its victims. Scott's plan was essentially a strategy of exhaustion. He wanted to impose a naval blockade to seal the Confederacy off from Europe and thrust down the Mississippi to isolate the trans-Mississippi west. The eastern half of the Confederacy would become a peninsula surrounded on three sides by Yankee naval power and bottled up on the landward side by massive armies. Having grasped the victim in the reptile's constricting coil, the North would wait for suffocation to begin, allowing southern Unionists to reassert control and bring the seceded states back into the Union. In focusing attention on the blockade and the Mississippi, Scott highlighted two essential elements of northern strategy. However, his plan contained a fundamental weakness: The anaconda dealt death slowly, and the public and prominent politicians wanted a rattlesnake-quick strike at Richmond.

Many generals also wanted more decisive action than what Scott proposed, and they spoke of ending the rebellion by destroying enemy armies in great battles. Lincoln realized that Confederate armies were vital Union objectives, urging his generals to "destroy the rebel army if possible" and expressing disappointment when they failed to do so. However, tactical problems made annihilation of an army in a single battle virtually impossible. As Union armies marched south, their numerical superiority dissipated as commanders had to detach troops for garrison duty and to guard ever-lengthening supply lines. Although generally outnumbering the South, the North rarely had *overwhelming* numerical superiority on the battlefield. And if Confederates assumed the tactical defensive, they could fight on more than equal terms, since the rifle made one entrenched defender worth several attackers. Ideally northern generals should combine a strategic offensive with the tactical defensive, but this prescription was easier stated than filled.

Even if the Union mauled a Confederate army, pursuit of the beaten foe was difficult. The retreating army moved through friendly country and along its lines of communications, destroying the railroads and bridges, denuding the region of supplies, and leaving rear guards to hinder the pursuer. Aside from having to reorganize after sustaining heavy casualties, the victorious army had to rebuild the communications lines, bring supplies forward, and frequently pause to deploy against the enemy rear guards. Even an army that was grievously hurt in battle usually managed to escape, rebuild, and fight again. An army could eventually be destroyed, but only through the cumulative effects of logistical deprivation and attrition in numerous battles.

To Scott's concepts regarding the blockade and the Mississippi and to the desire for war-ending climactic battles, Lincoln added an astute perception. He realized the Confederacy would be hard pressed to resist constant, simultaneous advances, which the North's greater manpower and material made possible. As he wrote to General Don Carlos Buell, the North must menace the enemy "with superior forces at *different* points, at the *same* time; so that we can safely attack one, or both, if he makes no change; and if he *weakens* one to *strengthen* the other, forbear to attack the strengthened one, but seize and hold the weakened one, gaining so much." However, the concept of simultaneous advances had two impediments, one conceptual and the other geographic. The president's strategic insight ran counter to the prevailing military principles of concentration and mass, which demanded only one offensive at a time. For example, in the winter of 1861–1862 the Army of the Potomac's commander developed a plan that called for a single army of 273,000 men and 600 artillery pieces to operate as a juggernaut that would flatten the South in one campaign. Any other operations would be decidedly secondary, designed solely to support this massive force. The geographic constraint was that although rivers were relatively secure routes of invasion, once the North reached the source of the Cumberland and Tennessee and controlled the Mississippi, it would have to depend on railroads, which were fragile; wherever they supported Union penetrations, Confederate cavalry units and guerrilla bands raided the vulnerable tracks and bridges, creating nearly insuperable logistical problems.

Late in the war Ulysses S. Grant added one last element to Union strategy: Sending army-sized raids to devastate the rebels' remaining logistical base. The raiding strategy not only eliminated the necessity to garrison more territory and to protect supply lines, but it also meant Union forces could avoid costly battles against Confederate armies deployed on the tactical defensive. The raiding force departed one point in occupied territory, moved rapidly through a region living primarily off the land, destroyed everything of military value in its path, and emerged at a different locale. Grant's foremost subordinate, William T. Sherman, perceived that these raids also had a psychological impact, undermining the South's morale by demonstrating its incapacity for effective defense. By 1865 the Union had virtually ceased trying to capture more Southern territory and instead relied almost exclusively on raids against enemy logistics.

Four key tasks dominated northern strategy after the war's first year. Control of the Mississippi would deprive the Confederacy of valuable supplies, such as Texas beef and grain. An offensive through middle and east Tennessee and then along the Chattanooga-Atlanta axis would liberate loyal east Tennesseans, deny the rebels access to Tennessee's resources, cut the South's best east-west railroad, and make possible a further movement toward Mobile or Savannah, slicing the Confederacy again and further disrupting its communications routes. Incessant military activity in Virginia would destroy Lee's army and, secondarily, capture the enemy capital. Finally, as land forces opened the Mississippi, cracked the Appalachian barrier, ravaged southern logistics, and hammered Lee's army, the Union Navy would tighten the blockade and support amphibious coastal assaults.

With limited resources to protect an enormous country, how could the Confederacy forestall a northern victory? In trying to answer this question, Confederate strategists wrestled with two fundamental problems. One was a matter of priorities. With enemy pressure in several places at once, which area was most crucial for survival, the eastern or western theater—and within the broad spaces of the latter, the Mississippi line or Tennessee? Since both theaters had prominent advocates, especially Lee for the eastern and Beauregard for the western, the Davis administration vacillated instead of making hard choices. The other question was whether the South should invade the North or stand behind its borders fending off Union assaults. Lee was the foremost proponent of an offensive defensive, arguing that winning battles on northern soil would hasten enemy demoralization and European intervention, allow hungry southern armies to feast on northern crops, and bolster home-front morale. A passive defensive policy would yield the initiative by giving the Union time to mobilize and the choice of when and where to fight. Others disagreed. Invasion might rally the northern population to the war effort and weaken the South's appeal to world opinion by making the Confederacy seem the aggressor. Tenacious defense better served Confederate purposes, particularly considering the advantage firepower conferred on the defense. Buffeted by conflicting advice, Davis advocated defending southern boundaries, but on three occasions he sanctioned invasions.

For defense Davis adopted the traditional American system of geographic departmental commands. The system, which the president hoped would reconcile the needs for both local and national defense, meshed with Confederate political and logistical realities. Every Confederate state felt threatened, since each one faced potential invasion from either the land or sea. States' rights oratory aside, all the southern states wanted the central government to bear the major defense burden. Wide distribution of Confederate forces placated state and local politicians. Since the South's transportation network made the centralization of logistical resources difficult, Davis's system required each department to protect the resources of its geographic area, and it gave the department a virtual monopoly on that region's raw materials, munitions, factory production, and food.

The departmental system also permitted strategic flexibility, since boundaries could be redrawn as the logistical and strategic situation changed. In 1861, for example, when military intelligence regarding the strength and objectives of Union forces was often inaccurate, Davis created a patchwork of small departments. However, as the strategic picture clarified in 1862–1863, Davis consolidated the departments into four major regional commands: the trans-Mississippi; the Department of the West, embracing the Mississippi and Tennessee subtheaters; the Department of South Carolina, Georgia, and Florida; and Lee's command in Virginia and North Carolina. No matter what the departmental boundaries were, the Confederate high command could conduct an active defense through interdepartmental troop concentrations, either to exploit strategic opportunities or to parry enemy thrusts. To facilitate these periodic concentrations, the government maintained a railroad pipeline at least partially filled with reserves. The pipeline concept involved sending troops from garrisons nearest the point of concentration and replacing them with units from more distant garrisons.

Although essentially sound, Davis's departmental system and the strategy of dispersed forces capable of concentration contained flaws. One problem was that Davis granted departmental commanders considerable autonomy on the assumption that they best understood the local situation. Having drawn the boundaries, selected the commanders, and granted discretion, Davis usually refused to *order* interdepartmental cooperation, relying instead on requests and friendly collaboration. All too often, however, departmental commanders became possessive of their men and resources and, without positive orders, refused to cooperate. Sometimes department boundaries were inappropriate. As one example, the belief that the Mississippi marked a natural division between departments ensnared the Confederacy's river defense in command squabbles. Finally, the South had to preserve its rail lines to maintain the ability to deploy reserves between departments rapidly.

Even as the belligerent governments grappled with strategic problems, troops were mobilizing. On March 6, 1861, the Confederate Provisional Congress authorized Davis to call out the militia for six months and to accept 100,000 twelve-month volunteers. Between March 9 and April 16 Davis called for 60,200 volunteers. Responding to Fort Sumter, the Confederate congress passed several laws authorizing more volunteers, some for "any length of time" the president prescribed and others for the war's duration. Under these various measures six-month, one-year, and long-term recruits entered Confederate service. Meanwhile, on April 15 Lincoln called for 75,000 three-month militia, basing his proclamation on the Militia Act of 1792. Throughout the North most states responded with alacrity to the quotas assigned by the War Department and overrecruited. The government accepted 91,816 men, but governors clamored for the War Department to take still more troops. Acting without legal authority, Lincoln increased the regular Army by 22,714 men and the Navy by 18,000 and called for 42,034 three-year volunteers. Again more men responded than the government called for, and governors urged the administration to increase their troop quotas. When Congress convened on July 4, the president asked sanction for his extralegal action and for authority to raise at least another 400,000 three-year volunteers. Congress assented to both requests, even raising the president's figure to 500,000 men.

Early northern and southern manpower mobilization was similar in four respects. First, both sides relied on newly raised volunteer armies rather than existing military institutions. The northern regular Army, which remained a distinct organization from the volunteers, expanded very little during the war. The Confederacy established a regular army that attained an authorized strength of 15,000, but few men ever enlisted in it. Most northern states refurbished their militias, which served as internal security forces, garrisoned forts and prisoner-of-war camps, guarded communications lines and industries, and patrolled the Canadian and Indian frontiers. During invasion scares states mobilized thousands of militiamen. But the militia's primary role was, as the Indiana adjutant general admitted, to serve "as the nursery from which the old regiments and batteries of volunteers were to be recruited and new ones organized." Southern militias performed similar functions in some states. However, they also played a harmful role that had no northern equivalent: States' rights governors utilized their state forces to challenge Richmond's centralized authority, hindering efficient manpower mobilization.

Second, prewar volunteer militia units supplied many recruits, giving each side a core of partially trained and equipped men. Third, the states, not the national governments, controlled mobilization, exhibiting far more vigor than the overburdened, understaffed war departments. State authorities and, in some cases, glory-seeking individuals enlisted the men, formed the regiments, and sent them off to war. Finally, more troops rallied to the colors faster than the governments (state or national) could provide for them. As one Indiana volunteer remembered, all his "regiment lacked of being a good fighting machine was guns, ammunition, cartridge boxes, canteens, haversacks, knapsacks, blankets, etc., with a proper knowledge of how all these equipments could be used with effect."

Amid massive administrative confusion, with both sides trying to organize and provision hectically raised troops, the war's first skirmishes occurred. The South's victory at Fort Sumter was largely symbolic, but within a few days it gained two more substantive successes; and to the worried Lincoln administration Confederate forces appeared close to an even greater achievement, the capture of Washington. Confronted by Virginia militiamen on April 18, the small Union garrison guarding Harpers Ferry abandoned the arsenal. The Yankees left it ablaze, but southerners salvaged much priceless equipment before they withdrew farther up the Shenandoah to Winchester. Three days later Virginia militiamen occupied the Norfolk Navy Yard, gaining intact the nation's largest naval base, with hundreds of modern artillery pieces, construction and repair facilities, and several ships under repair, including the *Merrimack,* which burned to the waterline during the Yankee evacuation. Teeming with Confederate sympathizers and situated between slave states, Washington was practically defenseless. Fearing an enemy coup d'état, Lincoln waited with mounting anxiety for militia to arrive. Fortunately, less than forty-eight hours after receiving his call, Massachusetts Governor John Andrew had four regiments commanded by Benjamin F. Butler heading for Washington. No state had a better volunteer militia, and on April 19 the 6th Massachusetts Regiment arrived. Other units quickly followed, and on May 24 troops undertook the North's first southward advance. Crossing the Potomac, they occupied Alexandria and Arlington Heights.

The Union had not only saved the capital but gained western Virginia. In late May General George B. McClellan, commanding the Department of the Ohio, ordered a force to aid the area's Unionists and protect the

Baltimore and Ohio Railroad. In a six-week campaign, McClellan's men maneuvered the Confederates out of western Virginia. McClellan's reputation soared, and with Federal guns inspiring confidence, the loyal mountaineers eventually formed a separate state (West Virginia), which entered the Union in 1863. Three months of war produced no big battles, and neither side gained an appreciable advantage. The preservation of Washington and the occupation of western Virginia counterbalanced the South's successes at Fort Sumter, Harpers Ferry, and Norfolk. However, within a three-week midsummer span the Confederacy won two stunning victories, one on the banks of a meandering Virginia stream, the other 800 miles to the west along a Missouri creek. Yet in 1861 the South would lose the most important struggle, the struggle for the border states.

Early Battles

General Irvin McDowell, a husky man with a prodigious appetite, was not yet hungry for a battle. He had never commanded so much as a regiment in action, yet he now led 35,000 officers and men stationed at Alexandria. Organizing the mixture of militia, three-year volunteers, and a few regulars took time, and like most professional soldiers, McDowell believed troops should be thoroughly trained and disciplined. The general did not want to fight, but he could not avoid it. Sentiment increased daily for an offensive, and Lincoln felt the pressure. The ninety-day militia enlistments expired soon, a demonstration of northern vigor would discourage European intervention, and northern morale needed a boost. Although General Scott supported his subordinate in counseling delay, general impatience overrode the generals' prudence. The president ordered McDowell to advance, resulting in the First Battle of Bull Run (or First Manassas) on July 21.

McDowell's objective was Richmond, but first he had to get through Manassas Junction, where Beauregard had 22,000 Confederates posted behind Bull Run. The southerners had several advantages. First, the rebel general learned when Lincoln had ordered McDowell to move forward. Thus alerted, Beauregard received reinforcements from Joseph E. Johnston's Army of Shenandoah, which was able to elude a larger Union army commanded by Robert Patterson and withdraw from the valley via the Manassas Gap Railroad. This was the first time railroads played an important role in a strategic maneuver. Although the Confederates were as untrained as their opponents, they fought on the defensive. Tired and thirsty after their long march, northern troops became disorganized as they attacked. Despite these southern advantages, McDowell's battle plan almost produced a Union victory. An assault on the enemy left flank initially drove the gray line back. But resistance stiffened around the Henry House

Hill, where one of Johnston's brigades, commanded by Thomas J. Jackson, fought ferociously. "Look!" cried a fellow general to rebel stragglers. "There is Jackson standing like a stone wall! Rally behind the Virginians!" Jackson bought enough time for Beauregard to bring reinforcements from his right flank and for Johnston's last brigade to arrive. Literally stepping out of the railroad cars and into the battle, Edmund Kirby Smith's troops spearheaded a counterattack. The bluecoats gave ground grudgingly at first, but the retreat became a rout, the jaded men fleeing toward Washington. Disorganized by their own attack, the Confederates could not immediately pursue. That night it rained, turning the roads to mud and making an advance toward Washington impossible.

While Confederates in Virginia were mired in mud and dispirited Yankees huddled behind the capital's defenses, armies were on the move in Missouri. A whirlwind campaign by Nathaniel Lyon, the commander of the St. Louis federal arsenal, saved St. Louis from militia raised by secessionist Governor Claiborne Jackson and drove an enemy army commanded by Sterling Price out of Jefferson City. Retreating into the southwest corner of the state, Price received reinforcements and turned northward. Having advanced to Springfield with 6,000 men, Lyon found himself outnumbered at least two to one. Rather than retreat, he launched a dawn attack on August 10. Catching the Confederates by surprise along Wilson's Creek, Union forces achieved initial success. However, the Confederates rallied, and when Lyon took a bullet through his heart the leaderless bluecoats retreated. Lacking sufficient strength to attack St. Louis, Price marched due north, placing the western half of Missouri in Confederate hands.

The casualty figures from the war's first major battles sent a shudder across the land. At Bull Run the North had about 3,000 casualties, the South 2,000. Wilson's Creek produced another 1,317 Union and 1,230 Confederate casualties. Small by later standards, these figures seemed ghastly. For southerners, success took the sting out of the losses, and they crowed about their martial ability. But the Confederacy was unable to capitalize on its victories. The capture of Washington and St. Louis might have produced a decisive political and diplomatic impact, but tactical battlefield successes without permanent strategic implications did not shatter northern morale or earn European recognition. Although some northerners believed Bull Run proved enemy invincibility, the defeat spurred Congress to greater war preparations. It passed a bill for another 500,000 volunteers. Added to the 500,000 authorized earlier in the month, Congress had voted for a million-man volunteer army! In response, Confederate legislators authorized 400,000 volunteers.

While weathering battlefield setbacks, the North achieved an important strategic victory by keeping the three crucial border states out of the

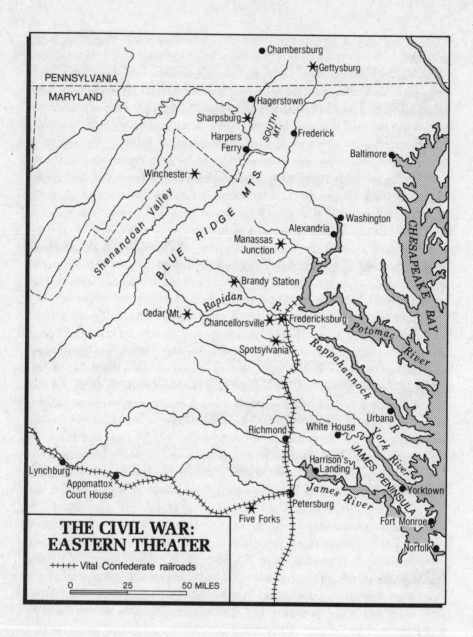

THE CIVIL WAR:
EASTERN THEATER

+++++ Vital Confederate railroads

0   25   50 MILES

Confederacy. The Lincoln administration prevailed in each state by a different course of events. The government used drastic measures in Maryland, suspending the writ of habeas corpus in parts of the state, occupying Baltimore and other pro-South areas, and arbitrarily arresting hundreds of citizens. If Lincoln's iron hand grasped Maryland, the president put on a velvet glove for Kentucky. Hoping to avoid a painful choice between North and South, Kentucky formally proclaimed neutrality in mid-May. Initially both belligerents respected Kentucky's neutrality. But a Union force at Cairo under Ulysses S. Grant alarmed Confederate General Leonidas Polk, who feared the Federals would occupy the strategic bluffs at Columbus, Kentucky. Grant had orders to take the city on September 5, but Polk moved faster, occupying it on September 3. Grant then took Paducah and Smithland at the mouths of the Tennessee and Cumberland Rivers. In rapid sequence both sides had violated Kentucky neutrality, but the South had done so first. The angry state legislature demanded Confederate withdrawal and openly sided with the Union.

Lyon's offensive had shattered Missouri's efforts to achieve a Kentucky-like neutrality and plunged the state into four years of civil war within the larger Civil War. When Lyon drove Confederate forces into the state's far corner, a Unionist-dominated state convention met in Jefferson City and appointed Hamilton R. Gamble as governor. In retaliation, Governor Jackson's government passed a secession ordinance—and in November the Confederacy admitted Missouri—but the secessionists lacked sufficient military power to control the state. Baffled by Missouri's politics, distracted by its rampant lawlessness, and surrounded by a fawning staff, John C. Fremont, who commanded the Western Department, brought little stability to the chaotic situation. The renowned Pathfinder was also unable to launch a thrust down the Mississippi as Lincoln had hoped, but in October he finally mounted an offensive that pushed Price toward the Arkansas border. As in Maryland, superior military strength kept Missouri in the Union.

Union control could not save the border areas from the special agony of a true brothers' war, as approximately 160,000 whites from Maryland, Kentucky, and Missouri served in Union blue and perhaps 85,000 in Confederate gray. Moreover, especially in regions where Unionists and secessionists lived side by side, guerrilla warfare ravaged the land as both vied for control over local communities. Although few in numbers, the irregulars cast a squalid pall of barbarism wherever they roamed, fighting with malignant fury for the Union or the Confederacy but also for personal gain, revenge, and other parochial agendas. The guerrilla conflict blurred the distinction between war and murder and soldier and civilian and brought terror and misery to those caught in its path.

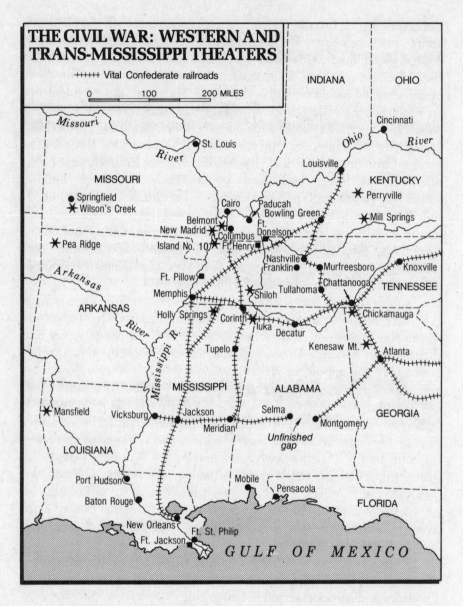

THE CIVIL WAR: WESTERN AND
TRANS-MISSISSIPPI THEATERS

++++ Vital Confederate railroads

0   100   200 MILES

Guerrillas were of two types. The Confederacy organized some units under the Partisan Ranger Act of April 1862. With a guerrilla warfare tradition dating from the Revolution and an exaggerated notion of the romanticism associated with irregular operations, southerners formed dozens of ranger units. The most famous was John S. Mosby's. Operating in Union-occupied areas of Virginia, the "Gray Ghost" kept his men under military discipline and bedeviled the Yankee invaders. But most rangers were less disciplined and less effective. Other guerrillas arose spontaneously in response to local conditions, especially in the Kansas-Missouri region. For the Confederacy William C. Quantrill deservedly earned an infamous reputation. But he was not alone. Among many others, "Bloody Bill" Anderson rode with enemy scalps dangling from his horse's bridle, and Coleman Younger and Frank and Jesse James displayed the thuggery that made them postwar outlaws. Nor did southern supporters have a monopoly on bestiality. Unionist Jayhawkers such as James H. Lane, Charles R. Jennison, and James Montgomery and Tennessee loyalists under Fielding Hurst matched them atrocity for atrocity. Other irregulars like Champ Ferguson, "Tinker Dave" Beatty, and Martin Hart terrorized enemy soldiers and civilians alike and brought the war to doorsteps far removed from conventional battlefields.

Although they maintained a rebel presence in border areas, Confederate guerrillas could not win Maryland, Kentucky, Missouri, or western Virginia for the South, and this northern domination of the border had momentous consequences. It deprived the South of men and resources. Washington remained linked with the North, and southern armies were stretched across southern Kentucky and northern Tennessee rather than along the Ohio River's south bank, which would have been a more easily defended border. Had the South controlled Missouri, it would have outflanked the Old Northwest and dominated a much longer stretch of the Mississippi. In winning the border, the Union established essential preconditions for ultimate success.

By late fall the North also had an array of new commanders. McDowell's defeat, Patterson's incompetence, and Fremont's ineptitude demanded changes. The day after Bull Run a telegram summoned McClellan to Washington to succeed McDowell; Nathaniel Banks soon replaced Patterson; and in late October David Hunter took Fremont's place. After his ungracious maneuvering forced Winfield Scott's retirement, McClellan also became commanding general. When Lincoln wondered whether his duties as an army commander and as the commanding general of the army might be too burdensome, McClellan assured him that "I can do it all." One of his first acts was to reorganize the high command west of the Appalachians. Henry W. Halleck replaced Hunter in the Department of the West, and Buell assumed command of the Department of the Ohio. Their principal subordinates were, respectively, Grant at Cairo and George H. Thomas at Lebanon, Kentucky.

These officers represented almost a typology of Civil War generalship. All but Banks were West Pointers, and Academy-trained officers dominated high command positions, North and South. Although some officers of southern background put nation above state—Scott and Thomas were Virginians—many resigned their United States commissions to receive new ones from the Confederate States. Lee was only the most famous of 313 regular Army officers (and more than 300 Navy officers) who joined the Confederacy. While professionals monopolized the highest levels of command, the majority of generals were nonprofessionals appointed for their political influence or—at least in the North, with its more heterogeneous population—their leadership of ethnic groups. For the Union, Banks, Butler, and John A. McClernand were powerful politicians, Franz Sigel and Carl Schurz were prominent German-Americans, and Thomas Meagher was an important Irish-American. Confederate politician-generals included John Floyd, Gideon Pillow, and Robert Toombs. West Pointers detested the nonprofessionals. As Halleck wrote, "It seems but little better than murder to give important commands to such men." Although most nonprofessional generals were inept, this had not always been true: Pepperrell, Washington, Greene, Jackson, Taylor—none had professional training. Furthermore, numerous Civil War professionals were also incompetent, while some amateurs, such as John A. Logan and Benjamin M. Prentiss for the North and Nathan B. Forrest for the South, performed creditably. Even had the failure of many nonprofessionals been predictable, neither Lincoln nor Davis would have dispensed with them. In a people's war requiring mass armies and high morale, using popular leaders made military and political sense. Rallying diverse constituencies, they strengthened national cohesion and determination.

Broadly speaking, two types of Union generals emerged. Some emphasized their difficulties and the enemy's opportunities and had little stomach for fighting. They often made their opponents look better than they were. Although unique in several respects—no other general had such a well-developed messianic complex or such an aura of patronizing arrogance—McClellan epitomized this category. McClellan was generally overcautious. A superb organizer and administrator, he strove for perfect arrangements down to the last percussion cap before beginning a campaign. Since perfection could never be achieved, he always planned to move but rarely did so—and then only slowly. McClellan chronically overestimated enemy strength, another deterrent to precipitate activity. He seemed to believe that the South, being more militant and led by a West Pointer, *must* be better prepared than the North.

McClellan was also reluctant to fight battles. Perhaps he recognized that technological developments made battlefield decisiveness difficult. Maybe he sincerely believed that maneuvering against the enemy's communications and occupying enemy terrain would win the war without much fighting. More likely McClellan feared taking risks and was paralyzed by the prospect of carnage. As he wrote to his wife, "I am tired of the sickening sight of the battlefield, with its mangled corpses and poor suffering wounded!" Although admirable humanity, this attitude often makes for poor generalship. Finally, the "Young Napoleon" despised political "interference" in military affairs, especially by such amateurs as Lincoln and Secretary of War Edwin M. Stanton. By mid-1862 McClellan regarded both men with contempt. Ignoring the nation's civilian leadership as much as possible, he misunderstood the political currents that drove and shaped a people's war, especially when Lincoln considered adding the destruction of slavery as an official Union war aim. Rejecting any shift toward a "hard war" policy of confiscation and emancipation, McClellan remained wedded to a war of moderation and conciliation toward the South, even as events were revealing the inadequacies of that approach.

In his defense, McClellan may have suffered from rising too high too fast. Caught in the transition from the limited war of 1861 to the total war of 1862 and organizing a truly large army for the first time, he lacked precedents. Staff, communications, and logistical techniques had not yet adjusted to the new complexities posed by mass and distance. Only trial and error, under circumstances in which error could be fatal, produced the necessary adjustments. Furthermore, he commanded at a time when Confederate armies were at their peak in strength and spirit.

Generals in the second category, personified by Grant, saw their opportunities and their opponent's problems and, while not exactly relishing battle, never hesitated to fight. Grant had the advantage of moving gradually up the chain of command, but he also exhibited intellectual flexibility and learned from mistakes, including his own. He realized that only complete conquest—including the destruction of slavery—would subdue the South, and he was determined to get on with the task. His philosophy left little time for perfecting arrangements. What counted was marching and fighting, even if it involved great risks. Unlike McClellan, who fluctuated between excessive optimism and acute pessimism in a crisis, Grant remained calm. His humility equaled McClellan's arrogance. He engaged in none of McClellan's peacock-like displays, preferring to sit quietly on a stump whittling sticks or smoking a cigar. Yet this ordinary-looking midwesterner waged war with a relentlessness beyond McClellan's ken.

But McClellan, Halleck, and Buell commanded in 1861, and northerners who expected decisive action did not get much. McClellan rejuvenated the Army of the Potomac and put it on display at public reviews. The well-ordered columns and bustling staff officers inspired confidence—and questioning. When would McClellan hurl his impressive host toward Richmond? Not this year, as it turned out. However, McClellan did order a reconnaissance in force toward Leesburg, resulting in a humiliating defeat at Ball's Bluff on October 21. Insignificant militarily, the battle had important political consequences. Radical Republican congressmen were demanding a stern war, including emancipation and arming of the slaves, that would fundamentally reconstruct southern society. McClellan's inactivity, proslavery sentiments, and Democratic politics aroused their suspicions. Would he fight their kind of war? Was he even loyal to the Union? Dismayed by Ball's Bluff, Radicals convinced Congress to create a Committee on the Conduct of the War. Using secretive procedures, the committee asserted Congress's right to exercise war powers, praising generals who agreed with the Radicals' philosophy and badgering those who seemed unwilling to wage war to the hilt.

Halleck and Buell also failed to make progress. Lincoln wanted Halleck to open the Mississippi line, Buell to invade east Tennessee. Considering the logistical problems in east Tennessee insurmountable, Buell eyed Nashville and asked Halleck to cooperate in an advance on the city. Preoccupied with the chaos in Missouri, Halleck declined. Nor would Buell assist Halleck. Refusing to cooperate with each other, neither achieved Lincoln's objectives, though Halleck made major strides in pacifying Missouri. As in the East, only one minor battle occurred. On November 7 Grant led a 3,100-man force down the Mississippi in transports to attack Belmont, Missouri, across the river from Columbus. In a repetition of Bull Run and Wilson's Creek, Union retreat followed initial success, the Federals barely escaping to their transports. While other Union forces were immobile, Grant had fought hard, demonstrating remarkable poise despite his army's perilous escape.

Still, Belmont was a loss, reinforcing the North's sense of failure as the South won every battle. Yet the northern situation was promising. Although its successes were less spectacular, they had greater long-term potential. Along with holding the border states, the Union began to benefit from its sea power, blockading the South and, in cooperation with the Army, cleaving coastal enclaves out of enemy territory. Lincoln proclaimed the blockade in April, but the Navy had only forty-two ships in commission, and all but fourteen were on foreign stations. Secretary of the Navy Gideon Welles undertook an expansion program, recalling the distant ships, refitting old vessels, building new ones, and buying or chartering merchantmen for conversion to warships. Welles also appointed a Strategy Board that considered ways to make the blockade more effective.

It recommended the capture of advanced bases to supplement the Navy's existing southern bases at Hampton Roads and Key West. In late August a joint Army-Navy expedition captured Hatteras Inlet, two weeks later the Navy took Ship Island in the Gulf, and in early November another combined operation captured Port Royal between Charleston and Savannah. By December the blockade still leaked, but with more ships becoming available and the southern coast proving vulnerable, it promised to become much tighter. As 1861 ended, the war had already lasted longer than most people expected, and it showed signs of becoming much larger and longer. Neither side was winning, and neither was quitting.

A Year of Indecisive Battles

Frequent and generally inconclusive battles, several of monstrous proportions, characterized 1862. From January to June dramatic Union victories occurred in all four theaters, and Confederate defeat appeared certain. But inept Union generalship and better southern leadership halted the Federal advances. The Confederacy launched late-summer counteroffensives that the North blunted during September and October. Then late in the year the South smashed renewed Union offensives on three fronts.

As the year began, gloom pervaded the Confederate high command. In Virginia a few small forces guarded the Shenandoah Valley and Joseph E. Johnston, wondering if he could stop an offensive by McClellan's 150,000-man army, commanded 50,000 men at Centerville. Equally anxious was Albert S. Johnston, who commanded all forces from the Appalachians to Indian Territory, a vast domain containing only a few widely dispersed troops over whom Johnston exercised only nominal control. His subordinate in the trans-Mississippi, Earl Van Dorn, had 20,000 men to oppose 30,000 Federals. In the western theater Johnston had troops at four positions. Polk held the Mississippi line with 17,000 men at Columbus, confronting Grant's 20,000 at Cairo. Anchoring the right flank, Felix K. Zollicoffer commanded 4,000 men in front of Cumberland Gap, watching Thomas's 8,000 at Barbourville. In the center the North could invade along the Louisville & Nashville Railroad or up the Cumberland and Tennessee Rivers. William J. Hardee at Bowling Green with 25,000 troops sat astride the railroad, facing Buell's 60,000 soldiers stationed southwest of Louisville. Perhaps 5,000 men garrisoned Fort Henry on the Tennessee and Fort Donelson on the Cumberland.

Confederate defenses in the middle and east Tennessee subtheater collapsed first. Prodded by McClellan, Buell ordered Thomas to attack Zollicoffer. At the Battle of Mill Springs (or Fishing Creek) on January 19, the South suffered its first significant battlefield defeat. In late January

Grant suggested that he could capture Fort Henry, and Halleck consented to the expedition. The next day Grant was underway with 15,000 troops and the Western Flotilla, which consisted of river steamers covered with heavy wooden planking (timberclads) and ironclad gunboats. A Navy captain, Andrew H. Foote, commanded the flotilla, although it was under Army control until transferred to the Navy Department in October. When Foote's gunboats attacked on February 6, the Confederates surrendered even before Grant's infantry arrived. With Foote's gunboats roaming up the Tennessee, the Federals had cut Johnston's army in half and outflanked both wings. Johnston retreated from Bowling Green, sending half his men to Donelson and the rest to Nashville. He also dispatched Beauregard to Columbus to withdraw that wing of the army, leaving only enough men to garrison New Madrid, Island No. 10, and Fort Pillow.

Meanwhile, Halleck ordered Grant to move against Fort Donelson, a more formidable position than Fort Henry. The Confederates repulsed attacks by Grant's infantry on February 13 and Foote's flotilla on the 14th, and the next day attempted a breakout, tearing a gap in Grant's right flank. With the door to Nashville wide open, Gideon Pillow, who commanded the attack, inexplicably ordered the troops back to their original positions. With sure instinct Grant counterattacked, breaching the enemy lines. The next day the fort surrendered. Grant's victories were a disaster for the South. The loss of men and material in the forts was serious, and Donelson's capitulation made Nashville untenable, forcing Johnston to retreat again. He established a new defensive line from Memphis through Corinth to Chattanooga that, like his original positions, lacked natural defensive barriers. Worse, it left the region drained by the Tennessee and Cumberland Rivers in Union hands, crippling Confederate logistics.

Southern woes increased when Van Dorn lost the Battle of Pea Ridge. During a winter campaign Samuel Curtis's 12,000-man Union army pushed Price into Arkansas, where he received reinforcements. Before he could attempt another Missouri invasion, all Confederates in the trans-Mississippi came under Van Dorn's command. Leading 20,000 men northward, Van Dorn attacked Curtis at Pea Ridge. The Confederates mauled the Federals on March 7, but Curtis counterattacked the next morning, shattering Van Dorn's army. The battle secured the North's hold on Missouri and made Arkansas vulnerable to invasion.

The southern situation was desperate, but the Union was unable to exploit its successes, giving Johnston time to rally his demoralized forces and to receive reinforcements. Halleck, whom Lincoln promoted to overall western commander on March 11, had ordered Grant up the Tennessee River but warned him not to fight a battle until Buell joined him. With his 40,000 men concentrated near Shiloh, Grant waited as Buell advanced from Nashville with 35,000 soldiers. While the Federals wasted most of March, Johnston benefited from the South's first great strategic concentration in the west. Braxton Bragg brought 10,000 men from Mobile and Pensacola, and Daniel Ruggles came from New Orleans with 5,000 more. Combining the reinforcements with the troops from Columbus and Bowling Green, Johnston had 45,000 men. He had also ordered Van Dorn to cross the Mississippi, but he could not wait for him since the Confederates had to strike Grant before Buell arrived. The twenty-mile march to Shiloh was mass confusion, and although the Confederate plan depended on surprise, troops test-fired their rifles and buglers practiced their calls. Yet when the rebels came screaming out of the woodlands on April 6, they achieved surprise. Grant's overall assessment of the situation was so deeply flawed that on the previous day he assured Halleck no attack was imminent.

The attack smashed into divisions commanded by Sherman, McClernand, and Prentiss, driving them back. However, Prentiss's men reformed along a sunken country lane, where the Union line held temporarily. Absent when the attack began, Grant reached the scene to find his army apparently wrecked. Coolly he organized ammunition trains, ordered Lew Wallace, whose division was camped five miles away, to come immediately, and requested Buell's advance elements to hurry. Recognizing the importance of Prentiss's position, dubbed the Hornets' Nest, he ordered the former militia colonel to hold at all costs. Prentiss did so, aided by a serious tactical error by the Confederate generals: Instead of outflanking the Hornets' Nest, they sent repeated frontal charges against it, in effect killing off their own men. Not until early evening did they force Prentiss to surrender, and the Confederate advance soon halted due to darkness, ammunition shortages, and disorganization. That night Beauregard, who succeeded the fatally wounded Johnston, telegraphed Richmond that the South had won "a complete victory." It had—almost. But Grant used the time bought with blood to organize a new line closer to the river. During the night Wallace arrived, and 20,000 of Buell's men crossed the Tennessee. Grant had more men at dawn on April 7 than when the battle began, and after a morning of hard fighting the southern forces retreated. Like the Confederates after Bull Run, Grant's victorious soldiers, as disorganized and exhausted by the fighting as the vanquished, were unable to pursue. The inability to follow tactical success with effective pursuit characterized almost every Civil War battle.

"War," as Confederate cavalryman Nathan B. Forrest observed, "means fighting. And fighting means killing." Shiloh proved it. The first massive battle, Shiloh dwarfed every previous engagement. Minimally trained citizen-soldiers fought with a savage tenacity befitting veteran regulars. Each side had more than 1,700 killed and 8,000 wounded, but Confederate losses were harder to bear. The South not only lost irreplaceable men but also failed to restore the balance of power in the middle and east Tennessee subtheater.

Serious southern losses occurred almost simultaneously along the Mississippi, where John Pope captured the Confederate garrison at New Madrid on March 13 and, with help from Foote's gunboats, Island No. 10 on April 7. Foote turned the Western Flotilla over to Captain Charles H. Davis in early May. A month later the gunboats caused the evacuation of Fort Pillow, and on June 6 Memphis fell. Southern defenders on the Mississippi were driven to Vicksburg, which in midsummer 1862 was vulnerable from both directions since the Union had also captured New Orleans.

While Confederate defenses in the trans-Mississippi and western theaters crumbled, Federal operations along the coast achieved victories at Roanoke Island, Fort Pulaski, and New Orleans. On February 8 an expedition commanded by Ambrose Burnside and supported by the Navy overran Roanoke Island and, in the next few weeks, captured North Carolina's inland seaports, depriving the South of blockade-running outlets. Two months later Fort Pulaski, guarding the entrance to Savannah, Georgia, surrendered, and the blockading fleet had one less port to watch. The North won an even greater triumph at New Orleans, the South's most vital port. Forts Jackson and St. Philip, located seventy miles below New Orleans, protected the city. Just below the forts a submerged barrier of hulks and logs would supposedly stop approaching ships, giving the forts' artillerymen stationary targets. Gunboats and fire rafts supplemented these defenses. The citizens of New Orleans believed they lived in the Confederacy's safest city, but they did not reckon with David G. Farragut.

Commanding eighteen warships and twenty mortar schooners and accompanied by Butler's 18,000 soldiers aboard transports, Farragut sailed up the Mississippi. On April 18 the mortar schooners opened fire on Forts Jackson and St. Philip, but after six days of constant shelling the defenses remained virtually intact. Rather than admit failure, Farragut decided on a daring plan. Northern gunboats punched a hole in the barrier, and in the predawn hours of April 24 his warships steamed past the forts. The enemy bombardment was so fierce the water seemed ablaze and the Southern gunboats fought heroically, but the Union fleet endured the artillery fire, fought off the enemy gunboats, and dodged the fire rafts. About noon the next day Yankee warships arrived at New Orleans, which was defenseless since most of its garrison had joined Johnston. A naval landing party accepted the city's surrender, and on May 1 Butler's occupation troops arrived.

The loss of New Orleans, with its factories, ordnance complex, and shipbuilding facilities, was worse than the loss of Nashville. Another entry-way for blockade-runners was slammed shut, and the South lost control of the lower Mississippi, allowing Farragut to take Baton Rouge and Natchez without resistance and steam to Vicksburg before going back downriver. In June Farragut brought his saltwater fleet back upriver, meeting Davis's freshwater ironclads a few miles above Vicksburg. The entire Mississippi was in Union hands, but only briefly. Although the combined naval forces pounded Vicksburg, the city could not be captured without a large land force. Farragut appealed in vain to Halleck for assistance, and the North lost an opportunity to gain permanent control of the river. Instead, Davis returned to Memphis, Farragut dropped downriver to New Orleans, the Confederates turned Vicksburg into a bastion and fortified Port Hudson further to the south, and the Yankees frittered away the summer.

Arriving at Shiloh after the battle, Halleck spent three weeks amassing a 120,000-man army. Intent on avoiding a Shiloh-like surprise, he moved toward Corinth at a snail's pace, averaging about a mile a day. When the Federals reached Corinth in late May, Beauregard retreated to Tupelo with-out giving battle. Halleck had excellent possibilities for further action. He could pursue the Confederate army or, holding a vital railroad crossroads, he could strike toward Vicksburg, Mobile, or Chattanooga. "Old Brains" chose Chattanooga as the next target. He retained a substantial force at Corinth, used aggressive Grant to occupy territory northward to Mem-phis, and sent cautious Buell toward Chattanooga. Entrusted with Hal-leck's sole offensive mission, Buell moved slowly, and enemy cavalry raids by John H. Morgan and Forrest caused further delays as they destroyed supply dumps and railroad bridges, tore up track, and captured Union outposts. Buell's unhurried pace, rebel depredations against his commu-nications lines, and Halleck's passive strategy in west Tennessee forfeited the initiative to the South.

Just as improbably, the Confederacy gained the initiative in the east-ern theater after McClellan's spring campaign carried his army to within sight of Richmond's church spires. Throughout the fall and winter McClel-lan's inactivity and reticence in divulging his plans strained the president's patience. When McClellan finally explained his strategy, Lincoln did not like it. The general proposed a waterborne movement to Urbana, which would place his army behind Johnston's. McClellan would defeat the enemy force as it retreated to protect Richmond and then occupy the city, ending the war. Lincoln preferred an overland advance to shield Washing-ton with the army and more readily force Johnston to fight. But McClel-lan was a professional and Lincoln an amateur. Reluctantly, the president accepted McClellan's plan.

However, Lincoln issued several orders indicating his distrust of the general and his strategy. On March 8 he divided the Army of the Potomac into four corps, a reorganization McClellan opposed, and appointed the corps commanders. Three of them favored Lincoln's overland approach, and as a group they leaned toward the Radicals in Congress, who despised McClellan. The president also ordered McClellan to leave Washington "entirely secure" and insisted that the movement down Chesapeake Bay begin by March 18. With bold action tearing open Confederate defenses in the west, Lincoln demanded a simultaneous advance in the eastern theater. On March 11 he demoted McClellan by removing him from the position of commanding general. The president named no replacement; he and Stanton would perform the commanding general's duties. Finally, Lincoln created a Mountain Department embracing western Virginia and east Tennessee, commanded by Fremont. Since the Radicals supported Fremont, his resurrection after his Missouri fiasco indicated the prevailing political currents, especially when viewed in conjunction with McClellan's demotion. During the upcoming campaign McClellan became convinced that he confronted two enemies: The gray army in his front and politicians to his rear. Lincoln and Stanton, he feared, had joined the Radicals in a conspiracy to engineer his downfall.

While still reeling from Lincoln's unsettling orders, the Union commander received more dismaying news. On March 9 McClellan learned the Confederates had fallen back to Culpeper, a move that dislocated his Urbana scheme, since a landing there would no longer be in Johnston's rear. However, McClellan decided he could still go by sea, landing at Fort Monroe and marching toward Richmond up the Peninsula, the southeastern Virginia district formed by the York and James Rivers. As he examined this prospect, McClellan preferred it. Union troops already held Fort Monroe, and the Navy could protect both flanks. Lincoln did not like this amphibious operation any better than the Urbana plan, but he acceded to it.

An armada of 400 vessels had barely started transporting troops to Fort Monroe when McClellan's army began to shrink. As Banks's army redeployed from the Valley to protect Washington, Stonewall Jackson's 3,500-man army attacked Banks's last remaining unit, James Shields's 9,000-man division, at Kernstown. Although Shields defeated Jackson, who had underestimated enemy strength, the Confederacy won a strategic victory, for the attack deranged Union troop movements. Would Jackson have attacked Shields without an equal or larger force? Were the Confederates preparing a thrust at Harpers Ferry, or even Washington? The War Department ordered Banks back to the Valley and detached a division from McClellan's command, sending it to Fremont. And what troops remained to protect Washington? In Lincoln's estimation, not enough.

Stanton ordered McDowell's corps not to move to the Peninsula. Believing that Union forces were on the verge of winning the war, Stanton also closed the volunteer recruiting service. McClellan lost not only a third of his men but also the prospect of receiving replacements. Yet McClellan still outnumbered Johnston about two to one, though he refused to believe it.

Advancing in early April, the Union army encountered the rebels' Yorktown line. Defended by a minimal force and fake cannons, the line appeared strong to McClellan, who considered a frontal assault risky. He resorted to siege operations, which consumed a month. Just when McClellan was ready to smash Yorktown with enormous siege guns, the Confederates withdrew. As they retreated, they had to abandon Norfolk, a severe blow to the Confederate navy. Plodding up the Peninsula, McClellan found that the Chickahominy River presented a problem. With his base at White House on the York River, the Union commander kept his army north of the Chickahominy, but he would have to cross it to attack Richmond. He also believed he would need reinforcements and beseeched Lincoln for McDowell's corps, stationed at Fredericksburg. On May 17 the president agreed, but he insisted that McDowell move overland. Stanton ordered McClellan to extend his right flank to meet McDowell. Thus McClellan had to straddle the Chickahominy, maintaining communications with his base and awaiting McDowell while at the same time advancing on the Confederate capital.

The Confederates considered McDowell's movement a potential calamity, as Johnston could be crushed between McClellan and McDowell. In desperation Johnston planned to attack McClellan, who had reorganized his army into five corps, before McDowell arrived. McClellan had pushed two corps across the Chickahominy, which, swollen by recent rains, separated the unequal halves of his army. Johnston would strike the three corps on the north bank to drive them away from McDowell. Meanwhile, acting as Davis's military adviser, Robert E. Lee proposed sidetracking McDowell by unleashing Jackson in the Shenandoah. Lee's advice initiated one of the war's most brilliant campaigns.

On May 23 Jackson pounded a Union garrison at Front Royal and moved down the Valley, simulating an advance on Washington. After momentary panic Lincoln recognized Jackson's thrust as a diversion, not an invasion. He also realized the North had an opportunity to trap Stonewall's 17,000-man army between Fremont, Banks, and McDowell. Ordering McDowell to countermarch away from McClellan toward the upper Shenandoah, Lincoln urged the three commanders to move swiftly and cooperate fully. They did neither, and Jackson, combining knowledge of the terrain with rapid marching, foiled the efforts of 60,000 Federals to spring the trap. Jackson's Valley campaign allowed Johnston to reorient his attack against McClellan. When news arrived that McDowell had reversed directions, Johnston decided to assault McClellan's weaker south wing. At the Battle of Fair Oaks (or Seven Pines) on May 31 the South came close to victory, but Union reinforcements crossed the Chickahominy on one half-destroyed bridge, and the advance stalled. The next day the Yankees pushed the rebels back to their starting point.

The strategically insignificant battle had momentous consequences. Johnston was badly wounded, and on June 1 Davis appointed Lee to replace him. Nothing in the new commander's previous Civil War experience foretold the fame he would achieve leading the Army of Northern Virginia to destruction, and to immortality in military annals. Like Grant at Belmont, Lee began on an unpromising note. He was sent to oust the Federals from western Virginia; his strategy miscarried, and troops derisively called him "Granny Lee" and "Evacuating Lee." While commanding the southern Atlantic coast, he earned another unflattering nickname, "the King of Spades," by ordering his men to dig entrenchments. No nicknames could have been less apt, because Lee's early wartime activities concealed his true character. No general surpassed him in audacity and aggressiveness. If McClellan took no risks, Lee perhaps took too many. He preferred the bold offensive, seeking in true Napoleonic fashion to destroy, not merely defeat, the enemy army. Dedicated to winning a battle of annihilation, he sometimes imprudently continued attacking beyond any reasonable prospect of success. Lee also needed to broaden his view of the war. Exhibiting a narrow parochialism, he believed Virginia was the most important war zone. He underestimated the problems Confederate commanders faced in the western and trans-Mississippi theaters and the significance of those theaters for southern survival. Yet Lee served the South well. Although costing the Confederacy dearly, his victories against great odds buoyed Confederate morale and depressed the North. Furthermore, Lee's emphasis on his native state was not entirely emotional. Richmond, the South's primary industrial center, acquired great symbolic value, and the Virginia countryside furnished men, mounts, food, and other logistical assets.

Lee's defense of Virginia through daring offensive operations began shortly after he assumed command. During June McClellan shifted all but Fitz-John Porter's 30,000-man corps south of the Chickahominy and repeatedly promised he would attack—as soon as he received more reinforcements. Although Lee had 85,000 men, McClellan thought he had 200,000. Not until June 25 did the Union commander launch a reconnaissance in force, but by then Lee had the Confederate army poised to strike. Learning from his cavalry commander, Jeb Stuart, that Porter's corps was vulnerable, Lee proposed holding off McClellan's four corps (70,000 men) with 30,000 soldiers and attacking Porter with 55,000, including Jackson's command. With Porter destroyed, McClellan would be cut off from White House. Lee believed McClellan would retreat toward the York River to protect his lines of supply and communications. The Confederates would then shred the Union army with constant attacks.

On June 26 the Confederates initiated the Seven Days Battles, which consisted of five engagements: Mechanicsville (June 26), Gaines' Mill (June 27), Savage Station (June 29), Glendale, or Frayser's Farm (June 30), and Malvern Hill (July 1). Throughout the week few things went right for Lee. Jackson invariably attacked late. Poor maps, deplorable intelligence, and inadequate staff work resulted in uncoordinated assaults. McClellan did not do what Lee expected. Instead of fighting toward White House, he shifted to Harrison's Landing on the James, executing a midcampaign change of base. Lee lost every battle except Gaines' Mill and failed to annihilate the Army of the Potomac. Particularly at Gaines' Mill and Malvern Hill he hurled his men against formidable defenses. As one division commander said after Malvern Hill, "It was not war—it was murder." The Seven Days cost the South more than 20,500 casualties, the North about 16,500. Yet Lee became a hero. His offensive battered the Federals away from Richmond and wrenched the initiative from the enemy. McClellan, who did not consider his change of base a retreat, believed he had conducted a brilliant campaign, especially since he thought he was fighting against a larger army without any help from the Lincoln administration. "If I save this army now," he wrote to Stanton during the furious combat, "I tell you plainly that I owe no thanks to you or to any other persons in Washington. You have done your best to sacrifice this army."

Lee soon gave the South more reason to believe in him. On the day Lee attacked at Mechanicsville, Lincoln consolidated the commands of Banks, Fremont, and McDowell into the Army of Virginia under Pope. On July 11 the president brought another westerner east, elevating Halleck, who had been so successful in the west, to the post of commanding general (or, as it was also called, general in chief). Lincoln had hoped Halleck would take responsibility for command and strategic decisions, but Halleck disappointed him, refusing to give orders on his own authority since he considered himself as "simply a military adviser to the Secretary of War and the President," who "must obey and carry out what they decide upon, whether I concur with their decisions or not." However, Halleck was an efficient administrator, a valuable talent in mass total war, and generally a source of sound advice. The first major question Lincoln asked Halleck was what to do with the armies of Pope and McClellan. Should they be concentrated? If so, on the James under McClellan or the Rappahannock under Pope? Acting on Halleck's recommendation, Lincoln decided that McClellan should evacuate the Peninsula. Bitterly resenting this decision, detesting Pope, and convinced "that the dolts in Washington are bent on my destruction," McClellan moved with inexcusable slowness, wasting more time than Pope had to spare, for Lee was hurrying north.

Having organized his army into corps commanded by Jackson and James Longstreet, Lee moved toward Pope before McClellan's withdrawal began, leaving Richmond sparsely defended but confident that McClellan would miss the opportunity. Jackson led the advance, defeating Banks's corps at Cedar Mountain on August 9, and within two weeks Lee's 55,000 men faced Pope's 65,000 across the Rappahannock. Violating every military maxim, Lee divided his army, sending Jackson with 23,000 men far to the west around Pope's right flank and into his rear. Jackson destroyed the Union supply depot at Manassas Junction and assumed a defensive position near the First Bull Run battlefield. Pope found Jackson late on August 28 and erroneously assumed that the retreating Confederates were trapped. Longstreet and Lee were following in the footsteps of Jackson, whose task was to hold on until they arrived. As the Yankees assaulted Jackson on the 29th, Lee and Longstreet reached the battlefield and took up a position lurking on Pope's left flank. The next afternoon, when renewed enemy attacks nearly overwhelmed Stonewall's position, Longstreet crushed the Union flank and sent Pope in disarray toward Washington. Another humiliating defeat, the Second Battle of Bull Run (or Second Manassas) cost the Yankees 16,000 casualties. But Lee, whose casualties were 9,200, had failed to destroy Pope's army.

After his successive victories over McClellan and Pope pushed the invaders out of most of Virginia, Lee prepared to carry the war into enemy territory. But he would not move northward alone. During the fall the South made its only coordinated offensive of the war, attempting simultaneous invasions of Pennsylvania, Kentucky, and western Tennessee. The Confederacy wanted to "liberate" Maryland and Kentucky and allow its armies to live off the enemy countryside. Many southerners believed victories beyond the Potomac and along the Ohio would foster northern war-weariness and inspire British intervention. The prospect of foreign aid was not fanciful. In May 1861 the British government had issued a neutrality proclamation granting the Confederacy belligerent status. In mid-July 1862, Parliament debated a motion for Confederate recognition, and two months later Foreign Secretary Lord Russell and Prime Minister Palmerston considered offering to mediate the conflict. But as the North's ambassador to the Court of St. James noted, "Great Britain always looks to her own interest as a paramount law of her action in foreign affairs." Recognition would best serve British interests if the Confederacy looked like a sure winner. As Palmerston told Lord Russell, "The Iron should be struck while it is hot" *if* "the Federals sustain a great Defeat."

As it splashed across the Potomac in early September, Lee's 50,000-man army was not in good condition. Many soldiers suffered acute diarrhea from eating green corn; others hobbled on shoeless sore feet. The high command was also in poor health. Lee's hands were in splints, Jackson had a sore spine, and Longstreet was in pain from a raw heel blister. With this bedraggled force Lee planned to sever the Baltimore and Ohio Railroad and the Pennsylvania Railroad and destroy the Union army. He was sanguine, for he knew that Lincoln had reappointed McClellan to command. McClellan's behavior during Second Bull Run incensed the president, who believed McClellan wanted Pope to fail. Yet Lincoln needed someone who could whip Pope's dispirited troops into fighting shape, and, he said, if McClellan "can't fight himself, he excels in making others ready to fight." "Little Mac" felt vindicated, writing that "I have been called upon to save the country" again, just as after First Bull Run.

McClellan actually did have the chance to save the country. When the Federals did not evacuate Harpers Ferry as Lee expected, the Confederate commander decided to eliminate this potential trouble spot threatening his lines of supply and communication. In Special Order No. 191 he detailed a daring dispersion of his army. Under Jackson's overall command, three columns would converge on Harpers Ferry while Longstreet remained at Boonsboro just west of South Mountain. On September 13 Union soldiers found a copy of Lee's order, which they sent to McClellan. Few generals have had so much good luck and done so little with it. With exact knowledge of Lee's deployments and with his own 88,000-man army at Frederick, McClellan could crush the enemy piecemeal if he moved rapidly. Unbeknownst to the Union commander, the situation was even more favorable, because Lee had sent Longstreet to Hagerstown, leaving only Daniel H. Hill's division at Boonsboro. Instead of marching immediately, McClellan waited until the 14th, when, despite a Thermopylae-like fight by the rebels, the Union army gained two gaps in South Mountain. Lee, who had recalled Longstreet, contemplated retreat. But the next day, learning that Jackson had captured Harpers Ferry, he decided to fight. Assuming a position behind Antietam Creek, he awaited Jackson, who arrived on the 16th. Straggling had thinned Lee's ranks to about 40,000 men. Believing Lee had at least 100,000, McClellan spent a day and a half preparing to attack, giving Lee's army time to concentrate.

The Battle of Antietam (or Sharpsburg) on September 17 unfolded from north to south. Initially Joseph Hooker's command struck the Confederate left, where the fighting raged with demoniacal fury, men screaming and laughing hysterically at the frenzy of death. Then Edwin V. Sumner's corps smashed into the southern center, where, wrote a Union colonel, "it seemed as if heaven and earth vibrated with the stunning roar" of battle. Finally Ambrose Burnside's corps crunched Lee's right, breaking the Confederate line. Dramatically, Jackson's last division arrived on the double-quick after a grueling forced march from Harpers Ferry, filling the breach and hurling the Yankees back. The disjointed attacks negated Union numerical superiority, allowing Lee to shift men from one threatened sector to another. Furthermore, McClellan refused to commit 20,000 reserves, fearful that *somewhere* out there Lee was massing the rest of his troops for a counterattack. Actually, every Confederate division was on the firing line. Antietam was the war's bloodiest day. As darkness encased the melancholy field, more than 24,000 men lay dead and wounded, 13,000 of them in gray. Despite his severe losses, Lee not only held his position on the 18th but contemplated an attack! However, his discouraged subordinates convinced him that an offensive would be foolhardy. Even more incredibly, McClellan did not attack. That evening Lee retreated, and McClellan did not pursue. The Federal commander took complete pride in his success, but Lincoln was angry that McClellan's success was not more complete.

Although tactically indecisive, Antietam had important consequences. Five days after the battle Lincoln issued the Preliminary Emancipation Proclamation, transforming a war for the Union into a war for freedom. The basic document was ready in July, but Lincoln delayed issuing it until the Union cause looked more hopeful, as it did after the Antietam half-victory. Paradoxically, in July McClellan had urged the president to follow a moderate policy, arguing that neither the confiscation of rebel property nor political executions nor "forcible abolition of slavery should be contemplated for a moment." Contrary to the Lincoln administration's expectations, the emancipation policy initially *increased* the chances of British intervention. Several leading British statesmen believed that the Union's conversion to emancipation was hypocritical, a desperate move to salvage victory by inciting servile insurrections throughout the Confederacy. Appalled by the prospect of a brutal race war, they argued that England should intervene not only to preserve its economic interests but also for humanitarian reasons. But in early November, the British secretary for war explained to the ministry the dire consequences for England if war erupted with the Union, and interventionist sentiment quickly abated. By early 1863, with the British population increasingly supporting the North's antislavery position, an alliance between England and the South was most unlikely.

The western theater invasions also ended in repulses. Angered by Beauregard's retreat to Tupelo, Davis replaced him with Braxton Bragg, an excellent organizer but a poor tactician. Watching Buell's slow progress toward Chattanooga, Bragg left Van Dorn holding Vicksburg with

16,000 soldiers and Price at Tupelo with another 16,000. With 32,000 men Bragg "raced" Buell to Chattanooga. The Yankees had a six-week head start, but by utilizing a circuitous railroad route to Mobile, Montgomery, and Atlanta, Bragg got there first. In conjunction with Edmund Kirby Smith, commanding a smaller force at Knoxville, Bragg planned a Kentucky invasion. Since each commanded a separate department, neither could command the other. In mid-August Smith moved into central Kentucky, capturing Lexington and Frankfort. Bragg entered Kentucky in late August along a more westerly parallel track, getting ahead of Buell, who was hurrying toward Louisville. Capturing Munfordsville, Bragg stood between Buell and the Ohio and was astride the Federals' supply and communications lines. However, Bragg foolishly moved to Bardstown, allowing the Union army to slip past him to Louisville.

In early October Buell headed southeast, stumbling into a Confederate force at Perryville on the 8th. Buell thought he faced Bragg's entire army, but only three gray divisions were on hand. Bragg, meanwhile, believed he confronted only a small Federal force, but almost 40,000 bluecoats were on the field. The rebel commander attacked and outfought Buell, but he retreated after learning the enemy's true strength and linked up with Smith at Harrodsburg. The failure to coordinate operations earlier in the campaign may have deprived the Confederates of success. Now Smith wanted to fight, but Bragg retreated to Chattanooga. Coming on the heels of Antietam, Perryville depressed the South and boosted northern morale, but Lincoln felt frustrated. Emulating McClellan, Buell went to Nashville instead of pursuing the enemy. Based on past performance he would be there for some time, reorganizing and preparing, before moving again.

Bragg wanted Van Dorn and Price to strike northward in conjunction with his invasion but allowed them to work out the details. Commanding separate departments, they could not agree on joint plans. Price preferred an advance toward Nashville and perhaps Paducah, while Van Dorn looked toward Memphis and St. Louis. Price captured Iuka, but Grant counterattacked with converging columns under Edward O.C. Ord and William S. Rosecrans. Price narrowly escaped on September 19, his invasion plans foiled. He joined Van Dorn for an attack on Corinth, commanded by Rosecrans, where a savage battle occurred on October 3–4. As at Antietam and Perryville, an indecisive struggle ended with a Confederate retreat.

After repelling the Confederates on three fronts, the Yankees renewed their advances, stalled since spring, in Virginia and in both western subtheaters. As Lincoln perceived the strategic situation, the North needed unrelenting simultaneous offensives against three cities: Richmond to destroy Lee's army; Chattanooga to protect Kentucky and Tennessee and open the gateway into the South's interior; and Vicksburg to secure the Mississippi. The president believed McClellan and Buell would never do the hard fighting necessary to achieve these objectives. They feared defeat more than they craved victory, detested emancipation, and, as Lincoln said about McClellan, "did not want to hurt the enemy." Burnside replaced McClellan, and Rosecrans replaced Buell. The commander in chief made one other change, sending Banks to New Orleans to succeed Butler. The one Army commander who remained in his post was Grant, about whom Lincoln said, "I can't spare this man. He fights." Both Banks and Grant had Vicksburg as their target. Unknown (at least officially) to Grant or Banks, a third force would also converge on the South's river Gibraltar. In October Lincoln secretly gave John McClernand, one of Grant's divisional commanders and a powerful prewar Democrat, authority to recruit an army in Indiana, Illinois, and Iowa. With the assistance of Davis's gunboats, he would move downriver against Vicksburg.

Although proclaiming his own incapacity for high command, Burnside seemed an admirable choice. Personally brave, he had conquered Roanoke Island and fought at Antietam, where he urged McClellan to renew the battle on September 18. Tragically, he assessed his abilities accurately. When he assumed command, the Union army was at Warrenton. Instead of advancing against Lee's forces at Culpeper, Burnside proposed an eastward movement to Fredericksburg followed by a drive on Richmond. While Lincoln opposed substituting the capital for Lee's army as the main objective, he approved the plan. Success depended on rapid marching to sidestep Lee and the timely arrival of pontoon bridges to cross the Rappahannock. Burnside's army covered forty miles in two days, leaving Lee temporarily baffled as to its destination. However, unpardonable errors caused by Halleck delayed the pontoons a week. By then Lee had reacted, getting his army into a stout defensive position along a series of ridges west and south of Fredericksburg. On the left, Longstreet held Marye's Heights; on the right, Jackson's corps occupied Prospect Hill. Recovered from Antietam, the Army of Northern Virginia numbered 75,000 men.

Burnside's army, 113,000 strong and divided into grand divisions under Sumner, Hooker, and William B. Franklin, crossed the Rappahannock on December 11–12. Franklin's division opened the battle on the 13th, temporarily breaching Jackson's line before a furious counterattack closed the gap. Meanwhile Sumner's men hurled themselves futilely against Marye's Heights. With Sumner's division wrecked, Burnside ordered Hooker to storm the Heights. Hooker, known as "Fighting Joe," prophetically protested that the task was suicidal, but Burnside would not retract the order, and the Yankees, said Longstreet, "were swept from the field like chaff before the wind." Darkness finally ended the massacre. In the one-sided killing match the North suffered 12,600 casualties, the South fewer than 5,000. This was not Lincoln's idea of hard fighting. "If there is a worse place than Hell, I am in it," he said when told of the battle's outcome.

News from the Mississippi River did not elevate Lincoln from the nether world. While McClernand recruited his army and forwarded regiments to Memphis, Grant began an overland advance on Vicksburg. But, suspicious of McClernand's activities, he requested clarification of his authority. Halleck, who favored professionals over nonprofessionals, replied that Grant had "command of all troops sent to your Department, and have permission to fight the enemy where you please." Grant immediately ordered Sherman to Memphis, where he commandeered McClernand's troops and made a riverborne descent to Vicksburg. Both prongs of Grant's offensive ended badly. Forrest destroyed long stretches of Grant's main rail line, and on December 20 Van Dorn wrecked his supply base at Holly Springs. His communications with the North broken and deprived of supplies, Grant withdrew to Memphis, abandoning forever any idea of taking Vicksburg by the overland route. The frailty of railroads made prolonged campaigning deep in enemy territory too difficult. Without Grant to worry about, the Confederates easily repulsed Sherman's assault against Chickasaw Bayou on December 29. Meanwhile, snarled in Louisiana's administrative problems and confronted by Confederates at Port Hudson, Banks came upriver no farther than Baton Rouge.

Rosecrans also failed to attain his objective, though at least he won a battle. On December 26 his 44,000-man Army of the Cumberland moved from Nashville toward Murfreesboro, where Bragg had concentrated his 36,000-man Army of Tennessee. The night of December 30 found the armies encamped within earshot of each other. Southern bands blared "Dixie," Federals countered with "Yankee Doodle," and then one band struck up "Home Sweet Home." Soon the cedar thickets rang with dozens of bands playing the tune, accompanied by thousands of voices with southern drawls and northwestern twangs. In the morning the killing began. Bragg crumpled the Union right, the combat roar becoming so loud that men paused in midcharge to stuff their ears with cotton plucked from open bolls. Although jackknifed into a tortured position, the Union lines held. Neither side attacked on New Year's Day, but on the 2d Bragg tried to settle the issue, hitting the Union left. After initial success the attack stalled, and on the evening of the 3d Bragg withdrew to Tullahoma. Approximately one-third of the men on each side were casualties. For the North the Battle of Stones River (or Murfreesboro) helped offset the Fredericksburg disaster and Vicksburg debacle and gave Lincoln a much-needed win to coincide with the official enactment of the Emancipation Proclamation on January 1. But the victory was not decisive. Success so mangled Rosecrans's army that it would remain at Murfreesboro for six months recuperating. Bragg's army, battered but intact, still blocked the pathway to Chattanooga.

The year of nearly continuous indecisive battles that ended at Stones River proved one point decisively: The war would not be short. Neither side derived comfort from this realization. The North's inability to make better progress in subduing the South fostered discontent across the political spectrum. Radicals demanded harsher war, while Peace Democrats preached conciliation. Antiwar sentiment was particularly strong in the northwest, where some Democrats came close to treason in their criticism of the administration's war effort. Actually the North had made considerable progress during the year, especially in the west. When 1861 ended, Union forces were poised along a line from southern Missouri to Cairo and up the Ohio to western Virginia. As 1863 began, Union armies held new positions from northern Arkansas to Memphis, Corinth, and Murfreesboro. Although the Yankees were still at bay, a ripple of defeatism twinged the South. The western territorial losses and the death and maiming of tens of thousands of the Confederacy's bravest men discouraged even the most resolute rebels. A drastic decline in the home-front standard of living resulting from the twin evils of commodity shortages and monetary inflation fueled the discontent. As the South assessed its prospects for independence, the future was perhaps more discouraging than the past. No one perceived this more clearly than Davis. "Our maximum strength has been mobilized," he told the secretary of war, "while the enemy is just beginning to put forth his might."

SEVEN

The Civil War,
1863–1865

"In considering the policy to be adopted for suppressing the insurrection," Lincoln wrote in December 1861, "I have been anxious and careful that the inevitable conflict for this purpose shall not degenerate into a violent and remorseless revolutionary struggle." Yet the president always emphasized that he would employ "all indispensable means" to preserve the Union and that he would "not surrender this game leaving any available cards unplayed." By the winter of 1862–1863 his conciliatory policies had failed to preserve the Union, and Lincoln began laying his unplayed cards on the table. He issued the final Emancipation Proclamation, armed black troops, supported conscription, and continued to suppress civil liberties in the North in order to control antiwar activities. The war's length and intensity had spawned the "violent and remorseless revolutionary struggle" that Lincoln wanted no more than did McClellan.

Black Recruitment and Conscription

January 1, 1863, was a Day of Jubilee. One hundred days earlier Lincoln had issued a Preliminary Emancipation Proclamation promising to release a final Emancipation Proclamation on this date. But would he? Pressure to rescind the promise was intense, and the president's racial views remained ambiguous. True to his word, Lincoln signed the final Proclamation, basing it on his war powers as commander in chief rather than on humanitarian grounds. The president took grave risks issuing the document.

Fighting for the Union *and* emancipation might fragment northern support for the war while uniting southerners behind the Confederate cause. Conservatives in the North considered the Proclamation unconstitutional and feared it would precipitate a race war. The new war aim might provoke even fiercer southern resistance, push the border slave states into the Confederacy, and alienate southern Unionists. Yet few other acts had such important military advantages. The prospect of European intervention ultimately waned further. If emancipation outraged some northerners, others considered freedom a great moral battle cry, infusing new vigor into the war effort. Since slavery supported the South's economy and social system, freeing the slaves was an excellent method of economic and psychological warfare. As the trickle of slaves responding to freedom's lure by crossing over behind Union lines became a torrent, southern white men had to serve in agriculture and industry instead of in the ranks. "Every slave withdrawn from the enemy," Halleck wrote Grant, "is the equivalent of a white man put *hors de combat.*"

Perhaps the greatest military asset flowing from the Proclamation was the large-scale recruitment of black men. Utilizing blacks for military purposes was not unprecedented. The Navy had always employed blacks, and black soldiers served in the colonial wars, the Revolution, and the War of 1812. Furthermore, by 1862 the Union Army was exploiting black labor, and some generals, without official approval, had organized black regiments. In occupied territory Union officers acted virtually as new masters over fugitive slaves, forcing them to build fortifications and abusing them unmercifully. Black people also aided the Army in less onerous ways—as scouts and spies, teamsters and carpenters, cooks and nurses. Meanwhile, ignoring government policy, James H. Lane organized the 1st Kansas Colored Volunteers, composed of Missouri fugitive slaves and northern free blacks; Butler raised the 1st, 2d, and 3d Louisiana Native Guards from among the free blacks and escaped slaves in New Orleans; and Hunter recruited the 1st Regiment of South Carolina Volunteers from blacks on the Sea Islands.

The government hesitantly moved toward black recruitment during the last half of 1862. The Second Confiscation and Militia Acts of July 17, 1862, authorized the president to employ black soldiers at his discretion, and on August 25 Stanton officially sanctioned raising black troops for the first time. The secretary of war ordered Rufus Saxton, who had replaced Hunter in South Carolina, to arm and equip up to 5,000 former slaves. The Emancipation Proclamation was the final step, indicating Lincoln's intention to employ black soldiers to the maximum extent. Dual motives of exploitation and idealism had irresistibly converted a white man's war into a black man's war as well. "The colored population is the great *avail-*

able and yet *unavailed* of, force for restoring the Union," Lincoln wrote. A song written by a Union staff officer best expressed the element of crass exploitation in black manpower mobilization:

> Some tell us 'tis a burnin' shame
> To make the naygers fight;
> An' that the thrade of bein' kilt
> Belongs but to the white:
> But as for me, upon my sowl!
> So liberal are we here,
> I'll let Sambo be murthered instad of myself
> On every day in the year.

Yet many people supported black recruitment for noble reasons. Soldiering would give blacks a claim to not just freedom but also equality. "Once let the black man get upon his person the brass letters, *U.S.*; let him get an eagle on his button, and a musket on his shoulder and bullets in his pocket," said the black abolitionist Frederick Douglass, "and there is no power on earth which can deny that he has earned the right to citizenship in the United States."

The organization of black regiments began in earnest during the first half of 1863. Initially the War Department authorized state governors and enterprising citizens to enlist regiments, just as they had organized white units. However, the national government soon exercised a near monopoly over black recruitment. In March it sent Adjutant General Lorenzo Thomas to the Mississippi Valley to organize as many black regiments as possible, and in May it established the Bureau of Colored Troops in the War Department to administer recruitment nationwide. Officially 178,892 blacks, commanded by approximately 7,000 white officers, served in the Army and at least 10,000 more in the Navy. Approximately 9 percent of all men fighting for the Union were black. Although black army units did a disproportionate share of fatigue duty, they bore an increasing combat responsibility as the war neared its end, fighting in thirty-nine major battles and dispelling the myth of black docility and cowardice.

National conscription was an even more profound assertion of centralized authority. On April 16, 1862, the Confederacy enacted the first national draft law in American history. Fighting for freedom and states' rights, the South paradoxically forced individuals to serve under central authority. The Confederate congress understood that conscription, although distasteful, was necessary. Casualties were high, few men volunteered, and the 1861 one-year enlistments soon expired. The law made all white males between the ages of eighteen and thirty-five members of the army for three years, automatically reenlisting the one-year volunteers for two more years. Subsequent legislation extended the age limits to seventeen and fifty, and in February 1864 the congress ordered all men already in the army to serve for the duration. Compulsory reenlistment meant that southerners served until they were killed or discharged due to disability, they deserted, or the war ended.

Two features weakened Confederate conscription. First, the law permitted substitutes. The substitute market was discriminatory and fraudulent. Prices soared to more than $5,000, which only the rich could pay, and many substitutes were unfit or soon deserted. When the Confederate congress later abolished substitution and made men who had provided substitutes liable for service, the rich felt betrayed. Second, although the original law contained no exemptions, a mere five days later congress began to correct this "oversight" by providing for several exempt categories; subsequent legislation expanded the exemption list. Exemptions included a large number of state and national government officials, militia officers, workers in critical war-production occupations, professional men, and one white man for every twenty slaves. Southerners abused many of these categories, and ultimately the Confederacy exempted about 50 percent of the men called out by conscription.

The North also felt a manpower squeeze during 1862. Realizing his error, Stanton reestablished Federal recruiting in June, and on July 2 Lincoln called for 300,000 three-year volunteers, but the response was slow. Like the South, the North turned to compulsion, though less directly. The Militia Act of July 17, 1862, authorized the president to "make all necessary rules and regulations" for states without adequate militia laws. Broadly interpreting that provision, on August 4 the government called for a draft of 300,000 nine-month militia. A proviso stated that a special militia draft would be conducted to meet the deficiency of three-year volunteers in those states failing to reach their quotas. Governors protested their quotas were too high and that the date for the special draft was too soon, and antidraft disturbances occurred in Wisconsin and Pennsylvania. Under pressure Stanton postponed the militia draft, which never went into effect. However, the threat of conscription brought forth 421,000 volunteers and 87,500 militiamen. Since the government considered one volunteer equivalent to four nine-month militiamen, the states more than met the July and August calls. But it had not been easy.

Confronted with the grievous casualties of the 1862 fall and winter campaigns, the likelihood of even greater losses in the upcoming campaigns, and the growing reluctance of volunteers to come forward, the North needed a more certain method of obtaining men. On March 3, 1863, Congress adopted a Conscription Act (also known as the Enrollment Act) based on the constitutional clause permitting the government "to raise and support armies." The law established a bureaucracy for administering and enforcing the draft that gave primary responsibility to military officers. At the apex was another new War Department bureau, the Provost Marshal General's Bureau headed by James B. Fry. At the base were 185 enrollment boards, one for each congressional district. To compile a list of eligible men, a board divided its district into subdistricts and for each one appointed an enrollment officer who went from house to house writing down the names and addresses of draft-age men. Between the apex and the base Fry appointed one or more acting assistant provost marshal generals for each state who would coordinate district affairs and serve as intermediaries between himself and local officials.

In important respects the Conscription Act contained features similar to militia laws. First, it maintained the principle of universal military obligation, imposing it on all able-bodied male citizens and alien declarants between the ages of twenty and forty-five. It divided enrollees into two classes: Class I, including all men between twenty and thirty-five and unmarried men between thirty-five and forty-five; and Class II, containing all men not in Class I. No Class II enrollees would be drafted until the Class I pool was exhausted. If a man was drafted, the term of service was three years or the duration, whichever ended first. However, as in militia laws, universal military service was theoretical, not actual. Congress intended to raise men indirectly, using the threat of conscription to spur volunteering. The president set draft quotas for each enrollment district based on population and the number of men from a district already in service. Districts had about fifty days to fill their quotas with volunteers. If too few volunteers entered service, a draft would be held to meet the deficiency. Ironically, Confederate conscription was a more forthright exertion of national authority. Southern lawmakers designed their act to raise troops directly, not to stimulate volunteering.

Second, the northern law contained exemptions. The list was unusually brief, consisting of the physically or mentally unfit, convicted felons, a restricted number of state and national officials, only sons of dependent widows, and sole supporters of infirm parents or orphaned children. The North did not allow the occupational exemptions that southerners so successfully manipulated to evade the draft. However, more than 50 percent of northern draftees found a way to gain an exemption, with physical disability being a sure avenue of escape. Some men practiced self-mutilation, while other draftees fabricated disabilities, buttressing their claims with testimonials from unscrupulous friends and doctors.

Third, a drafted man who was ineligible for an exemption, legal or otherwise, had two traditional means of evading service. He could provide a substitute or pay a $300 commutation fee. By setting a fixed commutation rate, Congress kept the price of substitutes under $300, since no one would pay more than that for a substitute. As in the South, substitutes were often of poor quality and likely to desert at the first opportunity; but unlike the Confederacy the North did not abolish the practice. However, in July 1864 it abolished commutation for everyone but conscientious objectors, and substitute prices rapidly increased. Since the South needed men more than money, Confederate conscription contained no provision for commutation.

Finally, to entice volunteers, the North resorted to the traditional method of offering bounties. Although providing a substitute or commuting carried no stigma, being conscripted did for both the draftee and his community. Wards, cities, and counties collected money for bounties through voluntary contributions, real estate taxes, and special fundraising events. States tacked on an additional bounty, as did the national government. The nation spent more than $700 million on bounties, which equaled the entire wartime pay for the Army! Since localities competed for volunteers, local bounty rates spiraled upward, giving richer cities and counties an advantage in avoiding the draft. With bounty piled upon bounty, a man could collect a substantial sum for volunteering, and he could become even richer if he volunteered more than once. "Bounty jumping" became a national scandal. A man would volunteer, collect the bounties, desert, volunteer in another district collecting more bounties, and so on. Not all volunteers were jumpers, but there were so many that the Army detailed armed squads to escort groups of them to the front. The Confederacy, with its more direct method of raising men and its limited financial resources, avoided the bounty problem.

Surprisingly, among those who volunteered, both North and South, were hundreds of women who—for reasons including the desire to be near a husband or brother in the ranks, patriotism, love of adventure, or the lure of a soldier's paycheck—rejected the battlefield exclusion that being female ordinarily provided them. Moreover, women who had been living as men before the war may have felt the pressure to enlist to prove their "manhood." In an age when medical exams were cursory and superficial, and when individuals did not carry personal identification papers (such as a driver's license), enlisting was fairly easy. Hiding one's identity could be more challenging as a woman made the difficult dual transition from a female to a male persona, and from a civilian to a soldier. Some women were discovered when hospitalized for illnesses or wounds and some when they had babies. At the Battle of Antietam, for example, two were killed in action and three more suffered wounds, including one who had to have an arm amputated. "There was an orderly in one of our regiments & he

& the Corporal always slept together," wrote a soldier in a Massachusetts regiment. "Well, the other night the Corporal had a baby, for the Corporal turned out to be a woman! She has been in 3 or 4 fights [battles]." Many females served lengthy enlistments without being discovered and, at least in some cases, continued living as men long after the war. When an accident in 1911 required "his" hospitalization, it turned out that Albert Cashier, who had served in the 95th Illinois Regiment, was really Jennie Hodgers.*

If northern conscription remained dependent on the colonial past for some of its operative features, it also represented a radical change from previous manpower mobilization policies. The draft law made the principle of universal military service an obligation to the national government rather than the states. Both in the Confederacy and in the Union the conscription procedure ignored the states. Another significant change was from voluntary to compulsory enlistments as the basis for mobilization. In one respect these changes weakened the war efforts of both North and South. With their intense localism and a strong tradition of voluntary associations, Americans identified with and took pride in regiments drawn from a limited geographic area. These bonds of kinship and friendship between the folks at home and the regiment in the field began to dissolve as the national government put conscripted "outsiders" into the ranks. However, the changes permitted more efficient use of manpower. States had rarely channeled volunteers into old regiments, since governors preferred to create new regiments, earning the loyalty of men appointed as officers. As a unit in the field became more experienced, it shrank from battlefield losses and disease, the numerical decline offsetting any increase in military skills. At Stones River, for example, Rosecrans commanded 139 regiments, representing a theoretical strength of approximately 139,000 men, but he actually had only one-third that many soldiers. Commanders believed that one new man in an old regiment was worth two or three in a new regiment, for, as Sherman wrote, "the former, by association with good experienced captains, lieutenants, and non-commissioned officers, soon became veterans, whereas the latter were generally unavailable for a year." Although the North and South continued to form new volunteer units, by assigning at least some draftees to experienced regiments both governments increased the fighting effectiveness of their units.

* Women successfully passed as males because uniforms were ill-fitting and loose; like many men, women attended to bodily functions in private areas instead of going to the disgusting latrines; the numerous adolescent boys in the ranks had high-pitched voices and little or no facial hair; females could readily emulate typical masculine behaviors, such as drinking, gambling, swearing, and chewing tobacco; and in many cases the menstrual cycle ceased because of the intense physical activity, poor nutrition, and severe psychological stress that all soldiers endured.

In October 1863, Halleck wrote to Sherman regarding the Conscription Act. "A more complicated, defective, and impracticable law could scarcely have been framed," he said. Twentieth-century authorities agreed and revamped the process in 1917. The act of 1863 showed them what to do fifty years later: omit substitution and commutation; outlaw bounties; increase civilian participation in administration; and instead of using enrolling officers, make it an obligation of citizenship for men to come forward to enroll. Despite the judgment of the general in chief that northern conscription was a failure, it worked exactly as its authors intended. The government held four drafts, and altogether enrollment boards examined 522,187 men, exempting 315,509 of them. Of the 206,678 men held to service, 86,724 commuted, 44,403 hired substitutes before they were drafted, 73,607 furnished substitutes after being drafted, and only 46,347 were actually drafted. Combining all substitutes and draftees, only 13 percent of Union Army enlistments came directly from the draft. Yet during the war's last two years the North enlisted more than 1 million men. Some of these were veterans who reenlisted, but most were new volunteers motivated in varying degrees by the fear of conscription and the lure of bounties. Southern conscription more directly augmented the gray armies. It kept veterans in the ranks and produced approximately 120,000 draftees and 70,000 substitutes, representing 20 percent of Confederate manpower. Inevitably the South's draft also had an indirect effect: Anxious to avoid the odium associated with conscription, an undetermined number of Confederates volunteered.

Although conscription filled the ranks, it also created internal dissension. Long accustomed to limited government, people in both sections considered conscription an un-American and despotic exercise of national power. To the lower classes it seemed especially unfair, since exemptions, substitution, and commutation appeared to make the conflict a rich man's war but a poor man's fight. Although opponents of the Davis and Lincoln administrations vigorously cultivated the charge of class favoritism for political purposes, this accusation was unfair. The Confederate and Union armies rather accurately mirrored their respective populations. If anything, unskilled laborers were proportionally underrepresented and white-collar workers proportionally overrepresented. To states' rights adherents, conscription was unconstitutional. In the South, Governors Brown and Vance obstructed its enforcement by expanding the number of civil and militia offices that qualified for exemption, and state judges issued writs of habeas corpus preventing the arrest of unwilling draftees. Northern Peace Democrats, often as state-oriented as southerners, fanned antidraft sentiment, sparking widespread evasion, bitter hostility to draft officials, and riots. More than 161,000 men who were not exempt and did not provide a sub-

stitute or commute failed to report when summoned by their local enrollment boards. The number of these illegal draft evaders nearly equaled
those who obtained substitutes or paid the commutation fee. Enrollment
officers discovered their duty was dangerous, since they were assaulted by
irate individuals and mobs, threatened and intimidated, attacked by dogs,
scalded with boiling water, and bombarded with everything from eggs to
bricks. The worst antidraft riot (which included a strong element of racist, antiblack sentiment) occurred in New York City, where four days of
arson, looting, lynching, and shooting erupted in mid-July 1863, resulting
in about 120 deaths. Grim troops coming from the Gettysburg battlefield
finally quelled the outbreak. Lesser mob violence against the draft took
place throughout the North.

The Lincoln administration not only freed and armed the slaves and
countenanced conscription but also suppressed civil liberties, permitting
the occasional repression of newspapers, the censorship of reporters' telegraphic dispatches, and the military arrest of perhaps as many as 15,000
people. The vast majority of those arrested were from the border states or
the Confederacy and included blockade-runners, smugglers, spies, defectors, and refugees. The only large group of Northerners arrested came in
the wake of the militia draft and the Preliminary Emancipation Proclamation, which generated tremendous opposition among Peace Democrats
(reproachfully known as Copperheads). These antiwar advocates urged
resistance to both emancipation and the draft, discouraged volunteering,
and encouraged desertion. Primarily to deal with resistance to the militia
draft, the administration suspended the writ of habeas corpus nationwide.
Suspension of the writ, the final Emancipation Proclamation, and the Conscription Act intensified opposition to the government's war policies. Copperheads accused "King Lincoln" of military despotism and vowed they
would not support his "wicked abolition crusade against the South," but
would *"resist* to the *death* all attempts to draft any of our citizens into the
army." But Republicans countered charges of tyranny with accusations of
treason. Congress passed a Habeas Corpus Act in March 1863 sanctioning
the practices established by the executive branch, and the president vigorously defended his administration's actions. Under the guise of freedom
of speech and press and the right of habeas corpus, he said, the Confederacy "hoped to keep on foot amongst us a most efficient corps of spies,
informers, suppliers, and aiders and abettors of their cause in a thousand
ways." Ordinary legal processes did not restrain these disloyal persons,
but courts-martial and military commissions would. Furthermore, the
infringements were only temporary. Military arrests during the rebellion
did not mean that Americans would be denied their constitutional liberties
"throughout the indefinite peaceful future which I trust lies before them."

Drawing the line between disloyalty and legitimate expressions of free speech, press, and assembly is not easy, and Lincoln did not draw it perfectly. Although innocent men suffered injustice, the administration's use of the Army against civilians resulted in no reign of terror. Moreover, just as Polk established bold precedents of strong executive wartime leadership, Lincoln created equally far-reaching precedents for the wartime interference with basic civil liberties. To conquer the South, he exercised new presidential powers that many people believed he did not and should not have, for liberty squelched in war might be lost in peace.

1863: Year of Decision

As the 1863 campaigning season approached, Union forces stood poised at five critical points. The Army of the Potomac, under a new commander, held the Rappahannock line. Following Fredericksburg, Burnside tried to redeem his reputation with a mid-January movement around Lee's left flank, but torrential rains turned the countryside into a swamp and the army sank to its knees and axles in muck. The "Mud March" destroyed what little confidence the army still had in Burnside, and on January 25 Lincoln replaced him with "Fighting Joe" Hooker. In the western theater Rosecrans's Army of the Cumberland occupied Murfreesboro, Grant's Army of the Tennessee was north of Vicksburg, and Banks's Army of the Gulf held the lower Mississippi. At sea Samuel DuPont had an ironclad squadron off Charleston. The South viewed these enemy hosts with alarm but for the first half of 1863 had reason to be optimistic. Northern antiwar sentiment surged, the drive to clear the Mississippi seemed stalled, Rosecrans remained inert, and the Confederacy won victories at Charleston and Chancellorsville. Then in midsummer and fall disaster struck. The North mangled Lee's army at Gettysburg, captured Vicksburg and Port Hudson, and expelled the rebels from Tennessee.

The Union public expected DuPont to achieve a victory at Charleston akin to Farragut's at New Orleans. But the tactical problems were not comparable. Once beyond the river forts Farragut could continue upstream, but Charleston was a cul-de-sac protected by powerful batteries. DuPont had a mere thirty-two guns on his eight monitors and the flagship *New Ironsides*. Moving on the noontime ebb tide of April 7, the vessels came within range of enemy batteries about three o'clock. To DuPont's chief of staff, "It seemed as if the fires of hell were turned upon the Union fleet," as Confederate gunners badly damaged all the ships. The repulse was a naval Fredericksburg, and its impact on northern morale was similarly depressing.

Surely Hooker would redeem Union fortunes! Fighting Joe performed wonders in reviving the dispirited army. For example, he abolished the "grand divisions" and reestablished the old corps, insisting that the men of each wear a distinctive insignia to enhance esprit de corps. Hooker also reorganized the cavalry into a single corps. Previous commanders assigned cavalry regiments individually to infantry divisions, a practice that hampered Union cavalry operations, since Lee and Stuart kept their cavalry concentrated. Properly organized and, after midsummer, increasingly armed with Spencer repeating carbines, Union troopers soon demonstrated that they were not inferior to their Confederate counterparts. Finally, the general's fighting spirit was contagious. When he proclaimed that he commanded "the finest army on the planet," people expected imminent victory.

Hooker was a skillful commander as well as a proficient organizer. Outnumbering Lee two to one, he planned to leave 40,000 men under John Sedgwick at Fredericksburg and take the remainder of the army upstream to turn the enemy left flank. Crossing the Rappahannock River simultaneously, the two wings would crush the Army of Northern Virginia. Initially the plan went well. By April 30 both Sedgwick and Hooker were across the river, the latter near Chancellorsville, a crossroads in an extensive area of tangled brush and second-growth timber called the Wilderness. "The rebel army," exulted Hooker, "is now the legitimate property of the Army of the Potomac."

Hooker's strategy placed Lee in a precarious position, but he responded with tactical daring. As he had done against Pope, the Confederate general divided his army, containing Sedgwick with 10,000 men and taking 50,000 troops to assail Hooker. Lee then further divided his army, sending Jackson's corps around Hooker's right flank on May 2. A vigilant commander would have crushed Lee's scattered army. Hooker, however, lost his nerve. When Jackson's men smashed the Union flank, Lee also attacked and the southerners initially drove the Yankees back. But stiffening resistance and nightfall halted the attacks, with Lee's army still divided. Most of Hooker's subordinates urged him to counterattack on May 3, but he refused. Instead, Lee attacked again, reuniting his army's wings after fierce fighting. Meanwhile, Sedgwick seized Marye's Heights and advanced toward Chancellorsville. Running another incalculable risk, Lee divided his army yet again. A fraction watched Hooker while the remainder assaulted Sedgwick on May 3–4, forcing him north of the Rappahannock. Lee then returned to confront Fighting Joe, who ordered his army to recross the river on the night of May 5–6.

Although the Battle of Chancellorsville was Lee's most dazzling victory, two factors tempered the rejoicing. First, Lee's 13,000 casualties, while fewer than the North's 17,000, represented a much higher proportion of his army. One of those casualties was especially costly: In the twilight after his flank attack, Jackson rode beyond his lines to survey the situation. As he returned, a jittery Confederate unit fired, fatally wounding him. His death forced Lee to reorganize the army, from the successful two-corps structure into three corps under Longstreet, Ambrose P. Hill, and Richard Ewell. Whether Hill or Ewell could match Jackson's genius for long marching and tough fighting was questionable. Second, the Union army had again been humiliated and hurt but not destroyed. Accustomed to suffering and surviving, the Army of the Potomac still manned the Rappahannock line.

Lee was eager to capitalize on his latest success by carrying the war into the North. Since early spring he had asked for permission to invade, but a great strategic debate snared his request. With the Yankees pressing hard on all fronts, which front was most vital for Confederate survival? The investment of Vicksburg, where Grant was closing in on John Pemberton's garrison, caused special concern. Some men suggested that Lee send reinforcements to Bragg, so that the Army of Tennessee could defeat Rosecrans, threaten Kentucky and Ohio, and save Vicksburg. Lee opposed any scheme for western reinforcement, however, because he could not reduce his army without sacrificing Virginia. Southern railroads were so dilapidated that the North could shift troops more rapidly than the Confederacy; Confederate reinforcements would always arrive too late. Lee also argued that since northerners could not survive a deep south summer, Grant would soon retreat anyway. The solution to Confederate difficulties was an invasion of Pennsylvania, which would dislocate Federal plans, force Grant and Rosecrans to send reinforcements eastward, save Virginia, and allow Confederates to obtain supplies from northern farms and storehouses. Victories on northern soil might gain foreign recognition and foster Copperhead sentiment. Lee's arguments convinced Davis that southerners should again wade the Potomac.

On June 9, as Lee shifted his 75,000 troops toward the Shenandoah, Union cavalry surprised Stuart at Brandy Station, resulting in the war's largest cavalry action. Although Confederate troopers forced the bluecoats to retreat, the victory margin was thin. Eager to refurbish his reputation, Stuart suggested a raid into Hooker's rear, and Lee consented. Departing on June 25, Stuart promised to rejoin the army in a few days, but unexpected difficulties delayed the cavalry's return a week and Lee advanced blindly. With his men at York, Carlisle, and Chambersburg in Pennsylvania, Lee still believed Hooker was in Virginia. The Federal army was actually at Frederick, and Fighting Joe no longer commanded it. Hooker's unwillingness to tangle with Lee as the gray column marched from the Rappahannock to Pennsylvania dismayed Lincoln, and on June 27 the president replaced him with George G. Meade. The new commander believed he could stand on the tactical defensive, since Lee would not retreat into Virginia without fighting. Meanwhile, learning that the Federals were dan-

gerously close, on June 28 Lee ordered his forces to concentrate at Cashtown. Three days later men from James J. Pettigrew's brigade went to seize a supply of shoes in Gettysburg. They bumped into a Yankee advance unit, John Buford's cavalry division, which held off the graycoats until infantry support arrived. Although nobody planned to fight at Gettysburg, once the shooting began both armies converged there.

Fighting on the first day was chaotic and fierce, as the Union I and XI Corps tried to hold ground west and north of Gettysburg, but the Confederates drove them through the town and onto Cemetery Hill and Culp's Hill. As more Federals arrived, the line extended southward along Cemetery Ridge to Little Round Top and Round Top. The position resembled a four-mile-long inverted fishhook running from the barb at Culp's Hill, along the shank of Cemetery Hill and Cemetery Ridge, to the eye at the Round Tops. The Confederate line ran roughly parallel from east of Gettysburg, through the town, then south along Seminary Ridge. Not only were the Federals dug in on high ground, but in terms of maneuver and communications they held interior lines. Reaching the battlefield at midnight, Meade saw enough by moonlight to know his 88,000-man army held formidable terrain. If only Lee would attack!

Longstreet opposed fighting at Gettysburg. The army, he told Lee, should slide around the Federal left flank, get between Meade and Washington, find good defensive terrain, and force the Army of the Potomac to attack. Rejecting the advice, Lee issued attack orders for Longstreet to deliver the primary blow against Meade's southern flank and Ewell to launch a secondary assault against Culp's Hill and Cemetery Hill. Longstreet hammered but did not break the main Union line, and Ewell made only slight headway, securing a lodgment on the lower slope of Culp's Hill. That evening Meade met with his subordinates to decide whether the army should retreat, attack, or hold its ground. Almost all agreed that the Federals should maintain their defensive posture. Where was Lee most likely to hit? Meade reasoned that the enemy, having tested the flanks, would attack the center. He was correct. Lee planned an assault, preceded by a massive barrage, aimed at the middle of the fishhook. The striking force would consist of approximately 13,500 men stretching across a mile-long front. Lee again entrusted the attack to Longstreet, who again protested his superior's plan. But the southern commander waved off his subordinate. "The enemy is there, General Longstreet," said Lee, indicating Cemetery Ridge, "and I am going to strike him."

Lee's plan was almost Burnside-like in its simplicity, and it produced a Fredericksburg with the roles reversed. The artillery barrage shattered the sultry stillness at one o'clock and continued for almost two hours before the Confederates emerged from the woods on Seminary Ridge and advanced as if on a parade ground. Pickett's Charge, named after George Pickett, who commanded the largest of the three attacking divisions, pitted gallantry against firepower. Forty minutes decided the issue. Yankee batteries rained grapeshot and canister on the exposed ranks. Federal infantry unloosed volley after volley, while punishing fire from the flanks engulfed the column. The storm of hot metal shredded the attacking column, which suffered 50 percent casualties.

"It is all my fault," Lee told the survivors, urging them to rally in case Meade counterattacked. Within a few hours the Army of Northern Virginia had regrouped, but Meade did not leave his lines. As after Antietam, Lee held his ground for a day before retreating. Battle casualties amounted to one-third of his army, and thousands of men straggled during the withdrawal. Meade did not pursue vigorously. With his army having suffered 23,000 casualties, he seemed content to escort the invaders off northern soil. By late July both armies were again on the Rappahannock, and a long stalemate ensued in the eastern theater. Lincoln was disconsolate when he learned that Lee's army had reached Virginia soil, and he penned a harsh letter to Meade, which he never actually sent. "I do not believe you appreciate the magnitude of the misfortune involved in Lee's escape," the president wrote. "He was within your easy grasp, and to have closed upon him would, in connection with our other late successes, have ended the war." The "other late successes" occurred in the western theater, where Vicksburg and Port Hudson surrendered and Bragg was in retreat.

A muddled command system exacerbated normal Confederate problems in the west: Too many places to defend, too few troops, and too little logistical support. In November 1862 Davis appointed Joseph E. Johnston, recovered from his wound at Fair Oaks, to command a newly formed Department of the West that included the armies of Bragg in Tennessee and Pemberton in Mississippi. The command difficulties were threefold. First, the extent of Johnston's authority was unclear. Retaining the right to correspond directly with Richmond, Bragg and Pemberton could circumvent him. Second, Johnston could not effectively coordinate the two armies due to the distance between them, the South's primitive transportation system, and Federal control of the Tennessee River. Third, Johnston and Davis disagreed on a fundamental issue. The department commander believed middle and east Tennessee were more important than the Mississippi, but Davis stressed holding the river.

Following his unsuccessful overland campaign toward Vicksburg, Grant went to Young's Point to oversee the river campaign. Both geography and man had made Vicksburg difficult to attack. Only the high ground south and east of the city offered suitable terrain for military operations. Grant's problem was to get there. The bayou country fanning northward from Vicksburg was impenetrable, as Grant learned after months of searching for a feasible route. Powerful batteries lining the river presented a barrier seemingly as impassable as the bayous. Grant admitted that the "strategical way according to the rule" would be to return to Memphis and try the overland route again. But in the Union's grim springtime mood people would have interpreted the move as another defeat, so Grant determined upon a plan as daring as any that Lee devised. His army would slog down the Mississippi's west side and cross below the city. David D. Porter, commanding the river flotilla, would simply have to run the gauntlet with gunboats and transports. Grant knew he might have a difficult logistical problem once he left his supply base north of Vicksburg. For supplies he would depend in part on a wagon road coming down the river's west bank and on the Navy's ability to run additional transports past the Confederate batteries. But the road was tenuous and the Navy's task risky, and Grant would have to live primarily off the country until he got back to the Mississippi above Vicksburg—if he could.

In early April Grant started his men marching south, and on the night of April 16–17 a dozen of Porter's ships slipped downriver. Confederate gunners hit all twelve ships, but only one sank, and on April 30 the army crossed at Bruinsburg. The next day Grant brushed aside rebels at Port Gibson and then paused for more than a week to stockpile supplies and organize a wagon train before resuming his advance. His first task was to keep Pemberton and Johnston, who had patched together a force near Jackson, from uniting. Grant headed for Jackson, winning another minor battle at Raymond and forcing Johnston to retreat. Then Grant turned toward Vicksburg, defeating Pemberton's main force at Champion Hill and his rear guard at the Big Black River. The Confederate commander retreated into Vicksburg's earthworks. Reluctant to undertake a siege during the summer months, Grant twice stormed the fortress, but the Confederates bloodily repulsed the assaults. The only way to take the city was by siege.

Throughout the campaign Johnston and Pemberton never agreed on a common strategy. Johnston had urged Pemberton to abandon Vicksburg and join him for a joint attack on Grant, but Pemberton refused, since he believed Vicksburg was a "vital point, indispensable to be held." Thus Grant was successful even though Confederates in the vicinity outnumbered him until mid-June. By then, however, he had 71,000 troops closing in on Vicksburg. Shelling went on night and day as the inhabitants huddled in basements or caves, subsisting on mule meat and rats, and on July 4 Pemberton surrendered. Four days later Port Hudson capitulated to Banks, who had besieged it since mid-May. "The Father of Waters," Lincoln happily wrote, "again goes unvexed to the sea."

As the Vicksburg siege entered its final stage, Rosecrans launched an offensive with his 60,000-man army. Moving with speed and skill, he maneuvered Bragg out of middle Tennessee. Bragg took refuge in Chattanooga, and Rosecrans paused to regroup. When he resumed his advance in mid-August, Burnside's Army of the Ohio marched simultaneously from Kentucky toward Knoxville. Burnside forced Simon B. Buckner's Knoxville defenders to withdraw and entered the city on September 3. Six days later Rosecrans took Chattanooga after clever maneuvering again forced Bragg to retreat. Rosecrans plunged southward in pursuit, each of his three corps pouring through mountain gaps twenty miles apart. Bragg prepared to pounce as the South effected another far-flung strategic concentration similar to the one preceding Shiloh. He received reinforcements from Buckner and Johnston, and he anxiously awaited two divisions under Longstreet coming from Lee's army. But the Union occupation of Knoxville severed the direct rail link between Virginia and Bragg, compelling Longstreet to take a roundabout route. Before he arrived, Bragg tried three times to strike Rosecrans's dispersed forces. The attempts miscarried but alerted Rosecrans, who hastily concentrated his army along Chickamauga Creek. At the ensuing Battle of Chickamauga, the Confederates had a numerical advantage of about 10,000 men. On September 18, as Longstreet's first troops detrained, the Confederates fought their way across the creek. The next day Bragg delivered an all-out attack but made little progress. He renewed the attack the next morning and rolled up the Union right flank. One-third of the army, including Rosecrans, fled to Chattanooga, and it appeared Bragg might annihilate the remaining two-thirds. But George H. Thomas rallied the Federals and repulsed attacks until dark, earning the sobriquet "the Rock of Chickamauga." That night Thomas retreated to Chattanooga.

Chickamauga was another dearly bought Confederate victory devoid of strategic consequences. The rebels suffered 18,400 casualties, the Yankees 16,100. Furthermore, the Union army retained Chattanooga even though Bragg besieged it. Since the only supply route Rosecrans utilized was circuitous and subjected to rebel cavalry raids, by mid-October his army was starving. With Rosecrans acting, in Lincoln's memorable phrase, "confused and stunned like a duck hit upon the head," the administration responded decisively by sending reinforcements and changing the command structure. Stanton ordered two corps from the Army of the Potomac under Hooker to Chattanooga. In the war's greatest railroad operation, 23,000 men covered 1,200 miles in twelve days. The War Department also ordered four divisions under Sherman to the beleaguered city. On October 17 Lincoln appointed Grant as commander of all forces (except Banks's army) between the Appalachians and the Mississippi and directed him to assume personal control at Chattanooga. He replaced Rosecrans with

Thomas, opened up a direct supply route, and developed plans to break the siege. Meanwhile, Bragg committed a blunder. At Davis's behest he sent Longstreet to recapture Knoxville just as the Union army was seizing the initiative under Grant's energetic generalship. On November 24–25 Union attacks drove the Confederates from their siege positions, forcing the Confederates to retreat to Dalton. Shortly thereafter Longstreet retreated from Knoxville, although he remained in a position to menace east Tennessee. Bragg admitted that Davis had erred in keeping him in command, since, as both men knew, he had lost the confidence of his generals. In October Davis had visited Bragg's headquarters and in the commander's presence asked each subordinate whether the army needed a new leader. All said yes, yet Davis retained Bragg! Now, after one failure too many, Davis replaced Bragg with Johnston.

Grant planned for a significant winter campaign, hoping for permission to advance from New Orleans to Mobile and then to "make a campaign into the interior of Alabama, and, possibly, Georgia." Concern in Washington for the security of east and middle Tennessee prevented Grant from undertaking the campaign. Lincoln and Halleck wanted him to drive Longstreet completely out of east Tennessee and to push Johnston farther back into Georgia. Although unable to undertake his Mobile campaign, Grant did send Sherman from Vicksburg to Meridian, Mississippi, in what was the first example of his raiding strategy. Departing Vicksburg in early February 1864 with 25,000 men, Sherman devastated the railroads and resources of central Mississippi and then withdrew to Canton before returning to Vicksburg in early March.

The North's achievements during the last half of 1863 gave it a firm strategic position for winning the war. Augmenting the substantial gains in the eastern and western theaters was a success along the coast. Following DuPont's failure, Lincoln replaced him with John A. Dahlgren, who cooperated with Quincy A. Gillmore's army forces to seal off Charleston by capturing Morris Island. Although the city remained in Confederate hands, blockade-running became doubly dangerous since ships had to escape Dahlgren's cordon and avoid Union artillery on Morris Island. The North had tightened the blockade one more notch. Indeed, less spectacularly than the land battles but more steadily, the blockade was strangling the Confederacy.

The Civil War at Sea

The most important aspect of the sea war was the blockade, which the North tried to tighten and the South struggled to break. The blockade's architects were Secretary of the Navy Welles and his assistant secretary,

Gustavus V. Fox. They helped plan and organize the amphibious operations that captured bases in enemy territory and closed southern ports, and oversaw the Navy's expansion to 671 ships by December 1864, including 236 steam vessels built during the war. With steam dominating the building program, in July 1862 Congress restructured the five naval bureaus into a new system of eight bureaus. The most significant change was the addition of a Bureau of Steam Engineering, headed by Benjamin F. Isherwood. Working closely with John Lenthall, chief of the Bureau of Construction and Repair, Isherwood did more than any other individual to design the Union's steam navy.

The steam navy's growth created special problems. Prices for labor and materials rose during the war, and cost overruns played havoc with the Navy Department budget. As Isherwood and Lenthall supervised the construction of vessels, they often changed specifications, leading to what Fox called "those horrible bills for additions and improvements and everlasting alterations." The biggest problem, however, was finding capable steam engineers. Although their numbers increased from 192 to 1,805, many were inexperienced. To compensate for the novices, Isherwood designed power plants for simplicity, reliability, and durability. But he achieved these admirable qualities by building machinery that was often heavy, underpowered, and inefficient, resulting in many slow, deep-draft ships with limited cruising ranges.

Whatever problems the Union Navy encountered, they were minor compared to those of the Confederate navy. Secretary of the Navy Stephen R. Mallory faced obstacles that made even a modest naval effort appear impossible. The southern population contained few sailors, and at its peak naval manpower was 25 percent below requirements. The South suffered more than the North from a shortage of engineers, and many of the skilled workers went into the army. Fuel, lubricants, iron, and other raw materials were scarce. The Confederacy initially had major naval facilities at Norfolk, Pensacola, and New Orleans, but the Union captured them in 1862, forcing the South to utilize small yards or build new ones in isolated locations beyond the reach of enemy amphibious operations. The transportation system often could not get even small quantities of materials to these far-flung facilities. Since Davis favored the army, the navy received inadequate funding. Money shortages crippled the effort to purchase foreign-built ships. Furthermore, constructing warships for a belligerent violated the neutrality laws of various European nations. The South's achievement was remarkable, considering the difficulties, for it built or acquired at least 130 ships.

The Confederate navy undertook two major activities intended to weaken the blockade. First, utilizing an array of technological innovations, the navy tried to protect southern harbors. With technology in rapid flux, Mallory hoped to pit southern ingenuity against northern ships. The navy department had a Torpedo Bureau and a Naval Submarine Battery Service to develop torpedoes (mines). Specially designed fifty-foot-long, cigar-shaped boats called "Davids" carried contact mines at the end of bow-mounted spars. Torpedoes sank or damaged forty-three Union warships. The Confederacy built the world's first successful submarine, CSS *Hunley,* which destroyed USS *Housatonic* off Charleston in February 1864, though *Hunley* also sank after the explosion. Torpedoes, "Davids," and submarines induced a well-founded fear in Union naval officers, who approached enemy harbors and river mouths with increasing caution.

The most ambitious effort to utilize new technology was the ironclad program. Prompted by Mallory, the government converted the captured *Merrimack* into the ironclad *Virginia,* authorized construction of two ironclads at Memphis and two at New Orleans, and appropriated $2 million to purchase ironclads abroad. The original purpose of the ironclads was to raise the blockade by sinking the Union's wooden ships and challenging the Federal Navy for control of the southern coast. The *Virginia* started the process spectacularly. On March 8, 1862, it steamed out of the Norfolk Navy Yard, destroying *Cumberland* and *Congress.* Three other Union ships ran aground trying to escape the iron-skinned beast. The day's events demonstrated that an unarmored ship could not fight an armored one. Fortunately for the Union, it had an antidote. When Welles learned of enemy plans for *Merrimack,* he appointed an Ironclad Board to study the problem. It recommended that the Navy Department authorize contracts for three different experimental ironclads, one of them designed by John Ericsson and known as *Monitor.* The *Monitor*'s most revolutionary feature was a revolving gun turret: Only the turret, not the ship, need turn in battle. On the night of March 8 *Monitor* arrived at Hampton Roads, and the next day, when *Merrimack* ventured forth to finish off the blockading squadron, the world's first fight between ironclads occurred. Armor against armor produced a tactical stalemate that worked to the North's strategic advantage. Union ironclads could prevent southern armored ships from directly lifting the blockade. Henceforth, the South primarily used ironclads to supplement harbor defenses, leaving Yankee sea power unchallenged along the seaboard.

The Battle of Hampton Roads touched off a *Monitor*-mania in the North and convinced the South that it should devote a major portion of its naval energies to acquiring ironclads. However, the Confederate ironclad program was not successful. The effort to buy foreign armored vessels yielded minimal results, and the domestic building program fared little better, as indicated by the fate of the four armored ships authorized in

1861. The two at New Orleans fell into Union hands after Farragut's triumph, the rebels destroyed one of the Memphis ironclads in August 1862 to prevent its capture, and the Federals captured the other one two years later. Although the South laid down or contracted for about fifty armored ships, only twenty-two ever became operational. Moreover, the South learned that once it built a novel weapon, the North, with its superior industrial capacity, could produce more of them. Before the war ended, the North had seventy ironclads in service.

The other Confederate naval activity was commerce raiding, which the South hoped would hurt the northern economy so badly that Welles would withdraw ships from the blockade to hunt down the raiders. Commerce raiders included privateers, converted merchantmen, and English-built steam cruisers. Davis issued a call for privateers in April 1861, and the government granted the first commission to the schooner *Triton* on May 10. A few more ships received commissions, but privateering soon ceased, since privateers had no place to take prizes. The blockade closed off southern ports, and the major European nations had signed the Declaration of Paris of 1856, outlawing the practice. The South possessed few merchant ships, but the government refitted about a dozen and commissioned them as regular navy vessels. But far more important than privateers or refitted merchantmen were three specially built cruisers bought in England. The CSS *Alabama* covered 75,000 miles under sail and steam in less than two years, capturing sixty-four prizes before the *Kearsarge* sank it. Its sister ship, *Florida,* took thirty-eight prizes before the sloop *Wachusett* captured the vessel as it refitted in a neutral port in Brazil. The South purchased the *Shenandoah* to replace the *Alabama,* and it practically destroyed the Yankee whaling fleet in the Bering Sea during the summer of 1865 before learning the war was over.

The direct losses from Confederate raiders amounted to about 250 ships, but the indirect costs were much higher. Hundreds of vessels lay in port fearing to put to sea, and shipowners transferred at least 700 more to foreign registry to avoid rebel depredations. Insurance rates skyrocketed for those ships brave enough to put to sea flying the American flag. However, though the commerce raiders practically drove the United States merchant marine from the oceans, they did not affect the war's outcome. Foreign shipping carried northern commerce, and Welles, recognizing the blockade's cardinal role in the war effort, refused to divert many ships from the southern coast.

Unable to weaken seriously the blockade with ironclads or commerce raiders, the South relied on blockade-running, an enterprise involving private individuals, foreigners, state governments, and the Confederate government. The allures of the business were adventure, patriotism, and money. Initially blockade-running was dominated by opportunistic captains, primarily interested in profit, who brought in high-value, low-bulk items such as perfume and silk that civilians craved but that did not noticeably help the army. In 1863–1864 the Confederate government began regulating the business by buying blockade-runners, taking control of half the cargo space on other ships, and banning a long list of nonessential goods. As the blockade tightened, blockade-running became more skillful and organized. The British yards at Clydeside built special ships. Fast, drably painted, and burning practically smokeless anthracite coal, they were nearly invisible during nighttime runs in and out of port. The business centered in Bermuda, Nassau, Havana, and the Mexican cities of Tampico and Veracruz, where cargoes shipped in bulk from Europe arrived for transshipment to blockade-runners.

In the deadly hide-and-seek game played nightly along the coast the blockade-runners had great advantages. They chose the port, time, weather, and other circumstances to maximize their chances, and even if spotted they were invariably faster than the blockaders. However, the number of ships penetrating the blockade declined as Federal warships became more numerous and amphibious operations closed Confederate ports, until by 1864 only Mobile and Wilmington remained open. In 1861 nine out of ten blockade-runners were successful, but by 1865 only one out of two made it. These ships brought in impressive quantities of war materials, such as 600,000 small arms, 624,000 pairs of boots, and millions of pounds of lead and meat. Yet this supply line was always tenuous: Union blockaders, storms, mangled propellers, blown cylinders, cracked steam pipes, limited cargo space, and intense competition made it unpredictable and expensive, vastly complicating the Confederate war effort. And, of course, the important question is not how much got through, but did enough? The answer is no. Although leaky, the blockade was one of the Union's most effective weapons, contributing significantly to the decline in the South's home-front standard of living and in the Confederate army's logistical support.

The Sinews of War

By the winter of 1863–1864 the disparity in strength was obvious, as the Union became stronger while the Confederacy, besieged by land and sea, grew weaker. In the North, order and organization replaced the chaos of 1861, manpower and material resources appeared inexhaustible, and industrial and agricultural output increased. In the South, raw materials were difficult to obtain, industrial production lagged, facilities deteriorated, the armies shrank, famine conditions occurred, and defeatism stalked the land. Compared to the Union, the Confederacy faced grave crises in supply, transportation, manpower, and home-front morale.

In the North an improvised logistical effort characterized by shortages and corruption soon gave way to a centralized, organized mobilization that abundantly supplied the Army. When the war began, the Army's rapid expansion overwhelmed the War Department's supply bureaus. Understaffed, headed by aged officers, dedicated to technical routine, and uncoordinated, the bureaus were initially as much hindrance as help. As expedients the North depended on cities and states to supply the men they raised and turned to foreign markets. Federal, state, and local purchasing agents and private speculators competed feverishly at home and abroad (where they also bid against southern agents), buying an assortment of arms and equipment. With a desperate demand for great quantities, buyers paid too little attention to quality—and to honest dealings. Lobbyists, contractors, and speculators descended on Washington and the state capitals like a cloud of locusts, devouring the national and state treasuries. Although the Army's unprecedented expansion made some logistical chaos inevitable, Lincoln's original secretary of war, Simon Cameron, contributed to the frenzy and corruption with deplorably lax administration.

By mid-1862, however, most of the inefficiency and deficiencies had disappeared. Congress established investigative committees to uncover fraud and passed laws regulating the letting of contracts. The forces of centralizing nationalism that brought manpower mobilization under federal control also returned logistical mobilization to the War Department's Ordnance, Subsistence, and Quartermaster Departments. The personnel in these bureaus expanded dramatically. For example, when Quartermaster General Montgomery C. Meigs assumed office in June 1861, he had only thirteen clerks, but by 1865 he had almost 600 civilian employees. War Department organization also became more elaborate. To use the same example, the Quartermaster Department initially had one subdivision (clothing), but Meigs created eight more, dealing with specialized logistical functions such as forage and fuel, barracks and hospitals, and wagon transportation. At a higher administrative level Stanton established a War Board composed of the bureau heads and chaired by Major General Ethan Allen Hitchcock, whom Lincoln and Stanton appointed as their personal military adviser. Acting as an embryonic American-style general staff, the board facilitated logistical coordination. Although it soon ceased meeting formally, Halleck inherited a budding tradition of interbureau cooperation when he became commanding general, which made his task easier. The Union was also blessed with honest administrators in high places, particularly Secretary of War Stanton, who replaced Cameron in January 1862, and Meigs, who spent $1.5 billion and could account for every penny.

Industry responded to the necessity and opportunity presented by the war, quickly converting to wartime production and expanding its output. The war demanded plan, order, and system, transforming what historian Allan Nevins called "a loose, inchoate, uncrystallized society" into an organized one. The war intensified business trends already evident in the antebellum era as industries became increasingly concentrated and coordinated. Truly national industries arose that utilized mass, mechanized production techniques and more sophisticated managerial methods. Without any economic controls, American industry geared up so successfully that foreign purchases ceased in mid-1862, and surpluses rather than shortages became the rule. By the end of 1862 Lincoln believed logistical excess *hampered* the war effort. "My dear General," he wrote in exasperation to Banks, "this expanding, and piling up of *impedimenta,* has been, so far, almost our ruin, and will be our final ruin if it is not abandoned."

Northern acquisition of weapons exemplified the evolution from hectic improvisation to an efficient system. When the war commenced, the North turned to European markets, buying 738,000 firearms in fifteen months. Most of the foreign weapons were dependable but some were inferior, and agents scouring the Continent paid premium prices for all of them. Meanwhile, the government stimulated the private arms industry by offering profitable contracts, and it increased production at government arsenals. The private and public armaments industries that produced fewer than 50,000 firearms in 1860 turned out more than 2.5 million during the war, and after 1862 foreign purchasing stopped.

While the North's logistical mobilization expanded, the South's peaked in early 1863 and then declined. Fundamental interlocking problems beset southern logistics. The Confederacy had few preexisting industries to expand and lacked sufficient raw materials upon which to build an industrial base. The South did have an existing agricultural foundation, dominated by tobacco and cotton. Efforts to convert to grain and meat production did not completely succeed. Northern conquests eroded the South's ability to make a sustained logistical effort, forcing it to draw raw materials and food from an ever-smaller area. The inability to meet the army's needs from domestic sources increased Confederate dependence on hazardous blockade-running. Economic difficulties, produced in large part by inflation, crippled both domestic and foreign procurement. Skilled labor remained scarce, and the transportation system faltered, ruining the essential link between procurement and timely distribution. While the North added 4,000 miles of track, increased its rolling stock, and captured or disrupted critical southern railroad lines, the South barely kept a few lines operating by cannibalizing less important lines, and it could not replace worn-out rolling stock. Furthermore, the Union occupied the upper south horse- and mule-breeding region, making wagon transport difficult.

Nothing hurt the supply services as much as the failure of decisive action and hard-headed planning by the Davis administration. The South needed a careful weighing of assets and liabilities, the setting of strict priorities, and centralized direction in order to use its resources efficiently. But Confederate leaders allowed events to control planning, resulting in uncoordinated, tardy, and generally impotent centralization of the logistical effort. The government gave no overall direction to the supply bureaus, which often bid against each other for materials and labor. Davis never permitted the military to utilize the railroads to best advantage and was slow to exert even moderate control over blockade-running. The Confederacy could have developed an extensive trade through Union lines, but the president at first prohibited it and then shackled the trade with so many regulations that it never fully developed. In sum, Davis's defective supply management made unavoidable problems worse.

The efforts of Lucius B. Northrop, the Commissary General of Subsistence, and Josiah Gorgas, chief of the Bureau of Ordnance, illustrate Confederate problems. In a rich agricultural region like the South, food should have been the least of difficulties. But the North soon overran or isolated its most productive areas, such as Tennessee, and in states remaining under rebel control labor shortages appeared as white men went into the army and slaves fled to Union lines. Farm machinery broke down, with no spare parts available. As Confederate currency depreciated, farmers became less willing to sell, since they rightly believed future prices would be higher. Confronted by massive hoarding, the government resorted to impressment and a tax in kind. The War Department published a price schedule for impressed goods, but the prices were far below prevailing market rates. Under the tax in kind the Subsistence Bureau confiscated one-tenth of a farmer's produce. The forcible seizures of food caused outraged protests, especially when much of the produce rotted before the transportation system could move it to the army. Evasion and outright resistance became common. In desperation Northrop tried to import meat—a bulky and hence expensive item—adding to the bureau's financial woes. By the spring of 1863 the food situation was critical. Lee's pickets along the Rappahannock shouted to their enemy counterparts that they had a new, tough general. When the Yankees asked for his name, the pickets replied, "General Starvation, by God."

Gorgas performed wonders in arming the South from three sources: Blockade-running, battlefield captures, and domestic manufacturing. He bought blockade-runners for his bureau's use, importing large quantities of firearms, saltpeter, lead, and percussion caps. Organized battlefield

The 1622 Virginia massacre touched off the first large-scale Indian war. Indian-fighting remained a central theme in U.S. military history for the next two and one-half centuries. *Théodore de Bry*, America, *Part XIII. Reproduced from the Collections of the Library of Congress.*

The English and their Indian allies attack the Pequot Indians in their Mystic River fort in 1637. To fight Indians successfully, whites invariably needed the cooperation of friendly Indians. *John Underhill*, News From America, *1638. Courtesy of The New York Public Library, Astor, Lenox and Tilden Foundations.*

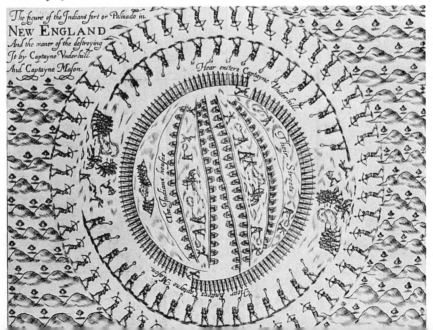

The cornerstones of American military policy from the Revolutionary era through the 1880s were citizen-soldiers; a small regular army; a small navy that cruised on distant stations; and coastal fortifications.

Citizen-soldiers at the Battle of Lexington in April 1775. *Engraving by C. Tiebout. Courtesy of The New-York Historical Society.*

The Continental Army, America's first regular army, at the Battle of Monmouth in June 1778. *Painting by H. Charles McBarron. U.S. Army Art Collection. U.S. Army.*

The 44-gun frigate *President* on station in the Mediterranean in the early nineteenth century. *Painting by Antoine Roux. Courtesy of The New York Public Library, Astor, Lenox and Tilden Foundations.*

Fort McHenry, built about 1800, defended the harbor of Baltimore. *Courtesy of the National Park Service.*

One important factor in the Union's victory over the Confederacy was the superior organizational and administrative abilities of these four Northern leaders.

President Abraham Lincoln, with practically no previous military experience, became a strong and resourceful Commander-in-Chief. *Reproduced from the Collections of the Library of Congress.*

Secretary of the Navy Gideon Welles mobilized the North's naval forces, which blockaded the South, assisted the Army in capturing coastal enclaves, and cooperated with the Army in operations along inland waterways. *Reproduced from the Collections of the Library of Congress.*

Secretary of War Edwin M. Stanton oversaw the growth of the Union Army to more than 1 million men and ensured that it had ample logistical support. *National Archives (111-B-4559).*

Henry Wager Halleck exhibited superb administrative skills as the commanding general from July 1862 until March 1864 and then as Chief of Staff. *Reproduced from the Collections of the Library of Congress.*

Railroads were indispensable logistical arteries and played a large role in shaping Civil War strategy. Raiders in blue and in gray often made them a prime objective, because overturned locomotives and torn-up tracks could frustrate enemy plans as decisively as a battlefield defeat. *Reproduced from the Collections of the Library of Congress.*

Approximately 180,000 black troops served in the Union Army, playing a vital role in the North's victory and, consequently, in the liberation of their race from slavery. This photo shows Company E of the 4th United States Colored Troops. *Reproduced from the Collections of the Library of Congress.*

These four military intellectuals fostered crucial developments in armed forces professionalization and theorizing during the late nineteenth century.

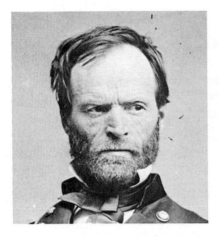

William T. Sherman, although best known for his Civil War exploits, made his most enduring contributions to the Army in the postwar era. *Reproduced from the Collections of the Library of Congress.*

Emory Upton wrote *The Military Policy of the United States* setting forth the simplistic thesis that the country was always unprepared for war. *Reproduced from the Collections of the Library of Congress.*

Stephen B. Luce, who hoped to apply scientific methods to the study of naval warfare, helped establish the Naval War College in 1884. *U.S. Navy Photograph.*

Alfred Thayer Mahan simply codified the big-navy philosophy of his age in *The Influence of Sea Power upon History, 1660-1783. U.S. Navy Photograph.*

Secretary of the Navy Benjamin F. Tracy, who proposed a "command of the sea" strategy based on battleship fleets, was instrumental in the dramatic transition in American maritime strategy in the late nineteenth century *U.S. Navy Photograph.*

The three battleships authorized in 1890, including the *Oregon* shown here, marked the advent of the new maritime strategy advocated by Tracy and Mahan. Once begun, battleship construction dominated the Navy for the next half-century. *U.S. Navy Photograph.*

The War with the Philippine Republic was America's first large war in Asia. Filipino soldiers ultimately submitted to an American pacification program that combined effective colonial government with vigorous campaigning. *National Archives (111-RB-1258).*

As in all of America's wars, hastily mobilized citizen-soldiers played an instrumental role in the War with the Philippine Republic. This picture shows Oregon Volunteer Infantry in the Philippines in 1899. *National Archives (111-RB-1047).*

scavenging yielded about 80,000 weapons during the 1862 spring and summer campaigns alone. But the domestic arms industry was Gorgas's most remarkable accomplishment, as he expanded or constructed armories, arsenals, and depots throughout the South. Yet shortages prevented Gorgas from doing more. Lack of money retarded the work of his European purchasing agent, Caleb Huse. Minerals remained scarce despite the abilities of Isaac M. St. John, who headed the bureau's Nitre and Mining corps, which became a separate bureau in April 1863. Charged with finding and developing mineral resources, St. John strove imaginatively to supply them. For example, when Bragg withdrew from Tennessee, losing the mines that produced 90 percent of the South's copper, St. John salvaged copper from apple-brandy stills. But he could not perform miracles. The scarcity of pig iron, for instance, prevented the South's largest manufacturing establishment, the Tredegar Iron Works in Richmond, Virginia, from operating at more than one-third capacity. The loss of a single skilled worker could be disastrous. When Yankee raiders killed John Jones, an expert barrel straightener, the Richmond Armory's production dropped by 369 rifles per month, and it took several months to train a replacement. Finally, Gorgas wanted to centralize operations at a few secure locations, but the railroads could not haul raw materials or finished products great distances.

If Confederate logistical support diminished after 1863, so did southern armies, and the two phenomena were not unrelated. The "present for duty" total was 253,208 on January 1, 1863, but only 154,910 two years later. Casualties and disease accounted for part of the shrinkage, but two other factors were more important in the Confederate army's disintegration. The feeble conscription enforcement machinery all but collapsed and was unable to provide a steady flow of new recruits. Meanwhile, the number of deserters, which would total more than 100,000 during the war, increased dramatically. Although the Union Army had twice as many deserters, the effect on the larger Federal force was less severe. To the South the absence of 100,000 men was of paramount importance, especially since the army had to detail men to track down the deserters, further reducing available manpower. Deserters also invariably took their arms and equipment, which the South could ill afford to replace.

Both sides tried to control desertion by similar means: Stationing guards at fords, ferries, and bridges; offering rewards for capturing deserters; appeals by officers, politicians, and editors; amnesty offers; and drastic punishment. Nothing worked. Many Confederate deserters entered Union lines, but most took to the hills, caves, and swamps, often joining draft dodgers to form armed bands that defied authorities. A few Federal deserters went over to the enemy, some fled to Canada or Mexico, but like southern deserters most sought refuge in inaccessible areas in their home section. Why did men desert? Some reasons were exactly the same for Billy Yank and Johnny Reb, such as cowardice before a battle or lack of devotion to the cause among conscripts and substitutes. Other reasons, although similar, varied in degree. The hardships of soldiering and worry about the family back home influenced men in both armies, but more so in the Confederacy, where the privations were *much* greater in the service and behind the lines. Some causes were unique to each army. The northern bounty system encouraged desertion, while rising defeatism on the southern home front, conveyed to soldiers through letters and rumors, motivated deserters, who knew they would get a sympathetic reception from their families and friends.

"The people are soul-sick and heartily tired of the hateful, hopeless strife," wrote a prominent Georgian. "We have had enough of want and woe, of cruelty and carnage, enough of cripples and corpses. There is an abundance of weeping parents, bereaved widows, and orphaned children in the land." Such sentiments represented the collapse of civilian morale that preceded, and contributed to, the army's defeat. Between 1861 and 1864 the South managed to maintain effective armies, but it failed to preserve the population's well-being. Shortages and inflation, the fear of a centralized government impinging on individual and state liberty, and the hopelessness arising from losses on the battlefield and in the international arena fostered a southern peace movement. People carried money to market in a basket and brought home their purchases in a purse—or so people said—and when Davis called for a day of fasting and prayer in March 1863, one man wrote that the president had asked for "fasting in the midst of famine!" That spring bread riots occurred in five cities, and everywhere gaunt-looking people wore dingy clothes. The knowledge that the North was virtually untouched by the war's ravages made the privations especially unbearable. The contrast was so stark that some southerners urged soldiers to desert to the Yankees "whear you can get plenty and not stay in this one-horse barefooted naked and famine stricken Southern Confederacy."

The Confederate government, wrote a North Carolina congressman in 1863, is becoming "a consolidated military despotism." Defining liberty as freedom from an arbitrary government, many southerners agreed with him. For popular liberty to survive, civil power must control the military, and state governments must protect the populace from the inevitable authoritarian tendencies of a central government. Yet the dual safeguards of civilian control and strong states seemed to be disappearing. Conscription, the periodic suspension of the writ of habeas corpus, arbitrary arrests, the impressment of private property, and novel taxes all spurred doubts about the justness of the Confederate cause. The government defended its actions on the grounds of temporary military necessity, but more and more civilians attested to the evils without acknowledging the necessity.

Had the South been winning, the privations and infringements might have been endurable. But even when the South won a battle the North became more powerful, and when the North won a battle the South became permanently weaker. By 1864 all hope that foreign aid would redress the imbalance was gone. Skillful northern diplomacy prevented an internal conflict from becoming an international war. Many reasons accounted for British nonintervention: English dependence on northern foodstuffs, access to new cotton supplies, turmoil in Europe, fear of what might happen to Canada and to British commerce in a war with the Union, and an unwillingness to side with slavery. The British government also wanted to establish precedents by respecting the blockade, a weapon that it often used. Most important, the South did not earn recognition on the battlefield. Realizing that England would never intervene, in August 1863 Davis canceled the diplomatic mission to London, and in December he told the Confederate Congress that European powers had become "positively unfriendly."

Incipient peace sentiment found organized expression in the Peace and Constitutional Society, the Peace Society, the Order of the Heroes of America, and other smaller societies. Dedicated to ending the war, these organizations resisted Confederate authority, discouraged enlistments, and assisted invading Union armies. Yet if some southerners despaired, most remained committed to independence. Tenacity among civilian leaders, the fighting prowess of rebel soldiers, and a dash of luck might reverse the war's adverse course. Northern Copperhead sentiment was by no means dead, and although the South could no longer win an outright military victory, it might forestall Union conquest long enough that the Yankees would give up in frustration.

The Final Campaigns, 1864–1865

"There is no enthusiasm for Gen. Grant; and on the other hand, there is no prejudice against him. We are prepared to throw up our hats when he shows himself the great soldier in Virginia against Lee and the best troops of the rebels." So wrote a colonel in the Army of the Potomac upon learning that Grant had been commissioned a lieutenant general on March 9, 1864, and replaced Halleck as general in chief. Eastern soldiers were skeptical about this westerner who now held a rank that only George Washington had previously held on a permanent basis. Yet they were ready to embrace him if he could duplicate his western successes against the Army of Northern Virginia, which they thought superior to any army that Grant had defeated beyond the Appalachians.

With Grant's promotion an awkward but workable command system with modern overtones emerged. To facilitate communications between Lincoln and Grant and between the commanding general and his department commanders, the War Department established the position of chief of staff. Halleck, who had been functioning informally as chief of staff since the summer of 1862, filled the new post. His ability to translate civilian thoughts into military language and vice versa ensured that Lincoln and Grant never misunderstood each other. The chief of staff also relieved Grant of the burden of personally corresponding with his department commanders. Halleck's position was especially important since Grant did not establish his headquarters in Washington but took the field with the Army of the Potomac, though he left Meade in tactical command of the Army.

Grant's plan for the spring campaign demonstrated a grand strategic design that would put simultaneous pressure on as many fronts as possible, working "all parts of the Army to-gether, and, somewhat towards a common center." In the east, Meade would assail the Army of Northern Virginia, assisted by smaller forces operating on the strategic flanks. Moving from Fort Monroe toward Richmond via the James River, Butler's Army of the James would capture the capital if possible but at least sever Lee's supply lines running south to Petersburg. Franz Sigel would move up the Shenandoah, depriving the south of the Valley's resources. Without supplies and threatened in the rear and on the flanks, Lee would have to move into the open to fight. In the west, Grant wanted Banks to move against Mobile and then thrust toward Georgia to cooperate with Sherman, whose task was to move against Johnston's army and then "to get into the interior of the enemy's country as far as you can, inflicting all the damage you can upon their War resources." While ravaging the countryside Sherman was also determined to strike at civilian morale. "My aim, then," he wrote, "was to whip the rebels, to humble their pride, to follow them to their inmost recesses, and make them fear and dread us."

From the start the plan went awry. Banks did not advance toward Mobile. Instead, Lincoln ordered him up the Red River to shore up the reconstructed pro-Unionist governments that had been organized in occupied portions of Arkansas and Louisiana, to warn the French in Mexico not to become too ambitious, and to seize the region's cotton supplies. Since it pointed away from Sherman and Grant, the Red River campaign was a strategic blunder, made worse by Banks's inept generalship. When a Confederate army defeated his advance divisions at Mansfield on April 8, Banks retreated to New Orleans. The two other political generals performed no better. Sigel confronted an outnumbered Confederate force at New Market on May 15. When the rebels attacked, Sigel excitedly issued orders in German to his English-speaking staff, contributing to a Union debacle. Butler initially outnumbered the scratch force facing him by six or seven to one, but he avoided capturing Richmond or Petersburg or cutting the vital rail lines. The Confederates penned up his army inside Bermuda Hundred, "as completely shut off from further operations directly against Richmond," wrote Grant, "as if it had been in a bottle strongly corked."

Grant had a very costly encounter with Lee. As the Army of the Potomac moved into the Wilderness on May 4, the commanding general believed he could defeat the Confederates somewhere between the Rapidan and the James. He had a two-to-one numerical superiority, the subsidiary attacks by Butler and Sigel would supposedly provide diversions, and the Federals had the initiative. Lee, however, also had advantages. The terrain provided defensive positions, morale remained reasonably high despite austere conditions and civilian backsliding, and a sense of desperation honed his fighting instincts. "We must destroy this army of Grant's before he gets to the James River," Lee wrote. "If he gets there, it will become a siege, and then it will be a mere question of time." Lee awaited Grant not far from where he had humiliated Hooker a year earlier, and on May 5 the Battle of the Wilderness began. After two days 17,000 Federals and 11,000 rebels were casualties. Grant had been jolted as badly as Hooker, and when the wagons moved rearward, soldiers thought that, as usual, they were retreating. But orders came for the army to move south. No retreat! Troops sang with joy, even though another cauldron awaited them in the near future.

What followed was a five-week ordeal in which a battle and a campaign became synonymous. Previous battles lasted several days and then the armies disengaged to recuperate. Now the fighting was continuous. Incessant skirmishing and shelling accompanied the almost weekly battles. Grant kept moving southeast, trying to outflank Lee, but the Army of Northern Virginia anticipated each move, raced along interior lines, and repeatedly blocked the way. The first flanking movement brought the armies to Spotsylvania Court House, where ferocious fighting occurred on May 10 and 12. Then Grant looped to the southeast, but Lee met him on the North Anna; the Federals again shifted, only to run into the rebels at Totopotomy Creek; still another flanking movement ended at Cold Harbor, where Grant launched an all-out attack on June 3. Grant always regretted ordering this ill-conceived frontal assault, which gained little but cost thousands in dead and wounded.

After more than a week of nasty trench warfare around Cold Harbor, on the night of June 12–13 Grant crossed the James heading for Petersburg, the railroad hub serving the capital. Seize Petersburg and Lee would have to come out from behind his entrenchments to fight for his supply lines. Grant conducted the maneuver brilliantly, leaving Lee mystified as to his destination and intentions. By June 15 the Federal army was below the James, while Lee was still north of it, and only a thin gray line manned the Petersburg defenses. But Beauregard's heroic defense, and the Union forces' conflicting orders and ill-coordinated attacks, allowed the rebels to hold the city until Lee awoke to his danger and moved the Army of Northern Virginia into the defenses. The armies then settled into a siege that would last nine months.

The Wilderness-to-Petersburg campaign earned Grant the reputation of a plodding butcher who resorted to slaughterhouse tactics, knowing that even if he lost two men to every rebel, the North would still win. True, the campaign extracted a terrible toll: 64,000 Union and 30,000 Confederate casualties. But Grant did not want a head-on killing match. With skill and ingenuity he tried to flush Lee into the open, but subordinates poorly executed good orders, and Lee parried each thrust by waging a stolid defensive struggle, refusing to risk his dwindling manpower outside the protecting trenches. Although Grant did not destroy Lee, he pinned the Army of Northern Virginia down in the strategic arena. Unlike Pope or Hooker, Grant did not disengage and let Lee seize the initiative. Remorselessly and at great cost he prevented Lee from launching an offensive that could restore the strategic balance.

Lincoln recognized this considerable achievement and urged Grant to "Hold on with a bull-dog grip, and chew and choke as much as possible." Grant needed no special prompting as he sought to snap Lee's defenses either by a breakthrough or by overextending them. The most famous breakthrough attempt was the Battle of the Crater on July 30. The Yankees dug a long tunnel and placed tons of powder under a Confederate redoubt. When the explosion went off, the position disappeared in a geyser of mud, timbers, and mangled Confederates, creating an enormous gap in Lee's lines. However, tragic blundering, including sending men into the crater instead of around it, gave Lee time to recover. "Such opportunity for carrying fortifications I have never seen," Grant sadly wired to Washington, "and do not expect again to have." Meanwhile, Grant pushed his lines westward, trying to cut Lee's supply arteries, spreading the Confederate defenders more thinly in the ever-extending trenchworks.

While Grant fought to Petersburg, Sherman maneuvered to Atlanta. Coordinating his offensive with Grant's, Sherman faced difficult problems. Supply depended on the railroad back to Nashville, which, said Sherman, "takes a whole army to guard, each foot of rail being essential to the whole." The rugged terrain, which Johnston knew how to utilize, was ideal for defense. Rather than attack at every opportunity, Johnston preferred to concede territory and conserve manpower. He wanted to draw the Federals deep into southern territory, inviting them to make frontal assaults against prepared positions, and await that supreme moment to unleash a lethal counterstroke. But Sherman refused to attack and instead flanked the Confederate left, never leaving an opening for Johnston to exploit. The armies engaged in a minuet, dancing from Johnston's initial position along Rocky Face Ridge to Kennesaw Mountain, where, mistakenly assuming Johnston had overextended his lines and left his center vulnerable, Sherman attacked on June 27. Suffering 3,000 casualties for his effort, he resumed the indirect approach, inducing Johnston to withdraw behind the Chattahoochee River. Then for the first time the Yankees flanked to the east and Johnston fell back to Peach Tree Creek.

President Davis watched the campaign with dismay. He had opposed retreating, and his confidence in Johnston waned in proportion to the length of the retreat. When the commander refused to give a firm commitment to defend Atlanta, Davis's tolerance snapped. The city had a symbolic significance second only to Richmond's, contained invaluable war industries, and was the last important railroad link between the west and Virginia. Losing it, especially without a fight, would be a severe blow, and on July 17 Davis placed John B. Hood in command of the Army of Tennessee. Hood had an arm mangled at Gettysburg and lost a leg at Chickamauga, but his fighting spirit remained intact. As both Sherman and Davis expected, Hood assailed the Federals. At the Battles of Peach Tree Creek, Atlanta, and Ezra Church, fought between July 20 and 28, Union troops had the advantage of entrenchments and inflicted 13,000 casualties at a cost of 6,000. Hood poured out the army's lifeblood to no effect, except to decrease morale and increase desertions. Davis ordered him not to attack again, and the army assumed a defensive stance in the trenches surrounding Atlanta. Like Grant at Petersburg, Sherman undertook a siege.

With the war degenerating into a protracted siege in both theaters and apparently stalemated, the northern public's determination wavered. The North expected imminent victory, anticipating that the Confederacy could not survive for long after the 1863 defeats; but instead of collapsing, the South seemed capable of prolonging the war indefinitely. Lincoln knew that the enemy armies retained little of their former striking power, but most people did not share his appreciation for his generals' accomplishments. Civilians saw that Meade and Sherman had failed to crush Lee and Johnston or to capture Richmond and Atlanta. They also saw the grisly casualty lists, especially from Grant's theater, and the South's ability to fight back: In July, Jubal Early's corps rampaged down the Valley, unbeknown to Grant for several weeks, reaching the outskirts of Washington on July 11. Early soon withdrew, but he did not go far and remained a threat.

As frustration increased, the 1864 election became a referendum on the war. The Democrats, who nominated McClellan, adopted an anti-emancipation, pro-peace platform. As the public feeling that the South could never be defeated increased, Lincoln received such pessimistic reports that he predicted his own defeat. Ironically, a dramatic reversal in the war was already underway; it began at Mobile Bay in a three-week August campaign. Farragut led a fleet through the minefields and past the forts protecting the bay's entrance, defeated an enemy naval squadron, and helped capture the forts, sealing Mobile off from the outside world. A week after the last fort capitulated, Sherman captured Atlanta. Although Hood's army escaped, the North exploded in celebrations. Further good news came from the Valley, where Grant ordered Philip H. Sheridan to destroy Early's army and turn the Shenandoah into "a barren waste." With a large numerical advantage, Sheridan defeated Early at Opequon, Fisher's Hill, and Cedar Creek and systematically destroyed the Shenandoah's resources, ending organized military operations in the Valley. Military success paved the way for Lincoln's overwhelming reelection, dashing southern hopes that McClellan's election meant independence. People everywhere realized that the election demonstrated the North's resurrected dedication to victory.

Although the South had no chance of winning after Lincoln's reelection, the war continued for another six months. In Georgia the armies that had waltzed together for months parted company. After he evacuated Atlanta, Hood moved north, threatening Sherman's railroad line, and for a month the Federals futilely chased him. Sherman finally decided to avoid dependence on vulnerable supply lines and undertake a massive raid through Georgia, while Hood planned an invasion into Tennessee. Sherman's purpose was primarily logistical and psychological: To cripple southern resources and to show even diehard rebels that the Confederacy was powerless. He left Atlanta with 62,000 men in mid-November. Foraging off the land, they cut a 250-mile swath against token resistance and captured Savannah on December 21. Only the veteran character of Sherman's army allowed it to complete the march. Nearly four out of five enlisted men and nearly 100 percent of the noncommissioned officers had been in service since 1862. Consequently they were campaign-toughened, inured to hardship and disease, self-reliant, and deeply committed to Union victory. They had also developed a ruthless, callous attitude toward enemy civilians that characterized so many experienced troops on both sides by 1864–1865, so they embraced their commander's goal of instilling fear in noncombatants as a means to hasten the war's end.

While Sherman's veterans advanced through the Confederate heartland, the Army of Tennessee marched to its death. At the Battle of Franklin on November 30, Hood made another suicidal Confederate assault against an entrenched force under John M. Schofield, losing 6,252 men to Schofield's 2,326. When Schofield pulled back to Nashville to join Thomas's army, Hood pursued and nominally besieged the strongly fortified city. In mid-December Thomas attacked and virtually annihilated Hood's army, which by then numbered only 25,000 demoralized men.

As the 1865 campaigns began, northern morale was unshakable, Federals controlled the Shenandoah, Sherman's march to the sea had bisected the Confederacy again, and one of the South's two major field armies had been obliterated. Furthermore, in January Union forces captured Fort Fisher on the Cape Fear River, bottling up Wilmington, which had been the last blockade-running port. All that remained of the shriveled Confederacy was Lee's army manning the Richmond-Petersburg trenches and a small army forming in North Carolina under Johnston, who was recalled to duty. Yet hardened rebels such as Davis and Lee were unwilling to quit. An indication of their determination and desperation was the South's decision in March to arm its slaves. Aside from the question of whether blacks would fight for the South, the law authorizing black enlistments came too late to do any good. The final acts already unfolding were not heroic drama, but needless tragedy.

In early February Sherman resumed his campaign against the South's resources and morale, heading north through the Carolinas. Though less well known than the march to the sea, the Carolinas trek was a more stunning accomplishment. The journey was longer, the terrain and weather were worse, and resistance was stiffer. Since the army burned "with an insatiable desire to wreak vengeance upon South Carolina," the birthplace of secession, the devastation was greater and more vindictively inflicted than in Georgia. On February 17 the army entered Columbia, causing the Confederates to evacuate Charleston, since the Federals had severed its communications to the interior. A month later the combatants fought the campaign's one large battle at Bentonville. Johnston tried to rout Sherman's left wing but failed, and on March 23 the Yankees entered Goldsboro, where they found Schofield's corps, which Grant had transferred from Tennessee, awaiting them. Although Sherman refitted for an advance against Lee's rear, it was unnecessary, for Grant drove the Army of Northern Virginia from its trenches and forced it to capitulate.

During the winter Grant undertook no major offensives, letting disease and desertion weaken Lee's army. Lee's only hope was to unite with Johnston, for combined they might push back Sherman, then turn on Grant. To make Grant contract his left flank and thereby open an escape hatch, on March 25 Lee struck at Fort Stedman in the Union center. Disastrous failure followed initial success, and Grant seized the initiative, massing Sheridan's cavalry and 43,000 infantry against 11,000 Confederates at Five Forks on Lee's extreme right. When the Federals routed the rebels on April 1, Grant ordered an attack against the Petersburg line on April 2, which overran long stretches of Confederate trenches. That night Lee abandoned Richmond and retreated westward, with Sheridan and several infantry corps in pursuit. Sheridan got in front of Lee's dwindling band on April 8, and after an unsuccessful breakout attempt on the 9th Lee surrendered at Appomattox Court House. Like the Army of Tennessee, the Army of Northern Virginia had been practically annihilated. Offering rations for Lee's starving army, Grant asked if 25,000 would be enough. "Plenty; plenty; an abundance," replied Lee, for he had fewer than 8,000 effectives.

Recalling the night of April 9, a Union cavalryman wrote that the "thought that I was certain, yes, certain of having a quiet night, the idea of security, was ineffable." All over the South, men soon experienced the same sense of relief, for by late May all other Confederate armies had surrendered. The immediate fears of neither the South nor the North came true. Southerners thought the victors might engage in mass reprisals, but no postwar bloodletting occurred. Grant, Sherman, and others worried that Confederates would form guerrilla bands and continue fighting, but this did not happen either. Many southern officers advised against it. No place existed for guerrillas to use as bases, since the North occupied much of the South, and Unionists and deserters ruled the mountains and swamps. Partisan bands would get little sympathy from the population, whose morale had cracked long before the army's. Finally, the average soldier was sick of war. The troops knew better than anyone that by *force majeure* the North had crushed the Confederacy.

The Final Reckoning

In Margaret Mitchell's famous novel *Gone With the Wind,* heroine Scarlett O'Hara's first husband, Charles Hamilton, rushes off to war in 1861 with romantic visions of glory. In less than two months he is dead—from measles followed by pneumonia. While hardly heroic, Charles's death was typical, since twice as many soldiers died from disease as from battle. Diseases swept through regiments in two waves. Shortly after a unit assembled, infectious childhood diseases such as measles and mumps thinned the ranks. Those who survived this wave then endured the camp diseases, primarily dysentery, malaria, and typhoid fever. Since these often occurred in epidemics, leading to unexpected reductions in fighting force, camp diseases were of great military significance.

The number of battle casualties was enormous, even though the theoretical long-range killing power of rifled weapons rarely came into play.

Two significant factors limited the rifle's impact. One was that few troops received training in estimating ranges, setting rifle sights, and firing live ammunition. Yet such practice was essential if a soldier hoped to hit a target—especially one that was moving—at more than a hundred yards. To counter both the minie ball's low velocity and gravity's tug at that distance, a shot would have to be aimed well above the target and come plunging down at a steep angle. If a rifleman aimed *at* the target, the bullet would plow into the ground well short of the intended victim. The second limiting factor was that many battles occurred in places like Chickamauga and the Wilderness, where the rugged terrain and dense foliage greatly reduced the killing range because combatants could not see each other at more than a few dozen yards' distance. Only in a few engagements such as Pickett's Charge, when a massed force advanced over a long expanse of relatively open ground, did rifled firepower and artillery quickly inflict fearsome losses.

Unlike Pickett's Charge, most battles rapidly degenerated into prolonged firefights between two "entrenched" forces, which were often so close to each other that old-fashioned smoothbores would have been just about as effective as rifles. The close-order ranks that an attacking army used so that soldiers could hear or see their officers giving orders rarely survived the opening moments of combat. Traversing stream-laced, heavily forested, steep terrain in tight formations was impossible. And the first few shots frequently impelled the attackers to take cover, since they invariably confronted defenders who enjoyed both the physical and psychological advantages of being protected by entrenchments and field fortifications. "The truth is," wrote one soldier, "when bullets are whacking against tree-trunks and solid shot are cracking skulls like egg-shells, the consuming passion in the breast of the average man is to get out of the way." But how? Fear of death or injury told a soldier he should not go forward; fear of being considered a coward restrained him from retreating. So an attacking force simply stopped, with each soldier seeking safety behind a nearby fence, rock, or tree stump or else digging a shallow, sheltering hole. Casualties accumulated slowly because the soldiers on both sides were dug in, but the final toll could be quite large, since these slugging matches often lasted for hours.

For attackers and defenders, losers and winners, a battlefield was a melancholy scene. Hundreds of men would be blasted into shapeless masses of pulpy gore. In warm weather the bodies and parts of bodies bloated, turned black, and putrefied rapidly, filling the air with a pungent stench. Though the guns might be still, the battlefield remained noisy with the anguish of the wounded. Perhaps the most chilling description came from Joshua Chamberlain, commander of the 20th Maine Volunteers, regarding the night of December 13–14 at Fredericksburg:

But out of that silence from the battle's crash and roar rose new sounds more appalling still; rose or fell, you knew not which, or whether from the earth or air; a strange ventriloquism, of which you could not locate the source, a smothered moan that seemed to come from distances beyond the reach of the natural sense, a wail so far and deep and wide, as if a thousand discords were flowing together into a key-note weird, unearthly, terrible to hear and bear, yet startling with its nearness; the writhing concord broken by cries for help, pierced by shrieks of paroxysm; some begging for a drop of water; some calling on God for pity; and some on friendly hands to finish what the enemy had so horribly begun; some with delirious, dreamy voices murmuring loved names, as if the dearest were bending over them; some gathering their last strength to fire a musket to call attention to them where they lay helpless and deserted; and underneath, all the time, that deep bass note from closed lips too hopeless or too heroic to articulate their agony.

And in the rear of each army the same grisly scene took place: temporary hospitals where bare-armed surgeons in blood-stained aprons and with bloody instruments worked to save the gashed and dying, invariably creating a mound of amputated limbs, the slicing and sawing more often than not done without the benefit of anesthetics.

Using round figures that are educated estimates, total Civil War casualties for soldiers and sailors on both sides were 1,095,000. Of these, 640,000 were Federals: 112,000 killed or mortally wounded in action; 227,500 dead of disease; 277,500 wounded; and 23,000 dead from miscellaneous causes such as drowning, murder, execution, sunstroke, and suicide. The remaining 455,000 were Confederates: 94,000 killed or mortally wounded in action; 164,000 dead of diseases; 194,000 wounded; and at least 3,000 deaths from miscellaneous causes. To put these figures in perspective, American deaths in World War I, World War II, and Korea totaled 564,000, but still do not reach the Civil War total of 620,000.*

Although war involves killing, killing is not the object of war. Men fight for vital reasons, as defined by their country's political leadership. The North fought for the preservation of the Union and the destruction of slavery, while the South fought for independence and the preservation of its "peculiar institution." In saving the Union and freeing the slaves, Lincoln believed the North would be achieving goals of cosmic significance, transcending national boundaries into the infinite future. Like many of America's leaders, he thought the United States had a special destiny to

---

* Though 620,000 remains the accepted figure, new research in pre- and postwar census data tentatively indicates that as many as 750,000 men may have perished during the war, an increase of 20 percent.

safeguard and foster its democratic institutions as an example for the world. The North, he said in December 1862, "shall nobly save, or meanly lose, the last best, hope of earth." And in the Gettysburg Address he urged his fellow citizens to take increased resolve from the northern soldiers who had given "the last full measure of devotion" on the battlefield. Let us ensure "that these dead shall not have died in vain—that this nation, under God, shall have a new birth of freedom—and that government of the people, by the people, for the people, shall not perish from the earth."

Those northerners who fell at Gettysburg and elsewhere did not die in vain, since the North achieved its dual war aims. The conflict delivered a deathblow to the doctrine of secession and considerably weakened (though it did not destroy) the idea of states' rights. Within the American federal system, the balance of power shifted from the states to the national government. People no longer said "the United States *are*" but instead "the United States *is*." In the process of saving the Union, the North also destroyed slavery. Advancing Union armies and the Emancipation Proclamation undermined the institution, and the Thirteenth Amendment killed it.

Southerners had seemingly died in vain, since the Confederacy achieved neither of its war aims. And yet merely saying that the Union lived and slavery died left several crucial questions unanswered. What was the status of the defeated states? How and when were they to return to "their proper practical relation with the Union"? Who would control the restored states, former secessionists or southern Unionists, perhaps in league with the freedmen? And what was the status of the former slaves? Although pledged to black freedom, the North had not adopted a third war aim of equality, and between freedom and equality lay a vast middle ground. As solutions to these perplexing problems emerged during Reconstruction, southerners salvaged much that looked like victory from their apparent defeat. Former secessionists regained effective control over the former Confederate States and maintained unquestioned white supremacy. Furthermore, southerners soon took as much pride in the legend of the Lost Cause as northerners did in the fact of Appomattox. Ironically, even perversely, by 1877 both North and South could proclaim success. How and why the North lost so many of the fruits of victory is a complex story in which the Army played a central role.

EIGHT

From Postwar Demobilization Toward Great Power Status, 1865–1898

T he weather on May 23 was beautiful for campaigning, and the Army of the Potomac was on the move. Under cloudless skies the soft spring sun glinted off the steel sabers and bayonets of 100,000 men. But this was May of 1865, the war was over, and the Union's saviors were marching down Pennsylvania Avenue to the cheers of jubilant spectators. Meade's cavalry stretched seven miles and took more than an hour to pass the reviewing stand. Marching twelve abreast, the general's infantry consumed another five hours. The next day six corps from Sherman's army repeated the performance, the rangy westerners swaggering past the crowds "like the lords of the world!"

Following the two-day victory festivities the Union military forces underwent a rapid demobilization. By November 1866, only 11,043 of the 1,034,064 volunteers in the service in May 1865 were still in uniform. As the volunteers departed, the regular Army remained. It temporarily benefited from lingering martial enthusiasm when, in July 1866, Congress authorized a peacetime strength of 54,302. Included in the table of organization were four black infantry regiments (reduced to two in 1869), two black cavalry regiments, and 1,000 Indian scouts. Although these black units and Indian scouts were an innovation in the peacetime Army, which historically had been composed exclusively of whites, they became a permanent feature of the postwar military establishment. However, Congress soon slashed the Army's overall size, and by 1876 the maximum strength was 27,442.

The Navy also underwent drastic reduction. Within five years it declined from a wartime peak of about 700 ships to 52. By European standards most of the ships were obsolete, for they were made of wood, moved by sails, and carried muzzleloading smoothbores. The mobilization accompanying the *Virginius* crisis showed how far the Navy had deteriorated. After war broke out in Cuba in 1868, *Virginius* made repeated voyages to the island carrying contraband to the revolutionaries fighting against Spanish rule. Although it sailed under the U.S. flag, the Spanish captured the ship in October 1873 and executed approximately fifty crewmen and passengers, many of them Americans. The result was a war scare with Spain. The Navy concentrated all available ships at Key West, but the assembled fleet (about two dozen ships, only six of them ironclads) was feeble compared to that of any major naval power, and diplomacy soon eliminated the likelihood of war. In early 1874 the fleet held maneuvers, which were unimpressive. Logistical support was nil, gunnery training was inadequate, and the ships' boilers were so decrepit that the fleet's top speed was only 4.5 knots. The fleet, declared one newspaper, was "almost useless for military purposes" because the vessels belonged "to a class of ships which other governments have sold or are selling for firewood."

Although Army and Navy officers naturally lamented the extent of the demobilization, the reductions actually made sense considering the nation's relative security and the missions that American policymakers wanted the armed forces to undertake. As even Generals Sherman and Sheridan realized, an invasion was unlikely. No European nation had a navy capable of transporting and sustaining a substantial expeditionary force across the Atlantic. Continental rivalries restrained any of the great powers from making a significant New World military commitment, and America's vast size and immense military potential made foreign conquest impossible. Geography and European balance-of-power considerations gave the United States virtually total security. Moreover, through the 1880s a foreign policy with limited goals required little mobilized military power.

The Postwar Navy

In the post–Civil War era the Navy and Army returned to their traditional missions in support of national policy. Two aspects of postwar policy particularly affected the Navy. First, since "continentalist" assumptions dominated thinking about the national interest into the 1880s, the United States did not need a large, modern navy. Lacking a desire to compete with Europeans in an imperialistic struggle, the nation needed no navy to challenge them. Defense of the continental domain dictated only a modest naval force that in wartime could raid enemy commerce and supplement the fortifications protecting the coast. Secretary of the Navy George M. Robeson correctly noted that the small and outdated postwar Navy was sufficient for the "defensive purposes of a peaceful people, without colonies, with a dangerous coast, and shallow harbors, separated from warlike naval powers" by the Atlantic.

Policy also required that the Navy protect lives and property abroad and, especially, foster trade by maintaining unimpeded access to foreign markets. Thus the Navy Department revived its prewar system of distant patrols. Although the European Squadron (successor to the old Mediterranean Squadron) had often been paramount in Navy planning, it declined in importance. Since European navies ensured stability in the Mediterranean, the United States made its major naval commitment to Latin America and Asia, where chronic instability provided ample opportunity for "gunboat diplomacy." The Navy suppressed piracy, transported diplomats, stopped vessels flying the American flag to verify their nationality, provided a haven for missionaries threatened by "savages," evacuated citizens endangered by war or epidemic diseases, and dispatched landing parties to deal with recalcitrant "barbarous tribes." On numerous occasions marines and sailors went ashore to protect American merchants, investments, and strategic interests in Asia and in South and Central America. Naval officers also continued a diplomatic-commercial role, in the image of Matthew C. Perry. For example, in 1882 Commodore Robert W. Shufeldt negotiated the first treaty between Korea and a Western nation. Officers performed these missions partly to achieve personal glory and to preserve national "honor," but they also shared the policymakers' belief that expanding commerce and the nation's welfare were inseparable.

The Navy's deployment on distant stations required a return to wooden sailing ships. Advances in armor, rifled guns, and marine engines appeared with dizzying rapidity, but the debt-ridden U.S. government was not inclined to expensive naval experiments. Prolonged voyages could not be made with steam-powered vessels. Since even engineers did not perfectly understand thermodynamics, costly steam engines remained inefficient and consumed enormous amounts of expensive coal. Ships could not carry much coal and still have room for the crew and supplies. Although European navies could refuel at their colonial stations, the United States had few such bases. Finally, obsolete ships were sufficient to intimidate most Asians and Latin Americans, who were even less well armed.

Reinforcing these technological, financial, and military imperatives were sociological and psychological factors. The struggle between staff and line officers raged with new intensity, and steam symbolized the conflict. Believing they had made a substantial contribution to Union victory and that steamships would rule the oceans, engineers demanded equal rank with line officers. Considering the extreme flux in naval technology, engineers often uncritically hailed innovations in steam engineering to enhance their position. But line officers were not eager to share their authority aboard ships, and they opposed steam to assure their own prominence. Still, they were not blind reactionaries; most realized that ultimately steam would replace sails. They also understood an important political and strategic factor: National policy made steam ironclads temporarily unnecessary. Line officers prevailed, and in 1869 Vice Admiral David D. Porter, acting in the secretary of the navy's name, ordered that all vessels "be fitted out with full-sail power" and that ships' commanders justify any use of auxiliary steam power. He also dismissed Benjamin F. Isherwood, the chief of the Bureau of Steam Engineering, and reduced the relative rank of other engineers.

The Frontier "Constabulary"

After a hasty post–Civil War concentration in Texas to help convince the French to withdraw from Mexico, the Army, like the Navy, resumed its traditional tasks. Taking advantage of America's domestic war, French Emperor Napoleon III had established the Archduke Maximilian of Austria as the Emperor of Mexico in 1864 and supported him with an army. The Union ineffectually responded with diplomatic protests against this violation of the Monroe Doctrine. When the Civil War ended, the government dispatched General Schofield to Paris to demand withdrawal, and, before the volunteer armies dissolved, 52,000 troops mobilized in Texas to buttress the demand. Faced with continuing guerrilla warfare in Mexico, with fear of Prussian ambitions in Europe, and with the military might of a reunited United States, Napoleon withdrew in 1867.

With the continent saved from monarchy and the volunteers returned to their homes, the regulars aided the nation's territorial and economic growth, manned the coastal forts, and fought Indians. The Army protected railroad construction crews, opened new roads, charted unexplored regions, briefly occupied Alaska, and improved rivers and harbors. The coast artillery stood guard in old masonry forts that rifled guns had made obsolete. The War Department planned a postwar program of earth, brick, and concrete barbette batteries, but reduced funding, and the relentless technical advances in artillery, soon killed the program. Given the country's security, why waste money on unnecessary defenses?

Regulars redeploying to the west found Indian wars engulfing the Great Plains. When the regulars marched eastward in 1861, western state and territorial militia and volunteers assumed the frontier constabulary mission. Indian-white conflict actually intensified, since citizen-soldiers were often extremely brutal toward both hostile and friendly Indians. Violence first flared in August 1862 with an uprising among the Santee Sioux of Minnesota, who had endured years of insults, greed, and deceit from whites. Erroneously believing that Confederate agents had provoked the outbreak, the Lincoln administration dispatched General Pope, fresh from his humiliation at Second Bull Run, to the scene. But Pope was no more successful against the Indians than he had been against Lee. The war spread westward into the Dakota and Montana Territories, engulfing all the powerful Sioux tribes, and merged with other conflicts that flared across the prairies farther south. The situation in the west became so critical that the Union had to divert troops, including six regiments composed of former Confederate soldiers, from the major battlefields east of the Mississippi. The worst incidents occurred in 1863 at the "Battle" of Bear River, near the present-day Utah-Idaho border, and in 1864 at the "Battle" of Sand Creek. California volunteers launched a near-dawn surprise attack on Chief Bear Hunter's Shoshone village camped along Bear River, killing approximately 250 men, women, and children. At Sand Creek, Colorado volunteers attacked Black Kettle's Southern Cheyenne village. An advocate of peace, Black Kettle raised American and white flags over his tepee, but this did not prevent the whites from massacring 200 Cheyennes, mostly women and children. As one observer wrote, the Indians "were scalped, their brains knocked out; the men used their knives, ripped open women, clubbed little children, knocked them in the head with their guns, beat their brains out, mutilated their bodies in every sense of the word."

The government signed a series of Indian treaties in 1865, blanketing the West in temporary peace. But gold and silver strikes, the Homestead Act, and railroad construction quickened the pace of settlement even during the Civil War. The idea of a permanent Indian frontier died under the deluge of land-hungry and gold-seeking whites, so the government devised a policy of concentrating the Indians on reservations, usually in areas that whites did not covet—at least immediately. The reservation system combined blatant greed and misguided philanthropy. Confined to unwanted land, the thinking went, the Indians would not interfere with white settlement. Denied their nomadic lifestyle, they could be "civilized"—taught the white man's language, turned into sedentary agriculturalists, and Christianized. The policy's flaw was that many tribes or tribal factions hated reservation life and rebelled against it. Then the Army had to force compliance.

The Army's task was thankless and difficult. One problem was white society's ambivalence about Indians. The opinions of frontiersmen and eastern humanitarians highlighted the ambiguity. "There are two classes of people," Sherman wrote, "one demanding the utter extinction of the Indians, and the other full of love for their conversion to civilization and Christianity. Unfortunately the army stands between them and gets the cuff from both sides." If the Army killed too many Indians, humanitarians cried "Butchery!" But if it killed too few, frontiersmen scorned the troops as cowards. Yet philanthropists demanded the forced acculturation that drove Indians onto the warpath, and westerners demanding "protection" often provoked violence by insisting that Indians move to smaller reservations.

Reflecting society, Army officers were often ambivalent about fighting for "civilization" against the "savages." Many of them despised pontificating humanitarians, disliked rapacious frontiersmen, and lamented their government's record of broken treaties. They viewed some aspects of Indian behavior (torturing captives and mutilating the dead) with revulsion. Yet they found much about the Indians commendable and commiserated with their fate. They lauded the Indians' fighting abilities. Such praise served professional and psychic needs, since the Indians' superb skills justified the Army's frequent failures, but many officers genuinely admired the Indians as warriors. They also praised the Indians' defiant fight for freedom. "We took away their country and their means of support, broke up their mode of living, their habits of life, introduced disease and decay among them and it was for this and against this they made war," wrote Sheridan. "Could anyone expect less?" Holding such sentiments, many officers preferred negotiations to bloodshed and took an active interest in Indian welfare. However, officers fulfilled national policy, insisting that Indians stay on their reservations and fighting them when they did not.

Divided responsibility for Indian affairs was another difficulty. The Interior Department's Bureau of Indian Affairs administered the reservation system, but the War Department enforced it, leading to confusion over the respective roles of civil and military officials. The government never imposed a clear solution to this problem, but the Army inevitably assumed increased authority because of Indian resistance. "Peace by kindness" could not make them accept the reservations.

It did not help that the Army campaigned at the outer rim of the American empire; projecting military power at an empire's edge is never easy. In the hostile western environment, the small number of troops and their inadequate training and weapons were severe handicaps. Extremes in topography, drought, cold, and vast distances made campaigning an ordeal. The lack of navigable rivers and the rugged terrain created logistical problems that the extension of the railroads only partially eased. The Army relied on wagons, horses, and mules, but boulders and gullies shattered axles and wheels, forage was scarce, and animals collapsed from hard usage. Always too few to police the west properly, regulars were often poorly trained and armed. Based on European-style tactical manuals, what little training they received left them ill-prepared to fight an unconventional foe who sometimes had superior shoulder arms. In 1873 the Army adopted the single-shot, breechloading, black-powder Springfield rifle. Not until 1892, when the Indian campaigns were over, did it adopt a repeating rifle, the smokeless-powder Krag-Jorgensen. Long before then some Indians had acquired repeaters, especially Winchesters. Whether armed with repeaters or bows, the Indians were worthy adversaries. In the east Indians moved on foot, but in the west they rode ponies, giving them greater mobility. With no towns to defend, no encumbering supply trains, and an uncanny ability to live off the land, the western Indians were adept at guerrilla warfare. Relying on stealth and ambushes, they appeared to be everywhere without being anywhere and generally refused to engage in pitched battles. On those few occasions when they did stand and fight, the Army had its hands full.

The factors that shaped colonial Indian wars, and the subsequent two centuries of native-white conflict, still prevailed. First, microbes continued to inflict a biological catastrophe, killing far more Indians than bullets did and thereby eroding their ability to resist. Since diseases were recurring—in the northern Plains an epidemic occurred about every six years in the eighteenth and nineteenth centuries—a tribe barely recovered from one epidemic before a new wave of death and anguish swept over it. The Comanche population, for example, peaked at 40,000 in the 1770s but, ravaged by periodic outbreaks of smallpox and cholera, dwindled to no more than 10,000 by the 1850s. Second, whites retained an advantage in their superior discipline and organization. While Native Americans were excellent strategists and tacticians, they primarily relied on transitory cooperation among tribes and tribal factions to achieve their goals. On the other hand, the Army's high command planned comparatively far ahead and campaigned relentlessly. Third, the primary problem was making the Indians stand and fight. The Army utilized converging columns, sending several forces into an area simultaneously, which occasionally forced the Indians into battle. Although the columns invited defeat in detail, officers assumed they would not encounter a large enemy force. The grass and game in any one region would normally not support substantial Indian concentrations.

A fourth theme was that to achieve decisive results, whites had to wage ruthless total war against the Indians' fixed camps. Since Indians dispersed into hunting and war parties during the summer, this often required winter campaigns. When the regulars found a winter encampment, the occupants were doomed. The Army invariably surprised the Indians, who were notorious for their lax security and thus could not put up a successful defense. The elements, the grass-fed ponies' weakened condition, and the presence of women and children made escape difficult. If the Indians fled, the Army destroyed their shelter and food supplies, leading to death from starvation and exposure.

Finally, the Army compensated for its weaknesses by the time-honored method of employing friendly Indians. At times the Army linked a tribe to a fort, forming a symbiotic military colony. The Tonkawas at Fort Griffin, Texas, and the Northern Cheyennes at Fort Keogh, Montana, were examples of this. Friendly Indians represented at least half the Army's strength in some encounters, and in a few instances the *only* U.S. soldiers engaged with the enemy were Indian allies. A general estimated that one Indian scout unit was more valuable than six cavalry companies. Yet many officers hesitated to rely on Indians. Within the context of American-style war they were not good soldiers, lacking discipline and refusing to sacrifice themselves in mini-Gettysburgs. Doubts lingered about their loyalty, though scouts turned on white soldiers only once, at the Battle of Cibicu Creek in 1881. Depending on Indians reflected badly on the Army, tainting the regulars' prestige. But the most successful officers utilized Indian allies.

For three centuries the conflict between whites and Native Americans followed the course of white settlement, which is why the final campaigns occurred on the Great Plains and in the intermountain west rather than the west coast. The tide of white settlement flowed steadily westward to the Mississippi, then inched across that mighty waterway to form a belt of well-watered states running from Minnesota to Louisiana. From there the Americans jumped across the west's interior and settled in California and Oregon. Only as the Civil War came to an end and in the succeeding quarter century did they backfill the Great Plains and intermountain west, and they did so by approaching from both the east *and* west.

The Indian "wars" between 1866 and 1890 consisted of little more than pursuits and skirmishes; only an occasional incident involved enough men to classify it as a "battle." Conflict flared intermittently in three zones. The regulars' nemesis in the arid southwest was the Apaches. In the Rocky Mountains and the northwest, the foremost adversaries were Utes, Bannocks, Sheepeaters, Paiutes, Shoshones, Modocs, and Nez Perce. And on the Plains the Army fought Comanches, Cheyennes, Arapahos, Kiowas, and, especially, Sioux.

The most deadly conflict in the final stage of the Native Americans' defeat throughout the continental U.S. was the so-called Snake War, a dreary, sputtering guerrilla conflict against Shoshones, Northern Paiutes, and Bannocks (whites collectively referred to these groups as "Snakes") who roamed the Great Basin where Oregon, Idaho, and Nevada converge.

Lasting from 1864 to 1868, the war claimed 378 soldiers, civilians, and Indian scouts, while 1,254 Indians died or were wounded. Although the Snake War was the deadliest, the Great Sioux War was the most famous, even though it had only about half the Snake War's total casualties. Among the Army's approximately 950 engagements in the post–Civil War West, the best known, by far, occurred during the Great Sioux War: The Battle of the Little Bighorn (known to the Indians as the Battle of the Greasy Grass), where the Sioux, reinforced by Northern Cheyenne and Northern Arapaho allies, defeated George A. Custer's 7th Cavalry.

Conquering the Sioux was not easy because they were stronger than many other tribes. Not only did their nomadic lifestyle protect them from the worst ravages of the epidemics that swept the Great Plains, but the government had also inoculated some Sioux bands against smallpox in 1832. Fortunately for the whites, the Sioux had been such aggressive expansionists that they alienated many weaker tribes; before the Great Sioux War ended, Crows, Assiniboines, Shoshones, Arikaras, Pawnees, Utes, and Bannocks fought for the Americans. Moreover, by the early 1870s the Sioux and their Northern Cheyenne allies had purposefully shifted from an offensive to a defensive strategy. They would no longer attack whites outside the region between the Yellowstone River and the Black Hills, but they would do all they could to defend themselves if the whites invaded that area. In order to put up the most effectual defense, they tinkered with new forms of centralized command to overcome the factionalism that so often sundered tribes. Sitting Bull became the foremost chief, with Gall and Crazy Horse his foremost subordinates. Perfect unity among the Sioux remained impossible to achieve, but strategic thinking underlay the effort.

The Custer fight demonstrated most of the themes of Indian warfare but also had unique features. Provoked by treaty violations and angered by efforts to confine them to reservations, large numbers of reservation Sioux joined the so-called "hunting bands" of Sitting Bull, which had never been on a reservation. In 1876 Sheridan planned an expedition of three converging columns to force all of the Sioux onto their reservation. Commanding more than 1,000 troops and 262 Crow and Shoshone allies, George Crook marched north from Fort Fetterman. John Gibbon with 450 soldiers and 25 Crow auxiliaries moved east from Forts Shaw and Ellis. Westward from Fort Abraham Lincoln came Alfred H. Terry leading 925 soldiers, including the 7th Cavalry, and 40 Arikara scouts. The commanders directed their attention to *catching* the enemy, giving little thought to then *defeating* him, since each column could deal with more warriors than anyone expected to fight in any single encounter. However, the Indians were concentrated in unprecedented numbers, perhaps 1,000 lodges (wigwams) in all, which meant about 2,000 warriors. They had no intention of fleeing, and many carried repeaters. They attacked Crook's column on June 17 at the Battle of the Rosebud, where fighting raged for six hours, with Crook's Indian allies repeatedly saving his position from being overrun. The battle badly mauled Crook's command and forced it to retreat.

Unaware of the Indians' uncommon determination and of Crook's repulse, Gibbon, Terry, and Custer planned to trap the Indians in the Little Bighorn Valley. Custer would ascend the Rosebud, cross to the Little Bighorn, and descend it. Gibbon and Terry would go up the Bighorn River and assume a blocking position at the Little Bighorn's mouth, bottling up the enemy. As soon as either force encountered Indians, it should give battle to prevent them from escaping. Custer declined to take a Gatling gun platoon, which would limit his mobility, and refused 2d Cavalry reinforcements, believing that he could "whip all the Indians on the Continent with the Seventh Cavalry."

Approaching the Little Bighorn on June 25, the day before Gibbon and Terry could be in position, Custer fragmented his regiment into four battalions. He sent Captain Frederick W. Benteen off to the south with three companies to ensure the Indians did not flee in that direction. Locating a village, he ordered Major Marcus A. Reno's three-company battalion to charge it immediately, perhaps assuming the Indians were surprised. Directly commanding five companies, Custer moved to the north, and one company stayed to the rear with the pack train. But instead of running, the Indians attacked, forcing Reno to withdraw and dig in and wiping out Custer's battalion. Reinforced by Benteen and the pack train, Reno held out until the Gibbon-Terry column arrived on the 27th. The postbattle reactions of Indians and whites showed much about their respective warmaking abilities. The Indians were unable to sustain collective action, drifting apart into bands to celebrate, hunt buffalo, and find fresh grass for their ponies. But the Army poured troops into Sioux country by rail, steamer, foot, and horse. Crook and Nelson A. Miles, aided by Indian spies and scouts, spearheaded a winter campaign that ferreted out enemy camps and virtually ended Indian resistance.

Although the Army's role in subduing the Indians should not be minimized, other factors were perhaps more important. By 1890 railroads crisscrossed the west, bringing new settlers. In 1866 fewer than 2 million whites lived in the west; twenty-five years later there were 8.5 million, planting crops, raising cattle, and depleting the timber, grass, and game that sustained Indian society. For the Plains Indians the buffalo's destruction was especially harmful, for they depended on its hide and meat for almost every want. By the late 1880s commercial hunters had reduced the buffalo herds from 13 million to a thousand, and Sheridan believed that did more than the Army to pacify the Indians. In other regions of the west, white settlement and activity also severely reduced other types of game. The frontier was gone, and Indians had nowhere to go but the reservations.

The conquest of the Indians ended an era in the Army's history. Indian fighting had been its primary function since the formation of the 1st American Regiment. Now the Army no longer needed to remain in the far-flung garrisons, and consolidation took place rapidly. By 1891 the Army had abandoned one-fourth of the posts occupied in 1889. Even before the troops settled into their fewer, more permanent installations, officers began debating a disturbing question: What was the Army's purpose now that its foremost traditional mission was gone?

The Army and Reconstruction

"Of the slain there were enough to furnish forth a battlefield . . . all killed with deliberation," wrote Albion W Tourgee in his 1879 novel *A Fool's Errand,* "shot, stabbed, hanged, drowned, mutilated beyond description, tortured beyond conception." Tourgee was not describing a frontier massacre. Having been a Republican judge during Reconstruction, he was explaining the fate of many blacks and their white political allies. Allowing for literary license, the judge told the truth. Appomattox was only a truce that ushered in two years of nominal peace before the south renewed the conflict at a guerrilla level. President Grant refought many of the men he had already defeated once and whose purpose had been little changed by Lee's surrender. Confederate veterans dominated the irregular warfare between 1867 and 1877, continuing the struggle against federal authority in order to preserve white supremacy and regional political powers. The renewed war forced the Army to participate in low-intensity military operations and to assume an untraditional duty. Garrisoning the south during Reconstruction was a deviation from its customary apolitical role.

During the Civil War the Army became involved in developing loyal governments in the seceded states and working out the freedmen's place in society. Lincoln appointed military governors with civil and military powers for occupied states, hoping they could mobilize loyal electorates, and Army officers initiated educational and free labor programs for exslaves. To support the Army's work with blacks, in March 1865 Congress created the Bureau of Freedmen, Refugees, and Abandoned Lands (Freedmen's Bureau) in the War Department. Staffed primarily by Army personnel, the bureau represented a unique social welfare experiment and an unprecedented extension of federal power into the states, since it had authority over the economic, legal, and political affairs of the former slaves.

Northerners assumed that martial law and the military's role in the south would end in 1865. They expected southerners to acknowledge defeat by treating blacks justly, rejecting Confederate leaders, and embracing southern Unionists. None of these things happened. Encouraged by President Andrew Johnson's Reconstruction policy, which imposed no severe penalties on the south, unrepentant southerners elected former Confederates to state, local, and national offices, formed militia units composed of exsoldiers, passed "black codes" restricting the freedmen's rights, slaughtered blacks in race riots, refused to ratify the Fourteenth Amendment, and bullied loyalists. Most important from the Army's viewpoint, southerners frequently insulted and sometimes assaulted soldiers and filed scores of damage suits in state courts against federal military personnel. In these suits claimants asked for damages for actions that the soldiers had taken under martial law during and after the war. Since the claimants, judges, and jurors were inevitably former rebels, the courts were unsympathetic to the defendants. Army personnel, whose legal status in the south from 1865 to early 1867 was ambiguous, were reluctant to exercise authority under martial law or support the Freedmen's Bureau for fear of provoking damage suits.

The problem of protecting the Army from vengeful southerners and establishing its legal position was one of the main factors that drove a wedge between Johnson, on the one hand, and Congress, Secretary of War Stanton, and Commanding General Grant, on the other. Johnson's position, expressed in proclamations issued in April and August of 1866, was that the rebellion was over, the southern states were restored to the Union under his lenient policy, and the civil authority was ascendant over the military. He wanted the Army out of the reconstructed states since, he said, "standing armies, military occupation, martial law, military tribunals, and the suspension of the writ of *habeas corpus* are in time of peace dangerous to public liberty" and incompatible with free institutions. In the *Milligan, Garland,* and *Cummings* decisions, the Supreme Court agreed with him that continued martial law was unconstitutional. But from the perspective of the Army and a growing number of Republican congressmen, if prevailing conditions did not change, the wartime sacrifices would have been in vain, for only loyal people would suffer any penalties.

Rather than see Appomattox reversed, Army personnel and white Unionists suffer further abuse, and blacks returned to virtual slavery, Stanton and Grant defied the president and turned to Congress for help, resulting in an alliance between the Army and Congress that wrested Reconstruction policy from Johnson's hands. In 1866 Grant, with Stanton's concurrence, issued orders permitting military personnel who believed the south's civil courts denied them justice to have suits transferred to federal courts or the Freedmen's Bureau's tribunals. He also issued a secret circular urging commanders to act discreetly but authorizing them to employ martial law when necessary despite Johnson's proclamations. Congress further protected the Army by amending the 1863 Habeas Corpus Act to provide for federal jurisdiction in suits against soldiers and to assist the defendants with government legal aid.

Laws passed in March 1867 signaled a complete victory for the Congress-Army alliance over the president and in essence established a separate army for Reconstruction duty. The Command of the Army Act and the Tenure of Office Act kept Grant and Stanton in their positions and enhanced the commanding general's authority over the entire Army. Although frontier garrisons remained under executive control and the precise extent of the president's loss of authority over the occupation forces remains subject to debate, Grant and Stanton, acting in concert with Congress, were the dominant voices affecting the Army in the south. To prevent organized resistance, Congress disbanded southern militia units and prohibited new ones from being raised without its approval.

Finally, Congress passed the First Reconstruction Act setting forth its own policy. The act legalized Army occupation, reinstated martial law, and divided the south into five military districts, each commanded by a general. The Army became a political instrument, a role that it did not relish but undertook as a means of self-preservation. Under the act the Army had the power to remove and appoint officials, register voters, hold elections, regulate court proceedings, and approve state constitutions. Grant interpreted the law to mean that commanders had "entire control over the civil governments" and were not responsible to any United States civil officer, and Congress agreed. Thus a general's political inclinations were important. A few lacked zeal for the goals of congressional Reconstruction and worked with Conservatives (Democrats) to limit its impact. But others favored the Republican Party, and their tutelage fostered Radical Republican governments. By 1871 Congress had readmitted most of the states, Conservative or Republican. After a state's restoration military rule ended and civil government began. However, southerners so detested most of the new regimes that, having created Republican governments, the Army had to help defend them.

White racists considered three organizations besides the Army provocative. Although the Freedmen's Bureau helped plantation owners by keeping blacks tied to the land as agrarian laborers, it also enhanced the freedmen's political and civil rights. The Union League, a northern patriotic society, spread to the south, where freedmen comprised the bulk of its membership and its main purpose was to mobilize black voters. To provide for local protection, most of the governments received congressional permission to raise militias. Composed of both blacks and white Unionists, the militias undertook general police and specific election duties, ensuring that freedmen voted and that ineligible former rebels did not. Paradoxically, the militias weakened rather than strengthened the Republicans. Congress used their formation as a pretext to reduce the Army, and the sight of armed black men intensified the white southerners' reaction to Republican rule.

The southerners' violent answer to Reconstruction was the Ku Klux Klan. Begun as a social fraternity in Tennessee, that state's leaders made it into a paramilitary arm of the Conservative Party. The Klan spread to every state between the Potomac and the Rio Grande and spawned a host of similar organizations, such as the Knights of the Rising Sun and the Knights of the White Camellia. Manned by undemocratic Democrats and racist reactionaries, the terrorist groups beat, whipped, raped, and murdered lone blacks and white Republicans, especially those active in the Freedmen's Bureau, Union League, and militias. Many incidents were simple brutality. But the violence also served a counterrevolutionary purpose, undermining the reconstructed governments by inducing some Republicans to leave the South and assassinating and intimidating others. Wherever the terrorists were active, Republican voting drastically declined.

"The Ku Klux organization is so extensive, and so well organized and armed, that it is beyond the power of any one to exert any moral influence over them," wrote a general serving in Tennessee. "Powder and ball is the only thing that will put them down." But who would supply the powder and ball? The reign of terror was so extensive that state governments were powerless to control it. Only the national government and its Army had the resources to quell the south's challenge to federal policy. Most Army officers were willing to engage the rebels again—even those who sympathized with southern goals deplored the lawless terrorists—and whenever the beleaguered state governments requested aid, they responded as best they could. But severe problems hampered the Army's war against the Klan. Too few regulars were available. In 1868 only 17,657 men were on occupation duty, and three years later the number was only 8,038. While numbers are not necessarily an indication of power, the Army was nevertheless too small to quash the violence. Constitutional and legal safeguards against military power also restricted the Army. When Congress readmitted a state, the Army could intervene only upon the application of, and in subordination to, state civil authorities. These officials, either afraid of or in sympathy with the terrorists, often inhibited effective action. Moreover, even when officials called upon the Army to assist in enforcing the law, its legal authority was as murky as it had been in 1865–1867. Thus officers facing a delicate political situation often hesitated to act decisively.

Perhaps the most fundamental problem was the north's flagging determination. Representing a minority in each southern state and utterly dependent on federal support, were the Republican governments worth saving? Increasing numbers of northerners thought not, and erstwhile backers of congressional policy gradually retreated. An important test between northern resolve and southern resistance came in the early 1870s, when Congress passed the Enforcement Acts. The most important one, called the Ku Klux Klan Act, outlawed the Klan and similar groups, permitted President Grant to declare martial law and suspend the writ of habeas corpus, and gave federal officials and troops unprecedented authority of enforcement. However, the enforcement record in the south was pitiable, and by 1874 the program retained little vitality. In nine South Carolina counties, where Grant for the first and only time suspended the writ of habeas corpus, the act did achieve measurable success and demonstrated what might have been achieved. The commander there, Major Lewis M. Merrill, deployed the 7th Cavalry so effectively that he broke the Klan's grip on the state. But South Carolina was the exception.

Despite the Enforcement Acts, not because of them, the Klan's activity declined as it lost the community support essential for irregular operations. The grosser Klan outrages repelled simple humanity, and the exile and demoralization of the black labor force hurt the economy. More important, Democratic leaders, unable to control the Klan, could not mobilize it to help them win elections. With the KKK, violence spawned violence, all too often unharnessed to political purpose.

But southerners did not give up their war for white supremacy and home rule. The north's obvious desire for peace and its growing indifference to the fate of southern Republicans encouraged Democrats to act boldly. In the mid-1870s a new white terror arose to "redeem" those states still under Republican rule. Openly directed by Democratic leaders, such well-armed organizations as the White League of Louisiana and the Red Shirts of South Carolina were essentially Conservative militias formed to counter Republican militias. Although relying heavily on economic pressure and threats, which were unlikely to provoke federal intervention, they resorted to violence when it served political purposes. Democrats planned race riots and battled Republican militias prior to elections, in time to keep Republicans from the polls but too late for Washington to send regulars to police the voting. What occurred between 1874 and 1877 was not indiscriminate Klan-style violence, but a calculated insurrection as the last unredeemed states fell to Democrats.

One unexpected result of Reconstruction was the difficulty in enacting legislation to reform and modernize the armed forces. The Democratic triumph in the south led to a reunited national Democratic Party. Based on its experiences between 1861 and 1877, it became an antimilitary party, giving new birth to the attitudes of the Jeffersonian and Jacksonian eras. For the next generation congressional Democrats, especially those from the south, generally opposed forward-looking military legislation. At times Democratic intransigence threatened the Army's operational ability. For example, in 1877 Congress appropriated no money for the Army until November 30, forcing soldiers to rely on loans from bankers, who were often usurious. Frequently joining the antireformist Democrats were the War Department's bureau chiefs, whose political power had been enhanced during Reconstruction. With the Army responsive to Congress's direction, the chiefs exerted even greater independence from their traditional superior, the secretary of war, and developed closer ties to Congress, thus gaining political leverage in fighting line-sponsored reforms.

In 1865 Sherman predicted that "no matter what change we may desire in the feelings and thoughts of people [in the] South, we cannot accomplish it by force. Nor can we afford to maintain there an army large enough to hold them in subjugation." He was right. Force failed to transform southerners. But northern public opinion never permitted the use of much force. A massive, sustained intervention might have produced more favorable results. But budgetary restraints, fear of standing armies, and concern for the consent of the governed (as long as they were white) prevented a significant commitment of indefinite duration. By 1877 the north was so anxious for sectional reconciliation that it gave up the effort to preserve the gains of 1865. It had won the conventional war but lost the unconventional war of 1867–1877. White supremacy prevailed, and the south's wartime leaders dominated a distinct section within the United States. As one man wrote in 1877, "Status quo ante bellum or things as they were before Lincoln, slavery excepted: such is the tendency everywhere." True, formal slavery died, but whites imposed informal servitude on blacks, making them the most cruelly deceived of all by Appomattox. The north got peace in 1877, but the peace lacked justice.

The Army's duty in the south was onerous. Subjected to political crossfires, it turned in a performance that seemingly pleased no one, north or south. Radicals argued that it did too little to support the congressional program, while Conservatives complained that it did too much. As the Army redeployed, most men were probably glad to leave the south. Avenging Custer or chasing the Nez Perce would surely be more satisfying (if also more deadly) than playing a thankless political and civil role. But the Army was about to march into another civil-military cauldron, for in 1877 a nationwide labor strike rocked the government, which ordered the Army to undertake another untraditional task: policing labor strikes.

The Army and Strikebreaking

In the last half of the century American society underwent rapid change. Immigration threatened its identity, urban growth compromised its agrarian past, and the rise of corporate capitalism altered the relationship between management and labor. Hard hit by recurrent depressions and stressing the rights and needs of individuals, laborers went on strike, raising the specter of class warfare. Capitalists demanded that the government intervene to preserve order, and presidents responded by ordering the Army to enforce the law. Essentially middle class by birth, Army officers shared the capitalists' ideology. Both groups were concerned about social stability and the sanctity of private property but little understood the conditions that drove workers to strike.

The 1877 strike began with railroad workers, but coal miners and the urban unemployed soon made common cause with them. Local law enforcement agencies and private industrial police were unable to restore order. Management appealed to governors for National Guard (militia) assistance, but some states found they had no militia, and those that did discovered their Guardsmen often sympathized with the strikers. Worried state officials and capitalists called for federal aid, and President Rutherford B. Hayes sent about 2,000 regulars to troubled areas, some arriving after forced marches from Indian country, "all tanned and grizzled, and with unwashed faces and unkempt hair, and their clothes covered with dust an inch thick in some places."

Military intervention in labor disputes was not unprecedented (in 1834 President Jackson used troops in a labor disturbance), and Reconstruction familiarized Americans with using regulars upon a governor's application. Still, Hayes's action marked the beginning of a wrenching experience for the Army. During the next twenty years it participated in several other shattering labor upheavals and several minor ones. Three characteristics marked the Army's role in labor troubles. First, in each situation the government and Army responded on an ad hoc basis. The government devised no policy, and the Army no contingency plans, for strike duty. Second, despite this handicap, the Army was effective. It not only restored order but also broke strikes, to the dismay of workers and the delight of capitalists. Third, the Army acted with restraint. Although sometimes met with abuse and rocks, regulars refused to respond with violence. In 1877, for instance, local police, hired guards, and National Guardsmen killed 100 strikers, but regulars did not kill a single man.

"In reality, the Army is now a gendarmery—a national police," wrote a colonel in 1895. The Army's participation in labor strife *apparently* convinced a few officers that this was true. Arguing that the nation needed an enlarged Army to restrain the industrial proletariat, they requested increased appropriations and manpower. Actually, such appeals may have been consciously spurious. By 1890 the thrust of professionalization was toward creating a modern Army prepared for war, and the money and men allegedly needed to control "white savages" could be used for this primary mission. Strikebreaking was no more edifying than Reconstruction duty: One alienated southerners and the other antagonized labor, which trumpeted the old arguments against a standing army. In any event, the officers' appeals did not work. Southern congressmen, remembering the army's "tyranny," obstructed Army legislation, and many other Americans were receptive to labor's warning about despotism. Moreover, state officials no longer needed to rely on regulars. After an inept start in 1877, National Guard units became more efficient and assumed a greater role in quelling labor strife.

The need for a police force for strike duty was only one stimulus that revived the volunteer militia, which almost universally assumed the name National Guard in the postwar era. After the war southern militias, first Democratic and then Republican, reformed immediately, but northern units briefly deteriorated. The exhaustion with war and the sense of security that led to the Army's reduction also sapped militia vitality. But by the early 1870s the traditional attractions of militia service began to resuscitate the institution. Spontaneous martial enthusiasm, the social prestige of belonging to an elite group, and the appeal to physical fitness, discipline, and duty sparked the renaissance.

Following the 1877 debacle the pace of the National Guard's revival quickened. Between 1881 and 1892 every state revised its militia code, and in 1879 militia leaders formed the National Guard Association to lobby Congress for favorable legislation. However, the association's only success came in 1887, when Congress doubled the annual appropriation begun in 1808 to $400,000. By the early 1890s the Guard contained more than 100,000 men, predominantly from the middle class. Its foremost activity was preserving order in industrial disputes. Between 1877 and 1903 governors called out the Guard more than 700 times, and about half of the calls were for the Guard to perform strike police duty. Since many working people viewed the Guard as a capitalist tool and disliked it intensely, serving as strike police was no more rewarding for Guardsmen than for regulars. Indeed, when the National Guard Association asked for federal aid, it emphasized the Guard's role as a reserve force, not as policemen. Thus neither regulars nor citizen-soldiers avidly pursued strike duty as a primary mission. But both groups sought other missions that armed forces modernization and professionalization offered.

Imperialism and Naval Modernization

Stimulated by America's emerging imperialist impulse, technological developments, and officers' career concerns, the armed forces started to modernize during the 1880s. A steam and steel "new navy" eased down the slips and onto the seas, and Congress appropriated funds to commence a new coastal fortifications program. To build ordnance and armor for the modern ships and coastal defenses, linkages developed among the military, government, and industry. During the century's last two decades, America shifted from isolation to imperialism, its outward thrust combining idealism, cultural arrogance, and economic expediency. A resurgent Manifest Destiny proclaimed the white man's moral responsibility to spread civilization, and Social Darwinists gave Manifest Destiny a "scientific" veneer, arguing that nations behaved like biological organisms. Only the fittest survived, so strong nations inevitably extended their power over weaker ones. And since Darwin described a *struggle* for survival, a nation must be prepared to fight. Some civil and military leaders actually glorified war. One congressman announced that "there are no great nations of Quakers," and a naval officer wrote an essay in the *North American Review* extolling "The Benefits of War."

The fusion of destiny, Darwinism, and a glorification of war was not the only cause of American imperialism. Some people thought the closing of the frontier, industrial overproduction, and labor unrest portended a crisis. They believed that America's history was one of expansion, the frontier (in theory) providing a "safety valve" for the discontented, raw materials, and a market for manufactured goods. With the frontier gone, was it coincidence that the nation suffered from excess production, depressions, and labor unrest? Policymakers sought a new frontier, primarily commercial rather than territorial, by channeling expansionist energies into an aggressive search for overseas markets to absorb the industrial glut, restore prosperity, and preserve domestic tranquility. The United States, however, did not have unfettered access to foreign markets. European empires controlled much of Asia and Africa, and some Europeans cast covetous eyes upon Latin America. President Chester A. Arthur had defined America as the "chief Pacific power" and the U.S. considered the Caribbean its private lake, but if the country did not enter the imperial quest, the great powers might foreclose its opportunities to sell exports in either region. Thus policymakers urged a strategy of preemptive imperialism: The United States should seize or dominate desirable areas before rivals gobbled them up.

Two imperatives flowed from the search for foreign markets. First, America must acquire more bases as trading and naval way stations to protect its interests and encourage commerce. Between 1867 and 1889 the United States purchased Alaska, occupied Midway, and acquired the right to build naval bases at Pearl Harbor, Hawaii, and Pago Pago, Samoa. (Few expansionists thought this was enough.) Second, the country must strengthen its coastal defenses and Navy, and broaden its definition of national security. Since the U.S. was becoming part of an interdependent world economic and political system, a commercial struggle might flash into an outright war, necessitating the protection of the continental domain *and* its overseas interests.

Rearmament advocates initially stressed traditional defensive strategies. An expanded Navy and modern fortifications would prevent an enemy from raiding the coast, bombarding wealthy port cities, and effecting a close blockade. By the mid-1880s the increased capabilities of European steam fleets made these prospects seem frightening. The Navy would also engage in single-ship operations, defending the merchant marine and foreign bases and destroying enemy commerce. However, a growing number of strategists questioned the viability of the traditional maritime strategies. They perceived that the telegraph and fast steam cruisers would make commerce raiding difficult. Moreover, instead of sailing singly or hovering near the coast to defend important harbors, the ships of a modern Navy might be massed for offensive fleet actions at sea. As one congressman said in 1887, we want a Navy "with which we may meet the foe away from our coast when he comes."

Technology joined imperialism as a spur to modernization. For twenty years Americans congratulated themselves for not following European nations that built the costly experimental weapons that soon became outmoded. But the technological advances had been tremendous. Delaying modernization much longer might mean falling irretrievably behind in the technological race. More important, European naval architects had eliminated much technical confusion, blending steam, armor, and improved guns into acceptable ship standards. Navies could dispense with full sail rigging, since better engines increased speed and range. Steel was superior to iron for hulls and armor, and hull compartmentalization would keep a damaged ship afloat. Guns came to be breechloading rifles using slow-burning powder that enhanced velocity. Compound barrels permitted lighter yet stronger guns, which hydraulic recoil mechanisms automatically returned to their firing position. In 1883 a naval commander summed up an increasingly universal feeling: "The present time is very favorable; it is possible after twenty years of experiments, mainly by foreign nations, the results of which are known to us, to build a fine fleet, of such numbers as may be judged necessary, and equal to performance and wants now well understood; a fleet that shall be superior ship for ship to the same kind of vessels elsewhere."

Army and Navy officers, particularly junior ones, pushed modernization for national security reasons, but also for narrow career interests. Promotion remained slow; larger, modern forces with important missions would break the logjam. With the ending of the Indian wars, the Army had lost its most active mission. Police duty was an unsatisfactory substitute, and no strategists envisioned sending large expeditionary forces abroad. At most the nation might require small Army forces to help the Navy temporarily defend a few points on foreign soil. The Army embraced a new fortifications program, for coastal defense seemed its sole remaining significant function. While reminding the public of the Navy's role in aiding businessmen abroad, naval officers propagandized for the new Navy among selected groups. They lobbied among shipbuilders, steel firms, and weapons manufacturers who would benefit from naval construction. Navalists also supported an expanded merchant marine, hoping they could convince the business community that more commerce justified more warships.

Ever since the *Virginius* affair of 1873–1874, navalists had lobbied intensively for a revitalized Navy, but it took a decade for them to achieve even modest results. The Navy's serious rebuilding effort began in 1882–1883 under Secretary of the Navy William H . Hunt, who persuaded President Chester A. Arthur that new construction was necessary. "Every condition of national safety, economy, and honor demands a thorough rehabilitation of the Navy," the president told Congress, which responded in 1882 with an act authorizing two steel cruisers, though it failed to appropriate funds to build them. The same law limited repairs on existing ships, which ensured an early retirement for the "old navy," and authorized the secretary to appoint a Naval Advisory Board, which recommended four steel cruisers and a dispatch boat. Congress eliminated one cruiser and in the Naval Appropriations Act of 1883 authorized and funded the protected (armored) cruisers *Atlanta, Boston,* and *Chicago* and the dispatch vessel *Dolphin* (known as the ABCD ships). The cruisers were transitional vessels, sail-rigged but with steel hulls, compartmentalization, steam engines, screw propellers, electric power plants, and breechloading rifles using slow-burning powder. Between 1884 and 1889 Congress authorized eight more protected cruisers (including *Charleston,* the first modern U.S. ship without sails), three unprotected cruisers, six steel gunboats, three armored cruisers (two of them, *Maine* and *Texas,* were originally classified as second-class battleships), and a few monitors. The new Navy initially remained wedded to the old mission of showing the flag and protecting commerce. The ships still lacked the armor and armaments to engage European fleets, yet they were ideal for intimidating nonindustrialized peoples and could carry out attacks on enemy commerce.

A fundamental change in naval policy occurred in the early 1890s, prompted by Secretary of the Navy Benjamin R. Tracy, who believed that the "sea will be the future seat of empire. And we shall rule it as certainly as the sun doth rise!" To do so, the United States needed bases (perhaps even colonies) and a great Navy, and Tracy was an avid expansionist and an ardent navalist. He cast his imperialist eye on several islands, but all his schemes failed. He had more success with the development of the Navy. His first annual report in November 1889, which reflected increasingly widespread professional naval thought, represented a clear break with past strategy. Instead of emphasizing coastal defense and commerce protection and raiding, he called for a new doctrine of command of the sea based on battleships capable of destroying an enemy's fleet in midocean. "The country," he said, "needs a navy that will exempt it from war, but the only navy that will accomplish this is a navy that can wage war." The present force of cruisers and gunboats did "not constitute a fighting force." He recommended building eight battleships for the Pacific and twelve for the Atlantic, all of them "the best of their class in four leading characteristics: armament, armor, structural strength, and speed." He also suggested a complementary force of sixty cruisers (thirty-one of which were already built or authorized) and twenty coastal defense vessels. He believed the U.S. could easily afford such a Navy and that its construction would benefit labor.

Tracy's recommendations for 100 modern warships might have seemed excessive had not the Policy Board's report of January 1890 been leaked to the press. Appointed by Tracy to study naval requirements and prepare a long-range plan, the board called for more than 200 ships! With the Tracy and Policy Board reports before them, congressmen engaged in an acrimonious debate. Many recognized that battleships marked a radical departure and hesitated to embark on an uncharted voyage. Some wanted only monitors and coastal fortifications, others preferred cruisers and gunboats. The resulting naval bill was a compromise. It authorized three battleships, but designated them "sea-going coastal battleships" and limited them to a 4,500-mile range. Traditionalists could thus consider *Oregon, Indiana,* and *Massachusetts* as little more than updated monitors with an enhanced ability to break a blockade. Yet the battleships *did* mark a departure, the starting point for a new maritime strategy that strove to gain command of the sea. Once begun, Congress did not reverse the trend. In 1892 it funded *Iowa,* a battleship with no statutory range limit; in 1895 it authorized two more battleships and in 1896 another three.

Tracy not only introduced battleships into the Navy but also formed a "squadron of evolution" in 1889 that was the precursor of a concentrated battlefleet. Comprised of the ABC cruisers and a steel gunboat, it practiced steaming in formation and tactical maneuvers, which were faster and more complex than under sail. In 1892 the Navy Department merged the squadron into the North Atlantic Squadron, which by 1897 developed into a fighting fleet. With good reason Tracy could claim in 1892 that progress made during his tenure marked "an epoch in the naval development, not only of this country, but of the world."

A well-defended coast was an essential adjunct to a strong navy. Both Army and Navy officers realized that "the navy is the *aggressive* arm of the national military power." However, it could undertake an offensive mission only if it had secure home ports and if relieved of defensive duties. The Chilean bombardment of Callao, Peru, in 1880 and the British bombardment of Alexandria, Egypt, in 1882 were vivid reminders of an undefended port's fate. American cities must be secure from similar attacks and from the prospect of a squadron holding them ransom, extracting money and exerting diplomatic leverage in return for immunity from shellings. In 1883 President Arthur called congressional attention to the obsolete coastal defenses, and the next year Commanding General Schofield's annual report spoke of "the perfectly defenseless condition of our seaboard cities." Sparked to action, in the Fortifications Appropriations Act of March 1885 Congress directed the president to appoint an Army-Navy civilian board, headed by Secretary of War William C. Endicott, to investigate the problem.

The Endicott Board report of 1886 painted a grim picture of the seaport defenses and proposed a massive fortress program estimated at $127 million. It recommended large numbers of breechloading rifles and rifled mortars, supported by floating batteries, submarine mines, torpedo boats, rapid-firing guns, machine guns, and electric searchlights, for twenty-six coastal localities and three Great Lakes sites. In 1888 Congress created a permanent Army Board of Ordnance and Fortifications to test weapons and make proposals for implementing the program. Funding for construction began in 1890, though at a more modest level than the Endicott Board had suggested. The work fell behind the original projections from the start, yet new defenses to match the new Navy were underway.

Building the ships and ordnance inextricably linked the government, the military, and industry. When the new Navy began, a fundamental question arose: How should the nation acquire the tools of war? Should it rely upon the private economic sector, which might lead to monopolies with respect to designs and prices? Or should it depend on government arsenals, an arrangement that smacked of socialism and might be less efficient than profit-motivated private enterprise? Or would some combination of private and public facilities be better? To study this problem, the Naval Appropriations Act of 1883 created a Gun Foundry Board composed of six Army and Navy officers. After investigating arms manufacturing in

Europe, the board recommended a mixed system. The government should offer contracts to private firms to supply basic steels and forgings, which government-owned plants would fabricate into finished guns and ships. The officers suggested the Army's Watervliet Arsenal and the Washington Navy Yard as excellent assembly plants.

The government accepted the Gun Foundry Board's report. The 1886 law authorizing *Texas* and *Maine* stipulated that they be built with domestic steel and machinery, and that at least one of the ships be constructed in a navy yard. To entice firms to bid, the secretary of the navy pooled orders for *Texas, Maine,* and four monitors into one $4 million contract, and in mid-1887 awarded it to the Bethlehem Iron (later Steel) Company. Subsequent contracts also went to Carnegie, Phipps and Company (later Carnegie Steel).

By the mid-1890s construction of the Navy and the coastal fortifications had intertwined private and public policy in a mutually beneficial relationship. Manufacturing armor and ordnance required expensive plants employing skilled workmen; to cease construction would idle the factories and create unemployment or disperse the workers into other endeavors. Thus economic depressions no longer meant decreased government expenditures but increased expenditures to keep factories operating and workers employed. This motive may have influenced the 1895–1896 battleship authorizations during the depression that began in 1893. Military contracts certainly allowed the Bethlehem and Carnegie firms, and their supporting subcontractors and shipbuilders, to survive while other establishments went bankrupt. In short, armed forces modernization bound together the public welfare, private interest, and national security.

Reforming the Armed Forces

"History does not countenance the idea that an untroubled assurance of peace is a guarantee that war will not come," wrote a naval essayist in 1879. "Lessons" drawn from history often rest upon feeble analysis and faulty analogy, but the writer had a point. Sooner or later, war came. To military reformers viewing the global great power rivalry, progressively involving the United States, a big war against a powerful adversary was not impossible. Indeed, the central theme in late-nineteenth-century military theorizing was that in peace the armed forces should prepare for war against even the most formidable potential enemy. While seemingly a truism, this postulate represented a rejection of past policy.

Traditionally the nation maintained small peacetime constabularies—the Army on the frontier and the Navy on its stations—and then extemporized fighting forces during wartime. Such a policy, professionals argued, would no longer suffice. The potential foes were too strong, the lead time in producing modern weapons was too long, and warfare had become so complex that hastily mobilized amateurs could not master it. In determining the composition and strength of the Army and Navy, the U.S. should look beyond Indians and pirates to the leading European nations, especially Germany and England. Officers also thought that preparing for war required the ability to wage it "scientifically." In their quest for efficiency they reflected a societal trend. During the initial stages of the Progressive movement in America, captains of industry applied scientific managerial techniques to the problems of production. "Progressives in uniform" sought similar expertise and bureaucratic forms, which would allow them to utilize prewar preparations in the most "scientific" wartime manner.

The reformers' greatest success was creating a more complete educational system. This success was due in large part to General Sherman (the commanding general between 1869 and 1883) and Rear Admiral Stephen B. Luce, two men who epitomized the professional spirit. Each was responsible for establishing an important school and both supported other schools, journals, and institutes, all fostering the expertise and corporate spirit essential for professional identity. Sherman and Luce also each nurtured a protégé (Emory Upton and Alfred Thayer Mahan, respectively) whose writings profoundly influenced military affairs.

A man of great intellect, Sherman vigorously pushed for Army education. He believed West Point was only the beginning of military education, envisioning it at the base of a pyramid consisting of advanced schools where officers gained specialized knowledge; at the apex he hoped for a "war college." Sherman sustained the 1868 revival of Calhoun's old Artillery School, encouraged the development of an Engineering School of Application, and, most important, founded the School of Application for Infantry and Cavalry at Fort Leavenworth. It began as a training school for junior officers that emphasized small-unit tactics, but two outstanding officer-instructors, Eben Swift and Arthur L. Wagner, stressed an analytical approach to learning rather than rote memorization and redirected the school toward a true staff college devoted, as Sherman said, to "the science and practice of war." Meanwhile, creative officers formed additional schools for the field artillery and cavalry combined, the Signal Corps, and the Hospital Corps, plus an Army Medical School. Sherman was also instrumental in the founding of the Military Service Institution in 1878, a professional society that brought together officers with a common interest in acquiring specialized knowledge. The Institution promoted writing and discussion about military science by publishing a bimonthly journal. It also spawned the formation of branch associations for the infantry, cavalry, artillery, and military surgeons, each publishing its own journal.

Perhaps Sherman's greatest contribution to military education was the encouragement he gave to Emory Upton, whose writings dominated Army thought well into the twentieth century. An 1861 West Point graduate, Upton had a meteoric Civil War career. Beginning as a second lieutenant, he was a brevet major general before his twenty-fifth birthday. Yet the war disturbed him. "I am disgusted with the generalship displayed," he wrote during the Wilderness campaign. Too many men had been "wantonly sacrificed" in frontal assaults. "Thousands of lives might have been spared," he continued, "by the exercise of a little skill; but, as it is, the courage of the poor man is expected to obviate all difficulties." In 1867 he published *Infantry Tactics,* which adapted tactics to rifled and breechloading shoulder arms, and the War Department immediately adopted the book for use in the Army and militia. The book emphasized simplicity in drill, specially trained and more numerous skirmishers, less dense attacking formations, and the need for soldiers to exhibit an intelligent initiative.

Upton, however, believed the major problem was a defective military policy. Appointed commandant of cadets at West Point, Upton developed a close relationship with Sherman, who, in 1875, appointed Upton to a commission assigned to propose Army reforms based upon its studies of foreign military systems. After the world tour Upton wrote two books, *The Armies of Asia and Europe* and *The Military Policy of the United States.* The latter, one of the most significant books in American military history, was a clarion call for drastic policy changes.

As Upton perceived it, U.S. policy contained near-fatal weaknesses. Excessive civilian control was a fundamental flaw, since most congressmen, presidents, and secretaries of war were inexperienced in military matters. The nation as a whole had an "unfounded jealousy of not a large, but even a small standing army." Thus America relied upon unreliable citizen-soldiers. Although volunteers and militiamen could be brave, Upton considered their short enlistments, lack of discipline, dual state-federal control, and untrained officers as crushing liabilities, making them useless as a reserve force. Since these defects prevented adequate preparations, the country's wars usually began with failures, were longer than they should have been, and entailed "enormous and unnecessary sacrifices of life and treasure." "Ultimate success in all our wars," warned Upton, "has steeped the people in the delusion that our military policy is correct and that any departure from it would be no less difficult than dangerous." Nothing, he argued, could be further from the truth.

While in Europe, Upton studied the German military, which offered a stark contrast. The Germans had a General Staff that operated in comparative freedom from civilian restraint. Unlike America's staff, which was simply an aggregation of the bureau chiefs, the German staff made peacetime preparations for war, gathering information about foreign armies, drawing up war plans, and controlling an educational system that ensured competent collective leadership. The regular Army was large and proficient and organized on the cadre, or expansible, principle. Germany relied on conscription and assigned its veterans to seven years' service in the reserves, which were under national control. With these sound practices, Upton said, Germany defeated Austria in six weeks and humbled the vaunted French in just three and a half months.

Upton proposed revolutionary reforms to prevent a repetition of America's past folly. Although he claimed that the United States "can not Germanize" and that it would not be desirable to do so, Upton's reforms had a definite Teutonic ring. The country should abolish its present General Staff and create a Germanic one, enhancing the powers of professionals relative to the president and secretary of war. An enlarged regular Army, organized on the expansible principle, should be at the center of military planning. To flesh out the Army in wartime, the United States should rely on "National Volunteers" controlled and led by regulars. Although he admired conscription and considered it a "truly democratic doctrine," Upton only obliquely advocated it, knowing the public would not accept peacetime conscription. The militia would be a force of last resort, used solely to execute the laws, suppress insurrections, and repel invasions.

Upton's ideas collided with America's most revered traditions, ran counter to the prevailing aversion to spending more money on an Army already performing its duties satisfactorily, and suffered from problems as fundamental as those he thought existed in America's policy. In unreservedly praising regulars and denigrating militiamen and volunteers, Upton misused history. Regulars were not uniformly successful, and citizen-soldiers were not always pathetic. As Washington, Jackson, Forrest, Lincoln, and others demonstrated, superb leaders could be created in arenas other than the Army. Nor did Upton understand that policy cannot be judged by any absolute standard. It reflects a nation's characteristics, habits of thought, geographic location, and historical development. Built upon the genius, traditions, and location of Germany, the system he admired could not be grafted onto America. In essence, Upton wrote in a vacuum. He began with a fixed view of the policy he thought the U.S. needed, and he wanted the rest of society to change to meet his demands, which it sensibly declined to do. Thus, for example, his plan for a large expansible Army faltered for obvious reasons. No peacetime nucleus big enough to avoid being swamped by a wartime influx of citizen-soldiers was politically, economically, or strategically feasible or necessary.

Despite the fallacies in his reasoning, Upton spoke for a generation of officers. He simply presented the ideas in systematic form, buttressed them with "scholarship," and "proved" the professionals' case. However, the Burnside Committee of 1878 showed how unrealistic the Upton reforms were within the context of late-nineteenth-century American society. Established by Congress to study Army reform and chaired by former general (now senator) Ambrose Burnside, the committee heard testimony from generals as diverse as McClellan and Sherman. All but one urged the expansible Army plan and other Upton proposals. Yet Congress defeated a bill incorporating these suggestions. Discouraged by his professional failures and suffering from violent headaches (for which doctors could find neither a cause nor a cure), Upton committed suicide in 1881. Many officers, realizing that the United States would not soon change its command and manpower policies, viewed the future pessimistically. But some began searching for sounder policy alternatives that would strengthen the Army without Germanizing it.

While the army had Sherman and Upton, the Navy had Luce and Mahan. Encouraged by Sherman and Upton, Luce was the foremost proponent of naval education and the driving force behind the formation of the United States Naval Institute in 1873. Analogous to the Army's Military Service Institution, the Naval Institute began publishing its *Proceedings* on a regular basis in 1879. But Luce's greatest achievement was persuading Secretary of the Navy William E. Chandler to begin the Naval War College at Newport, Rhode Island, in 1884. "No less a task is proposed," wrote Luce, who was the college's first president, "than to apply modern scientific methods to the study and raise naval warfare from the empirical stage to the dignity of a science." Since the Navy had no authoritative treatise on naval warfare fought under steam power, he proposed to discover the requisite principles through a comparative approach. By studying the conduct of warfare on land, he believed that naval officers could establish parallel principles for sea warfare. Realizing that the key faculty member would be the lecturer on naval history, Luce looked "for that master mind" who would do for naval science "what Jomini has done for military science." As he later wrote, "He appeared in the person of Captain A.T. Mahan, U.S.N."

Nothing in his previous career foretold greatness for Mahan. The son of West Point's Dennis H. Mahan, he attended the Naval Academy against his father's wishes, graduating in 1859. During the following years of uneventful service, he developed a hatred of the sea and maneuvered for shore duty whenever possible. He hoped to win renown through intellectual performance, and in 1883 he published a competent study of the Civil War Navy. Accepting Luce's offer to teach at the Naval War College, he spent the winter of 1885–1886 preparing his lectures. Published in 1890 as *The Influence of Sea Power upon History, 1660–1783,* the lectures established his reputation as the world's foremost naval historian.

The book, supplemented by Mahan's article titled "The United States Looking Outward" that also appeared in 1890, set forth a philosophy of sea power linking national greatness, prosperity, and commerce to imperialism and navalism. From his research Mahan concluded that England became a great nation by controlling the seas and the commerce they bore. Britain could attack an enemy's colonies, blockade its ports, and choke off its trade routes. Enumerating six elements of sea power based primarily on England's experience, Mahan emphasized the applicability of these factors to the U.S. and concluded that it possessed the ingredients to become a world sea power.

To achieve greatness, the United States must abandon its "continentalist" policy in favor of more aggressive competition for world trade, which required a strong merchant marine, colonies, and a big navy. The merchant marine would carry foreign trade and serve "as the nursery of naval attitudes," while colonies provided raw materials, markets, and naval bases. Mahan especially wanted to annex Hawaii as a bridge to Asia and to control any future Central American canal, which would be a funnel for world trade and inevitably attract Europeans bent on defiling the Monroe Doctrine. An avowed missionary for Manifest Destiny, Mahan also perceived colonies as toeholds for extending Western civilization. A powerful navy would protect the merchant marine and colonies, but not by the traditional *guerre de course*. Mahan considered it useless as a primary strategy, since history "taught" him that commerce raiding never won a war. A navy's purpose was to gain "command of the sea" by defeating the enemy fleet in a decisive battle. Only battleships, not cruisers and destroyers, could fight such battles. A concentrated battleship fleet was "the arm of offensive power, which alone enables a country to extend its influence outward."

Mahan preached a gospel of armed aggressiveness that won him world acclaim (and healthy royalties). His writings took England by storm. He received honorary degrees from Oxford and Cambridge, dined with the First Sea Lord of the Admiralty, and was the first foreigner ever entertained at the Royal Navy Club. Germany's Kaiser tried to learn Mahan's book by heart and ordered translations put aboard every ship in the Imperial fleet. In Japan the Emperor, government leaders, and the officer corps received copies. In the United States Navy his writings became holy writ, sanctifying its requests for more and better ships. Mahan's main purpose in writing *The Influence* was to provide a rationale for naval expansion, and he succeeded admirably.

Like Upton, Mahan achieved fame even though his ideas were not novel and his arguments contained weaknesses. Numerous officers and informed civilians had understood the sea power concept before Mahan put pen to paper. During the late 1870s and 1880s, Porter, Schufeldt, Luce, and many other officers expressed Mahanian ideas, as did expansionist civilians such as Tracy. Mahan merely codified the big-navy philosophy of his age, but he had the advantages of writing eloquently and at the moment when imperialism and navalism were in full flower. Mahan also used history as badly as Upton and drew a false analogy between the U.S. and a European country. Relying on the Royal Navy's example, he believed that a similar American navy would yield comparable diplomatic and military benefits. However, Mahan was careless with his facts, studied a unique era when no rival navy matched England's, and only paid lip service to Britain's geographic position and fortuitous control of crucial narrow seas. He never really understood that America was a continent not an island, that the Atlantic was not the Channel, and that the Caribbean was not the Mediterranean. Intellectually rooted in the age of sail and convinced that the principles of strategy did not change despite evolving technology, Mahan ignored technological developments, such as submarines, self-propelled torpedoes, floating mines, airplanes, and expanding networks of railroads and all-weather roads, all of which in part modified his battleship/command-of-the-sea thesis. Although some of these innovations were not evident in 1890, most were by Mahan's death in 1914. Immensely influential yet doctrinally conservative, Mahan hastened the building of a battleship navy designed to fight decisive battles for "command of the sea."

Along with the growing sophistication of military education, another professional triumph for the reformers was the creation of embryonic intelligence organizations. In 1882 the Navy Department established the Office of Naval Intelligence (ONI), and in 1885 the War Department formed a similar organization, eventually known as the Military Information Division (MID). These groups served almost as European-style general staffs, creating at least a rudimentary foundation for rational planning. Through Washington-based staffs and attachés assigned to America's principal embassies, ONI and MID gathered data about foreign military affairs, began to prepare war mobilization plans, and disseminated maps, charts, and specialized military reports. Predictably, a rivalry developed between ONI and MID. When ONI's chief discovered an Army intelligence officer borrowing a report, he was incensed. "Such an incident as this served to make me doubly cautious," he wrote, "especially in dealing with these army people, who in matters of tact or discretion seem to me to be a lower order of intellect than the mule." In spite of the bickering, ONI and MID were vital steps toward the professional's foremost objective, the preparation for war in time of peace.

Armed forces progressives had mixed success in reforming their personnel, reserve forces, and command systems. Since conditions for enlisted men had not improved since before the Civil War, few well-adjusted, native-born Americans enlisted, and the services included many criminals, outcasts, and foreigners. At times more than 50 percent of the men in both services were foreign-born, though some were naturalized citizens. For relief, enlisted personnel resorted to "watered whiskey and wayward women," suicide, and especially desertion. At times the Army's desertion rate climbed as high as 33 percent. The Navy averaged 1,000 desertions a year out of an authorized strength of 8,000, which made its manpower problems acute since naval modernization required more men.

By the late nineteenth century authorities were so concerned about the large number of foreigners in the Army and the high desertion rate that they made a conscious effort to Americanize the Army and improve the living conditions of enlisted men. The adjutant general ordered recruiters into rural areas to reduce the proportion of enlistees from northern cities with large immigrant populations, which were the Army's traditional recruiting grounds. And Congress passed a law declaring that enlistees must be citizens (or have made a legal declaration of their intent to become citizens) and know how to read, write, and speak English. Moreover, reformers in both services maintained that tolerable treatment of enlisted personnel would attract better men and reduce the desertion rate. They proposed a number of improvements, such as better food, clothing, and living quarters, higher pay, greater promotion opportunities, and an equitable legal system. But progress was slow and uneven, hampered by public apathy, congressional economy, and opposition from conservative officers who believed these changes ruined discipline.

Personnel reform extended to the officer corps, where reformers also achieved modest progress. One demand was for promotion on ability rather than seniority. To determine ability, reformers suggested rigorous examinations and annual fitness reports. Although conservatives argued that politics and social influence would pervert selective promotion, in 1890 the Army required examinations for officers below the rank of major, and in the mid-1890s it instituted efficiency reports for all officers. In 1899 the Navy acquired a rudimentary system of promotion by merit that allowed for the "selecting out" of ineffective officers reaching the grade of captain. Neither service's promotion system worked very effectively, but the systems established the principle of selection by merit. Reformers also wanted a compulsory retirement system, on the assumption that aged officers lost their initiative and energy. Older officers disagreed, but in 1882 Congress enacted mandatory retirement at age sixty-four.

One of the Army's most troublesome problems was whether a national reserve or the state-controlled National Guard would be its first line of support. Almost all regulars preferred an Upton-style national reserve, separate from the militias and under federal control. They wanted militias to perform auxiliary duties as short-term local defense units and to serve as manpower reservoirs for national forces. In the regulars' eyes the Guard was not battle-ready, and its mobilization would raise perplexing questions: Could federalized militias serve more than three months, and could they serve overseas? State authorities and National Guardsmen opposed a federal reserve, but Guardsmen disagreed on what their role was. Militiamen from the Atlantic coast and Canadian border states accepted the Army's definition of their function, since proximity to important ports and fortifications guaranteed them a vital local defense role. However, they were reluctant to serve for more than a few months and opposed overseas service. Guardsmen from inland states, whose homes would not be threatened, rejected the regulars' definition. Wanting recognition as the organized cadre of any wartime volunteer force, they were willing to undertake extended campaigns, even overseas. Despite their differences over the composition and control of reserve forces, regulars and Guardsmen moved toward closer cooperation. The Army loaned cannons and mortars to militia units, detailed officers to inspect National Guard encampments and assist in training, and occasionally participated in joint maneuvers. However, the basic issue of the Guard's military function remained unresolved.

The Navy faced a similar problem concerning the naval militia. Encouraged by the National Guard's example, in 1888 Massachusetts established the first naval militia, and by 1898 fifteen state militias had a combined strength of 4,215. Many professionals viewed the new organizations warily, preferring a national naval reserve. Since militias were under state control and had elected officers, the Navy could not ensure their quality. Officers also questioned whether technology had not made amateur sailors an anachronism and feared that the naval militia might distract attention from more important matters, like building battleships. Still, in the absence of a national reserve, militias provided a second-line force that might be useful for coastal defense. Federal and state forces began to cooperate, beginning in 1891 with an annual $25,000 appropriation for the "arming and equipping of the Naval Militia." The Navy loaned warships for militia training and conducted joint summer cruises, a few militia officers attended the Naval War College, and the Navy Department created an Office of Naval Militia. But as with the Guard, the fundamental question of the naval militia's role in national defense remained unanswered.

The progressives' biggest failure in the last third of the nineteenth century was their inability to reform the military's command structure. The Army discarded the Civil War chief of staff and Army Board, leaving the prewar structure intact. At the top was the secretary, usually a civilian lacking military knowledge and burdened with routine detail. Below the secretary were the bureaus, each headed by an independent Army chief.

Although proficient and even progressive within their own individual areas of highly technical activity, the bureaus remained woefully deficient in overall planning and coordination. Standing somewhere in the organizational chart (no one knew exactly where) was the commanding general, whose authority was uncertain. Having achieved his position through seniority, he and the secretary were often incompatible. These three disconnected power centers spent much time in bureaucratic conflict at the expense of coordinated effort, the strife manifesting itself in the ongoing line-staff feud. The secretary received no united professional advice, and no agency had clear responsibility for studying problems of wartime high command and mobilization. The Navy Department lacked a position analogous to the commanding general, but the secretary and bureau chiefs managed to foster similar bureaucratic confusion.

Both services tried expedients to solve their command problems. When Sherman became commanding general, President Grant promised that he would be the Army's professional head and ordered all segments of the Army to report to Sherman. However, Grant soon rescinded the order when the bureau chiefs rebelled and Congress complained that subordinating the bureaus to the commanding general violated the law. When Schofield became commanding general in 1888, he solved the problem by relinquishing all pretense of commanding the Army. Realizing that Upton's call for military independence from civilian control was unacceptable, he served the secretary as a military adviser, or de facto chief of staff. Schofield's solution worked well, but his successor, Nelson A. Miles, refused to subordinate himself to anyone. His ambitions shattered the harmony of the Schofield years and revived the command muddle. Navy secretaries sought control over their bureaus by creating ad hoc boards. Usually formed for a specific purpose, the boards reported and then dissolved, leaving no permanent imprint.

By the 1890s progressive officers, usually from the line, unanimously wanted a general staff for each service and rotation between staff and line. The staffs would undertake planning and coordinating functions, while rotation would temper the line-staff imbroglio. But the reformers failed. Congress had scant interest in reform, bureau chiefs resisted, and conservative officers objected. Under the current system the United States had won its wars, so why change?

In 1897 the German General Staff published a survey of world military forces. Although it detailed such "powers" as Portugal and Montenegro, the study excluded the United States Army. The omission was logical; compared to European armies, the Americans' 28,000 officers and men did not represent an "army" in any operational sense of the word. Yet the Army was not somnolent. Its external appearance was little changed, but reformist officers had established the basis for a modern force. If Europeans could safely ignore the Army, the United States Navy was another matter. By 1898, with four first-class battleships (and five more building), two second-class battleships, two armored cruisers, and more than a dozen protected cruisers, the Navy was ascending toward European standards. Supported by the new seacoast emplacements, an expanding specialized industrial base, and the writings of Mahan, the Navy was on the brink of its debut as a world sea power.

NINE

The Birth of an American Empire, 1898–1902

O n the night of February 15, 1898, a Marine bugler played "Taps" aboard USS *Maine,* anchored in Havana's harbor since late January. Captain Charles D. Sigsbee, the ship's commander, finished writing a letter as the notes drifted off into the evening stillness. Just as he reached for an envelope, "a bursting, rending, and crashing roar of immense volume" rocked the ship, which trembled, listed to port, and settled into the mud. Out of 354 officers and men on board, 266 died in the explosion. What caused the disaster? No one knew for sure, but one thing was certain: The incident made war between the United States and Spain more likely.

Relations between the two countries had gradually deteriorated after the Cuban Revolution began in 1895. Commanded by Maximo Gomez, the revolutionary army relied on guerrilla warfare and devastation of the island's economy to expel the Spanish. Eventually, Gomez thought, either Spain would cede independence or the U.S. would intervene on the rebels' behalf. But Spain had no intention of granting independence to the last remnant of its New World empire and poured troops into the island. A "reconcentration" policy, initiated by Governor General Valeriano Weyler, involved herding the rural population into specified towns and areas while Spanish forces systematically devastated the countryside. Weyler hoped that the rebels, deprived of food, recruits, and timely information regarding enemy movements, would capitulate.

Americans watched the savage war with growing concern. Humanitarianism swelled for the Cubans' suffering, as thousands died under Weyler's reconcentration program. By disrupting trade with Cuba and threatening American investments there, the war touched not only Americans' hearts but also their pocketbooks. The U.S. proclaimed neutrality in the summer of 1895, but enforcing it was hard, and maintaining coastal patrols and prosecuting offenders was expensive. Moreover, American expansionists considered Cuba in a larger perspective. Stressing the virtues of world power, they were eager to intervene as a means of propelling the nation into an active international role.

Imperialist aspirations collided with President William McKinley's aversion to war and emphasis on domestic economic affairs. Having served in the Civil War, the president had seen enough death and destruction. With the country in a depression, he concentrated on tariff reform and maintaining a sound currency. Desiring a diplomatic solution, he refused to recognize Cuban belligerency or make preparations for possible intervention. Yet McKinley hinted that his patience was not inexhaustible and that Spain must end the suffering in the "near future." He was also an astute politician who valued public opinion, which became increasingly pro-intervention. Pressed by McKinley, in late 1897 Spain initiated reforms, suspending the reconcentration policy, granting amnesty to political prisoners, and adopting an autonomy plan that gave Cuba greater home rule but left Spanish sovereignty intact. But the rebels rejected the scheme, and the Spanish garrison in Havana rioted in protest against it. The war continued, with neither side able to win.

Events in early 1898 drove Spain and the U.S. to war. On February 9 a stolen letter from the Spanish minister in Washington appeared in the press. It contained insulting comments about McKinley and revealed that Spain was not serious about its reformist policy. A week later *Maine* sank. Although an accidental internal explosion probably destroyed the ship, many Americans blamed Spain for the disaster, an impression heightened when a naval board of inquiry—hardly an objective group of inquisitors— concluded that a submarine mine had caused the ship's forward magazines to explode. Just prior to the board's report, Senator Redfield Proctor recounted his impressions from a recent tour of Cuba, detailing the human tragedy with dispassionate yet compelling language. Vividly described in the press, these events created a "sort of bellicose fury" among the public, which demanded intervention.

Ultimately responsive to public opinion, in late March McKinley informed Spain that it must grant Cuban independence. Confronted with this ultimatum, Spain stalled for time, hoping to avoid a crisis by indefinitely delaying it and trying (unsuccessfully) to mobilize European support to deter American intervention. Spain also made further concessions, declaring an armistice on April 10. But it would not concede independence. On April 11 McKinley asked Congress for authority to intervene to stop the misery and death, protect American lives and property in Cuba, curtail the damage to commerce, and end the onerous task of enforcing neutrality. Congress responded with a joint resolution that called for independence, immediate Spanish withdrawal, and, if necessary, use of armed force to attain these goals. The Teller Amendment to the resolution disclaimed any intention of annexing Cuba. On April 23 Spain declared war, as did the United States two days later.

Mobilizing for War

Although he went to war reluctantly, McKinley was a strong commander in chief. He controlled strategy and diplomacy through a White House "war room" replete with large-scale maps studded with colored flags showing the location of troops and ships, telephones linking McKinley to cabinet officers and Congress, and telegraphic hookups giving him rapid overseas communications. The president devised an appropriate, limited-war strategy that effectively utilized force to further the nation's limited political objective of compelling Spain to grant Cuban independence. He pursued a peripheral strategy, directing attacks against Spain's colonies, hoping that many small victories, even if far from the enemy homeland, would have a cumulative effect. The president also served as liaison man between the Army and Navy and became involved in the details of Army operations. Understanding that overseas operations required joint planning, Secretary of War Russell A. Alger and Secretary of the Navy John D. Long organized an Army-Navy Board, composed of one officer from each service. However, the board was ineffectual, leaving McKinley as the interservice mediator.

The personalities of Alger and Commanding General Miles exacerbated the inherent difficulties in the command structure. Affable yet egotistical, Alger knew little about modern warfare, while Miles's vanity, political ambitions, and desire to control Army operations made him ill-suited for his position. Alger and Miles quarreled incessantly, and McKinley learned to distrust them. For professional advice, the president initially turned to Schofield, who had retired in 1895, but increasingly relied on Adjutant General Henry C. Corbin. Discreet and committed to civilian control, Corbin became the president's de facto chief of staff, assisting him with decisions that Alger and Miles should have made but did not.

Spain was poorly prepared for war, both militarily and psychologically. It had a large army, with 150,000 regulars in Cuba, 8,000 in Puerto Rico, 20,000 in the Philippines, and another 150,000 at home, but the figures were deceptive. Hard fighting against Cuban and Filipino revolutionaries, plus the debilitating effects of tropical diseases, had drained the colonial forces. The home army could not be deployed unless Spain controlled the seas, and its navy was small, in serious disrepair, and lacked trained crews. In the Atlantic, Spain kept part of its navy at Cadiz and assembled a squadron, commanded by Admiral Pascual de Cervera, at the Cape Verde Islands. Its destination was the Caribbean, but each of America's battleships was capable of single-handedly defeating the squadron. In the Philippines, Spain had another antique squadron, commanded by Admiral Patricio Montojo. Many Spanish statesmen and officers were pessimistic, knowing they had little chance to win. At best, they hoped for a gallant and resourceful defeat.

The initial strategic principle for United States military preparations was that the war would be mainly a naval conflict, with little Army activity. The Navy would destroy enemy squadrons and merchant shipping, and perhaps bombard or blockade Spanish cities and colonies. No one contemplated dispatching large expeditionary armies to invade Spain or to conquer its colonies, although almost everyone assumed that the Army would send small forces to aid the Cubans. The Army's paramount duty would probably be manning the coastal fortifications against possible enemy raids. The disposition of a $50 million military appropriation, approved by Congress on March 9, reflected strategic thinking: The Navy received three-fifths of the funds.

With their share of the appropriation, Long and Assistant Secretary of the Navy Theodore Roosevelt readied the naval forces. Orders went out for commanders to retain men whose enlistments were about to expire, and the Navy stockpiled ammunition and fuel. The Navy Department ordered the battleship *Oregon* from the Pacific coast to the Caribbean. Rear Admiral Horace Eban received orders to prepare for the mobilization of a "mosquito flotilla" (later called the Auxiliary Naval Force) manned by the naval militia, which provided 4,000 officers and men during the war. The Navy also purchased or chartered warships and suitable merchant vessels and pleasure boats. In late February, Roosevelt sent orders to the European and Asiatic Squadron commanders to prepare for war. Finally, in March Long established a three-man Naval War Board, which included Mahan, to give him strategic advice.

All of these preparations had a sharp focus, for beginning in the mid-1890s the Navy had developed war plans against Spain. At Luce's suggestion, the Naval War College began studying the strategic implications of a war with Spain, and in 1896 Lieutenant William W. Kimball completed a document titled "War with Spain." Although several subsequent plans materialized, the basic features of the Kimball plan remained intact. Kimball assumed that the war would be fought to achieve independence for

Cuba, that the U.S. did not contemplate major territorial acquisitions, and that command of the sea would determine the outcome. The main objective should be Spanish forces in and around Cuba, with attacks on the Philippines and Puerto Rico being secondary. Only if these assaults against the Spanish empire failed to achieve results would the Navy shift its attention to the Iberian peninsula. Kimball envisioned limited land operations only in the Caribbean, where the Army would assist Cuban rebels and perhaps attack Havana and occupy Puerto Rico. However, expeditionary forces would not be dispatched until the Navy had gained mastery in the Atlantic.

Acting in accordance with these plans, modified by public concern for coastal protection, Long and Roosevelt deployed the Navy in five squadrons. The Asiatic Squadron, commanded by George Dewey, was at Hong Kong poised to descend on the Philippines. A Northern Patrol Squadron guarded the waters between Maine and the Delaware capes, the Auxiliary Naval Force watched numerous ports, and a Flying Squadron, based at Hampton Roads under Winfield Scott Schley, provided additional protection for the east coast. The bulk of the North Atlantic Squadron was at Key West under the command of William T. Sampson. On April 23 Sampson began a blockade of Cuba, initially concentrating on Havana, other points on the northwest coast, and Cienfuegos on the south shore, in order to prevent Spain from resupplying and reinforcing its largest troop concentration on the island. Almost all naval leaders opposed the division of the Atlantic fleet, wanting it concentrated for blockade duty and to defeat a Spanish naval relief expedition in a decisive battle. As one officer complained, the fragmentation "was the badge of democracy, the sop to the quaking laymen whose knowledge of strategy derived solely from their terror of a sudden attack by Cervera."

Compared to the Navy's preparations, the Army's initial mobilization was chaotic. One problem was the diffusion of responsibility within the War Department. A second difficulty was that the Army lacked the money and streamlined procedures for advance preparations. The Army spent most of its share of the $50 million appropriation to improve the coastal fortifications. Only small amounts went to the Medical, Quartermaster, and Signal Departments. With their meager allotment, these departments began to stockpile supplies, but congressional regulations choked their activities in red tape. The Army's greatest handicap was the belief that it would need only about 100,000 men under professional command to serve as a compact striking force for its limited overseas missions. The War Department assumed that once the Navy controlled the Caribbean, it would send a small force to secure a Cuban beachhead and perhaps dispatch smaller forces to attack other Spanish possessions. If these measures did not secure peace, then the Army might attack Havana with 50,000 men.

To meet the contingencies, the Army had Representative John A.T. Hull introduce a bill in Congress. Intended as a permanent reform, the Hull bill proposed an expansible 104,000-man Army that would eliminate the need for state manpower. The National Guard would simply garrison coastal defenses and serve as a manpower pool. Eastern Guardsmen supported the measure, but unfortunately for the Army's hopes for a modest but orderly mobilization, inland Guardsmen protested. Joined by southern Democrats, Populists who feared the Army, and a few regular officers with technical objections to the legislation, they defeated the Hull bill. Bowing to this strong indication that any manpower legislation must fully utilize the Guard, the administration introduced a new bill to create a volunteer army. Passed on April 22, the law permitted the president to limit an initial call-up of volunteers to National Guard members, with state quotas based on population. McKinley could appoint all volunteer staff officers and general officers, but governors would appoint lesser officers. The law also forbade states from sending new regiments into federal service under a second call unless their existing units were at full strength. With their position secure, Guardsmen did not oppose an April 26 law establishing a 65,700-man regular Army. New recruits would augment existing units and serve only for the duration of the war. As usual, the regular Army could not compete against volunteer service and remained below authorized strength.

Despite the necessity of mobilizing state volunteer regiments, the Army achieved some success in establishing an Upton-styled federally controlled volunteer force. The April 22 law authorized 3,000 federal volunteers (three cavalry regiments). Subsequent legislation established a 3,500-man brigade of federal Volunteer Engineers, a 10,000-man force of Volunteer Infantry (ten regiments in all) with presumed immunity to tropical diseases and known as the "Immunes," and a Volunteer Signal Corps. The most famous of these federal volunteer units was the 1st United States Volunteer Cavalry, popularly known as the Rough Riders. Its commander was Colonel Leonard Wood, and its lieutenant colonel was Roosevelt, who resigned from the Navy Department. Combining the regulars and the state and federal volunteers, the Army contained 11,108 officers and 263,609 men when the war ended. All of the new troops were to be discharged upon the proclamation of peace, leaving just the 28,000-man prewar Army.

Manpower mobilization began before anyone had a clear idea of how many troops would actually be needed, and it was on a far larger scale than the War Department anticipated. Expecting McKinley to call out 60,000 Guardsmen, Army planners were shocked on April 23 when he called for 125,000! The president wanted to avoid Lincoln's mistake of mobilizing too few troops at the outset and hoped that the spectacle of an arming host might break Spain's will to resist. More important, the 125,000 figure was close to existing National Guard strength. Calling out fewer troops would alienate those Guardsmen unable to volunteer, dampening martial enthusiasm and courting political disaster. In late May, with most of the initial 125,000 men in the service, McKinley called for another 75,000 volunteers, 40,000 of whom were used to fill existing regiments.

Miles proposed that volunteers remain in state camps for prolonged training, but this was impractical. Too few regulars were available to supervise training at scattered locations, troops and officers needed practice in large-scale management and maneuver, and the War Department was anxious to avoid the "disturbing influences of home locality" that interrupted serious preparations. The War Department had already ordered the regular Army concentrated at Tampa and Camp Thomas at Chickamauga Park, Tennessee; and now as fast as volunteers could be sworn into federal service (as individuals, not as units, to bypass the constitutional uncertainty about overseas service), they moved to large camps. Many joined the regulars' encampments, while others moved to San Francisco, Key West, New Orleans, Mobile, and Camp Alger near Washington. As the Army concentrated, the War Department completed its command structure, organizing seven corps, each commanded by a major general. In June it created an eighth corps.

As in past wars, manpower mobilization preceded logistical mobilization. Combined with the magnitude of the call-up and the Guard's lack of readiness, the emphasis on men over material created difficulties for the supply bureaus. Assurances from state and Guard officials led federal authorities to believe Guardsmen would have basic drill and musketry skills and would be equipped by the states. But the states and Guard failed to fulfill their promises. On the average, one-third to one-half of the men in peacetime Guard units refused to enlist or failed their physical examinations. The Guard regiments filling the volunteer army contained many new recruits "who fancied they were soldiers because they could get across a level piece of ground without stepping on their own feet." Volunteers were also unequipped, streaming into the camps without basic items such as tents and mess kits. What equipment they had was broken or obsolete. Ill-prepared in almost every respect, save for typical volunteer enthusiasm, 125,000 men arrived within six weeks of McKinley's call.

The National Guard mobilization temporarily overwhelmed the Army's supply capacity. Confusion should not have been unexpected, since the bureaus were geared to supply only the small peacetime Army. Moreover, line officers and civilian policymakers had not consulted the chiefs regarding mobilization plans. In coping with the crisis, the bureaus encountered fundamental problems, none of them the War Department's fault. It took time for government arsenals and private industries to retool to manufacture large orders for specialized equipment. The number of regular staff officers was inadequate, and many newly appointed volunteer staff officers did not arrive at the camps until midsummer, requiring additional weeks to learn their jobs. Cumbersome procedures for making contracts and regulating funds, which Congress had designed to prevent peacetime fraud, inhibited the bureaus' wartime efforts. One crippling procedural difficulty was the bureaus' reliance on requisitions from unit commanders before forwarding supplies, which precipitated a flood of paperwork and caused interminable delays. Poor transportation facilities hindered distribution. Camps lacked adequate sidings, resulting in railroad traffic jams. A mid-1890s government economy drive had forced the Army to sell its six-mule wagons, which it now needed to move material in the sprawling camps. Finally, the bureaus' task of simultaneously preparing small expeditions and a large volunteer force was difficult, especially since policymakers gave them no guidance on which had priority.

The War Department struggled rather successfully to overcome the logistical problems. Alger met daily with the bureau chiefs to coordinate activities and pressed for freer spending and the suspension of restricting rules. The bureaus improvised, and when one expedient failed, they tried another. Everyone labored long hours, somehow getting done what needed to get done. Chaos yielded to order, system, and purpose as arsenals and industries geared up, new staff officers learned the ropes, red tape got snipped, and transportation snarls were disentangled. Within three months material mobilization caught up with manpower mobilization. Meanwhile, the War Department also launched expeditions on opposite sides of the globe. Considering the conditions prevailing in April and May, its achievement in equipping a quarter of a million men was remarkable. Unfortunately for Alger, the administration dispatched the expeditionary forces *before* the mobilization crisis had been resolved and *before* the improvements became apparent. Thus, to the press and public, which were caught up in the muckraking of the Progressive era, bungling and inefficiency seemed the War Department's hallmarks.

The Spanish-American War, 1898

George Dewey hoped to attend West Point, but no vacancy was available so he went to Annapolis. Neither Civil War service nor his postwar duties distinguished him from dozens of other officers. Although he idolized Farragut, four decades of naval life gave him no opportunity to emulate his hero. One thing Dewey did was to acquire powerful friends, such as Theodore Roosevelt and Senator Redfield Proctor. His political connections

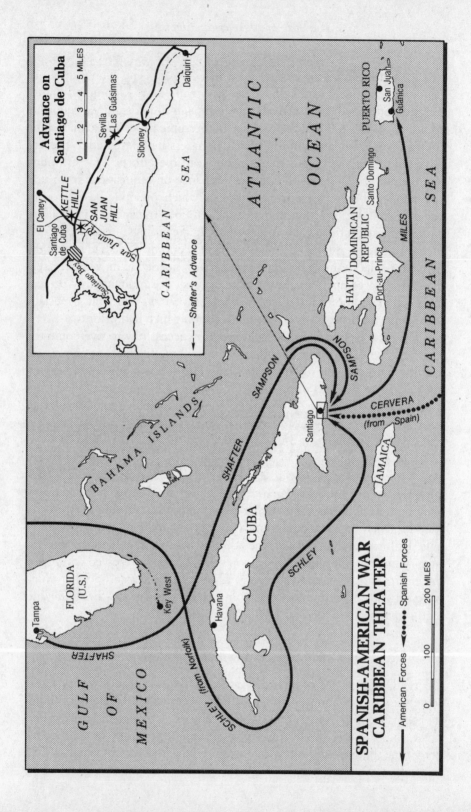

Advance on Santiago de Cuba

0 1 2 3 4 5 MILES

El Caney
Santiago de Cuba
KETTLE HILL
SAN JUAN HILL
San Juan R.
Santiago Bay
Sevilla
Las Guásimas
Siboney
Daiquiri

CARIBBEAN SEA

-- -- -- Shafter's Advance

ATLANTIC OCEAN

PUERTO RICO
San Juan
Guánica

DOMINICAN REPUBLIC
Santo Domingo
HAITI
Port-au-Prince

MILES

CARIBBEAN SEA

SAMPSON

SAMPSON

CERVERA
(from Spain)

Santiago

SHAFTER

BAHAMA ISLANDS

SCHLEY

JAMAICA

CUBA

Havana

Key West

SCHLEY (from Norfolk)

SHAFTER

Tampa

FLORIDA (U.S.)

GULF OF MEXICO

SPANISH-AMERICAN WAR CARIBBEAN THEATER

American Forces •••• Spanish Forces

0   100   200 MILES

gained him command of the Asiatic Squadron, which was at Hong Kong when Roosevelt's late-February message warned Dewey to prepare for war. On April 24, when McKinley sanctioned an attack on Manila, Dewey was ready.

With orders to destroy the Spanish fleet, Dewey entered Manila Bay before dawn on May 1. His squadron had far greater firepower than Montojo's ships, which lay at anchor off the Cavite naval base. Just as light was breaking, Dewey gave the order to fire, and in the next few hours the Asiatic Squadron demolished Spanish sea power in the Pacific with naval-review efficiency. The next day the Cavite garrison surrendered, but Spanish forces still held Manila and the rest of the Philippines. Naval power, said Dewey, could "reach no further ashore. For tenure of the land you must have the man with a rifle." Alerted to Dewey's predicament, the McKinley administration devised plans to send 5,000 volunteers to the Philippines.

Meanwhile, as a virtual hysteria of Dewey hero worship swept the country, strategic attention shifted from the Far East to the Caribbean, where, as in the Philippines, naval action prepared the way for Army operations. Gloomily expecting total destruction, on April 29 Cervera left the Cape Verde Islands, heading west. Thinking that Cervera would steam to San Juan, Sampson proceeded there with the bulk of his squadron. But the Spanish admiral, learning of Sampson's movements, went to Martinique and Curaçao before steaming to Santiago Bay. By June 1 Sampson's squadron, united with the Flying Squadron, had clamped a blockade on Santiago harbor. Although bottled up, Cervera's ships constituted a fleet-in-being that restrained other American land and sea operations for fear they might escape. With orders not to risk his armored vessels against land batteries, Sampson could not go in and attack Cervera: Spanish forts guarded the harbor mouth, and two lines of electrical mines blocked the channel, which was so tortuous that ships could enter it only in single file. Another option was to sink a ship in the channel so that the Spaniards could not come out. Sampson tried, but the effort failed. A third course of action was to rely on Army assistance, which the Navy requested. If troops captured the forts, the Navy could sweep up the mines and venture into the harbor. While awaiting the Army's arrival, the Navy maintained a tight blockade. To establish a nearby coaling base, Sampson sent a battalion of Marines to seize Guantanamo Bay. Aided by eighty Cuban insurgents, they captured it after four days of sporadic combat in mid-June, the first fighting by Americans on Cuban soil.

Before it received the Navy's request, the Army's strategic planning evolved through two stages. Initial strategy was to supply the Cubans and annoy the Spanish with small incursions. On April 29 the War Department ordered Major General William R. Shafter to Tampa, where he assumed command of the nearly all-regular 5th Corps. He was to organize a brief reconnaissance in force to the south side of Cuba, designed to carry arms and supplies to Gomez. This strategy avoided a large commitment during the rainy yellow fever season and did not make undue demands on the volunteer army. But Cervera's departure from the Cape Verdes forced cancellation of the reconnaissance, and in its second stage Army strategy focused on Cuba's north coast. With McKinley anxious to exert pressure on Spain, a White House conference on May 2 recommended attacking Havana with 50,000 men no later than mid-June, without regard for the rainy season. Shafter continued preparations for this new task. However, reacting to the Navy's need for assistance, another war council again modified Army strategy, deciding on May 26 to send the 5th Corps to Santiago.

The decision set off feverish activity at Tampa. Shafter assured Washington that "I will not delay a minute longer than absolutely necessary to get my command in condition," but readying the command was difficult. The obese Shafter, who looked like "a floating tent," had no experience in organizing a large force. The expedition's size depended on the number and capacity of transports, but the quartermaster general could not find many. The Navy had acquired most available auxiliary cruisers, shallow Cuban waters precluded use of deep-draft ships, and international law forbade the transfer of foreign vessels to American registry. The Army had to rely on small, run-down coastal steamers. Tampa had only two rail connections to the north and lacked storage facilities. Railroad cars were backed up as far as Columbia, South Carolina. Boxcars reaching Tampa arrived before the bills of lading, so no one knew what they contained, and the 5th Corps had too few staff officers to sort out the mess. Only one rail line ran from Tampa to the embarkation point at Port Tampa, creating an even narrower bottleneck.

His patience worn thin by the delays, on June 7 McKinley ordered Shafter "to sail at once with what force you have ready." The next day, after a disorganized scramble to get aboard ships, the expedition was nearly out to sea when an urgent War Department message stopped it. An erroneous report of two Spanish warships near Cuba caused the halt. For a week the Navy searched for the ghost ships while the soldiers remained on the transports, living in compartments "unpleasantly suggestive of the Black Hole of Calcutta." The convoy finally sailed on June 14. Although expected to number 25,000 men, the expedition contained just under 17,000 soldiers, dangerously overcrowded aboard the miserable transports. The troops consisted primarily of regulars, plus the Rough Riders and two volunteer regiments.

The disembarkation might have been a disaster without assistance from the Cubans and the Navy. After conferring with Sampson and Calixto Garcia, the insurgent commander in the area, on June 22–23 Shafter landed at Daiquiri and Siboney. Although still in reasonably good health, the Americans had spent nineteen days on the transports, sweltering in blue woolen uniforms and eating unappetizing travel rations. They were not in the best condition to fight their way ashore. Fortunately, the Navy provided small boats for the landings and naval gunfire support. Moreover, Miles had initiated contact with Garcia in early April, and by mid-June cooperation between Americans and Cubans was routine. Now Garcia's men and the Navy's guns drove the few and scattered defenders away from the landing beaches. The Cubans also besieged every major Spanish garrison in eastern Cuba, preventing the Spanish commander, Arsenio Linares, from reinforcing Santiago.

Shafter and Sampson held divergent views of the expedition's purpose. The naval commander saw it as a limited operation to capture the batteries at the harbor entrance. But Shafter's orders were discretionary, authorizing him to move against the forts or toward Santiago. The orders also specified two tasks for his command: capturing the Spanish garrison and assisting the Navy against Cervera, listed in that order. Reading between the lines, Shafter realized that the War Department expected a major land campaign, and he made Santiago his objective. Once ashore, he virtually ignored the Navy, striking obliquely inland along the road from Siboney to Santiago.

Three miles northwest of Siboney, 1,500 Spaniards occupied Las Guásimas, a strategic gap on the Santiago road. On June 24, Major General Joseph Wheeler, a former Confederate general now commanding Shafter's dismounted cavalry division, attacked the position with 1,000 men. After a sharp fight the Spanish "retreated"; unbeknownst to the Americans, Linares had previously ordered his men to withdraw. The skirmish had several important effects. The Americans assumed they had routed the foe, and their morale soared. Control of Las Guásimas allowed the Army to reach Sevilla, the only good camp site near Santiago. Finally, the skirmish opened the way to the main enemy position just east of the city.

After Las Guásimas, Shafter planned a delay to make preparations for a final assault, but an immediate attack became essential. On June 28 he learned that Spanish reinforcements had broken through a Cuban covering force and would soon reach Santiago. Shafter had to race not only against the arrival of enemy reinforcements but also against a collapse of his logistical "system." The entire 5th Corps relied on one lighter to move supplies from the transports to the beaches. Although food had priority, Shafter had difficulty stockpiling more than one day's supply. Many vital items, such as medical stores, remained aboard ship. If supply from the transports to the beaches was bad, supply from the beaches to the soldiers was worse. The road to Santiago was little more than a rutted trail. Hemmed in by the jungle, the path was barely wide enough for a single wagon and passed through deep ravines and across several unbridged streams. Streams flooded and the soil turned to mud when it rained, which it did often. Wagons got stuck and broke down, pack trains could not ford the swollen streams, and tropical diseases incapacitated teamsters and packers. Gaining access to Santiago's wharves to ease the logistical crisis reinforced Shafter's primary concern over enemy reinforcements, prompting him to attack sooner than he had planned.

The campaign's one hard day of fighting came on July 1, when Shafter's troops attacked El Caney, a hamlet to the northeast of Santiago, and the San Juan Heights, which rise along the Santiago road east of the city. Flanking the road were Kettle Hill to the north and San Juan Hill to the south. Although the enemy positions were within range of Sampson's naval guns, Shafter did not ask the admiral for fire support.

Shafter's attack plan unraveled from the start. Troops were slow getting into position, and some high-ranking commanders, including Shafter, were too ill to participate. El Caney's 500 defenders tied down more than 5,000 Americans for the entire day instead of the two hours Shafter expected. Planned to commence when El Caney fell, the attack on the heights began late and took place without assistance from the division engaged at El Caney. While deploying in the jungle terrain, the two divisions assigned to storm the heights endured a galling fire that caused many casualties and demoralized the troops. The movement up Kettle and San Juan Hills was no romantic charge, with streaming flags and cheering men. A few brave soldiers led the advance into the hailstorm of Mauser bullets, which went "chug" when they found flesh. Behind these stalwarts came two single lines of men, spreading out like a fan, who drove the badly outnumbered defenders from the heights.

"Another such victory as that of July 1," wrote correspondent Richard H. Davis, "and our troops must retreat." Davis expressed the belief of many officers and men that the Battles of El Caney and San Juan Heights had brought the 5th Corps to the edge of disaster. After the unopposed landings and success at Las Guásimas, Americans assumed the Spanish would not fight well. The battles of July 1 proved otherwise, as enemy troops, outnumbered more than ten to one, held back the Army's best corps for the better part of a day, inflicting 1,385 casualties. Among many others, the normally irrepressible Roosevelt, who led the Rough Riders up Kettle Hill, felt discouraged. "We have won so far at a heavy cost, but the Spaniards fight very hard and charging these entrenchments against modern rifles is terrible," he wrote. "We *must* have help—thousands of men, batteries, *and food* and ammunition." Even more dismaying, El Caney and San Juan Heights were mere outposts in advance of the main defensive position.

Believing the situation was desperate, Shafter telegraphed Washington that he was considering a withdrawal to a position where he could be supplied by railroad. Preoccupied with his difficulties, the 5th Corps commander overlooked his adversary's even worse condition. Coming on top of three years of warfare against the insurgents, the 600 Spanish casualties were a severe loss. Short of ammunition, food, and water, the Santiago garrison was near collapse. Shafter also failed to understand the implications of a retreat. Depending on a strong show of force, McKinley's peripheral strategy could not stand such a setback. Thus Shafter's retreat message created consternation in Washington. Although leaving the final decision to Shafter, his civilian superiors tried to stiffen the general's resolve, urging him to hold his position, promising reinforcements, and ordering Miles to Cuba should a change in command be necessary.

On July 3, the day Shafter sent his alarming telegram, the situation changed dramatically. First, convinced that Santiago was about to capitulate, the Cuban governor general ordered Cervera to make a sortie rather than surrender. Cervera's escape attempt surprised the blockading squadron, which was below full strength and under Schley's immediate command. One cruiser had taken Sampson to Siboney to confer with Shafter, and other ships were refueling at Guantanamo. Still, Schley's broadside was triple the weight of Cervera's, and the Americans easily destroyed the enemy squadron. The victory produced no hero comparable to Dewey. An acrimonious debate soon developed over whether Sampson, who commanded the squadron, or Schley, who was in tactical control during the battle, deserved paramount credit. The squabble tainted both their reputations.

One important result of Cervera's defeat was the Spanish government's recall of Admiral Manuel de la Camara's squadron. Spain had sent Camara toward the Philippines after Dewey's victory, creating a strategic dilemma of whether to save Dewey or maintain unchallenged superiority in the main theater of war. Including a battleship and an armored cruiser, Camara's force would be a stern challenge for the Asiatic Squadron. With all its battleships and armored cruisers committed in the Caribbean, the Navy Department ordered two powerfully armored monitors from the west coast to Manila, but strategists worried whether they could beat Camara to the Philippines. The department also organized the Eastern Squadron from Sampson's fleet to pursue Camara or, by attacking the Spanish coast, force his recall. However, dispatching the Eastern Squadron would weaken Sampson, perhaps allowing Cervera to escape. Fortunately, Cervera's defeat resolved the knotty problem. Recognizing that the

Battle of Santiago Bay freed the Eastern Squadron to sail without endangering Sampson, Spain recalled Camara. The Navy Department never sent the Eastern Squadron to European waters but held it in readiness, exerting pressure on Spain to come to an agreement.

July 3 was also important because even as Shafter contemplated retreat, he boldly demanded Santiago's surrender. General Jose Toral, who replaced the wounded Linares, refused but indicated an interest in further discussions. Buoyed by Cervera's defeat and the prospect of negotiations, Shafter wired Washington that he would not retreat. During the talks between Shafter and Toral, which went on for two weeks, the rivalry between Sampson and Shafter sank to the nadir. Shafter urged the Navy to attack the harbor entrance forts and steam into the bay, taking the Spanish garrison in the rear. Sampson would gladly oblige, if only the Army would capture the forts. Claiming he needed all his men for the siege, Shafter refused. Although the stalemate with Sampson continued, Shafter achieved a breakthrough with Toral, who formally capitulated on July 17. Since he surrendered *all* the troops under his command, not just those inside Santiago, Spanish resistance in eastern Cuba ended.

In his moment of glory, Shafter was petty. He allowed no naval officer to sign the capitulation document. In callous disregard of the Cubans' contribution, he did not permit them to participate in the surrender negotiations or ceremonies. Shafter's ungracious behavior marked the final stage in the deterioration of Cuban-American relations that began immediately after the landings. The Americans' prewar image of the Cuban army was that it fought in conventional style and contained many whites. But black men filled the ranks, kindling race prejudice, and without their rifles and cartridge belts the rebels "would have looked like a horde of dirty Cuban beggars and ragamuffins on the tramp." Forgetting the privation Cuban soldiers had endured, American soldiers considered them "human vultures" when they begged or stole food and other items. Yet without the Cubans, Shafter probably could not have taken Santiago. Not only were they valuable allies in an immediate sense—helping at Guantanamo, covering the landings, preventing or delaying the arrival of reinforcements, digging trenches, and acting as scouts and guides—but they had also severely weakened Spain before America entered the war.

The day after Toral's surrender, the War Department authorized Miles to launch his long-contemplated invasion of Puerto Rico. Departing on July 21, he landed at Guánica four days later and on August 9 launched a four-column offensive toward San Juan. Unlike Shafter's hastily dispatched expedition, Miles's had excellent logistical support and encountered little resistance. Events at Santiago sapped the enemy's will to resist, the Puerto Rican militia deserted in droves, and civilians cheerfully cooperated with

Miles. In six minor engagements the Americans suffered forty-one casualties before Miles received an August 12 telegram informing him that the U.S. and Spain had signed a peace protocol.

The peace message did not reach the Philippines in time to prevent a "battle" after the war was over. McKinley selected Major General Wesley Merritt to command the 5,000 volunteers that the administration planned to send to Manila. Merritt insisted that the expedition be enlarged and include regulars, and the War Department agreed, assigning him 20,000 men, including regulars. Designated the 8th Corps, the expedition assembled at San Francisco and deployed to Manila with little confusion. A more skilled administrator than Shafter, Merritt also had the advantage of time to prepare methodically and benefited from a more complete logistical mobilization. The general's first contingent departed on May 25, captured Guam in the Spanish-held Marianas on the way, and arrived at Cavite on June 30. Another contingent left on June 15, a third later that month, and two more in July.

Merritt departed without a clear understanding of his purpose and entered into a confused political and military situation created by the presence of a Filipino army. "I do not yet know whether it is your desire," Merritt wrote to McKinley, "to subdue and hold all of the Spanish territory in the islands, or merely seize and hold the capital." The president's formal instructions did not clarify the matter, although they implied an extensive campaign. The Filipino army resulted from a revolution against Spain, similar to the Cuban insurrection, that began in 1896. The Spanish had forced the revolutionary leader, Emilio Aguinaldo, into exile, but with the encouragement of Dewey and American consuls at Hong Kong and Singapore, he returned. Reorganizing his army, he soon controlled most of the Philippines, besieged Manila, issued a declaration of independence, and established an American-style Philippine Republic—all before American troops arrived. Dewey and Merritt had instructions to avoid entangling alliances with the insurgents "that would incur our liability to maintain their cause in the future." Aguinaldo initially viewed the Americans as friends, but he became suspicious that the U.S. might annex the islands when soldiers arrived and officials refused to recognize his government.

The "Battle" of Manila exacerbated tensions between Americans and Filipinos. Knowing the futility of resistance, Governor General Don Fermin Jáudenes negotiated with Dewey and Merritt to surrender Manila after a mock battle that would save Jáudenes's reputation and Spain's honor. His troops would defend only the outer line of trenches and blockhouses, not the inner citadel, and would not use their heavy guns. In return the Americans agreed not to blast Manila with naval gunfire and to keep the Filipinos out of the city, for Jáudenes feared they might retaliate for past

Spanish atrocities. After this collusion with an enemy against a presumed friend, the play unfolded pretty much according to the script. Some fighting occurred along the outer defenses, but the Spanish caused less trouble than the betrayed insurgents. Serious conflict threatened when Filipinos spontaneously joined in the attack and occupied several suburbs. However, both sides wanted to avoid an open break, and at the end of the day Americans controlled most of the city. But they faced outward, surrounded by angry Filipinos demanding joint occupation. Hostile Americans and Filipinos still glared at each other on August 16 when word arrived that the war had ended four days earlier.

Aftermath of the "Splendid Little War"

As prewar strategists predicted, the war at sea was decisive. When Spain signed the August 12 protocol its main garrisons at San Juan, Havana, and Manila were intact, but with the losses at Manila Bay and Santiago Bay they could no longer be maintained. Under the protocol's terms, hostilities ended, Spain granted Cuban independence and ceded Puerto Rico and Guam, and the combatants agreed to decide the Philippines' fate at a postwar peace conference, which began at Paris on October 1. The United States had many options regarding the islands: Grant independence, return them to Spain, acquire only a naval base, annex only Luzon, establish some form of protectorate, or annex the entire archipelago. For moral, economic, political, and military reasons, McKinley decided on complete annexation, and by the Treaty of Paris of December 10, 1898, Spain ceded the Philippines.

The decision to annex the Philippines touched off a wave of protest, spearheaded by the Anti-Imperialist League. Most anti-imperialists were not against expansion, favoring acquisitions within the Western Hemisphere and the retention of naval bases elsewhere. But the annexation of a distant, sprawling archipelago inhabited by diverse and alien peoples aroused their opposition, for it represented a clear break with past policies. The U.S. had never acquired territory that could not be eventually admitted as states, and if it meddled in the Far East, it could not reasonably forbid others from meddling in the Americas. Defending the colony would be difficult and costly, creating a large military establishment and leading to militarism abroad and despotism at home. A huge land grab tarnished the crusade to liberate Cuba. Despite these arguments, on February 6, 1899, the Senate consented to the treaty. Spain and the U.S. exchanged ratifications on April 11, 1899.

"No war in history," exalted one American, "has accomplished so much in so short a time with so little loss." The United States acquired a colonial empire, annexing Puerto Rico, Guam, and the Philippines and establishing a limited protectorate over Cuba. During the imperial outburst, it also annexed Hawaii, Samoa, and Wake Island. A nation born more than a century earlier in a reaction to imperial domination had become an imperial power, joining the maelstrom of international politics. During the 1880s, Europeans spoke of six great powers (France, Germany, England, Russia, Austria-Hungary, Italy). They now added a seventh, computing the United States into balance-of-power combinations. A German cartoon expressed the new sentiment, showing Uncle Sam reaching out to encircle the globe, saying, "I can't quite reach around—but that may come later."

Yet for the Army it had been far from "a splendid little war," as Secretary of State John Hay called it. A storm of controversy caused by medical disasters in the 5th Corps and in the volunteer camps engulfed the War Department as the war ended. The death toll explained the calamity's magnitude: Out of 5,462 deaths in the armed services in 1898, only 379 resulted from combat. The 5th Corps' ordeal was severe. During the siege men lay in their tents, which were steaming mudholes during downpours and ovens when the sun blazed down, without adequate food. Exhausted and filthy, they were susceptible to disease even as the opening of Santiago Bay remedied their material deficiencies. Malaria, dysentery, and typhoid began their death march through the ranks. The Americans also greatly feared an outbreak of yellow fever, although doubts remain as to whether it actually afflicted any of the troops.

By late July almost a quarter of the men were sick, and so many died that Shafter suspended rifle volleys and bugle calls at burials for fear of undermining morale. On August 3, with the concurrence of his general officers and medical staff, Shafter finally alerted the War Department, writing that he commanded "an army of convalescents." The corps must be immediately transferred home, or it would perish. When the news leaked to the press, it further discredited the War Department, already under mounting criticism for its seeming ineptitude in preparing for war, threatened to undermine the peace negotiations then underway, and hastened the corps' withdrawal to Camp Wikoff at Montauk Point, New York. By August 25 the veterans had departed, replaced by volunteer regiments and "Immunes" who, as it turned out, were not immune.

The survivors arrived at Montauk "mere shadows of their former selves," with pale faces, sunken eyes, staggering gaits, and emaciated forms, many of them candidates for premature graves. They wobbled ashore into a welter of confusion. Alger had planned a reception camp *before* he received Shafter's August 3 report, and given enough time a fine facility would have awaited the troops. But the sudden emergency caught the camp with inadequate transportation and shortages of equipment, medical supplies, and laborers. As during the mobilization in April and May, the War Department's heroic efforts, plus the goodwill of private relief agencies, resulted in rapid improvements. However, the press and private citizens had flooded into the camp in its early weeks and spread tales of suffering, convincing citizens that the government had neglected the victors of Santiago.

Events in the volunteer camps reinforced the belief that the War Department had ill-used its soldiers. Most volunteers remained in camp for the duration, bored and homesick, engaging in endless military routine, enduring shortages of all types since overseas expeditions had supply priority, and wallowing in pervasive filth caused by their own carelessness and indiscipline. Under these conditions epidemic diseases swept the camps. In combating them, the Medical Department labored under crippling handicaps. It had little prestige or authority, low priority in terms of men and money, too few trained personnel, no power to enforce its recommendations (which were often excellent but ignored by the volunteers), and, like medical science as a whole, it did not know how the killer diseases were transmitted. Only when the crisis was at hand did the Army react, rushing doctors and supplies to the camps and ordering a massive redeployment that placed the men in healthful new camps where officers enforced strict cleanliness. The improvements, plus the onset of winter, rapidly dropped the disease mortality rate, but the public did not easily forget the sight of hundreds of men dying on home soil.

Demobilization and an investigation of the War Department's alleged mismanagement began almost simultaneously. In October Shafter formally disbanded the 5th Corps, and in May 1899 the last of the original seven corps was demobilized. Spurred by the outcry caused by the Army's chaotic mobilization and the tragedies in the 5th Corps and the volunteer camps, on September 26 McKinley appointed a commission, chaired by Grenville M. Dodge, to investigate Army administration. The commission questioned numerous witnesses, including Alger, the bureau chiefs, officers of every grade, enlisted men, nurses, and concerned citizens. Miles was the most spectacular witness, charging that troops had been fed beef injected with harmful chemicals, causing much of the sickness. The commission thoroughly studied the "embalmed beef" issue and, when it reported on February 9, 1899, correctly pronounced Miles's accusations as false. When Miles persisted in his charges, McKinley appointed a military board of inquiry that came to the same conclusion.

The Dodge report also exonerated the War Department of charges of stupidity, deliberate negligence, and major corruption, drawing a picture of conscientious officers struggling "with earnestness and energy" to overcome problems primarily not of their own making. However, it did indict the department for excess paperwork and declared, in a tactful criticism of Alger, that "there was lacking in the general administration of the War Department . . . that complete grasp of the situation which was essential to the highest efficiency and discipline of the Army." Although Alger was not a strong secretary, and inefficiency and poor coordination dogged the war effort, the real causes of the War Department's difficulties were the hasty mobilization of too many men, primitive medical knowledge, and the country's long neglect of the Army.

Most citizens found the Dodge report's detailed analysis of staff organization and Army administration boring and did not want the facts to interfere with their perceptions. They were sure something was rotten in the War Department, and Alger became the scapegoat; "Algerism" became synonymous with government corruption and incompetence. Despite the public's lack of confidence in the secretary, McKinley owed Alger a moral debt, knowing that he had loyally followed orders and was taking the blame for decisions imposed upon him. McKinley also worried that firing Alger would be an admission of military mismanagement, which would reflect badly on his presidency. Not until Alger sided with an anti-administration senatorial candidate did McKinley ask for his resignation; on August 1, 1899, Elihu Root replaced him. The widespread sentiment that the war had been conducted unscientifically, the lack of interservice cooperation, and the new international responsibilities allowed Root to institute Army reforms.

Most of the overseas acquisitions posed few problems. The Navy Department governed Samoa, Guam, and Wake without difficulty. Puerto Rico remained under military government only until May 1900, when the first American civil governor assumed his duties, and Hawaii was quickly placed on the road to eventual statehood. But Cuba was different. The United States had never recognized the Cuban Republic. Now the question was whether it should grant independence, establish a protectorate, or annex the island despite the Teller Amendment, which imperialists argued had been a great mistake. While the nation wrestled with this problem, Cuba remained under military government, headed by Major General John R. Brooke until December 1899, when Wood succeeded him. Wood tried to Americanize the island, hoping to pave the way for eventual annexation. A man of great administrative talent and imbued with Progressive ideals, he did much to rebuild the devastated island and restore its economy, and he promoted reforms in education, municipal government, the legal system, and sanitation and health care. Although his emphasis on centralization and urban development ran counter to the Cubans' desire for more local autonomy and rural traditions, many of Wood's programs were of lasting value.

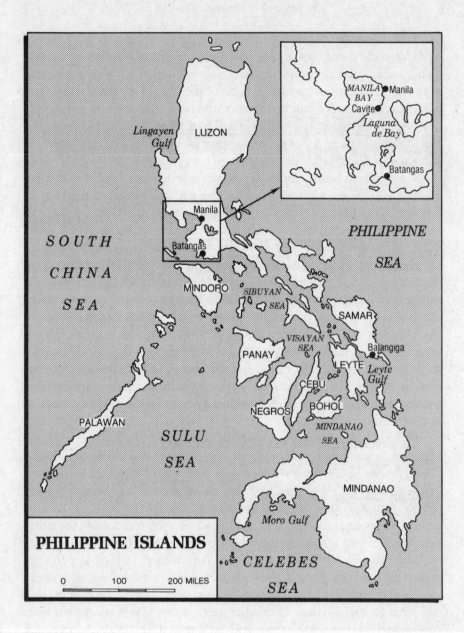

PHILIPPINE SEA

SOUTH
CHINA
SEA

MANILA
BAY
Cavite
Laguna
de Bay
Manila
Batangas

Lingayen
Gulf
LUZON

Manila

Batangas

MINDORO

SIBUYAN
SEA

SAMAR

Balangiga

VISAYAN
SEA

PANAY

LEYTE
Leyte
Gulf

CEBU

NEGROS
BOHOL

MINDANAO
SEA

PALAWAN

SULU

SEA

MINDANAO

Moro Gulf

CELEBES

SEA

PHILIPPINE ISLANDS

0   100   200 MILES

In May 1902 the United States recognized Cuban independence. Expansionists could not overcome the idealism expressed in the Teller Amendment or the fear that Cubans might rebel against annexation. However, the U.S. established a semiprotectorate and maintained de facto dominance through the Platt Amendment and the Reciprocal Trade Treaty of 1902. Incorporated into the Cuban constitution, the amendment was a compromise between altruism and annexation, allowing Cuban internal self-government while protecting America's special interests. It forbade Cuba to sign treaties that might infringe its independence, limited its capacity to get into debt, preserved America's right to intervene to maintain stability, and forced Cuba to sell or lease naval stations to the U.S. The trade treaty tied Cuba's principal export, sugar, to the American market, thus giving the United States considerable economic influence.

Cuba, however, was not the most troublesome of the overseas possessions, for in annexing the Philippines the United States annexed a war.

War in the Philippines, 1899–1902

"Is Government willing to use all means to make the natives submit to the authority of the United States?" Merritt and Dewey asked Washington as the Filipinos pressed for the joint occupation of Manila. McKinley replied that there must be no joint occupation, that the insurgents must recognize U.S. authority, and that Merritt could "use whatever means in your judgment are necessary to this end." The president realized that war was possible, although he sincerely wanted to avoid fighting the Filipinos. While awaiting the outcome of the Paris peace conference, the Filipinos also prepared for war. Merritt's successor, Elwell S. Otis, convinced the Filipinos to withdraw from the suburbs they had occupied, but Aguinaldo's men strengthened their besieging positions and their *sandatahan* (militia) inside Manila. In this festering situation the American troops began referring to Filipinos with derogatory terms, such as "niggers" and "gugus," and the number of violent incidents increased.

Since the United States was determined to exercise sovereignty and the Filipinos were equally determined to be independent, the Treaty of Paris created an impasse solvable only through war. Fighting began on the night of February 4–5, 1899, along the Manila perimeter. Aided by gunfire from Dewey's squadron and gunboats on the Pasig River, the next morning the Army attacked, driving the Filipinos from their trenches after several days of combat. Later in the month the Manila *sandatahan* rose in rebellion, but the Americans quashed it. In March and April, Otis launched attacks north and east from Manila, continually defeating the Filipinos. Aguinaldo favored guerrilla warfare but one of his generals, the European-educated Antonio Luna, persuaded him to fight in conventional style; this ill-suited the Filipinos, who lacked artillery and sufficient modern rifles. However, Otis's spring offensive achieved few permanent results before the rainy season began in May, halting large-scale campaigning.

As Otis waited for better weather he confronted severe problems. The Eighth Corps had an unprecedented task, for Americans had never before engaged in a colonial war of conquest. The Indian wars were not analogous: Indian resistance was always on a smaller scale, and the Army had the assistance of railroads, settlers, and buffalo hunters. Once defeated, Indians could be confined to reservations, but no Philippine reservation system was feasible. For pacification to succeed, the Army had not only to defeat Aguinaldo's army but also to make Filipinos *want* American rule or at least tolerate it peacefully. But the proper mix between coercion and benevolence was not easily discovered.

Another difficulty was that Otis underestimated Aguinaldo's support, the fierce resentment against Americans, and the Filipinos' fighting skills. Consequently, he sent Washington optimistic assessments that slowed the necessary troop buildup. After ratification of the Treaty of Paris most of his soldiers were eligible for discharge, and McKinley insisted they be returned home as soon as possible. Foreseeing this demobilization, the administration introduced a bill calling for a 100,000-man regular Army. On March 2, 1899, Congress passed a bill keeping the regular Army at 65,000 but authorizing the president to enlist 35,000 volunteers, organized into twenty-five regiments and recruited from the country at large, for the Philippine emergency. The volunteer enlistments expired July 1, 1901; on the same date the regular Army would shrink to 28,000.

In contrast to his actions during the war with Spain, McKinley wanted the force sent to the Philippines kept "within actual military needs." For immediate reinforcements he dispatched regular regiments. But since Otis claimed he needed only 30,000 men, which could be drawn entirely from regulars, the president delayed organizing the volunteers. Responding to an upward revision by Otis, in late June McKinley authorized the creation of twelve volunteer regiments, and another increased estimate from Otis soon prompted organization of the remainder. Largely due to his own misjudgment, Otis endured what Washington and Scott had experienced: exchanging one army for another in the face of the enemy. Fortunately, War Department procedures perfected during the war with Spain permitted the expeditious shipment of well-equipped volunteers; by February 1900 all of them were in the Philippines.

In November 1899, as the first volunteer regiments arrived, Otis attacked Aguinaldo's main army on the Luzon plains, shattered it, and drove Aguinaldo into northern Luzon's mountainous wilderness. Otis then sent a secondary thrust into Cavite Province and the Laguna de Bay region, which fragmented the Filipino forces there. As soldiers marched over Luzon from one end to the other and then occupied virtually every other island of consequence in the archipelago, Otis reported to Washington that "we no longer deal with organized insurrection, but brigandage."

While smashing the Filipinos' conventional forces the Army also instituted civic action programs similar to Wood's in Cuba. Wanting Filipinos to "bless the American republic," McKinley ordered the Army to prove "to them that the mission of the United States is one of benevolent assimilation, substituting the mild sway of justice and right for arbitrary rule." Recognizing the value of benevolence as a pacification technique, officers undertook the task with enthusiasm. Beginning in Manila and then fanning outward, they inaugurated reforms, especially in transportation, education, and public health, to convince the Filipinos that the Americans would raise their standard of living. New railroads, bridges, highways, and telegraph and telephone lines strengthened the economy and forged a new interdependence among the islands. Convinced that education "can be more beneficial than troops in preventing future revolutions," the Army created a school system, which reduced illiteracy. The military's public-health assault on disease virtually eliminated smallpox and the plague and reduced the infant mortality rate. Although conducted with an arrogant ethnocentrism and often interfering with local customs, these (and other) programs gained an increasing number of Filipino collaborators, reinforcing Otis's perception that the war was over.

But instead of being over, the war entered a new phase. With their army shattered, the Filipinos turned to guerrilla warfare to counter America's conventional firepower. Although they had used guerrilla tactics before, these now became the primary means of resistance. What Otis thought was the enemy's collapse was simply a reorganization into small units at the local level. Instead of a single nationalist struggle directed by one commander, Aguinaldo, the conflict became decentralized, a collection of local conflicts that varied from region to region depending on ethnic and religious differences, the terrain, and the revolutionary leadership's caliber. During this phase local guerrilla officers were much like Andrew Jackson during the War of 1812, acting like regional warlords who obeyed higher authorities only when it suited their region's needs. Most leaders came from the economic and political elite rather than the masses; many of the latter loathed Americans but also had scant enthusiasm for a war directed by the prewar Filipino upper class, which had demonstrated little interest in social justice or land redistribution.

In some cases guerrilla warfare merged with the traditional banditry that Filipino *ladrones* had perpetrated since time immemorial, the political "cause" of independence merely providing a cover for age-old practices. Indeed, many U.S. Army officers initially underestimated the guerrilla threat because they blamed the endemic violence wholly on *ladrones* and other social outcasts. Yet leading Filipinos such as Aguinaldo and Miguel Malvar, a high-ranking officer in Batangas Province, understood guerrilla-warfare techniques and strategy. They believed that a protracted war might result in two possible favorable outcomes. It might undermine the morale of the American Army and populace, leading to victory for the anti-imperialist Democratic Party in the presidential election of 1900. Filipino propagandists attached great importance to this eventuality. As one American officer noted, the insurgents watched American politics closely, and "every disloyal sentiment uttered by a man of prominence in the United States is repeatedly broadcast through the islands and greatly magnified." Or the Filipinos might receive foreign aid, perhaps from a European nation but more likely from Chinese republicans or Japanese pan-Asianists.

Guerrillas increasingly fought only when victory was certain, usually ambushing small patrols. When confronted by a superior force they hid their weapons and dispersed to their homes, where they greeted Americans with a friendly smile and a hearty *"Amigo!"* They also engaged in sniping and sabotage, inflicted hideous tortures on prisoners, and set trailway traps, such as pits filled with sharpened stakes. Soldiers learned that a "pacified" area extended no further than the range of a Krag-Jorgensen.

While their guerrilla operations nullified America's earlier military success, the insurgents employed terrorism to defeat what they called the enemy's "policy of attraction." Directed primarily against Filipinos holding positions in American-sponsored municipal governments, terrorism (the guerrillas called it "exemplary punishment on traitors to prevent the people of the towns from unworthily selling themselves for the gold of the invader") took many forms. Lucky "traitors" were fined or had their property destroyed; unlucky ones were hacked to death with bolos or buried alive. To mete out punishment and control the villagers, the insurgents established shadow governments in the *barrios.* Many officials who worked openly with the Americans for civic improvements also worked secretly for the insurgents, spying on their townsmen, collecting taxes, recruiting men, and supplying information. The system of terror and invisible governments was successful in many locales, where fewer and fewer people cooperated with the Americans.

The deteriorating situation provoked an ugly reaction among some American soldiers, who committed atrocities such as torturing prisoners. Official policy forbade these cruelties. But authorities argued, with some plausibility, that the very nature of guerrilla warfare led to excesses, and imperialists insisted that anti-imperialists exaggerated troop misconduct for political purposes; indeed, the number of verifiable atrocities was only fifty-seven. However, since soldiers do not publicize their illegal acts, the actual number of misdeeds was certainly higher.

By May 1900, when Arthur MacArthur succeeded Otis, the military situation had become frustrating. Although the Americans were not in immediate danger of losing the war, the guerrillas were holding their own and Filipino terror sapped much of the civic action program's appeal. Furthermore, although MacArthur needed more troops, he was obliged to send men to China to help suppress the anti-Christian and antiforeign Boxer Rebellion. When the Boxers besieged the Legation Quarter in Peking, McKinley ordered U.S. forces to participate, for the first time, in an international relief expedition. He wanted to save the beleaguered Americans in the Legation Quarter and to protect national interests as expressed in the "Open Door" policy, which called for equal trade privileges in China for the major European powers, Japan, and the United States, as well as the maintenance of Chinese sovereignty. A small naval squadron assembled and the U.S. committed 10,000 men commanded by Adna R. Chaffee to the relief force, which included troops from several European nations, Russia, and Japan. Prior to the legations' mid-August relief, Secretary of War Root got 5,000 troops to China, and more were on the way. Some went directly from the U.S. and others from Cuba, but many came from MacArthur's command. When the crisis ended Root ordered those soldiers en route to China to proceed to Manila instead, and most of the men already in China eventually followed them.

Meanwhile the American position in the islands had deteriorated. Making matters ever more difficult, at least from MacArthur's perspective, was the arrival of the Taft Commission, headed by William Howard Taft. McKinley ordered the commission to establish civil government in the Philippines, and in September 1900 it began exercising legislative authority, while MacArthur exercised executive power. Since the president had failed to define the division of authority between MacArthur and Taft, jurisdictional squabbles soon arose.

Unlike Otis, MacArthur realistically assessed the war and devised an appropriate strategy that combined "a more rigid policy" toward guerrillas, greater efforts to protect the civilian population from insurgent terrorism, and continuing benevolence. In December 1900 he invoked General Orders No. 100. Issued during the Civil War, the orders had gained international acceptance as an ethical code for the conduct of warfare. War should be fought in conventional style between uniformed armies; guerrillas deserved little mercy, being subject to imprisonment, deportation, or execution. Although an army should respect the rights of civilians, two loopholes—"military necessity" and "retaliation"—allowed commanders to employ harsh measures against those who continued to resist. MacArthur also insisted on vigorous offensive action, and to carry it out his troop strength approached 70,000 by early 1901. Before the 1899 enlistments expired, Congress passed a bill in February 1901 increasing the regular Army to 100,000 men. For the second time a veteran volunteer force departed while a new force, this one of regulars, arrived. But close coordination between MacArthur and the War Department allowed the drawdown and buildup to occur simultaneously without hindering the war effort.

MacArthur also pursued an old Indian-fighting tactic by recruiting pro-American Filipinos, emphasized military intelligence, and called on the Navy for greater assistance. Otis had recruited a few Philippine scout companies but MacArthur expanded the program to compensate for the Americans' inadequate knowledge of local languages, customs, and terrain. As had many officers in the American west who had worked with Indian scouts, MacArthur turned to indigenous soldiers reluctantly. By June 1901 he had organized 5,400 scouts (plus 6,000 Filipino police who performed semimilitary duties), but the February 1901 Army Act had authorized more than double that number. The Army organized a Division of Military Information in Manila to collect and disseminate timely intelligence data. MacArthur asked the Navy to intensify its patrolling to sever the insurgents' interisland communications and the flow of arms from abroad.

While stressing more vigorous military measures, MacArthur realized that government based on force alone was not sufficient, that permanent pacification required the consent of the governed. Thus he continued the benevolent action program. To nurture pro-American sentiment, officials formed the Filipino Federal Party, which offered a political alternative to Aguinaldo's independence movement. Working closely with the Taft Commission, the new party organized village committees to combat the influence of the guerrillas' shadow governments and helped to pave the way for civil rule.

Between the fall of 1900 and the spring of 1901, the guerrillas suffered three stunning blows. In a spirited campaign in which anti-imperialists accused him of conducting an undeclared (and hence unconstitutional) war of "bare-faced, cynical conquest," McKinley won reelection against anti-imperialist William Jennings Bryan. His victory demoralized the guerrillas, who could no longer hope that America would soon withdraw. With carefully calculated timing, MacArthur then initiated his stiffer policy. Instead of releasing guerrilla leaders, the Americans deported, imprisoned, or executed them. In the field, Army patrols hounded insurgent bands, allowing them no rest or sanctuary and isolating them from their village bases, where larger and better-organized garrisons provided security. Finally, in March 1901 General Frederick Funston, leading a company of Filipino scouts, staged a daring raid that captured Aguinaldo. The next month Aguinaldo issued a proclamation accepting American sovereignty and calling on his compatriots to end resistance. Thousands of guerrillas began surrendering monthly, while others simply gave up the fight and went home. By summer only two sizable guerrilla units remained active, Malvar's in Batangas and Vicente Lukban's on Samar.

Capitalizing on the insurgent collapse, on July 1 McKinley transferred executive authority from the military governor to civil authority, designating Taft as the civil governor; legislative power remained with the commission, which now included three Filipinos. Concurrently, Chaffee replaced MacArthur as commanding general and continued to exercise control in the remaining unpacified areas. One of the civil government's first acts was to establish a Philippine Constabulary, officered by Americans but manned by Filipinos and separate from the Army's scouts and the municipal police. By January 1902 the constabulary had 3,000 enlisted men, who maintained order in pacified regions and allowed the Army to concentrate where guerrilla bands were still active.

The final pacification campaigns on Samar and in Batangas were brutal. The ghastly massacre of a U.S. infantry company at Balangiga, Samar, in September 1901 whipped Americans into a vengeful fury. Chaffee believed that "false humanitarianism" was responsible for the massacre; now, he said, if the troops followed his instructions "they will start a few cemeteries for *hombres* in Southern Samar." The commanding general gave the pacification task to Jacob H. Smith, known for good reason as "Hell Roarin' Jake." Smoke from burning villages and crops marked the progress of Smith's troops on the island. Meanwhile Chaffee ordered J. Franklin Bell to pacify Batangas. Believing that "it is an inevitable consequence of war that the innocent must generally suffer with the guilty," Bell rigidly enforced General Orders No. 100 and kept up to 4,000 troops scouring the province, fighting Malvar's men, destroying crops and livestock, and herding more than 300,000 civilians into concentration zones. "General Bell does not propose to starve these people as Weyler did the Cuban reconcentrados," editorialized a pro-administration newspaper, and imperialists echoed the theme. But one commander called the zones "suburbs of hell," and widespread suffering occurred in them as people lived without adequate food and shelter and thousands died of disease.

By April 1902, Lukban and Malvar had surrendered and Samar and Batangas had been pacified. These final campaigns were atypical of the pacification effort, which, like the Filipinos' guerrilla warfare, varied from place to place. While none were pretty, no previous regional pacification efforts rivaled this late-war ugliness.

However, persistent charges throughout the war that American troops had committed atrocities, reinforced by the Samar and Batangas episodes, provoked an anti-imperialist backlash and prompted Senator George F. Hoar to request a special investigating committee. The Republican majority persuaded him that the Senate's standing committee on the Philippines should undertake the investigation. Chaired by the imperialist Henry Cabot Lodge, who had faint patience with those who criticized American soldiers, the committee held sporadic hearings between January and June 1902. The committee ensured that friendly witnesses predominated, badgered hostile witnesses, barred the public, issued no final report, and allowed only pet reporters access to its findings. The hearings did expose some instances of American misconduct, as even friendly witnesses sometimes made damaging admissions, but Lodge was generally successful in limiting the investigation's scope in order to prevent a full-scale review of the administration's war policy, and the antiwar furor quickly subsided. An era of romantic nationalism made sustained criticism of the nation's "duty" to spread civilization difficult, and most Americans had trouble remaining morally indignant about events seven thousand miles away involving a nonwhite race. People also found it difficult to criticize success, and on July 4, 1902, President Roosevelt proclaimed a successful end to the war.

The United States had crushed Aguinaldo's dream of an independent republic. The successful conquest resulted from a combination of strong military force and wise political action. As American soldiers soundly defeated the guerrillas, benevolence and the Federal Party won popular support. The Americans swiftly integrated the revolutionary leadership into the civil government, while the constabulary, assisted by the scouts and the greatly reduced American garrisons, maintained peace. But the cost had been high. The financial tab was $400 million, twenty times the price paid to Spain for the islands. More than 125,000 troops saw service, of whom approximately 4,200 died (approximately 1,000 of them in action) and another 2,900 were wounded. Approximately 20,000 Filipino soldiers also died.

Combatants were not the only ones who suffered. Civilians in certain regions, such as Batangas, endured a demographic catastrophe for which the war was only partly responsible. An outbreak of rinderpest (a disease that killed cattle and carabaos) not only reduced the number of agricultural workbeasts but also compelled malaria-carrying mosquitoes that preferred bovine-blood meals to bite humans instead. The workbeast shortage and wartime disruptions reduced rice production, so the people ate imported thiamine-deficient polished rice rather than nutritious home-grown varieties. Malnourishment weakened their immune systems, making the populace unusually susceptible to malaria and other potentially fatal diseases. Bell's concentration policy fueled the death rate, since microparasites were rapidly transmitted from one host to another in the overcrowded conditions.

Although most officers wholeheartedly embraced the war, a few questioned its justness and wisdom. One general referred to it as an "unholy war" and another believed that the United States had "ruthlessly suppressed in the Philippines an insurrection better justified than was our Revolution of glorious memory." Others feared that expansion weakened rather than strengthened American security, and the question of how to defend the islands baffled strategists for decades to come. Even Teddy Roosevelt soon perceived that the Philippines were America's "heel of Achilles."

TEN

Building the Military Forces
of a World Power,
1899–1917

With uncharacteristic restraint, Theodore Roosevelt assessed American military policy at the dawn of a new century: "I believe we intend to build up a good navy, but whether we build up even a respectable little army or not I do not know; and if we fail to do so, it may well be that a few years hence . . . we shall have to learn a bitter lesson. . . ." Even though he had more insight into world politics than most of his countrymen, Roosevelt could not have predicted in 1900 that in less than two decades the United States would be embroiled in a world war or even that the nation would enter that war with standing forces beyond the imagination of policymakers in the nineteenth century.

However inadequate those forces were, they represented a fundamental change in American policy. The shift in policy produced an essential dependence upon a standing battlefleet to protect the United States from foreign invasion and reduced dependence upon coastal defense artillery and fortifications, backed by military forces. It also increased dependence upon the Navy and the regular Army for military tasks beyond the continental United States. At the same time, the political elite gained increased confidence in the skill and political neutrality of the Army and Navy officer corps and became more willing to institutionalize military advice and accept military professionalism as compatible with civilian control. Both groups shared an interest in the reform of the militia as the nation's reserve force for land operations and the creation of federal reserve forces for both naval and military mobilization in case of a major war. They also urged the accelerated application of new technology to military operations, especially improved ordnance, the internal combustion engine, the airplane, and electronic communications. The reasons for increased American military preparedness in the early twentieth century can be reconstructed with some certainty. The nation's political elite feared that great power international competition (largely, but not completely, economic) had increased the likelihood of war. Imperial rivalries around the globe threatened to involve any number of major nations. Although such rivalries were hardly new, the introduction of efficient steam-powered warships and large passenger liners and merchant vessels made transoceanic military operations a possibility. In an era of rampant nationalism when "insults" to the flag, the destruction of private property, and physical assault upon foreign citizens could stir both elite and popular demands for punitive military action, small conflicts in Asia, Africa, and Latin America became more common and carried the seeds of larger wars. Imperial rivalries over the creation and protection of colonies offered similar perils.

The cornerstone of American military policy remained, however, the defense of the United States. Unlike their European contemporaries, American policymakers did not worry excessively about land invasions, since the United States enjoyed amicable relations with Great Britain, which meant that the Canadian border did not require more than routine policing. Mexico until 1910 was ruled by a friendly dictator, Porfirio Diaz; when his regime collapsed, so too did the Mexican armed forces. Even though the Mexican revolutionaries bore no love for the United States, they used their limited military forces against one another with few exceptions. Whatever major threats the United States faced had to come from the sea and from naval powers like Great Britain, Germany, and Japan. The worst threat (but least likely) was that a major power would launch a naval assault, perhaps accompanied by a limited land campaign, against a major American seaport city like San Francisco or New York and then hold the city for diplomatic advantage. The more likely threat was that a major power would penetrate the northern half of the Western Hemisphere, a fear traditionally expressed in the Monroe Doctrine. In specific geographic terms, American policymakers worried about the newly annexed Hawaiian Islands, the Isthmus of Panama, where they intended to build a canal, and the unstable nations of the Caribbean. They saw Alaska as relatively safe, since its weather and terrain made it unappealing to foreign powers searching for bases. Revolutionary Mexico drew more concern because various Mexican factions flirted with Germany as a source of military support against possible American intervention.

The defense of the continental United States, then, seemed to rest on the ability to mount immediate military operations to defend Hawaii, the Canal Zone, and Puerto Rico or to preempt any foreign power that attempted to establish a *new* military presence in places like the Virgin Islands, Cuba, Haiti, and the Dominican Republic. Entangled with issues of economic advantage, republican sentiment, and the belief in national self-determination, the policy of the United States toward nations of the hemisphere did not rest entirely upon military considerations. Nevertheless, it required military forces that did not depend upon mobilization and formal declarations of war. Therefore, the American government had to assume that military action beyond the nation's borders—whether those operations were limited or became the opening moves of a general war—would require larger and more effective regular forces. One of the primary concerns of American defense policy before World War I became the creation of a ready reserve force that could be sent beyond the nation's borders.

American military policy in the Far East had two challenges: The defense of the newly annexed Philippine Islands and support of the "Open Door" diplomacy designed to preserve the political and territorial integrity of China. In the face of European competition and the militancy of a modernizing Japan, the two concerns were linked. Although American policymakers viewed Russia, Great Britain, and Germany as diplomatic problems in Asia, they were most concerned with Japan, especially after the Japanese upset the balance of power by signing a mutual security treaty with Great Britain in 1902 and then defeated Russia in the war of 1904–1905. Adopting British and German military equipment and techniques but grafting these modern military capabilities upon modified *samurai* traditions, Japan defined its new international role as one of economic expansion in China and the liberation of Asia from European (and American) colonialism. The mistreatment of Japanese immigrants in the United States provided an additional irritant. The United States, on the other hand, viewed itself as the champion of an independent and reformed China. It also had no intention of surrendering the Philippines to another foreign power, Asian or not, particularly after making sizable financial, human, and emotional investments in governing the islands. American imperial impulses—a strange amalgam of humanitarianism and cultural arrogance—dictated that the future of China and the Philippines follow an American path.

The difficulty with backing the "Open Door" policy with military forces stationed in the Philippines and China was that the national stake in Asia did not seem worth the cost. At least, so it seemed to a substantial portion of Congress, the attentive public, and the officer corps of the Army and

Navy. Since the United States could not find a suitable way to divest itself of the Philippines or to sever its missionary and economic ties with China, it faced an unsolvable strategic problem: How could it extend its limited military forces-in-being across six thousand miles of ocean to defend interests its citizens probably regarded as insufficient to fight for? The "Philippine problem" was to distress military planners for decades to come.

The Rise of American Military Strength
1899–1917

Department of the Navy

	EXPENDITURES (IN MILLIONS)	STRENGTH NAVY	STRENGTH MARINE CORPS	MAJOR COMBATANT VESSELS*
1899	$64	16,354	3,142	36
1904	$102	32,158	7,584	29
1908	$118	42,322	9,236	62
1912	$135	51,357	9,696	64
1916	$153	60,376	10,601	77

War Department

	EXPENDITURES (IN MILLIONS)**	STRENGTH U.S. ARMY	STRENGTH NATIONAL GUARD
1899	$299	80,670	100,000 est.
1904	$165	70,387	115,937
1908	$175	76,942	111,000
1912	$184	92,121	121,852
1916	$183	108,399	132,194

*Battleships and cruisers with 6-inch or larger main batteries. Monitors not included.

**Civil projects by the Corps of Engineers included in the budget.

The United States probably would have had to readjust its military policies without the war with Spain in 1898 and the territorial annexations that accompanied the war, but the nation's imperial spasm dramatized both the utility of military force and the nation's relative unpreparedness to face any state more formidable than Spain. The defense of the Philippines and the Caribbean (and the projected canal) demanded that military reform come quickly. Certainly, the new possessions complicated defense planning and forced the pace of naval expansion and the emphasis on ready land forces. The result was two decades of accelerated military change.

Building a Great Power Navy

Halfway through the nation's two-decade drive toward "a Navy second to none," President Theodore Roosevelt in 1907–1909 sent the American "Great White Fleet" on a dramatic, globe-circling cruise. Although the voyage had some bearing upon America's disputes with Japan and the president's request for more battleships, the cruise had greater symbolic purposes. Although TR's sixteen battleships did not send up the appropriate signal flags, the message to the world could not have been clearer: The United States had come of age as a world naval power and viewed the battlefleet as the nation's first line of defense and primary military instrument of great power diplomacy.

Like its potential adversaries, the United States Navy was a battleship navy. By the outbreak of World War I, the American battlefleet, which had undergone both modernization and expansion, was superior to all other naval forces except the Royal Navy and the German High Seas Fleet. From a force of eleven battleships in 1898, the battleline of the U.S. fleet had increased to thirty-six vessels by 1913. With fluctuations tied to congressional perceptions of the available money and the international situation, American battleship building held a relatively steady course for almost twenty years. During Roosevelt's administration, Congress normally authorized at least two new battleships a year. It cut the program to one ship only once and often authorized as many as four (and once five) new vessels. During the presidencies of William Howard Taft and Woodrow Wilson the authorizations up to 1916 focused on replacing the older battleships at a rate of one or two a year, which stabilized battleship numbers but increased the fleet's capability.

Battleship construction in the same period reflected the quickening pace of technological progress, especially in the strength of armor plating, the fabrication of heavy naval guns, the destructiveness of explosives, and the power of marine engines. Battleships became larger, more lethal, and more expensive. In size American battleships began the century in the 10,000- to 15,000-ton range but reached 31,000 tons in 1914; their cost soared from $5 million to $15–20 million each. With larger bunker capacity (first for coal, then oil), their ranges became transoceanic. Their main batteries increased in numbers and caliber until the standard battleship mounted ten or twelve guns of 12 or 14 inches in diameter; the larger guns both increased the weight of a broadside and improved ranges from 6,000 to 20,000 yards. Since the technological improvements of the era were shared by all the naval powers, the American building program also shared the universal insecurity about obsolescence and relative effectiveness. This insecurity was fed in 1906 when Great Britain launched the first true all-big-gun capital ship, HMS *Dreadnought.* Demonstrating dramatic improvements in speed, firepower, and armoring, *Dreadnought* accelerated the naval arms race. Naval analysts divided the world's battlefleets into pre-*Dreadnought* and post-*Dreadnought* categories. The United States, which was already shifting to the all-big-gun ship in 1906, more than kept pace. In 1914 the American fleet boasted fourteen post-*Dreadnought* battleships.

The growth of the American battlefleet also demonstrated significant changes in the political and strategic foundations of American naval policy. The political coalition that supported the "new Navy" of the 1890s broadened and deepened in the federal government and the public. At the point of political attack strode Roosevelt (and, more reluctantly, Taft and Wilson), a coalition of internationalist Republican and Democratic senators and congressmen, industrialists with an economic stake in navalism, Navy officers, and several public interest groups, especially the Navy League, formed in 1903.

Of particular significance within the Navy Department was the institutionalization of professional advice from line officers, who were enthusiastic naval builders but also critics of many aspects of fleet modernization. Before 1898 and to some degree thereafter, such long-range planning as occurred came from officers assigned to the Naval War College, the Office of Naval Intelligence, and the Bureau of Navigation. In 1900 Secretary of the Navy John D. Long created a General Board of senior officers to consolidate professional advice, and the General Board became the central agency for coordinating war-planning and building programs. The General Board consistently requested more vessels than its civilian superiors would approve; between 1900 and 1914 it asked for 340 vessels but received only 181. In 1910–1913 it caused a public stir by setting American modern battleship strength at forty-eight, more ships than the government thought it needed or could afford. Presided over by Admiral George Dewey, the hero of Manila Bay, the board emerged as a force for fleet modernization and expansion.

To some Navy officers, collectively labeled the "Young Turks," the General Board did not provide sufficient line influence over Navy policy, and the period of naval expansion was accompanied by bitter arguments over Navy Department organization. On some issues there was consensus. The naval reformers, for example, agreed that sea power meant a battle-fleet-in-being, ready for a decisive ocean duel with its enemy. By 1907, the Navy had abandoned its traditional far-flung squadron deployments and concentrated most of its battleships in Atlantic waters. The only units deployed outside the hemisphere had old battleships, a few cruisers, and smaller vessels.

The Young Turks, led by such aggressive officers as Henry C. Taylor, A. O. Key, William S. Sims, William F. Fullam, Bradley Fiske, Ridley McLean, and Washington I. Chambers, lobbied for line-reformer influence. By 1915 the organizational reformers had made some limited progress in the face of civilian skepticism and Navy conservatism. In 1909 they scored a minor victory when Secretary of the Navy George von Lengerke Meyer created a group of "naval aids," staffed with Young Turks, to give advice, spur the General Board, and evaluate fleet readiness. Meyer's Democratic successor, Josephus Daniels, reluctantly approved the creation of the post of chief of naval operations to replace the aids in 1915, but he filled the job with a traditionalist admiral, William S. Benson. Nevertheless, the CNO's immediate staff continued to be a focal point for improved fleet efficiency and replaced a system of personal influence with bureaucratized policy advising.

The reformers' demand that the line officers who would command the fleet in war receive more power reflected concern about real problems. For all its dramatic appearance, the Great White Fleet was not as effective as it might have to be. The battleships themselves showed distressing technical deficiencies. Their armor was often placed too low on the hull, and turrets received too little protection. The vessels had too little freeboard, which meant that heavy seas made manning the lower turrets and aiming guns difficult. The turrets did not have effective baffles to keep burning debris from reaching the powder magazines below; catastrophic explosions in 1904 and 1906 on American battleships caused a clamor for naval reform and temporarily threatened TR's building program. Line officers were equally aware that the fleet lacked adequate numbers of sailors to man the new vessels. Despite a dramatic increase in the size of the Navy from 16,354 (1899) to 60,376 (1916), each ship normally lacked about 10 percent of its complement. The shortages were especially acute among petty officers and the skilled technicians needed to operate the new machinery. The recruiting service did not have enough manpower, money, or authority; the efforts of Secretary Daniels to sell the Navy as a great vocational education school and laboratory for social uplift did make recruiting somewhat easier. Naval planners also worried that the Navy did not have a "balanced" fleet for wartime operations. Although Congress would buy battleships, it would not fund adequate numbers of smaller vessels. By 1916 the General Board calculated the fleet was short 125 cruisers, destroyers, and auxiliary vessels.

The whole question of battlefleet support—especially the issue of bases—demonstrated the political limits to naval planning. In sum, the Navy had too many bases in the United States and too few bases abroad, measured by the projected war plans. Traditionally, a major naval base had the necessary dry docks, machinery, and workshops needed to overhaul a battleship completely. By such criteria, the United States had ten major continental bases before World War I, while the much larger Royal Navy had only six. Navy planners knew that American facilities were excessive, but Congress regarded base building and manning as attractive patronage. New bases at Charleston and Bremerton, Washington, supplemented by smaller facilities at San Pedro and San Diego, California, gave the Navy more than enough shore support by 1916. The continental base structure was dramatically enhanced in 1914 when the Panama Canal opened, since the canal cut transit time from coast to coast by two-thirds.

The Navy's search for bases abroad was frustrated by the State Department, which thought base building bad diplomacy, and Congress, which thought base building bad spending. Although the Navy sought a base in China, the diplomats ruled that this policy did not conform to the Open Door and stopped the movement. Interservice disputes stopped plans to build a major base in the Philippines. The Navy chose Subic Bay on the west coast of Luzon as its preferred site. The Army reported that it could not defend the base from a land attack; Subic Bay would be another Port Arthur, the "impregnable" Russian port in Manchuria that had fallen to the Japanese army in 1905. The Navy rejected the Army's choice, Cavite peninsula in Manila Bay, since the old Spanish base had neither adequate base facilities nor anchorages for the fleet. Although the Navy eventually maintained facilities at both Subic and Cavite, it agreed in 1909 to build its major Pacific base at Pearl Harbor, Oahu, Hawaii. This decision did not immediately loosen congressional purse strings, and it further limited the Navy's enthusiasm for defending the Philippines.

Since the Caribbean was close enough to the Navy's Atlantic coast yards to make major bases unnecessary, the Navy sought instead a system of operating bases and stations there that would support wartime operations against either Britain or Germany. It was only partially successful in enacting its plans. Although the United States had the rights to two bases in Cuba, it built only one at isolated Guantanamo Bay, since the diplomats vetoed as too provocative plans for another at Havana. Diplomatic considerations also stopped plans for a base in Haiti or Santo Domingo. The annexation of Puerto Rico in 1899 and the Virgin Islands in 1915 gave the United States uncontested access to base sites in the eastern Caribbean, but the harbor at San Juan, Puerto Rico, and the Virgin Islands' coves were not suitable for major fleet use.

Unable to secure forward bases in either the Pacific or the Caribbean, the Navy considered an alternative tactic, establishing temporary, or "advanced," bases in the early stages of a naval campaign. Although the Navy was not satisfied with the numbers or sizes of its auxiliaries (colliers and oilers, ammunition ships, supply vessels, transports, and floating tenders and machine shops), it thought it might find such vessels in wartime in the American merchant fleet. It could not, however, completely extemporize a force to defend a forward operating base. In 1900 the General Board turned to the Navy's sister service, the Marine Corps, and asked that the Corps reorganize and train for advanced base operations. Despite some modest experiments in emplacing harbor defenses, the Corps did not establish an Advanced Base Force until 1910, and it did not conduct major exercises until 1912. Marine traditionalism and the manpower and financial demands of garrisoning the increased number of naval stations abroad dampened Corps interest. The limited exercises and theoretical studies done by Navy and Marine officers, however, demonstrated the need for such a force. In theory, the Advanced Base Force would occupy an undefended harbor and then defend it from sea attack with stationary heavy guns and mines. Its mobile infantry and artillery would stop a land attack. The Navy would provide monitors, torpedo boats, and a few cruisers to assist the sea defenses. Convinced that the advanced base concept offered the Corps an important wartime role, a cadre of Marine officers became articulate spokesmen for improving the Navy's ability to establish forward operating bases, but the actual forces for such operations did not develop rapidly.

Elsewhere in the Navy, other officers and civilian innovators examined the potential of new technology to reshape naval operations. Two novel developments—the submarine and the airplane—suggested that future naval warfare might occur above and beneath the seas, not just between rival battlefleets dueling upon the ocean's surface. Although the first submarines appeared in experimental form in the late eighteenth century and the first successful submarine attack on a warship occurred in 1864 during the American Civil War, the Navy did not commission its first submarine until 1900. Naval conservatism in this case did not rest on a lack of mission, since the submarine (more properly, the "submersible") was an attractive weapon for close-to-shore coast defense. The difficulties were largely technological, primarily the development of adequate powerplants and torpedoes. The difficulty was that technological progress depended upon government funding, since submarines had no special commercial attractions. In the United States the submarine champion, the aging eccentric John R. Holland, took some twenty years and six models to prove that he had an answer to the propulsion problem. Essentially, Holland coupled the internal-combustion engine for surface cruising with battery-powered electric engines for submerged attacks. Attendant problems in designing pressure hulls and ventilation systems slowed adoption of the submarine; early crews seemed to have little choice between carbon monoxide and chlorine gas asphyxiation. Submariners were constantly in fear of a break in their hull, which could submerge their vessel permanently. Nevertheless, the submarine remained a relatively cheap coastal defense weapon, and the Navy had thirty-four boats by 1914, twelve of them modern diesel-powered vessels of 500 to 700 tons, or five times larger than Holland's experimental boats. At the time, the United States was the world's fourth-strongest submarine power.

Although the Navy watched the often comical and futile efforts to fly with detachment, its interest increased after the Wright brothers' flight in 1903 and flowered in 1910 when Captain Washington I. Chambers and inventor Glenn Curtiss formed an effective coalition of naval aviation enthusiasts. In terms of mission, the aviation champions thought of airplanes as reconnaissance and naval gunfire scouting craft. Technically, this role meant that some method had to be found to fly an airplane off a ship and then recover it. In 1911 Congress gave the Navy $25,000 for its first three experimental planes after a civilian test pilot successfully flew a Curtiss aircraft off a warship the year before. With pontoons and a hoist, an airplane could also be recovered. Nevertheless, the "hydroaeroplane" force developed slowly because aircraft themselves were expensive, and the development of a force of pilots, bases, and supporting establishment suggested costs that naval planners and Congress were not willing to pay. Part of their reluctance stemmed from the fact that the airplanes of the day did not have the power to drop bombs that would sink a warship. Although experiments with the electric torpedo (used by both surface ships and submarines) suggested that an airplane might someday have an attack capability, aviation enthusiasts did not have much success in selling the airplane as the future ultimate weapon of naval warfare. Even though they proved that an airplane could land on a warship with the help of arresting gear, which suggested that heavy bomb carriers could be developed free of the seaplane-hoist mode, naval aviators could muster support only for an aviation force linked to the reconnaissance mission. On the eve of World War I the Navy had only eight aircraft and thirteen officer-pilots. In fact, public and official interest supported the use of dirigibles for naval aviation tasks. With the responsibility for aviation policy divided between several of the traditional technical bureaus, the future of Navy flying ranked well below other Navy Department concerns.

In 1915, however, the Navy's aviators and their civilian colleagues had made sufficient progress to win General Board and congressional support for a more ambitious commitment to naval aviation. Its interest heightened by the world war, Congress appropriated $1 million to create and support a force of fifty airplanes and three dirigibles. This program was still in its earliest stages when the U.S. Navy went to war in 1917.

The U.S. Navy between 1898 and 1917 increased its capability to engage the fleet of any other major power, but it could do so only if the decisive fleet action occurred north of the equator, close to the Navy's bases in the continental United States. The United States did not have the resources to conduct major wartime naval operations in the western Pacific, and its dominance in the Caribbean might be secure in peacetime but not, perhaps, in wartime. Holding the Panama Canal remained critical to operations in either ocean. In addition, the Navy retained its battleship orientation, since naval politics within the service and the federal government produced no other consensus. The fleet-in-being was not balanced for wartime needs and required augmentation with merchant vessels and wartime construction in order to provide sufficient numbers of cruisers, destroyers, submarines, and auxiliaries. Neither submarine nor aviation development had yet reached the point of challenging the great fleet engagement as the essence of naval warfare. While the Navy's line officers, whose principal interest was war preparedness, had gained some influence in the Navy Department, they did not yet dominate policymaking. The Navy of Manila Bay and Santiago had changed, but so had its potential adversaries and missions.

Reforming the Land Forces

Despite its victory in "the splendid little war" against Spain, the U.S. Army entered the new century conscious that its campaigns in 1898 were "within measurable distance of a military disaster," as Theodore Roosevelt characterized the siege of Santiago. For the public, the press, and much of the Army officer corps the war felt like a defeat, for it had revealed all the flaws of American land force policy and had dramatized the institutional weaknesses of the regular Army and the militia (or National Guard) of the states. Both major components of the wartime Army showed they had not made the transition from frontier constabulary and strike police. Nor had the War Department yet reorganized in order to make the wartime mobilization of citizen-volunteers more efficient. Although the War Department's failure, investigated by a special presidential commission headed by railroader and former general Grenville Dodge, seemed worse than it really was, most War Department officials and critics believed that some reform was necessary. Over the content of the reform movement there was continuous disagreement. Nevertheless, by 1917 the reform movement had worked fundamental changes in American land force policy.

Assisted by a close group of Army officer-advisers, Secretary of War Elihu Root (1899–1904) led the reform movement, which rallied sufficient congressional and Army supporters to give it momentum beyond Root's tenure. Upon taking office, Root accepted the key concept of military professionalism: "The real object of having an army is to provide for war." This axiom became the basic measure of land force reform. Giving this idea institutional expression proved far more difficult, for the American political tradition remained hostile to increased military preparedness and professionalism. An astute negotiator and corporation lawyer, Root knew and the Army was to learn that the sense of disaster was short-lived. Before the impetus for reform ebbed, only to be stimulated again by World War I, the reformers had scored several limited victories in the name of mobilization readiness.

Coached by Adjutant General Henry C. Corbin and Major William H. Carter, Root quickly learned that the War Department had to become a unified center of policy direction rather than three conflicting alliances based upon the office of the Secretary of War, the office of the commanding general, and the heads of the various administrative, technical, and logistical departments and bureaus. Until the War Department had a single "brain of the army," as British writer Spencer Wilkinson characterized a general staff, the planning for war and the direction of war when it came would continue to be plagued by poor coordination, jurisdictional battles, and inertia. In an ideal sense, the model for military management was the German *Grosse Generalstab,* or Great General Staff, which military analysts credited for the German victories in the wars of unification in the 1860s and 1870s. Such a staff, dominated by line officers, would advise the president and secretary of war, prepare Army legislation and policies, supervise the activities of the departments and bureaus, and direct training. Politically, however, a general staff conjured up visions of German militarism, regular Army arrogance, and executive branch tyranny.

Outflanking his opponents, Secretary Root advanced steadily toward a general staff until Congress accepted the organization in limited form in the General Staff Act of 1903. Aware that the general staff concept had powerful enemies within the Army, especially Lieutenant General Nelson A. Miles, the commanding general, and Brigadier General Fred C. Ainsworth, chief of the Record and Pension Office, Root moved with caution. First, he had a board of officers study the question of establishing an Army War College; the board's positive report was endorsed and the war college created in 1900. Root immediately assigned the war college faculty duties much like those of a general staff and used its officers to develop and advocate the general staff concept. Then, mustering support from Roosevelt, a prestigious group of Civil War generals, and reformist civilians, Root persuaded Congress to accept an Americanized version of the Great General Staff. The new law replaced the commanding general with a chief of staff, who would rotate in office every four years, and a staff of forty-five officers. Some of these General Staff officers, who would also rotate, would serve in Washington while others served in the headquarters of the Army's geographic departments, which supervised the field forces. The law, however, gave the General Staff only "supervisory" and "coordinating" authority over the War Department departments and bureaus, and it did not consolidate the logistical bureaus as Root advocated. In fact, the law and its subsequent implementation and modification gave Ainsworth, who became the adjutant general, real power equal to the chief of staff's.

Once established, the General Staff did bring some improvements to the Army's organization for wartime mobilization, but its power did not increase rapidly enough to please Army reformers. Among the staff's accomplishments were the improvement of officer education, field maneuvers, contingency planning, intelligence collection and analysis, tactical organization, and theoretical mobilization planning. When the United States sent regular troops to the Mexican border in 1911, the movement was not especially well organized; a similar deployment in 1913 went much more smoothly. An expedition to Cuba in 1906 by 5,000 regulars showed a managerial competence absent in 1898.

Nevertheless, the General Staff suffered many wounds in its early days, some from enemies, some self-inflicted. For example, the bureau chiefs still proved fractious and insubordinate, encouraged by their Army friends and congressional allies. Several chiefs of staff had great difficulty enforcing policy until Chief of Staff Leonard Wood (1910–1914) and Secretary of War Henry L. Stimson (1911–1913) challenged General Ainsworth's power in 1912. Maneuvering Ainsworth into retirement with the threat of a court-martial for insubordination, the imperious Wood and Stimson seem to have established the chief of staff's position as the principal source of professional advice and command authority, but Ainsworth and Congress immediately curbed Wood and the staff with inhibiting legislation. When Wood's tenure ended, he was replaced by less assertive generals. With the Wilson administration and Congress hostile to the General Staff, the "brain of the Army" did not prosper. When the United States entered World War I, the staff had only twenty-two officers in Washington, mired in routine paperwork and theoretical war plans of limited usefulness.

If the Army's "brain" needed fresh blood, its body—the tactical units with which it would fight future wars—needed more muscle, principally manpower. Postponing permanent legislation until the end of the Philippine insurrection was in sight, Congress waited until 1901 to enlarge the regular Army to 3,820 officers and 84,799 men, and it did not appropriate enough money to maintain even this force, which fell below War Department estimates. Clearly some sort of reserve force would be required to reinforce the regulars in the early stages of war while the United States mobilized and trained a citizen-soldier army. The reinforcement mission meant that the first-line reserves would have to mobilize quickly and be available legally for expeditionary duty abroad. Ideally, the War Department preferred a reserve force raised, organized, and controlled only by the national government. Its model was the German system, which required conscripts to serve first with the standing army and then in various reserve units for a total of twelve years. Americans, however, thought compulsory service militaristic and foreign to their society and institutions, whatever its military benefits. As Secretary Root and his advisers realized, any reserve system had to rely on volunteers, and the only expression of military voluntarism in peacetime was the National Guard.

As it proved in 1898 when it served as the principal recruiting base for volunteers, the National Guard could provide ardent recruits for wartime service and some existing tactical structure for their training and employment. In 1899 Congress rewarded the Guard by increasing its annual subsidy from $400,000 to $1 million. The Guard's shortcomings were equally obvious. Politically, there were as many National Guards as there were states and territories, all influenced more or less by state patronage politics, which tolerated aged, infirm, and incompetent officers to a degree the regular Army (at least the reformers) would not. In terms of mission and political theory, the Guard tended to fall into four camps: states' rights units, "social" units, "law and order" units, and reservists-for-war units. For two decades, National Guard reformers, represented by the National Guard Association of the United States, had attempted to persuade state legislatures to increase Guard subsidies for military training unrelated to state missions, which were principally suppressing labor and racial violence. Although the governments of New York, Pennsylvania, and New England proved supportive, reform at the state level did not flourish. Disappointed at the limits of state support for the wartime reserve mission, the Guard reformers turned to the federal government and found the War Department and Congress sympathetic.

From 1903 to 1912, militia reform flourished in Washington, spurred by Roosevelt (an ex-Guard officer), Root, Assistant Secretary of War William Cary Sanger (also an ex-Guardsman), the National Guard Association, part of Congress, and even regular Army officers. The final laws disappointed uncompromising Uptonian officers, states' righters, and the antimilitary clique in Congress, but they did provide the foundation for an improved Guard for the reinforcement mission. In 1903 Congress passed a new Militia Act, whose principal legislative sponsor was Representative Charles W. Dick, an Ohio Republican and Guard general. The Dick Act essentially exchanged federal dollars and equipment for increased Army control of the Guard's training and organization. The law recognized two militias: the Organized Militia (National Guard) under dual federal-state control, and the unorganized mass of males (ages eighteen to forty-five) that retained both national and state military obligations in emergencies. Only the Organized Militia, however, would receive federal monies and then only in relationship to the degree that its units met federal standards in commissioning officers, recruiting enlisted men to Army physical and mental standards, organizing units like their Army counterparts, and undergoing field training. For example, Guard units could increase federal support by going to summer camp and participating in maneuvers with the regular Army. Under a complex funding formula, the more the Guard trained, the more money it received to pay the trainees and the more free arms and equipment it could requisition through the Army. In addition, the president could call up the Guard for nine months rather than three months, but the geographic limitation to continental service remained. As a beginning, however, especially when the Guard subsidy increased to $2 million in 1906, the Dick Act heartened the reformers.

The Dick Act left many issues unresolved, but a second Militia Act of 1908 appeared to address most of the remaining problems. The most important change was that the time and geographic limits for Guard service disappeared, but only in return for a provision that Guardsmen would go to war as units, not individual replacements for Army regiments. One might have interpreted the original Dick Act to mean that Guard regiments might be federalized as units, then reorganized as federal volunteers for overseas service. Guardsmen argued persuasively that hometown officers and local loyalties gave the Guard its peacetime vitality and wartime mobilization potential. To check Guard fears that the General Staff saw it primarily as a pool of individual replacements, Congress established a National Guard Bureau in the War Department, whose chief reported directly to the secretary of war, not to the General Staff.

The Guard reform movement, however, slowed in 1912 when the attorney general ruled that the provision for compulsory overseas service included in the 1908 law was unconstitutional. Ironically, the ruling actually came from the office of the judge advocate general, the Army's chief lawyer. Reflecting General Staff–bureau antagonisms, the conservatism of the Taft administration, and the Uptonianism of regular officers, the ruling turned attention away from the Guard and back to the issue of an independent federal reserve force. One effort at this alternative, the Reserve Act of 1912, allowed regulars to shorten their obligated active service by joining a federal reserve. Two years later this "force" numbered sixteen enlisted men. Clearly the United States did not have an adequate system for wartime mobilization.

The General Staff and reserve force issues tended to dominate land force policymaking, especially in the civil-military political arena, but the

Army at the same time made halting steps to organize itself for modern warfare and to come to grips with the new military technology offered by a mighty host of civilians and its own uniformed inventors. Although America was rich in inventors, the absence of external threat and public urgency limited the Army to experimentation and testing. Spurred by the world war, the European armed forces soon took the lead in finding more efficient ways to destroy each other with new weapons and organizational techniques. The U.S. Army shared the exploration for new ways to wage war.

Organizationally, modernization took many forms. The tactical units of the Army, principally the thirty infantry and fifteen cavalry regiments, gradually shifted to posts that could accommodate a regiment or more in order to improve training. Congressional reluctance to close bases, however, impeded troop concentration. On paper—and occasionally for maneuvers and service on the Mexican border—the Army formed brigades (two or more regiments) and divisions (two or more brigades), and even the National Guard had a theoretical grouping of twelve divisions, organized on a regional basis. The Army school system proliferated in order to accommodate more detailed technical training for regular officers and enlisted men. After much debate and political infighting, the artillery separated in 1907 into two separate arms, field artillery and coast artillery. Field artillery regiments reappeared on maneuvers, while the new Coast Artillery Corps enjoyed its status by establishing a separate staff in Washington and successfully lobbying for increased money for new guns and fortifications. In 1912 Congress finally accepted the wisdom of logistical consolidation and created a Quartermaster Department that absorbed the functions of the Subsistence and Paymaster Departments. The law also provided for a separate Service Corps of 6,000 men for field and base operations.

To some degree the growing revolution in military technology posed a bewildering range of organizational and doctrinal problems. Like other armies, the U.S. Army experienced an era of technical anxiety. In terms of ordnance, improved metallurgy, machine tooling, and chemistry made it possible for small arms and artillery to increase their ranges, rates of fire, and accuracy by a factor of three. In rifles and field guns, the United States kept pace by adopting the Springfield M 1903 and the M 1902 3-inch gun. The artillery piece had shells, a recoil mechanism, and optical sights comparable with the French 75-mm gun, the premier European fieldpiece. In 1905 the Army opened its first plant to produce the most advanced smokeless powder. The Ordnance Department also tested a wide variety of machine guns, including the models offered by John M. Browning, Hiram Maxim, and I.N. Lewis. Emphasizing the need for light weight for field mobility, the Army adopted a substandard automatic weapon, the Benet-Mercie, primarily because it thought the inventors would soon produce lighter models of their machine guns. In the meantime, Browning, Maxim, and Lewis guns turned the Western Front of World War I into a slaughter pit.

The revolution in military firepower posed serious problems for the battlefield control of tactical units, but the changes in communications did not keep pace. The telegraph, telephone, and radio had already improved administrative and strategic communications, but tactical communications depended upon visual signals and written messages until the Army adopted battery-powered field phones. With the development of an indirect fire capability, the artillery led the way in creating phone systems to link its forward observers, fire detection centers, and firing batteries. Wire, however, could be laid only as fast as men could walk or drive (both slow under fire), and it was vulnerable to enemy fire and careless teamsters.

The smell of oil and exhaust fumes around a few posts announced, too, that the Army had begun its love affair with the automobile. The military advantages of marrying the internal combustion engine to wheeled carriages had impressed the Army as early as the 1890s, but only after two years of limited tests did the Quartermaster Department in 1906 purchase its first six cars. More experiments followed, now including the use of trucks and cars in the field. When one colonel covered the same distance in three hours by car that he had traveled on horseback in three days, he vowed he would never again get into a saddle when a car was available. In 1912 an auto-truck test unit drove 1,500 miles and proved that it could average speeds twice those of mule-drawn wagons. Nevertheless, motorization faced substantial barriers. Army conservatives feared that their soldiers would use the vehicles for personal errands and would not maintain them properly. These proved reasonable concerns. The tradeoffs in cost and availability of gasoline and spare parts versus forage and harness perplexed quartermaster planning. Given the primitive state of American roads, horses looked like a better option than trucks, especially in the west, where much of the Army still trained and patrolled the borders. In addition, War Department requirements for field cars and trucks discouraged commercial builders, who saw no future in small Army orders. Nevertheless, the field experiments continued until 1916, when Army trucks got their first real test during the Punitive Expedition into Mexico. In a daring buy of 500 commercial vehicles valued at $450,000, the War Department formed twenty-two truck companies, which proved their worth carrying supplies. The Army stood on the curb of the motor age.

Like the motorization movement, the Army's earliest experiences with airplanes were long on promise and short on performance, but the operations of 1916 in Mexico revived a flagging commitment. Discouraged by its fruitless donations to aerial inventor Dr. Samuel Langley, the War

Department's Board of Ordnance and Fortification avoided subsidizing the Wright brothers even after 1903 and believed that dirigibles offered more military potential than rigid-wing aircraft. In 1907, however, with President Roosevelt's encouragement, the Signal Corps formed an aeronautical division and reopened negotiations for a test aircraft, which the Wrights eventually delivered in 1909. Army-dictated performance standards proved difficult to meet, but the potential use of the airplane for reconnaissance purposes kept Army interest alive. The Army demanded an aircraft powerful enough to carry two persons (one to fly, one to observe) for 125 miles at 40 miles an hour. Deterred by the cost and danger of manned flight (the first American fatality was an Army lieutenant), the Signal Corps conducted its tests cautiously in both the financial and operational sense. Although Army officers successfully rigged primitive bombing systems and machine guns on the test planes, most aviation pioneers (including Billy Mitchell) did not think aviation technology would soon produce anything other than reconnaissance planes. Nevertheless, by 1913 the Army could organize a 1st Aero Squadron in Texas, equipped with eight primitive Curtiss biplanes. In 1916 the squadron deployed into Mexico and performed yeoman service conducting scouting missions and carrying messages, but soon lost all its aircraft to crashes or maintenance problems. The squadron's performance, however, broadened support for a more ambitious Army aviation program.

Aviation experimentation, funded by congressional appropriations for the Army and Navy, sailed along with relative safety and success, then crashed in both aircraft and funding terms. No one considered pioneer flying risk-free. Between 1903 and 1910 thirty-four pilots died in flying accidents. In one two-year period, 1911–1912, however, more than 200 pilots died, many of them pioneers. Control systems and engine mountings did not keep pace with engine power and the aerodynamics of faster flight. Aviation development in the United States stalled as Congress and aircraft designers became risk-averse. The opportunity to exploit the Lewis machine gun, Speery gyroscopes, and optical bombsights passed. Between 1909 and 1925 no American aircraft or aviation technology won a prize at the Paris air show, the showcase of international aviation.

Even without the stimulus of the world war, the Army and the National Guard by 1916 showed distinct signs of modernity despite the absence of a significant threat or any widespread public interest in military affairs. There was no "Great Khaki Army" to excite support, like the Great White Fleet. With the exception of a few civilian military enthusiasts, the heart of modernization was the regular Army officer corps, which depended upon fragile coalitions with civilian political leaders and technologists to make organizational changes. Modernization, moreover, could not break free from the expectation that the only war the United States would fight would occur either in the Pacific or in the Western Hemisphere. In either theater the enemies could be defeated by the regular Army and National Guard in the war's early stages or overwhelmed eventually by America's vast industrial and manpower resources. In any event, the battlefleet might decide the issue before the land forces even became engaged. While such assumptions proved naïve in 1917, they rested on political realities that Army officers themselves shared. In the face of such popular notions, the wonder is not that land force reform accomplished so little, but that it accomplished so much.

The Armed Forces and Imperial Defense

A major barrier to the modernization of the American armed forces before World War I was the military's constant involvement with overseas interventions. Despite the fact that reformers argued that the Army, Navy, and Marine Corps should concentrate upon their wartime missions, all the armed forces found themselves busy with constabulary duties beyond the borders of the United States. These duties may have provided some favorable publicity, usually romantic nonsense, but by and large they distracted the armed forces from training for modern war. As European military observers noted, the United States had a declaratory policy of military modernization and national defense, but it had a military establishment still wedded to imperial policing.

Surveying the wreckage of the Spanish empire in the Caribbean, to which the United States had administered the *coup de grace* in 1898, American policymakers committed their own armed forces in order to reshape the destiny of the nations in "the American lake." In the strictest terms of self-interest, the primary concern was building and protecting an isthmian canal. But this self-interest did not exclude other rationales for interventionism, which included curbing European influence, protecting American loans, stimulating economic growth and international trade (primarily for American merchants), and encouraging the development of republican, democratic governments and private and public institutions much like those in the United States. Although American cultural imperialism fell short in reality, it kept substantial portions of the armed forces occupied in reformist occupations.

After the Treaty of Paris in 1898, the Army made Cuba and Puerto Rico its laboratory for reform but soon surrendered its mission to the Marine Corps. Since Puerto Rico was an annexed territory, the Army's administrative functions passed quickly to a civilian government, but not before Army officers had begun to reshape the island's public services. In addition, the

War Department formed the Puerto Rican Regiment, a regular Army infantry regiment, to provide federal authorities with a military response to civil disturbances and minor foreign threats. In Cuba the War Department ran a military government from 1898 until 1902, when Cuba officially became an independent nation. During the transition period the Army successfully found a way to curb yellow fever, pioneered public health and public works projects, reformed the island's educational system, and introduced novel governmental practices like efficiency, justice, and honesty. None of these accomplishments proved transferable, however, and in 1906 the United States again assumed control of the island's government when corrupt elections sparked a civil war. Again, Army officers led a drive for administrative reform, which ended with the American withdrawal in 1909. Disillusioned with the tool of reformist military occupation, the United States took a more limited role in subsequent Cuban civil wars.

The military also served as the spearhead of American action in Panama. When the Roosevelt administration decided to exploit Panamanian nationalism and investors' cupidity in 1903 and take direct control of the isthmian canal route and construction, it blocked Colombian military intervention with Navy squadrons at Colon and Panama City and landed Marines to protect the Panamanian revolutionaries. When a highly favorable treaty created the Canal Zone and heralded the beginning of American construction, the Roosevelt administration gave the military principal roles in making the canal program work. The Corps of Engineers—under the eventual guidance of Brigadier General George W. Goethals—and the Medical Department, represented by Colonel William C. Gorgas, received the mission to overcome the engineering and disease problems that had frustrated earlier canal builders. Both groups of officers succeeded, and the canal opened in 1914. Small naval units and a Marine regiment assumed the initial responsibility for ensuring order and defense, but the Marines were replaced by World War I with a mix of Army coastal defense and mobile troops. In the meantime, the Marines and Navy supported State Department policies in nearby Nicaragua, another possible canal location and site of American political and financial commitments. In 1912 American expeditionary forces intervened in a Nicaraguan civil war and waged active military operations to crush the revolt. A Marine legation guard remained in Managua to dramatize American concern with Nicaraguan politics.

Across the sun-kissed Caribbean, the green island of Hispaniola also concerned the State Department, primarily because its governments courted foreign intervention and failed to establish effective, democratic administrations. The neighboring countries of Haiti and Santo Domingo both proved running sores in American Caribbean policy. Justified by the Roosevelt Corollary to the Monroe Doctrine, which stated that the

United States would intervene to preempt European intervention, various formulas for diplomatic pressure and fiscal supervision for both countries proved unsuccessful in reducing governmental instability. Civil wars in Haiti in 1915 and the Dominican Republic in 1916 drew Navy squadrons and Marine expeditionary brigades to both countries, first to break up the rebel armies and then to impose reformist occupations. In both countries Marine units, assisted marginally by Marine-created native constabularies, fought vicious guerrilla wars with rural terrorists. The twin occupations, which lasted in the Dominican Republic until 1924 and in Haiti until 1934, absorbed many of the Marine units assigned to Advanced Base Force training and brought no special credit to the Corps, which was accused of atrocities. The general effectiveness of American military administration in both countries did not prove publicly appealing or lasting, and both nations lapsed into dictatorships after American withdrawal.

Willingly ceding the pacification mission in the Caribbean to the Marine Corps ("State Department troops," soldiers called Marines), the Army did not escape the toils of America's Latin diplomacy, for from 1911 until 1917 much of the Army's attention focused upon the possibility of war with Mexico. While the Mexican Revolution twisted its way to eventual success, American diplomacy followed the same complex path. Under the Taft administration, the government tried to seal the border to gun-runners and guerrilla organizers with scant success. When cavalry patrols proved insufficiently impressive to the Mexicans, the administration in 1911 and 1913 formed an entire division of combined arms in Texas. The first mobilization had little clear direction, but the second was the first stage in War Plan Green, which included an overland campaign (à la 1847) from Veracruz to Mexico City. The Wilson administration considered military intervention seriously, since it feared German and Japanese penetration in Mexico and found the counterrevolutionary Heurta regime (1911–1914) distasteful. Favoring a rebel victory, Wilson committed a Navy-Marine task force to Veracruz in 1914, where the Americans fought their way through the city and established an occupation zone. An Army brigade from Texas soon followed, but, assessing the unexpected bloodshed, the Wilson administration chose to talk, not fight. The American forces withdrew by the end of the year, but not before the Huerta regime had collapsed.

The Veracruz expedition did not end the Mexican deployment, since the civil war—now waged between two revolutionary factions led by Venustiano Carranza and Pancho Villa—spilled over the American border and spawned lesser political and racial violence along the Rio Grande. Frustrated by American support for Carranza, Villa's band raided Columbus, New Mexico, in March 1916, and killed fifteen American civilians and soldiers. Wilson ordered the Punitive Expedition of 10,000 soldiers under the command of Brigadier General John J. Pershing, a very hard task-master, into Mexico to destroy Villa's army. When the Mexican government sent troops to seal the flanks of the expedition, which it had tacitly accepted but disliked, Wilson mobilized most of the regular Army along the border and reinforced it with 112,000 National Guardsmen. Despite two battles between American and Mexican regulars, both nations backed away from war, since the Americans had also dispersed Villa's mounted columns. As the threat of war with Germany mounted in early 1917, the Punitive Expedition returned across the international border, rich in field experience and disgruntled with the ambiguities of Wilsonian diplomacy.

Across the Pacific other American soldiers guarded the Philippines from external attack (an unlikely threat) and internal violence (an ever-present possibility). To discourage any invader, Army engineers began to fortify and arm the islands at the mouth of Manila Bay, principally Corregidor and El Fraile, which became the "concrete battleship" known as Fort Drum. North of Manila, the Army formed a composite brigade of two infantry regiments, two cavalry squadrons, an artillery battery, and an engineer detachment as its mobile defense force. These troops, however, did not bear much of the burden of insular peacekeeping, which fell to the American-officered regiment of Philippine scouts and the paramilitary Philippine Constabulary. The most active operations occurred on the Moro islands of Mindanao and the Jolo archipelago, where Muslim Filipinos resisted civilization American style. Unassociated with the *insurrectos* of 1899–1902, the Moros defended their traditions of slavery, tribal warfare, and religious frenzies. Some American generals like Leonard Wood and John J. Pershing enhanced their reputations as the civil governors and military commanders of the Moro territory, largely by conducting campaigns to disarm the Moros or to break up dissident bands. The American "bamboo army"—usually a combination of regular Army, Scout, and Constabulary companies—began operations against the Moros in 1902 and fought them through a series of arduous campaigns: Lake Lanao and Jolo (1903), the Cotabato Valley (1905), Bud Dajo Mountain (1906 and 1911), and Bud Bagsak Mountain (1911 and 1913). While these campaigns tempered a whole generation of Army officers, the battles with the Moros harked back to the nineteenth-century clashes with the American Indians.

The World War and the Preparedness Movement

The roar of the guns of August 1914 reached the United States in indistinct tones, but a year after the outbreak of World War I, the European conflict brought a major reconsideration of American military policy. By the autumn of 1916 the Preparedness Movement had become a force in a presidential election and had produced ambitious legislation that reshaped naval and land force policy. Like all American mass political phenomena, the Preparedness Movement contained policy contradictions and antagonistic goals and represented the diverse interests of many political groups. Nevertheless, it represented the first time that defense policy in peacetime influenced American politics and involved more people than a limited policymaking elite. On the other hand, its legislative products came too late to have any substantial impact on American military readiness, either to fight World War I or to avoid intervention by imposing a peace before American entry into the war.

Concerned by the early indecisiveness of the European war and the German conduct of submarine warfare, American internationalists (largely eastern, Republican, and pro-Allied) formed a complex network of preparedness lobbies and began propaganda programs in order to build support for increased military spending. The Germans cooperated in the organizing phase of the movement by sinking the British liner *Lusitania* in May 1915 and killing over 100 Americans. The *Lusitania* crisis shifted American animus toward Germany, awakened a larger audience to military affairs, and converted President Wilson to preparedness, if only to stay in front of public opinion. German submarine warfare also focused public and congressional attention upon American naval policy, since freedom of the seas was a concept relatively free of political division that transcended the wisdom of intervention. Americans who found no attractions in aiding the Allies could support naval preparedness because a larger fleet could still be an instrument of unilateral action, foreign trade, and protection of the Western Hemisphere during and after the war. Interventionists, on the other hand, saw a new building program as a useful way to mobilize public opinion, coerce Germany, and hearten the Allies. Building upon a generation of public faith that the fleet would protect the United States from foreign unpleasantness, the uneasy coalition of navalists fashioned an ambitious new plan to give the nation a "Navy second to none."

As pressure for some sort of naval legislation increased, the Wilson administration and Congress designed a new fleet-building program. Abandoning 1914 plans to modernize but not enlarge the fleet, the administration essentially proposed a five-year program drafted by the General Board that would have brought the fleet by 1925 to numbers second only to the Royal Navy and in quality superior to even the British. After much internal bargaining, Congress approved the General Board's plan in August 1916, with the major change that the shipbuilding should be completely started within a three-year period, thus ensuring a "Navy second to none" earlier than 1925. Approved by the Senate by a vote of 71 to 8 and by the House by 283 to 50, the Naval Act of 1916 provided for the construction of ten battleships, sixteen cruisers, fifty destroyers, seventy-two submarines, and fourteen auxiliaries. The strategic rationale for the program did not depart from the assumptions of prewar contingency plans, largely focused on deterring or fighting Japan in the Pacific and Germany in the Caribbean. The law, however, stated that the United States would forgo the program if it could find some way to negotiate freedom of the seas and secure its interests in the Western Hemisphere and the Pacific through mutual nonaggression pacts. Given the development of the naval campaigns of World War I, the act had little relevance to the war itself, since it paid no special attention to antisubmarine warfare.

Land force reform followed a more controversial course. Discouraged by the limits of National Guard reconstruction and encouraged by the enthusiasm of Secretary of War Stimson and Chief of Staff Wood, the General Staff completed a comprehensive analysis of land force policy in 1912, released in an executive document, *The Organization of the Land Forces of the United States.* The General Staff study had two novel aspects: It was made public, and it focused on the lack of an adequate reserve force with prewar training. Reflecting Stimson's and Wood's faith in the effectiveness of the American citizen-soldier, the report stressed that the United States could not fight a major war without reserves drawn from the citizenry, but it warned that the nation might not be granted sufficient time to train volunteer forces in a future war. But the idea of voluntary peacetime training in a federally sponsored reserve system found no champions in an election year despite its military wisdom.

Coming to office in 1913, the Wilson administration and its Democratic Congress did not view land force reform as a pressing national issue. Recognizing General Wood's preference for the Republicans and professional commitment to reserve reform, the administration nevertheless allowed the aggressive Rough Rider to finish his full term as chief of staff. Wood used the opportunity to sponsor a pet project: summer military training camps for college students. Surveying the public sentiment for voluntary peacetime training, Wood saw hopeful signs in the cadet training programs of the land-grant colleges established by the Morrill Act of 1862. Even without any promise of a postgraduation commission, such programs in 1911 had 29,000 male participants. Wood also knew that the most critical shortage of soldiers in the wartime volunteer armies was company-grade officers. Therefore, he established two summer camps for college students in 1913. So successful was the response from students and educators that Wood held four camps in the summer of 1914, enrolling nearly 1,000 students. Not accidentally, the summer trainees, who paid their own expenses, represented the elite of the east coast and received as much citizenship and policy indoctrination as technical military training.

The outbreak of World War I gave the voluntary training movement a welcome stimulus, and Secretary of War Lindley M. Garrison and Wood, now commander of the Eastern Department, exploited the new sense of urgency in land force reform. Converted to preparedness by the General Staff, Garrison sponsored an updated report on readiness, *Statement of a Proper Military Policy for the United States* (1915), which proposed the creation of a federal volunteer reserve force of 250,000 men trained before war broke out. But Garrison's "Continental Army Plan" did not impress Congress, since it smacked of intervention in the world war and relegated the National Guard to a lower order of federal support. Both characteristics were politically unattractive, even to preparedness advocates. In the meantime Wood, manfully supported by new Chief of Staff Hugh L. Scott, enlarged the summer training program to include college students and civic-minded business and professional men from the east coast. Although the summer camp movement took its name from Wood's encampment at Plattsburgh, New York, the 1915 camps were held at four different locations and enrolled nearly 4,000 volunteers. Despite official and Democratic criticism that the camps were a hotbed of Republican interventionism, the summer camp movement prospered under the sponsorship of an impressive array of business, labor, professional, and religious groups. As Wood himself became more controversial and outspoken on the issue of compulsory military training, the leadership of the movement shifted to civilians, especially the Military Training Camp Association (1916), led by New York lawyer Grenville Clark.

Nourished by Clark's astute guidance and heightened public concern for military preparedness, the Plattsburg Movement reached a new apogee of popularity in the summer of 1916, when 10,000 volunteers attended ten different camps held across the country. Although the War Department supported the camps with training cadres and equipment, the trainees still paid their own way or received "scholarships" and had no guarantee that they would be commissioned in wartime. Nevertheless, the Plattsburg Movement demonstrated the depth of interest in military training and presented Congress with irrefutable proof that influential portions of the public were willing to make personal commitments to peacetime preparedness. In addition, the movement stressed values that no true Progressive could reject: Increased civic awareness and public responsibility; the role of military service in reducing class, ethnic, and regional antagonisms; and the preparation of American youth for leadership.

Having scuttled the "Continental Army Plan" and thrown Wilson's War Department into disarray when Garrison and his assistant resigned,

Congress seized the initiative in drafting new land force legislation. Correctly reading public sentiment toward some form of peacetime training, Congress patched together a set of proposals drawn from the General Staff, the National Guard lobby, citizen preparedness groups, and a technical-corporate elite concerned about economic mobilization. The intense cloakroom bargaining reflected not only ideas about preparedness but also Democratic determination to seize the military reform issue away from the Republicans and to accommodate the National Guard. As passed finally on June 3, the National Defense Act of 1916 represented the most comprehensive effort to organize a land force structure for future mobilization, but it made no special provisions for a crash preparedness program. Any reform hinting at intervention in the European war was still too controversial. To interventionists, the act was "either a comedy or a tragedy," as one critic described it.

The National Defense Act of 1916, however, contained ambitious plans for future land force expansion. The regular Army was to grow to 175,000 over a five-year period. Its first-line reserve force would be the National Guard, which was supposed to grow with the aid of federal drill pay to a maximum of 400,000. By taking a dual oath (federal and state) upon enlistment, Guardsmen could be compelled to serve abroad for unlimited periods of time in a national emergency, but they would go to war as Guard units, not as individuals. Guard units, however, would not receive federal subsidies unless they drilled forty-eight times a year at their armories and attended a two-week summer camp. The War Department would establish physical and mental standards for Guard enlistees and retained the right to screen Guard officers for fitness. Behind the Guard the law did not establish a federal reserve like the "Continental Army," but it did provide opportunities for college students and Plattsburg enthusiasts to receive reserve commissions through the Reserve Officers Training Corps at universities and through summer training. The reserve officers would form an Officers Reserve Corps prepared to provide junior line officers and technical specialists for the enlarged wartime Army.

The new law for the first time also recognized that the federal government required substantial emergency powers over industry and transportation if it was to supply a mass wartime Army. The president could compel any business to give government orders first priority in wartime. In the meantime, he should begin to study the problems of economic mobilization, a charge further strengthened with additional legislation that created a Council of National Defense from within the cabinet. Although Wilson did not use the council, he permitted Secretary of War Newton D. Baker to appoint an advisory committee of industrial experts in December

1916. This committee provided the early direction of mobilization planning upon America's entry into World War I.

Together the Naval Act of 1916 and the National Defense Act of 1916 culminated two decades of unsteady but consistent growth and modernization of the American armed forces. Certainly the two acts appalled antimilitarists and noninterventionists, primarily because they believed the legislation was a frightening national affirmation of bellicosity. Some believed peacetime compulsory service would soon follow. On the other hand, militants like Theodore Roosevelt and Leonard Wood recognized that paper reform did not mean real increases in military capability unless Congress funded the shipbuilding plans and the expanded, improved Army and Guard. Whether or not Congress would do so depended upon political events beyond the control of the military establishment. As commentators of all persuasions debated the meaning of the acts, German submarines prepared to resume unrestricted warfare against Allied and neutral shipping. As silent and deadly as a running torpedo, the European war approached a United States rich with paper plans and woefully unprepared for the one war it had not foreseen.

☆ ELEVEN ☆

The United States Fights
in the "War to End All Wars,"
1917–1918

During the green April of 1917, as America entered the "Great War," a United States senator cornered a General Staff officer and asked the critical strategic question of the intervention: "Good Lord! You're not going to send soldiers over there, are you?" Some eighteen months later, the answer was clear as the American Expeditionary Forces (AEF) of over 2 million men, cooperating with the armies of France and the British Empire, bludgeoned Imperial Germany into an armistice. Supporting the AEF stood a Navy and Marine Corps of over 600,000. In the United States and in places as far separated as northern Italy, polar Russia, and Siberia, another 2 million American soldiers served the war effort and diplomacy of the Wilson administration. World War I was the debut of the United States as an international military power. Like most debuts, the war brought its share of high anticipation, major disappointment, dogged accomplishment, and exaggerated exhilaration.

The American role in World War I derived its character less from strategic thinking in the United States than from the geopolitical notion that the future well-being of the United States depended upon the balance of power in Europe and the outcome of the war. Discarding the hallowed assumption that Europe's affairs did not involve the United States and the security of the Western Hemisphere, the Wilson administration decided that the nation had a critical stake in an Allied victory. American involvement stemmed from economic self-interest as well as an emotional commitment to support "democracy" (France and Great Britain) against "autocracy" (Germany). After a brief economic dislocation when the war began in 1914, American bankers, farmers, industrialists, and producers of raw materials exploited British naval control of the Atlantic and Allied financial strength to make the war the biggest profit-making enterprise in the history of American exporting. Before American entry, the balance of trade, already favorable to the U.S., jumped by a factor of five; the Allies liquidated $2 billion of American assets and privately borrowed another $2.5 billion to pay for their purchases. In contrast, Germany secured only $45 million in American loans.

The patterns of trade depended upon the relative strength of the Royal Navy and the submarine force of the Imperial German Navy, whose operations had to cope with American conceptions about neutrality and freedom of the seas. Despite some minor German successes at surface commerce raiding early in the war, the Royal Navy controlled the Atlantic—except its cold, green depths. The Germans could keep about thirty submarines on stations around the British Isles to intercept trans-Atlantic merchantmen. This force proved an important threat to the Allied war effort, which was dependent on American and Latin American imports. The German submarine campaign, however, had limitations. Despite mutually declared blockades by both the Allies and Germany, the Americans became more upset about submarine warfare than about British interference with neutral trade. While the British blockade cost money and irritated shippers, German submarines killed American citizens with their unannounced torpedo attacks. The *Lusitania* incident of May 1915 was only one of several well-publicized episodes in which American passengers died. Although the German U-boat (*Unterseeboot*) campaign, characterized by periods of "restricted" and "unrestricted" operations, could not halt American trade, it produced a groundswell of anti-German outrage in the United States.

Deprived of decision in its ground war, the German military planned one more massive, unrestricted effort against all shipping in 1917. Even though this campaign was likely to bring open belligerency from the United States, the Germans thought the prospect of victory outweighed the risks of American entry. The German General Staff had carefully analyzed the potential military threat from the United States and decided that the Americans could not influence the ground war in Europe for at least two years. General Erich Ludendorff, the major architect of the German war effort after 1916, summed up the German position on the United States: "What can she do? She cannot come over here! . . . I do not give a damn about America."

Despite its global reach, the war remained in 1917 a war to be won or lost on the three major fronts of Europe. From the American political and military point of view, two of these three fronts did not appear attractive. From the Baltic to the Balkans, the armies of the Austro-Hungarian Empire, reinforced with German troops, continued to bleed the Russians, but with such losses that both belligerents stood on the verge of collapse. Although the first phase of the Russian Revolution in March 1917 made the Russians more "democratic" allies, few American policymakers saw profit in a commitment to the Eastern Front. In northern Italy the Italian army remained locked in the mountains with other Austro-Hungarian and German ground forces after two years of futile offensives.

Although it was crucial to avoid defeat in both Russia and Italy in order to prevent the release of the German armies there, the British and French commanders regarded the Western Front—stretching from Belgium to Switzerland—as the theater of decision. Already the muddy graveyard of Allied and German armies, the Western Front had become the ultimate test of the belligerents' political and military will and capability. Both had run thin by 1917. Nevertheless, as the United States entered the war, the Allies made one more effort against the German barriers of barbed wire, machine guns, artillery, fortifications, and skilled infantry. The results of the Allied effort, launched in conjunction with an equally desperate Russian offensive, could not be tallied until the late summer of 1917. It was an unequivocal failure that cost the British and French an additional million casualties. The French army mutinied and refused to participate in any further offensives. Under the command of a new general, Henri Philippe Petain, the French army manned its trenches and waited for better times. The Russian army simply dissolved as the Russian Revolution moved in more radical directions. The British Expeditionary Force (BEF), commanded by General (later Field Marshal) Sir Douglas Haig, lapsed back into a defensive posture, riven by command and civil-military conflicts and deprived of reinforcements by Prime Minister David Lloyd George. Having exhausted their own armies, the British and French stood ready to fight to the last American.

Declaring war on April 6, 1917, the Wilson administration, prodded by British and French diplomats and military missions, reluctantly concluded that the American military effort had to focus on the Western Front. American war aims, articulated later by President Wilson as the "Fourteen Points," required maximum effort in the theater of decision with minimal political and military integration with the Allies, whose own war aims remained suspect and decidedly nonidealistic. The Allies sought such practical goals as dissolving the German and Austro-Hungarian Empires, annexing territory, eliminating German military power, and collecting monetary reparations. Wilson, on the other hand, thought in terms of a new world order based on principles of national self-determination, democratic government, freedom of the seas, an end to imperialism, open diplomacy, disarmament, and free economic development. Administration slogan makers told the public that the United States would make "the world safe for Democracy." French Premier Georges Clemenceau wondered why Wilson needed Fourteen Points when God required only Ten. More practically, the volatile state of American public opinion seemed to justify only a commitment to free France from its German occupiers, since a direct alliance with Britain threatened to raise the ire of Irish-Americans and opponents of British imperialism. The War Department General Staff urged that an American army go to France, since only such a commitment would break the military stalemate and thus provide the diplomatic leverage Wilson sought. The Western Front, for all its horrors, was the only "over there" that counted.

The American Mobilization

"We want men, men, men," insisted Marshal Joseph Joffre. Part of an Allied mission that came to Washington as soon as the United States declared war, the former French commander shocked American officials with his frank discussion of affairs on the Western Front. The rest of the Allied mission supported his emphatic demands for American troops. By World War I standards, however, the size of the United States land forces was pitiful. In April 1917, the regular Army numbered 133,111, reinforced by another 185,000 National Guardsmen. Another 17,000 officers and men had joined one or another of the federal reserve forces established by the National Defense Act of 1916. The War Department General Staff agreed that the Army would have to be enlarged and that the equitable, efficient way to raise a mass force was by conscription.

Aware that forced military service was distasteful to Americans, President Wilson and Secretary of War Newton D. Baker characterized their call for men as "selective service." Conscription evoked memories of the Civil War experience: evasion, violent resistance, communal hostility. With those perils in mind, the General Staff officers who crafted the Selective Service Act of May 18, 1917, created a manpower policy and administrative system that demonstrated political deftness, flexibility, and efficiency. Since Congress, particularly the House of Representatives, proved reluctant to accept conscription as the price of intervention, the Wilson administration did everything it could to soften the draft and place its execution with local civilians rather than federal military authorities. It also surrounded the draft with a flood of patriotic symbols and civic rhetoric that stressed voluntarism. Even as Congress voted for conscription, the Army and National Guard launched recruiting drives to bring themselves to war strength. By the end of 1917 they had enlisted nearly 700,000 volunteers. Weighed against the War Department's estimated manpower needs and complex quota system, nearly 500,000 of the volunteers could be counted as substitutes for potential draftees. The result was that the 1917 draft did not bear heavily upon the American male population. In June nearly 10 million men in the draftable age range of twenty-one to thirty registered for conscription. Although 3 million were called to service in 1917, one-third were found physically unfit and another million were exempted from service on the grounds of dependency, alien status, critical occupations, and religious beliefs. Of the remaining draftable men, only half a million were called into the service by the end of 1917. As intended, the draft "selected" those men the Army wanted and society could best spare: 90 percent of the draftees were unmarried, and 70 percent were farm hands or manual laborers.

The organization of the draft diffused resistance and hostility toward the national government and applied the full majesty of the local community—"your friends and neighbors"—to make the draft work. At the national level the War Department administered the draft through the Office of the Provost Marshal General, headed by Major General Enoch H. Crowder, a crusty lawyer and former opponent of conscription. Crowder's staff, ever sensitive to civilian advice, established national policy, issued general orders, and held the lottery that established the order of call-up. It did not select or exempt individuals. Supervised by state officials and district boards, the actual task of inducting draftees rested with the members of some 4,600 local boards. Additional committees of citizens groups gave medical and legal advice and assisted the inductees until they departed for the training camps. Of the nearly 200,000 participants in the system in 1918, only 4,000 were Army officers and enlisted men, most of whom served in Washington. State officials, not the federal government, appointed the members of the district and local boards. The result was a system attuned to local occupational needs, personal problems, and community attitudes.

One reason conscription moved with all deliberate speed was that the War Department in 1917 did not think it would need an army of more than 2.2 million men. Given supply shortages, it was not sure it could equip such a force in less than eighteen months. For the first six months of its war, the War Department, assisted by varied military missions to France, wrestled with mobilization plans. By early autumn 1917, the planning initiative shifted to the General Headquarters (GHQ), American Expeditionary Forces (AEF), which had sailed for France in late May, followed by one token division to boost Allied morale. Major General (soon General)

John J. Pershing, the ambitious, austere, politically adept commander of the AEF, had no intention of sharing the critical decisions of forming his army with either the General Staff or the Allies. Actually, GHQ AEF and the General Staff drafted similar plans, although Pershing's program had a specific strategic rationale. After surveying the wreckage of the Western Front and assessing Allied troop and logistical deployments, Pershing decided to mass his army in Lorraine between Verdun and the Moselle River. Across no man's land in this inactive sector lay the fortress city and railhead of Metz and the coal and iron fields of the Saar. An offensive against these objectives, Pershing's staff reasoned, would break the German defenses throughout France and force a peace on Allied terms. Even though a general offensive might not be possible until 1919, GHQ AEF wanted to have twenty combat and ten training and replacement divisions in France by December 1918. With all its supporting units, the AEF would require 1.1 million men. This "thirty division program" governed the Army's planning and shaped the execution of the draft.

Raising men for war had been a traditional government task, but World War I introduced Americans to a new, poorly understood aspect of twentieth-century war: Economic mobilization and regulation. In 1917 few policymakers realized the accuracy of the observation of automotive executive Howard E. Coffin: "Twentieth century warfare demands that the blood of the soldier must be mingled with from three to five parts of the sweat of the man in the factories, mills, mines, and fields of the nation in arms." The Allies had already learned this lesson by 1917, but Americans, with the notable exception of a few businessmen and Army officers, had not paid much attention to the economic implications of a national mobilization. For almost a year the United States struggled to find the political-administrative system best suited for industrial and agricultural mobilization and the productive capacity to meet the war's demands.

In the broadest economic terms, American entry into the war meant that demands for goods and services far exceeded supply. In peacetime the economy normally served American consumption and domestic investment with an important second function, serving foreign consumers. With World War I foreign demand increased dramatically, both to maintain the English and French civilian economies and to supply the Allied armies. The foreign demand by 1917 had pulled the economy out of a recession, but it had also committed much of the American economic effort to the war. For example, American munitions and firearms companies were already fully committed to Allied orders. In April 1917, therefore, the United States could not form a wartime Army and Navy of its own without expanding and regulating its economy.

The short-term effects of wartime mobilization put unforeseen strains on the economy. Military forces are prodigious consumers of both civilian supplies and specialized military equipment, largely because military training and wars tend to make weapons and supplies disappear. In World War I the United States eventually put 4.8 million men in uniform; this force represented about one-twenty-fifth of its total population. As wage earners, these men would have contributed to and consumed a larger fraction of the gross national product. As a wartime Army and Navy, however, these Americans eventually absorbed an estimated $32 billion. During two years of wartime spending, the American armed forces consumed about one-quarter of the entire gross national product.

Any form of strict economic calculus would not include another factor that inhibited American economic mobilization: the federal government did not trust concentrations of power, either in the government or in business. From the dominant coalition in Congress, made up of small-town and rural Progressives of both parties, to Secretary of War Baker and Secretary of the Navy Josephus Daniels and President Wilson himself, the government was a bastion of hostility to big corporations and powerful government bureaucracies. The military reinforced the bias against centralized, collaborative relations with business. The Army and Navy bureaus responsible for material procurement did not want to deviate from peacetime practices and relationships, although they recognized that speed required a change in contracting procedures. For the Navy, wartime expansion proved to be manageable within the existing bureau system and did not place special strains upon the Navy's peacetime system of shipbuilding and supply procurement. The Army was quite another matter. During the course of the war, the Army placed $14 billion in orders, and for more than a year these orders came from eight separate agencies that had not considered priorities and limited supplies. Moreover, the Army tended to think in terms of "outputs" (rifles, planes, tanks, blankets, shoes) rather than "inputs" (raw materials, skilled labor, and production technology). Therefore, the War Department was not organized to work efficiently with industry. Waste, artificially high prices, and inefficiency characterized Army procurement throughout the war.

The federal government need not have suffered the mobilization fiascos of 1917, since, in the technical sense, it had adequate information about the challenges of economic mobilization. Anticipating American entry into the war, the Navy Department and the Chamber of Commerce (and belatedly the War Department) formed advisory committees in 1915 and 1916 to examine the problems of industrial mobilization. In an institutional sense these actions had produced a Naval Consulting Board, an Industrial Preparedness Committee of the Chamber of Commerce, and, most important, the Advisory Committee to the Council of National Defense.

The council, organized by statute in 1916, included the principal cabinet members who would guide a wartime mobilization. These committees—which eventually led to a General Munitions Board and the War Industries Board (WIB) in 1917—viewed the potential impact of a total economic mobilization with alarm. By and large the committee leadership included public-spirited businessmen and professional managers. They feared that a wartime economic crisis would bring the nationalization of some industries; they also feared a continuation of Progressive antitrust legislation. They preferred instead a system of industry self-regulation with some governmental participation, and they argued that, with military support, such a system was also most likely to produce the material needed for a major war. Led by Coffin, AT&T executive Walter S. Gifford, management educator Hollis Godfrey, advertising executive Grosvenor B. Clarkson, financial speculator Bernard Baruch, construction executive Benedict Crowell, and manufacturer Frank A. Scott, these men argued for more centralized governmental control of economic mobilization, but designed to preserve the existing character of American industry.

Despite the establishment of the War Industries Board in July 1917, the Wilson administration and the War Department for different reasons resisted giving it full powers to regulate the economy and to allocate scarce raw materials and goods between the Allied, domestic, and military claimants. Wilson and Baker would not relinquish their own (largely unused) authority and did not trust the WIB, dominated by businessmen in temporary government service. The General Staff and logistical bureaus did not want civilians interfering with the determination of military requirements or contracting procedures. The latter had already been modified to ensure the speedy letting of contracts. Instead of public bidding and fixed-price contracts, the War Department had shifted to contracts negotiated with sole-source suppliers on a cost-plus-fixed-fee basis. This practice allowed the Army to deluge the economy with orders and money in 1917. It also created opportunities for businesses to control pricing and profits through some sixty "commodity committees" of business representatives, provided the cooperating industries did not have to fear conflict-of-interest and antitrust laws. In 1917, however, the federal government would not suspend these laws and thus stifled productivity. The industrial mobilization progressed, therefore, without firm central direction.

In some critical areas the government had to accept more centralized control. Two separate administrations assumed the responsibility for production, pricing, and distribution of food and fuels. A Shipping Board and Emergency Fleet Corporation in 1916 expanded the American carrying trade and allocated vessels to meet Allied and military needs. To increase production and encourage domestic conservation, Congress passed a

Food Production (Lever) Act and Food and Fuel Act in August 1917. In December 1917, with railroad traffic tangled throughout the eastern United States, the government temporarily took over the management of the nation's railroads. To handle Allied orders, Congress created a War Trade Board, but it too had difficulties dealing with parochial industries and the weak WIB. Despite the movement to greater centralization, the American economy did not respond rapidly to the military's demands, and by the winter of 1917–1918 shortages of civilian goods and military supplies plagued the nation.

The War Department's wartime procurement efforts had a mixed effect. Military construction produced thirty-six major cantonments for training full divisions of almost 30,000 each. These military boomtowns of tents and barracks were largely completed by the winter of 1917–1918. Ordnance problems proved more intractable, and the Army decided to arm the AEF with British-model rifles already being produced in the United States and accept Allied machine guns, mortars, artillery pieces, and tanks. American soldiers in France used more Enfield rifles than Springfields, more French automatic weapons than new Browning automatic rifles and machine guns, more French 75-mm field guns than American 3-inch cannons. The aviation program was especially disappointing. Announcing its intention to build 10,000 warplanes, the government turned to the automobile industry, which had a deserved reputation for mass production miracles. The automobile manufacturers, in fact, produced a sturdy, dependable engine—the Liberty—but airframes proved more difficult to produce. Although the manufacturers eventually adopted Allied designs, aircraft production never met requirements, and Army aviators flew to glory in French and British aircraft.

The fitful performance of the Wilson administration and the national economy in 1917 might have been excusable if the strategic situation had improved while the Allies awaited the AEF. Instead, the three-front European war changed to a one-front conflict. In the autumn of 1917 the Russian war effort collapsed, and the Bolsheviks sued for peace. German divisions immediately entrained for the Western Front. In Italy a German-Austrian offensive shattered the Italian army at Caporetto and drove the remaining Italian troops back toward Venice. Although the front stabilized with an infusion of Allied reinforcements, additional German troops were freed for transfer to France. From the council chambers in London and Paris to the headquarters of the Allied armies, General Pershing found unrelieved pessimism. Allied commanders knew the Germans could now shift to the strategic offensive for the first time since 1914, and they doubted that they could stop a general attack without American troops. But in December 1917 the AEF numbered fewer than 200,000 men and could provide only four divisions, none of which had completed their training. The Americans would have to provide more than promises, but it was uncertain that they could do so in time to prevent German victory.

The Navy's War

For the American army three thousand miles of cold Atlantic Ocean led to the war, and in 1917 passage along this highway of waves was perilous. Unless the U.S. Navy, in league with the Royal Navy, could win the war against the German submarines, the conflict in Europe might end before the great American "reinforcement" arrived. Some German admirals predicted that the U-boats would ensure that the American soldiers would feed the Atlantic fish, not fill the Allied ranks in France.

In February 1917 the German navy started its second flurry of unrestricted commerce raiding with a force of only 133 U-boats. This force, never to expand appreciably, was deployed from the North Sea to the Mediterranean. In operational terms the Germans could keep about 32 to 36 U-boats positioned to intercept merchantmen approaching British ports. With this meager force the German navy almost brought the British Empire to its knees. German planners believed that if their U-boats could sink 600,000 tons of shipping a month for six months, they would force Britain to sue for peace or accept economic collapse. In March, the estimated tonnage sunk passed the magic 600,000-ton mark. From April to August, the U-boats kept up the torrid pace of sinkings. Although it juggled tonnage figures to hide the fatal attrition of the transoceanic merchant fleet, the Admiralty staff confessed to its civilian superiors that Britain faced its greatest peril of the war.

The first contribution of the U.S. Navy in the war against the U-boats was the weight of professional opinion. It was an important contribution, for it encouraged the Admiralty to adopt the convoy system and eventually break the U-boat menace. The force behind the American position for convoys was Admiral William S. Sims, stormy petrel of naval affairs and the commander of American naval forces in European waters. Arriving in London on a fact-finding mission before the declaration of war, Sims assessed the U-boat war and immediately supported those Royal Navy officers who argued for the formation of convoys. The opposition was unmoved: The proper way to fight U-boats was to seek them out with patrols, not wait for them to attack merchantmen. Moreover, merchant vessels would not hold formation, maintain adequate speed, or submit to naval commanders. As the sinkings mounted, the conservatives' arguments weakened. The forceful Sims insisted: "The mission of the Allies must be to force the submarines to give battle." The convoy system offered the best chance for decision, since the U-boats *had* to come to the Allies to accomplish their mission. The convoy escorts—primarily destroyers—could sink or drive off the U-boats. When two experimental convoys crossed the Atlantic in May with slight losses, the Admiralty made convoying the new policy. By the autumn of 1917 the rate of sinkings had slowed, and U-boat losses began to mount.

The convoy issue quickly created tension in the Navy Department over the extent of the American naval effort. President Wilson, Secretary Daniels, and Chief of Naval Operations William S. Benson favored convoying, but they were not so sure as Sims that the U.S. Navy had no other mission than to fight U-boats. Examining the location of most of the sinkings (the eastern Atlantic) and the meager force of fifty-one modern American destroyers, Sims cabled, "We cannot send too soon or too many." The Navy Department, examining its deployments to the Pacific and planning to hold a balanced fleet in American waters, decided to retain most of its vessels in the western Atlantic. Sims, however, kept up the barrage of cables until his escort force grew. From the first six destroyers that arrived in Ireland in May, Sims's antisubmarine force climbed to thirty-six toward year's end and to sixty-eight in 1918.

With Sims aligning himself with Admiralty positions, the Navy Department often found itself at odds with its impatient field commander. For example, Sims emphasized the protection of the merchantmen bringing critical supplies to England. The Navy Department, on the other hand, stressed using American vessels outside British control to protect the troop transports sailing directly to France. Largely under Navy escort and using high-speed passenger liners, the stream of transports reached France without an inbound loss and only three outbound losses while merchantmen continued to sink. Committing the major American effort to troopship protection increased the burden on the British economy, but the Wilson administration regarded American troops as more important than Kansas wheat, Texas oil, Argentine beef, and British sailors. It was the sort of choice imposed by a hard war. In the face of the submarine menace and the Allied need for troops, the United States had to find more ships. One of the nation's major contributions was its creation of an emergency merchant fleet that doubled the prewar American tonnage. By 1918 the federal government had become the largest American shipper, accumulating a fleet of 1,700 vessels. The government merchant fleet of 3 million tons was but a fraction of the Allies' some 15 million tons; the American fleet, however, was absolutely critical for carrying the AEF and its supplies to France. Under the direction of the War Shipping Board and Emergency Fleet Corporation, the government confiscated, bought, and chartered 700 vessels. It built 1,000 bulk cargo carriers in record time. This new fleet

either plied the Atlantic or shuttled men and supplies across the English
Channel—and lost 200,000 tons in the effort. The American emergency
fleet, however, did not appear overnight, and shipping shortages and cargo
priorities bedeviled all military planners well into 1918.

Swelling the convoys required a larger Navy escort fleet. It also
required a dramatic change in Navy shipbuilding policies, and in July 1917
the Navy Department suspended its 1916 capital-ship program and turned
its resources to building antisubmarine warfare (ASW) vessels. Characterized by aggressive contracting and technical virtuosity, the Navy's management of its shipbuilding and procurement programs showed such
spectacular successes that they proceeded with minimal WIB participation. They also captured raw materials and skilled manpower the War
Department needed in 1917. In any event, the ASW vessels flowed down
the ways and into the war. The destroyer force grew by fifty-one new, swift
four-stackers of 1,200 tons. Construction time for destroyers fell from a
year to an average of seventy days. Light cruisers and converted yachts
also performed escort duties. The wonder of the wartime Navy, however,
was the "splinter fleet" of 400 wooden subchasers. Modeled after New
England fishing vessels and manned by wartime sailors without maritime
experience, the subchasers probed the waters from the North Sea to the
Adriatic with acoustic sounding gear, searching for U-boats lurking along
the shipping lanes. By the Armistice the ASW fleet numbered nearly 800
vessels. Although Admiral Sims continued to believe that too few American warships arrived in European waters, the Navy Department's material
mobilization was one of the bright spots in the American war effort.

The ASW fleet demanded men as tough and durable as their vessels,
since convoy duty meant long days at sea in weather and living conditions that tested the most phlegmatic sailors. The Navy found such men
throughout American society. The junior officers came from abbreviated
Academy classes, the merchant marine, and Navy officer candidate schools
created on the Plattsburg model. From an officer corps of 4,400 the Navy
expanded to 23,000, of whom only a few thousand held regular commissions. The enlisted force grew from 56,000 to almost 500,000. Since the
Navy Department until August 1918 kept the administration convinced
that it should be excluded from the draft, volunteers (true and draft-
inspired) composed the bulk of the enlisted Navy. Given the popularity of
the Navy, its reputation as a school for vocational training, and its demand
for a wide variety of technical skills and the ratings such skills justified, the
Navy probably recruited more than its share of highly motivated, trained
young men.

Service aboard convoy escorts or in gun crews on merchantmen did
not exhaust all the possibilities for service against the Germans. Some sail-

ors found their way to Europe aboard the eight battleships added to the British Grand Fleet; other sailors served heavy railway guns in France. The antisubmarine war, however, dominated American naval deployments. Despite Sims's protests over diverting resources from the convoy escort squadrons, President Wilson and his naval advisers sympathized with the Admiralty's desire to strike at the U-boat bases. Wilson set the tone of the ASW offensive: "We are hunting hornets all over the farm and letting the nest alone." Offensive operations centered on two alternatives: using mines to sink or discourage U-boats sailing to and from their bases and launching direct attacks upon the bases themselves, principally those in Belgium.

Navy Department planners chose to create a North Sea mine barrage between Scotland and Norway as the principal American ASW offensive. The whole scheme rested upon the inventors' ability to produce a mine that did not depend upon direct contact with a U-boat to explode. To cover a field 250 miles long and 15 to 35 miles wide would require an estimated 400,000 contact mines, whose cost to manufacture and to plant exceeded the field's likely value. It was also unlikely to be planted in time to affect the submarine war. In 1917, however, inventors created a mine that could be detonated by electrical impulses from a 70-foot antenna. Any U-boat that brushed these copper wands would find its voyage rudely interrupted. Although the unit cost of each electrical mine was much higher than that of a contact mine, the planners decided 100,000 of the new mines could cover the projected field, thus making the campaign (in theory) cost-effective. A joint American-British task force began operations in the summer of 1918 and had planted 70,000 mines by the time the war ended. The results were controversial. The mines sank four subs and may have sunk four others; they may have damaged others; and they may have complicated sub operations and demoralized German crews. But the submarine menace had largely passed as a decisive influence by the time the North Sea mine barrage became effective.

Lukewarm about the prospects of the North Sea mines, the Admiralty in 1917 mounted a series of blocking operations against the Belgium submarine bases, but these direct naval and amphibious attacks proved ineffective. Disappointed, American naval planners turned to the alternative of bombing the German bases. Naval aviation was already contributing to the antisubmarine campaign, largely by providing aircraft and dirigibles for scouting duties. When the United States entered the war, the Navy Department began an ambitious program to build 700 aircraft; six months later the planned force had expanded to 1,700 aircraft. The naval aviation force eventually reached more than 2,000 planes and 37,000 officers and men, 19,000 of whom reached Europe. The initial purpose of this force was convoy protection and related reconnaissance duties, but in November 1917 the Navy Department placed the bombing offensive first on its list of priorities. This decision eventually required the Navy to switch its planned force from seaplanes to land-based bombers, principally British-built DeHavilland biplanes. Slowed by earlier Navy programs and disputes with the Army over the allocating of aircraft, the Northern Bombing Group did not begin operations until the autumn of 1918. Composed of a night wing of Navy pilots and a day wing of Marine aviators, the group eventually flew 5,691 sorties against Continental targets. The ASW flights, on the other hand, numbered 22,000. The Northern Bombing Group's contribution came too late to influence either the naval or the land campaign. But the entire Navy aviation effort proved the usefulness of aircraft to all sorts of wartime operations. It also created a group of aviators ready to expand their programs within the peacetime Navy.

Relying primarily on escort convoys, the Navy accomplished its wartime mission, which was to ensure that the American army and supplies and raw materials from the Western Hemisphere reached the Allies. From beginning to end, however, the naval war was Great Britain's to win or lose. Its surface control uncontested after 1916, the Royal Navy carried the burden of the antisubmarine war, and its escorts and subhunting patrols dispatched the vast majority of the 132 U-boats sunk in 1917–1918. American escorts and aircraft participated in only five kills, while Allied submarines alone sank eighteen of their German counterparts. On the other hand, the Navy's principal mission was to escort Army troopships. Confounded by the aggressive escorts and the transports' high speeds, U-boat commanders instead sought slower merchantmen, whose cargoes and numbers could be more easily replaced. Like the Army, the Navy required more than a year to hit full mobilization for a war for which it had not prepared. Despite conflicts between Sims and the Navy Department over the course and speed of the Navy's war effort, the Navy joined the antisubmarine war as rapidly as it could. Looking past the war to the postwar naval balance in both the Pacific and Atlantic, the Navy Department had no intention of abandoning its goal of "a Navy second to none." Meanwhile, the Navy fought well a naval campaign it had not foreseen and had not shaped.

Forming an Army in France

Assessing the erratic state of America's mobilization in January 1918, an official of the Chamber of Commerce admitted to his colleagues that "we are at sea without a chart." Matching the chill of winter, storms of public dissatisfaction swept over Washington, threatening to bury the Wilson administration in political disaster and Allied condemnation. The president fought back. During the same month that the evidence of failed mobilization mounted, Wilson announced his Fourteen Points. But the idealistic words did not sweep away the fact that the Allied cause was in crisis. From Europe came discouraging news: Allied intelligence sources confirmed that the German army had begun to shift more than forty divisions to its western army and to retrain and reequip it for major offensive operations. With an estimated 200 divisions available on the Western Front, the Germans for the first time since 1914 enjoyed a clear superiority in numbers. Moreover, they had perfected new tactics. By using short, intense bombardments, they could penetrate enemy lines with fast-moving infantry battlegroups, whose assignments were to avoid strongpoints and disrupt enemy command and supply arrangements. These tactics produced unit disintegration. Tested in Russia and Italy, the new tactics promised battlefield victory. Dominated by Field Marshal Paul von Hindenburg and General Erich Ludendorff, the German high command decided a land campaign was the only hope for victory in 1918, the last year before the Americans would influence the war. Aware of the German plans, the Allies clamored for a greater American effort.

Embarrassed by the gap between its public promises and its actual performance in 1917 and threatened by a series of congressional investigations, the Wilson administration intensified its direction of the wartime mobilization. It also increased its efforts to crush dissent and encourage patriotic commitment by manipulating opinion. In 1917 the government thought largely in terms of preventing the Germans from collecting information on the war effort; the Espionage Act of 1917 and government control of overseas communications, as well as censorship actions at home, did not bear heavily on the public. The administration, however, also created the Committee on Public Information (CPI), directed by publicist George A. Creel. When it hit its stride in 1918, the Creel Committee bombarded the public with anti-German and pro-American propaganda notable for its multimedia virtuosity and its loose connection with truth. CPI writers, cartoonists, and moviemakers applied their considerable skills to such topics as Teutonic "barbarism," American altruism, and governmental competence. In 1918 the positive appeal of CPI propaganda did not seem a sufficient counter to the antiwar efforts of native-born radicals, alien dissenters, some labor leaders, and draft evaders. No longer confident that the anti-German vigilantism of 1917 would sustain the war effort, Congress in May 1918 passed a Sedition Act characterized by a generous definition of seditious activity. Enforced enthusiastically by Justice Department agents, the Sedition Act gave the 1918 mobilization a vicious edge.

At the core of the flagging mobilization remained the administration's reluctance to centralize economic regulation and force the War Department to reorganize itself and cooperate with the War Industries Board. Under congressional and public pressure, Wilson and Baker partially overcame their fears of industrial self-regulation, corporation-military collusion, and profiteering. The German offensive of March 1918 destroyed the procrastination. Faced with forming a larger AEF than anticipated in 1917, the government delegated enhanced executive authority to a new chairman of the WIB, Bernard Baruch; and a new chief of the War Department General Staff, General Peyton C. March.

Using new broad authority to reorganize the executive branch, granted by Congress in the Overman Act (May 1918), Baruch and March made the WIB and War Department more effective organizations. The key reorganization occurred in the War Department, where March merged the logistical planners of the General Staff with the managers of the Army bureaus. Headed by Major General George W. Goethals, the hard-driving engineer who had completed the Panama Canal, the Purchase, Storage, and Traffic Division of the General Staff brought much-needed efficiency and energy to the Army's war effort. On its own part the WIB moved aggressively to determine supply priorities, fix prices, plan procurement and shipping schedules, mollify labor and farmers with improved wages and profits, and reassure industry that it would retain the major voice in economic regulation. Relieved of most fears of nationalization and antitrust prosecution, American corporations began to produce much-needed military supplies.

The revived mobilization brought more men into uniform and changed the Selective Service system. In early 1918 the organization of the Army remained marked by equipment shortages and personnel turnover. No sooner had the situation improved than the draft calls escalated. From a January low of 23,000 the draft calls climbed to 373,000 in May and averaged around 275,000 a month for the rest of the war. The War Department feared that it would run short of men, while the WIB became concerned that the draft would strip the economy of skilled labor, whose absence could only be partially offset by hiring women war workers. One solution was to assign registrants to five general categories of priority for call-up; introduced in May 1918, the classification of registrants by national category eased the burdens of the local boards by making equity issues more manageable. It did so by adjusting local draft quotas to the number of men in each classification, not the total number of men registered. Classification alone, however, did not produce more men. In 1918 the government held two more general registration periods to catch men not registered in 1917. When the first 1918 registration produced less than a million new registrants, Congress extended the age limits of draftables down to eighteen and up to forty-five. Drafting teenagers was not popular with mothers, the schools, and the churches, but its threat probably made drafting twenty-year-olds easier. If, however, the war had continued into 1919, the Army would have had to fill its ranks from the 13 million younger and older men who registered in September 1918.

Facing the prospect of a German offensive in 1918, Allied leaders coveted the masses of new American soldiers. In December 1917 and January 1918, they eyed the thirty-seven divisions still assembling and training in the United States and examined the AEF's plans for bringing this force to Europe. They did not like what they saw The Allies wondered whether the United States could equip and ship an independent army; they doubted that American commanders and staffs could organize and direct such a force against the skilled Germans. Moreover, they feared that they could not stop the Germans without American troops. Essentially, the Allies wanted to amalgamate American units—from battalions of 1,000 to divisions of 26,000—into the existing structure of the French and British armies. This policy would prevent the diversion of American troops into all the supporting units an independent field army required. The Allies had powerful weapons with which to negotiate amalgamation, for the British had shipping and the French military equipment. These resources were interrelated. To ship a full American division with all its organic equipment (including guns, trucks, and wagons) required four times as much shipping as was needed to bring the men and their personal weapons and equipment. With time of the essence and shipping scarce—and the American military procurement program in disarray—the Allies urged a change in the War Department's shipping plans.

The shipping-amalgamation controversy continued through two phases, the period before the German offensive (December 1917–March 1918) and the period during which the Germans attacked and then lost the strategic initiative (March–July 1918). At the center of the controversy stood the stubborn commander of the AEF, John J. Pershing, who took his orders to create an independent army even more seriously than the civilians who gave him the orders. When Wilson and Baker wavered on the issue, influenced by the Allies and their own advisers, Pershing stood fast. He shared Wilson's assumption that an independent army would be essential to the president's war aims. He also doubted that Allied command procedures, operational concepts, training, and leadership would be acceptable to American troops. He knew that Allied charges of incompetence were unacceptable to the Army's career officer corps.

The first phase of the controversy began with a British proposal to ship all the infantry battalions of ten divisions to France in British vessels. Although he had no objection to having his troops train with the British, as they were already doing with the French, Pershing insisted that this plan was unacceptable since the battalions would have to be amalgamated into the BEF to be combat-effective. After some heated conferences and cable traffic, the AEF and the British agreed to bring six full divisions to Europe on British vessels not already committed to carrying American troops. While the Americans trained with the BEF, American cargo vessels would bring their equipment, and the divisions would return to the AEF in the summer. Under this plan, although it was modified, ten American divisions served with the BEF at some time in 1918 under the control of the U.S. II Corps headquarters. From Pershing's standpoint, the agreement had real advantages: It brought more troops more rapidly to Europe than he expected, and it seemed to end the amalgamation controversy.

Even before the six-division plan was well underway, the German March offensive drove the Allies back to the bargaining table with amalgamation on their minds. In a series of tense negotiations, Pershing agreed to postpone the formation of his own field army, but he would not accept anything but the emergency use of American troops by Allied commanders. He extracted agreement in principle that an American army would be formed and that it would have a sector of its own in Lorraine, the site of the AEF's planned 1918 and 1919 offensives. Again, the key was British shipping. Diverting more vessels from other missions, the British proposed that the Americans bring nothing but infantrymen and machine gunners to Europe at a rate of 120,000 a month for three months for service in the BEF. Unbeknownst to Pershing, the War Department accepted this proposal in April 1918. Pershing and the unreinforced French viewed the pact with displeasure, and the negotiations continued. At a conference at Abbeville, France, in early May, Pershing insisted upon another modification of the shipping plans that would allow the shipment of full divisions. In exchange for French support, he argued that British vessels might bring these troops but that they should be shared with the French. Despite British pleas that they had thus far suffered the greatest losses in the 1918 battles, the new Allied high commander, French General Ferdinand Foch, argued that the French army also needed reinforcement. The temporary resolution of the dispute was that the infantry and machine gunners would receive priority shipment to Europe but would shortly be followed by the rest of the troops of six divisions. If the British released even more ships, they could carry more infantry. This agreement covered only the months of May, June, and July.

The final phase of the shipping-amalgamation controversy occurred against a background of French defeat and American assertiveness. Having restudied the shipping schedules, Pershing's staff found that even though almost a million men were on their way to the front, the AEF would still be short the almost 400,000 support troops necessary for an independent army. In the meantime, the Germans had struck the French army and sent it retreating toward Paris. In another conference at Versailles (June 1–2, 1918) Pershing and the desperate French again collaborated to change the British-sponsored shipping schedules. In exchange for more British shipping, Pershing agreed to bring the combat troops of ten more divisions to Europe, but he also gained both British and American vessels to bring additional support troops. Essentially what occurred was that in May through July 1918 an average of 270,000 American troops arrived in Europe each month. The emergency deployment brought the AEF to more than 1 million men and included enough support troops to bring an independent army closer to reality. The AEF was not yet ready to fight as an independent field army, but it had avoided amalgamation and had gathered its units as full divisions, not as fillers in Allied divisions. This triumph for American policy was Pershing's.

The rush of Americans to France once again reduced War Department plans to shambles. At Versailles General Foch estimated that the United States must provide 100 divisions (big divisions by European standards) to ensure victory in 1919, and he persuaded the Allied political leaders to cable this demand to Washington. Pershing endorsed the new American program, in part to galvanize what he regarded as a halfhearted war effort. The Allied request confounded the War Department, and General March asserted he would "need an Aladdin's lamp" to meet the demands for more troops. During June and July 1918, as the battle continued in Europe, the War Department and WIB studied the problem and concluded that in terms of shipping and supplies the United States could not provide more than 65 divisions. With additional promises of more British shipping and more Allied equipment, the War Department revised the ceiling to 80 divisions. From July until the end of the war, the 80-division program shaped the draft calls and equipment orders.

Although the amalgamation controversy and the rapid expansion of the AEF established the general shape of the American effort in France, General Pershing's headquarters faced a wider variety of organizational problems. Most of them stemmed from the flaws in the American military system and interservice and Allied politics. For example, relations between GHQ AEF and the War Department General Staff deteriorated badly during 1918, and Generals Pershing and March ended the war as chiefs of rival factions. To some degree the problems rested in personality: Both men were hard-driving West Pointers with enviable combat records in the Philippines and vast staff and foreign experience. More important, their disagreements stemmed from the fact that each believed he was the principal commander of the wartime Army. They quarreled over shipping schedules, the training program in the United States, the assignment and promotion of officers, the management of the AEF's supply system, and the procurement of weapons. Secretary Baker adjudicated their disputes but, characteristically, did not decide whether the chief of staff or the expeditionary force commander would be the Army's dominant voice. That decision awaited another war.

Pershing's problems in France did not end with the cables to the War Department, for his force lacked skilled officers at every level of activity. Unless Pershing improved the AEF's leadership and staff efficiency, he faced more demands from the Allies to amalgamate American troops. Only one in every six of the 200,000 American officers who served in World War I had prewar commissioned service in the Army or National Guard. The level of professional competence among the AEF officer corps, particularly among the new officers, concerned Pershing throughout the war. Before the combat of 1918 swamped the AEF, Pershing established an elaborate system of officer schools in France, with courses ranging from weapons employment to staff functioning. These courses, however, stripped units of leaders during their training and could not meet all the AEF's demands in 1918. The wide variety of professional competence in the AEF often meant that operation plans from higher headquarters allowed little flexibility and were executed with little skill, particularly in the use of supporting arms. The Army emerged from the war convinced that it needed a better system of training citizen-officers.

As demanding as he was with his officers, Pershing did not ignore his enlisted men. He insisted that the standards of the AEF would be the standards of West Point, and to the best of his ability he enforced rigid standards of discipline, drill, military courtesy, and dress. It was largely a losing battle. In some ways Pershing kept his promise to run a "clean" army. He would not authorize supervised brothels (as the Allies did), and his medical officers waged a desperate (and largely successful) battle against venereal disease. The war against *vin ordinaire* and demon cognac was less successful; the friendly French, chill weather, and American drinking habits were on the other side. A more basic problem was relations between officers and enlisted men, relations characterized by mutual tolerance and familiarity and casual attitudes toward performance of duty, particularly behind the lines. French and British officers found the Americans warrior-like but unmilitary. They also noted the traditional American profligacy with equipment and supplies; logistical discipline was not an AEF triumph. American units exhausted cars, trucks, and horse-drawn transport at rates that amazed the Allies. From the AEF's standpoint, it never had enough transportation, and its troops' strongest memories were of long hikes under crushing packs.

Two categories of troops bothered AEF headquarters. The first were the Marines. Bowing to Navy Department pressure, Pershing had allowed two Marine infantry regiments and a machine-gun battalion to join the AEF by early 1918. Organized as the 4th Brigade in the 2d Division, the Marines proved excellent in discipline and, eventually, crack assault troops. The trouble was that they wanted to organize an entire Marine division, and they had powerful friends in Washington. Pershing would not allow a Marine division. Although his staff cited administrative problems as the principal barrier, Pershing's primary concern was Navy Department meddling and the Marine Corps' ability to publicize its own accomplishments and thus presumably demoralize the rest of the AEF.

A more vexing question was the role of black American troops in France. By the end of the war the Army had sent 200,000 black soldiers to Europe, most of them draftees. Three-quarters of these men served in labor units, where their work was essential to the AEF. For GHQ AEF these labor units presented one major problem: Fraternization with the French, particularly women. Following their own racial biases and fearing black-white clashes among American troops, AEF commanders established "Jim Crow" practices in France, much to the amazement of the Europeans and the distaste of black Americans. The question of black troops in combat—mostly led by black officers—proved even more tense. Largely as a convenience, Pershing assigned four black infantry regiments, built on prewar National Guard units, to the French army. These regiments fought with distinction throughout the war. Pressed at home by racial equalitarians, the War Department also forced the AEF to form the black 92d Division. Plagued by divisions between its white and black officers and the poor training of its uneducated men, the 92d Division did not perform well and poisoned Army attitudes toward all-black combat units.

Training the AEF brought further strain to the American war effort in France. After his exposure to Allied tactical techniques, Pershing stressed that the AEF should not adopt European "trench warfare" tactics, but should stress "open warfare" maneuvers. He urged the War Department to curtail the activities of the 800 Allied officers and enlisted men in American training camps, and he ordered his division commanders to minimize their dependence on Allied instructors. Pershing wanted his men to practice large-unit assaults with principal emphasis on rifle fire and artillery support, while the Allies stressed small-unit raiding with emphasis on grenades, mortars, and automatic weapons. Since Pershing planned to use the AEF to break through the German defenses, he wanted his troops prepared for battles in the open countryside. A student of warfare who appreciated the firepower of modern armies, Pershing knew the value of troop dispersion, fluid tactics, and punishing artillery support, but his own impatience and the amateurishness of many of his officers often led to a too literal interpretation of his tactical doctrine. Allied observers despaired in the AEF's early battles when they found lines of dead Americans mowed down in windrows like their French and British predecessors of 1914 and 1915. Only late in 1918 did the veteran American divisions show the same degree of tactical skill as their Allied and German counterparts, and the lessons came by bloody experience.

Winning the War, 1918

Against a background of growing famine and political unrest and the serious attrition of the German armed forces, General Erich Ludendorff and his planners designed the great offensive of 1918 to force a negotiated peace before the Americans could affect the war on the Western Front. From March 21 until mid-July, the German army launched five separate major attacks and inflicted serious tactical defeats upon the Allies. Nevertheless, fighting with minimal American participation, the Allied armies proved sufficiently resilient to blunt the German attacks and set the stage for the final victory.

The initial German offensive struck two British armies in the valley of the Somme and drove a 40-by-60–mile salient in the BEF's lines in one week's heavy fighting. Although the Germans began the attack with a local superiority of three to one in artillery and 47 to 29 in divisions, the Allies eventually contained the assault. To draw off Allied reserves, the Germans launched a more modest attack in Flanders on April 9. After a week's heavy fighting, which involved several hundred Americans training with the BEF, the second offensive also stalled. Both sides by now had over 250,000 casualties.

During the opening phases of the German offensive, General Pershing in a moment of high drama offered all he had to the Allied cause. "All" meant the AEF's four divisions that had reached some semblance of combat readiness. One of these divisions joined the French army in Picardy holding the point of the German salient. In late May the 1st Division launched the first major American attack of the war and recaptured the village of Cantigny, impressing both the Germans and Allies with its skill and *élan*.

Before the AEF could make any additional dispositions, the Germans mounted another major offensive against the weakly held Allied lines between Noyen and Reims. In one week (May 27–June 5, 1918) two German armies of seventeen divisions drove fifteen weak French and British divisions away from the Aisne River and then back across the Marne River. The point of the German attack reached Chateau-Thierry and access to the roads to Paris, only forty miles away. In Paris elements of the French government and civilian population began to evacuate the city as the Allied high commanders hurriedly shifted scarce reserves to contain the German offensive. Among the available troops were the American 2d and 3d Divisions. For three weeks these two American divisions helped hold the Marne River line. The 2d Division actually launched a local counterattack that recaptured Belleau Wood and Vaux, and the 3d Division met the fifth German offensive (July 15) and prevented any serious penetrations south of the Marne in its sector. In both division sectors the Americans fought with such suicidal stubbornness that the Germans began to revise their low esteem of the AEF.

If training the AEF concerned Pershing, the American army's logistical requirements dazzled AEF planners with their scope and complexity. The manpower requirements of the Services of Supply (SOS) taxed American resources; at the end of the war there were as many soldiers, civilians, and prisoners supporting the AEF as there were soldiers fighting the Germans. Even this million-man force had difficulty moving the tons of supplies the AEF needed. Most of the AEF's supplies came from ports between Brest and Bordeaux, and these ports suffered from crowded facilities and problems of accounting for all the shipments. Supplies moved forward by rail to a series of depots that maintained levels of supplies for forty-five, thirty, and fifteen days of operations. Matching the flow of supplies to the needs of the fighting divisions demanded ingenuity and administrative skill. As the AEF burgeoned in 1918, the Allies complained that Pershing's staff and the SOS headquarters could not manage their supply system. After the War Department suggested that it send General Goethals to France to run the SOS as an independent command, Pershing gave SOS more independent authority and appointed Major General James G. Harbord, a trusted associate, to command it. Harbord's drive and intellectual grasp helped improve logistical management, but the key reforms came from sheer experience, a reduction of reserve supplies, more careful management, and more realistic estimates on troop usage of different types of supplies. As with so many other aspects of the AEF's experience, the American army learned by doing and did not reach its full potential until near the end of the war.

The problems of combining skilled men and effective equipment in France found no more dramatic expression than the formation of the Air Service, American Expeditionary Forces. Early in the war the Allies told the Wilson administration that it would have to provide 5,000 pilots and as many planes if the Allies were to hold air superiority over the Western Front. Such a program was staggering and beyond America's capacity before 1919. Yet, for all the agonies of the aircraft production program, the United States almost met all its goals. By the end of the war the Army Air Service, a branch nominally under Signal Corps direction, numbered

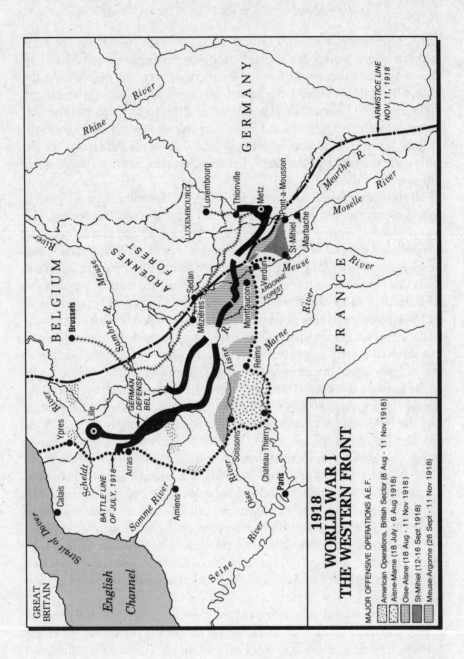

GREAT
BRITAIN

English
Channel

Strait of Dover

Calais

Ypres

Lille

Arras

Amiens

Somme River

Scheldt

Oise River

Seine River

BELGIUM

Brussels

Sambre R.

Meuse River

ARDENNES
FOREST

LUXEMBOURG

Luxembourg

GERMANY

Rhine River

Mézières

Sedan

Soissons

Reims

Chateau Thierry

Paris

Aisne R.

Marne River

Meuse River

Verdun

Montfaucon

ARGONNE
FOREST

Meuse

Thionville

Metz

St-Mihiel

Marbache

Pont-a-Mousson

Moselle River

Meurthe R.

FRANCE

ARMISTICE LINE
NOV. 11, 1918

GERMAN DEFENSE
BELT

BATTLE LINE
OF JULY, 1918

1918
WORLD WAR I
THE WESTERN FRONT

MAJOR OFFENSIVE OPERATIONS A.E.F.

American Operations, British Sector (8 Aug - 11 Nov 1918)

Aisne-Marne (18 July - 6 Aug 1918)

Oise-Aisne (18 Aug - 11 Nov 1918)

St-Mihiel (12-16 Sept 1918)

Meuse-Argonne (26 Sept - 11 Nov 1918)

12,000 pilots and 183,000 officers and men in aircrews and ground support roles. Of this aerial host 58,000 were serving in France. This massive air effort, however, produced only forty-five operational squadrons in contact with the Germans, and the burden of combat flying fell upon only 1,500 aviators. The Air Service, not really committed to combat until the spring of 1918, included 740 planes, one-third of them made in the United States, the others in Europe.

The organization of the Air Service posed special problems for Pershing. Still in its infancy, Army aviation had no senior officers and no institutional base. Until early in 1918 three strong-willed men dominated AEF aviation development: Brigadier General William "Billy" Mitchell, Brigadier General Benjamin D. Foulois, and Colonel Raynal C. Bolling. All young for their rank, Mitchell, Foulois, and Bolling had immense talents, but personal diplomacy was not among them. Plagued by contentiousness, the Air Service buildup led the AEF in waste and confusion until Pershing appointed Major General Mason D. Patrick, an elderly engineer, to the senior Air Service post. Bolling died in 1918, but Mitchell remained as the air combat commander and Foulois as Air Service, AEF, logistical administrator. Unlike Foulois, who learned to fly from the Wright brothers, Mitchell was a latecomer to Army aviation, but his energy and personal magnetism made him a popular commander and primary spokesman for the AEF's aviators.

Led by the Army's few veteran aviators and American pilots who had flown with the Royal Flying Corps or the Lafayette Escadrille, the Air Service joined the war for the use of the air space above the Western Front. The aviators' mission was largely to observe and photograph enemy troop dispositions and movements. This observation mission, which included the use of balloons, required a pursuit force to drive off enemy attackers. Air operations could also be offensive: Strikes at enemy air bases, attacks on enemy troops and depots, bombing runs on enemy trains and trucks. But the Air Service organization reflected its role: Twenty pursuit squadrons, eighteen observation squadrons, and seven bombing squadrons. At a loss of 235 men and 289 planes, this force destroyed 781 German aircraft and 73 balloons. The air effort still left its participants dissatisfied with the focus on observation and air superiority operations and convinced that Army conservatism had constrained their effectiveness.

Although Pershing committed his divisions to the Allies' desperate defensive operations, he and his staff estimated that the Allies could stop the Germans with their own reserves. Establishing corps headquarters to control his scattered divisions, Pershing ordered the consolidation of his best divisions around the Marne salient for the counteroffensive planned for mid-July by the French high command. Pershing had become convinced that French generals had no special expertise, and he feared that the "temporary" use of American divisions in French corps might become a permanent arrangement. When the Allied Aisne-Marne counteroffensive (July 18–August 6) began, the AEF made its first appearance in major strength. Eight American divisions operating primarily in American corps launched many of the attacks that drove the Germans back to their defensive positions along the Aisne and Vesle Rivers. In the meantime, the reinforced BEF launched a series of punishing attacks that continued into early September. The first attack on August 8 produced an unusual event, the complete rout of the defending German divisions. It was, as Ludendorff noted, "a black day" for the German army. The subsequent days were little better, as the attacking BEF inflicted twice as many casualties on the Germans as it received, another new experience that signaled a precipitous decline in German effectiveness and morale.

Even as the Aisne-Marne counteroffensive flickered out along the poison-gas-choked banks of the Vesle, Pershing declared the U.S. 1st Army operational and assembled its five French and fifteen American divisions around the St. Mihiel salient, southeast of the Aisne-Marne battlefields. Pershing intended not only to reduce the salient, but, if German resistance faltered, to drive against the major defenses in front of Metz. The Allies had other ideas. Encouraged by the BEF's successes, Field Marshal Haig proposed a giant "compressing" envelopment against the German army. One wing would be the BEF driving directly eastward through Belgium and northern France; the other wing would be the U.S. 1st Army and French forces driving north through the Meuse River–Argonne Forest region. If this right wing of the Allied attack could penetrate five German defensive zones and fight its way across some forty miles of inhospitable terrain, it could cut the major German railroad supply lines at Sedan and Mezieres and force the Germans to fall back along either side of the mountainous Ardennes region. Without any better plan of his own, Marshal Foch adopted Haig's scheme and persuaded Pershing to reduce the objectives of the St. Mihiel offensive. Pershing agreed to redeploy his army and be ready to begin the Meuse-Argonne offensive in late September.

The St. Mihiel offensive (September 12–16, 1918) produced mixed results. In terms of ground recaptured, the American attack achieved its objectives, and the Air Service, AEF, coordinated its support of the ground assault with ardor and skill. The bag of Germans killed and captured did not meet Pershing's expectations, for the enemy had already begun a tactical withdrawal to strong defensive positions across the base of the salient. The Germans also brought up reinforcements, and Pershing's staff doubted that the 1st Army could have continued the attack. Pershing thought otherwise, but he conformed to his promise to Foch to limit the offensive.

The St. Mihiel offensive confirmed some characteristics of war on the Western Front and American tactical practices that did not bode well for the Meuse-Argonne offensive. Basically, an attacking infantry force could sustain its momentum for about four days and/or a distance of about ten miles. Then the strength of the defenders (presumably reinforced) grew as the power of the attackers diminished. The factors that limited sustained offensives were numerous. As the infantry began to outdistance the range of the prepositioned artillery, casualties—inflicted largely by artillery, gas, and machine guns—climbed. The fire support for infantry attacks became limited to mortars, machine guns, and the few light tanks that survived mechanical breakdowns, tank traps, and enemy fire. Unit effectiveness dwindled with the losses among officers and NCOs, fatigue, anxiety, thirst, and hunger. While the exhausted, overburdened infantrymen collapsed into defensive positions, the rest of the army struggled forward. Units found it difficult to move along clogged country roads turned into quagmires by the autumn rains and intense shellfire. It was particularly difficult for artillery batteries to move forward with adequate ammunition for more heavy barrages. Allied observers found an enormous traffic jam of field kitchens, ammunition carts, supply trucks, horse- and tractor-drawn field guns, and logistical units behind AEF lines. Normally it took the hard-pressed engineers, reinforced by infantry reserves, about four days to repair the roads from the original line of departure to the front. It took another four or five days to organize another attack. The Germans exploited this grace period by preparing another defensive position.

Aware of the 1st Army's limitations but determined to use it to the best of its ability, Pershing massed his forces for the Meuse-Argonne offensive, the most ambitious American military effort in history. From as far distant as sixty miles, 600,000 American troops and 4,000 guns moved toward the new front. Depots behind the front swelled with 40,000 tons of ammunition and similar quantities of other supplies. The movement alone showed a degree of skill in staff planning and logistical management that brought the AEF up to European standards. Huddled over maps and accompanied by the roar of typewriters and mimeographs, division, corps, and 1st Army staffs drafted the complex operational plans that had become a feature of modern warfare.

Emerging from the pages and pages of map overlays, artillery fireplans, and troop lists came a vision of the offensive marked by unwarranted optimism. Pershing approved a three-corps attack (nine divisions) between the Meuse and the Argonne Forest. French troops would support the Americans west of the forest and east of the river. The central American corps would mount the main effort, a head-on drive through Montfaucon into the third German defensive line at Romagne and Cunel.

The left-flank corps would clear the forest and the Aire River Valley to Grandpre, also a major bastion in the third German line, or *Krimhilde Stellung*. The right-flank corps would fill the area between Cunel and the river. The offensive was supposed to cover eight miles and penetrate the main defenses, manned by five divisions, in only two days' time.

Following an intense three-hour barrage the U.S. 1st Army moved in infantry waves against its first objectives on September 26, beginning the AEF's most sustained offensive effort. Only the Armistice on November 11 halted the American attack. The offensive did not, however, move with mechanical smoothness. Only four of the assault divisions had seen serious combat, and four had not worked closely with their artillery. Although the right-flank corps accomplished most of its missions, the center and left-flank corps immediately found themselves tangled in woods and deep ravines or punished in the open hills by machine guns and converging artillery fire. Two days of heavy assaults did not reach the main German defensive position, and two more days of local attacks did not change the situation. In the meantime, the Germans hurried six reinforcing divisions into the Grandpre-Romagne-Cunel line. On October 1, Pershing admitted the original plan had failed and called for his own reserves. The halt allowed the artillery and supplies to creep forward along the ruined roads. The French, meanwhile, argued that the U.S. 1st Army should commit its reserves to the French flank armies. Some French officials, including Premier Clemenceau, suggested also that the AEF needed a new commander.

Determined neither to lose his independent army nor surrender the AEF's hard-won influence on the course of the war, Pershing mounted a series of attacks throughout October. The new attacks, which began on October 4, initially profited by the commitment of Pershing's most veteran divisions. The German reinforcements were equally veteran, and the fighting raged at close quarters. As one artillery corporal recorded, "We are pouring over all sorts of hell on Fritz's head. No wonder he is suing for peace. Nevertheless, he is putting up a terrible resistance. Half the infantry of the First Division in our front have become casualties . . . and we are being shelled day and night." The relative stability of the lines, however, allowed the Americans to mass overwhelming artillery and feed more divisions into the line. Position by position, the key German bastions fell. To the east and west additional American divisions assisted the parallel French advances against such strongholds as Blanc Mont and the heights east of the Meuse. The major American tactical innovation during this phase of the fighting was to launch several night attacks, which, mounted without preliminary bombardments, surprised the Germans and allowed the Americans to penetrate their lines and force several sudden withdrawals. The Americans had discovered through hard experience the same tactics the Germans had introduced in March 1918. In addition, the best American divisions showed considerable skill in combining artillery fire, close air support, poison gas, and tanks with their infantry attacks. The terrain, weather, and German defenses, however, seldom provided opportunities for tactical imagination at the division level, and uneven leadership at lower levels ensured that American casualties remained high.

Having bludgeoned its way through the *Krimhilde Stellung,* the U.S. 1st Army, now commanded by Lieutenant General Hunter Liggett, exploited its success in another series of attacks that began on November 1 and ended with the Armistice. During this exploitation phase of the Meuse-Argonne operation, Pershing opened another front on the approaches to Metz with the U.S. 2d Army, commanded by Lieutenant General Robert L. Bullard. On November 6 the U.S. 1st Army reached the heights above the Meuse at Sedan and bombarded the German railroad. Some of its divisions pushed units across the river east of Sedan, while on November 10–11 the U.S. 2d Army launched a limited advance. Joined with French divisions that bridged the gap between the two American armies, Pershing's army group ruptured the entire German position between Sedan and Metz. In the meantime the BEF had hammered the northern German army groups backward toward the Rhine. At the same time the Central Powers' fragile lines in Italy, the Balkans, and Palestine broke. Faced with global disaster and the defection of the Austrians and the Turks, the German government accepted the Allied armistice terms. On November 11 the fighting dwindled and ended on the Western Front. The exhausted, numbed soldiers of the AEF climbed from their holes. Lighting warming fires, they savored the silence.

Measured by their own national experience, Pershing and his staff viewed the AEF's accomplishments with awe and pride. When the war ended, 1.3 million Americans had served at the front in twenty-nine combat divisions. These troops had provided the margin in numbers that allowed the Allies to grind the German army into surrender. In 200 days of combat, the Americans had lost 53,402 men killed in action or died of wounds. Over 200,000 more were wounded in action. Disease deaths, largely associated with the flu epidemic of 1918, claimed the lives of another 57,000 soldiers at home and abroad. As amateur Civil War historians, some of Pershing's officers could not help drawing comparisons with their Army's heroic past. In area and type of terrain, the Meuse-Argonne operation resembled the Battle of the Wilderness in 1864. There the similarities ended, as the AEF's struggle made the Wilderness pale by comparison. The Wilderness lasted four days, the Meuse-Argonne forty-seven. The Union Army fought with 100,000 men, the AEF with 1.2 million. In the course of the campaign Pershing's artillerymen fired a tonnage of munitions that exceeded the totals fired by the entire Union Army during the course of the Civil War. About half the total AEF casualties occurred in the Meuse-Argonne.

As Woodrow Wilson learned at Versailles, however, the Allies did not view the American achievements and sacrifices with similar reverence. In a four-and-a-half-year war that claimed the lives of 8 million soldiers, the United States fought late and at relatively small cost. Despite its profligate mobilization, the United States bore only one-fifth of the Allies' war costs. Quickly forgetting their relief at the arrival of the AEF's big divisions in 1918, Allied generals minimized the American contribution to the final victory. The Germans convinced themselves after the war that they had been defeated by the war-weary revolutionaries at home and the British at the front. As the AEF's generals expected, few of their countrymen appreciated the scope and complexity of the American war effort. Yet for all the AEF's problems, its role in the Allied victory was crucial, and the Americans who fought in France, professionals and citizen-soldiers alike, knew they had participated in a critical turning point in their nation's military history. They had gone to Europe, and they had fought a mass, industrialized war with allies against a modern national army noted for its expertise. "Over there," they had seen the face of future war.

TWELVE

Military Policy Between
the Two World Wars,
1919–1939

Like the lights of Europe that winked out in 1914, Woodrow Wilson's hopes for peace dimmed during the negotiation of the Treaty of Versailles. By the time his internationalist foreign policy died in the presidential election of 1920, the outlines of postwar American diplomacy and national security policy had emerged. In strategic terms the Fourteen Points and associated idealistic sentiments shrank to three goals: Defending the continental United States and its overseas possessions from foreign attack, deterring European intervention in the affairs of the Western Hemisphere, and preserving China's sovereignty and territorial integrity.

The exhaustion of the European powers in World War I did much to ensure that the United States could achieve its strategic goals without increasing its military power. Germany had disappeared as an imperial power; revolutionary Russia could not muster the forces to do much more than wage civil war; Great Britain, France, and Italy did not have the resources to expand their influence and instead chose to further exhaust themselves by defending their weakened hold on their existing foreign possessions. The collapse of the Austro-Hungarian and Ottoman Empires, in fact, set off a wave of wars of independence and decolonization and the creation of new nations that went on unabated into the 1990s.

Caught between its sympathy for national self-determination and its distaste for great power politics, as well as its desire for expanded international economic influence, the American foreign policy elite returned to traditional notions of unilateralism and noninvolvement in Europe's affairs. After rejecting membership in the League of Nations, the United States focused on foreign trade policy, which became increasingly protectionist in the 1920s, and the collection of war debts assumed by the European nations. Rejecting any commitment to collective security through the League of Nations or any less binding defensive ties to its former partners in World War I, the United States made it less likely that Great Britain and France would find the will and resources to maintain the European balance of power. Even before the end of the 1920s some astute Americans observed that the First World War had simply planted the seeds of a second, even greater, global struggle. They also predicted that the United States would be no more successful in avoiding the second world war than it had the first.

Surveying the political wreckage of 1919, the planners of the Joint Army-Navy Board realized that the most immediate strategic problem was the enhanced international ambition and strategic power of Imperial Japan. More than a decade earlier, Japan's victory in the Russo-Japanese War and deteriorating U.S.-Japanese diplomatic relations prompted the joint board to formulate a contingency plan for conflict with the emerging Asian power. In 1911, the board formalized Plan ORANGE, which called for defending the Philippines and Guam while concentrating U.S. naval forces for an offensive through the central Pacific to isolate Japan. Joining the Allied cause in 1915, the Japanese had extended their military power on the Asian mainland and across the reaches of the central Pacific. Japanese domestic politics, economic weakness, and European-American resistance had snuffed out the Japanese enclaves in China and Siberia by 1921, but the world war left the Japanese the dominant power in the Pacific as far east as the international date line. Securing its conquest of Germany's Pacific holdings, Japan placed itself in a favorable position to return to mainland Asia free of American and European interference. By developing bases in the Caroline Islands, the Marianas (with the exception of American Guam), and the Marshall Islands, Japan made it unlikely that the U.S. Navy could steam to the defense of the Philippines or stop either another incursion into China or attacks on the rich but weak colonial regimes of the Dutch East Indies, French Indo-China, and British Malaya. With the U.S. Navy's trans-Pacific reach blunted by the potential Japanese naval-air-defense system in the central Pacific, a continued Russian military presence in Siberia became even more important in deterring Japan. Should, however, the Soviets become involved in a European war, their ability to involve Japan in a two-front Asian war was likely to disappear. As the Navy's General Board recognized when it reviewed War Plan ORANGE in 1919, Japan did not menace the continental United States and the Western Hemisphere, but it now stood in a favorable position to close the Open Door and deal a deathblow to the imperial system in Asia, which was still critical to the economic reconstruction of Great Britain and France.

American policymakers saw that the world war had not made the world safe for democracy, let alone for narrower American political and economic interests. The disappointments of peacemaking after World War I, however, reduced American will to match the strategic challenges of the postwar world with enlarged, improved military forces. With little popular appetite for "foreign wars" and increased peacetime military spending, the United States, especially the staffs of the Army and Navy, attempted to design a postwar military policy that reconciled the nation's muted internationalism and its commitment to "normalcy." For twenty years the United States relied again on its military potential rather than standing forces.

Postwar Defense Policy

Between 1919 and 1922 the United States government tried to digest all the real and imagined lessons of World War I and establish the legislative base of a military policy compatible with both foreign policy and domestic concerns. The period began with the Versailles Peace Conference and ended with the Washington Conference treaties on naval limitation and security in the Pacific. If the policies of the early 1920s did not survive the rise of international military crises in the 1930s and the disaster of the Great Depression, they did, nevertheless, represent a reasonable response to the risks of the 1920s.

The cornerstone—or the keel—of American defense policy remained the fleet. Although the German U-boat war upon Allied commerce suggested that Mahanian specifics on sea power needed some rethinking, neither the Navy nor civilian navalists saw any reason to abandon the Naval Act of 1916, which foresaw a "Navy second to none" capable of meeting simultaneous naval threats from Great Britain and Japan. Even as the Navy Department phased out its wartime building programs and demobilized emergency sailors, Congress agreed to duplicate the 1916 building program in the Naval Act of 1919. The salvaged 1916 program, however, immediately ran aground. Although naval advisers still viewed Great Britain as a potential adversary, the Wilson administration's civilian negotiators at the Versailles conference suggested to their British counterparts that the United States would abandon another naval arms race if the existing naval powers could negotiate some ceilings on fleet size, type, and modernity. The British proved interested in the proposal. Another restraint upon the Navy came from Congress, which was faced with paying the nation's war debts and cutting government spending in order to check inflation and end a postwar depression. By 1920 Congress had already failed to appropriate money to continue the 1916 program, justified in part by a Senate investigation of the Navy Department's performance in the world war. Encouraged by charges from Admiral William S. Sims that the Navy was organizationally flawed and technologically backward, Congress found ample excuse to cut the battleship building program. The impulse to cut naval spending found diverse support among the reborn peace movement, domestic lobbies like organized labor and reform groups, and the advocates of international agreements to control military spending. Even within the Navy, reformist officers wondered if a renewed commitment to the battleship might be an obsolete response to the potential havoc submarines and airplanes might cause the surface fleet. In sum, the concept of sea power remained largely intact. The instrument of that concept—the battleline of the U.S. Navy—might, however, be altered by a combination of international agreement and organizational-technological change.

The Washington Conference, an international meeting held during the winter of 1921–1922, shaped naval policy until the eve of World War II. Led by Secretary of State Charles Evans Hughes, the American delegation hammered out an agreement on capital-ship numbers and characteristics for the United States, Great Britain, Japan, France, and Italy, assisted by full knowledge of the Japanese position from compromised communications. The Five Power Treaty created a tonnage ratio for battleships and battle-cruisers (a faster, more lightly armored battleship mutant) at 500,000 tons for the United States and Great Britain, 300,000 tons for Japan, and 175,000 tons for France and Italy. The tonnage ceilings were accompanied by a common agreement to limit battleships to 35,000 tons each and main batteries to no larger than 16-inch guns. For ten years the signatories would take a building "holiday" and then replace ships only under treaty agreement.

In more specific terms, the United States fared very well when the tonnage ratios became real battleships. The U.S. Navy battleline would number eighteen vessels, ten of them completed after 1906 and eight of them completed since 1916. The larger Royal Navy battlefleet (twenty ships) was not nearly so modern; the Japanese force numbered only ten battleships. If the Anglo-Japanese alliance of 1902 had remained intact, their combined fleets might have been overwhelming, but the Washington treaties effectively ended the Anglo-Japanese treaty. This strategic uncoupling had been a major American goal and allowed the Navy to preserve a policy it had already adopted. In 1919 the Navy had split the battleline and assigned the most modern battleships to the new Pacific Fleet. Although American commentators made much of the fact that the United States had scrapped fifteen capital ships and stopped work on eleven others, the former were pre-*Dreadnought*s of dubious utility, and the latter were battleships and battlecruisers that Congress had proved reluctant to complete. Moreover, the treaty allowed two battlecruiser hulls to be converted to aircraft carriers, *Lexington* and *Saratoga*. When the two 33,000-ton carriers joined the fleet, they were the best of their type in the world.

At the insistence of the restive Japanese, the Washington treaty on limiting naval armaments also included a provision that the signatories would not add to their base facilities and fortifications in the western Pacific. Much to the Navy's dismay, this provision prevented converting any base west of the Hawaiian Islands into a major facility for supporting fleet operations. Japan had already agreed not to develop bases in the mandated islands and now extended this pledge to Formosa, but its geographic proximity gave it an assumed advantage if war occurred.

The base provision of the Five Power Treaty took on lesser significance, however, when weighed against two other Washington agreements, the Four Power Treaty and the Nine Power Treaty. The former pledged Japan, the United States, France, and Great Britain not to interfere with each others' Asia-Pacific possessions. The latter pledged all the nations with some claim to special privileges in China to respect its political and territorial integrity. Presumably these two treaties made the Five Power Treaty acceptable by eliminating the most likely causes of a Pacific war.

For a Navy already becalmed by budget cuts, the Washington treaties allowed ample room for modernization of the remaining battleships and the use of other funds to develop a "balanced" fleet complete with submarines, a naval air arm, and a scouting force of cruisers (limited to 10,000 tons and 8-inch guns by the Five Power Treaty) and destroyers. Since the Five Power Treaty required comprehensive review within ten years, the naval policy could be changed if the political arrangements for Pacific and Asian security collapsed. If the treaty regime later appeared to pave the road to naval inferiority, the source of difficulty was not the Five Power Treaty itself, but subsequent naval budgets.

Like the creation of the "treaty" Navy, the postwar reorganization of the nation's land forces blended the lessons of the world war and more traditional elements of military policy. The fundamental postwar legislation, the National Defense Act of 1920, created an "Army of the United States," a force of many parts designed to mobilize and expand in wartime around a cadre of regulars and part-time soldiers. Regardless of the manpower formulas it heard from advocates of peacetime military training, Congress rejected compulsory service. It also rejected any appreciable increase in the standing forces. The law, nevertheless, refined the legislation of 1916 in useful ways and eventually provided a sounder basis for wartime mobilization than existed in 1917.

The core issue of postwar military policy focused on manpower mobilization and the relationship of the elements of the Army of the United States to the federal government and each other. In 1919 the War Department General Staff submitted a plan to Congress that called for a regular Army of 500,000 men and a program of universal military training (administered by the regulars) that would provide a reservoir of 500,000 trained reserves. These reserves would fill the ranks of existing units in wartime. In theory this system—unabashedly Uptonian—would have been the quickest way to reach combat effectiveness in an emergency, assuming a parallel state of materiel preparation. The plan, however, appeared Germanic and militaristic—and expensive—to Congress, one of whose members called it "an outrage." Another congressman announced that everyone had had "a bellyful of the damn Army." Searching for an alternative system, Congress borrowed the services of Colonel John McAuley Palmer, historian, experienced staff planner, author, and Pershing protégé. No Uptonian, Palmer was instead Utopian. He urged universal military training on the Swiss model, arguing that a mass army of citizen-soldiers raised by compulsion would be true to American traditions and civilian control of the military. The latter point was dubious and the former point silliness, since the United States had not had compulsory peacetime training since the Militia Act of 1792 had gone unimplemented. Congress, in fact, accepted Palmer's view that the nation did not need a large regular Army, but it rejected the recommended substitute, a citizen reserve force raised through universal military training. Instead the National Defense Act of 1920 built a multi-tiered system based on voluntary participation and diverse degrees of readiness.

The new legislation envisioned a regular U.S. Army of 280,000 officers and men, whose primary mission was to provide tactical units for overseas defense, expeditionary duty, and border protection. It also trained the army's civilian components. Heavily influenced by the National Guard lobby and the Guard's local popularity, Congress designated the Guard the first federal reserve force and strengthened Guard influence on War Department planning. Depending upon citizen interest and federal dollars, the Guard might reach a peacetime strength of 435,000. The next source of soldiers would be the organized reserves, a federal force of officers and enlisted men drawn initially from World War I veterans, who would maintain the headquarters of tactical units as large as divisions. These skeleton divisions would absorb and train wartime conscripts; other federal reservists from the Officers Reserve Corps and Enlisted Reserve Corps would fill the ranks of the active formations in wartime. General Staff planners estimated that the Army of the United States could number 2.3 million men after sixty days of intense mobilization. To manage peacetime training and wartime expansion, the army would be organized into nine corps areas, and each corps would have a regular Army division, two National Guard divisions, and three reserve divisions.

In one particular area the National Defense Act of 1920 proved especially valuable: The provision for commissioning reserve officers on a continuing basis. The War Department and Congress agreed that a critical weakness in America's wartime armies had been the quality and quantity of junior officers in combat units. Since the World War veterans would quickly age—and those with reserve commissions reach field-grade rank—the legislation institutionalized the peacetime training and commissioning of new lieutenants, primarily through a campus-based Reserve Officers Training Corps and a system of summer training camps for non-ROTC participants. Whether ROTC was compulsory or not remained the decision of individual campuses, but the War Department favored compulsion despite the fact that fewer than 10 percent of ROTC cadets took the four-year program that qualified them for a commission. Presumably, two-year compulsory participants would accept wartime commissions rather than serve in the ranks. When the United States once again mobilized in 1940, the War Department could call 80,000 reserve officers to active duty, most of whom were ROTC products.

Manpower mobilization had always fascinated military policymakers, but the experience of World War I showed that industrial mobilization plans equaled manpower policies in importance. Influenced by civilian and military participants in the World War I economic mobilization, especially Bernard Baruch, Congress assigned the duty of industrial readiness to the assistant secretary of war. The assistant secretary's office, staffed by both civilians and officers, became responsible for matching the wartime Army's procurement needs with the nation's production capacity. Although the law did not give the War Department the specific responsibility for designing a mobilization plan for national economic regulation, the National Defense Act of 1920 implied that military procurement could not be divorced from the more comprehensive problems of wartime economic policy.

Planning for Another War

Although the size and composition of the fleet, the structure of the Army of the United States, and the unanswered questions of wartime industrial mobilization brought a new complexity to strategic planning, no single issue so complicated policymaking as the future role of aviation. The airplane challenged traditional definitions of Army and Navy doctrine and functions and stimulated complex patterns of interservice cooperation and conflict. It also set off sharp internal power struggles within both the Army and Navy, consumed scarce personnel and funds that otherwise would have gone to the land army and the surface fleet, and provided an additional weapon for civilians who wanted to prod the military bureaucracies toward new ways of waging war and saving money. The airplane obsessed technological visionaries, who imagined that air war would deter or decide quickly all future conflicts among the industrialized nations. The airplane bonded together an important new political coalition for policy shaping: Military aviators, scientists and engineers, private airplane builders, and those civilians who saw the potential of the airplane for carrying commercial freight and passengers. In sum, the airplane had a far-reaching impact upon interwar military policy in virtually every way except one: It did not offer a cheap and decisive way to protect America.

Fascinated with the potential of the airplane, only partially exploited in World War I, the military missionaries brought the air power gospel to the government and public in 1919. By 1926 both the Army and Navy had made giant strides in establishing military aviation establishments and creating the basic concepts for the airplane's wartime use. Within the Army, Brigadier General William Mitchell led the campaign. The Navy had no Mitchell, and it did not want one. It had instead a trio of aging Young Turks—Admirals William F. Fullam, Bradley Fiske, and William S. Sims—for public education, and in Rear Admiral William A. Moffett the Navy had one of the most talented organizers and lobbyists in its history. Both services also had a tightly knit, dedicated cadre of flying officers who firmly believed that national defense required the aggressive exploitation of the airplane, even to the exclusion of other ways of waging war.

The War and Navy Departments did not ignore military aviation. In 1919 the Joint Board of Aeronautics, an offshoot of the Army-Navy Joint Board, issued its first doctrinal statement on air warfare. The board stressed the importance of air operations to land and sea campaigns but rejected the radical notion (associated especially with Mitchell) that air power might itself win wars. In the future the Army would develop air forces appropriate for the support of all phases of land warfare. As Mitchell defined them, these missions were winning air superiority over the battlefield by destroying the enemy's air force (pursuit), the destruction of ground targets away from the battlefield (bombardment), the destruction of enemy forces on the battlefield (attack), and fire direction and information gathering (observation). The Navy would develop the air forces, based either on carriers or land stations, essential to the conduct of a naval campaign. Naval aviation analysts already believed that future fleet operations would require air superiority. They also recognized that land-based naval aviation might be critical to several phases of a naval campaign, particularly convoying, reconnaissance, and the attack upon enemy naval bases. The knottiest problem, however, was the joint responsibility for coastal defense. The doctrinal statement of 1919 said that both Army and Navy planes might be involved in attacking an invading fleet. Although a sea-borne invasion of the United States seemed a remote threat, naval attacks on the Philippines, Alaska, Hawaii, and the Canal Zone did not appear so unlikely. Whatever the threat, the Joint Board on Aeronautics did not define in any detail the division of labors in aerial coastal defense, thus recognizing (if not solving) an intricate interservice problem.

From his post as director of training and operations for the postwar Army Air Service, Mitchell challenged 1919 doctrine both publicly and privately. Supported by Army and civilian true believers, some of whom were congressmen, Mitchell argued that the airplane would replace the battlefleet as the ultimate weapon of coastal defense. In colorful and unrestrained language, he challenged the government to substitute "Air Power" for "Sea Power" as the nation's basic security policy. Mitchell also urged the creation of a separate air force and department of aviation within a department of defense that would unify all military aviation. He wanted the Navy to have only those land air stations required to train for carrier duty. Although he had not yet developed a full-blown theory of strategic bombardment, Mitchell thought that only organizational autonomy would ensure the full exploitation of aviation.

Military aviation policy did not suffer from official neglect, but the consensus within Congress and the executive branch—argued most vehemently by the General Staff—was that the aviators had not discovered an independent mission for themselves. The only concession to aviators came in 1920 when an Army reorganization elevated the Air Service to coequal status with the other combat arms of the Army. The Navy Department created a Bureau of Aeronautics the following year, with Admiral Moffett as its first chief. The Navy also accelerated its tests of bomb damage to warships, begun in 1920. Exercising his contempt for organizational discipline and his flair for publicity, Mitchell challenged the Navy to let the Air Service participate in its tests. The chief of the Air Service, Major General Charles T. Menoher, a nonaviator, found himself trapped between Mitchell and his disciples and a public clamor to test Mitchell's theories about battleship vulnerability. Confident that Mitchell's claims were exaggerated, the Navy allowed a special Army bombardment force to join its 1921 test program. Mitchell grasped the opportunity, sure that at the least he could make his case that land-based bombers could destroy "unsinkable" battleships and thus enlarge the Army air role in coastal defense.

The bombing tests of 1921 off Chesapeake Bay gave Mitchell his public relations coup, but under circumstances that hardened official opinion against his own leadership and radical reforms. Disregarding Navy rules for the experiments, Mitchell's pilots dropped eleven 1,000- and 2,000-pound bombs on and around the former German battleship *Ostfriesland* and sent it to the bottom. Mitchell crowed over the act and then leaked his own analysis of the tests to the press. Unfortunately, several admirals had implied that bombs would not sink even an anchored, undefended battleship, and Mitchell seized upon their statements to discredit the Navy's leadership and assert that bombers could also sink enemy warships in real combat. Naval aviators had mixed reactions to Mitchell's air theatrics. Although they appreciated the boost to their own cause—that fleet aviation needed increased attention—they did not share Mitchell's enthusiasm for either organizational autonomy or the future of bombing. The Navy position was amply stated in the Washington Conference negotiations: Naval aviation development should not be curbed in international agreement. Congress approved this position in 1922 by authorizing a five-year program to modernize and increase naval aviation to 1,000 modern airplanes and by funding the completion of *Lexington* and *Saratoga.*

Within the War Department Mitchell's insurgency had wide impact. When the exhausted Menoher requested reassignment, General Pershing replaced him with Major General Mason M. Patrick, who had already curbed Mitchell once when they had served in the AEF. Patrick immediately learned to fly (at the age of sixty) and broke up Mitchell's cabal in Washington. He also brought new order and discipline to Air Service affairs. Mitchell himself departed on a tour of Europe, where he renewed his friendship with General Sir Hugh Trenchard of the RAF and may have met General Giulio Douhet, the Italian air chief and author of *Command of the Air* (1921). Mitchell and his disciples understood Douhet's theory that heavy bombers could defeat an enemy by bombing urban civilian populations into demoralization and political upheaval. They did not think that Douhet's strategy suited America's needs, since they still thought largely of the coast defense mission. They agreed with the Europeans, however, that air force autonomy would bring the optimal utilization of military aviation.

If the War Department thought that Mitchell's crusade for an independent air force had slackened, it was mistaken, for even Patrick and other moderates in the Air Service urged the accelerated development of Army aviation. A General Staff study of air power in 1923 found no justification for severing air war from land campaigns or creating an independent air force, but it acknowledged aviation's future importance. The following year a special congressional investigating committee reviewed air policy and reached similar conclusions. Although unhappy over official refusal to allow the creation of an air force freed from the control of field army commanders, Patrick accepted the current belief that air power still served the land campaign. Mitchell did not, and he said so publicly. Patrick transferred Mitchell to a field post, which meant that Mitchell also lost his brigadier generalship. Mitchell continued to charge that the government's inattention to air power bordered on "treason." In the face of Mitchell's continued agitation and public interest in his charges, President Calvin Coolidge ordered another review in 1925, led by Dwight W. Morrow. The Morrow Board also rejected air force independence but urged increased attention to aviation development. The board's findings overlapped Mitchell's court-martial conviction for insubordination and stole some of the aviator's public impact. Disgusted, Mitchell left the Army in 1926 rather than be suspended from duty.

The American love affair with military aviation flowered in 1925–1926 and set both Army and Navy aviation on a stable course. In 1926 Congress passed the Air Corps Act, which changed the Air Service to the Air Corps and gave it equal access to the Chief of Staff. It also provided for a force of 1,514 officers, 16,000 men, and 1,800 planes, which would be modernized by a five-year expansion and modernization program. The War Department would also add an assistant secretary of war (air), a post duplicated in the Department of the Navy. Faced with lessened resistance to aviation within its own ranks, the Navy in 1925 and 1926 adopted policies designed to integrate naval aviation into the mainstream of Navy affairs. By law only naval aviators could henceforth command carriers, seaplane tenders, naval air stations, air squadrons, and aviation training commands. Naval Academy graduates would receive compulsory aviation training after an initial tour of sea duty. In both the Army and Navy, aviation duty no longer carried a stigma, and ambitious officers more eagerly sought certification as pilots. The first phase in the development of postwar military aviation closed with the Army and Navy committed to giving their pilots a chance to prove their separate theories about air operations.

Naval Arms Limitations and War Plan ORANGE

Much to the amusement of the audience—and the irritation of the naval officers present—the male chorus of the 1929 Washington Gridiron Club variety show lampooned the military and its travails with disarmament. Taking their melody from *HMS Pinafore's* "Little Buttercup," the chorus lamented:

> I'm off to the Conference
> That London Conference
> Though I can scarcely tell why;
> Sadder and wiser, of

Diplomats I'm very shy
Our ships they are slighting,
They say, "No more fighting."
We scarcely dare think what it means;
The Navy they're sinking
The Army they're shrinking—
Thank God, we still have the Marines.

Caught between the shoals of budget cutting and the storms of international diplomacy, the "treaty" Navy steered a delicate course into the 1930s. Although still skeptical about the friendship of Great Britain, the Navy deployed the weight of its battleline along the Pacific coast in accordance with the assumptions of War Plan ORANGE. Annual fleet exercises, however, brought the battleships into the Caribbean and Atlantic through the Panama Canal, demonstrating the fleet's flexibility. Small squadrons of light cruisers, destroyers, and gunboats protected American interests in the Far East and Caribbean. When *Lexington* and *Saratoga* joined the fleet in 1928, they went to home ports on the west coast.

Still seeking a margin of offensive superiority that would overcome Japan's geographic advantages in case of war, the Navy Department, especially the General Board, advocated modernization of its battleships and the construction of a balanced fleet within the constraints of the Five Power Treaty. Congress in 1929 approved the construction of a small carrier (14,500 tons) to replace *Langley,* which still allowed three more 23,000-ton carriers within treaty limits. The major concern, however, was the state of the cruiser force. Navy planners argued that the ten light cruisers on duty did not meet the long-range requirements of a war with Japan. Congress approved a force of eight heavy or "treaty" cruisers (8-inch guns, 10,000 tons) in 1924. After another naval disarmament conference at Geneva failed to set any tonnage limits on other naval powers' cruiser forces, Congress again responded to the Navy's pleas for more ships and authorized fifteen more cruisers.

The Great Depression, the Hoover administration, Great Britain, and Japan came between the Navy and its cruiser-building program. As the nation's economic crisis worsened in 1930, the Hoover administration asked the Bureau of the Budget to review the Navy's plans. Exercising the budget-setting powers it had wielded since 1921, the bureau estimated that the Navy's current building program to expand the cruiser force and modernize the rest of the fleet would cost $1.1 billion over a twelve-year period. In annual terms this meant a Navy Department budget around $450 million a year, or at least $100 million a year *more* than the Navy was already spending. When Britain and Japan reported they were ready for another round of negotiations, the Hoover administration promptly sent a pliant delegation to London to solve the cruiser problem on paper.

The London Conference of 1930 produced the last set of diplomatic constraints upon the U.S. Navy before World War II, but its limitations only ratified the Hoover administration's reluctance to support the 1929 building program. Neither Great Britain nor Japan wanted to match the American heavy-cruiser program. Preferring investments in more numerous light cruisers, they agreed to tonnage limitations that they were already predisposed to follow unilaterally. The United States agreed to cut its heavy-cruiser program to eighteen ships within a 180,000-ton ceiling. Light-cruiser ceilings were set at around 140,000 tons for Great Britain and the United States and 100,000 tons for Japan, figures that could accommodate British and Japanese building plans. In addition, the conferees limited submarine tonnage to 52,700 tons and extended the "holiday" on capital-ship construction to 1937. Carrier limitations went unmodified—as the United States wished. The cruiser limitations did not satisfy Navy planners but still allowed some expansion should Congress choose to provide the funds for new heavies and lights. On an extended schedule, Congress authorized the heavy cruisers. It did not fund the light cruisers during the life of the Hoover administration. It also declined to modernize the aging destroyer force, approving only eight of the twenty-eight destroyers the Navy wanted to replace the eighty-seven four-stackers authorized during World War I. In summary, the surface Navy made limited progress toward a balanced fleet structured for the special problems of a Pacific war.

Budgetary constraints affected the fleet in other ways. Funding for manning the fleet, operations, maintenance, and modernization fell well below the recommended levels and dropped about 20 percent below the funds actually authorized in 1922. The Navy's enlisted strength hovered around 80,000 sailors, or 20 percent less than 1922 projections. As new ships joined the fleet—despite some vessel retirements—the manning problem worsened. The Navy attacked both the manning and operations problems by proposing to eliminate a number of marginal bases, but Congress proved reluctant to close bases that provided constituents employment. It also refused to appropriate adequate funds for the development of a major fleet base at Pearl Harbor.

Nevertheless, the "treaty" Navy could point to some bright signs of progress. After *Lexington* and *Saratoga* participated for the first time in fleet maneuvers in 1929, some farsighted battleship admirals could see the potential of air strikes against enemy vessels and land targets. Whether carrier aircraft should strike the enemy's fleet, especially his carriers, or simply protect the American battleline from air attack divided naval tacticians, but the evidence of consecutive fleet exercises pointed inexorably toward the carriers' offensive potential. (The Navy also began to appreciate the importance of rapid-fire antiaircraft batteries and fire direction systems aboard ship.) In addition to the steady development of new types of carrier aircraft, the Navy won an increase of its air forces to 1,625 aircraft in 1933 and ensured a broader appreciation of air power by requiring all lieutenant commanders of the line to take ten hours of flying instruction and to then win wings if they could. Some of the latecomers, like Ernest J. King and William F. Halsey, proved marginal pilots but unlimited enthusiasts for naval aviation.

Below the ocean's surface and the public's general awareness, the "treaty" Navy also created a submarine force designed to participate in fleet operations against Japan. As part of the postwar reassessment of the details of War Plan ORANGE, the Navy started building and experimenting with submarines designed for other than coast defense. Ironically, the submarines the Navy built were admirably suited for commerce raiding, although Navy doctrine declared that long-range or "fleet" submarines fought in support of the battlefleet by scouting and attacking enemy warships. The first fleet boats or "S" Class submarines started a decade-long trend to larger boats whose surface speed, habitability, and fuel capacity would allow them to accompany the surface fleet across the central Pacific. The initial results were not promising. The first trans-Pacific cruise in 1921 took seven months; the subs' surface speed did not reach the required levels; underwater speeds and handling problems discouraged submariners when they submerged and practiced torpedo attacks. Submarine service also proved dangerous. The crews risked substantial dangers even without enemy action. Faulty diesel engines offered carbon monoxide poisoning during surface cruising; saltwater and electric batteries produced deadly chlorine gas when a sub submerged; and propulsion and diving control difficulties sent several subs to the bottom. Rescue and escape procedures—real and simulated—took up a considerable portion of submarine operations.

By the 1930s the fleet submarine program had dropped from fifty-one boats to twenty-six, but design and technological advances had made a true fleet submarine possible. With policy largely set by a conference of aggressive submarine officers, the Navy Department adopted a fleet boat of 1,400 tons with six to ten torpedo tubes. The fleet boats should be capable of patrols lasting seventy-five days and a cruising range of 12,000 miles. Although submarine numbers dropped from a 1930 high of ninety-three to forty-two in 1935, the smaller force was far more capable. Moreover, naval planners and Congress viewed the submarine as an important naval weapon, at least in part because it was cheaper to build and man than surface vessels.

Of all the problems presented by War Plan ORANGE, none proved more troublesome than the absence of a defensible American base system in the Pacific. Even though the fleet retained technical and numerical superiority over the Imperial Japanese Fleet, it could not operate for long beyond its west coast bases, let alone beyond Pearl Harbor. The fleet's appetite was large for spare parts, fresh water, oil, ammunition, food, and repair facilities. In theory the Navy found a solution: To create a "fleet train" of auxiliary vessels capable of mobile support, even underway. In reality, the fleet depended upon an auxiliary force inadequate in numbers (fifty-one ships in 1939) and most notable for its advanced age. For example, it had only two ammunition ships, seventeen oilers, three repair ships, and four stores ships. Only one of these vessels had been commissioned after 1922. Naval planners, who chose to build warships with their limited funds, assumed that the American shipbuilding industry could produce the necessary auxiliaries once war began.

One part of the naval establishment, however, committed itself with enthusiasm to solving the basing problem: The U.S. Marine Corps. During the postwar review of War Plan ORANGE, Major General Commandant John A. Lejeune ordered his erratic protégé, Major Earl H. Ellis, to study the implications of a war with Japan. Casting aside the conventional wisdom that amphibious assaults upon defended positions were impossible, Ellis wrote a study—Operation Plan 712D, or "Advanced Base Force Operations in Micronesia"—which Lejeune endorsed in 1921. With a brilliant fusion of faith and realism, Ellis thought he had identified and solved the fundamental problems of seizing a defended island. Naval gunfire and air strikes would provide the fire superiority that conventional artillery could not, while waves of landing craft brought infantry, machine guns, light artillery, and tanks to the beaches. The concentrated violence of the beach assault should carry the Marines through the beach defenses, provided the Navy could keep the reinforcements and supplies coming in the ship-to-shore movement. Henceforth the Marine Corps would make the impossible amphibious assault possible, since the Navy could not advance across the central Pacific without the bases the Marine Corps would seize for it.

As part of the fleet exercises in 1924 and 1925, small Marine air and ground units tested some of Ellis's theories and found them woefully theoretical, since the Navy did not have the transports and landing craft and the Marine Corps the specialized equipment to make an amphibious landing a bearable risk. The Navy's General Board wanted an amphibious capability, but the available funds did not allow the development of ready forces. Nevertheless, the Army-Navy Joint Board in 1927 declared that the Marine Corps had the basic responsibility for developing amphibious techniques and providing the forces for the base-seizure portion of a naval campaign. With most of its field forces deployed to Nicaragua and China to support American diplomacy in the midst of two civil wars, the Marine Corps reduced its work to more theoretical studies, centered at the Marine Corps Schools, Quantico. By 1934 the Corps had produced a doctrinal publication, *Tentative Manual for Landing Operations,* which in 1938 became the basic Navy guidance for landings. The appearance of the *Tentative Manual* coincided with two other important developments: The return of most of the Marine field forces from abroad and the official announcement that these forces would become the Fleet Marine Force (FMF). Although a new commandant, John H. Russell, was firmly committed to developing the FMF, he reported that a total Marine Corps of 16,405 officers and men could provide only about 3,000 Marines for a projected wartime FMF of 25,000. Materiel development, largely dependent upon Navy and Army commitments, lagged as well. Nevertheless, the concepts that proved so important in all theaters in World War II had been created.

Finally, the Navy Department recovered some of the leadership it had lost during World War I in the field of radio communications and electronics. By the 1930s it had forged a collaborative relationship with the new Radio Corporation of America and initiated an aggressive program to modernize ship-to-ship and ship-to-shore radio communications, both essential to successful operations. Operational communications programs profited by their relationship to general maritime navigation and rescue problems. In addition, Navy intelligence experts joined with communications officers to develop radio intercept techniques and equipment that would allow them to record Japanese messages. Although codebreaking was still an arcane, imprecise, and officially ambivalent activity, the Navy communications-intelligence experts added an invaluable dimension to naval operations. In the related field of radio detection and ranging (radar), however, the Navy did not make parallel progress, largely because of low funding and technical equipment problems.

In 1934 the Houghton Mifflin Company published a second edition of Hector C. Bywater's 1924 bestseller, *The Great Pacific War.* As in the first version of his fictional account of an American-Japanese war, Bywater described a bleak campaign characterized by early American naval defeats. An informed student of naval affairs, Bywater saw no reason to temper his earlier pessimism despite both negotiated naval limitations and fleet modernization and diversification. Like many of his navalist contemporaries, Bywater believed that the United States and Japan had charted collision courses over Asia's future, yet American naval policy had not yet adjusted to the provocative nature of American diplomacy. Bywater had few doubts that the United States could eventually overwhelm Japan with its industrial might, a conclusion shared by Japanese planners as well, but he wondered if the United States could muster the will to reverse the defeat of the "treaty" Navy. Bywater's skepticism reflected the private views of a series of chiefs of naval operations. From the Navy Department's perspective, the future of the Navy depended less upon the flaws in War Plan ORANGE and fleet readiness than upon the political determination to increase naval appropriations. That determination appeared to depend primarily on two incongruous friends of the Navy: A crippled yachtsman from Hyde Park, New York, and a rural Georgia lawyer. The former, however, was now president of the United States and the latter the new chairman of the House Naval Affairs Committee. On the shoulders of Franklin D. Roosevelt and Carl Vinson rested the responsibility of ensuring that Hector Bywater's fiction did not become reality.

Mobilizing and Modernizing the Army

In September 1924 the War Department staged a "Defense Test Day," its first rehearsal of the plans based on the National Defense Act of 1920. The exercise was a farce. Since the War Department wanted to show "that every unit is a part of its own community," the series of patriotic rallies and base open houses must have represented success of a sort, but veteran officers knew that the affair was less a mobilization test than a social gala to honor General Pershing on his retirement. Although regulars, Guardsmen, and reserves manned their mobilization posts, the great muster day produced no new soldiers, since the law had not created a mass citizen army trained in peacetime. Spending only 2 percent of each tax dollar on the Army, the United States had disarmed itself more effectively than the Versailles Treaty disarmed Germany.

For a decade after the passage of the National Defense Act of 1920, the War Department attempted to nurture the Army of the United States. Budgetary pressures kept the half-strength regular Army at around 130,000 officers and men, backed by a National Guard of 180,000. General Staff studies in the 1920s grappled with organizing an army of the future, but the mobilization plans had little success in reconciling a series of critical problems. The General Staff perfected its organizational schemes only by divorcing them from actual contingency plans and ignoring logistical problems. The War Department's basic goal was to weight its plans toward total mobilization and to maintain as many cadre units and individual fillers as the Army of the United States could afford. In reality all elements of the land forces entered the 1930s in a pitiable state of readiness.

In 1931 a new chief of staff, the charismatic Douglas MacArthur, began to shift War Department priorities toward modernizing and training only the most active portions of the Army of the United States. A controversial officer noted for his imperious treatment of existing Army plans and values, MacArthur directed the General Staff to focus on specific war plans or "probable conflicts" and to increase the president's ability to order a partial mobilization on a discretionary basis, meaning free of congressional interference. By 1934 the General Staff had consolidated the paper army active and reserve into a twenty-two-division force, organized into four field armies, of regulars and National Guardsmen. Instead of emphasizing the organization of a mass army to protect the United States from invasion, MacArthur wanted the War Department's funds to go to an "Initial Protective Force" of 400,000 soldiers that could respond to a real crisis, especially a war with Japan. Continued by his successor, Malin Craig, MacArthur's approach—the Protective Mobilization Plan—included a series of six-year programs designed to modernize the regular Army and Guard. The latter force made steady progress in the interwar period, for in 1924 the federal government began to pay the Guardsmen for weekly drills. In 1933 additional legislation ensured that mobilized Guard units would not be broken up and required that Guard officers hold federal reserve commissions and meet regular Army standards in order to draw drill pay.

The War Department foray into peacetime planning for industrial mobilization posed new challenges and produced minimal progress. The constraints on economic planning were political, not technical. Taking its charge from the National Defense Act, the office of the assistant secretary of war created a planning staff for assessing the relationship of the nation's industrial capacity and the Army's projected wartime needs. In 1924 this staff received assistance from a new institution, the Army Industrial College, whose faculty and students collected and analyzed industrial data. Formed in 1922, the Joint Army-Navy Munitions Board reviewed and coordinated industrial planning from the interservice perspective. Although Army and Navy officers did not regard industrial mobilization planning as a pressing matter, industry and trade associations took the War Department's primitive studies seriously, and some 14,000 industry consultants, many of them reserve officers and World War I mobilization veterans, provided information and advice. Among the most influential was Bernard Baruch. After several false starts, the War Department produced its first official, comprehensive Industrial Mobilization Plan (IMP) in 1930.

When the War Department finally published an IMP, it found that the plan stirred interest and substantial criticism. The first plan largely duplicated the World War I system, emphasizing the decentralization of power and minimal interference with the existing economic system. When Congress created a War Policies Commission in 1930 to review economic mobilization planning, industrial spokesmen and veterans' lobbies criticized the IMP's pro-business treatment of corporate profits, industrial wages, consumer prices, and the allocation of the labor force between nonmilitary civilian jobs and military service. Responding to these critics, the planners revised the IMP to provide more centralized direction of the wartime economy, rigorous wage and price fixing, and even the hint of a wartime labor draft. Although the IMP did not place the military in control of the economy, another set of critics thought they saw a conspiracy to give large corporations huge "war profits" for military orders and a concerted effort to "militarize" the economy and destroy organized labor. Although it focused on the export of weapons and the effect of foreign loans on causing wars—especially ones the United States entered—the Senate munitions inquiry by the Nye Committee further eroded the legitimacy of the IMP by pursuing the "military-industrial" conspiracy theme. The result was that the initial appropriations to test portions of the IMP, to encourage raw-materials stockpiling, and to finance a small enlargement of industry's war production capacity all became politically impossible until 1938.

The War Department's planners responded to the IMP's critics by reducing direct Army-Navy participation in making broad wartime economic policy, but their organizational solution of more comprehensive civilian control found little favor. In 1936 the planners designed a War Resources Administration, to be headed by a single director, with powers substantially greater than those of the War Industries Board in World War I. Although Army and Navy planners and corporation executives supported the War Resources Administration concept, virtually no one else did. Satisfied that the WRA would curb high wages and profits, the American Legion accepted the proposal, but peace groups, consumer lobbies, farm groups, organized labor, and the rest of the federal bureaucracy resented their lack of a voice within the WRA's inner circle. Speedy, cost-effective, rational military procurement did not impress the IMP's critics, whom Assistant Secretary of War Louis A. Johnson unfairly characterized as "semi-Communistic wolves." More important, President Roosevelt had no intention of alienating the critics or sharing presidential power with some future economic czar. The 1936 and 1939 revisions of the Industrial Mobilization Plan brought the United States no closer to a wartime system. Instead, the administration turned to the existing agencies, principally the Army-Navy Munitions Board, whose powers and functions were both limited and conservatively administered.

As the Army's mobilization planners realized, all of the General Staff's complicated studies brought no measurable improvement in the Army's readiness to fight. Even when General MacArthur chose to emphasize modernization instead of maintaining all the elements of the Army of the United States, the six-year programs brought little improvement. Army dollars did not stretch far enough. From 1925 until 1940 the War Department spent about $6.2 billion. Of this sum $854 million (roughly two years' appropriations) went to weapons procurement and research and development; the ground forces received only $344 million of these appropriations, or an annual average of $21 million for new procurement.

The Army knew what it needed. In 1934 the General Staff established its modernization priorities: Tank and artillery mechanization, field force motorization, aircraft, communications equipment, and a new semi-automatic rifle. Three years later it placed antiaircraft artillery and target location equipment at the top of its list. Nevertheless, the available funds limited the Army to developing weapons prototypes; it did not have enough money to reequip its field forces to contemporary European standards. Some of the model weapons were first rate: The 60-mm and 81-mm mortars, the 105-mm howitzer, the M1 Garand rifle.

Saddled with World War I weapons and ammunition surpluses, the Army had difficulty winning modernization funds from Congress until it had exhausted its obsolescent stocks. It also chose to maintain its personnel strength when pushed to the fiscal wall; even MacArthur fought to hold trained soldiers rather than buy new weapons. In addition, the Army damaged its own case for modernization by intense, if honest, disputes over modernization priorities and the future use of new weapons. Some congressional critics—for example, Representative Ross A. Collins—hectored the General Staff for its supposed conservatism, but the Army's vague missions made modernization decisions difficult. If the most likely opponent was Mexico, the two divisions of horse cavalry and horse artillery would be more useful than all the tanks in Europe. If the Japanese attacked the Canal Zone or the Philippines, coast artillery would have more importance than either tanks or horse cavalry. In sum, the regular Army and the National Guard hedged against the future by maintaining a wide variety of units, all minimally equipped.

The Army's halting development of armored forces typified all the problems of interwar modernization. By 1920 the wartime Tank Corps of some 5,000 vehicles and nearly 20,000 officers and men had shrunk to 700 French- and British-model tanks and 2,600 soldiers. Despite some interesting exercises by two small tank battalions stationed at Fort Meade, Maryland, the Tank Corps disappeared after the National Defense Act of 1920. (The two battalion commanders, George S. Patton Jr., and Dwight D. Eisenhower, returned to the cavalry and infantry, respectively.) Congress and the General Staff agreed that tanks should support infantry, the decisive arm in combat, so tank units joined the regular infantry for training. The doctrine for tank use remained wedded to the concepts (and speed) of infantry combat. Building on World War I experiments, European forces in the meantime explored new ways of using tanks to wed firepower and mobility and thus restore the decisiveness of offensive ground operations. The fundamental theories were simple to understand but difficult to execute. British theorists argued that future armies could penetrate or flank enemy positions with true armored forces. These forces would combine tanks, mechanized and motorized artillery and infantry, reconnaissance elements, and supporting aircraft. Once through enemy positions, the armored forces would wreak havoc on command and logistical units and so demoralize the enemy that his combat units would retreat or disintegrate.

When the Army began a major motorization program in 1926, it allowed too much innovation, which produced 360 different types of vehicles and maintenance problems. In 1939 it settled on six basic vehicles, all superior performers in World War II. Meanwhile, between 1927 and 1931 the Army flirted with armored warfare but eventually abandoned the experiment, largely because of cost, doctrinal disputes, organizational politics, and technological limitations. After observing the maneuvers of a primitive British armored force in 1927, Secretary of War Dwight Davis ordered the General Staff to create a similar unit. After exhaustive study, the Army assembled two different armored forces, which conducted exercises in 1928 and 1930–1931. Only the most enthusiastic officers, especially Adna R. Chaffee and Sereno Brett, recognized the potential of an armored force, for the tanks themselves were so technologically limited. In addition, the Army's senior officers disagreed about the value of mechanization, and few of them thought armored warfare doctrine justified organizing a separate force for its application. When MacArthur ordered all arms of the ground forces to begin mechanization in 1931, the experimental mechanized force disappeared from the troop list.

While the infantry continued to see the tank as a supporting weapon, some senior cavalry officers welcomed mechanization, since modern weapons had already demonstrated the limitations of horse cavalry. Still prohibited by law from having tanks, the cavalry reformers created a highly experimental mechanized brigade in 1933–1937. The cavalry forces, built around light tanks or "combat cars," emphasized the traditional cavalry virtue of mobility and shock action rather than mobile firepower. They also undervalued the importance of integral infantry and artillery units, also mechanized. Compared with contemporary European armored forces, the mechanized cavalry was long on *blitz* and short on *krieg*. In the meantime the War Department decreed that a medium tank could not weigh more than fifteen tons, the load limit of the army's temporary bridges.

Armor experts put the likely weight of a medium tank at twenty-five tons. The first U.S.-designed tank, the M1921, weighed twenty-three, but subsequent 1930s models dropped to under fifteen tons. The Army dropped a project with J. Walter Christie, who built a tank that could exceed 25 mph, because the tank weight exceeded fifteen tons. Christie sold his chassis design to the Russians, who turned it into the T-34, an exceptional tank of World War II. On the eve of World War II, the Army had made some progress on integrating tanks into its field forces; both infantry and cavalry doctrine dictated that tanks be used in mass to provide shock action. Nevertheless, the Army's four mechanized regiments did not yet represent a new form of ground warfare.

For aviators of the new Army Air Corps, the modernization of the ground forces had no more relevance than buying more horses, since they believed air power would make land forces obsolete. As one ardent lieutenant testified to a presidential commission in 1934, "the defeat of the enemy results from breaking his will to resist and . . . this is most quickly accomplished, in the scheme of modern war, by disruption, by direct action, of his means of prosecuting war . . . . An Air Force is an arm which without the necessity of defeating the armed forces of the enemy, can strike directly and destroy those industrial and communications facilities, without which no nation can wage modern war." Although its post-1926 progress did not satisfy Army aviators, the Air Corps in the decade after the Air Corps Act of 1926 took giant strides in winning an important, nearly independent position in Army strategic planning and force structure. With about one-tenth of the Army's manpower, the Air Corps spent about one-fifth of the War Department's appropriations and built a strong base of public support. By the eve of World War II the air fleet had virtually supplanted the battlefleet as the uniquely American first line of defense—at least in the popular imagination.

The development of the Air Corps depended upon the complex, fragile interrelationship of strategic thought, military planning, aviation technology, tactical doctrine, and organizational politics. As aviators learned in the Mitchell era, the future of military aviation was not exactly self-evident to Congress, the General Staff, and the U.S. Navy. Mitchell's vision was particularly cloudy when he and his disciples argued that airplanes alone would win future wars by strategic bombardment. Nevertheless, Air Corps strategic theorists argued that independent air action would be critical to the next victory—or defeat. The center of Air Corps doctrinal development was the Air Corps Tactical School (ACTS), which drafted field manuals for the Office of the Chief of the Air Corps. Although the General Staff did not approve of severing air operations from land operations, the conventional wisdom of Air Corps planners by the early 1930s centered on the primacy of bombing enemy industrial targets. The ACTS faculty predicted that a future war would require, first, bombing strikes upon the enemy's air forces (built or building), then a concentrated attack upon his war production base in order to destroy his military materiel. Aware of Douhet's concepts of attacking the morale of urban populations by bombing with high explosives, gas, and incendiaries, American air war theorists rejected such notions as wasteful and too unpredictable.

The difficulty with air war theory was its inapplicability to America's specific strategic situation—unless one planned to bomb Ottawa and Mexico City. The immediate fate of the Air Corps rested with the coastal defense mission. Tacitly sharing the aerial responsibility of coastal defense, the Army and Navy had difficulty defining just how they would divide all the possible coastal defense functions. Under presidential pressure, General MacArthur and Admiral William V. Pratt (the chief of naval operations) agreed in 1931 that the Air Corps bore the principal responsibility for conducting land-based attacks upon an enemy invasion fleet. Two years later MacArthur directed the Air Corps to create long-range patrol and bombing squadrons to be stationed in the Philippines, Hawaii, and the Canal Zone. Like other phases of military planning, the Air Corps mission found rationalization in the worst-case possibility of a war against Great Britain and Japan. The new emphasis on coastal defense emerged in the Army's planned structure of the Air Corps, which gave increased emphasis to the bombardment mission. In 1926 the War Department wanted an air component of twelve bombardment squadrons, twenty-one pursuit squadrons, four attack squadrons, and twenty-three observation squadrons. In 1934 this force structure changed to twenty-seven bombardment squadrons, seventeen pursuit squadrons, eleven attack squadrons, and twenty observation squadrons. The coastal defense mission also stimulated the Air Corps to search for long-range navigational equipment and a precision bombsight, the latter developed by the Sperry Corporation and adopted by the Air Corps as the Norden bombsight in 1933.

The Air Corps took the coastal defense mission seriously and conducted many bombing exercises that influenced its tactical doctrine. One of its principal conclusions was that bomber formations could fly farther, higher, and faster than the pursuit aircraft sent to shoot them down. Flying in formations that provided mutual protection, armed and armored bombers would penetrate enemy defenses with acceptable losses and reach their targets. The Air Corps thought it could hit stationary targets and moving ships with decent accuracy with high-altitude, level-approach bombing attacks.

The coastal defense mission gave the Air Corps a reason to stress the creation of large, long-range aircraft. As early as 1927 Major General James Fechet, an aviation pioneer and Patrick's successor as chief of the

Air Corps, ordered that bomber development receive the highest priority in research and development. This decision grew in part from the Douglas, Martin, and Boeing corporations' interest in building long-range aircraft for commercial purposes. Aeronautical engineers tackled the critical problem with enthusiasm: To increase the power of aircraft engines while proportionately reducing aircraft weight. Attacking the payload, lift-to-weight problem, the engineers produced spectacular successes. Shifting to all-metal monoplanes utilizing lightweight composition metals like aluminum, the engineers predicted in 1936 that they could build a bomber that could fly 8,000 miles at 230 miles an hour. They demonstrated the art of the possible for the Air Corps by producing two airplanes that gladdened the hearts of bombing enthusiasts: The twin-engined Boeing B-9 and Martin B-10. The engineering successes in the bomber program so encouraged the Air Corps that in 1934 it offered contracts for the development of a bomber with a 2,000-mile range. From the prototypes, the Air Corps selected the four-engined Boeing XB-17 in 1935 for further development and eventual procurement. By 1937 the Air Corps had wedded its future to the XB-17, despite some early testing frustrations and the lack of funds for a full bomber force.

Bomber development fueled the Air Corps' campaign for additional autonomy from the ground forces and the General Staff. In turn, the General Staff worried about the cost of aviation and the future of air support for the field armies. Banking on congressional and public support, a series of Air Corps chiefs argued for the creation of an "air force" as distinct from an "air corps." The former would conduct offensive operations against a wide range of targets; the latter would support ground units with observation aircraft. Between 1933 and 1935 a series of General Staff, War Department, presidential, and congressional reviews of the Army's aviation policies gave air officers the opportunity to argue forcefully for additional freedom. A series of crashes, some related to the emergency use of the Air Corps to carry the air mail in 1934, galvanized public interest and dramatized the shortcomings of the five-year expansion program authorized in 1926. More important, the General Staff recognized that the Air Corps had a persuasive political case for more independence and feared that Congress would give it the status of a separate service, which would further erode the aviators' commitment to missions related to ground campaigns.

As a compromise the War Department approved in 1934 the creation of a peacetime command labeled General Headquarters (GHQ) Air Force, which would control all bombing, pursuit, and attack squadrons based in the United States. Commanded by an Air Corps general, this force would train in peacetime and fight in war directly under the operational control of the Army chief of staff or an expeditionary force commander, but not field army commanders. Ably commanded by Brigadier General Frank M. Andrews, GHQ Air Force continued to experiment with bombing missions and to influence aviation research and development. The General Staff curbed bomber development by deemphasizing the coastal defense mission (with Navy approval) and stressing ground attack missions. Nevertheless, the Air Corps had by 1938 reached a position to make strategic bombardment an important part of American military doctrine.

Rearmament for Hemispheric Defense

After more than a decade of limiting its armed forces through international agreement and unilateral fiscal action, the United States in 1933 began to rearm. The course change was slight and the increase in speed modest, for the nation still regarded the fleet as the first line of defense and viewed its maritime security system as a bulwark against foreign troubles, not a tool for interventionism. The strategic focus of rearmament remained a minimal effort to deter Japanese adventurism in Asia and the western Pacific and the defense of the Western Hemisphere against foreign military incursions. As always, nonstrategic factors influenced military policy. Coping ineffectively with the Great Depression, the federal government wanted to reduce spending. Yet it also had an inclination to assist some embattled businesses with government orders. One of these industries was shipbuilding, another was aircraft production. Another influence was that the coalition of disarmament advocates and noninterventionists continued to argue that international agreements and congressional action could keep the United States out of another war. Until 1936 the nation participated in international conferences on arms limitation, and between 1935 and 1939 Congress passed five different neutrality acts inhibiting official and unofficial participation in "foreign wars." Only toward the end of the decade did military policy bear any direct relationship to the threat of war.

Naval rearmament required a change of attitude in Congress and a new face in the White House. Unlike Herbert Hoover, Franklin D. Roosevelt did not boast that he had never approved a new vessel and had purposely kept the Navy well below treaty strength. Like his cousin Theodore, FDR had grown up close to the sea, ships, and Navy social circles, and he had few illusions about the force of good intentions in world affairs. Roosevelt, however, promised in his first two presidential campaigns that he would cut government spending, including the military budget. The initiative for naval rearmament rested in Congress, especially Carl Vinson's House Naval Affairs Committee. But at least congressional navalists could depend upon a more sympathetic president. The first test came with the National Industrial Recovery Act of 1933, a modest attempt to stimulate economic recovery by giving businesses increased freedom for self-regulation. A provision of the act allowed the president to use public works funds to build naval vessels, and Roosevelt soon issued an executive order that allocated $238 million for warships. The thirty-two-ship, three-year program provided for two carriers, four cruisers, and twenty destroyers as well as smaller vessels. Congress, however, changed its mind about military public works when the Army and Navy requested more "welfare" spending and forbade similar presidential initiatives.

Undeterred by the protests of critics that the United States had started another naval arms race, Vinson, a legislator of consummate skill, designed another shipbuilding program in 1934. Although it did not meet specific Navy recommendations, the Vinson-Trammell Act authorized the Navy to build up to treaty strength by 1942. Under the act the Navy could build 102 warships, which brought the new authorizations up to 134 vessels. Yet Congress did not rush to modernize the fleet. In 1937, a year after Japan renounced its adherence to all treaty limitations, the Navy had three carriers, ten cruisers, forty-one destroyers, and fifteen submarines under construction. Given the long lead times for warship construction, most of the new ships would not join the fleet until the end of the decade.

After the clear demise of naval arms limitation and the Japanese invasion of China in 1937, Congress reconsidered the fleet's projected strength and returned to a "Navy second to none" policy. The Naval Act of 1938, again piloted through the legislative process by Vinson, expanded the fleet past treaty limits for the first time. The ten-year $1.1 billion program represented a tonnage increase of 20 percent over treaty limits and authorized construction across every category of warship: Three battleships, two carriers, nine cruisers, twenty-three destroyers, and nine submarines. In addition, Congress approved a naval aviation force of 3,000 aircraft, almost doubling authorized airplane strength. The ambitious legislation, however, did not give the Navy any real superiority over Japan, which had also embarked upon a fleet expansion program.

Comparative Fleet Strengths
1939

	UNITED STATES	JAPAN
Battleships	15	10
Carriers	5	6
Cruisers	36	37
Destroyers	104	122
Submarines	56	62

As the Navy Department consistently reminded Roosevelt and Congress, the shipbuilding programs did not exhaust the Navy's pressing needs. A 1938 study of the Navy's base system produced predictable results: The Navy could not operate at any distance from its continental bases, which were themselves inadequate to support the growing fleet. It recommended a $238 million program to expand or build twenty-six bases and assigned "immediate strategic importance" to nine bases, six of which were in the Pacific. Roosevelt and Congress did not respond to the plea for overseas bases. Critical to the execution of War Plan ORANGE, the naval station on Guam, for example, received only sufficient funds to develop its seaplane facilities. In 1939 the Navy reported that the base system could not support fleet operations beyond the hemisphere.

The Navy and Marine Corps also lacked adequate manpower. Although both naval services received increased funding for personnel after 1933, their 1939 numbers were still 20 percent short of estimated peacetime needs. The Navy had 125,202 officers and men, the Marine Corps 19,432. When the Navy's General Board prepared a special report, "Are We Ready Now," in the summer of 1939, the answer was a resounding "No." Manpower shortages inhibited war readiness as much as warship and base shortcomings.

Naval rearmament did not end the Roosevelt administration's interest in military preparedness, for the president recognized that Hitler's Germany posed an additional threat to American security, if only because the Third Reich would limit Britain's and France's ability to deter Japan. Shortly after the Munich crisis in the autumn of 1938, FDR called a special conference of his military advisers to consider aviation policy. Like many of his fellow Americans, FDR tended to think that naval and air forces represented the ultimate answer to the nation's military problems. He also had become expert in political symbolism and believed that words were as useful as weapons in demonstrating international resolve. Much to the consternation of his military advisers, the president ended the aviation conference with the announcement that the United States would expand its military force by 10,000 aircraft at a cost of $500 million. This program would create an aviation industry capable of producing 24,000 aircraft a year sometime in the indefinite future. The difficulty was that FDR did not indicate that he would also call for the money necessary to train pilots, build bases, and procure the equipment and supplies for this force. Skeptics recalled Woodrow Wilson's romantic notion in 1917 about darkening the skies with American planes. Even the numbers had an uncomfortable similarity.

The War Department General Staff and the planners of the Army Air Corps took the president's vague guidance and produced a "balanced" program in time for FDR's annual message to Congress in January 1939. The president, however, would not approve the plans, especially the suggestion that he also support ground force modernization. Three months later Congress passed FDR's reduced request for $300 million and authorized the Air Corps to create a total force of 5,500 aircraft, of which 3,251 would be new planes. It also approved an increase of the Air Corps' pilot strength by 3,000 men. This emergency air-defense expansion act was justified in strategic terms by the fear that the Germans might create air bases in South America. It was also supposed to complement FDR's 1938 decision to create a permanent Atlantic Squadron, dramatizing American concern in the Caribbean.

As the omens of global war mounted, the United States held to its traditional interest in unilateralism, neutrality, and hemispheric security. Even the modest rearmament of the 1930s did not reflect any serious consideration of a two-front war—except among the Army's and Navy's contingency planners. In the words of Admiral Isoroku Yamamoto of the Imperial Japanese Fleet, the United States remained "a sleeping giant" whose massive military potential still required mobilization. Its active forces had marginal influence upon the designs of German and Japanese expansionists and the weak resolve of the British and French governments to meet the aggressors on the battlefield. Yet the interwar period had been especially rich in ideas within the armed forces—ideas about the use of naval aviation, amphibious forces, mechanized ground armies, and strategic air power. United States military policy now faced its greatest challenge.

THIRTEEN

The United States and World War II: From the Edge of Defeat to the Edge of Victory, 1939–1943

On the evening of November 28, 1943, the leaders of the Allied war effort—President Franklin D. Roosevelt, Prime Minister Winston S. Churchill, and Premier Josef Stalin—discussed the world's most destructive modern war. Dining at the Soviet embassy in Tehran, Iran, the "Big Three" moved quickly from a review of their current military operations to an animated exchange of views on the political organization of the postwar world. The choice of subject spoke volumes, for Roosevelt, Churchill, and Stalin assumed that they—and not the Germans and Japanese—would dominate the peace. At different times and in different ways the Allied anti-Axis coalition had moved by the end of 1943 from the edge of defeat to the edge of victory.

Four years earlier the visions of victory came from meetings in Berlin and Tokyo. The momentum for changing the world's map rested with Nazi Germany, the Japanese Empire, and fascist Italy. Pursuing their visions of a new world order, the Axis states had tested the resolve of the Western democracies and the Soviet Union and found that resolve wanting. Between 1936 and 1939 Adolf Hitler, disregarding the cautious advice of his senior military officers, defied the Allies by remilitarizing the Rhineland (1936), annexing Austria (1938), and occupying Czechoslovakia (1938–

1939). The Italians under Benito Mussolini had extended their African empire into Ethiopia without Western resistance, and the Germans and Italians had supported the victorious fascists in a civil war in Spain (1936–1939). In the Far East the Japanese government, dominated by the military, had used its armed forces to create a puppet state in Manchuria (1931) and had then opened a war of conquest against the Chinese Nationalist government (1937) in the name of civilizing China, ending European imperialism in Asia, and forming an Asian economic sphere that would feed and supply Japan.

Much to the glee of the Axis leaders, the aggression of the 1930s threw the potential anti-Axis coalition into disarray. The simultaneous pressure in both Europe and Asia seemed to present insoluble political and military problems for Great Britain, France, the Soviet Union, and the United States. After disappointing talks with the Western Allies, the Soviet Union signed a nonaggression pact with Hitler in August 1939. The Tri-Partite Pact (1940) between Germany, Italy, and Japan pledged mutual assistance if an uncommitted nation (i.e., the United States) entered a war with any of the signatories, and in 1941 Japan and the Soviet Union signed a neutrality agreement. For the Axis powers the great imponderable in their strategic calculations was the United States, whose manpower and industrial resources for war they recognized. They assumed, however, that the United States could not muster the national will to fight a global, two-front war. The dinner conversation in Tehran would prove how wrong these calculations were, but in 1939 Hitler and his Japanese allies had every reason to doubt that the United States would disrupt their plans for a Thousand Year Reich and a Greater East Asia Co-Prosperity Sphere.

Despite tentative efforts by President Roosevelt to alert the American public to the danger of Axis aggression, Congress best represented public opinion when it passed a series of neutrality acts after 1935, acts designed to limit public and private financial and economic assistance to any belligerent. The acts assumed that the United States could follow isolationist policies that would prevent its entry into "foreign wars" and still protect its national interests and physical security. Reexamining their war plans in 1938, Army and Navy planners saw no political support for any strategy but the defense of the Western Hemisphere. In practical terms this area was the hemisphere north of the equator, the Pacific Ocean west to the International Date Line, the Atlantic Ocean east to Greenland, and the approaches to the Caribbean basin. In a new set of war plans, labeled RAINBOW, the planners examined a wide range of contingencies. Although the planners considered the possibility of having allies, they focused on the problem of hemispheric defense without allies against attacks by both the Japanese and Germans. It was an unhappy exercise.

The Philippines and Guam could not be defended, and the planners concluded that the United States—even if it mobilized immediately—could defend its hemispheric security zone by itself only with great difficulty.

The German invasion of Poland in September 1939 and the subsequent declarations of war by Great Britain and France ended the uncertainty about a European war, yet for a year the conflict did not sharply alter American defense policy. Although Roosevelt issued a declaration of national emergency on September 8, 1939, the administration supported programs to improve the readiness of only the regular Army and Navy, for it assumed the public would support no larger mobilization and that the Allies would finally stop Hitler by force and diplomacy, even without Russian assistance.

The stunning German conquests of Norway, Denmark, the Low Countries, and France in June 1940 brought a dramatic change to American policy. With only a battered Britain still in the war, the United States could no longer count on a balance of power in Europe to protect its own interests. After June 1940 the Roosevelt administration, always aware of the divisions in American public opinion, moved cautiously in the name of hemispheric defense toward policies that assisted Great Britain. The United States agreed to consult with Canada, an active belligerent, on the defense of the hemisphere's northern frontier. It then wrested an agreement from its Latin American neighbors that a hemispheric coalition should block the transfer of French and British possessions in the Caribbean basin to the Axis, which might convert these colonies into military outposts. Sensitive to Churchill's pleas for arms, Roosevelt in September 1940—with the reluctant approval of his military advisers—transferred fifty overage destroyers to the Royal Navy in exchange for base rights to eight naval stations from Newfoundland to Trinidad. The agreement increased the Royal Navy's antisubmarine convoy force and improved the coverage of the U.S. Navy's air and surface neutrality patrols. Less to the military's liking was the president's demand that the British be allowed to purchase scarce military equipment—including aircraft—originally ordered by the Army and Navy.

The fall of France and the start of the air-naval Battle of Britain brought new urgency to programs to improve America's military strength, but the emergency actions did not immediately strengthen the nation's military position or bring much assistance to the embattled British. Inhibited by divided opinion about intervention, Roosevelt, military planners, and Congress took only minimal or clearly popular steps to mobilize. Within a clear tradition of emphasis on hemispheric defense, Congress approved in July 1940 an emergency, expansionist "Two Ocean Navy" act to double the tonnage of the Navy's combatant fleet. Although none of the new vessels could join the fleet until 1943, the 1940 authorizations included nine battleships, eleven *Essex*-class carriers, and forty-four heavy and light cruisers. Relying upon the fleet as the bastion against foreign troubles had been American policy since the days of Mahan. The complementary reliance upon air power was newer but no less compelling. In 1940 the Army Air Corps drafted plans to expand to fifty-four groups and 4,000 combat aircraft, then revised its estimates up to eighty-four groups and 7,800 combat aircraft. These plans also received governmental approval.

The most dramatic and controversial programs of 1940 were designed to enlarge the Army's ground forces. Initially, the War Department General Staff, dominated by Chief of Staff George C. Marshall, did not favor a major manpower mobilization, since the regulars to train new units and adequate equipment were in short supply. Roosevelt and Congress, however, saw manpower mobilization as an essential act to awaken the public to the possibility of war, even if the immediate results of mobilization would be decreased readiness. Alerted for active duty in June 1940, National Guardsmen began to enter federal service for additional training in September. By June 1941 nearly 300,000 Guardsmen had swelled the ranks of the active Army. In the meantime, over 600,000 draftees joined them, for in September 1940 Congress passed the Selective Service and Training Act, the nation's first peacetime draft. Supplemented by mobilized reserve officers and other new officers and enlistees, the new Army—the Army of the United States—mustered 1.2 million men by the summer of 1941. It was a force weakened, not strengthened, by manpower expansion and materiel shortages.

Hectored by strident advocates both for and against intervention in the European war, Roosevelt also found himself at odds with his senior military advisers (Marshall and Chief of Naval Operations Harold R. Stark) over the course of the readiness program. Aware that his own urge to help Britain was stronger than the public's and deep in his third presidential election campaign, the president searched for acceptable ways to keep Britain in the war against Germany, the only alternative he saw to direct American participation. The consummate politician, FDR realized that military mobilization could not substitute for the possible deterrent effect of other American policies. When he ruled that the Army Air Corps should share new aircraft production on a fifty-fifty basis with the British, the AAC staff protested that this decision endangered the nation. The president replied simply, "Don't ever let me see those charts again!"

Confident that his seven years as assistant secretary of the navy had made him a qualified strategist, the president concluded in June 1940 that American interests would be served if he deterred the Japanese from advancing upon the Allies' colonial empires in Southeast Asia. Correctly guessing that the European war would prove too great a temptation to the Japanese, who coveted Asia's oil and raw materials, Roosevelt ordered the fleet to the unfinished base at Pearl Harbor, Oahu, Hawaii. When the admiral commanding the fleet later protested that permanently basing the fleet at Pearl Harbor actually reduced its readiness, FDR replaced him. Searching for some way to contain Japan—a policy that served the Allied war against Germany and also protected China and the Philippines—the president risked both increased criticism at home and Japanese belligerency abroad. In 1940 there were no good choices.

As 1941 dawned, the fragile anti-Axis coalition, still based on the continued belligerency of Great Britain, received several encouraging developments. In the United States FDR won reelection, and public opinion, however fatalistic, swung toward more active support of Great Britain, even at the risk of war. The Royal Navy and the Royal Air Force had made the invasion of England a risk Hitler would not accept, and the Third Reich had once more turned its attention to *Lebensraum* in the east and an attack on the Soviet Union, its nominal ally. Despite savage submarine attacks upon its maritime commerce, Great Britain survived and even frustrated Italian designs for African hegemony. The British also destroyed part of the French fleet and ended the French military presence in the Middle East, thus retaining access to the resources of India and the oil-rich Arab lands. American planners watched these developments and soon shared FDR's assessment that the British Empire had not yet lost the war. With the president's approval, the time had come to talk with the British about America's role should it become a belligerent.

From January to March 1941, the principal planners of the United States Army and Navy met with their British counterparts and hammered out the broad contours of an Allied strategy for victory in a war the United States had not yet entered. The Americans had already examined the relevant issues in drafting the Navy's Plan DOG, which assumed a war with allies against all the Axis powers. The British planners, reflecting the judgment of Winston Churchill, had made a similar analysis. The major challenge was Hitler's Germany, for only Germany had the manpower, industrial might, and military capability to ensure an Axis victory. Italy and Japan could not long survive with Nazi Germany destroyed. The defeat of Germany, therefore, received the highest priority. The ABC-1 Staff Agreement (March 1941) represented a military strategy that meshed with the established policies of the United States and Great Britain: i.e., that the course of world politics depended upon the mastery of Western Europe and the northern half of the Western Hemisphere. "Germany First" would be the centerpiece of Allied strategy.

Although FDR did not formally approve ABC-1, Army and Navy planners worked out the details of a "Germany First" strategy in War Plan

RAINBOW 5. Without being precise about the place and timing of specific campaigns, the planners foresaw an offensive war that included naval operations to secure control of all critical seaways and to ruin the enemies' seaborne commerce, strategic bombardment to destroy their air forces and warmaking capacity, the encouragement of resistance movements to erode their political control, and land campaigns to destroy the Axis ground forces. In its Victory Program plan completed in September, the Army estimated that the United States would require a wartime Army of 8.7 million men, divided into a ground army of 6.7 million capable of fielding 213 divisions (half armored or motorized) and an Army air force of 2 million and 195 air groups. The Army planners believed that three-quarters of this force would be available for overseas service. Planners of the Air Corps (soon to be renamed the U.S. Army Air Forces, or USAAF) drafted their own supplement to RAINBOW 5, known as AWPD-1. The planners listed all the tasks they expected the USAAF to perform but put their emphasis on the strategic bombardment of Germany, mounted from England and the Middle East. To conduct all the air tasks, the planners predicted an air force of 64,000 aircraft and 239 air combat groups, about half of which would be bombers. The highest priority in aircraft development was the creation of a very long-range bomber with a 4,000-mile range, a decision that eventually produced the B-29.

The war and FDR, however, confounded the buildup of the American armed forces, since the president still hoped he could avoid war by supporting the Allies and deterring Japan. Recognizing that Britain could not pay for American munitions, the administration and its congressional allies, buoyed by polls that the public favored military assistance to the British, won approval of the Lend-Lease Act in March 1941. Despite repayment provisions, the act further fused the United States to the Allied war effort and gave the British a claim to American war production uninhibited by their inability to pay. In May the administration extended Lend-Lease to the Chinese Nationalists with the faint hope that the Chinese would pin the Japanese army to the mainland of Asia. By November 1941, the cost of Lend-Lease programs had mounted to $13 billion, ten times the amount originally appropriated, and had disrupted delivery schedules to the American armed forces.

The war's major development came in June, when Hitler gave the Allies their greatest strategic gift by invading the Soviet Union. Other than extending Lend-Lease aid to the Russians (transporting was quite a different problem), the United States could do little to assist the Soviet armed forces, whose introduction to the *Blitzkrieg* resulted in one of history's most dramatic military disasters. Riding its euphoria and panzers as far as the approaches to Leningrad, Moscow, and the Donets river basin, the

Wehrmacht had locked itself in battle with a foe of greater numbers and equal tenacity. His mind awash with historical analogies to the war against Napoleon, Churchill lauded the Russians despite their Communism, but Allied military analysts doubted whether the Soviets could stay in the war. They also warned that the Russo-German war removed the last real check upon Japanese expansionism into Southeast Asia. In fact, Japanese military planners were already hard at work on strategic concepts that included the United States' possessions and forces as objectives.

The most immediate strategic challenge, however, was getting Lend-Lease equipment to England across an Atlantic Ocean patrolled by German U-boats (*Unterseebooten*), commanded by officers determined not to lose another Battle of the Atlantic as they had done in 1918. Although the British had formed convoys from the start of the war, the Royal Navy's beleaguered escort forces could not stop U-boat "wolfpack" attacks from producing shocking losses of merchantmen. In the ABC-1 talks the Royal Navy asked for help, and, in the guise of defending neutral rights at sea, FDR gave it. Throughout 1941 the president expanded American naval operations in the Atlantic, and by December the United States was in an undeclared naval war with Germany. Roosevelt expanded the Navy's patrol force to full fleet status, reinforced it from the Pacific Fleet, and gave Admiral Ernest J. King the command. To assist the British, the U.S. Navy began to convoy merchantmen as far east as Iceland and reported U-boat sightings to the Royal Navy; to protect its reconnaissance operations from Iceland, the United States garrisoned the island with a brigade of Marines. Despite Hitler's demands for caution, German submarines in October hit one American destroyer and sank another.

The United States' major strategic concern in November 1941 remained deterring Japan. Roosevelt believed he had warned the Japanese against attacking Malaya and the Netherlands East Indies. His military advisers and critics thought he had done nothing but provoke the war he wished to avoid. America and Japan moved toward war in the summer of 1941 when, against continued American warnings, Japan occupied critical military positions in southern French Indochina. Similar moves in 1940 had brought weak economic sanctions, but this time FDR froze Japanese assets and embargoed oil exports. Negotiations accelerated in activity but declined in hopefulness. American military planners believed the Japanese would strike, and they considered a naval raid on Pearl Harbor a possibility. Polishing their war plans, their Japanese counterparts went further and made the Pearl Harbor strike on the Pacific Fleet an essential part of their opening attacks, which included simultaneous campaigns against Hong Kong, the Philippines, and Malaya. Championed by the brilliant, indomitable commander of the Combined Fleet, Admiral Isoroku Yamamoto, the Pearl Harbor strike summed up Japan's basic strategy: a quick, limited war of conquest between India and the International Date Line, followed by a strategic defense and a negotiated peace with the Allies. The Japanese assumed that the Allies would exhaust themselves in the war with Germany and that the anti-imperialist United States would not wage total war to recover Asian colonies when it had not rescued China and had renounced its own claims to the Philippines.

Assessing FDR's diplomacy and the mounting fear of a Japanese attack, American strategists in Washington worried most about the Philippines, whose defense rested upon the fragile capabilities of the Asiatic Fleet and an American-Philippine army, commanded by Douglas MacArthur. The planners doubted that the Philippines could be defended, but in July 1941 Roosevelt mobilized the Philippine armed forces and ordered the military chiefs to reinforce MacArthur's command and the Asiatic Fleet. MacArthur unleashed his own persuasive prose to urge that the Philippines be defended. Despite "Germany First," the Army and Navy in November 1941 had a reinforcement program underway; B-17s, additional submarines, artillery and antiaircraft units, and munitions were on their way to the Philippines. Japanese domination of the central Pacific highlighted the importance of the Hawaii-Australia-Malay Barrier route south of the equator. British and American planners estimated that any strategic defense of Allied interests in the Pacific would require holding the Malay Barrier-Australia line, although the Americans would not make a firm commitment to defend Singapore. Heated discussion on these matters in Washington, London, Manila, and Hawaii distracted American leaders from the dangers to Pearl Harbor. Faced with ambiguous political reporting and incomplete radio intelligence, the Roosevelt administration foresaw war but not its exact opening acts. Sailing in radio silence along the northern Pacific route, the Japanese navy brought its carrier strike forces undetected into Hawaiian waters.

Enduring Defeat, Planning for Victory

After the Allied rout in Burma in May 1942, General Joseph W. Stilwell spoke of the disaster in his theater, but his words applied to the entire American experience in the first six months of World War II: "I claim we got a hell of a beating . . . and it is humiliating as hell." From the Sunday-morning attack on Pearl Harbor (December 7, 1941) until the naval victory in the Battle of Midway (June 4–5, 1942), the United States saw its armed forces in the Pacific reel from one defeat to another as the Japanese conducted an Asian version of the *Blitzkrieg* and seized every one of their planned objectives at minimal cost and almost exactly according to schedule. The attack on Pearl Harbor was so stunning that its impact sent a shudder throughout America, unifying a confused public ("Remember Pearl Harbor!") and propelling the nation into war with Japan. Germany and Italy then declared war on the United States, convinced that the new enemy would spend itself in the Pacific.

Whatever its shortcomings in political acumen and technical execution, the Japanese attack on Pearl Harbor ensured that the Pacific Fleet—the only major threat to Japan's strategic design—would not interfere with operations in Asia and the western Pacific. Columns of oily smoke and flame rose above the blasted anchorages and air stations of Oahu; in one morning the United States lost 2,500 servicemen, 200 aircraft, five battleships, and three other ships. Eight more vessels suffered battle damage. The only comforts were that American soldiers, sailors, and Marines had fought back with ferocity and that the Japanese had missed three carriers and their escorts, which had been at sea convoying reinforcements to the island outposts around Hawaii; furthermore, the Japanese had not done serious damage to the fleet's fuel farms and maintenance facilities. But the physical wreckage was bad enough, and the psychological wreckage reached all the way to Washington.

Japan's simultaneous attacks on other Allied targets proceeded with shocking speed, especially since uninformed Americans thought the Japanese armed forces were inferior copies of their European models. Strategic and tactical skill, significant advantages in both the numbers and quality of aircraft and warships, and eleven divisions of hardened soldiers gave the Japanese offensive the appearance of invincibility. British Commonwealth forces lost Hong Kong, Malaya, Singapore, and Burma, while outmatched Allied naval forces could only delay the conquest of the Netherlands East Indies. Fanning out from military bases in the central Pacific, the Japanese seized Guam and Wake Island and moved south toward Australia through New Britain and New Guinea and the Solomons to the east. For the United States the fall of the Philippines produced special agonies, for, in the face of disheartening odds, the Filipino-American forces actually resisted until early May 1942, but they could be neither withdrawn nor reinforced.

The defense of the Philippines depended upon the Asiatic Fleet, the Far East Air Force (FEAF) of about 140 aircraft, 31,000 American and Filipino regulars, 100,000 Filipino levies, and the fertile brain of Douglas MacArthur. None proved adequate to meet the Japanese invasion. Through command lapses that still defy explanation, the majority of the FEAF bomber and fighter force burned to junk on the ground from a bombing attack on December 8. The remaining planes and the Asiatic Fleet could not stop invasions throughout December in both northern and southern Luzon, and the Navy fell back to join the Anglo-Dutch squadron defending the Malay Barrier. MacArthur himself did not enjoy one of his finest hours in command, for, alternating between romanticism and despair, he threw his feeble ground forces against the Japanese army rather than retreat immediately to the Bataan peninsula according to plan. By the time his battered forces eventually reached Bataan, they had already suffered serious losses; more important, they had abandoned the food, supplies, and munitions that might have prolonged their resistance or at least reduced their subsequent suffering. Under field conditions that beggar the mind, the Philippine army fought until early April 1942. Disease, malnutrition, and ammunition shortages doomed Bataan's staunch defenders. Their comrades on Corregidor Island resisted an additional month, and then General Jonathan Wainwright, who assumed command after FDR ordered MacArthur to Australia, surrendered the remaining forces throughout the Philippines. Thousands of American and Filipino servicemen and civilians faded into the mountains to form guerrilla units that harassed the Japanese for four years. Wainwright cabled Washington: "With profound regret and with continued pride in my gallant troops, I go to meet the Japanese commander. Good-bye, Mr. President."

As the Philippines fell, the Japanese and the Allies raced toward the last unconquered outposts along the periphery of the eastern line the Japanese intended to defend. The U.S. Army had already dispatched over 100,000 ground and air troops to the island line from Hawaii to Australia, and its planners foresaw using Australia as the base for an advance against the islands of the Malay Barrier, the "soft underbelly" of the Japanese Empire. Having promised "I shall return," MacArthur had begun to organize the counteroffensive, but his forces and those of his Australian counterparts needed time, and only the Navy could buy it. After Pearl Harbor, FDR changed the Navy's leadership, appointing Admiral King to the dual position of fleet commander and chief of naval operations. FDR sent Chester W. Nimitz to Pearl Harbor to command the Pacific Fleet and all other naval activities in the Pacific. Nimitz's ability to stop the Japanese centered on only four carriers and their escorts. This force raided Japanese islands in the central Pacific, and two carriers delivered a squadron of AAF B-25 medium bombers close enough to Japan to stage a dramatic raid on Tokyo on April 18. The initiative, however, remained with the Japanese. The Navy had one closely guarded advantage: its radio interception, decoding, and radio traffic analysis skills gave it special insights into Japanese plans and deployments.

In the spring of 1942 the Japanese moved simultaneously in three directions—toward the Aleutians in the northern Pacific, across the central Pacific, and against the remaining Allied outposts on New Guinea and in the Solomon Islands. The grand design was to cut the supply line to Australia and engage the U.S. fleet in decisive battle. (The Aleutian attack was a ruse.) At the Battle of the Coral Sea (May 3–8, 1942) a U.S. Navy task force with two carriers fought a confused battle with a Japanese invasion force in the first major sea engagement in which airplanes bore the offensive burden and the fleets never saw one another. The Americans lost one carrier, but the Japanese called off their fleet. A month later Admiral Yamamoto sortied with the Combined Fleet to capture Midway and draw Nimitz's three remaining carriers into a decisive battle. Forewarned by his intelligence experts, Nimitz committed his naval aviation against the Japanese carrier force on June 4. The Japanese fleet proved difficult to locate, and the squadrons arrived over their targets at varied times and already low on gas. Three torpedo squadrons attacked without fighter cover and perished, but their attack diverted the Japanese fighters, which did not intercept three following divebomber squadrons. The Americans caught the Japanese carriers in the process of refueling and rearming their planes and turned three of them into exploding, sinking pyres. The battle later cost each fleet another carrier. Japanese losses in pilots, planes, and carriers meant that the Combined Fleet no longer had any appreciable offensive edge over the Pacific Fleet, however reduced. For the moment the Pacific war hung in the balance.

As the American armed forces and public opinion reeled under the news from the Pacific, the Roosevelt administration rallied to build the diplomatic, political, and strategic foundations for ultimate victory. A cautious Wilsonian, FDR wanted a clear statement of Allied war aims that would appeal to the American people. In August 1941, he negotiated with Churchill an idealistic document, known as the Atlantic Charter, that branded fascism a menace to all mankind. FDR's own "Four Freedoms" further identified the basic human values for which the Allies were fighting. In January 1942, he persuaded the British, Russians, and Chinese to sign the Declaration of the United Nations, a statement that pledged the Allies to pursue total victory (and no separate peace treaties) to the limits of their means in order "to defend life, liberty, and religious freedom, and to preserve human rights and justice in their own lands as well as in other lands." The foreign signatories viewed the statement as part of the price of American participation, but FDR viewed it as not only an instrument to mobilize home-front support, but a guide for American diplomacy and strategy.

Translating a policy of total victory into strategic plans proved difficult for the Americans and British and nearly impossible in collaboration with the Russians and Chinese. The ABC-1 statement about defeating "Germany First" seemed sensible, and neither the Americans nor the

British ever strayed far from this position. Nevertheless, the orchestration of the war against Germany and Japan in terms of the timing and geographic emphasis of military operations provided ample opportunities for disagreement and strategic negotiations. These opportunities received their first full examination at an Anglo-American conference in Washington in December 1941–January 1942, a conference attended by Roosevelt, Churchill, and their principal military advisers. The British had a far more precise strategic vision than their American counterparts: defeat Germany by bombing, internal subversion, aid to the Russians, and military operations along the vulnerable frontiers of *Festung Europa*. Reverting to their traditional approach to defeating continental enemies, the British wanted to avoid a direct confrontation with a full-strength Wehrmacht in northern Europe until this confrontation carried little risk of a 1914–1918 stalemate. Instead they urged operations in the Mediterranean theater, where they were already engaged and where their scarce naval, air, and ground forces had shown some ability to check the Germans and Italians. Churchill stressed that the Mediterranean theater offered many strategic opportunities, since the African littoral could be wrested from the Vichy French forces in Morocco and Algeria and the German-Italian army campaigning in the Libyan-Egyptian area against the British 8th Army. Churchill argued that a 1942 campaign in this area would divert German troops from Russia and strengthen the British war effort. What he did not say was that this campaign would be British-commanded (thus presumably using the greatest Allied expertise in generalship) and help restore the integrity of the British Empire, which Churchill desperately wanted to preserve.

The American military planners found the British position unappealing and pressured FDR not to accept Churchill's strategy. The Army representatives, equally knowledgeable about World War I, doubted that the Allies could avoid a major campaign against the Wehrmacht in France, accepting even the most optimistic estimates of the Russian contribution. Strategic bombing, which the Army planners favored, was an unproved war winner, but at least it would support an invasion. The impact of subversion by resistance movements was equally uncertain. And operations in Scandinavia and the Mediterranean seemed unlikely to bleed the Wehrmacht in quantities that justified the commitment. The Army planners, with the notable exception of Dwight D. Eisenhower, also warned FDR that British strategy seemed designed more to preserve the empire than to defeat the Germans, and they feared that the British would fight only for narrow national interests. In addition, Admiral King, an Anglophobe, urged that the war against Japan should not be delayed by the "Germany First" strategy.

The Washington conference produced no firm commitments to future operations other than that the Allies should work together to mount a bombing campaign and antisubmarine effort. In principle the Americans agreed to Churchill's "tightening the ring" strategy of limited operations, but they approved no specific operations. After the conference, however, the Army's planners proposed a more detailed strategy for 1942–1943. The U.S. Army ground and air forces would deploy to England (BOLERO) in order to prepare for two possible expeditions to the Continent. An invasion in 1942 (SLEDGEHAMMER) would occur if the Russians appeared to be on the verge of defeat or the Hitler regime was weakened by internal upheaval. More likely was a 1943 invasion (ROUNDUP) that would throw forty-eight divisions (thirty American) onto the Continent for a massive campaign against the Wehrmacht. Examining the implications of these operations, the British responded that they did not think Allied cargo and amphibious assault shipping could meet the demands of this strategy; and, equally perceptive, they did not believe that the U.S. Army could raise and train an air and ground force adequate to give the Allies the necessary edge to guarantee victory without prohibitive losses.

In deciding where to strike first and in what force, FDR's viewpoint proved critical. From his perspective, coalition and domestic politics played a larger role than strategic theory. First of all, FDR recognized that his commitment to a "second front" (wherever it might be) would play a role in the Allies' continued will to fight, and he placed the highest priority on Allied solidarity, both in waging the war and designing the peace. Always the man of action rather than of theory or long-range planning, FDR wanted to commit the American armed forces in 1942 against both Japan and Germany and in ways more dramatic than weak bombing raids and naval warfare. His politico-strategic sense was sound, sounder than his military advisers', who recognized the role of "politics" but thought it meant elections and party advantage. FDR had no desire for the Democrats to lose the congressional elections of 1942, but his purposes were larger. He feared that inaction in 1942 would produce domestic pressure to abandon the "Germany First" strategy and endanger the administration's ability to mobilize the home front for total war. Influenced by Churchill's golden rhetoric and alarmed by his Army planners' insistence on a real SLEDGEHAMMER, the president in July 1942 made two critical commitments: to send American divisions to French North Africa along with the British and to allow a modest counteroffensive in the south Pacific. In effect, FDR's decision meant that a major invasion of France would have to wait until 1944. His decision pleased the British, the Navy, and General MacArthur, who had his own strategic designs and his own political base among the Republican Party and the press.

Dealing with the British in 1942 forced the Americans to organize themselves for coalition operations and for interservice cooperation, neither skills in which the American armed forces were very advanced. The organizational arrangements they created lasted beyond the war. To advise the president, the senior service commanders created the Joint Chiefs of Staff (JCS), which included obvious members like General Marshall and Admiral King. When Admiral Stark lost his post as chief of naval operations to King, the new CNO became the only Navy representative, but FDR soon appointed a personal chief of staff and ad hoc chairman of the JCS, Admiral William D. Leahy, a former CNO and trusted friend. On the Army side, General Marshall urged the equal participation of General H.H. "Hap" Arnold, his deputy chief of staff for air and commanding general, USAAF. Arnold's participation seemed justified by the assumed role of air power and the independent status of the Royal Air Force. When the American military "big four" met with the British, the JCS became part of the Combined Chiefs of Staff; more important, the CCS created its own Anglo-American staff system to study plans and operations directed by the CCS. For actual management of operations—and for strategic recommendations—the CCS agreed on further integration. The American and British organized their field forces as both *combined* (all Allied) and *joint* (all services) in each geographic theater. The commander's nationality and service would be determined by the nature of the war in the theater and which nation would provide the bulk of the forces.

In practice, only in the European-Mediterranean theaters did the Allies create a truly cooperative command system, and even there national and civilian-military divisions on strategy surfaced throughout the war. On the mainland of Asia the two principal Allied commanders, Admiral Lord Louis Mountbatten and Generalissimo Chiang Kai-shek, dominated strategy, with minor (and frustrated) American influence exercised by General Stilwell and the air commander, General Claire Chennault. In the Pacific, where only the Australians and New Zealanders provided significant non-American forces, the CCS accepted two American commanders, MacArthur in the southwest Pacific area and Nimitz in the Pacific Ocean areas, which included the south Pacific, central Pacific, and northern Pacific. Neither MacArthur nor Nimitz proved very ecumenical in their management of the war. Although both commanded joint and combined forces at some point in the war, MacArthur and Nimitz ran their theaters with Army and Navy staffs respectively. Their personal preferences reinforced service predispositions on strategy. Selectively encouraged by Marshall and King, MacArthur and Nimitz both urged additional American commitments to the war upon Japan, but they had different ideas about just what sort of war that should be. MacArthur favored an Army-USAAF advance through the large jungle islands toward the Philippines, in which ground-based air and Army and Australian divisions would carry the war. Nimitz thought in terms of fleet actions and amphibious operations across the central Pacific in the best War Plan ORANGE tradition. By appeasing both MacArthur and Nimitz, the JCS remained decisive in shaping Pacific operations, while FDR ensured that the war on Japan did not jeopardize "Germany First" by holding a veto over JCS plans.

Mobilization and Opportunity

America's entry into World War II meant that the world's most powerful economy had joined the Allied cause, and from the beginning of the war the Roosevelt administration intended to make the United States the anti-Axis coalition's "Arsenal of Democracy." In crude terms the United States preferred to spend dollars, not lives, and to place forces in the field that enjoyed superiority in both the technical quality and quantity of their military equipment and supplies. America's farms and factories could support not only the nation's own armed forces but those of the British Empire, the Soviet Union, Nationalist China, and any other ally (like the Free French and Free Poles) who wanted to take the field. In the case of the British, the United States also bolstered a domestic economy stretched to poverty levels by the war effort, for British civilian morale and industrial productivity were important to the Axis defeat. In the broadest national terms the "Arsenal of Democracy" approach was successful, for the United States spent more money on the war ($350 billion in direct expenditures) than the other major belligerents but suffered the fewest war-related military deaths (405,399) among its allies and foes. Removed by distance from the fighting as it was, its civilian casualties were trivial. During the war it placed a smaller proportion of its population in uniform than the other major belligerents, and in 1945 in both absolute and relative terms its economy remained the world's strongest.

American strategy for a two-front war, of course, required a manpower mobilization that in absolute numbers exceeded all previous national experience. Between December 1941 and December 1946, more than 16 million Americans wore uniforms, approximately 11 million as members of the Army, 4 million as sailors, 669,000 as Marines, and 350,000 in women's military units. When the war ended, around 12 million Americans were still serving, of whom 266,000 were women. The major instrument for mobilizing manpower was the Selective Service System; it was already functioning on the day of Pearl Harbor, and a year later all formal volunteering for the armed forces ended by law. The draft legislation by the end of 1942 required that all males ages eighteen to sixty-four register, but in practice the upper age limit for service was set at forty-four, then dropped to thirty-eight. The Selective Service System registered 36 million males but inducted only 10 million members of the military pool. The majority of men rejected (6.4 million) had medical defects that would not have spared them from service in other nations. The draft officers found only 510,000 registrants absolutely disqualified for service. In sum, the United States put about one-sixth of its total male population into uniform.

The manpower mobilization forced the armed services under political pressure to drop or modify their policies on the admission and assignment of ethnic minority males, who could be drafted, and women, all volunteers. The largest minority in service was African-American. Before the war's end, 650,000 African-Americans had joined the air and ground armies. Another 167,000 black men became sailors (and thirteen naval line officers), and 19,000 joined the Marine Corps. Americans of Latino descent served throughout the armed forces, including senior officers, and numbered an estimated 350,000. Mexican migrant workers added 125,000 men to the ranks. Chinese, Koreans, and Filipinos of American citizenship joined all the services and often joined special forces and intelligence units.

Americans of Japanese ancestry born in the mainland states and Hawaii (*Nisei*) prized their citizenship and bristled at accusations of disloyalty, accusations that sent 110,000 family members (about 62 percent citizens) to barren relocation camps in 1942. Hawaiian Japanese in 1943 rushed to join a token unit, the 100th Infantry Battalion, raised in part to send young, dissident *Nisei* to the mainland. The battalion grew to become the 442d Regimental Combat Team, which won unparalleled honors in the war against Germany. The "Go For Broke" *Nisei* provided an estimated 10,000 officers and men for a unit of 4,500 authorized billets. The regiment suffered 717 combat deaths and collected almost 10,000 Purple Hearts for wounds. Many GIs bore more than one wound and hospital trips, which explains some of the soft statistics. (A monument to all *Nisei* service personnel lists 16,163 individual names, including 37 women.) Members of the regiment received over 5,000 decorations for valor, and the 442nd RCT received eight unit citations.

For multiculturalism, the 298th Infantry Regiment, Hawaiian National Guard, set the standard. It included prewar Guardsmen and new soldiers from the Chinese, Filipino, Portuguese, Mexican, Polynesian, *haoli* (white) and *hapa* (mixed race) communities of the islands. The regiment served on security duties in the South Pacific during 1943–1944.

Between 1906 and 1935 more than 150,000 Filipinos came to the United States, principally to serve as farm workers in Hawaii and California. Ineligible for naturalization under the existing laws, Filipinos could not join the armed forces unless born in the United States. Ironically, Filipinos could enlist in the Philippine Scouts, part of the American colonial army. The valiant service of the Scouts in a losing cause convinced Congress to change the law in 1942 and allow Filipino "aliens" to enlist and in 1943 to use service as a path to citizenship. Although the Army created an infantry regiment, separate infantry battalion, and airborne reconnaissance battalion, between 1943 and 1945 Filipino soldiers could be found throughout the Sixth and Eighth Armies in the southwest Pacific. They performed valuable service in the liberation of the Philippines, 1944–1945. An estimated 400,000 Filipinos served in the U.S. armed forces, the Army of the Commonwealth of the Philippines, in the Philippine Scouts, and in the guerrilla units formed by the U.S. Army Forces Far East.

Federal personnel planners urged the services to recruit women for an estimated 400,000 jobs that would free males for combat service. Before the war ended an estimated 350,000 women had donned uniforms for temporary, noncombat jobs. About half of them served in the Women's Army Auxiliary Corps (WAAC), the only service units other than nurses to go overseas. More than 6,500 WAACs were black women. The Army and Navy expanded their nursing corps to 14,000, who served in all overseas theaters. The Navy and Marine Corps enlisted almost 100,000 women auxiliaries. Although not technically military, the 1,900 female aviators of the Women Airforce Service Pilots (WASPs) ferried USAAF aircraft between stateside bases, and thirty-eight died in crashes.

Native Americans, most of them volunteers from reservations, added 25,000 warriors to the services, with 22,000 going to the Army. One-fifth of the 45th Infantry Division, Oklahoma National Guard, came from residents of the former Indian Territory, populated by the displaced "civilized tribes" from east of the Mississippi. Texas and southwestern National Guard units included Pimas, Kiowas, Apaches, Comanches, and Navajo. The 32nd Infantry Division, Wisconsin National Guard, included hundreds of Great Lakes tribal members.

In theory, the armed forces assigned members on the basis of character, education, trainability, aptitude, and physical qualifications. African-Americans faced racial prejudices that limited assignments. These racial assumptions held that blacks could not and should not command whites. Blacks lacked technical aptitudes. Either because of slavery or racial characteristics, blacks would not fight and die for the United States, which ignored a good deal of history. Educated blacks served only to challenge Jim Crow barriers, which was partially true. Most blacks could serve usefully in labor units. The war put a lie to all these assumptions, although it is also true that in 1941–1945 black enlisted personnel, mostly drafted, came from the undereducated south.

Only one-third of black GIs served abroad, the largest number (132,000) in Europe, 1944–1945. About 50,000 black soldiers served in 22 combat units in Europe, the bulk of them in the 92d Infantry Division in Italy, 1943–1945, with uneven success and poisoned by interracial friction among its officers. The most notable service came from all-black tank, tank destroyer, artillery, and truck battalions of the "Red Ball Express." In the infantry replacement crisis of 1944–1945, 4,500 black GIs volunteered to serve as replacement infantry platoons in white companies in ten different divisions. The experience did not test real integration, which would have been the color-blind assignment of black officers and NCOs.

The most telling experience was the formation of the four-squadron 332d Fighter Group ("The Red Tails") and the 477th Medium Bomber Group. Both groups came from the USAAF pilot-training school at Tuskegee Institute, Alabama. The USAAF did not welcome this "experiment," but it faced stubborn pressure from white, urban northern Democrats and black civil rights leaders. A handful of white officers, notably Colonel Noel Parrish, supported the mission. Eventually, 450 Tuskegee fighter pilots flew 15,000 sorties against the Luftwaffe. Sixty-six died in aerial combat over Germany and Italy. The 332nd group commander, Colonel Benjamin O. Davis Jr. (USMA 1936) became the first black general in the U.S. Air Force.

The Navy and Marine Corps made more limited steps in opening their ranks to ethnic minorities, but blacks faced the greater challenges toward integration. In principle, the Navy could assign black sailors to any billet, not just as stewards, but in reality the majority of black sailors served in shore depot, construction, and base service units. They also suffered the greatest casualties ashore: 202 sailors killed and more than 300 injured in the 1944 ammunition dump explosion at Port Chicago, California. Nevertheless, pressured by Secretary of the Navy James V. Forrestal, the Navy created all-black crews for a destroyer escort, a patrol craft, and twenty-five service ships, to demonstrate the broad skills of black sailors. The Marine Corps organized two defense battalions and sixty-two depot and ammunition companies, many of which saw rear area combat on Pacific islands during 1944–1945.

The armed forces exploited cultural diversity against foes that worshiped "purity." One innovation by the Marine Corps was to use Navajo tribesmen to send rapid, secure tactical radio voice messages. The U.S. Army had experimented in World War I using Choctaw "codetalkers" and employed Comanches in the same role in the European war, 1944–1945. The Marine Corps created its "codetalkers" after Japanese and Navajo linguists, most of them missionaries, convinced Navy-Marine Corps communications security officers that no Japanese could understand or duplicate Navajo, an archaic tonal language with no alphabet. Some Japanese, however, could speak some variety of American English. Eventually, 429

Navajo "codetalkers" directed air and artillery strikes and made urgent position reports in the Pacific war. The U.S. Army Military Intelligence Service recruited and trained more than 6,000 Americans of Japanese and Chinese descent to serve as interpreters and translators for the war with Japan. All the services benefited from their courage and imaginative missions from Burma to New Guinea.

The "Arsenal of Democracy" policy meant that the armed services did not have an unlimited call upon the nation's manpower (even those who met service standards), for the policy required a motivated, capable industrial and agricultural work force. Manpower experts in the federal government in 1942 estimated that the war effort would require a military and civilian work force of around 60 million from a total population of 135 million. (The actual work force in 1945 numbered 73 million.) Enlarging the work force—as long as the armed forces did not exceed 15 million— did not prove especially troublesome. When the munitions industry began to expand in 1940, there were 7 million unemployed American workers. As these Americans entered the military and civilian war work, they were joined by another 7 million Americans who had not worked before. The prospect of war work produced a vast national internal migration; retirees, women, and blacks appeared in vast numbers on the assembly lines, and impoverished farmers and agricultural workers from the south and prairie states moved to industrial complexes in the east, the midwest, and Pacific states. The industrial work force expanded by 10 million, and the agricultural work force declined by 5 million.

Placing the right numbers of people with the right skills in war work taxed the Roosevelt administration, however, since it and Congress refused to conscript war workers. The government, instead, depended upon wage incentives to attract workers. Uncontrolled, this approach did not work well, for war industries bid against one another for skilled workers, and worker turnover early in the war damaged productivity in critical industries. The strongest element of compulsion in mobilizing civilian labor was the provision for the Selective Service System to grant occupational deferments, and in the course of the war it provided deferments for over 5 million workers. The inefficiency of wage incentives, however, convinced the government to take greater direct control of manpower policy, and in early 1942 two new agencies, the War Manpower Commission and the National War Labor Board, assumed responsibility for coordinating government-industrial relationships and policies. Both agencies established programs to train, attract, and keep war workers on the job, but neither succeeded in injecting any substantial compulsion into the labor supply system.

The government rejected "work or fight" programs and refused to approve laws to outlaw strikes or the right of individual workers to choose

their own jobs. Labor unions and the farm lobby proved powerful influences upon national policy; for example, the tobacco industry managed to
have itself labeled "critical" to the war effort, thus securing deferments for
2 million workers. The civilian labor managers enjoyed two limited successes, curbing military demands for more men and bringing some uniformity to wage policies, which dampened labor pirating. They were more
successful in establishing training programs for undermanned trades (e.g.,
metalworking) and in securing better working conditions. Fortunately, the
unmobilized labor force of 1941 and the wage incentive policy combined
to provide the "Arsenal of Democracy" with adequate war workers. World
War II provided a boon for the American worker, whose wages during the
war increased 68 percent while the cost of living increased only 23 percent. On the basis of income distribution changes within the population
during the war, fully one-third of Americans moved into the middle class,
and their reborn optimism, new skills, and unspent savings provided the
foundation of postwar prosperity.

Mobilizing labor for war provided ample challenges for the Roosevelt
administration, but industrial mobilization and the production of war
materiel made labor problems pale by comparison. Nevertheless, the government hammered out its basic policies by 1943. Many of the technical
problems of military procurement were well known from the World War I
experience. The barriers to effective mobilization were more political than
technical, although shortages of both raw materials and industrial plants
slowed mobilization. The war did not end the deeply held beliefs about the
American economy that had characterized the New Deal years and shaped
national politics in the 1930s. Economic planners, farmers, labor and consumer groups, and the intellectual coalition of government administrators
and academics feared that America's corporate and financial leaders would
use the war to curb the federal government's power to push the economy
toward full employment and a wider distribution of wealth. Some business leaders and their Republican allies did indeed see the war as such an
opportunity, but the majority of business leaders simply did not want the
wartime emergency to be an excuse for extending permanent government
control, which they thought would ruin their postwar ability to do business as market-oriented, profit-making corporations. The War and Navy
Departments tended to favor the business point of view, since they wanted
industry to provide the weapons of war as quickly as possible in enormous
quantities, and they believed that reform of the American economy would
inhibit the war effort. Civilian analysts estimated that the Army's "Victory
Program" would cost $150 billion. The Navy's early wartime estimates
were no less breathtaking. FDR himself changed his own appreciation of
the military's needs. Before the fall of France he saw no need for urgency,

but in January 1942 he told Congress that the United States would need to produce in the next two years 185,000 aircraft, 110,000 tanks, and 55,000 antiaircraft guns. Lend-Lease produced additional demands upon the "Arsenal of Democracy," and before the war's end the United States had provided its allies with 37,000 tanks, 792,000 trucks, 43,000 aircraft, and 1.8 million rifles.

Amid much political bargaining the government established its basic policy for industrial mobilization before Pearl Harbor. That policy assumed that the war effort would depend upon the profit motive and corporate leadership to spur industrial expansion. Government regulation would be minimal and come only when political pressure or business uncooperativeness demanded action. Certainly the military would not determine economic policy, since such an approach was politically unacceptable and neglected the importance of national interests beyond victory in World War II. Instead, nonmilitary agencies would determine the relationship between immediate military requirements (American and Allied), domestic needs, the available resources, and the structure of the economy. Tested in 1940–1941, when munitions production doubled, the government thought it had found a formula for spurring the conversion of an expanded industrial plant to war production. Essentially, the government promised to relieve war industries of financial risk by buying weapons on a cost-plus-fixed-profit basis, with additional incentives to exceed time and quantity goals. It provided attractive tax write-offs for plant expansion and modernization, purchased and leased factories to private companies, provided scarce raw materials, and helped recruit and train labor. Large industries also could assume freedom from antitrust prosecution. Despite numerous problems, the World War II industrial mobilization proceeded without the degree of inefficiency and waste that had characterized World War I, and corporate profits during the war mounted from $6.4 billion to $10.8 billion, which kept business cooperative. Industrial productivity drove the gross national product up from $91 billion in 1941 to $166 billion in 1945.

The federal government, however, could not surrender economic mobilization to American business, since the war was too important to be left to management. Before Pearl Harbor the Roosevelt administration followed a modus operandi it had developed in the 1930s. When an economic problem cried for government intervention, the administration created a special agency to deal with the problem, but the agency seldom had clear power or authority, sharing its mission with others. This system (or lack thereof) drove politicians and bureaucrats to distraction, but it preserved FDR's power and allowed all the competing political interests to seek accommodation or annihilation. They usually compromised, as the president wanted.

In January 1942 the administration finally decided that its current way of doing business would not suffice and created the War Production Board (WPB), headed by retailing executive Donald M. Nelson.

FDR could have granted Nelson a "czar's" powers, since in March 1942 Congress in a second War Powers Act gave the president the authority to allocate materials and facilities to war production, an implied charge to centralize economic mobilization. He did not do so. Temperamentally, Nelson was no Bernard Baruch, and he faced powerful competitors in the Army and Navy (who coordinated their own plans through the Joint Munitions Board), the Lend-Lease Administration, the Maritime Commission, the Office of Civilian Supply, the Office of Price Administration, and five different Anglo-American supply coordination boards. Without a clear political mandate from FDR and nearly friendless in Congress, Nelson had little success in controlling military orders or pressuring industry to cut domestic production. Unsettled strategic plans and unresolved conflicts over scarce raw materials brought increased demands for central control by *somebody*. The military departments did not relish the role, but they would have taken it since equipment scarcities were still epidemic. In May 1943, FDR finally created the Office of War Mobilization and persuaded James F. Byrnes, an astute former senator and Supreme Court justice, to take the job. With increased authority, expanded production, and clear strategic plans, Byrnes made OWM the central coordinator of a mobilization kingdom that continued to be peopled by fractious bureaucratic barons and political interests.

Selected Items, American War Production
July 1940–August 1945

Tanks	86,000
Artillery pieces	120,000
Shoulder weapons	14 million
Trucks and jeeps	2.4 million
Combatant vessels	1,200
Landing craft and ships	82,000
Bombers	96,000
Fighters	88,000
Transports	23,000
"Liberty" ships	2,600
Tankers	700

The actual instruments for producing materiel for the war effort were as varied as the agencies created to direct the mobilization. When economic incentives and some degree of self-regulation stimulated producers, they found ways to increase production of such critical items as food and petroleum products, assisted by rationing and pricing policies that restricted domestic consumption. The same approach applied to rubber, with the additional provision that the chemical industry found it attractive to produce synthetic rubber. The voracious need for metals could be only partially served by increased production, so durable consumer goods disappeared from the marketplace and manufacturers moved to paper and plastics as substitute materials in both military and civilian consumables. The scarcity of raw metals and steel also furnished the government with the most effective tool for settling priority disputes among war industries. Designed by Ferdinand Eberstadt, a Baruch protégé and leader of the Army-Navy Munitions Board, the Controlled Materials Plan went into effect in late 1942 and allowed the WPB to adjust production schedules to FDR-JCS strategic decisions by allocating steel, aluminum, and copper to the twelve principal government contractees rather than the thousands of contractors. Each claimant, therefore, had to persuade a Requirements Committee chaired by Eberstadt on the virtues of its raw-materials needs. The WPB further influenced the process by also controlling the delivery of scarce raw materials and components, thus shaping production schedules.

The federal government used its war powers over the nation's financial system to pay for the war, reduce domestic consumption, and control inflation. Increased income and corporate and excise taxes financed the war and checked civilian spending; the government paid 40 percent of the war's costs from current revenues, a percentage never before approached in American war financing. It also borrowed $187 billion from its own citizens in the form of war bonds and from itself by regulating credit and the money supply through the Federal Reserve System and the Treasury Department. The national debt increased from $49 billion in 1941 to $260 billion in 1945. Money and credit controls supplemented price controls as a check on consumption and inflation, which the administration correctly identified as a threat to public morale and productivity.

The "Arsenal of Democracy" policy also assumed that the American scientific-engineering community would ensure that the armed forces enjoyed technological superiority over the Axis. After some pulling and hauling between the various military and civilian components of the research and development (R&D) community, the administration established the Office of Scientific Research and Development under Dr. Vannevar Bush, president of the Carnegie Institution. An active lobbyist for war-related research, Bush won an important early battle by winning draft exemptions for 10,000 critical scientists and engineers. He also designed the basic R&D system by using liberal government contracts to turn university and industrial research laboratories to critical war projects. Bush successfully argued that government-controlled laboratories would not utilize scientific talent effectively and would stifle technical creativity. Bush and his associates decided which labs would tackle which projects by evaluating the labs' specialties and arranging close civilian-military collaboration in equipment design. Using their own and British inventions, the American developers produced an impressive list of military innovations: radar, antitank rockets for aircraft and infantry launchers, amphibious vehicles, bombing guidance systems, sonar for detecting submarines and a variety of rocket-propelled weapons for destroying them, improved shells, a radar-controlled proximity fuse for all kinds of ground and naval antiaircraft artillery, drugs to combat infection and tropical diseases, and, ultimately, the atomic bomb. Although German achievements in artillery and tank design—as well as jet aircraft and long-range rockets—proved that the Americans had no monopoly on developmental expertise, the United States created a research and development effort that balanced technical sophistication with mass production and time-urgent deployment.

The Allied accomplishments in the electronic "wizard war" complemented the performance in the mass production war. The use and abuse of the radio wave shaped many military operations. During the course of the war the Allies developed radio signals as guides to long-range air and naval navigation; the use of radar dramatically improved the ability of airplanes and warships to find targets when eyesight failed because of distance, darkness, and weather. Long-range radio communications allowed senior commanders to coordinate the movement of forces far from their headquarters. The widespread use of radio signals, however, opened a whole arena of military operations, and the Allies eventually emerged as victors in the signals intelligence war that resulted. With equipment capable of receiving enemy radio messages, both sides could exploit radio intercepts in several ways. With high-frequency direction-finding receivers, the Allies could locate enemy forces (especially warships) whenever those forces sent radio messages within range of Allied monitoring stations. A careful analysis of radio messages, even when encoded, often allowed Allied intelligence officers to identify the message sender and to track enemy deployments. Finding the location and identity of enemy forces permitted intelligence analysts to make astute guesses about enemy intentions.

One especially significant Allied advantage in signals intelligence was in high-level codebreaking, which often reduced the guesswork involved in assessing the enemy's intentions, numbers, deployments, equipment, and morale. By midwar, the British and Americans had broken their adversaries' most important codes, occasionally through pure cryptanalysis utilizing sophisticated mathematical theories, but often only with the help of captured cryptography equipment and codebooks and careless errors by enemy radio operators. Even before Pearl Harbor the United States had penetrated Japan's foremost diplomatic code, which the Americans read fluently until Japan surrendered. The resulting intelligence, codenamed MAGIC, was vital in the battle against both Japan and Germany; messages from the Japanese ambassador in Berlin to Tokyo reporting his interviews with Hitler and other leading Nazis were an invaluable source of information regarding the Germans. In the Pacific theater, the Americans generated ULTRA, which was intelligence gleaned from breaking Japan's military codes, including its primary navy code, Army Water Transport Code, military attaché code, main army code, and several army air force codes. In the European and Mediterranean theaters, the British Government Code and Cipher School at Bletchley Park also produced ULTRA, but in this case it denoted intelligence obtained from messages transmitted by the Germans over their supposedly secure Enigma machines. Fortunately for the Allies, the Germans were wrong; from late 1943 until war's end Bletchley Park produced nearly 84,000 Enigma decrypts per month. Military intelligence resulting from even the best codebreaking effort was rarely perfect or complete, and it would have been useless if it had not been utilized in battle by determined commanders and brave soldiers, sailors, airmen, and Marines. Still, codebreakers made an indispensable contribution to Allied operational planning. In the arcane world of coding and codebreaking, and of deceiving the enemy with bogus radio signals, the Allies enjoyed far more success than their enemies.

Maritime Victory

"The Arsenal of Democracy" could do nothing to defeat the Axis unless the Allies could ship American manpower, supplies, and weapons to the theaters of war across the world's oceans. In 1940–1943 Allied shipping had to run a gauntlet of German U-boats to reach England, and Admiral Karl Donitz and his determined, skillful submariners believed that they stood on the edge of victory even as the United States entered the war. Without a triumph over the U-boats there would be no victory over Germany. As Winston Churchill wrote FDR, "the spectacle of all these splendid ships being built, sent to sea crammed with priceless food and munitions, and being sunk—three or four a day—torments me day and night. Not only does this attack cripple our war energies and threaten our life, but it arbitrarily limits the might of the United States coming into the struggle. The oceans, which were your shield, threaten to become your cage."

In 1942 the balance in the Battle of the Atlantic swung toward the Germans, who profited immediately from American belligerency. Since the Royal Navy included surface commerce raiders and the Luftwaffe's anti-shipping campaign menaced only the convoy routes to northern Russia, the U-boats alone held the initiative in the Atlantic. The Allied antisubmarine warfare (ASW) campaign suffered from shortages of everything: escorts, land-based and carrier-based ASW aircraft, and information, for British codebreakers had lost their ability to read Atlantic U-boat radio messages, which used a new code. Donitz deployed his U-boats in 1942 in two kinds of operations: "wolfpack" attacks against Allied convoys in the North Atlantic and individual patrols against the unconvoyed American ships along the Atlantic seaboard and in the Caribbean. The results were devastating. With only about forty U-boats in combat at any one time, the Germans sank an average of 100 ships (around 500,000 tons) a month for most of 1942. They did so at a cost of only 21 U-boats, easily replaced by the 123 submarines the Germans built in the same period. The Allies lost another 700,000 tons of shipping to German and Italian raiders and mines, while the Japanese onslaught deprived the Allies of an additional million tons. With many defeats from which to choose in 1942, Churchill and Roosevelt regarded the losses in the Battle of the Atlantic as the worst of the year.

Although Anglo-American shipbuilders came close to replacing the 1942 losses, Allied planners had to face the fact that they could not mount any major operations in the European theater unless they defeated the U-boats. The very ability of Great Britain to fight the war rested in the balance, since its merchant fleet had suffered an important net loss by 1943. British imports had dropped by half, producing grave shortages of raw materials, food, and consumer goods. American visitors to England in 1942 were shocked by the widespread poverty of their ally and worried about British war-weariness. The depressing mathematics of 1942 showed that shipping shortages would limit the American buildup in England and further stretch the British economy.

The greatest concentration of wartime shipbuilding was in the San Francisco bay area, the home of fourteen major shipyards that produced merchant ships. All but two of the yards did not exist in 1939, and they were underutilized. The pioneer in efficiency and productivity in building Liberty and Victory ships was a six-company consortium led by Henry J. Kaiser, an industrial visionary of quick, massive production. Using a newly trained work force, including women and minorities, and modular construction, Kaiser's shipyards could assemble a 10,000-ton Liberty ship in ten days (1942), then seven and a half days. Four shipyards in Richmond, California, built 747 ships, 519 of them Liberties. Kaiser's workers received pioneering attention in healthcare, wages, plant safety, housing and skilled training. Two thousand miles away, Andrew J. Higgins used many of the same assembly-line innovations to produce 9,000 landing craft in an instant, sprawling empire around New Orleans, Louisiana. In the Mississippi Valley, corporations that specialized in building bridges, factories, and railroad engines as well as tugs and barges built over 1,000 Landing Ships, Tank (LSTs), an essential beaching vehicle carrier for amphibious assaults. Much of this production sacrificed financial cautiousness for speed of delivery, a recognized strategic trade-off.

Oil and gasoline powered the American armed forces, and POL (the military designation for fossil fuels) moved overseas by ship. These ships came in two broad categories, tankers and, for the U.S. Navy, fleet oilers capable of underway refueling. Tankers were the POL workhorses, and the German U-boats made them prime targets in 1942, sinking 97 U.S. tankers in Western Hemisphere waters. Such losses did indeed cripple Great Britain and Japan, but not the United States. Of the 5,777 ocean-going vessels built by American shipyards, more than 700 were tankers. One prime tanker supplier, the Marineship Corporation of the Bechtel-McCone construction empire of California, could build a 22,800-ton tanker (6 million gallon capacity) in thirty-three days and make it operable in two more months. The construction required 17,000 welds and 10,000 cuts and bends to sixteen miles of piping in the ship. The Navy oiler fleet expanded from twenty-nine to nearly one hundred, easily replacing the nine lost to the enemy. In the meantime, tanker losses dropped to twenty-five in 1943, ten in 1944, and six in 1945.

The shipping crisis required an unprecedented American effort to increase production of merchantmen and tankers, and in 1943 the United States tripled its deadweight tonnage (the carrying capacity of ships) in new vessels from 3 million to 9 million tons. To do so, however, meant that the government had to assign lower building priorities to all warships except escort vessels, thus slowing the construction of the vessels the Navy needed to win control of the Pacific and to carry amphibious invasion forces to both the war's theaters. The U-boats also put enormous strains upon Anglo-American cooperation and upon interservice and civil-military relations among America's war managers, since "Japan First" strategists like Admiral King argued that the Battle of the Atlantic would prevent SLEDGEHAMMER and ROUNDUP and justified a shift in theater priorities. Navy and Army planners clashed over the allocation of long-range aircraft and the organization of ASW land-based air operations. Military planners complained bitterly whenever Roosevelt committed new vessels to carrying imports to Britain rather than military supplies for American operations abroad. The torpedo explosions in the Atlantic sent concussions throughout the Allied war effort.

Building upon the hard-learned lessons of World War I and the ocean battles of 1940–1941, the Royal Navy, Canadian navy, and U.S. Navy bore the brunt of the war against the U-boats. They received some assistance from the RAF and USAAF, which mounted some long-range reconnaissance operations (useful) and bombed submarine bases and construction yards (largely futile). For victory there was no substitute for convoying. Only troop-carrying transoceanic liners could maintain sufficient speed to outrun U-boats, and even these normally had destroyer screens. Merchantmen formed into convoys off North America, divided into "fast" and "slow" groups. A convoy averaged around fifty vessels, spread in parallel columns over twenty-four square miles of ocean. Bulk cargo merchantmen formed the outer ranks, with oil tankers, munitions ships, aircraft and tank carriers, and troopships clustered in the center of the formation around the convoy commander's ship. Around the convoy prowled the escorts, usually no more than six. Destroyers and smaller warships (destroyer escorts, frigates, corvettes, and even converted yachts) made up the escort, progressively reinforced with escort carriers, which provided critical air cover. At a 1942 rate of about six convoys a month the Allies plunged through the awaiting wolfpacks.

The Battle of the Atlantic produced some of the war's hardest service and grimmest experiences. Weather—arctic storms, fog, and heavy seas—plagued friend and foe alike. The U-boats attacked submerged by day and on the surface by night. Usually the first sign of an attack was the roar of a torpedo ripping open a merchantman; tankers and munitions ships often exploded and sank in a cloud of flames. Merchant seamen who escaped their vessels often perished from hypothermia in the frigid seas. Survivors who managed to find lifeboats and rafts might go days before a rescue vessel dared to pick them up. On the escorts the strain of long watches, wretched living conditions, and recurring contacts and searches for U-boats often brought crews to the point of collapse during every voyage. Moreover, the escorts seldom had the release of an obvious victory over the U-boats, unless a victim surfaced before sinking. In any event, the Navy bagged few U-boats in the battle's opening phases.

For eighteen months the Battle of the Atlantic hung in the balance, and it was not clear until the summer of 1943 that the Allies had won one of the war's critical campaigns. No single development, either in mass-producing escorts and ASW aircraft or inventing miracle weapons or electronics, spelled victory for the Allied navies. Rather, the ultimate victory rested upon a wide range of organizational, technical, and operational programs. To conduct his share of the campaign, Admiral King created a separate command—the 10th Fleet—from which he directed operations through a series of geographic commands that deployed the escorts, air patrols, and convoys. Intensive ASW training paid dividends as the Navy received more escorts (especially destroyer escorts) and aircraft. Shore-based long-range patrol planes like the PBY Catalina and the Navy's version of the B-24 and carrier-based search-and-attack aircraft eventually gave the Navy full aerial coverage of its areas of responsibility, including the "black hole" in the Atlantic between Iceland and the Azores that land-based planes could not reach. Since the U-boats had to surface to move rapidly, to recharge their batteries, and to take on fuel and supplies from their own U-boat-tankers, they were especially vulnerable to air attack. They also preferred to move at night on the surface from their European bases, a tactic exploited by RAF Coastal Command, which mounted intense night patrolling over the Bay of Biscay. The ASW campaign also profited from the use of mathematically based operations analysis by American and British teams, who developed optimal ways to use escorts, aircraft, and ASW ordnance.

The technological war at sea also swung against the Germans. Improved radar and sonar aboard escorts and aircraft made it more difficult for the U-boats to surprise a convoy; Allied high-frequency direction-finding equipment intercepted German radio traffic and allowed more accurate position locating. The Allies also invented an airborne radar system that the Germans could not foil with their radar-detecting "black boxes." The Allies developed and deployed more accurate, destructive ASW ordnance, including rocket-assisted depth charges and magnetic and acoustic antisubmarine torpedoes. In the codebreaking war the Allies used message analysis to discover that the Germans had broken the convoy routing codes, and the subsequent Allied code changes hampered U-boat operations. The Allies also again cracked the Germans' own U-boat code, which allowed hunter-killer naval support groups to locate and attack submarines before they closed upon a convoy, or to divert convoys around the U-boats. In April 1943, for instance, the Allies learned from ULTRA that the route Convoy SC 127 was sailing would take it into a wolfpack of 25 U-boats. Forewarned, authorities changed the convoy's route, sending it north of the lurking subs. Several subsequent changes allowed the convoy to avoid smaller U-boat concentrations that ULTRA revealed, and the entire convoy arrived safely in England.

Admiral Donitz's submarine force had, however, grown throughout 1942, and in early 1943 the admiral launched a major wolfpack effort against the North Atlantic convoys, and the U-boats sent record numbers of Allied ships to the bottom. But the Germans' own losses increased; they began losing one submarine for every Allied vessel destroyed. In one two-month period the Allies sank fifty-six U-boats. The Germans reached their peak of frustration in May 1943, when fifty-one U-boats attacked a convoy of forty-two vessels and the pack lost six U-boats in order to sink thirteen merchantmen. Donitz ordered his U-boats to safer waters, and in two months sixty-two convoys crossed the Atlantic without any losses at all. Although the German submarine force continued its war until the collapse of the Third Reich, it did so with appalling losses (753 of 863 patrolling submarines; 28,000 of 41,300 sailors) and diminished danger to the Allied war effort. In the meantime American shipyards, working on twenty-four-hour shifts and profiting by one engineering and managerial innovation after another, continued to send warships and merchantmen down the ways and into the war. Aboard those ships moved American troops and military materiel to places thousands of miles distant that had little in common except that they were now battlegrounds.

Opening a Two-Front War

In the face of depressing news about home-front mobilization failures, of Atlantic sinkings, and of German victories in southern Russia, FDR held fast to one politico-strategic conviction: "It is of the highest importance that the U.S. ground troops be brought into action against the enemy in 1942." Still unhappy about the diversion of American forces from the buildup in England to expeditions in North Africa, the JCS extemporized two major campaigns to meet the president's charge, a charge based primarily on FDR's desire to help Russia and to keep the American public committed to a total war effort. Until early 1944 these two campaigns—one in the Mediterranean and the other in the south Pacific—were the focus of America's battles with the armed forces of Germany, Italy, and Japan. The campaign in the Mediterranean pleased the British, who feared a premature return to France and who questioned American operational expertise. The broadened commitment to the war against Japan united a set of peculiar bunkmates: General MacArthur and all his domestic admirers, prewar isolationists, the pro-China public, most of the leadership of the U.S. Navy, and even part of the War Department General Staff, which could use the Pacific war to badger the British into a firm commitment to a cross-Channel offensive. The British provided the rationale for the Mediterranean: An Allied offensive there would sever Italy and Vichy France from German domination, divert the Wehrmacht from Russia, and provide air and naval bases for further operations against the heart of the European continent. MacArthur provided the Pacific analogue to Churchill's "soft underbelly" thesis, arguing that operations mounted from the Hawaii-Australia line would strike Japan's vulnerable southern defenses and destroy its major bases at Rabaul on New Britain Island and Truk in the Carolines.

Mounting the first offensives required hard bargaining regarding the command and distribution of the available American forces. For the North

Waiting to advance: American infantry in the Meuse-Argonne campaign, 1918. *Signal Corps No. 111-SC-24445 in National Archives (hereafter NA).*

Transportation problems: An AEF traffic jam in the Meuse-Argonne reflects the problems of coordinating an offensive. *Signal Corps No. 111-SC-24642 in NA.*

Artillery conquers, infantry occupies: A 75-mm. gun of the 6th Artillery Regiment fires for the 1st Division during AEF attacks, 1918. *Signal Corps No. 111-SC-27421 in NA.*

Air support for the AEF: Sopwith Camel pursuit planes of the 148th Squadron, American Air Service, AEF, prepare for a mission, 1918. *Signal Corps No. 111-SC-18846 in NA.*

The Navy prepared for a naval campaign above, on, and below the Pacific Ocean: The U.S.S. *Lexington* (CV-2) at anchor at Hawaii, 1933. *No. 80-A-416531 in NA.*

Submarines gave the U.S. Navy additional power for a Pacific war: "Fleet boats" like U.S.S. *Mackeral* (SS-204) provided the 1941 Navy with scouts and skirmishers—and commerce raiders after Pearl Harbor. *U.S.N. No. 19-N-23722 in NA.*

Amphibious warfare at inception: A detachment of Marines practices loading a landing craft, Quantico, Virginia, 1920s. *Defense Department No. 531602 in NA.*

Amphibious warfare at maturity: Beaching ships carry the heavy equipment of three marine divisions ashore at Iwo Jima, February, 1945. American amphibious assault operations provided the allies with an important offensive advantage in World War II. *Defense Department No. 110851 in NA.*

Attack on Fortress Europe: 8th Air Force B-17s bomb German oil refineries, November 1943. The Anglo-American bomber forces created a "Second Front" in the air. *Defense Department No. 55429 AC in NA.*

Attack on Fortress Europe: Soldiers of the U.S. 2nd Infantry Division clear a street of German defenders in Brest, France, August 1944. *Signal Corps No. SC 193705-S in NA.*

The ships that sank an empire: The carriers *Langley* (CVL-27) and *Ticonderoga* (CV-14) lead three fast battleships and four light cruisers into Ulithi anchorage after air strikes on Japanese bases in the Philippines, December 1944. *No. 80-G-301352 in NA.*

Limited war remains total for the infantry: Soldiers of the 1st Cavalry Division prepare to cross a rice paddy, Korea, 1951. *Signal Corps No. SC 368495 in NA.*

Air power helps save Korea: UN Command tactical air power, such as this F-80 taking off from Japan, provided an important advantage over the Communist armies in Korea, 1950. *U.S. Air Force No. 77201 in NA.*

Vertical assault in Vietnam: UH-1B "Huey" helicopters carry American soldiers into action in central Vietnam, 1966. Air mobility gave the U.S. Army and Marine Corps added effectiveness in the war with the North Vietnamese Army. *Signal Corps No. SC 634829 in NA.*

Ambush! Marines cross a creek under fire during a jungle patrol near Phu Bai, South Vietnam, 1967. Despite added helicopter mobility and close air support, American infantry still had to fight the NVA in Vietnam's wooded mountains. *Defense Department No. A188945 in NA.*

Air power in the Nuclear Age: A B-52 bomber, designed to carry nuclear weapons to deter attack by the Soviet Union, instead carries conventional bombs to targets in South Vietnam. *U.S. Air Force No. 94836 in NA.*

African operations, the CCS selected General Marshall's protégé Dwight D. Eisenhower but surrounded him with British subordinates. Aware of the tension between the British and the French, the Allies hoped a distinct American coloration to TORCH (the Moroccan and Algerian invasions) would confuse the Vichy defenders and improve the chance that Allied diplomacy would subvert French resistance. In the Pacific the JCS redrew theater boundaries to give Nimitz control of operations in the Solomon Islands and to limit MacArthur's direct command to the American and Australian forces aimed at New Guinea. The Navy distrusted the idea of any Army general conducting naval operations using scarce carriers, and MacArthur's performance in the Philippines had not won him any admirers in blue. The commitment of Army and USAAF units by the end of 1942 showed how dramatically TORCH and CARTWHEEL (the isolation of Rabaul) had redirected the deployment plans of "Germany First." In rough terms the Army and USAAF sent about 350,000 men to the Pacific and 350,000 to the Mediterranean and England. In terms of combat units the disparity became more striking: The departure of six divisions and eleven air groups for Africa and five divisions and fifteen air groups for the Pacific left only one division and sixteen air groups in England. The diversion of USAAF groups left the air effort against Germany with only one-third of the aircraft planned in early 1942. The naval services put even greater emphasis on the Pacific war. In all warship categories, including destroyers, the Navy deployed the majority of its vessels in the Pacific, building its striking forces in August 1942 around its four surviving large carriers and their cruiser-destroyer screens. Of its ten Pacific battleships, only two were new enough for fast cruising. For the south Pacific war the Marine Corps could provide two divisions and fifteen aviation squadrons.

The Navy–Marine Corps landings at Guadalcanal and nearby islands in August and MacArthur's Army-Australian advance on Buna, New Guinea, in September opened the south Pacific offensive and set off six months of bitter land-sea-air fighting that ended in a decisive Japanese defeat. Although the jungle war for Guadalcanal tested the fighting heart and skills of two Marine and two Army divisions before the Japanese remnants withdrew, the battle for the Solomons depended ultimately upon air and naval superiority. Admiral Yamamoto and Admiral William F. Halsey attempted to reinforce Guadalcanal and destroy one another's air units and warships. The U.S. Navy fought its most desperate battles of the war in the Solomons. In seven major fleet engagements and many minor skirmishes, Halsey's fleet lost twenty-four warships and 5,000 sailors. (In comparison, the ground and air forces had around half as many killed in action.) When the Japanese finally broke off the campaign, only two serviceable American carriers remained. The Japanese suffered even more grievous—and

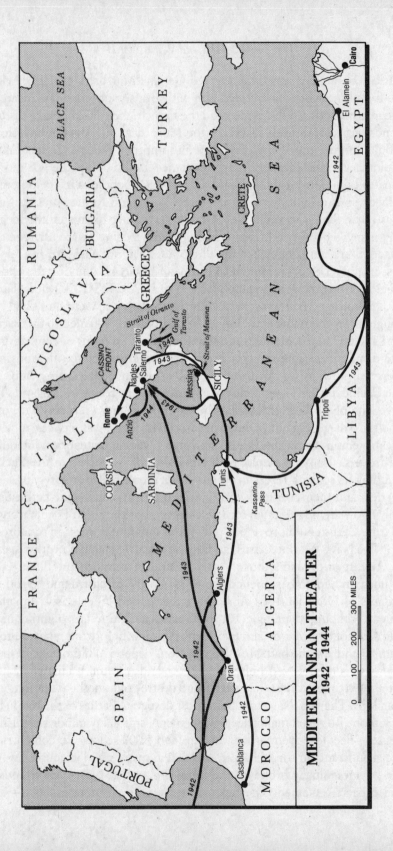

MEDITERRANEAN THEATER
1942 - 1944

0   100   200   300 MILES

FRANCE

SPAIN

PORTUGAL

MOROCCO

ALGERIA

Casablanca   1942

Oran   1942

Algiers   1943

1942

1943

1943

Tunis

TUNISIA

Kasserine
Pass

LIBYA   1943

Tripoli

EGYPT

El Alamein

Cairo

1942

MEDITERRANEAN   SEA

CORSICA

SARDINIA

ITALY

Rome

Anzio

Naples
Salerno

CASSINO
FRONT

1944

1943

1943

SICILY

Messina

Strait of Messina

Taranto

Gulf of Taranto

Strait of Otranto

1943

GREECE

CRETE

YUGOSLAVIA

BULGARIA

RUMANIA

BLACK SEA

TURKEY

less replaceable—losses: 30,000 soldiers and sailors, 24 warships, more than 100 merchantmen, and 600 aircraft. Among the casualties were many experienced pilots. Moreover, the U.S. Navy demonstrated its willingness to close with the Japanese, even when the flaws in its night-fighting techniques, gunnery, use of radar, and torpedo attack defense tipped the balance toward its more experienced foes. Only in naval air battles—attacks mounted and received—did the Americans show any clear margin of superiority. By the end of the campaign, however, the Americans could meet the Japanese on more than equal terms, whether the combatants were jungle patrols or night-fighting cruisers. The myth of Japanese invincibility died in the Solomons.

MacArthur's New Guinea offensive established the strategic pattern for Allied victories in the other part of the dual south Pacific advance. With only four American and Australian divisions to commit, MacArthur relied upon USAAF air support and, operating under this air cover, an Allied amphibious fleet composed of beaching ships and craft, cruiser and destroyer escorts, and supply vessels. Tropical diseases, monsoon weather, and jungled mountains conspired with the Japanese to make the Buna campaign a nightmare for the ground troops, but in January 1943 MacArthur's force held firm control of a lodgment on New Guinea's northern coast. Although the Buna campaign had been largely an overland epic, MacArthur's next thrust against the Japanese bases along Huon Bay threw both the 5th Air Force and 7th Fleet into the fray and drew a maximum Japanese air and naval response. The result was a series of disasters for the Japanese as USAAF aircraft, often directed to their targets by ULTRA, destroyed the enemy air cover and reinforcing convoys. By the end of the year MacArthur was prepared to leap the straits to New Britain Island to isolate Rabaul, which he and the JCS no longer thought required actual capture. In the meantime, the American forces in the Solomons had fought up the chain at New Georgia and Bougainville, completing the encirclement. Recognizing the dimension of their defeat in the south Pacific, the Japanese withdrew their fleet and their surviving air units to a new defense line that included the Marianas, the Philippines, Formosa, and Southeast Asia. Deprived of reinforcements, the remaining Japanese garrisons east of this line received orders to delay the Americans as best they could.

Half a world away from the rainforests of the south Pacific, other Allied forces entered the war for the Mediterranean in November 1942. A year later they had driven the Germans back to the approaches to Rome. As General Bernard L. Montgomery's 8th Army drove a German-Italian army back from El Alamein to Tunisia, an Anglo-American invasion force struck at three Moroccan locations and the Algerian ports of Oran and Algiers. Arrayed against confused Vichy French defenders and assisted by

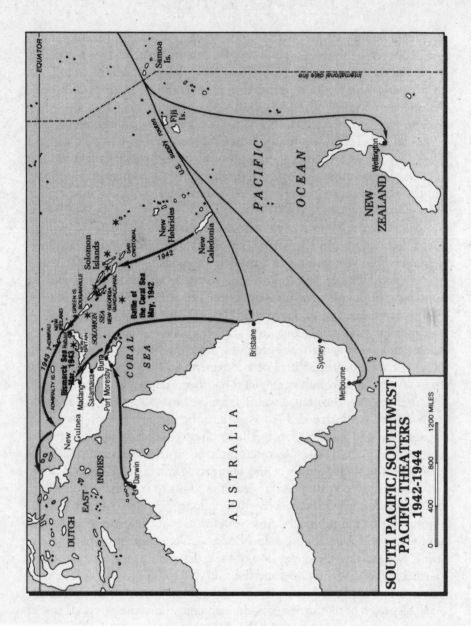

SOUTH PACIFIC/SOUTHWEST
PACIFIC THEATERS
1942-1944

0   400   800   1200 MILES

Free French rebels, the Allies plunged ashore in a combination of commando port assaults and nighttime beach landings. Adding tactical confusion to the political puzzle, the Allies overwhelmed the largely feeble French defenses, then negotiated an end to French resistance with the Vichyite military commander, Admiral Jean Francois Darlan.

Initially mistaken about the Allies' objectives, Hitler and the Wehrmacht responded quickly by occupying all of France and pouring another army into Tunisia. Eisenhower's command, plagued by poor transportation and rain, lost the race to Tunisia and soon received its first exposure to German tactical expertise in the Tunisian mountains. The results for the Americans were disheartening. In a series of battles—including a German counterattack at Kasserine Pass—the Americans did not measure up. General Eisenhower judged their leadership as "thin" and their discipline close to that of a "disorderly mob." American tactics and weapons did not match the Germans', and American operations showed striking defects in intelligence, reconnaissance, and air support. Only American logistics and artillery proved noteworthy. Smarting from criticism spoken and implied, the amateurish American divisions stuck with the task, prodded by a new corps commander, Lieutenant General George S. Patton Jr. As his deputy, Major General Omar N. Bradley, noted, the American soldier would improve only by "winning battles and killing Germans."

Despite the frustrations of the Tunisian campaign, the Allied high command (including Roosevelt and Churchill) assembled in Casablanca in January 1943 to examine their strategy for the coming year. The decisions and indecision had a marked Churchillian cast. The war upon Germany would continue to depend primarily upon strategic bombing, the war against the U-boats, subversion on the Continent, and active operations in the Mediterranean. The British argued that Italy could be driven from the war with the resources already committed to the Mediterranean theater, and the CCS approved planning for an invasion of Sicily. Additional meetings in Washington and Quebec extended and expanded the Mediterranean campaign to include a September invasion of Italy. Buoyed by the final success of the Tunisian campaign, which ended in May 1943 with the surrender of 240,000 Germans and Italians, the Allies had clearly deferred a cross-Channel attack until 1944. The Russians and some American planners wondered if there would be any attack at all.

The reasons in 1943 for expanding the Mediterranean campaign were many and persuasive. In strategic terms a campaign into Italy might divert German divisions from the Eastern Front and provide air bases for Allied bomber strikes against Germany and targets in Eastern Europe. Italy's collapse would wound the German cause politically and weaken it militarily. In logistical terms the Allies had made an irreversible commitment to the theater, building ports and airfields, establishing supply dumps and bases, and deploying an army of rear-echelon administrative and technical personnel that outnumbered the fighting troops. The Tunisian campaign had also established the fact that Anglo-American command relationships needed refinement. Another major concern was the shocking lack of air-ground cooperation.

The Sicilian campaign (July–August 1943) revealed both improvements and deficiencies in the Allies' ability to beat the Axis armed forces in battle. Enjoying tactical surprise because the Germans again misjudged the invasion objective, the American 7th Army (Patton) and the British 8th Army (Montgomery) established beachheads ashore, but German-Italian armored counterattacks on the American beaches came within a few kilometers of success. Only the suicidal bravery of American infantry (particularly the troopers of the 82d Airborne Division) and the timely massing of naval and artillery shellfire drove the Germans off. Luftwaffe attacks on the invasion shipping and beaches hindered operations and led Allied antiaircraft gunners to shoot down more friendly troop transports than they did German aircraft. The campaign developed as two operations, primarily because Patton and Montgomery so chose, and Eisenhower and General Harold R.L.G. Alexander, overall ground commander, did not impose their will upon the ambitious army commanders. The result was Patton's sweeping ground-amphibious envelopment of Messina through Palermo and Montgomery's plodding advance up Sicily's eastern coast toward the same objective. The Axis defense forces—built around only two German divisions—fought a skilled delaying action, then evacuated the island across the straits of Messina. Despite the Allied victory, the Sicilian campaign—marked by Anglo-American acrimony—did not bode well for combined operations.

Like the North African invasion, the Allied assault upon Italy began in a miasma of political intrigue. Mussolini's political and military failures had alienated King Victor Emmanuel and the Italian military high command, who conspired to remove *Il Duce* in July. The change actually worked to the Allies' disadvantage, for it removed the pretext for Italian-German cooperation. The Wehrmacht moved swiftly to send troops deep into Italy's "boot" and to intimidate the Italian armed forces, which either disintegrated or went into captivity. The Italians wanted out of the war, but they didn't want to fight Germans. This decision meant that an easy landing, especially at Rome or farther north, passed into the realm of might-have-beens. When Italy formally surrendered on September 8, the military results were negligible. The Allies would have to fight up the entire peninsula, a very hard underbelly in topographical and tactical terms. As one Allied general noted, "Wars should be fought in a better country than this."

The Italian campaign developed in ways that suggested that the Germans were diverting the Allies from other theaters rather than vice versa. Although the British 8th Army—an international force of British Commonwealth, Polish, and French units—managed to land against light resistance and fight up Italy's eastern coast, the Anglo-American 5th Army (Lieutenant General Mark W. Clark) had to fight a stiff battle at Salerno before it freed the port city of Naples on the western coast. Two months of hard campaigning brought the Allied armies only as far as the Germans' Gustav Line, a belt of mountain defenses a hundred miles south of Rome anchored in front of the Americans along the Rapido River and the heights above Cassino. Terrain and weather favored the German defenders, who again proved highly professional and definitely undefeated. In a war of rocks and rubble, air superiority and massed artillery could not spare Allied infantry the task of rooting out the Germans position by position. At the end of 1943 the Italian campaign had stalled, with eleven German front-line divisions confounding the best efforts of fourteen Allied divisions.

Assessing the actual course of the war at the end of 1943, FDR, Churchill, and their military planners had to face several strategic situations that carried elements of both promise and disappointment. The offensive war with Japan had developed with greater success than might have been expected, despite limited operations in the Pacific. The Mediterranean campaign had indeed accomplished its more limited objectives (eliminating Vichy France and Italy as Axis assets), but it had not brought excessive pressure upon the bulk of the Wehrmacht. The most impressive military victories, in fact, belonged to the Russians, who had turned the tide at Stalingrad and had begun offensive operations against the Germans. Although the Allied bombardment of Germany had forced the Luftwaffe to redeploy air units from the Russian front, it had not become a true "second front," at least in Russian eyes. The American mobilization, however, was reaching its productive peak, and the victory in the Battle of the Atlantic meant that American divisions and air groups could now reach England in accelerating numbers. In sum, the war was not yet won, but it would not be lost if the Allied coalition remained intact and applied its military might toward the goal of German and Japanese unconditional surrender.

FOURTEEN

☆   ☆

The United States and World War II: The Road to Victory, 1943–1945

For the embattled Allies the winter of 1943–1944 was the best of times and the worst of times. The prospect of ultimate victory had never been brighter, yet that prospect depended on operations not yet mounted, on campaigns not yet successful. Moreover, the strategic opportunism of 1942–1943 had not produced decisive victories comparable with the Allied effort. Only the campaign in the south Pacific had brought a major shift in enemy strategy dictated by the power of Anglo-American arms. The war's greatest change, in fact, had come in Russia, where the Soviet armored hosts had bludgeoned the Wehrmacht onto the strategic defensive. Josef Stalin complained that the two "second fronts" that the Allies had thus far created—the Mediterranean campaign and the strategic bombardment of Germany—had not produced wounds mortal for the Third Reich.

If the second-front issue weighed heavily upon the Russians, it also burdened FDR and his military planners, for the British—spearheaded by the persuasive Churchill—continued to argue for the expansion of the Mediterranean campaign, which could not occur without a diversion of American assets from the buildup in England. Churchill's fertile imagination and the dexterous British planning staffs produced offensive projects that extended from the Balkans to the Istrian coast at the head of the Adriatic Sea to the west coast of Italy. The only operation the Allied chiefs approved, an amphibious envelopment at Anzio in January 1944, did not alter the stalemate in Italy. Limited forces, tactical caution, and German combativeness ended Churchill's dream of a dramatic success. Although the Americans still saw some marginal advantages in continuing the Italian campaign, principally in opening additional air bases, they opposed any substantial reinforcements for the Mediterranean, especially troops and ships needed for a cross-Channel attack.

Despite persistent questions about the size and location of the invasion of France, the Tehran conference (December 1943) ended the debate about whether the offensive (OVERLORD) would occur in 1944. With General Marshall carrying the brunt of the argument, the Americans, seconded by the Russians, persuaded the British that the invasion should take the highest priority in allocating Anglo-American forces. As FDR boasted to Secretary of War Henry Stimson, "I have thus brought OVERLORD back to you safe and sound on the ways for accomplishment." Army ground and air units still held in strategic reserve in the United States would go to northern Europe, with only minimal reinforcements to the Mediterranean and the Pacific war. (In 1944 the Army sent twenty-six divisions to Europe, seven to the Pacific.) In addition, the preponderance of American forces in the Allied expeditionary force made the British concede that the commander of the invasion would be an American general. Marshall hoped he would be that commander, but FDR reluctantly concluded that he could not spare the chief of staff from his councils of war. He chose instead Marshall's most trusted subordinate and proven coalition commander, Dwight D. Eisenhower.

The accelerated preparations for OVERLORD did not end the often tense strategic discussions between the Americans and British about how a campaign in Europe should develop. While Eisenhower and his coalition staff wrestled with the tactical and logistical problems of OVERLORD, the Combined Chiefs of Staff argued about an American proposal for a simultaneous invasion of southern France (ANVIL). The military planners did not see how the Allies could find enough ships, transports, tactical aircraft, and divisions to mount two major invasions at the same time unless operations in the Pacific halted for the summer of 1944. That prospect was anathema to the American planners, especially Admiral King. Supported by Field Marshal Sir Alan Brooke, chief of the Imperial General Staff, Churchill lectured the Americans about using the forces for ANVIL (largely American and Free French) for intensified operations in Italy or other Mediterranean locales. The Americans, however, held fast to the ANVIL concept, for a second "second front" in France would force the dispersion of German divisions and perhaps cut some of them off if the Allies could quickly link their armies along the Rhine frontier.

Despite British claims that ANVIL was additional evidence of American naiveté, Roosevelt rejected Churchill's anti-ANVIL position for the same reasons he ultimately turned away from the entire Mediterranean strategy: He saw no reason to divert American forces from the war with Germany in France to other operations in central Europe, which the Allies would enter from the Adriatic. FDR did not think Churchill was pathologically opposed to the Russians, but he feared that the British would antagonize the Soviets by entering an area of Europe that the Russians seemed determined to dominate. FDR's political judgment coincided with his planners' preferred strategy. The president did not believe his constituency would support American military intervention in central Europe, let alone a postwar military presence. Moreover, he wanted to ensure that the Russians would enter the war with Japan, whose armies were still relatively strong. Superficially the eternal optimist, Roosevelt privately doubted that the United States had the political will and military resources to block the Soviets in central Europe at the same time it was fighting the Germans and Japanese.

The Pacific war exerted its pull upon America's military leaders, their commitment to OVERLORD notwithstanding. Through the end of 1943 the Army deployed almost as many divisions and air groups (heavy bombers excepted) to the Pacific as it did in Europe. Except for its antisubmarine escorts and support groups, the Navy built its forces for a climactic battle with the Japanese, assisted by the divisions and aircraft wings of the Fleet Marine Force. In the summer of 1943, pressed by King and all the Pacific commanders, the JCS authorized Nimitz to begin operations in the central Pacific, which meant a "second front" along the eastern edges of the Japanese defense perimeter. The Pacific theater and JCS planners crafted plans that would take the Navy's new carrier and amphibious task forces across the central Pacific through the Gilberts and Marshalls to the western Carolines, capturing or isolating the major naval base at Truk. Further negotiations between the planners produced an additional set of objectives: the large islands of the Mariana group (Saipan, Tinian, Guam), coveted by both the Navy and the Army Air Forces as naval and air bases. Hap Arnold—an apostle of strategic bombing—and King made strange allies, but both wanted to take the war to the Japanese homeland as quickly as possible. Arnold would have a new long-range bomber (the B-29) to use against the Japanese home islands, and King wanted to put his carrier groups and submarines between Japan and its raw materials in the south. The Marianas would provide bases for both forces, leading to economic strangulation and demoralization. In addition, the Navy believed the Imperial Japanese Fleet would have to fight again somewhere in the western Pacific, and it felt confident that it would finish the work it had begun at Midway and in the south Pacific.

U.S. Overseas Deployments
December 1943

	AGAINST GERMANY	AGAINST JAPAN
Personnel	1.8 million	1.8 million
Divisions		
U.S. Army	17	13
Marine Corps	0	4
U.S. Army Air Forces		
Strategic bombers	2,263	716
Tactical bombers	1,251	723
Fighters	3,456	1,897
Transports	849	545
Naval aviation		
Land-based aircraft	204	1,662
Carrier aircraft	366	1,941
U.S. Navy warships		
Battleships	6	13
Large carriers	1	7
Light carriers	0	7
Escort carriers	9	14
Heavy cruisers	2	12
Light cruisers	8	20
Destroyers	120	188
Destroyer escorts	112	57
Submarines	40	123
Amphibious transports	10	34
LSTs	92	125

Threatened with a shift of strategic priorities away from his own southwest Pacific theater, General MacArthur presented the JCS with a series of plans (RENO) that would take his command from the coast of New Guinea to the Philippines. As the south Pacific theater closed down in early 1944, MacArthur received additional Army divisions and air groups from the JCS. MacArthur unloaded his own strategic arguments on Nimitz, King, Marshall, and even FDR, whom he met in Honolulu in a classic confrontation of great egos. The recapture of the Philippines, MacArthur argued, would interdict Japan with land-based aviation as effectively as any naval blockade. At the root of MacArthur's persuasiveness, however, was the emotional appeal of wiping away the stinging defeat of 1942 and freeing both Americans and Filipinos from the harsh grip of their Japanese captors. Authorizing a dual drive into the western Pacific also allowed FDR and the JCS to postpone again the question of overall command in the Pacific, an issue neither wanted to resolve. As Nimitz's forces turned west across miles of ocean and low coral atolls, MacArthur aimed his own American-Australian divisions and air forces, supported by the 7th Fleet, toward the Philippines.

The dual Pacific drive also reflected the JCS's disillusionment with the Nationalist Chinese. Early in the war FDR and his planners envisioned Chiang Kai-shek's primitive but numerous army as the foundation of an offensive against the Japanese on the mainland of Asia. By the end of 1943 this optimism had gone aglimmering in a cloud of distrust, broken promises, wasted aid, and reciprocal contempt. If Chiang wanted to fight at all, he wanted to fight fractious warlords and his Communist rivals, not the Japanese. Having no confidence in Chiang, the British avoided extensive operations in Burma, which Chiang championed. Even a limited offensive in 1943 by the Anglo-Indian army along the southern Burmese border came to nothing.

The American interest in the China-Burma-India (CBI) theater changed from a war carried by the Nationalists to a war carried by American strategic bombers. The requirements for the bombing offensive against Japan (MATTERHORN) were disheartening. To maintain a B-29 force of 700 aircraft in China, so USAAF planners calculated, would require an airlift force of 3,000 transports to fly the awesome "Hump" of the Himalayas from India. The American air bases in western China would need both ground and air protection from Japanese attacks, which were sure to follow the first raids. Even if the Chinese provided the ground defense forces, the logistical requirements for MATTERHORN would probably exceed 15,000 tons a month, far in excess of American airlift capacity in 1943. The alternative was to open an overland route from Ledo, a railhead in India, to the Burma Road, but this option would require a ground campaign in northern Burma, since the Japanese held the Burma Road. Except for skilled (but small) Anglo-American "long-range penetration forces" and Burmese hill tribe guerrillas, the ground offensive depended upon the Chinese divisions organized and trained by General Stilwell's military mission in India and Yunnan, China. Aware that Chiang did not want them to waste their troops against the Japanese—as long as the USAAF would fly the "Hump"—Stilwell's Chinese generals showed minimal enthusiasm for a harsh jungle campaign.

Back in Washington, General George C. Marshall fretted about "local-itis" and "theateritis," a virulent condition of limited perspective that seemed to infect all the principal Allied commanders. But the war was still an odd lot of minimally connected operations mounted from an initial posi-tion of weakness. Whether all the theater campaigns could now be linked and pursued to victory remained the challenge to the Allied grand coalition.

The War Against Germany and Japan

If the cross-Channel attack was the future foundation for German defeat in 1944, the strategic bombing campaign against the Third Reich had been part of Anglo-American strategy since Pearl Harbor. In the uncertain win-ter of 1943–1944 it had not yet produced victory. Prewar theorizing sug-gested that an aerial campaign might make traditional warfare obsolete; under the press of actual experience strategic bombardment seemed less likely to defeat the Germans. The most enthusiastic bombardment cham-pions in the RAF and USAAF still believed that bombing might make an invasion unnecessary. The experience of the RAF's Bomber Command before 1942 did not, however, augur well for the Americans. Prohibitive losses in daylight bombing had forced the RAF to switch to nighttime operations and to change its targeting doctrine. Instead of striking spe-cific industrial and military targets, the RAF bombed the central areas of German cities on the theory that killing and "dehousing" civilians would demoralize the Germans and stir internal resistance to the Nazi regime. Against a progressively sophisticated German air-defense system, the RAF sent streams of bombers into the blackness above the Continent to blast and burn the Third Reich.

The forward elements of the USAAF 8th Air Force deployed to England with the American doctrine of strategic bombardment unmodified by the European air war. American airmen, led by prewar bombing advo-cates Carl "Tooey" Spaatz and Ira Eaker, believed that the B-17 could con-duct precision, daylight operations against specific industrial targets and do so beyond the range of escorting fighters. They also believed that their first task was to ruin the German air force by destroying its aircraft before they were ever assembled. Factories manufacturing airframes, engines, and specialized component parts should receive first attention. The next most important targets—whose destruction would cripple the German econ-omy—were electricity-generating plants, the petroleum industry, and the transportation system. While the bombing might affect German morale, the American air planners did not regard public demoralization as an appropriate objective. In this conviction they differed from the RAF, which wanted American bombers to join its city-busting campaign.

The initial American bombing efforts in 1942 were too modest to produce conclusive evidence on the ultimate success of the air campaign. With TORCH approaching, units assigned initially to the 8th Air Force went instead to North Africa for the Mediterranean campaign. In addition, the 8th Air Force changed target priorities, for the CCS demanded that it bomb U-boat pens and construction yards. Since most of their early targets were in France, the 8th Air Force bombers had fighter support on their raids, and the Luftwaffe, by its own admission, had not trained to attack mass formations of B-17s. Yet even in its limited early operations the 8th Air Force lost an average of 6 percent of its bombers per raid, a loss rate that had led the RAF to abandon daylight operations. The promise of the bombing campaign, on the other hand, still carried the B-17s forward into the fighters and flak. After a raid in which he had lost almost a third of his bombers, one wing commander asserted, "There is no question in my mind as to the eventual result. VIII Bomber Command is destroying and will continue to destroy the economic resources of Germany to such an extent that I personally believe that no invasion of the Continent or Germany proper will ever have to take place."

FDR, Churchill, and the Combined Chiefs of Staff did not share such unrequited optimism, but at Casablanca (January 1943) they included the strategic bombing of Germany among their most important offensive priorities. A "Combined Bomber Offensive" (POINTBLANK) appeared critical to any invasion and ground campaign, since the limited Allied ground forces would require clear air superiority and a weakened Wehrmacht. The CCS statement on POINTBLANK was modest and very general: "The aim of the bomber offensive is the progressive destruction and dislocation of the enemy's war industrial and economic system, and the undermining of his morale to the point where his capacity for armed resistance is fatally weakened." Arguing that limited bomber numbers and unperfected bombing techniques had made an assessment of the campaign difficult, the CCS said that larger raids would reduce bomber losses. They also thought that the bombing campaign would not win the war by itself or destroy German morale, but that "it already has an appreciable and will have an increasing effect on the enemy's distributive system and industrial potential." The bomber offensive also had its political dimension, for FDR and Churchill presented it to Stalin as a "second front in the air" that would cripple the German armies fighting in Russia: The British would bomb at night, the Americans by day.

Stripped of bombers and fighters for the North African operations, the 8th Air Force started POINTBLANK with attacks on targets in Western Europe, especially naval bases, airfields, and railroad marshaling yards. Usually the bombers had fighter escorts. The Luftwaffe's response was intense enough for General Eaker, who had succeeded General Spaatz as the 8th Air Force commander, to order his available medium bombers and fighters to attack German airfields and maintenance depots. Guided by British intelligence and JCS targeting orders, Eaker placed highest priority on attacking the German aircraft industry, especially fighter assembly plants, engine factories, and ball-bearing manufacturers. Petroleum targets and transportation systems dropped down the priority list, while submarine targets remained close to the top. Frustrated by erratic weather (which limited attacks to about ten a month) and crew and aircraft shortages, 8th Air Force did not mount a very impressive effort until the summer of 1943. It did, however, help to divert about half of the Luftwaffe's fighter force to antibomber operations.

When he received additional B-17 groups, Eaker ordered major missions into Germany, since the airfield bombings were not appreciably reducing German fighter strength. On August 17, the 8th Air Force launched its deepest raids against factories at Schweinfurt and Regensburg. The bombs destroyed some of the factory complexes, but the Luftwaffe destroyed and damaged much of the bomber force. The raids cost the 8th Air Force 60 of 315 bombers—and the ten crewmen in each bomber. After more raids on Luftwaffe airfields, the 8th Air Force made another massive effort the next month. Of 262 bombers sent against Stuttgart, 45 fell. Although the Americans proved—weather permitting—that they could put some of their bombs on target, their losses in unescorted raids suggested that the 8th Air Force might not find planes and crews to replace its losses and maintain efficiency and morale.

The 8th Air Force's frustrations had many authors. Allied intelligence had underestimated the resiliency and unmobilized capacity of German industry; in 1943 German manufacturing had yet to hit its peak wartime productivity. The dispersion and hardening of factories (some even went underground) made them less vulnerable, and, as the Allies would eventually learn, bombs might destroy structures but not necessarily machine tools and assembly lines. The Luftwaffe also proved a hardy, sophisticated foe. With radar warning systems and centralized control of interceptor forces, the Luftwaffe could mass its fighters along the bombers' routes. Once engaged, the German interceptors had a variety of techniques to blow holes in the B-17s' formations of interlocking machine-gun fire. Head-on and underneath attacks exploited gaps in the B-17s' firepower as daring German pilots, flying the agile Me-109 and FW-190, whirled through the American formations. Other stand-off German interceptors pummeled the bombers with rockets and cannonfire. The results were catastrophic.

Undaunted, General Eaker reorganized his force for another maximum effort into Germany in October 1943. Reinforced with bomber groups redeployed from North Africa, the 8th Air Force once again flew unescorted into the heart of industrial Germany. Losses in the second week of "Black October" climbed, until the second mass raid upon Schweinfurt capped the slaughter. On October 14 a force of 230 B-17s flew into Germany and lost 60 aircraft; of the survivors, another 138 bombers suffered damage and casualties. The loss trends spelled disaster, for 8th Air Force crews were disappearing at a monthly rate of 30 percent. Luftwaffe pilots perished at half that rate. At his Schweinfurt debriefing a pilot stated one clear solution: "Jesus Christ, give us fighters for escort!"

The combined effect of the bad weather and tenacious German air defenses created pressure upon the 8th Air Force to adopt urban-area bombing. The British, Eisenhower, and Arnold suggested that the USAAF should switch targeting concepts; but first Eaker, then Spaatz, still believed that industrial targets should be bombed. As one of their planners characterized terror-bombing, it was "a baby-killing plan of the get-rich-quick psychological boys." Although the USAAF did participate in city-area bombing in Germany before the war's end, most of its senior leaders held to the view that daylight precision bombing was the only sure way to defeat Hitler because it destroyed his ability to wage war.

The reform of POINTBLANK in 1944 came from several sources, and in the first six months of the year the USAAF turned the tide against the Luftwaffe. In October the USAAF activated the 15th Air Force, a strategic bomber force flying from Italy that could reach targets in south-central Germany and the oil-refining targets in the Balkans; 15th Air Force attacks forced the Germans to defend against two major bomber threats during daylight. American aircraft production was finally meeting the USAAF's needs, and the USAAF training establishment was producing increasing numbers of bomber crews and fighter pilots. In December 1943, the 8th Air Force mounted its first 600-plane raid.

The bombers also received fighter escorts in increased numbers and ranges. For three months Arnold ordered all new fighters to the 8th Air Force, which meant a force of 1,200 operational fighters for escorts. Building on engineering projects in 1943, the 8th Air Force mounted wing and belly tanks on its P-38 Lightning and P-47 Thunderbolt fighters. The USAAF also discovered that by placing a new engine in the P-51 Mustang, a ground attack fighter-bomber, it had an optimal long-range escort fighter. In the meantime, the 8th Air Force had redesigned its formations for more accurate bombing and mutual self-protection; it had also made strides in defeating the cloud cover by using radar-guided bombing.

With a new headquarters—U.S. Strategic Air Forces (General Spaatz)—coordinating 8th and 15th Air Forces raids, the American bombing campaign reached a new peak effort. Testing all its reforms in early February 1944, the 8th Air Force mounted a third Schweinfurt raid and lost only 11 bombers of 231; three other raids on the same day sent 600 bombers against Germany with minimal losses. The USAAF mounted six major raids during "Big Week," the last week of February. With fighters that could fly beyond the Rhine and both protect bomber formations and sweep ahead to engage the Luftwaffe interceptors, the 8th Air Force formations reversed the loss ratio with the German fighter force; bomber losses fell well below 10 percent of each raiding force, and German pilot losses mounted to around 25 percent a month for six months. American bombs hit their targets, but monthly German fighter production climbed from 1,000 to 3,000 in 1944. The difficulty for the Luftwaffe was that it was running short of skilled pilots, for it could man only one-quarter of the new planes. Moreover, the Americans changed target priorities in May 1944 and concentrated on the petroleum industry. Fuel shortages squeezed the Luftwaffe, which curtailed pilot training to save fuel. The German fighters and flak could still be dangerous: 69 of 658 bombers fell in a March raid on Berlin. But the Americans could now make good the losses in planes and crews, and the Germans could not.

Despite the hope that "Big Week" killed the Luftwaffe, the air battle over Germany continued with unabated ferocity through the first five months of 1944, but it produced the minimal objectives spelled out by the CCS. On D-Day the Luftwaffe did not menace the Normandy invasion, and the Allies enjoyed air superiority over the battlefield for the rest of the war. In the meantime, the remnants of the Luftwaffe fighter force battled with the RAF and the USAAF in the skies above the German industrial heartland. For American bomber crews the experience had a numbing sameness: pre-mission tension; the grip of cold and thin air; the scream of air battle as B-17s filled with machine-gun smoke and, too often, flames and electrical sparks; a safe return or a plunge to earth—all to be repeated in each mission. In 1944, however, the sacrifices seemed bearable and the risks diminished as German air defenses found fewer victims. Just the size of the American effort boosted confidence. From 600-plane raids, the 8th Air Force mounted first 1,000-plane, then 2,000-plane raids by the end of 1944. Surely, planners and aircrews reasoned, the Germans could not take the pounding.

Yet the Combined Bomber Offensive paid limited and costly dividends. It definitely ruined the Luftwaffe and forced the Germans to allocate much of their industrial production to air defense and their transportation system. The 8th and 15th Air Forces lost over 29,000 crewmen killed and 8,237 heavy bombers in order to destroy the German petrochemical and transportation systems and thus cripple the Wehrmacht, but the destruction came

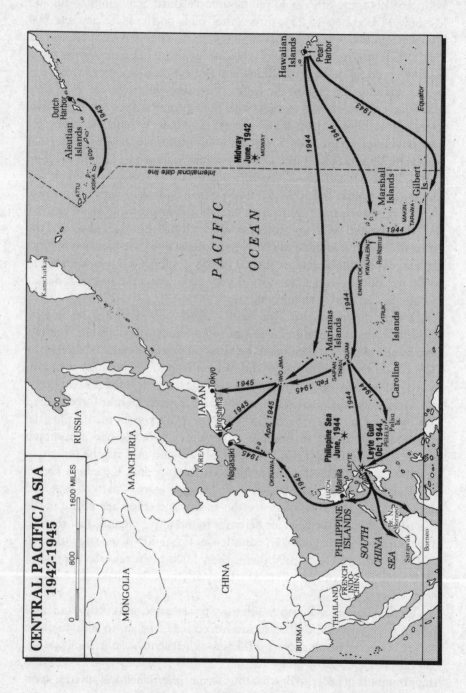

CENTRAL PACIFIC/ASIA 1942-1945

0   800   1600 MILES

MONGOLIA

MANCHURIA

RUSSIA

CHINA

KOREA

JAPAN

Kamchatka

Tokyo

Hiroshima

Nagasaki

PACIFIC

OCEAN

BURMA

THAILAND

FRENCH INDO-CHINA

PHILIPPINE ISLANDS

SOUTH CHINA SEA

Manila

LUZON

LEYTE

Br. N. Borneo

Sarawak

Borneo

Aleutian Islands

Dutch Harbor

ATTU

KISKA

1943

International date line

Midway June, 1942

MIDWAY

IWO JIMA

1945

1945

April 1945

1945

OKINAWA

Philippine Sea June, 1944

Leyte Gulf Oct, 1944

Feb 1945

Marianas Islands

SAIPAN

TINIAN

GUAM

1944

1944

Palau Is.

PELELIU

Caroline Islands

TRUK

ENIWETOK

KWAJALEIN

Roi-Namur

1944

Marshall Islands

MAKIN

TARAWA

Gilbert Is.

1944

1943

1944

1944

Hawaiian Islands

Pearl Harbor

Equator

too late to decide the battle for Europe. In sum, German war industry continued to produce war materiel until the last days of the war, but the Germans could not ship their fleets of Panzers and 88-mm guns to the front. Their munitions industry cried for chemicals and coal, and their vehicles ran low on gasoline. Weighed against its loss of 47,000 crewmen and 8,325 heavy bombers, RAF Bomber Command's contributions were even more limited. Its night campaign of city destruction brought untold suffering to urban Germans and drove the survivors underground. Under Nazi control and conditioned to a life of privation by the gradual escalation of the bombing, the German people did not crack under the explosions and firestorms that swept their cities. Strategic bomber commanders complained that they did not have ample men and aircraft soon enough to make their doctrine work. They also argued that German air defenses diverted men and weapons from the land battle. Critics of the campaign, who judged the 600,000 civilian deaths disproportionate to the military results, thought that POINTBLANK had not affected the war's outcome at all. Both extreme viewpoints ignored the doctrinal, organizational, and technical limitations of the Allied bomber forces as well as their ultimately awesome destructive power. In the war of attrition fought at 30,000 feet the Allies won another narrow victory that contributed to the final collapse of the Third Reich.

Strategic Change in the Pacific

With the general strategic outlines of the Pacific war established in 1943, the American armed forces massed in early 1944 for a year of climactic campaigning against the Japanese. As Admiral Yamamoto (killed by USAAF fighter pilots in April 1943) had feared, Japan could not stop the military might of an aroused United States. By the end of the year, the Americans had permanently ruptured Japan's mid-Pacific defense perimeter and destroyed its ability to fight a conventional air-naval-ground war. The dual advance toward the western Pacific mixed long-range plans and strategic opportunism, a combination made possible by the sheer size of the American forces and their increasing operational skill. In 1944 the Americans won the major campaign of the Pacific war but did not yet win the war itself.

General MacArthur and Admiral Nimitz organized their forces for extended and unrelenting operations in their theaters. MacArthur's ground forces combined American and Australian infantry divisions, supplemented by additional artillery and logistical units. MacArthur eventually formed two American field armies (6th and 8th), which he used for the western drive into the Philippines, while the Australians continued the ground operations against the isolated Japanese bases in the southwest

Pacific. MacArthur's land-based Far East Air Forces (FEAF) included Lieutenant General George C. Kenney's U.S. 5th Air Force and elements of the Royal Australian Air Force; this force provided the full range of air support from interdiction bombing to battlefield close support. MacArthur's navy was the U.S. 7th Fleet, task-organized for amphibious operations, but Admiral King made sure that MacArthur would not control the fast-carrier task forces. Instead Nimitz remained responsible for directing the major naval campaign, which would occur in the central Pacific theater. Although Nimitz's warships and amphibious task forces left the war only for essential refitting and brief rests, his naval forces fell under two different commanders, Admiral William F. Halsey (3d Fleet) and Admiral Raymond A. Spruance (5th Fleet). While one commander conducted operations, the other planned the subsequent offensive. Nimitz's command also included the USAAF 7th Air Force and land-based Navy and Marine aircraft. His ground forces for 1944 included four Marine divisions and a separate Marine brigade and four Army infantry divisions, all amply supported with artillery and other supporting arms, organized as two amphibious corps commanded by Marine generals.

The Americans in the Pacific had by 1944 also developed a logistical system capable of supporting continuous operations. In MacArthur's theater the system was traditional, for it depended upon eleven major fixed bases and the forward shuttling of supplies by ship and plane, which moved from island to island behind the fighting forces. Shipping shortages, exacerbated by limited port and storage facilities and inefficient management and manpower, plagued MacArthur. Working from fixed bases in the jungle islands, his forces had a voracious appetite for supplies. FEAF was an especially heavy consumer, since its commanders kept it in continuous action against Japanese shipping routes and isolated bases. In the central Pacific Nimitz's fleet depended upon a sea-based logistical system capable of replenishing warships at sea and of utilizing extemporized bases among the captured atolls of the theater. Islands with suitable anchorages and airstrips were the key objectives of the central Pacific war, first to deprive the Japanese of their use, then to develop them for fleet operations. The service force that supported the 3d, 5th, and 7th Fleets grew to 3,000 vessels in 1945. It included specialized ships of all sorts: tenders, fast oilers, ammunition and stores ships, floating dry docks, and hospital ships. The Navy also formed special construction battalions ("Seabees") to build new facilities with their bulldozers and scrapers as soon as the former occupants had ceased to exist. Logistical demands accelerated throughout 1944, but the Navy and Army service commands managed to keep pace, thus assuring a high tempo of operations the Japanese could not match.

Still uncertain about the intentions of the Japanese fleet and their own ability to operate without superior land-based air power, MacArthur and Nimitz opened their dual advance in conservative fashion. Nimitz started the campaign with amphibious assaults upon the Tarawa and Makin atolls in the Gilbert Islands in November 1943. Despite suicidal Japanese resistance, the two American divisions took their objectives in only four days; Japanese air and naval forces did not contest the landing except for sporadic air and submarine raids. The Marine landing at Tarawa demonstrated that amphibious assaults still needed refinement. Japanese fixed defenses needed the special attention of pinpoint, methodical air and naval gunfire bombardment if landing force casualties were to be reduced. In addition, the assault troops required amphibian tractors to cross the coral reefs that barred the way to troops and supplies. In February 1944 the central Pacific amphibious forces showed they were quick learners, for the assault on the Marshalls occurred with greater sophistication. One Marine division and part of one Army division overwhelmed Kwajalein atoll. Both divisions were relatively inexperienced, but both profited from improved fire support, more numerous "amtracs" (amphibian tractors), and their own enthusiasm for close combat. Again the Japanese fleet did not come out. Impressed by the 5th Fleet's ability in amphibious operations and confident that his fast carriers would best the Japanese, Nimitz scrapped his original timetable and ordered an additional February assault a thousand miles to the west. In a week's time a landing force of one Marine and one Army regiment seized Eniwetok, another anchorage and air base. The ratio of American to Japanese dead in these assaults climbed to well over one to ten, a more than acceptable price for the Americans. In addition, the seizure of Kwajalein and Eniwetok allowed Nimitz to isolate the four remaining Japanese base complexes in the Marshalls. These bases were bombed and starved into impotence by Marine and USAAF aircraft throughout the rest of the war.

In the southwest Pacific General MacArthur in early 1944 combined the final stages of the isolation of Rabaul with the first moves toward the Philippines. In February he too found the Japanese reluctant to fight more than a delaying action when he sent three American divisions into the Admiralty Islands. Covered by his own air strikes and deep raids by Nimitz's carriers, MacArthur accelerated his own operations along the coast of New Guinea. With relatively light casualties, he leapfrogged westward from Hollandia and Aitape (April 1944) to the island of Morotai (September 1944), which placed him within air range of the Philippines. The Japanese rushed aircraft south to contain the American advance, but the FEAF had become too numerous and skilled for the Japanese to best. In addition, the Japanese learned that the Americans had mounted simultaneous operations against the Marianas, so the force that might have inconvenienced MacArthur returned to the north to face the more menacing offensive.

In June–August 1944 the 5th Fleet dealt the Japanese armed forces another critical defeat by capturing Saipan, Tinian, and Guam and destroying the enemy's naval aviation force at the Battle of the Philippine Sea (June 19–20). As the American amphibious forces (523 vessels, 127,000 troops) approached the twin objectives of Saipan and Guam, Admiral Spruance sent Task Force 58, which included his fast carriers, west of the Marianas, since he expected a major effort by the Japanese against the invasion force. The four carrier task groups (fifteen carriers and their escorts) ranged north and west of Saipan. On June 15 the amphibious assault forces (two Marine and one Army divisions) plunged ashore at Saipan and engaged the Japanese army in a hard-fought ground battle that included mountain fighting, mass suicide attacks, and artillery barrages given and received in a magnitude not faced in the jungle and atoll fighting. So fierce was the fighting that Nimitz postponed the landing on Guam. In the meantime the Japanese fleet sortied from its western Pacific bases for another major engagement with the U.S. Navy. American radio intelligence and reconnaissance by aircraft and submarines prevented any surprise, and, despite Spruance's cautious conduct of the battle, the 5th Fleet's aviation annihilated its Japanese counterpart. With better aircraft and radar and more experienced pilots, the American carrier forces and escort vessels downed 480 Japanese aircraft and lost only 130 aircraft and 76 airmen. In addition, the Americans sank three large Japanese carriers of the nine engaged. "The Great Marianas Turkey Shoot" ended the threat of Japanese naval aviation in the Pacific. Secure from enemy attack from the sea, the amphibious expeditionary forces took Saipan, then Guam and Tinian. The USAAF immediately began to turn the Marianas into an air base complex for its B-29s.

The Pacific commanders moved quickly to exploit the Marianas victory, scrapping their previous timetables. Admiral King wanted a move directly to Formosa, but he lost the argument to MacArthur, who wanted the next effort (as planned) against the Philippines. The Americans did not have the fresh amphibious forces and logistical shipping for an operation so near China and the Japanese home islands. When Admiral Halsey's 3d Fleet raids into the western Pacific revealed the Japanese shortages of aircraft, the JCS and MacArthur agreed to bypass Yap in the western Carolines and Mindanao and to strike directly at Leyte in the central Philippines. In October 1944 MacArthur's 6th Army (six divisions) and the 7th Fleet—with Halsey's 3d Fleet carriers in support—attacked Leyte. The Japanese navy made one more effort to inflict a decisive defeat upon the Americans but failed at the Battle of Leyte Gulf (October 23–25). The Japanese fleet approached the Americans from three directions. The center force, running a gauntlet of submarines and air attacks, actually passed through the San Bernardino Strait and engaged the escort carrier groups of the 7th Fleet. Lured past Luzon by reports of large carriers in the Japanese northern force, the 3d Fleet could not rescue the invasion force, which fought back so fiercely that the Japanese retired. To the south an American task group of surface warships caught the Japanese southern force in the Suriagao Strait and demolished it in a classic night bombardment. Successive attacks by Japanese planes based in the Philippines could not turn the tide. The defeat spelled the end of the Japanese fleet, which lost four large carriers, three battleships, nine cruisers, eleven destroyers, and 500 more aircraft. The 3d and 7th Fleets, by contrast, lost only two small carriers and three destroyers. The Marianas pattern then reemerged ashore. The isolated Japanese army fought with skill and devotion and perished. True to his word, MacArthur had returned in considerably greater strength than he had left in 1942.

The first great American offensive in the western Pacific, however, brought a major change in Japanese tactics that did not bode well for the rest of the war. Recognizing that they could not match American firepower and tactical skill in the air, on the sea, and in conventional land warfare, the Japanese decided to fight on new terms. In island fighting they demonstrated their new tactics against the 1st Marine Division and 81st Infantry Division on Peleliu, a rocky island in the western Carolines, in September 1944. Exploiting an interlocking defense system of caves and concealed weapons bunkers, the Japanese turned what might have been another week-long battle into a bitter two-month campaign that ruined the 1st Marine Division. The Japanese defenders forced the Americans to kill and bury them with demolitions, flame-throwers, and close assaults. To eliminate about the same size force (6,000) they had faced at Tarawa, the Americans lost almost twice as many killed in action (1,800) as they had suffered at Tarawa. The battle was even more unpalatable, for Peleliu was part of the planned Mindanao operation, which had been canceled.

As a minor part of their counterattack at Leyte Gulf, the Japanese introduced the *kamikaze* corps, a fleet of new planes and novice pilots who did not need to master air-to-air tactics or return landings since their sole purpose was to crashdive into Navy vessels. As Admiral Nimitz admitted after the war, the *kamikazes* took the Navy by surprise, since designed suicide had not been a part of American air doctrine. It had not been in the Japanese repertoire until the summer of 1944, when the losses in experienced pilots doomed conventional Japanese air attacks. The Divine Wind Special Attack Corps made its auspicious debut on October 25, 1944, when fewer than twenty *kamikazes* sank one and damaged four escort carriers of the 7th Fleet. With no bombs to drop or torpedoes to launch, the *kamikazes* could penetrate the blanket of antiaircraft fire at any angle. As a floating bomb of aviation gasoline and ordnance, an American carrier needed only one *kamikaze* crash into its hangar deck to set off secondary explosions, which at the very least would halt flight operations. Escort vessels were somewhat less vulnerable but not immune. For the first time since the Solomons campaign, it looked as if the Navy faced prohibitive warship losses. The Japanese cave tactics ashore now had their counterpart at sea, giving the Japanese a faint hope that the war of attrition could be turned back to their advantage. Although the American public was only vaguely aware of the new tactics—obscured as they were by the great victories in the Marianas and Leyte—the war in the western Pacific had entered a new phase that increased the cost of a continued American advance.

From Normandy to the Rhine

The driving rain and whistling night winds were no more grim than the mood of the senior American and British commanders meeting in a manor house outside Portsmouth, England. The June 4, 1944, conference had one purpose: to decide if the weather would force another postponement of the cross-Channel invasion. At the cutting edge of months of preparation and years of planning, Dwight D. Eisenhower bore the responsibility for the decision. His ground commanders wanted to get on with the battle; the air and naval commanders were less enthusiastic. Eisenhower listened again to their advice, to familiar arguments about surprise, morale, and logistics. Promised a slight improvement in the weather—critical for air and naval gunfire operations—he made his decision without flair: "I'm quite positive we must give the order. I don't like it, but there it is. I don't see how we can possibly do anything else." D-Day in Normandy would be June 6.

Under serious consideration for more than a year, OVERLORD attempted to exploit Allied air and naval superiority and to mislead the Germans about the place of the actual landing. Only a substantial degree of surprise could prevent what the Allies feared most, a mass armored counterattack on the landing force. Even with additional amphibious ships and landing craft, the Allies could not hope to match the six German Panzer divisions in northern France if these were quickly committed. Yet the opportunity for surprise was limited by the iron demands of logistics and air basing. To wage offensive war with an expeditionary force of millions of men and hundreds of thousands of vehicles, the Allies required fixed port facilities. For example, the Allies' 250,000 vehicles burned more than 7,000 tons of gasoline in one operational day. American logistical planners, using wartime data, cut their estimates of the Army's needs but still produced awesome estimates: An infantry division needed one ton of supplies *per soldier* per month, and an armored division's needs were five times greater than an infantry division's. The Allies also counted upon fighter-bombers to give them a big edge in maneuver warfare, and the optimal use of tactical air meant not only high logistical requirements but also forward bases in France.

The location of the invasion narrowed inexorably to Normandy, since a landing there would allow the Allies to capture the port of Cherbourg at the tip of the Cotentin peninsula. An attack to the north around Calais was a bit too obvious, and the Germans had already emphasized the defense of the Atlantic Wall north of the Seine by reinforcing their 15th Army and fortifying the beaches. The Brittany coast to the south offered five major port facilities that the Americans knew well, since they had used them in World War I, but an attack so far south would slow the liberation of France and allow the Germans too much time to reinforce their western armies. The Allies planned to use the Brittany ports but only after they were safely ashore in Normandy. The German obsession with the Pas de Calais, on the other hand, could be exploited by a complex deception plan utilizing the full range of Allied capabilities: air attacks, dummy military installations and shipping, misleading radio communications, false agent reports, and other intelligence ploys. If the Germans did not redeploy before D-Day, the Allied invasion forces would face just six German divisions in Normandy, only two of which were first rate.

The success of the landings depended upon air superiority over the amphibious force and air interdiction to prevent German reinforcements. Three months before D-Day the Anglo-American air forces initiated the "Transportation Plan," a massive attack upon the French railway system and the bridges across the Seine and other major rivers. As part of the deception plan two-thirds of the bomb tonnage fell on targets in the Pas de Calais area. The 9th Air Force executed the American portion of the plan, joined in the last two months before D-Day by the 8th Air Force and RAF Bomber Command. The interdiction campaign also profited by the sabotage and espionage activities of the French underground. In all, rail traffic in northern France and western Germany fell by 70 percent before the invasion. The air campaign also had a special urgency, since the Germans had introduced the first of their "V" rocket-bombs, which might disrupt the invasion and discourage the British.

The actual assault placed more than 100,000 Allied troops ashore in France by the end of D-Day. Three American infantry divisions and two airborne divisions fought their way into positions behind two beaches at the western half of the Allied landing area; on "Omaha" beach the Germans inflicted shocking casualties, but on "Utah" methodical naval gunfire, weak defenses, and the confusion created by the massive airborne assault allowed the Americans to anchor the right flank. The British attack

American and German Divisions, Manpower and Equipment 1944

	U.S. INFANTRY	U.S. ARMORED	U.S. AIRBORNE	GERMAN INFANTRY	GERMAN MECH. INFANTRY	GERMAN PANZER
Men	15,768	11,581	8,533	12,700	13,800	13,700
Infantry	8,800	4,700	6,700	5,500	7,000	5,200
Machine guns	950	940	376	656	1,101	1,231
Antitank rocket launchers	663	669	182	108	—	—
Mortars	145	94	140	163	76	72
Towed antitank guns	93	—	46	21	30	—
Self-propelled antitank guns	—	36	—	12	44	44
Artillery howitzers	70	54	36	78	54	54
Artillery guns	—	—	—	12	83	82
Armored cars	49	80	—	—	35	35
*Tanks	76	307	—	48	92	150
Trucks and light vehicles	1,560	1,496	408	615	2,637	2,685
Horse-drawn wagons	—	—	—	1,466	—	—

*A U.S. and German infantry division often had one tank battalion attached to it.

seized the left flank with three divisions, three armored brigades, an air assault division, and various commando formations. Montgomery, however, did not take Caen, the city that controlled the road network south of the Seine and the gateway to open tank country, for the conservative British general feared a massive Panzer counterattack. It did not come, largely because Hitler thought the Normandy attack was only a diversion and would not allow his front-line commanders to commit the Panzer reserve or draw troops from the 15th German Army in the Pas de Calais.

The Normandy campaign quickly changed into a bitter, two-month slugfest, with the tide turning to the Allies' advantage. In the American sector the hedgerow country, characterized by narrow roads and textbook defensive terrain, slowed the advance to a bloody crawl to the south to link and expand the beachhead area. The only dramatic success was the seizure of Cherbourg, but even there the German defenders held long enough to destroy the port facilities. In the British sector, Montgomery's 21st Army Group took Caen and destroyed the German piecemeal armored counterattacks, but the British won no striking victories that allowed an Allied breakout. Moreover, the Allies had difficulty building their logistical base, for a severe storm ruined their extemporized port facilities along the beaches, and the land battle did not secure enough ground for adequate air bases and depots. Nevertheless, by early July the Allies had a secure lodgment on the Continent, packed with more than a million men and protected by superior air forces.

Frustrated by Montgomery's penchant for bold promises and weak accomplishment, Eisenhower looked to Omar Bradley's 12th U.S. Army Group to open the enclave to the west and south with an overwhelming attack by the 1st U.S. Army, to be followed by an exploitation by George S. Patton's 3d U.S. Army. In the last week of July, Bradley launched Operation COBRA, which used the full range of American armored and air capabilities, including saturation attacks by heavy bombers. Although the bombers had the unfortunate habit of dropping their loads on friend and foe alike, the one-corps attack slugged its way forward against weakening German resistance. With one flank on the ocean and the other in the Normandy hills, the American divisions penetrated the enemy positions, and within a week the 3d U.S. Army had plunged through the gap, sending one corps on to Brittany and another corps to the northeast to envelop the whole 7th German Army position around the Normandy enclave. Finally alert to the severity of the German position, Hitler ordered a major counteroffensive against the exposed American left flank in the Mortain area. But warned of the impending attack by ULTRA, the 1st U.S. Army and tactical air attacks ruined the Panzer assault. Although a fit of caution prevented the Allies from trapping the whole 7th German Army and Panzer

ATLANTIC

OCEAN

ICELAND

Murmansk

Archangel

SWEDEN   FINLAND

NORWAY

Leningrad

UNITED
KINGDOM OF
GREAT BRITAIN
AND
NO. IRELAND

DENMARK

ESTONIA

UNION OF SOVIET
SOCIALIST REPUBLICS

LATVIA

Moscow

EIRE

LITHUANIA

Supply route from U.S.

London

NETH.

EAST
PRUSSIA

D-Day
June 6, 1944

Antwerp
Brussels

RUHR 1945

Berlin

1945

Warsaw

POLAND

Kiev

ARDENNES
FOREST

1944

GERMANY

Paris

Metz

Rhine R.

1945

1944

FRANCE
Lyon

SWITZ.

HUNGARY

1945

RUMANIA

SPAIN

CORSICA

Rome

BELGRADE
YUGOSLAVIA

BULGARIA

BLACK SEA

SARDINIA

ITALY

ALBANIA

TURKEY

GREECE

**NORTHERN EUROPEAN
THEATER
1943-1945**

0   200   400 MILES

Group West, the battle ended with the Allies free to exploit their victory
for one ecstatic month. While the 21st British Army Group drove north
across the Seine into the Pas de Calais, the 12th U.S. Army Group drove
north and east on either side of Paris, which was liberated by the Resistance and French and American divisions on August 25.

Everywhere in Europe the Allies seemed close to victory. The German
high command was in disarray. In late July a group of German generals
and civilians attempted to kill Hitler and end the Nazi regime. Although
unsuccessful, the attempted coup, coupled with the Allied victories in
France and the Russian advances in the east, brought extensive confusion to the Nazi war effort. Two German field marshals committed suicide
rather than face Hitler's tender mercies, and Hitler sacked his supreme
commander in France, Gerd von Rundstedt. In Italy the Allies had finally

taken Rome (June 4) and moved north before the Germans could restore their position along another fortified belt. The new stalemate in Italy was no comfort to the Germans, for the Americans had at last overwhelmed Churchill's reluctance and their own shipping shortages to mount ANVIL, the invasion of southern France. On August 15 a Franco-American invasion force, built around divisions redeployed from Italy, landed without serious resistance and drove north as part of a vast double envelopment of all the German forces west of the Rhine. The drive up the valley of the Rhone River brought the new 6th U.S. Army Group up to the flank of the 3d U.S. Army in early September, which meant that the Allies now had a continuous front from the German frontier to the English Channel.

The race across France slowed in September. At the root of the Allies' problems was the voracious appetite of their highly mechanized and motorized armies. The American armies especially had outrun their supply lines. Patton, whose 3d U.S. Army had already reached Lorraine and the approaches to the Rhineland, argued that the rest of the Allied armies should surrender their gasoline and ammunition to his divisions. Montgomery was equally insistent that his army group receive highest priority in supplies, and he tried to reverse his reputation for conservatism with Operation MARKET-GARDEN, an airborne-armored thrust through Holland across the lower Rhine. Although MARKET-GARDEN brought the 21st British Army Group to the Rhine, the German counterattacks showed special ferocity and deprived the Allies of the bridge at Arnhem, which ended the operation. Eisenhower's logisticians extemporized as best they could as the two Allied army groups in the north cried for supplies. Nonstop truck operations (the "Red Ball Express") shuttled critical supplies forward, and transport aircraft performed similar services. Nevertheless, the Allied Expeditionary Forces could not maintain wide, continuous offensives without pipelines and railroads. The former took time to build, and the latter took time to repair. The Germans, on the other hand, profited from a shortened front and supply lines as well as the special ardor that comes from fighting for one's own national territory. Along the vaunted West Wall, or Siegfried Line, the Allied advance stalled.

As German resistance stiffened along the approaches to the Rhine, Eisenhower's command faced three major, interrelated problems. One was operational, one logistical, and one organizational, and all three influenced the character of the campaign. The operational difficulty occurred when Montgomery, promoted to field marshal and supported in Britain by even those who found him insufferable, urged Eisenhower to reinforce the 21st British Army Group with at least one American army and to give the British the Allied supply priority. Montgomery would then advance on a narrow front through Holland and the northern Rhineland to the north German plain in what he described as a "Schlieffen plan in reverse." Montgomery's plan had at least the advantage of strategic concentration, since he had pointed the 21st British Army Group at the heartland of the Third Reich. Patton's proposed offensive into Bavaria boasted élan in the pursuit of secondary objectives. The logistical crisis of autumn 1944 would not allow a full offensive all along the Allied front, so Eisenhower had to choose some concentration.

Eisenhower also had reason to worry about his ability to fight the Germans on even terms, for he could see an end to the number of divisions he could deploy in Western Europe. His shortage stemmed from decisions a year old, which limited the Army ground forces to 90 divisions. Assuming that Allied aviation and the Russians would compensate for limited ground forces, the War Department had cut division activations and in the autumn of 1944 had only twenty-four divisions left to deploy worldwide. In September Eisenhower had thirty-four divisions, and he received only fifteen more before the war ended. (Six American divisions remained in Italy.) The British had no more deployable combat divisions at all.

The administrative and logistical demands of the Army's overseas effort also limited the numbers of combat troops, a situation worsened by the Army's inability to manage its own manpower system. One general characterized the manpower pipeline as "an invisible horde of people going here and there but seemingly never arriving." In late 1944 the combat ground forces worldwide numbered 2.1 million, with another million men in supporting units, in an Army of about 8 million. Only about a quarter of the ground army's total strength at any one time was assigned to units engaged with the enemy; the infantrymen in these units suffered 90 percent of the casualties. The War Department took drastic action in late 1944 to meet the immediate crisis, which was finding replacements for the existing divisions. It deactivated units of marginal utility (e.g., antiaircraft battalions), stripped service units of combat-fit replacements, and shipped marginally trained (fifteen to seventeen weeks) eighteen-year-olds and physically limited older men to Europe.

If American divisions had consistently performed in battle with superior effectiveness, their limited numbers would not have been serious, but such was not the case. The best American divisions were as good as any in the war; several infantry and armored divisions and the 82nd and 101st Airborne clearly fell into this category. But the majority of American divisions needed overwhelming artillery support (another logistical drain) and close air support to best their German opponents. Operations at night and in bad weather thus were not good risks. An infantry division also had only one attached tank battalion, which limited tank-infantry operations. American armored divisions had more tanks than the Panzer divisions but were outgunned by most German tanks in 1944–1945.

Army personnel assignment policy also penalized the ground forces and limited American combat effectiveness. From the war's beginning the Army assigned people to military jobs on the basis of both intelligence and physical capability, but intelligence reigned supreme in allocating the physically fit to overseas duties. The most intelligent men went into technical billets, the others into the infantry. In 1944, 40 percent of the enlisted men in an American division were classified as below average in intelligence. This policy made it especially difficult to find and keep competent NCOs, who bore the brunt of combat leadership and suffered disproportionate casualties. The lack of small-unit leaders had not been a special problem in the divisions that had fought in the Mediterranean campaign, since they produced able leaders from their own ranks. The newer infantrymen, however, were younger and less intelligent than their 1943 comrades, which restricted the leadership pool. In France the rate of casualties among veterans and replacements alike eroded the quality of tactical leadership. Leadership problems, for example, contributed to a persistent American weakness: a minority of infantrymen fired their weapons in any one engagement.

Faced with such structural problems, Eisenhower was loath to attempt any dramatic battles in late 1944 until his American divisions (now two-thirds of his ground combat force) could regroup and his logistical system could catch up with the battlefield. He had no confidence that Montgomery would use his scarce combat troops with any greater competence than his American generals. His major adjustment was to adopt a variant of Montgomery's strategy by committing the new 9th U.S. Army and most of the 1st U.S. Army north of the Ardennes while curbing Patton's 3d U.S. Army and instructing the 6th U.S. Army Group to the south to limit offensive operations. With autumn mud and winter cold slowing forward movement and restricting air support, Eisenhower planned to capture at least a bridgehead over the Rhine before the year ended. With the once beaten Germans fighting with desperate effectiveness in the Hürtgen Forest, in Aachen, and the Roer Valley, the Allied campaign reverted to a war of attrition that resembled the Meuse-Argonne offensive of 1918. The battle for the Siegfried Line promised to offer nothing more than mounting casualties.

The Isolation of Japan

As its carriers and amphibious forces advanced to the western Pacific in 1944, the United States launched devastating attacks upon the economic life and morale of the Japanese people. The accumulative destruction ruined Japan's ability to maintain a wartime economy, but not its will to fight on. The American assault on the home islands came in two forms: submarine warfare against the Japanese merchant fleet and bomber attacks on Japan's highly flammable industrial cities. In a sense, the Japanese experienced the combined pain of the German U-boat attacks on Britain and the Allied bombing of Germany. So obvious were the effects of the submarine and bombing campaigns by 1945 that some American planners believed that economic collapse would make an invasion of the home islands unnecessary.

Beginning the war with no combat experience and limited numbers, the submarine force of the Pacific Fleet had every reason to be a "silent service." Despite the heavy demands placed upon the submarines to attack the Japanese fleet, virtually every phase of the submarines' early efforts was flawed. Despite its limited numbers (fifty boats, about evenly divided between Pearl Harbor and Cavite), the submarine force sortied against the entire periphery of the Japanese defensive area. When the Asiatic Fleet's boats fell back to Australia in 1942, they patrolled the full length of the Malay Barrier while the Pearl boats roamed the Pacific from the home islands to the equator. Too few submarines patrolled too much ocean.

Doctrine and tactics combined to limit the effectiveness of American submarine attacks. Since submarine forces were supposed to concentrate on attacking warships, they planned to launch their torpedoes from deep beneath the sea. Surface attacks, even at night, were officially discouraged. The difficulty with deep submerged attacks was that American subs did not yet have adequate ranging sonars and computing and tracking equipment. Instead, the Navy had attempted to develop a torpedo that made a near miss as good as a direct hit: the Mk XIV torpedo with the Mk VI exploder. This theoretically deadly combination was supposed to explode when the torpedo entered the magnetic field of its target; it also carried a contact exploder in case the magnetic detonation did not take place. Submarine commanders discovered that neither of the exploders worked very well. Their 1942–1943 patrols experienced a bewildering number of problems: torpedoes that prematurely exploded, others that did not explode at all, torpedoes that ran underneath their targets (the Mk VI's depth setting was also flawed), torpedoes that even circled back upon the submarines that had launched them. In a fit of anger at the designers, Rear Admiral Charles A. Lockwood, commander of the Pearl submarines, suggested that the Navy design a special boathook with which submarines could rip off the sides of Japanese vessels.

Even with the hardiest of souls, the early submarine offensive would have had problems, but the submarine force was not commanded by the Navy's fiercest warriors. Weighted down by the stress of command, the fear of losing their crews and boats, and their peacetime-bred operational conservatism, the submarine captains habitually failed to close with the enemy and sink ships. One-third of them were relieved in the war's first year. The submarine force, however, had attractions that allowed the Navy to man its boats with its finest sailors, officers and enlisted men alike. Submarine sailors were all volunteers, attracted by the force's elite standards, casual discipline, technical challenges, and extra pay. All volunteers had to pass rigorous physical, mental, and psychological tests to qualify for the demanding submarine training program, for the Navy knew that undersea warfare created stresses that weak personalities could not handle. With experience and the proper weapons, therefore, the submarine force had the human potential to carry the undersea war right into Japanese waters.

The Pacific submarine force spent much of 1942 and 1943 sorting out its problems and mustering its strength for a maximum effort in 1944. The size of the force doubled, and its commanders increased both the number and length of their patrols. The Navy finally fixed its errant torpedoes, and the quality of its boats and crews to endure and survive Japanese ASW attacks had been proved. Younger, more aggressive captains replaced their cautious seniors. Moreover, submarine planners had enough data to analyze operations and change them. With Admiral Nimitz's approval (Nimitz himself was an experienced submariner) and encouraged by the accuracy of their signal intelligence, especially ULTRA derived from the broken Japanese Army Water Transport Code, the planners massed their patrols along constricted shipping routes in the western Pacific. The destruction of the Japanese merchant fleet became the submarines' primary mission, and they deployed for fleet action only when a major engagement seemed likely. The submarine force also had sufficient influence to limit many of its secondary missions, like transporting guerrillas and raiders, carrying supplies to guerrillas behind enemy lines, and performing reconnaissance duties. One secondary mission that submariners actually relished was rescuing downed Allied airmen; daring snatches from underneath Japanese guns became an operational tour de force.

The statistics on operations for 1941–1943 demonstrated both the disappointments and achievements of the Pacific submarine force. In 700 patrols the Americans sank 515 ships of 2.25 million tons, but it required an average of ten torpedo firings to result in one sinking. The offensive, however, reduced Japanese merchant tonnage, which slipped from 5.2 million tons to 4.1 million tons by the end of 1943. In one critical vessel category— oil tankers—the Japanese actually increased their fleet from 686,000 to 863,000 tons with conversions and new construction. Oil tankers, then, were the optimal target for 1944. On the hopeful side—despite improved Japanese convoy operations—American submarine losses were bearable: twenty-two boats (and nineteen entire crews) in the war's first two years.

In the war's last two years the Pacific submarine force effectively ended the Japanese economy's ability to sustain a major war effort with imports from Southeast Asia. Operating from new forward bases in the Marianas and Philippines, patrolling submarines could saturate the straits and inland seas from the home islands to Malaya. Enjoying new technological improvements in torpedo operations, the Pacific subs exacted a rising toll on merchantmen. In total tonnage the Japanese merchant fleet declined from 5 million to just over 2 million. Heroic efforts kept tanker tonnage about even, but only at the expense of all other building programs. In the war's last year (September 1944–September 1945) the subs finally took out the tanker fleet, cutting it from almost 900,000 to under 200,000 tons. When the war ended, the Japanese merchant marine was reduced to less than 2 million tons, mostly wooden-hulled coasters and fishing boats of limited carrying capacity. By postwar reckoning based on Japanese figures, the submarine force destroyed 60 percent of the merchantmen and 30 percent of the Japanese warships sunk by the Americans. It inflicted these losses in exchange for 3,500 lives and forty-five boats lost on operational patrols. In no other part of the American war effort was the relationship between cost and great results so clear.

For all the statistics, submarine service in the Pacific remained a highly personal experience, filled with memories of the smell of sweat and oil, the wracking concussion of exploding depth charges, the controlled chaos of an emergency dive, the quick peek through a periscope at a flaming tanker or the peak of Mount Fuji, the bittersweet tension of a submerged attack amid a Japanese convoy. And, finally, there was the thrill of victory.

For the Japanese the growing signs of defeat in the maritime war—shortages of food and oil—paled in comparison with the direct impact of American bombs upon Japan's cities. From the war's earliest stages, American military planners viewed strategic bombardment as an essential element in Japan's defeat. The instrument of the bomber offensive was the very long-range bomber, the B-29, rushed into production without full testing in 1943. The B-29 was a giant. With a wingspan of 141 feet and 99 feet long, the four-engined bomber could fly 2,000 miles and drop 10 tons of bombs from 30,000 feet. It carried machine guns and cannon enough to intimidate all but suicidal fighter pilots. Although plagued by mechanical problems, inherent in its shortened testing period, the B-29 gave air-war planners their weapon. Their major difficulty was to place the aircraft in range of the home islands.

In 1943 the best available site for bases was China. Already in operation, the 14th Air Force had been conducting bombing operations within the range of its B-24s and B-25s. In June 1944 the "Superfortresses" of the XX Bomber Command, controlled directly by the JCS, bombed Japan for the first time, while other B-29s in India attacked targets in Southeast Asia. The difficulties of supply and relations with the Nationalist Chinese made

China an unattractive basing site, and after October 1944, B-29 operations in the CBI theater did not expand. Already in the process of redeploying to the Marianas, XX Bomber Command withdrew in greater haste in January 1945, when the Japanese launched a ground offensive that overran most of the USAAF bases in China. When the B-29s staged their last raid from China in March, they had mounted only forty-nine missions in all. Operation MATTERHORN ended as a molehill.

In 1944 the USAAF shifted the weight of its strategic air offensive against Japan to four major bases in the recently captured Marianas. At the same time that MacArthur waded ashore at Leyte, B-29s arrived on Saipan. XXI Bomber Command, whose parent 20th Air Force also controlled XX Bomber Command, began raids against Japan in November 1944. Using concepts borrowed from the air campaign against Germany, XXI Bomber Command ran precision-bombing, high-altitude raids against the Japanese steel and aircraft industries. Plagued more by weather and headwinds, engine problems, and low numbers than air defenses, the bombers did little damage. Poststrike analysis of the major raids showed that only 20 percent of the bombs landed on target. Impatient for results, General Arnold ordered Major General Curtis E. LeMay, a seasoned bomber commander from Europe and China, to the Marianas with orders to make the air war effective. After three months of experimentation and analysis, LeMay completely changed the character of the strategic bombing campaign.

Based on target analysis conducted in Washington and his own observations of B-29 operations, LeMay adopted—with Arnold's encouragement—the night area-bombing operations pioneered by the RAF against Germany. In part, the city busting and burning had an economic objective, for Japanese factories and assembly plants were dispersed throughout the cities. Incendiary bombs rather than high explosives appeared to be the optimal weapons to destroy Japan's military industries. The campaign also had larger purposes than weakening Japan's military forces as a prelude to invasion. USAAF planners believed that the air-submarine campaign against Japanese shipping and strategic bombing would bring the Japanese to such a low state of morale and general poverty that the imperial government would surrender. An island nation dependent on imports, its industrial work force and factories concentrated in six major cities, Japan appeared especially vulnerable to strategic bombing. In a war that had already killed millions, little patience remained for ethical arguments. As one USAAF explanation of the campaign stated in 1945, "There are no civilians in Japan. We are making War and making it in the all-out fashion which saves American lives, shortens the agony which War is, and seeks to bring about an enduring Peace. We intend to seek out and destroy the enemy wherever he or she is, in the greatest possible numbers, in the shortest possible time."

On March 9–10 XXI Bomber Command attacked Tokyo with incendiaries, passing over the city in a bomber stream of more than 300 B-29s. The low-altitude night attack devastated one-quarter of the city and killed 84,000 people. Despite its own growing losses, unavoidable in low-level attacks even with escort fighters, XXI Bomber Command expanded its raids until in June all of Japan's major cities lay in ruins. LeMay worked his crews to the point of exhaustion, with weather and bomb shortages the only factors affecting scheduling attacks. As XXI Bomber Command increased in size toward 1,000 B-29s, it ran both night and daylight operations, pulverizing cities and military targets throughout the summer of 1945. The Japanese air force no longer contested the raids, husbanding its remaining planes for *kamikaze* assaults on the Navy. For all the suffering they endured, including as many as 900,000 deaths and the destruction of 80 percent of their cities, the Japanese people had no direct influence over their government, whose military diehards had not yet accepted defeat. Instead, the Japanese military steeled itself for a suicidal resistance against the Allied invasion. It would take even greater shocks than B-29 fire raids to end the war.

The Axis Last Stand

Satisfied with the grand strategic designs they had created in 1943–1944, Roosevelt, Churchill, and Stalin saw no reason in late 1944 to rethink their approach to total victory. Even though he was predisposed to tinker with operations to the war's closing days—largely for postwar political advantage—Churchill reminded his collaborators in August 1944 that everything they "had touched had turned to gold." The war against Hitler had certainly taken its final shape, a vast east-west dual invasion compressing the Wehrmacht to its death within Germany's prewar borders. The war against the Japanese had the most loose ends, complicated by the potential role of the British and Russians and the Americans' divided command in the western Pacific. Nevertheless, in the autumn of 1944 the Allies saw victory ahead.

Given the overwhelming nature of their victories, the Allies had some reason to underestimate their foes' capacity to resist, even when that capacity became apparent in the Philippines and along the Siegfried Line. Both political and military calculations led the Anglo-American leadership to misjudge the resilience of the German army and unconventional strategic instincts of Adolf Hitler. Conceding irreversible strategic losses to the Russians, Hitler ordered his limited tank production and manpower reserves into the skeleton divisions that had fallen back to the Rhine. Drawing his inspiration from the desperate defensive campaigns of Napoleon and Frederick the Great, who also had faced implacable coalitions on two fronts,

Hitler planned a massive offensive against the Anglo-American armies in the west. His geographic goal was the port of Antwerp, his psychological goal to divide the Allies in the confusion of defeat. Under his personal supervision, his commanders formed two Panzer armies and one infantry army of twenty-five divisions (250,000 men) capable of offensive action and deployed them in the Ardennes, weakly held by the 1st U.S. Army.

Although some American intelligence officers found signs of a counteroffensive, the timing, size, and place of the German attack remained obscure. The Germans masked their preparations with an elaborate deception plan and benefited from the fact that their internal communications had become more secure. Moreover, Hitler deceived the Allied generals by calling Gerd von Rundstedt from retirement to command his western armies. Rundstedt's appointment pacified the German army high command, which favored (as did Rundstedt himself) a limited offensive to restore the breaks in the Siegfried Line. The Allies assumed that the aged *Feldmarschall,* a consummate professional, would fight a delaying action west of the Rhine rather than launch a major counteroffensive. German and Allied generals once more underestimated Hitler's fevered fascination with the bold stroke.

"The Battle of the Bulge" began in mid-December, and for two weeks it appeared as if the Germans might at least reach the Meuse River, if not Antwerp. Penetrating the extended front of four American divisions, the two Panzer armies broke the 1st U.S. Army's front and drove fifty miles toward the Meuse. Showing a desperate courage that surprised the Germans, the American infantrymen and tankers fought back with a ferocity fueled by true tales of SS atrocities and stark anger at their predicament. While many American service units clogged the roads with panicked convoys, combat units from isolated platoons to the better part of divisions ruined the German timetable and forced the penetration into a narrow corridor. Both shoulders of "the Bulge" held, and ferocious defenses at St. Vith and Bastogne cost the Germans precious time and troops. Starved for fuel and continuous air support, the Panzer divisions reached the limit of their offensive endurance, the best Christmas gift the Allies received in 1944.

As soon as he assessed the scope of the German attack, Eisenhower organized an overwhelming riposte against both flanks of "the Bulge." To simplify command arrangements and draw British armored divisions into the fray, he gave Montgomery temporary control of the 9th U.S. Army and all but one corps of the 1st U.S. Army along the northern flank. Montgomery's unfortunate manner and thirst for publicity irritated the Americans, but he managed the battle with skill, blunting the attacks of the right-flank Panzer army with the right mix of delaying actions and counterattacks. On the southern flank, which required less cautious action, Bradley unleashed Patton, whose 3d U.S. Army changed the direction of its operations and slammed into the left-flank Panzer army. As Eisenhower urged, his generals fought the battle as "one of opportunity for us and not disaster." Enjoying air superiority when the weather cleared, the Allies regained the initiative and by the end of January had driven the German remnants from "the Bulge" in a hard-fought campaign made more taxing by snow and bitter cold. When the battle ended, the Americans had lost 100,000 men, the Germans 120,000. The German losses in skilled troops, tanks, self-propelled artillery, and mechanized vehicles made their defeat a catastrophe. "The Battle of the Bulge" ended the Wehrmacht's ability to disrupt even a broad-front Allied offensive into the heartland of the Third Reich.

As the Allied armies in Europe beat back the last great German offensive, MacArthur's 6th Army and the 7th Fleet turned north toward Luzon to liberate the most populated island of the Philippines. With air support from USAAF fighters on Mindoro, captured in a follow-up of the Leyte operation, and from the carriers of the 3d Fleet, the 7th Fleet would have been undisturbed by conventional Japanese attacks. The *kamikazes,* however, made January 4–15, 1945, the worst period in the Navy's war since the battles in the southern Solomons in 1942. Intercepting the 7th Fleet (an armada of 164 vessels) on its way to Lingayen Gulf, the *kamikazes* sunk an escort carrier and damaged four other warships on January 4, damaged nine vessels the next day, and sank a destroyer and damaged eleven warships the next day. In three days the Navy suffered 1,100 casualties, many of them burned and dismembered by explosions. Despite concentrated air strikes on Luzon's airfields, the suicide attacks continued—with more sinkings and destruction—until the Japanese ran out of airplanes on January 15. When the raids ended, the Navy had lost five ships sunk, eighteen severely damaged, and thirty struck at least once; 738 sailors died and 1,400 had been wounded. Concerned about the *kamikazes'* effectiveness, the 3d Fleet's fast carriers doubled their fighter strength by disembarking their dive bombers.

The land campaign for Luzon showed no diminution of the Japanese willingness to die for the Emperor. In six months of combat, the 6th Army endured nearly 10,000 casualties while killing over 100,000 Japanese. When the war ended, another 50,000 Japanese were still holed up in Luzon's mountains. In conventional battle on the Luzon plains, the Americans crushed the Japanese with close air support, armor, artillery, and infantry assaults, but in the mountains the war became more equal, with Filipino guerrillas a plus for the 6th Army. The battle for Manila, however, demonstrated the dogged character of Japanese resistance. Although General Tomoyuki Yamashita had declared Manila an open city, some 20,000 Japanese naval and army service troops disobeyed his orders and fought the Americans block by block. It took three American divisions a month to capture the city at a cost of 1,100 dead; almost all the Japanese defenders perished in the rubble, for Manila became a shambles. Caught in the battle, more than 100,000 Filipinos died in the city, many massacred by the Japanese. The battle for Manila again demonstrated that the Japanese armed forces might be doomed by Western standards, but they would use every opportunity to kill Americans and Filipino civilians in the faint hope that their very ferocity would demoralize their enemy. As MacArthur's 8th Army liberated the Visayans and Mindanao, the Americans and their guerrilla allies showed little inclination to take prisoners, and the Japanese did nothing to attract mercy, often murdering wounded and prisoners as part of their thousands of last stands.

If the Luzon campaign dramatized the *kamikaze* danger, the capture of the volcanic island of Iwo Jima (February 19–March 26, 1945) proved the damage that Japanese cave and bunker defenses could deliver upon even the most determined, skilled American landing force. Three crack Marine divisions slugged their way with blast-and-burn tactics across and up the island. They seldom saw the Japanese, who shelled and machine-gunned them from belts of fortified positions hidden in thousands of caves and bunkers. Although the island had real value as a haven for stricken B-29s and a base for their escort fighters, Iwo Jima cost the Marines about 6,000 dead and 20,000 wounded. For the infantry regiments, the campaign was a nightmare of incessant shelling, sudden death from hidden positions, relentless attacks, and pestilence, for the island became infested with flies feeding on the dead. As one Marine despaired, "They send you to a place . . . and you get shot to hell and maybe they pull you back. But then they send you right up again and then you get murdered. God, you stay there until you get killed or until you can't stand it anymore." Although the 21,000 Japanese troops on Iwo Jima perished almost to a man in their caves, they had for the first time in the central Pacific campaign inflicted more casualties than they suffered. Their defensive system frustrated both naval gunfire and air attack, leaving the Marines no choice but to fight the battle with flame-throwers, hand grenades, and demolitions. Such tactics demanded that uncommon valor become a common virtue. It also meant that three Marine divisions had to be rebuilt with teenage replacements before they could fight again.

The war in Europe also reached a new frenzy as the Allies and the Russians opened the continuous offensives in January 1945 that would end the war against Hitler in May. Russian armies of nearly 7 million men pushed forward from the Baltic to the Balkans, and in the same month the 4 million men of the Anglo-American armies surged against the last strongholds on the Siegfried Line on their way, finally, across the Rhine.

Two-thirds of his divisions and tactical air wings were by now American, but Eisenhower gave the 21st British Army Group the place of honor in the offensive and used the 9th U.S. Army for reinforcement. Eisenhower accepted Montgomery's theory that the weight of the Allied attack should be north of the Ruhr; the Germans agreed and defended the Rhine River line in front of 21st British Army Group with fierce skill. As Montgomery organized a "big push" in his best World War I style, the 1st and 3d U.S. Armies to the south broke the German forces west of the Rhine into isolated pockets and punched across the last great barrier of the Third Reich. Exploiting success, Eisenhower planned to envelop the Ruhr and trap about half the remaining Germans on his front. Shuttling scarce Panzer reserves from one Allied penetration to another, German operations had become (as even Hitler recognized) "moving the catastrophe from one place to another."

The last month of the European war found the armed forces of the Grand Coalition mounting exploitation campaigns on three fronts. In Italy the Allies reached the Po Valley and soon received the first major German surrender. The Russians drove to within thirty miles of Berlin by April, only to face stiffening German resistance. Benefiting from the general collapse of the Wehrmacht and Hitler's last, desperate dispatch of reserves against the Russians, the American armies roared eastward from the Rhine to the Elbe, the prearranged place to meet the Russians. Some forces went even farther, as the 1st and 3d U.S. Armies crossed the Czech and Austrian borders. In the Ruhr the Americans captured over 300,000 Germans. So fluid had the front become that one German corps commander tried to reorganize a mass of Wehrmacht soldiers until an American MP politely informed him that he, too, had just become a POW. Only fierce national and military pride, the effectiveness of the Nazi police-security organization, and Hitler's mad determination preserved a semblance of resistance. After briefly celebrating FDR's death in April, Hitler made himself the Third Reich's most important war death before the month was out. His successors surrendered to the Allies on May 7 amid a ruin of death and fire Germany had not seen since the Thirty Years' War. The conflict in Europe had ended.

The Asian *Götterdämmerung* came at Okinawa, only 350 miles south of the home islands, in a campaign that pitted the 5th Fleet and the 10th Army against the most savage Japanese resistance of the war. For the Navy the campaign developed as a battle of attrition, pitting the fast carriers and their escorts against the *kamikazes*. In ten major attacks the Japanese threw 2,800 aircraft of all kinds against the fleet and lost most of them. In sheer numbers the *kamikazes* punished the Navy as the Imperial Fleet had not; when the battle ended in mid-June, the 5th Fleet had lost around 10,000 casualties (half of them killed) and 28 ships and craft sunk by air attack. Of the 325 ships damaged, 43 had to be scrapped. Six fast carriers took successive hits, two so many that they had to leave the war. Although the *kamikazes* sometimes reached the amphibious task force and destroyed American vessels, they poured their worst havoc upon the destroyers and smaller escorts along the antiaircraft picket line. The *kamikazes* that escaped the combat air patrols dove in succession at American warships, penetrating the curtain of antiaircraft fire often enough to turn destroyers into flaming junkheaps manned by bloody remnants of their crews. Although the *kamikazes* did not slow the land battle, they impressed the Navy and made the prospect of future amphibious operations grim.

The battle for Okinawa itself (April 1–June 21, 1945) again allowed the Japanese army to employ its cave-and-bunker defense system and forced the 10th Army to pay dearly for its victory. Defending only the lower third of the long, thin island, the Japanese (with one exception) fought from their prepared positions without major counterattacks. Rejecting the option of amphibious flanking attacks for reasons that remain arguable, the 10th Army's commander committed five Army and two Marine divisions to a series of bloody offensives against the Japanese defenses. Although the Americans enjoyed massive close air support and artillery superiority, the Japanese positions could not be eliminated except by infantry assault. Veterans of Peleliu and Leyte remembered the seesaw battles along the muddy ridges as the worst of the war. Before it had killed more than 100,000 Japanese soldiers, the 10th Army lost around 40,000 men, about a fourth of them killed in action. High and low shared the slaughter. Both the American and Japanese commanding generals perished, as did an estimated 100,000 native Okinawans. As the campaign staggered to a close, the Army began to redeploy divisions from Europe for the invasion of the home islands in late 1945. The Japanese defeat was inevitable, but the orgy of death seemed equally unstoppable if the war in the Pacific continued in its new form.

The American government, now led by President Harry S. Truman, had one unused weapon: the atomic bomb. Warned of the military implications of German nuclear research by two refugee scientists, Enrico Fermi and Albert Einstein, Roosevelt in 1939 had arranged minor government subsidies for similar research in the United States. Convinced of the theoretical possibility of causing an atomic chain reaction, scientists at five major universities pursued their basic research into the explosive properties of the uranium atom until the University of Chicago group created the first chain reaction in December 1942. Proven theory did not a weapon make. Throughout 1943 and 1944 the Office of Scientific Research and Development and the Army Corps of Engineers' "Manhattan Project" assembled thousands of scientists, engineers, and skilled craftsmen—at Oak Ridge, Tennessee; Hanford, Washington; and Los Alamos, New Mexico—to fabricate a working atomic bomb that could be dropped. Without knowing its mission, a special B-29 group practiced dropping a bomb that had not yet been built, let alone exploded. The organizational and security aspects of the project fell to Major General Leslie R. Groves, but Dr. J. Robert Oppenheimer provided the scientific leadership at Los Alamos that turned theory into reality. On July 16, 1945, the Los Alamos team exploded the first nuclear device in the desert. As he watched the mushroom cloud boil upward, Oppenheimer recalled a Hindu quote: "Now I am become death, destroyer of worlds."

To Harry Truman, a man of modest attainments and simple instincts, fell the task of deciding to use the bomb against Japan. Informed of the bomb's likely existence after becoming president, Truman arranged careful consideration of the issue by a civilian Interim Committee, which considered scientific and political opinion, and by the JCS. With the exception of a dissident group of scientists who counseled nonuse, the advisers assumed that the weapon would be used to end the war. Most of the arguments dealt with postwar concerns, especially relations with the Soviet Union. One group of scientists suggested a demonstration of the weapon, but Oppenheimer and others feared a misfire. With only two working bombs available in August 1945, there was little margin for miscalculation. Faced with the prospect of an invasion of Japan and millions of Japanese and American casualties, the JCS preferred the bomb, since economic blockade and the air war had not yet brought peace.

Truman had every reason to seek a quick end to war, for his advisers pointed out that the Soviet Union would soon enter the war with Japan, which promised to complicate peacemaking in Asia. According to an agreement made with FDR at Yalta in February, Stalin pledged to break his neutrality pact with Japan and enter the war three months after Germany's defeat. The Japanese government sensed Russia's new policy when it tried to find some third party to negotiate peace with the Allies after April 1945. All the principals saw only part of the politico-strategic problems of the period. Truman, for example, saw that the preservation of the institution of the Emperor did not endanger postwar reconstruction of Japan, but he knew that the American public saw Hirohito as a war criminal. His advisers thought unconditional surrender might in practice be modified, but only after a military capitulation. The Japanese peace faction around Hirohito wanted to retain the Emperor and saw their nation as an impoverished state with 13 million bombed-out refugees; their opponents (largely army generals) saw Japan as a nation with 2.3 million soldiers and 4 million paramilitary fighters ready to die fighting the Americans, rallied by their commitment to the Emperor's divine being. Already aware of the American bomb and committed to nuclear weapons development of their own, the Russians did not quail at Truman's hints about a "super weapon" when they again met the Americans at Potsdam in July. They instead hastened preparations for their planned offensive into Manchuria and Korea. An Allied declaration from Potsdam threatened the Japanese with worse war but also hinted at a negotiated settlement. The Japanese response was equally subject to misinterpretation. Although the Japanese intent was to explore the terms, the American government thought the response a contemptuous declaration of continued war.

With no presidential order to delay its atomic bombing attacks, XXI Bomber Command organized its last raids. The target list came from Washington; the exact cities to be bombed and the timing rested in the USAAF's hands. On August 6 the first bomb fell on Hiroshima, and the second exploded over Nagasaki three days later. The explosions killed 135,000 Japanese and razed the two cities. In between raids the Soviet Union abrogated its neutrality treaty and declared war on Japan. Despite a desperate attempt by army diehards to seize the government by capturing Hirohito and assassinating his advisers, the Emperor rallied the peace faction and in a rare demonstration of imperial action ordered his government to sue for peace on August 10. As the Truman administration had hoped, the two atomic bombs had shocked the peace faction into decisive resistance against the war faction. To save the remnants of the Japanese nation, Hirohito ordered his armed forces to surrender. Equally relieved by the sudden end of the war, the Allied high commanders in the Pacific met a Japanese delegation aboard the USS *Missouri* in Tokyo Bay on September 2 to bring an end to the modern world's most devastating conflict. As General MacArthur observed in his radio announcement of the surrender ceremony, "We have had our last chance. If we do not devise some greater and more equitable system, Armageddon will be at our door."

FIFTEEN

Cold War and Hot War: The United States Enters the Age of Nuclear Deterrence and Collective Security, 1945–1953

The end of World War II marked the beginning of a new era for the United States, for its foreign policy could no longer stand on the twin pillars of noninvolvement and commercialism and its defense policy on the dual concepts of maritime security and wartime mobilization. The second maiming of Europe and the collapse of its empires in Africa and Asia opened international relations to a bewildering array of conflicts that carried the potential for wider wars. Had the United States followed its diplomacy of the marketplace and relied on broad oceans to protect it, the nation might have avoided the traumas of foreign wars, military alliances, and higher levels of peacetime military spending. The United States might also have lost its political and economic power and mortgaged the safety of its population. The creation of nuclear weapons and their adaptation to intercontinental bombers stripped the shield of time and space from American security. Amid the casualties of World War II lay the corpse of traditional American defense policy.

Although the development of an alternative policy came slowly and with much agonizing, the United States government committed the nation—with public approval—to a new strategy. Instead of waiting for general war to engulf the United States or depending upon the nation's industrial and manpower potential to discourage potential enemies, the United States adopted the strategy of deterrence. To deter war, so policy-makers and theorists reasoned, the nation required ready military forces and the political will to threaten their use or to use them if deterrence failed. For sheer destructiveness, accomplished with shocking speed, nuclear weapons appeared to be the ultimate deterrent, and from the birth of the first atomic bombs, policymakers pondered the potential of nuclear weapons to make war obsolete. The more farsighted strategists like academic Bernard Brodie, Secretary of War Henry Stimson, diplomat George Kennan, and scientist J. Robert Oppenheimer wondered, however, if the threat of nuclear retaliation would be a truly credible deterrent, since the enormity of nuclear war might be out of proportion to the threat.

Drawing upon its experience in coalition warfare in two world wars, the United States complemented unilateral nuclear deterrence with a commitment to collective defense and nonnuclear deterrence. One instrument of collective security became the United Nations (UN), an international body championed by the United States and created by international agreement by forty-six nations on June 26, 1945. The second instrument was the regional military alliance, allowed by the United Nations Charter. The United States joined its first such alliance since its 1778 treaty with France when it signed the Inter-American Treaty of Reciprocal Assistance (the Rio Pact) on September 2, 1947, and bound itself with nineteen other nations for the defense of the Western Hemisphere.

The concept of nuclear deterrence and collective security did not develop in a political vacuum, for the United States found itself at odds with the Soviet Union over a wide array of international issues. Although American diplomats in Russia warned that the Soviet Union did not view the postwar world in terms acceptable to American interests, the Truman administration attempted to deal with the Stalin regime as if it had some interest in postwar cooperation. In one sense the United States and the Soviet Union shared similar characteristics. Both were latecomers to the arena of international politics; both had large populations and industrial resources that spanned entire continents; both had been drawn into continental rivalries that had produced two global wars; both had messianic visions about the nature of political organization and economic development; both had just demonstrated an awesome ability for military action; both had no intention of allowing the traditional European patterns of nationalism and imperialism to define the international system in the last half of the twentieth century.

At the heart of the American-Soviet rivalry lay an irreconcilable bond between national interest and ideology that ensured global competition. If the United States and the Soviet Union had behaved only according to the dictates of state interest, the course of history since 1945 might have been different. Such was not the case. The two nations tended to see their rivalry as a clash between principles, with their own national futures tied to the success of such concepts as capitalism and socialism, individual liberty and state security, religious freedom and scientific materialism, and international diversity and the ultimate victory of the Communist commonwealth. The opposing system represented the greatest threat to peace, for its very nature ensured war. Global conflict was inevitable and indivisible as long as the opposing system existed.

The primary arena of East-West competition was Europe. The rivals' sphere of concern ran from Great Britain to the borders of prewar Eastern Europe, but the rivals' writ ran along the borders of their occupation forces. By 1949 the United States had merged its occupation zone in Germany with those of Great Britain and France into a single West Germany that had all the attributes of an independent state except an armed force and a foreign policy. The Soviet Union took similar steps to ensure that its portion of divided Germany fell into its political orbit. In 1948 the only nation that had a coalition government that included non-Communists, Czechoslovakia, fell to a Russian-approved internal coup. The Russians then closed overland communications between West Germany and the jointly occupied city of Berlin, but an Allied airlift of nine months' duration saved West Berlin from Communist absorption. In Eastern Europe the Russians established Communist governments in Poland, Romania, and Hungary. Nationalist Communist resistance movements provided new regimes in Albania and Yugoslavia; the former remained under Russian influence, but the latter, governed by the guerrilla hero Josip Broz (Tito), did not fall entirely into the Soviet embrace.

The developing anti-Communist coalition in the West had its share of early "Cold War" victories during the same period. With the assistance of American funds, channeled through intelligence agencies and international labor organizations, France and Italy eliminated their Communist parties from their new republican governments by 1949. In military terms Great Britain created a new continental alliance system in 1946 by joining France in the Dunkirk Agreement, which joined those two countries in an alliance. In the Brussels Pact of 1948 the Dunkirk partners extended the alliance to the Netherlands, Luxembourg, and Belgium. Recurring crises in Greece and Turkey provided the Truman administration with an opportunity to meet the Communist challenge directly. Informed by the British that they could no longer support the Greek royalist government in its civil war against Communist rebels and responding to a Turkish plea for assistance against Russian pressures to revise the international convention on control of the Straits, the president requested $400 million in military and economic assistance for Greece and Turkey in March 1947. The program for Greece included a military mission to reform the Greek army. President Truman described his request in terms of a new diplomatic principle, labeled "the Truman Doctrine," which committed the United States "to help free peoples to maintain . . . their national integrity against aggressive movements that seek to impose upon them totalitarian regimes." To support the policy of "containment" described by Truman, Congress voted the aid package two months later. Again responding to a presidential initiative, Congress a year later approved a $13 billion program of economic assistance—the Marshall Plan—for Western Europe.

The widening domestic consensus to challenge the Soviet Union in international affairs drew much of its force from the conviction that Soviet agents or "fellow travelers" had infiltrated Western governments. The impetus of the concern over Communist subversion came from several highly publicized cases that linked American and British citizens with Soviet spying, primarily upon the wartime development of the atomic bomb. Although Soviet espionage had limited influence upon the development of a Russian military threat, the Truman administration and its Republican critics vied with one another to purge the federal bureaucracy—especially the State Department—of people they regarded as agents (few in number and quickly eliminated) or "Communist sympathizers," who could be variously defined and counted. Anti-Communism in every form became the rage of the time. The "Second Red Scare," unlike its predecessor of 1918–1921, popularized a more aggressive foreign policy, at the substantial cost of individual rights and sober analysis of the real Soviet threat. The issue of internal security, however, alerted otherwise complacent Americans to the fact that the Soviet Union had interests beyond its formal borders.

The collapse of European influence throughout the rest of the world added another dimension to the Cold War. In a sense the United States replaced Great Britain as the Western player in the "Great Game," as the Anglo-Russian competition of the nineteenth century had been called. From the Middle East to China, the world war had rewritten the terms of political competition, and those terms pitted the United States and Russia as the missionaries for two very different forms of postcolonial political organization. With few exceptions the resistance movements of World War II had fallen to native leaders dedicated or sympathetic to Communism, if not Russian domination. China provided the most conspicuous example of a new form of conflict: A Communist inspired "people's revolutionary war." Built on the foundation of rural-based partisan warfare, political indoctrination and organization, and subversion, the Chinese Communists under the leadership of Mao Zedong defeated the Nationalists (the Quomindang) in 1949 and chased Chiang Kai-shek and his surviving followers to Taiwan.

The "loss" of China suggested an international Communist conspiracy orchestrated from Moscow. Certainly there was real evidence of Communist activism in several guerrilla wars that blossomed after V-J Day. In French Indochina, the Philippines, Malaya, the Dutch East Indies, and Burma, anticolonial insurgents preached and fought for an Asian version of Marxism. In a divided Korea the Soviet Union adopted a Communist regime while the United States accepted a nationalist, anti-Communist government. Only the civil war that accompanied the division of independent India and Pakistan and the Jewish-Arab war of 1948, which created the state of Israel, fell outside the pattern of Communist revolution. In one way or another, largely through the provision of military and economic assistance or indirect political support, the United States became a party to most of the wars of decolonization. American policymakers feared that Communist victories meant losses to the "Free World," and their European partners insisted that containment in Europe depended upon continued access to the resources of the Middle East, Africa, and Asia. The Truman administration did not embrace the concept of indivisible containment, but it did not accept Communist victories in the Third World either, for to do so weakened the role of the United Nations and strengthened the position of those domestic critics (largely Republican) who held the administration responsible for the fall of China.

Foreign policy problems, then, abounded in the postwar world. As Secretary of State Dean Acheson repeatedly stated, the problems did not lend themselves to quick, easy, inexpensive solutions. Nor did a general policy of containment or a strategy of deterrence and collective defense translate themselves into military programs. Instead, the federal government moved from crisis to crisis, from budget to budget, extemporizing programs characterized by political controversy and public misunderstanding. Nevertheless, by the time the Truman administration left office in 1953, it had laid the foundations of an enduring national security policy and organization.

Groping for a New Strategy

The crises of the Cold War's first five years forced Harry S. Truman to look hard at American military capability, and he found very little. Driven by domestic politics, which focused upon the performance of the economy, the reduction and balancing of the federal budget, and the close rivalry of the Democrats and Republicans, the president shared with Congress the responsibility for the nation's pallid defenses. In April 1947, as Congress considered aid to Greece and Turkey, he learned that the United States had no ready atomic bombs and that the Strategic Air Command (SAC) might not hit its targets anyway. At the height of the Berlin crisis a year later, Truman told his advisers he would like to give the Russians hell, but Secretary of State George C. Marshall responded that he thought one American division in Europe was not an adequate instrument for even the threat of hell. Briefed in February 1949 on planned atomic bomb production, Truman exclaimed, "Boy, we could blow a hole clean through the earth." But he then soberly remembered that the stockpile of bombs would not be ready until 1951, and by then the Soviets might have nuclear weapons too. Truman doubted that he would ever again order the use of atomic bombs unless the Russians struck first. In September 1949 Air Force reconnaissance planes picked up the first radioactive evidence of a Russian nuclear explosion on August 29, in Siberia.

Although his intelligence advisers missed the end of the American nuclear monopoly by three years, Truman had been facing the nuclear future since 1945, when his own scientists and Secretary of War Stimson had urged him to provide a system of controls that would prevent the future use of the atomic bomb. In domestic terms, nuclear controllers wanted an organization for research and development outside military control; in 1946 Congress passed the Atomic Energy Act, which created a five-man civilian Atomic Energy Commission (AEC). The AEC included a military applications division, so military concerns were not slighted, but the agency became a cockpit of controversy about nuclear programs. A study directed by Dean Acheson and David E. Lilienthal urged that the United States establish an international regime for the control of nuclear weapons. As Congress considered the law that created the AEC, Truman approved a proposal to internationalize nuclear weapons and sent Bernard Baruch to the UN to present what became known as the "Baruch Plan." The plan asked that the UN create an international atomic energy commission that would control all aspects of atomic affairs, from the mining of fissionable materials to the use of nuclear power for peaceful purposes. The Security Council would mete out "condign punishment" to any nation that turned nuclear power to military purposes. Although the administration's commitment to the plan was at best modest, its proposal foundered on the provisions for on-site inspection. Already committed to its own nuclear program, the Soviet Union ensured that the Baruch Plan disappeared into the mire of UN debate and study.

In 1946 and 1948 the United States conducted atomic tests at the Pacific atolls of Bikini and Eniwetok and learned more about nuclear effects and weapons design. The 1946 tests did little to advance the deliverability of atomic bombs. The weight of each nuclear device remained in the five-ton range and the yield stayed below 50 kilotons [the explosive equivalent of thousands of tons of TNT]. Now working on reduced budgets, the nuclear engineers had a limited capacity to produce fissionable materials and bomb assemblies. In 1949 the United States could have assembled 169 atomic bombs for a war plan that required more than twice that number of weapons. The 1948 SANDSTONE tests at Eniwetok, however, produced important breakthroughs for bomb design by producing a re-engineered core of plutonium and uranium that dramatically reduced the cost and size of each bomb while increasing its yield. The available uranium, thought to be in short supply, could now be distributed to many more bombs of greater accuracy and explosive power. The AEC in 1949 believed it could meet a JCS program target of 400 atomic bombs by 1953; in fact, the bomb builders produced 429 bombs by 1951, and by 1953 the American arsenal of nuclear weapons had grown to 1,152.

To deliver the bombs, however, produced other challenges. Not until 1948 did the Air Force have a single team capable of assembling a droppable bomb, and the custody of nuclear weapons remained in the hands of the AEC until 1953. The Strategic Air Command, equipped with B-29s and the postwar improved B-29 (the B-50), had little ability to deliver nuclear weapons. In 1948 SAC had around thirty trained crews and properly equipped aircraft, but when SAC's new commander, General Curtis E. LeMay, tested his force, not one crew could place a weapon on target in conditions approaching those of wartime.

The nation's nuclear weakness did not prevent policymakers from putting the atomic bomb at the center of U.S. strategy. A presidential Air Policy (Finletter) Commission and a similar congressional committee both reported in 1948 that the threat of nuclear retaliation was the cornerstone of defense policy. Atomic warheads and intercontinental delivery systems would probably outstrip the ability of defensive systems to stop them, so ready offensive air forces seemed essential to deter war in the first place. After several false starts, the JCS approved its first postwar joint emergency war plan, HALFMOON, in 1948, followed by a more elaborate plan in 1949, DROPSHOT. These plans placed primary emphasis on the use of nuclear weapons to strike Russian urban-based industry, especially petroleum and electrical targets. The military planners believed that Western Europe could not be defended in a general war. Instead, the United States would have to depend upon air strikes mounted from Great Britain, the Middle East, and Japan to defeat the Russians. The only commitment of nonnuclear air and ground forces would be related to holding air bases and the oil resources in the Middle East. The difficulty with the war plans was that the number of bombs the planners required exceeded the supply of weapons and aircraft needed to deliver them. The JCS also recognized a further complication: The war plans demanded overseas bases for SAC, since the Air Force did not have an adequate intercontinental capability.

Truman paled at the prospect, but he approved the military's concept of fighting a nuclear war if deterrence failed.

Within the government, argument raged in 1949 on how to make nuclear weapons a credible deterrent. One obvious answer was to improve the size and effectiveness of Strategic Air Command, an Air Force responsibility pursued in the development of the B-36, an intercontinental bomber, and of an in-flight refueling capability for the B-29s and B-50s. Within SAC, General LeMay drove his crews to higher efficiency through morale-building programs and realistic, demanding training. The major issue, however, became the development of a more awesome weapon. A civilian-military coalition of advocates, led by scientists Edward Teller and E.O. Lawrence and AEC Commissioner Lewis Strauss, urged the government to give top priority to producing a fusion, or hydrogen, bomb. Fraught with both theoretical and engineering problems, the "super bomb" program, which promised to produce weapons in the megaton (a million tons of TNT) range, had taken a backseat to the perfection of fission weapons, largely through the influence of the AEC's General Advisory Committee, dominated by J. Robert Oppenheimer. In brutal bureaucratic infighting that eventually drove Oppenheimer from government service, the AEC recommended in 1949 that the "super" project go forward on a crash basis. Convinced by JCS and AEC studies that the H-bomb represented only a logical extension of nuclear strategy, Truman approved the new emphasis on the fusion weapon program in January 1950.

The advent of nuclear weapons sharpened interservice competition for military missions, since all the services wanted to develop forces capable of waging nuclear war while maintaining their ability to handle more traditional short-of-war tasks and general war mobilization. Within the budget ceilings imposed by the Truman administration—one-third of the federal budget, or roughly $10 billion to $13 billion—the military programs could not all be funded. In fact, the money, spread among the services, bought only skeleton forces, meager research and development, and a great deal of bitter controversy. In the War Department the postwar Army Air Forces sought complete service autonomy, built around nuclear weapons and the strategic deterrence/war role. The ground Army sought a comprehensive universal military training law that would allow it to mobilize a trained wartime force for the next war, based on compulsory citizen peacetime training. Both the AAF and the Army thought largely in terms of general war with the Soviet Union in Europe. The Navy and the Marine Corps, on the other hand, tried to integrate general war (nuclear or not) preparation with their traditional conceptions of sea power. The Navy Department sought to hold on to its full World War II force structure (carrier task forces, land-based antisubmarine aviation, the Fleet Marine

Force, the submarine force) while adapting it to nuclear weapons. By the late 1940s the Navy had cruise and ballistic missile experiments underway for both its submarines and surface ships. It had introduced the *Midway* class (45,000 tons) carrier for new attack jets, and in 1948 Congress approved plans for *United States,* a 65,000-ton carrier that could carry nuclear-capable bombers. In March 1949 Navy pilots flew a patrol bomber with a 10,000-pound simulated bomb from the east coast to California and back again without landing. This project dramatized the Navy's general war strategy, which was to launch air strikes against land air bases from 500 miles at sea, followed by additional attacks against Russian naval bases with shorter-ranged naval planes. The Marine Corps also looked to new aviation to preserve amphibious landing operations; close air support aircraft and helicopters would overcome the dispersion that nuclear weapons would force upon amphibious task forces.

Military missions joined the related issues of funding, defense organization, and strategy to produce five years of political upheaval in defense policy. The first round of controversy opened when the War Department in 1945 submitted to Congress a JCS-approved plan for reorganizing the armed forces. The Army plan, which granted autonomy to the Air Force, argued that national military policy would be improved by establishing a single defense staff headed by a single military officer, supervised by a single civilian defense secretary. The new organization, which reflected the War Department General Staff system and the World War II theater unified commands, would "unify" the armed forces by giving the single defense chief and defense secretary the dominant voice in deciding roles and missions and preparing annual budgets. The proposal assumed that interservice competition was the most important barrier to more effective defense planning.

The Navy Department, led by the redoubtable James V. Forrestal, fought the Army plan to a standstill in the White House and Congress, for it saw the War Department plan as a blueprint for the end of its maritime security mission. Forrestal knew the unpublished assumptions of the War Department proposal: Cuts in naval aviation, the transfer of land-based naval air to the Air Force, no Navy nuclear weapons, the reduction of the Marine Corps to minor peacetime security functions. A future war, probably with the Soviet Union, would not involve major naval campaigns, since the Russians did not have a global navy. Therefore, so the Army and AAF planners thought, the Navy should finally relinquish its role as the first line of defense, surrendering that function to the Air Force. Forrestal and his staff retaliated with an alternative plan, designed by Ferdinand Eberstadt, an expert wartime mobilizer. For interservice relations Eberstadt's plan continued the JCS and theater unified command system, which would prevent the arbitrary assignment of roles and missions by a single chief of staff. Moreover, Eberstadt argued that the major planning difficulty was not interservice rivalry but the lack of civilian-military, interagency coordination in the executive branch. He therefore proposed a new set of agencies to centralize broad planning, coordinate intelligence collection and analysis, conduct mobilization resource planning, sponsor scientific research and development, and supervise education and training. Eberstadt's plan, quickly adopted by Navy partisans in Congress, checkmated the War Department proposal, since it allied serious issues with considerable political emotion.

For almost two years (1945–1947) two coalitions of defense reorganizers battled until Truman and Congress, exhausted by the struggle and anxious about Russia, forged the National Security Act of 1947, the fundamental legislation on postwar organization. In the balance, the law represented a Navy victory. The president would set policy in consultation with a National Security Council, which drew its statutory membership from old and new agencies: The president, the secretary of state, the secretary of defense, the military department secretaries, and the chairman of the National Security Resources Board. Although the latter agency, along with similar R&D and munitions boards, did not last, another new organization—the Central Intelligence Agency (CIA)—prospered. The new defense organization—labeled the "national military establishment"—was not a centralized, "unified" system but a federation on the World War II model. The secretary of defense, aided by a small staff, had only general, coordinating powers. He was held hostage to three military departments (Army, Air Force, and Navy) with separate secretaries and staffs. The law also specified service roles and missions, particularly for the Navy and Marine Corps, which saved all naval aviation functions and the Fleet Marine Force by inspired lobbying with Congress. Interservice relations remained bound to the JCS system of military negotiation; the JCS did not even have a formal chairman. Navy partisans were even more pleased with what had been avoided. Secretary of War Robert Patterson would not accept the new defense post, and Forrestal became the first secretary of defense. General Eisenhower did not become a single, powerful military defense chief and could only function informally as a presidential adviser. Only Congress could approve the reallocation of basic service combat roles and missions.

The National Security Act represented the end of one battle, not the end of a war. Although Congress rejected the Army's proposal for universal military training (instead it reestablished a limited draft in 1948, mostly to stimulate recruiting), it showed high interest in enlarging the Air Force's budget. Secretary of the Air Force Stuart Symington and Air Force Chief of Staff Hoyt S. Vandenberg (whose uncle was a prominent Republican senator) bedeviled Truman and Forrestal with their successful congressional lobbying. Unable to reconcile the JCS's budget requests, which ran about twice the money Truman would allow, Forrestal gathered the chiefs at Key West, Florida, and Newport, Rhode Island, in 1948 to hammer out a gentlemen's agreement on roles and missions. The Navy could develop nuclear weapons for all phases of a naval campaign, and the Marine Corps could develop air-ground amphibious forces, but the Navy could not have a strategic air force and the Marine Corps a ground army. Forrestal, however, could not create defense consensus under service and congressional pressure. Suffering from a nervous breakdown that led to his suicide, Forrestal surrendered his office in March 1949 to Louis Johnson, a former Army officer and assistant secretary of war, Democratic national fundraiser, and Truman intimate. Directed to curb interservice dissent and hold the line on the defense budget, Johnson tried to impose a solution to the persistent roles and missions conflict. In drafting the fiscal year 1951 defense budget ($13.5 billion), Johnson struck a deathblow at naval aviation by canceling the supercarrier *United States,* cutting the active carrier force from eight to four, and reducing carrier air groups from fourteen to six. Another battle, "the revolt of the admirals," immediately blazed.

For most of 1949 Air Force and Navy partisans, in uniform and mufti, used Congress to conduct an erratic, bad-tempered review of defense policy and organization. The result was an administration victory for its nuclear strategy and low defense budget. A Navy attempt to discredit the B-36 bomber program foundered, for Johnson would not approve a Navy proposal to test fighter-interceptors against SAC's bomber force. The Navy made some prescient debating points about the dangers of pinning deterrence solely on nuclear weapons, but it could not destroy Johnson's barebones budget or convince Congress that Army and Air Force planners had a limited vision of the military future. The secretary of the navy resigned in protest, and Johnson removed Chief of Naval Operations Louis E. Denfeld in retaliation for the CNO's aggressive political offensive against the B-36. When Congress finally concluded its hearings in late 1949, the strategic issues remained unresolved.

In organizational terms, however, "the revolt of the admirals" contributed to a consensus that the "national military establishment" needed an overhaul. Even Ferdinand Eberstadt, who led an investigation of defense management in 1948, admitted that his handiwork of 1945–1947 needed refinement. The result was a 1949 amendment to the National Security Act that strengthened the powers of the secretary of defense. The secretary received a deputy secretary and three assistant secretaries to improve his managerial effectiveness. More important, the law created a single

Department of Defense with three constituent military departments; the law eliminated the military department secretaries from the National Security Council and the cabinet. In addition, presumably to curb interservice rivalry, Congress approved the position of chairman of the Joint Chiefs of Staff. Although the chairman did not yet have a vote on the JCS, he became the principal adviser to the secretary and the president. He did not become a statutory member of the NSC, which added only the vice president as a new formal member, but in practice the president could invite anyone he chose, and he often asked the chairman and the director of the CIA to attend and to advise him directly. In terms of influence, the 1949 amendment started a trend to centralize defense policy planning in the office of the secretary of defense. The secretary, presumably, could use his budgeting powers to decide disputes that the JCS could not reconcile as long as he could avoid a presidential or legislative veto.

For the armed forces, the functional and organizational disputes of the late 1940s helped create an environment that encouraged civilian intervention in military affairs, even in matters that might have been narrowly interpreted as "internal, professional" matters. The postwar years opened an era of controversy about the relationship of the armed forces to reform within American society. In 1950 Congress approved the Uniform Code of Military Justice (UCMJ), which extended civilian substantive and procedural legal principles to the armed forces. Influenced by legal reformers, veterans' groups, and other public lobbies, Congress accepted their testimony that "military justice" was an arbitrary tool to enforce discipline and strengthen the privileges of the officer corps. In concert with a presidential study of officer-enlisted relations and morale by the Doolittle Commission, the reform movement attacked the powers of commanding officers by reducing their disciplinary discretion and enhancing the powers of military and civilian lawyers. The ultimate appeals court, for example, became a three-man, all-civilian Court of Military Appeals. Although the armed forces eventually adjusted to the new, time-consuming jurisprudence, some officers used the UCMJ as an excuse to abdicate their leadership responsibilities, which did nothing to improve the efficiency of the postwar armed forces.

The armed forces also faced major changes in their social composition in the postwar period. As the World War II veterans left the service, the male enlisted force dropped dangerously in age, education, and class background, which made training it more difficult. The decline in recruit quality helped justify two far-reaching manpower reforms. In 1948 Congress passed the Women's Armed Services Integration Act, which gave women the prospect of a military career, largely in nursing, health services, and administrative fields. Similar manpower and political concerns moved Truman to order the racial integration of the armed forces in Executive Order 9981 (July 1948). The armed services viewed the reform with alarm, fearing that racial integration would further demoralize the troops and reduce white recruiting. Instead the Army, the Air Force, and the Marine Corps maintained token all-black units. The Navy in principle had integrated its enlisted force, but its recruiting and training policies in effect forced two-thirds of black sailors to the Steward's Branch. The services argued that unrestricted assignments on the basis of individual qualifications and the use of black career officers in integrated units jeopardized military efficiency, despite World War II evidence that at least this was not the case with the former policy. Senior military commanders battled with civilian reformers to retard the execution of 9981 through the use of quotas and slow-paced integration. In sum, the integration of women and blacks further upset the undermanned, marginally effective armed forces.

From every perspective postwar defense policy seemed calculated to widen the gap between military responsibilities and capabilities, a gap that could not be narrowed by nuclear weapons, defense reorganization, and social reform. As the sense of external threat mounted by 1949, the Truman administration sought additional ways to make deterrence work without a major upturn in military spending. After lengthy negotiations the United States committed itself to its most ambitious exercise in collective, forward defense—the North Atlantic Treaty Organization (NATO). NATO kept the Russians out, the Americans in, and the Germans down. In April 1949 the United States joined the signatories of the Brussels Pact and Canada, Iceland, Portugal, Italy, Denmark, and Norway in a pledge that every NATO nation would henceforth regard an attack on one member as an attack on the entire alliance.

The treaty could mean several things, a fact demonstrated when the Senate debated it. Members of the executive branch and the Senate, which approved the treaty by an 82–13 vote, had different conceptions about the extent of America's NATO participation. One faction argued that extending nuclear deterrence in principle sufficed; conventional forces should be a European responsibility. European leaders argued that their nations could not provide the social reforms demanded by their people and rebuild their shattered economies and still maintain forces that could match the Russians. The JCS led another American faction that took the Europeans' part. The United States should station conventional air and ground units in Europe as part of a NATO command, if only to secure bases for naval and air action against the Soviets. The only substantial action came in the form of adding arms to the European aid program. In October 1949 Congress approved the administration's Mutual Defense Assistance Act, which provided $1.3 billion in military equipment and services for NATO. A month later the new NATO Defense Committee approved its first "integrated" defense program, but this plan did little more than ratify the status quo, since it assumed that NATO nations would provide those forces in which they "specialized." For the United States this concept meant strategic nuclear air forces and naval forces to protect shipping lanes from Russian submarines.

Within the government a coalition of policy planners, led by Secretary of State Acheson, agreed that the Truman administration needed to reassess the military meaning of "containment." In January 1950 a group drawn from the State Department's policy planning staff and the JCS strategic planning staff conducted a three-month study and presented its findings to the National Security Council as NSC Memorandum 68 (NSC 68). The study concluded that the Soviet Union presented a long-term threat to the United States and world peace, a threat that would increase with Russian nuclear forces and continued deployments in occupied Eastern Europe. The United States had four choices: Continue its current policies, retreat into unilateral isolationism, wage preventive war, or increase its own and its allies' military strength in order to deter Soviet expansionism and war. The study group estimated that the latter alternative was preferable, even if it increased the defense budget to $40 billion a year. Without denying the logic of NSC 68, Truman, however, took no action on the memorandum, for he judged that Congress and the public would not support a more ambitious defense program. Without some additional crisis the United States would have to rely upon its feeble nuclear retaliatory capability. Little did the president realize that Asian Communists half a world away would give him the opportunity to do what he and his advisers already knew had to be done—rearm the United States for an extended Cold War.

A War in Korea

Much to the surprise of the Truman administration, the North Korean People's Army (NKPA) crossed the 38th Parallel on June 25, 1950 and opened a three-year war for control of the Korean peninsula. The Korean War brought a major shift in United States military policy, for it provided an atmosphere of crisis that allowed the nation to mobilize for one war in Asia and rearm to deter another war in Europe. By the time the conflict ended in an uneasy armistice in July 1953, the United States had tripled the size of its armed forces and quadrupled its defense budget. It had also redefined the Communist threat to a challenge of global proportions.

Korea had been a backwater of American postwar diplomacy, and it did not loom large as a military concern. Divided in 1945 by an arbitrary line at the 38th Parallel so that occupying Russian and American forces could disarm the Japanese and establish temporary military administrations, Korea had by 1950 become part of the Cold War's military frontier. In North Korea, the Russians had turned political control over to the Communist regime of Kim Il-sung. The American dilemma in South Korea centered on the lack of a legitimate political movement to turn into a government. The State Department complicated finding a successor by agreeing with the Soviets in December 1945 that Korea should pass through a short trusteeship period that would end in a unified, neutral, lightly armed Korea, an Asian version of the arrangements for occupied Austria. Every political faction except the South Korean Labor Party (the southern Communists) opposed trusteeship. The American zone became a battleground with an anti-occupation revolt in the autumn of 1946. The U.S. Army Military Government in Korea (USAMGIK) managed to beat back the center-left labor and agrarian protest movements, but only by forming alliances with Koreans suspected of collaboration with the Japanese, populist fascists linked to the Chinese Nationalists, westernized liberals, regional political bosses, veterans of Japanese military service, and rabid anti-Communist associations of refugees from North Korea. The leftist oppositionists, led by the SKLP, set up a shadow government in North Korea and started an insurrection in the American zone designed to frustrate UN-sponsored elections in May 1948.

Although political violence had plagued the USAMGIK since 1945, the insurgency of April 1948 became a nationwide guerrilla war. Kim Il-sung nurtured the conflict by arming the SKLP partisans and opening a border war in late 1948 that supported partisan infiltrations and mutinies in the South Korean armed forces. The 1948–1950 war in the Republic of Korea (as southern Korea became in August 1948) killed more than seven thousand ROK soldiers and policemen and at least thirty thousand partisans, SKLP supporters, and innocent bystanders. The Korean National Police and Korean Constabulary, which became the ROK army, survived defections and betrayals and conducted effective, if punitive, counterpartisan operations under the supervision of the U.S. Army Korean Military Advisory Group (KMAG). Despite the war, the Koreans elected delegates to a constitutional convention that adopted a republican constitution and, under that constitution, elected a National Assembly, which chose Syngman Rhee, a well-known anti-Japanese expatriate, age sixty-eight, as president. Rhee, American diplomats thought, was the least bad choice for his office.

Viewed from Pyongyang, the partisan war in South Korea offered the opportunity to create a unified Communist Korea, modeled after the Communist victory in China. Secure in his Soviet patronage, Kim Il-sung went to Moscow in March 1949 to seek Stalin's approval and assistance in invading the ROK, to aid SKLP guerrillas with the NKPA conventional forces. Stalin said "no" or at least "not yet." He set forth several preconditions for Soviet support of a North Korean invasion. The last U.S. Army combat troops had to leave South Korea, which occurred in June 1949. There should be no chance of a timely American intervention from Japan. The Rhee regime and the ROK army had to be near collapse or defection. The partisans must make a dramatic "Second Front" attack on ROK military bases throughout the country. The North Korean army must be enlarged, more heavily armed with tanks and artillery, and trained by a new Soviet military mission. And Mao Zedong must agree to assist Kim if the North Koreans needed military help. Kim agreed to these terms and worked for a year to meet them—or promise that they would occur. The key elements were Chinese support and American withdrawal, the latter a critical error by the United States. None of the suicidal conditions attached to the ROK came to pass, although Rhee did lose supporters in the National Assembly elections of 1950.

The South Korean security forces suppressed the SKLP partisans, but did not have the weapons and training to stop the NKPA armor and heavy artillery. The KMAG feared an invasion. It reported that only half the ROK army had enough weapons and training to be combat-ready and had no effective antitank weapons, no tactical air force, and no artillery capable of matching the NKPA. Within South Korea, an invasion seemed certain. The imponderables were its timing and the American response. The KMAG and ROK army generals predicted an invasion, but American leaders in Tokyo and Washington missed or ignored the reports.

The American position was that South Korea had no strategic value, which meant it could not be used as a base in a U.S.–U.S.S.R. World War III. The ROK army of about 100,000 was not a strategic asset, which meant it could not defend American air and naval bases in South Korea, should they be needed, which seemed unlikely. Interviews, news stories, and congressional testimony on the U.S. defense budget placed no value in holding South Korea. The ROK army looked too much like the Chinese Nationalist army, prone to surrender or abandon U.S. Army heavy weapons. Not arming the ROK army, diplomats and generals said, prevented it from attacking North Korea. Rhee and some of his generals did chant "pukjin tong-il" or "march north for freedom," but KMAG knew there was no ROK army ability to do so. The Pentagon did not want to send scarce and costly tanks, guns, and aircraft to Asia when NATO needed them.

The creation of the People's Republic of China (October 1949) forced the Truman administration to redirect its Asian foreign policy. Defending

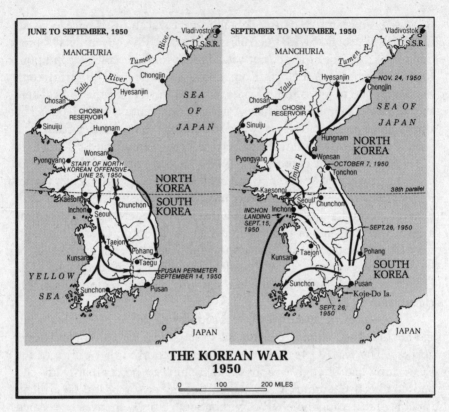

JUNE TO SEPTEMBER, 1950

MANCHURIA

Tumen River

Yalu River

Vladivostok
U.S.S.R.

Chongjin

Hyesanjin

Chosan

CHOSIN
RESERVOIR

Sinuiju

Hungnam

Wonsan

Pyongyang

START OF NORTH
KOREAN OFFENSIVE
JUNE 25, 1950

Kaesong

Inchon

Seoul

Chunchon

NORTH
KOREA

SOUTH
KOREA

SEA
OF
JAPAN

Taejon

Pohang

Kunsan

Taegu

PUSAN PERIMETER
SEPTEMBER 14, 1950

YELLOW

SEA

Sunchon

Pusan

JAPAN

SEPTEMBER TO NOVEMBER, 1950

MANCHURIA

Tumen R.

Yalu

Vladivostok
U.S.S.R.

Hyesanjin

NOV. 24, 1950

Chongjin

Chosan

CHOSIN
RESERVOIR

Sinuiju

Hungnam

NORTH
KOREA

SEA OF
JAPAN

Pyongyang

Wonsan

OCTOBER 7, 1950

Imjin R.

Tonchon

Kaesong

Seoul

Chunchon

38th parallel

INCHON
LANDING
SEPT. 15,
1950

Inchon

SEPT. 26, 1950

Kunsan

Taejon

SOUTH
KOREA

Pohang

Sunchon

Pusan

Koje-Do Is.

SEPT. 26,
1950

JAPAN

**THE KOREAN WAR
1950**

0   100   200 MILES

Japan seemed the only compelling strategic requirement. Taiwan would not be defended, at least in a U.S.–Quomindang alliance. South Korea had some residual value in the defense of Japan, but was not an essential ally. In a major foreign policy address in January 1950, Secretary of State Dean Acheson admitted that South Korea had no role in strict strategic terms. Its security was a United Nations responsibility, supported by the United States. Republican critics later charged Acheson with "selling out" South Korea, but their cause was really Taiwan's survival. To save South Korea, the administration had to save the Chinese Nationalists. No doubt Chinese and Soviet intelligence analyzed Acheson's speech, but it was not a determining factor in the North Korean invasion. Rather, Kim Il-sung profited from a Soviet-Chinese mutual security and economic assistance treaty accepted by Stalin in February 1950. The North Koreans could then exploit the U.S.S.R–PRC pact to their military advantage. For example, the Chinese People's Liberation Army (PLA) transferred two Korean divisions to the NKPA and released thousands of other PLA veterans to fill up Kim Il-sung's infantry divisions. Artillerymen and tankers came from training bases in the U.S.S.R. Eventually Kim fielded an eleven-division army of 135,000 soldiers seasoned by service in the Soviet and Chinese Communist armies. The NKPA was a pocket model of its Soviet counterpart, armed with T-34 tanks, heavy artillery, and attack aircraft, all of which were brought to bear in June 1950 along the 38th Parallel.

Within two weeks of the NKPA invasion—while the armies of the Republic of Korea (ROK) fell back in disarray—the Truman administration established the international and domestic political foundation for an extended and substantial American military commitment to Korea. Of highest importance was Truman's determination to use the war as a test of the United Nations' ability to meet aggression with collective military action. Assisted by Russia's temporary absence, the United States guided several resolutions through the Security Council that gave the intervention United Nations sanction. The aim of UN action in July 1950 was to restore the prewar border and stop the war, either by negotiation or battlefield victory. In popular interpretation the war became an international "police action" rather than a national conflict. Nevertheless, Truman also requested and received overwhelming congressional support for emergency, war-related measures: Supplemental defense funds, draft extensions, reserve mobilization, and expanded presidential powers. Truman consulted with congressional elders about the commitment of American ground troops and found them acquiescent. In the traumatic days of June 1950 the president might have received a formal declaration of war if he had so chosen, but he and his advisers regarded their actions as fully sanctioned by the United Nations charter. They also assumed the responsibility of fighting the war as part of a coalition whose ardor for the war waxed and waned outside American control.

In the Far East American military action did not stop the NKPA offensive until early September, and the UN forces—three scratch Army divisions from Japan and one from the United States—barely held on to a perimeter around the port of Pusan. Although air strikes and naval bombardments pummeled the NKPA, the ground actions produced one crisis after another for United Nations Command (General of the Army Douglas MacArthur) in Tokyo and the 8th U.S. Army (EUSAK) in the field, commanded by Lieutenant General Walton H. Walker, a sturdy tanker in the Patton mold. Critically short of essential weapons (e.g., less than one-fifth of its authorized tanks) and units, EUSAK entered the war a partially trained army that had just rotated about half its GIs back to the United States; it was critically short of trained infantrymen. Although it had a cadre of combat officers and NCOs, it did not rally until its ranks were reinforced with American soldiers and it received more artillery, tanks, and antitank weapons. (Korean conscripts shoved into American infantry units were of limited assistance.) EUSAK developed no offensive capability until it added units from outside the theater; the 5th U.S. Infantry Regiment, the 2d U.S. Infantry Division, and the 1st Marine Brigade. On Korea's hot, dusty hills the Americans learned about combat the hard way. They battled T-34s with inadequate weapons, fell prey to night attacks, retreated in disorder, fought with desperate but ill-organized valor, surrendered, and were shot by their captors.

UN Command, however, had Douglas MacArthur. His towering ego nourished by five years as the surrogate emperor of Japan, MacArthur seized the diplomatic and strategic initiative in the Far East, exploiting the uncertainties of collective decision-making in Washington. Basically, MacArthur wanted to make the Korean War a showdown with international Communism. Regarding Asia as more critical to America's future than Europe, MacArthur had few qualms about the risks of extending the war to Communist China or even to Asian Russia. He believed that the Nationalist Chinese, licking their wounds on Taiwan, could return to the fray with increased American assistance, a proposal immediately rejected by Truman. MacArthur also wanted to extend air and naval operations to North Korea (permission granted) and even to Communist bases in Manchuria (permission denied). To reverse the ground war, he planned an amphibious deep envelopment at Inchon and the recapture of the capital of Seoul, matched with a breakout from the Pusan perimeter. Drawing additional reinforcements from the United States—especially the 1st U.S. Marine Division—MacArthur launched the Inchon invasion on September 15. His plan seemed inordinately risky to every senior military officer who reviewed it, including the JCS and the Navy and Marine officers who commanded Operation CHROMITE. Nevertheless, MacArthur correctly assessed the weak NKPA resistance (more by faith than hard intelligence), and the Navy-Marine team found ways to overcome the physical perils of Inchon harbor, dominated by narrow channels and sharp tidal changes. A wealth of World War II experience prevailed, and in two weeks American troops had liberated Seoul. In the meantime EUSAK took the offensive and drove the NKPA back toward the 38th Parallel in disarray. Close air support and newly arrived artillery battalions reduced the NKPA by one-third in troops and two-thirds in tanks, artillery pieces, and trucks. The shift in military fortunes could have hardly been more dramatic.

The euphoria of victory brought the agony of decision. In October 1950, despite veiled Chinese hints of intervention, the United Nations, pushed by Harry Truman and ROK President Syngman Rhee, approved a change in war aims. Accepting MacArthur's request to cross the 38th Parallel to finish the destruction of the NKPA, the Truman administration and the UN expanded the goals of the pursuit to include the reunification of Korea under UN supervision. Truman imposed trivial limitations on MacArthur's offensive—keep American troops away from the Yalu River—in the hope that the Chinese would not intervene. MacArthur assured the president that the Chinese would stay out; and if they entered the war, he would bomb them to destruction. When Chinese troops first appeared on the battlefield in late October, punishing isolated American and ROK units, MacArthur wished away the threat as an inconsequential delay to his last grand offensive to the Yalu.

Exploiting the night and the worsening winter weather, 260,000 hardy light infantry of the People's Liberation Army (PLA) attacked EUSAK and the autonomous X Corps (the 1st Marine Division and two Army divisions on Korea's northeast coast) in late November and sent UN Command reeling back toward the 38th Parallel. The defeat was both militarily and psychologically stunning. Reporting that "we face an entirely new war," MacArthur asked the president to consider every option, from evacuating his forces from Korea to nuclear attacks on the Chinese. Truman agreed that the war had changed and issued a declaration of national emergency on December 15, accelerating reserve call-ups and rearmament programs with a fourth supplemental defense appropriation. With only one combat-ready division in strategic reserve, he had little to send MacArthur but replacements. In addition, Truman found his UN allies, especially Great Britain, reluctant to expand the war to China. Although the UN decided to fight on, it returned to its original war aims, the preservation of a free South Korea. It was a decision MacArthur could not accept.

Despite MacArthur's dire predictions, EUSAK stabilized the front south of the 38th Parallel in January 1951 and even mounted limited counterattacks. Rebounding under the firm leadership of a new commander, General Matthew B. Ridgway, EUSAK pulled itself together. X Corps, fighting its way to the coast and evacuated by ship, returned to the front, and Ridgway soon commanded a true international army, with professional troops from the British Commonwealth, Turkey, Greece, Colombia, the Philippines, Ethiopia, France, the Netherlands, Belgium, and Thailand. Harassed by UN air strikes, the PLA had increasing difficulty mounting sustained offensives, for it suffered serious supply shortages that its coolie-carrier logistics system could not meet. In addition, EUSAK soldiers now understood Chinese night attacks and mass-infiltration tactics and could defend against them in depth and with massive firepower. When the PLA launched its last grand offensive in April–May 1951, EUSAK fell back in good order, fighting hard, and halted the attack without the crisis of the preceding winter. EUSAK then counterattacked with deliberate advances and awesome artillery and air support, and the PLA began to fall apart, with Chinese soldiers surrendering by the thousands. Despite MacArthur's pessimism, the soldiers of UNC had proved they could hold South Korea.

In the meantime, Truman weathered the last and most serious test of his decision to limit the Korean War, a test mounted by Douglas MacArthur. Bitterly disappointed by his defeat at the hands of the Chinese, MacArthur pressured the administration to accept his own war aims. Marshaling heroic rhetoric—"There is no substitute for victory"—the general conducted a political campaign to open Communist China to direct attack by his own forces and the Chinese Nationalists. He continued to hint darkly about the use of nuclear weapons, an option Truman never seriously considered. Incident mounted after incident: Indiscreet press conferences, unauthorized contacts with Chiang Kai-shek, inappropriate challenges to the Communists, provocative correspondence with veterans' groups and Republican congressional leaders, dark hints of treason by the UN allies, especially Britain. With the full approval of Acheson, new Secretary of Defense George C. Marshall, and the JCS, Truman finally relieved MacArthur and ordered him home in April 1951. Buoyed by his enthusiastic public reception and bathed in martyrdom, MacArthur took his case to Congress. In a memorable public address to both houses, he accused the administration of appeasement and defeatism before promising to fade away like an old soldier in a barracks ballad. Like most MacArthur predictions, the promise to disappear proved flawed, since the Senate held hearings on the war and defense policy. MacArthur produced harsh words and limited enlightenment but could not reverse the administration's policy of limiting the war. As JCS Chairman General of the Army Omar Bradley stated, MacArthur's wider war was "the wrong war, at the wrong place, at the wrong time, and with the wrong enemy." The concept that a theater commander could dictate global policy seemed to endanger the principle of civilian control as well as the professional stature of the Joint Chiefs of Staff. Acutely aware that MacArthur's proposals endangered his rearmament program and the development of NATO, Truman summed up the issue: "General MacArthur was ready to risk general war. I was not." MacArthur faded away after his weak showing in the early presidential primaries of 1952. The war went on without him.

The United States Rearms

The Truman administration had an appropriate substitute for victory in the Korean War, and that substitute was the rearmament of the United States, the development of a collective security alliance based upon

NATO, and the strengthened deterrence of the Soviet Union with both nuclear and conventional forces. When Truman submitted his four supplemental budget requests for fiscal year 1951, he made his dual goals clear: "The purpose of these proposed estimates is two-fold; first, to meet the immediate situation in Korea, and, second, to provide for an early, but orderly, buildup of our military forces to a state of readiness designed to deter further acts of aggression." The president presented his priorities in reverse order, since the administration eventually spent 60 percent of the 1951–1953 defense budgets on general military programs and 40 percent on waging the war. In fiscal terms, defense outlays became two-thirds of all federal spending. Supplemental appropriations brought the 1951 defense expenditures to $48 billion, followed in the next two fiscal years by outlays of $43.9 billion and $50.3 billion. Although the budgets fell short of Department of Defense requests, the administration approached a "holiday" on defense spending in its relations with Congress that approximated the halcyon days of World War II.

Financially, the buildup was anything but orderly in its first year, but the Truman administration eventually patched together a program of increased personal income and corporate taxes and wage and price controls that checked inflation and preserved economic growth. Greater presidential authority over the economy, anathema to conservative Republicans, stemmed from several political adjustments. Warned by the defeat of several prominent liberal Democratic senators and representatives in the 1950 elections, the president backed away from his Fair Deal reform programs, especially those that cost money. Irritated by Louis Johnson's political ineptness and residual liability as the agent of pre-Korea defense austerity, Truman in September 1950 appointed George C. Marshall as secretary of defense and Marshall's trusted aide Robert A. Lovett his deputy. Truman agreed with Marshall's insistence that he serve only one year and that Lovett be his successor. Marshall's appointment gave the administration greater authority with Congress and pleased the JCS, who welcomed Marshall back to the Pentagon. Although Marshall and Secretary of State Acheson took their verbal lashings from the conservative wing of the Republican party, they gave the administration a tested, forceful team fully committed to the president's rearmament policy.

Amply funded and skillfully managed, the Korean War rearmament program nevertheless had its intrinsic confusions, since it was two mobilizations for two wars. The real war in the Far East required fast and large reinforcements in men and materiel, especially after the Chinese intervention. The Department of Defense, however, had a more compelling concern: The possibility of a war with the Soviet Union. The administration's military, diplomatic, and intelligence advisers estimated that by 1952 the

Russians would have an optimum opportunity to initiate a general war with the United States and its NATO allies. By that time the Soviets were likely to have sufficient nuclear weapons—including hydrogen bombs—and aircraft to carry them to launch an attack on the continental United States. Just the threat of such an attack might so intimidate the United States that it would not use its own nuclear weapons to meet a Soviet conventional attack on Western Europe, where the Russian forces still outnumbered Western forces on an order of three to one in manpower and weapons. Even if the Soviets did not actually attack, the threat of such an attack might bring Soviet-leaning neutrality to most of Europe. The Truman administration accepted the "year of maximum danger" concept, but its dilemma extended far beyond 1952. It had to weigh the immediate demands of proxy war with the Communists against the long-term requirements of deterring general war.

U.S. Armed Forces
1945–1953

	ARMY	USAAF/ USAF	NAVY	MARINE CORPS
Pre-1950 estimated required forces	14 divisions 940,000 personnel	70 groups 400,000 personnel	1,043 ships 560,000 personnel	3 divisions 3 aircraft wings 108,000 personnel
Actual forces, June 1950	10 divisions 5 regiments 591,000 personnel	48 groups 411,000 personnel	683 ships 382,000 personnel	2 divisions 2 aircraft wings 74,000 personnel
Actual forces, 1953	20 divisions 18 regiments 1.5 million personnel	93 wings* 974,000 personnel	1,130 ships 808,000 personnel	3 divisions 3 aircraft wings 246,000 personnel

*The Air Force changed from groups to wings to describe two or more squadrons and supporting elements.

Constructing some sort of rational policy on military manpower dramatized the administration's difficulties in weighing the conflicting demands of war waging and war deterring. In the Korean War's first year the most pressing demand was to enlarge the active armed forces, accomplished by drafting 585,000 men and calling to active duty 806,000 reserves and Guardsmen. Even the massive call-up caused controversy, since the reserves, the majority of whom had had limited military training since World War II, went into active units, including those in Korea. Although the emergency required the wholesale infusion of experienced air and ground officers and enlisted men into EUSAK, the Far East Air Forces, and the 7th Fleet, the assignments caused substantial personal hardships and real equity problems. The problem was that Truman also activated eight National Guard divisions and supporting Air National Guard and ground Guard units to restore the strategic reserve in the United States, which had been stripped of regulars to reinforce EUSAK. These organizations had been receiving drill pay and included large numbers of enlisted men who had not seen World War II service. Reserve officers and NCOs fighting for the second time in Korea noticed the difference. In part to appease them, the Department of Defense introduced in early 1951 a policy with long-term implications: i.e., it would rotate combat veterans out of the war zone (and usually out of active service if so desired) after one year. The limited-tour policy increased the manpower demands, met largely by drafting 1.2 million more men, but dampened military and public criticism of the war.

In the middle of a war, the government grappled with the prospect that it would require larger standing and reserve forces after the war. It moved haltingly toward some long-range policy for an extended Cold War. Led by Truman and Marshall, enthusiasts for universal military training (UMT) resurrected their earlier proposal for compulsory short-term active service for training, followed by obligatory reserve service. Although Congress passed a Universal Military Training and Service Act in 1951, the legislation fell far short of creating a comprehensive plan. The act reaffirmed the principle of universal obligation and accepted earlier decisions to extend active-duty periods to two years and include eighteen-year-olds in the military pool. The law dealt primarily with manpower issues created by the Korean War, not its aftermath. The Congress, for example, did not tamper with two Selective Service System policies: To defer college students from immediate call-up and to allow local draft boards to make decisions on occupational and educational deferments. The law provided that veterans who had served less than three years on active duty not only retained a total of eight years of service liability, but had to serve a total of five years in ready-reserve status before reverting to the standby reserve. The distinction was significant, since ready reservists could be called to active duty by the president in an emergency without congressional approval and standby reservists could not. In other words, military service and reserve participation still flowed from the draft, not from true universal military training. Outside of voluntary participation by veterans in the reserves, reserve service appealed most to youths who sought escape from the draft. The law provided, however, that universal military training might be erected upon the extemporized manpower policies of 1950–1951.

Congress reviewed the proposals for UMT in 1951–1952 and rejected the concept, substituting instead the Armed Forces Reserve Act of 1952. The little compulsion that remained was tied to the operation of the draft. Although servicemen—draftees or volunteers—had an obligation to belong to the ready reserve if they had served less than four years on active duty, they did not have to participate in a reserve unit.

Truman's rearmament policy rested upon the assumption that if deterrence failed, a war with the Soviet Union would be a protracted struggle in which nuclear weapons might open, but not close, the war. Although less than comprehensive, the administration's manpower policy expressed a need for conventional forces. It also paid new attention to the potential problems of resource mobilization, enlarging its purchases of strategic materials from $1 billion (1946–1950) to $7 billion (1950–1953). In the Defense Production Act (September 1950), Congress gave Truman the power to bend industrial production toward military needs if normal contracting procedures did not suffice. Its policy of subsidizing mineral exploration produced dramatic quantities of weapons-grade uranium in the United States and Canada. Increased funding for nuclear weapons development brought important progress in the size and composition of the American nuclear arsenal. In 1951 the United States tested two small thermonuclear devices at Eniwetok in Operation GREENHOUSE, followed the next year with two additional tests during Operation IVY. One of the tests, the MIKE SHOT, incorporating Edward Teller's experimental design for a thermonuclear bomb, produced a 10-megaton explosion. The second explosion, a fission weapon, produced a half-megaton explosion, which amply demonstrated America's nuclear virtuosity. The scientific and engineering portents of the tests were enormous: The United States could reasonably expect to increase the number and yield of its nuclear weapons while reducing their size. Although the Soviet Union tested its first fusion weapon in 1953, it fell behind in the nuclear arms competition.

As the principal instrument of both deterrence and general war offensive power against Russia, the Air Force, especially the Strategic Air Command, profited most from the rearmament program. When the Korean War mobilization fell into balance with the long-range program in fiscal year 1952, the Air Force received a third more funds ($20.6 billion) than the Army ($13.2 billion) and the Navy ($12.6 billion). The Air Force broke through its 70-wing program, creating 95 wings and winning theoretical approval of eventual expansion to 143 wings.* A third of the wings belonged to SAC, which doubled its personnel and aircraft in two years. In 1952 SAC put its first all-jet bomber, the B-47, into operation. To handle its expanded force and complicate Soviet targeting, SAC dispersed its forces from nineteen to thirty bases in the continental United States and from one to eleven bases abroad. In part dictated by the short range of the B-47 and the requirement for forward-based refuelers, the development of overseas bases in England and Morocco (and soon Spain and Libya) further committed the nation to a policy of forward, collective defense. SAC's targeting doctrine reflected the growing complexity of its missions. Initially it had focused upon military-industrial targets related to Russia's war-making potential. By 1953 it also had to target Soviet nuclear forces and weapons facilities and the Soviet air and ground forces that threatened NATO. As a series of strategic-scientific study groups reported, the proliferation of Soviet nuclear forces multiplied the target list and the number of aircraft and bombs SAC would need to make retaliation both a credible threat and plausible instrument for war fighting.

Although SAC received priority in funding, the rest of the Air Force expanded its role as the nation's first line of defense during the Korean War era. One high-level study, Project VISTA, concluded that the defense of Europe required a NATO force of 10,000 tactical aircraft, some nuclear-capable, to offset ground forces inferiority. This concern allowed the Air Force to increase to 106 planned wings in 1953. In addition, other studies convinced Truman that the nation required a real air-defense system to counter the Soviet bomber threat. In 1951 the Air Force created Air Defense Command to develop an integrated system of interceptors, antiaircraft artillery and missiles, and radar warning. After much internal debate and scientific analysis, Truman in 1952 ordered the Air Force to construct a distant early warning (DEW) radar line across the top of the North American continent. Although pessimistic about its ability to stop Russian bombers from hitting American cities, the Air Force pursued the air-defense mission primarily as a means for protecting its SAC bases from a disarming first strike. The logic of the era, whether it started with the defense of NATO or air defense, always ended with a critical role for SAC's bombers.

Complementing the strengthening of SAC and the extension of its protection to Europe, the Truman administration struck hard and fast to turn NATO into a formidable military alliance in 1950–1952. Truly alarmed at the prospect of additional Communist invasions, Truman, Acheson, Marshall, Bradley, and most of their advisers developed by the end of 1950 a

---

* The Air Force shifted to the "wing" instead of the "group" to identify an organization of two or more squadrons.

comprehensive program for NATO and formed an effective trans-Atlantic political alliance with most of NATO's senior statesmen. The NATO rearmers had five goals: Appoint an American as supreme military commander in Europe (SACEUR) and allow him to develop plans for an integrated NATO force; send more American forces to Europe; accelerate military assistance to the NATO nations; develop a forward strategy for defense at the borders of divided Germany; and create within NATO a West German army of twelve divisions. It was a large menu, and even the Americans sometimes disagreed on the method and timing for accomplishing their goals. Although the particulars of German rearmament brought the program to a temporary pause in 1953, the alliance had eighteen months of breathless accomplishment.

In December 1950 Truman nominated General Dwight D. Eisenhower to be the first SACEUR, a nomination hailed in Europe since the general brought vast experience and international prestige to the command. Truman also indicated that he would send more troops to Europe, and Acheson led a successful move to commit the NATO governments in principle to German rearmament. The prospect of sending more troops abroad set off a "great debate" in Congress that allowed isolationist Republicans to vent their ire but not stop the troops. Truman accepted a weak congressional prohibition that he could not send more than four divisions without further approval. By February 1951 the debate was over, and the Army began to move four divisions, which brought the 7th U.S. Army in Germany to six divisions. The United States example was followed by Great Britain, but France proved a reluctant ally. Although France was willing to risk a rearmed Germany if the Germans were integrated into a European Defense Community (EDC) structure, its foreign policy condemned ten divisions to service in Indochina, which left only nine in Europe. After the outbreak of the Korean War the Truman administration extended its aid to the French military effort in the Far East, in part to fight a two-front war against the Asian Communists, in part to subsidize a larger French NATO force and buy off French resistance to German rearmament. The policy was not an unvarnished success.

In the meantime, American policy toward Europe became increasingly linked to the carrot of military assistance. To the dismay of some State Department planners, the Truman administration sponsored a Mutual Security Act (1951), which severed economic aid from military assistance and put the administration of military assistance in the hands of the independent Mutual Security Agency. The reorganization eventually passed military aid into the hands of the Department of Defense, which used the Mutual Defense Assistance Program (MDAP) to influence foreign policy. Distributing over $20 billion in MDAP funds in 1951–1953, the United States championed the admission of Greece and Turkey into NATO in

1951 and improved diplomatic relations with fascist Spain and socialist Yugoslavia. None of these four nations was a military power, but they had attractive basing possibilities and gave NATO a southern frontier that might complicate Russian planning.

With General Eisenhower's planners hard at work, the Truman administration set progressively higher goals for NATO's forces. In September 1951 the Atlantic Council approved a forty-three-division force by 1954 and then escalated the alliance's plan five months later. In the Lisbon Agreement (February 1952) the NATO ministers set a 1954 goal of 10,000 aircraft and eighty-nine divisions, half of which would be combat-ready. Such heady plans had torn loose of political and economic reality, but by 1953—even without the Germans—NATO could field twenty-five active divisions, fifteen in central Europe, and 5,200 aircraft dispersed to around 100 airfields. In two years NATO had become at least equal to the Soviet forces deployed in East Germany.

The West German rearmament plan, however, remained unfulfilled. The enthusiasm of the French National Assembly did not match the vision of the statesmen who saw NATO as the foundation of a united Europe. Instead, the leaders of the Fourth Republic hoped to wedge more military assistance and other concessions from the United States in exchange for approving the EDC treaty. West German rearmers, led by Konrad Adenauer, did not relish assigning their troops to NATO without the right to conduct their own foreign relations and create their own national military establishment. Negotiations over the terms of German rearmament dragged on past the end of the Korean War.

For all the confusion created by programs that mixed war waging, long-range rearmament, and strategic deterrence, the United States used the passing crisis of Korea to close the gap between the rhetoric of containment and its actual military capacity. Critics of the "militarization" of American diplomacy believed the rearmament policy was an exaggerated reaction to an overestimated Soviet threat. But the Russia of 1950–1953 was Stalin's domain, and conventional wisdom gave Moscow the power to control its Communist collaborators in Europe and Asia. The Truman administration, buffeted at home by its political enemies and growing disillusionment over the war, had won a lasting victory for the Free World.

Korea: Settling for an Armistice

In 1951 United Nations Command won but could not end the Korean War. Guided by the revised war aims of the Truman administration and the Security Council, the UN international army restored the geographic integrity of the Republic of Korea by launching an offensive that captured the dominant terrain necessary to frustrate any further Communist attacks. After a false start at armistice negotiations in the summer of 1951, the Communists returned to the peace table, in part as a tactic to demoralize and divide the UN allies, in part to buy time to restore the shattered Chinese expeditionary force. Satisfied that his forces had established a line they could hold, General Ridgway, MacArthur's replacement as supreme commander, shifted to the strategic and tactical defense in November. Only another year and a half of war along a relatively static front made the UN accomplishment seem less than a victory.

In sustained, bitter fighting EUSAK—a force of seven American, one Commonwealth, and ten ROK divisions—won the war in 1951 the hard way. Although the Communist and UN forces in 1951 both numbered roughly half a million men, the Chinese and Koreans put more combat troops into the lines, and they fought hard in their massive spring offensive and on the defensive for the rest of 1951. Blessed with massive artillery and close air support, EUSAK nevertheless had to best the Communists in close infantry combat, and it did so. Shifting to the offensive in June, the UN divisions bludgeoned the Communists back across the 38th Parallel everywhere but in the extreme west, a militarily insignificant area. In consultation with the JCS and his field commander, Lieutenant General James Van Fleet, Ridgway established a defensive zone labeled the KANSAS-WYOMING line that he wanted EUSAK to hold. The key to establishing this line was a network of valleys and high ridges that dominated the terrain just north of the 38th Parallel in central Korea, an area designated "the Iron Triangle." Using primarily the American 2d Infantry and 1st Marine Divisions, EUSAK wrested the Triangle from the Communists in a series of wearing battles that took their names from the moonscape mountains: The "Punchbowl," "Bloody Ridge," and "Heartbreak Ridge." Divisions to the east and west reached the KANSAS-WYOMING line with somewhat less difficulty.

With a valor and skill that reached the highest standards seen during World War II, the American and other UN troops destroyed the myth of PLA invincibility, inflicting casualties in a ratio over ten to one. Even the ROK divisions showed a higher degree of professionalism as hard experience weeded out incompetent officers and trained the enlisted men. So fearsome had EUSAK become in the autumn of 1951 that Van Fleet believed he could hammer the Communists deeper into North Korea, but American policy did not anticipate a return to the reunification campaign of 1950. Instead the Truman administration allowed Ridgway to respond to a Soviet ceasefire proposal in June 1951 by opening direct negotiations with the Communists at Kaesong in July. The talks produced nothing but a presentation of extreme positions and propaganda parry and thrust, and

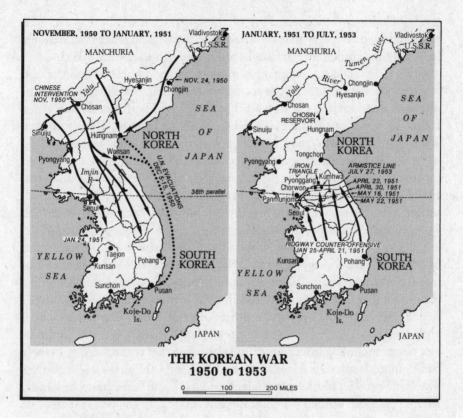

THE KOREAN WAR
1950 to 1953

0   100   200 MILES

the fighting continued until more Communist battlefield defeats brought on serious truce talks in November.

The rebirth of EUSAK in 1951 came from the converging influence of many mobilization policies and battlefield reforms. EUSAK benefited from the charismatic leadership of Matthew B. Ridgway and the solid professionalism of James Van Fleet. The test of battle eliminated the less effective corps, division, and regimental commanders, who could be replaced with proven leaders with World War II experience. Once past the emergency days of 1950, EUSAK incorporated well-trained and intelligent draftees and reserves into its combat units; it also improved performance by eliminating all-black units and making itself the first fully integrated combat formation in American history. As industrial mobilization hit full effectiveness, EUSAK received ammunition and weapons in quality and quantity that offset the Russian materiel supplied the Asian Communists and blunted the Chinese-Korean manpower superiority in the front lines. At the same time, the infusion of American advisers and equipment, especially more artillery, brought the ROK divisions to progressively higher levels of military efficiency. Part of the frustration of the Korean War stemmed from the fact that the front-line troops and their commanders believed they could have accomplished more than they were asked.

UN Command's air campaign, marked by geographic limitations and frustrations, contributed to the success of the allied war effort. In terms of offensive missions, the Far East Air Forces (FEAF) performed three major tasks: Air superiority, interdiction, and close air support. Except for the war's opening months, the UNC did not worry about enemy air attacks on its troops and installations, although occasional Communist planes slipped through on night attacks. Instead, the F-86 "Saber" jets of 5th Air Force, FEAF's major combat command, prowled the skies above North Korea, assigned the mission of destroying the Communists' interceptor force. The Communists' threat was substantial, since they kept about 1,000 MiG-15 jets deployed to bases along either side of the Yalu. With the exception of occasional MiG surges against UNC bombers, the F-86s kept the skies free for UN operations. Normally outnumbered three or two to one during air combat, the F-86s mastered the MiGs through greater pilot experience, tactics, teamwork, and sturdier aircraft. The MiG had excellent high-speed and high-altitude handling characteristics, but the Communist pilots, including hundreds of Russians, avoided combat far from their bases. In air battles FEAF jets downed 589 MiGs at a cost of 78 Sabres. The Air Force would have preferred to attack the MiG bases in China, where American airmen watched the MiGs flock up to "MiG Alley," but the Truman administration would not widen the war unless UNC air superiority was truly menaced. It was not.

Limited to targets within Korea, FEAF concentrated on interdicting the battlefield, destroying enemy units, equipment, and supplies before they reached the front. Air attacks in 1950 against both the NKPA and the PLA blunted the Communist offensives. The major interdiction effort began when the front stabilized along the 38th Parallel. Estimating that the Communists required 2,400 tons of supplies a day—and even more for sustained offensive operations—FEAF planners mounted Operation STRANGLE in early 1951, a maximum attack upon the North Korean railway system. Ten months of sustained attacks on bridges, tunnels, marshaling yards, and other choke points along the rail routes did not "strangle" the Communists, who responded with a massive railroad repair effort. The Communists also increased their truck and porter carrying capacity to offset their loss of 12,000 locomotives and railcars. UNC pilots sang "We've Been Working on the Railroad"; the Communists presumably could have sung the same refrain as they filled the craters, cleared the wreckage, and relaid the track. The UNC pilots also patrolled the highways, which became jammed with trucks after nightfall. The technology and techniques for night attacks did not match the Communist motorized effort; UNC pilots claimed 82,000 vehicles destroyed, but the supplies kept coming. Although FEAF dropped the name STRANGLE, it did not stop the campaign of air interdiction pressure. Its aircraft flew twice as many interdiction sorties as they did air superiority and close air support missions, and Air Force and Marine squadrons lost 816 of the 1,041 aircraft downed in action to groundfire. Naval aviation also participated in the campaign, flying from the carriers of Task Force 77 and losing 564 aircraft in the effort. In the war's last year FEAF received permission to broaden its target list, and it attacked the North Korean hydroelectric and irrigation dams with considerable success. The Communists howled about "genocidal" air attacks, a refrain picked up by other Third World nations and faint-hearted Europeans. The economic attacks came to a halt through political pressure, but also because North Korea had so few such vulnerable targets. To have been truly effective, interdiction would have had to reach into China and Asian Russia.

American aviators also provided EUSAK with close air support—i.e., air strikes against enemy troops and weapons engaged with friendly ground troops. The Air Force did not relish such missions because they required trained air control parties on the ground to put the bombs on target and not on friendly troops; such parties, the Air Force argued, demanded aviation personnel it could not spare. Air Force doctrine stressed the use of airborne spotter aircraft and limiting strikes to 1,000 yards from friendly troops. The 1st Marine Aircraft Wing and Navy attack squadrons, however, followed practices developed for amphibious warfare and delivered close strikes with a precision that gladdened the hearts of UNC infantrymen. Along a stabilized front, close air strikes also required precision artillery fire in order to suppress flak; such fire-support coordination demanded intimate air-ground collaboration, not common between EUSAK and FEAF. Marine and naval aviation assumed much of the burden for close air support for all EUSAK, but after 1950 UNC limited close air support sorties to an average of ninety-six a day, or about eight per division. Army and Marine ground commanders did not regard the sortie rate as adequate.

The close air support issue assumed even greater importance as the Army and Marine Corps introduced helicopters to combat for the first time during the Korean War. The limited size and power of 1950 helos limited their use to reconnaissance and casualty evacuation missions until the Marine Corps began troop-carrying missions in 1951 with its Sikorsky HRS-1, which could carry eight combat infantrymen. By 1952 helos had become a common sight above UNC's positions, but the concept of the vertical envelopment assault against defended positions went untested.

Battered by UNC ground and air assault, the Communists met the UN military negotiators at Panmunjom in November 1951 and opened the sustained, often acrimonious bargaining that eventually brought an armistice in July 1953. In four months of intense talks, the negotiators shaped an agreement, largely by identifying the provisions they would not accept. They agreed that they would establish a Demilitarized Zone along the line of contact when the fighting ended; both sides would have responsibilities and rights for inspecting the DMZ. The Communists, however, would accept few provisions for inspections beyond the DMZ and no formal limits on the forces stationed in North Korea. In light of Communist intransigence, UN Command rejected most provisions limiting the stationing of foreign troops in South Korea, and American planners had to accept the implications of the proposed truce: A massive buildup of the South Korean armed forces and the permanent stationing of American units in Korea. Nevertheless, the Truman administration, under intense pressure from its UN allies to end the war, decided it could accept a mere ceasefire, even if the Communist military threat remained immediate. The negotiating barrier to peace in early 1952 became the disposition of prisoners of war, a problem UNC underestimated because it did not view the issue from the same perspective as the Communists.

To UN Command, POWs were war's unfortunates, but to the Communists they were instruments of combat. The Communists had every reason to regard the POW issue as an important propaganda issue. When UNC surveyed the 170,000 Chinese and Koreans in its hands, it estimated that half of them would not be repatriated voluntarily, an enormous embarrassment to the Communists. UNC held fast to the principle of voluntary repatriation. In the meantime, the Communist high command infiltrated organizers into UNC camps to intimidate the nonrepatriators and harass their guards; a full-scale revolt on the island of Koje-do in May 1952 ended in combat operations and discomfited UNC. The Communists showed a similar callousness in handling UNC prisoners. Of the estimated 7,245 Americans who may have fallen into Communist hands, only 3,800 returned. As many as 600 may have been murdered, while 2,806 died of illness under degrading conditions. Communist POW administrators used turncoats to control the POWs, and political officers extracted confessions of germ warfare and other alleged atrocities, largely from airmen, by direct physical and mental torture. Political indoctrination ("brainwashing") sessions were common for all captives. The full nature of Communist POW treatment, of course, could not be investigated until the POWs returned, for escapes from the Communist camps were impossible for weak prisoners who found no assistance beyond the wire. UNC personnel attempted hundreds of escapes, but none succeeded. The Communists faced an even larger charge: Where were some 250,000 Korean soldiers and civilians under Communist control who disappeared during the war?

The most important strategic factor that delayed an armistice agreement, however, was the post-truce ability of the two rival Koreas to defend themselves against each other. The United States and China had one interest in common: They did not intend to keep large armies in Korea forever. The Chinese answer was to dig into North Korea's mountains and create fortified positions miles deep along the DMZ and both coasts. Hailed as the underground equivalent of the Great Wall, the barrier systems could check amphibious envelopments and the use of nuclear weapons. The Chinese completed their digging in the summer of 1953. For the United States the focus stayed on the enlargement and improvement of the ROK army, planned for twenty divisions on a troop base of 500,000 soldiers, or five times its 1950 strength. By the summer of 1953 the JCS judged the ROK army (at sixteen divisions) capable enough to defend the South Korean border with two or three UNC divisions and U.S. air and naval support.

Stalin's death in March 1953 accelerated the peace process because his successors-in-committee wanted the war, a drain on Soviet defense spending, ended and told Mao Zedong and Kim Il-sung to get an armistice in 1953. The Communists soon accepted a UN plan to allow POWs to refuse repatriation. The barrier now was Syngman Rhee, who thought a divided Korea, occupied in part by Chinese troops, would never survive. His tacit cooperation required more military aid, a $1 billion economic assistance package, a mutual defense alliance, and U.S. sponsorship as a UN member. It was a good deal at the time.

The war also continued along the Main Line of Resistance (MLR) established in the winter of 1951–1952. Although UNC and Communist numbers throughout Korea were comparable (700,000 to 900,000), the Communists enjoyed a trench advantage of two to one and used their manpower, improved artillery support, and the advantages of night and surprise to carry the battle to UNC. In many respects the fighting of 1952–1953 resembled the trench warfare of World War I without the "big pushes." The MLR and its combat outposts became warrens of trenches, bunkers, barbed wire, mines, and heavy-weapons positions. Firing an average of a million shells a month, UNC artillery helped hold back the Communist probes. The war was a siege, with the Communists most anxious to dig and tunnel up to the outposts along the Iron Triangle and north of the Imjin River. UNC beat back most of the Chinese attacks, but tactical commanders, reluctant to risk lives, often underestimated the situation and committed units piecemeal, normally protracting the battles and ruining the units actually fighting. This tactical pattern did not inspire UNC soldiers, especially when recaptured terrain was eventually abandoned. Between the promise of the peace talks and the prospect of individual rotation, the morale of American combat units slipped, but UNC as a whole—bolstered by the professionalism of UN troops and improved ROK performance—held fast until the armistice.

Between the autumn of 1952 and the spring of 1953 the international context of the Korean War shifted, pointing the way to a ceasefire. In the 1952 presidential elections the Republican candidate, Dwight D. Eisenhower, won handily, in part on the promise that he would investigate the war. Once in office, Ike sent signals to the Communists that he might widen the conflict with Nationalist Chinese reinforcements and nuclear-capable aircraft deployed to Okinawa. Stalin's death in March 1953 may have softened Soviet ardor when the surviving leaders turned to their rivalries and internal problems; in Asia the Communists were close to victory in Indochina and did not need a wider war in Korea. In political terms the principal American problem became convincing the hard-bitten Rhee government to accept a peace, for Rhee feared a sell-out. He softened his resistance when he received guarantees of increased military assistance, the presence of American troops, and a mutual security treaty with the United States. Of the negotiating issues, the Communists finally accepted the reality of voluntary repatriation, managed by an international commission. Rhee encouraged their cooperation by ordering his guards to turn loose 27,000 North Korean prisoners. In any event—in the midst of some of the heaviest action along the MLR—the truce talks moved rapidly, and the belligerents finally agreed to an armistice on July 27, 1953. With few emotions beyond relief and exhaustion, UNC troops along the MLR ceased fire—but held their positions with loaded weapons.

The Korean War marked a major turning point in post-1945 American military policy. It provided the political context for rearmament and the development of NATO. It also drew the United States into a more active military role in Asia, which now joined Europe as part of the Free World system of collective, forward defense. During the course of the war or shortly after its conclusion, the United States entered mutual security agreements with Japan (which began its own rearmament), the Republic of Korea, Taiwan, the Philippines, Australia, and New Zealand. More ominously, the Truman administration increased its support to the French war in Indochina, but it also demanded that the French develop Laos, Cambodia, and Vietnam as autonomous states. The costs of the Korean War itself were not inconsequential. The American government spent around $40 billion to fight the war and sent over 2 million men to the war zone. Of these servicemen 33,741 died in action, and another 2,835 perished in the war zone. America's allies, principally the South Koreans, had 61,000 killed in action, while the Communists lost between 1.5 and 2 million soldiers. If "limited" in the global sense, the war reached major proportions in north Asia. Only a later Asian war would diminish the legacy of the nation's only major victory in a war with Communists.

SIXTEEN

Waging Cold War:
American Defense Policy for Extended Deterrence and Containment, 1953–1965

After the Korean War, the United States turned from a crisis-oriented military policy toward concepts and programs designed to last as long as the rivalry with the Soviet Union. Presidents Dwight D. Eisenhower, John F. Kennedy, and Lyndon B. Johnson adopted policies suited for "the long haul." With Soviet-American competition accepted as the central fact in international relations, American policymakers regarded defense policy as a principal instrument for containing the parallel spread of Communism and Soviet imperialism. To check the extension of Soviet influence, the United States sought to reduce the chance that the Russians would threaten or use military force as a tool of international influence. For all the debate about the means and costs of defense, American policy rested upon consensual assumptions about the nature of the military challenge and the appropriate response. Supported by an activist coalition in Congress, the three Cold War presidents further refined containment, strategic deterrence, and forward, collective defense.

Nuclear weapons remained at the heart of American strategy. The era saw the extension of nuclear deterrence in both political and technological terms, for the changing nature of the Soviet threat, the requirements of alliance support, and the dazzling possibilities of technological change made the development of nuclear forces irresistible. By 1965 the United States and Soviet Union had both created the rudiments of the strategic "triad," a force of intercontinental bombers, intercontinental ballistic missiles (ICBMs), and submarines armed with intermediate-range ballistic missiles. These delivery systems bore warheads of increased destructive power, since they combined the explosive force of the hydrogen fusion process and improved missile accuracy. In raw numerical terms the United States enjoyed nuclear superiority over the Soviet Union, largely because of its sizable bomber force. The Soviet Union sought to counter this potential advantage by building a thick air-defense system of interceptors and missiles and by creating its own ICBMs, manned by the Strategic Rocket Forces (SRF). The direct threat to American nuclear forces and cities increased during the era. Acutely aware of this growing vulnerability, American policymakers tried to reduce the likelihood of general war by making deterrence more complex and awesome.

Another role of strategic deterrence was to extend it to America's alliance system. From its creation, NATO had enjoyed the ultimate protection of America's nuclear weapons, but the growing Soviet nuclear threat to the United States introduced doubt that SAC would come flying to Europe's rescue if war occurred. To defend Western Europe—and South Korea and Japan as well—the United States developed nuclear forces for forward deployment: Intermediate-range missiles stationed in NATO countries, Air Force fighter-bombers with the ability to drop nuclear weapons, and carrier-based aircraft. The option of regional nuclear war proved a mixed blessing. On the one hand, it demonstrated the indivisibility of the American nuclear umbrella and created nuclear alternatives short of general war. On the other hand, it tied American strategy to the behavior of its allies and opened the question of whether American guarantees had any meaning when the survival of the United States was at risk.

The intricacies of nuclear diplomacy brought strains upon the Free World and Communist alliance systems, opening fissures between the United States and Soviet Union and their allies. Unhappy with American reluctance to assist its modest nuclear weapons program, the French government went ahead on its own *force de frappe,* exploded a warhead in 1960, and withdrew from the NATO military system in 1966. The Soviets, however, faced an even greater dilemma in Asia. Invoking its 1950 alliance with Russia, the People's Republic of China demanded assistance with its nuclear program. When the Russians refused, the Chinese exploded their own nuclear device in 1964. Nuclear proliferation joined an ever-increasing set of international concerns.

The ominous shadow of nuclear war gave the United States and the Soviet Union an incentive to supplement their military programs with arms control negotiations. President Eisenhower appreciated the role arms control might play in preventing "the stupid starting of stupid war." Nikita S. Khrushchev regarded U.S.-U.S.S.R. arms talks as a weapon of Soviet policy, for they bought time for Russian strategic programs, offered international recognition of Russia's military strength, divided NATO, and encouraged the peace movement in the West.

As if the politics of strategic deterrence were not complex enough, the United States attempted to build a regional alliance system outside Europe that would contain Russian and Chinese intervention and subversion. The Korean War experience served as the model of what might be done and what should be avoided. "No more Koreas" served as a slogan for the deeply held belief that the United States should avoid another protracted land war for limited objectives. Instead, the NATO pattern of forward and collective defense, already extended to Latin America by the Rio Pact and applied on a bilateral basis in the Pacific, might work as well in Asia and the Middle East. In 1954 the United States decided not to use nuclear weapons or conventional forces to save French Indochina, but tried to salvage the anti-Communist position in Southeast Asia by forming the Southeast Asia Treaty Organization (SEATO). It extended SEATO's military guarantees to the new states of South Vietnam, Laos, and Cambodia. It sponsored a similar arrangement for the Middle East, the Baghdad Pact, in 1955. Much of American foreign policy found its stimulus in alliance reinforcement.

The United States did not rely solely upon its military alliances to contain Communist subversion. It also battled revolutionary insurgents with economic aid, military assistance, and covert action with success in Greece and the Philippines. The government then employed the CIA to topple governments with Communist participants in Iran (1953) and Guatemala (1954). When similar techniques did not prove feasible in Lebanon in 1958, the Eisenhower administration sent a Marine Corps–Army task force to stop a civil war and deter Syrian intervention. The policy of countersubversion flowered in the early 1960s in Allen Dulles's CIA, which mounted covert operations against Fidel Castro in Cuba and against Communist-influenced guerrillas in the Congo. Among the battlefields of covert action and military assistance, Laos and South Vietnam proved to be the most persistent problems.

American security policy required a high degree of presidential freedom of action. Although their successes varied, Eisenhower, Kennedy, and Johnson enjoyed relative freedom from congressional interference except in the annual budget process. Regardless of party, the presidents maintained the security policy initiative through the manipulation of a bipartisan, internationalist congressional coalition that included all the important floor leaders and committee members. When it came to a test of strength, the presidents prevailed. Eisenhower successfully beat back a congressional effort to curb his powers to make executive agreements with foreign governments. In 1954 he received congressional support to help the Chinese Nationalists defend the offshore islands of Quemoy, Matsu, and the Pescadores; the House vote was 410 to 3, the Senate vote 83 to 3. Copying Eisenhower's effort a decade later, Johnson took a blank check from Congress to use military force in Southeast Asia. The Gulf of Tonkin Resolution vote dramatized the president's ability to drive the political process.

Congressional enthusiasm for collective security depended upon public support. Until the end of the 1960s the opinion polls and the elections sent a consistent message to Washington: Beware of the Soviets and maintain American military superiority. Defense spending did not distress the public, since its share of the federal budget and gross national product dropped in the decade after the post-Korea demobilization. Some defense spending, in fact, seemed to have benefits beyond military security: interstate highways; improved public education; high-technology research and development; and the support of the aviation, electronics, shipbuilding, and transportation industries. To some degree the sense of national purpose that flowered in World War II persisted for another twenty years. When John Kennedy vowed at his inauguration that the nation would "pay any price, bear any burden . . . for the success of liberty," he expressed sentiments shared by his countrymen since 1941.

The "New Look"

In the year after his election President Dwight D. Eisenhower redirected American defense policy for the post-Korean era of neither war nor peace. Eisenhower's policy, labeled the "New Look," required redefinition of the Soviet threat. Essentially, Eisenhower believed that proxy wars like Korea and the pressure of defense spending would fatally weaken the American economy, and he pledged to cut the federal budget by $14 billion in his first two years in office. The major target for budget cutting was defense, and Harry Truman had already proposed similar cuts in 1952.

Announcing its intention to have "security with solvency," the Eisenhower administration designed the New Look between December 1952 and October 1953. The new chairman of the JCS, Admiral Arthur W. Radford, assumed the task of turning fiscal guidance into strategy. The administration lopped $5 billion in authorizations from the fiscal year 1954 defense budget and then submitted a 1955 proposal for $35 billion, a figure well below the $42 billion requested by the JCS. Although the administration never reached its fiscal goals, it held defense expenditures around the $40 billion level. During the two Eisenhower administrations, the defense budget fell from 64 percent of federal spending to 47 percent and averaged about 10 percent of gross national product. Even pressured by inflation in the late 1950s and the escalating real cost of high-technology weapons, the administration held to its New Look fiscal assumptions.

To stabilize defense spending, the Eisenhower administration deemphasized conventional forces and stressed the deterrent and war-fighting potential of nuclear weapons. Inheriting a standing force of 3.5 million, the government reduced it to 2.47 million by 1960, well below levels the JCS thought safe. The manpower cuts forced the services to cancel their Korean era expansion plans and eliminate six Army divisions, 15 Air Force wings, and 300 Navy ships by 1960. Alarmed by the New Look, the JCS argued that it needed more insight on Ike's strategic expectations. Assisted by ad hoc study groups and the newly established professional staff attached to the National Security Council, Eisenhower provided the guidance in NSC Memorandum 162/2 (October 1953), a study that directed the Department of Defense to arm all the services with nuclear weapons. Local wars of the Korean variety would have to be fought by America's allies, who would use their own ground forces, backed by American air and sea forces.

Anxious to link the New Look to its foreign policy goals, the administration tied the exploitation of nuclear technology to the more aggressive containment of Communism. Impressed by the development of small nuclear warheads, Eisenhower believed they could be directed at more precise military targets "just as you would use a bullet or anything else." Vice President Richard M. Nixon suggested that nuclear superiority gave the United States an exploitable edge over the Russians: "Rather than let the Communists nibble us to death all over the world in little wars we would rely in the future primarily on our mobile retaliatory power which we could use at our discretion against the major source of aggression at times and places that we chose." Following the 1953 review of American defense policy, Secretary of State John Foster Dulles announced in January 1954 that the administration would rely upon the threat of nuclear escalation to deter or stop Communist-inspired local wars. Russian adventurism would put at risk the very existence of the Soviet Union, for the United States would "depend primarily upon a great capacity to retaliate, instantly, by means and at places of our own choosing."

The New Look reflected the administration's belief that the Russians would do everything within their power to weaken the United States, disrupt NATO, and draw newly independent Third World nations into the Communist orbit. In assessing Soviet military capability, the administration faced greater uncertainty. Its difficulties in collecting information took on greater importance after the Russians exploded a fusion device in 1953, since the New Look depended upon an accurate judgment of the Russians' ability to destroy SAC's bomber bases and America's major cities. The administration made great strides in collecting information, but its problems allowed its critics to charge that Eisenhower was too optimistic. By 1960 the character of the Soviet threat had become a major political issue.

At the beginning of the Cold War, American intelligence experts, principally the Central Intelligence Agency, depended primarily upon human observers to report upon Russian scientific and military activities. Until the mid-1950s the flood of refugees, returning German prisoners, and Russian defectors provided reasonably good information, but improved Soviet internal security, directed by the ruthless KGB, soon made human intelligence scarce. The CIA tried to insert agents in Russia, exploit the network of spies run by the West Germans, and work with its British and French counterparts. The results were not altogether satisfactory, since the British, French, and German intelligence agencies had been penetrated by Russian agents. The CIA complicated its problems when it merged its intelligence collection and covert operations in a single Directorate of Plans, which was dominated by men who had more enthusiasm for covert action than information collection. The American government turned to technology rather than agents. Inheriting the new National Security Agency (NSA), created in 1952, the Eisenhower administration expanded its funding and staffing. NSA's mission was to listen. Intercepting radio communications and eventually radio-transmitted phone calls, NSA stations tried to translate and analyze millions of encrypted messages, with limited success. The CIA was more successful in communications interception, tapping Russian phone lines in Eastern Europe. Nevertheless, communications intelligence did not give the CIA much confidence that it had a good grip on Russian military developments. Its military collaborators, especially Air Force intelligence, shared its disquiet.

American intelligence agencies looked for other ways to peek at Russian programs. One technical means was to establish radar stations along the borders of the Soviet Union in order to monitor aircraft and missile test flights, and by the end of the 1950s such stations ranged from Europe through Turkey, Iran, and Pakistan. There was no substitute for penetrating Soviet air space for a direct look, but the operational problems of such overflights proved difficult. In Operation SKYHOOK, the Air Force launched high-altitude balloons to transit the Soviet Union, but erratic wind currents limited their usefulness. Manned aircraft were far more reliable—and more vulnerable. In 1952–1953 Russian interceptors contested fly-around and modest overflight penetrations in Europe and Asia by the Air Force and Royal Air Force. Unless the CIA could find an aircraft that could fly above Soviet air defenses, overflights could not be made. Developed by Kelly Johnson of the Lockheed Corporation, the U-2, a thin, gull-like plane, answered the CIA's needs, since it could fly across the Soviet Union above 70,000 feet. Making its first flight in 1956, the U-2 produced photographs from twenty to thirty flights in the next four years and gave intelligence analysts, according to one CIA official, about 90 percent of their hard data on Russian military developments. The National Photographic Interpretation Center became a key intelligence agency. In 1960 the Russians, outraged by the overflights, brought down a U-2 with an air-defense missile. Amid an international furor, Eisenhower canceled the overflights.

The administration had other collection means near at hand to replace the U-2. Eisenhower's scientific advisers, especially James R. Killian Jr., and the Air Force's research and development community joined forces with the CIA to win funding for reconnaissance satellites. Receiving high-priority funding after 1955, the satellite reconnaissance program produced an effective satellite equipped with high-resolution cameras from the Polaroid Corporation. Finding an adequate launch booster proved more difficult, in part because of bureaucratic competition within the armed forces, CIA, and the aerospace industry. To direct the satellite programs, Eisenhower authorized the creation of the National Reconnaissance Office in 1959 under the general supervision of the Air Force. By the end of 1960 the first satellite system was in operation. Through British intelligence, the CIA also in 1960 recruited a disaffected colonel in Soviet military intelligence, Oleg Penkovsky, who provided significant details about Soviet missile programs. In short, the administration's technical means of intelligence collection, supplemented by Penkovsky, gave it a clearer picture of the Soviet threat than it could admit to its critics for fear of compromising its sources.

The slim flow of hard data on Soviet aviation and missile development in the 1950s encouraged the Air Force to exaggerate the growth of Russia's strategic forces. The debate on the Soviet threat might have been contained to a dispute between the NSC staff, CIA, and the Air Force except for the fact that national security had become tempting partisan politics. Four Democratic senators with presidential ambitions—Lyndon B. Johnson, Henry Jackson, Stuart Symington, and John F. Kennedy—made sure that the New Look became a campaign issue. The first conflict was the "bomber gap" affair of 1954–1956. Using exaggerated assessments of Soviet aircraft productivity, supported by an alarmist count of an "Air Force Day" bomber flyover, Air Force experts projected that the Russian heavy-bomber force would grow from around 50 to 800 by 1961. Although this prediction receded by 1957 to a realistic prediction of around 200 bombers, the bomber gap affair left the impression that the United States faced a threat its air-defense system could not meet. The alarm became panic in 1957 when the Soviets used a liquid-fueled SS-6 missile to place a Sputnik satellite in earth orbit. Sputnik surprised intelligence experts, who did not expect the SS-6 to be operational before 1960. The next CIA estimate in 1958 was that the Soviets could deploy a force of 500 ICBMs by 1961. The "missile gap" set off another round of recrimination and criticism of "massive retaliation" and the New Look.

The Eisenhower administration pointed with pride to Strategic Air Command as the centerpiece of American defense. During the New Look, SAC adopted new aircraft and the nuclear weapons, expanded its base system, and improved its communications. In 1954 SAC's bomber force numbered about 1,000 B-36s and B-47s. By 1960 this force had increased to almost 2,000 bombers. Although the B-47 remained the backbone of SAC despite its range limitations, SAC supplemented it with 500 new bombers—the Boeing B-52. Operational in 1955, the B-52, loved by its crews for its dependability and handling ease, gave SAC the intercontinental jet bomber it wanted. To reduce its vulnerability, SAC placed 20 percent of its bombers on strip alert (1957–1960), then extended this program to airborne alert. SAC also continued to expand its base system to confuse Russian planners. Its continental bases increased from thirty-seven (1954) to forty-six (1960); its overseas bases climbed in the same period from fourteen to twenty.

The deterrent monopoly of SAC's bombers, however, eroded under the pressure of three developments: Soviet air defenses and ICBMs, civilian scrutiny of strategic deterrence and force structure, and interservice rivalry. The result was an acceleration of America's own intercontinental missile program. Although all of the services had experimented with missiles since 1945, no service had given its program top priority. Within the Air Force, scientific committee investigations and RAND Corporation studies cast doubt upon the future of the bomber force. Additional studies recommended that guided missiles—ballistic and cruise—join America's deterrent force, and this position received the strong approval of the Air Force's two most influential scientific consultants, Theodore von Karman and John von Neumann. A handful of Air Force generals urged a more aggressive missile program, prodded in part by the knowledge that the Army had assembled its own missile development team under the aggressive Wernher von Braun. The strategic part of the pro-missile argument was critical. If the United States expected to have a portion of its nuclear forces survive a Russian first strike, it needed something to complement the bomber force.

In 1955 Eisenhower assigned missile development the highest priority in military research and development. In part, the president had been persuaded by the report of his own Technical Capabilities Panel, chaired by Dr. Killian, which emphasized the growing Soviet nuclear threat and recommended a major American effort. The Air Force had already anticipated the change by establishing a special office to develop two ICBMs, the Titan and Atlas. The key specifications for the missiles were that they have a 5,500-mile range and carry a 1-megaton warhead. With Defense Department approval, the Air Force also went ahead with its intermediate-range missile and intercontinental cruise missile programs. Technically these programs were more advanced than the ICBM program and produced the Thor IRBM for deployment in 1958 and the Snark cruise missile in 1957. The Army pressed ahead with its own IRBM, Jupiter, which also passed its tests in the same period. The Air Force was already at work on a second-generation ICBM, called Minuteman, which was designed to use solid fuel, have a fully developed inertial guidance system, and be built strongly enough to place in deep, survivable concrete silos. The first-generation ICBMs, IRBMs, and Snark had the same disadvantages as the bomber force: They took time to ready for firing, and they had to be launched above ground, making a tempting target for a first strike. By 1960 the Air Force had twelve Atlas ICBMs and thirty Snarks based in the United States and four Thor squadrons stationed in England. Work on the promising Minuteman continued with ample funding.

The Navy slipped into the nuclear deterrence mission by winning official approval of its own IRBM program in the 1955 decision to give missiles high priority. The Navy, of course, had demanded nuclear weapons in the late 1940s but had thought primarily in terms of arming its carrier aircraft. Its post-Korea carriers, six vessels of the *Forrestal* class and the nuclear-powered *Enterprise,* had been designed for a flight deck compatible with a new aircraft, the Douglas A 3 D Skywarrior, a true nuclear bomber. In 1954 all the Navy's deployed carriers bore nuclear weapons to strike Soviet ports and naval forces.

In the mid-1950s the Navy changed course. For one thing, it had a launch platform that met the test of survivability—the nuclear-powered submarine. Driven by Hyman G. Rickover, an engineering officer of genius and irascibility, the Navy had built its first nuclear-powered submarine, *Nautilus,* operational in 1955. An expert at bureaucratic politics, Rickover had built a nuclear power coalition that included his own Navy staff, the Atomic Energy Commission (in which he also held office), Congress, and the Westinghouse and General Electric corporations. Rickover saw "his" nuclear submarines as weapons to attack ships, but a new chief of naval operations, Arleigh A. Burke, saw the nuclear submarine as a missile carrier for submerged strikes at land targets. The Navy, however, did not have a missile, since it had worked primarily on the Regulus cruise missile for both warships and surfaced submarines. In 1957 Burke redirected the Navy IRBM program toward a solid-fueled missile that could be launched from a submerged submarine. For the missile he followed the Air Force model and created a Special Projects Office, whose staff, the AEC, and the Lockheed Corporation produced the 1,500-mile Polaris missile by 1960. Because the missile had a limited payload and accuracy, its warhead could destroy only an area target. Nevertheless, the relative invulnerability of the launch platform made the fleet ballistic missile (FBM) an attractive addition to the deterrent force.

The White House and the Russians assisted Burke. To review the effectiveness of America's nuclear posture, the Science Advisory Committee to the Office of Defense Mobilization had established a special "security resources panel" in April 1957. When this group, known as the Gaither Committee, made its report the following November, the Sputnik crisis gave its study special importance. The Gaither Committee report emphasized the nation's vulnerability to a nuclear attack and the pitiable state of its air-defense and civil defense programs. The only thing that stood between the United States and atomic Armageddon was SAC's bombers. The Gaither Committee did not think SAC should bear the burden alone. When the Navy in 1957 proposed that it develop three missile submarines, the administration authorized five submarines and moved the operational date forward from 1962 to 1960. Rickover cooperated in supporting the construction of fleet ballistic missile submarines, as long as they were nuclear-powered. In 1960 the first *George Washington*–class fleet ballistic missile submarine (SSBN) went on patrol with sixteen Polaris sea-launched ballistic missiles (SLBM).

More military miracles occurred in the cloistered Lawrence Livermore and Los Alamos laboratories of the Atomic Energy Commission. In less than a decade after the first fusion explosion, nuclear scientists and engineers discovered ways to reduce dramatically the size of nuclear weapons. The first fusion device had been 22 feet long; the nuclear warhead for the Army's Davy Crockett mortar was only 2 feet long and 12 inches in diameter. The redesign of the gun-type trigger and the use of extremely dense metal alloys permitted chain reactions with diminishing amounts of radioactive material. At a time when the published minimal amount of radioactive material for a weapon was around 50 pounds, the real minimum was probably around 12 pounds of plutonium and 22 pounds of enriched uranium. Smaller warheads meant a wider variety of delivery vehicles— ground- and air-launched ballistic and cruise missiles, depth charges, torpedoes, artillery shells, rockets, and mines. Behind the imprecise rhetoric of "massive retaliation" rested an awesome fact: The United States could manufacture literally thousands of nuclear warheads for its armed forces.

Between 1953 and 1959 the number of warheads soared from 1,161 to 12,305.

The flood of nuclear weapons into America's arsenal did not exhaust the military efforts to blunt the Soviet threat, for both the Air Force and Army searched for ways to create an effective air-defense system. The search was expensive and frustrating. As one Air Force chief of staff mused, "active air defense is a can of worms." No one knew precisely how much the Defense Department put into air defense, but the figure probably reached $40 billion for the 1950s. When the Russian threat appeared to be a bomber strike, the air-defense planners managed to win sufficient funds for a plausible system, but the bureaucratic battle between the services for the mission gave air defense a sour flavor. In 1956 Secretary of Defense Charles E. Wilson ruled that the Air Force would handle area air defense, the Army point air defense. The decision actually reversed the services' interests, for the Air Force wanted point air defense of SAC bases, while the Army argued that sufficient numbers of its "Nike" family of conventional and nuclear surface-to-air missiles could provide effective area air defense if assisted by Air Force supersonic interceptors. The growth of the Air Force's own air-defense missile program, Bomarc, complicated the issue, which was then further confused when it became apparent that the threat would come from ICBMs, not bombers. The Army argued that a new missile, Nike-Zeus, could intercept ballistic warheads. The Air Force, however, wanted rapid development of a satellite-based air-defense system. The only clear area of agreement was that the nation needed a better warning system, and the administration started work on the Ballistic Missile Early Warning System (BMEWS) in 1957.

As the nation's nuclear forces proliferated, defense planners became increasingly aware that they had no single plan for using these forces should deterrence fail. More important, it had become difficult to judge the relative utility of SAC's bombers and missiles compared to the Navy's carrier aircraft and SLBMs against the targets they had to threaten to make deterrence credible. A gnawing sense of costly redundancy plagued defense analysts. In 1960 Secretary of Defense Thomas S. Gates created the Joint Strategic Target Planning Staff (JSTPS) and charged it with building one plan from SAC's "Emergency War Plan" and the Navy's comparable documents. In part the JSTPS had to reconcile two different visions of nuclear deterrence. The Navy stressed the importance of holding Soviet cities hostage; the Air Force argued that Soviet strategic forces should be the primary targets, a position that meant that warhead numbers and accuracies should expand in proportion to an ever-increasing number of Soviet military targets. When the JSTPS produced its first "Single Integrated Operational Plan" (SIOP) in 1961, the plan continued the Air Force emphasis on targeting Soviet nuclear forces. Russian war-related industry and its Warsaw Pact ground and air forces received lesser priority. In reality a SIOP strike would have also devastated many Soviet metropolitan areas, so "finite" or "countervalue" city-threatening deterrence might be assumed. No planner could predict what level of threat would really deter the Soviets.

The Eisenhower administration did not view the New Look's deterrent programs as the only method to assure the nation's security, for the United States might profit from international arms control agreements. The major issues the administration addressed were nuclear proliferation, surprise attack, and testing. In December 1953 Eisenhower proposed that the peaceful use of nuclear power be encouraged by international cooperation and monitored by an international organization, eventually created as the International Atomic Energy Agency (1957). While such an arrangement could encourage the construction of nuclear power plants, it might also inhibit the spread of nuclear weapons. The administration believed that nuclear power projects would absorb much of the world's uranium supply; new uranium discoveries confounded this hope. Inhibited by its fear of international verification, the Soviet Union slowed the UN-sponsored talks. The same problems impeded Eisenhower's second arms control initiative, the "Open Skies" proposal of July 1955. Concerned about the threat of a surprise first strike, Eisenhower proposed that reconnaissance overflights be protected by international agreement. When the United Nations proved uninterested in the proposal, the United States and the U.S.S.R. opened bilateral negotiations, which produced no agreement on aircraft overflights but tacitly accepted the future deployment of reconnaissance satellites.

The prospect of nuclear proliferation, plus growing evidence that atmospheric testing created health hazards, persuaded the administration to pursue UN talks on restricting nuclear tests. Once more the United States and the U.S.S.R. divided on the timing and extent of verification procedures. By 1958 the talks had shifted to international scientific meetings on the technical problems of detecting nuclear explosions. These meetings concluded that all but deep underground tests could be unambiguously identified, and seismograph experts believed they could soon tell the difference between an earthquake and even a small (20-kiloton) nuclear explosion. Frustrated by the complexities imposed by United Nations negotiations, the United States, Great Britain, and the Soviet Union pursued the talks on a trilateral basis in 1959 and within a year drafted a treaty banning atmospheric and water testing. The U-2 incident stalled the talks in 1960, but the United States and the Soviet Union stood on the threshold of their first major arms control agreement. As France and Communist China were quick to point out, the test ban imposed greater handicaps on the nonnuclear powers than the United States and Russia, but the limited test ban at least cleared the air of radioactivity, if not of international distrust. These negotiations introduced a new element in the U.S.-U.S.S.R. arms competition by suggesting that the risk of nuclear war might be reduced by agreement.

The growth and diversification of American and Russian strategic forces, paired with the administration's cautious arms control initiatives, popularized deterrence theory, developed largely by civilian writers. The accumulated effect of the civilians' analysis was to question the simple vision of deterrence by city-threatening retaliation inherent in massive retaliation. The Gaither Committee report was but one of a series of skeptical studies. Asked to examine SAC basing, the RAND Corporation questioned bombers' survivability and stressed the importance of invulnerable, nonprovocative second-strike weapons capable, if necessary, of destroying Soviet strategic forces. The doctrine of "counterforce-no cities" emerged in additional RAND analyses, a report by the secretary of defense's Weapons Systems Evaluation Group, some Air Force studies, and an open study of defense policy sponsored by the prestigious Rockefeller Brothers Fund. The president's Scientific Advisory Committee became part of the coalition of strategic revisionists, and within the military Army Chief of Staff Maxwell D. Taylor found common cause with the scientist-engineers and social scientists who emerged as the principal theorists. Among the latter were Bernard Brodie, Albert J. Wohlstetter, William W. Kaufmann, Paul Nitze, Henry Kissinger, Charles Hitch, Henry S. Rowen, and Herman Kahn.

The civilian "defense intellectuals" of the 1950s created a body of thought that became politically influential among the Senate critics of the New Look. The appeal of deterrence theory rested in part on the academic credentials of the principal theorists, almost to a man Ph.D.s in the social sciences. Another factor was the persuasiveness of analytical techniques based on economic theory; numbers spoke louder than words. An additional influence was the growing belief that traditional strategic thought, as developed by military professionals, had no application in a world of nuclear weapons. Some of the new deterrence theory did, in fact, make traditional defense calculations appear obsolete. One concept was that only force survivability really counted and that the Soviets had to perceive that survivability to make deterrence work. Yet the prestrike force should not appear threatening, thus inviting a preemptive attack. Just how a force could be large enough to survive and attack Soviet military targets and not also appear threatening proved an elusive calculation. Another concept was that should deterrence fail, the goal of strategic forces should be to limit the war, thus providing negotiating time. Phrases like "escalation control" and "damage limitation" soon entered the strategic lexicon. Analysis by game theory, psychological modeling, and the measurement of marginal utility further brought strategic analysis by analogy to a high art form. It also provided the intellectual foundation for the dramatic expansion of American strategic forces in the 1960s.

Reorganization and Alliances

From its first days in office the Eisenhower administration believed it could organize away some of its defense problems. Even moderate Republicans thought the "failures" of FDR and Harry Truman were linked to their "unorganized" leadership styles. Another article of faith was that the greatest obstacle to economical defense planning was interservice rivalry. Angered that the JCS had supported Truman's Korean War policies, congressional Republicans pressed Eisenhower to eliminate the "Democratic chiefs," a policy the president followed by not reappointing the incumbents when their terms expired. The thrust of the New Look's reorganizational efforts brought increased centralization to the office of the president, the office of the secretary of defense, and the Joint Staff that supported the JCS. But the reforms stopped well short of any true revolution in defense planning, for the Congress did not vote itself out of its shared constitutional responsibilities. The Eisenhower administration's two fits of reorganization did not make the hard decisions easier. They only increased the number of voices in the process.

No stranger to organizational problems, Eisenhower struck swiftly in 1953 to strengthen interagency coordination in national security planning. Although he could not announce all his goals, the president sought to limit congressional interference with what he considered presidential business. Eisenhower first institutionalized the National Security Council by making weekly meetings a fixture. More important, he gave his special assistant for national security affairs the power to create a staff. Part of the staff's function was to prepare weekly agendas and then manage the flow of NSC business through two interagency committees, the Policy Planning Board and the Operations Coordinating Board. The NSC staff in effect became a small, unofficial amalgam of the State Department, the Defense Department, and the CIA, emboldened by its proximity to the president.

From his experiences as an Army elder statesman during the Truman administration, Eisenhower concluded that the service departments presented the major barrier to effective defense planning and management. His predispositions received sanction from a Rockefeller Commission study that subsequently served as the basis for Reorganization Plan No. 6, a mix of executive and congressional reforms enacted in 1953. The Rockefeller study urged reorganization in the name of "maximum security at minimum cost, and without danger to free institutions." For the JCS the reform meant enhanced power for the chairman, who received control over the role of the enlarged Joint Staff. The office of the Secretary of Defense expanded its influence even more dramatically. Six new assistant secretaries of defense and a general counsel joined the secretary's deputy and existing three assistant secretaries, thus giving the secretary a staff that could contend with the service departments in all defense functions.

In five years of testing the Eisenhower administration found the 1953 reforms wanting, and in 1958, once again supported by the findings of a Rockefeller-sponsored study, the administration proposed even more centralization. The reforms bore heavily upon the JCS. The chairman received formal authority to vote on JCS matters, and the individual chiefs found themselves outside the operational chain of command, which now ran from the president to the secretary of defense to the principal military commanders in the field. (The latter were the heads either of "unified" geographic commands or single-function "specified" commands like SAC.) Congress, however, refused to designate the chairman as the principal military adviser to the president and the secretary, and it allowed the service chiefs to retain their right as individuals to see the president and testify before Congress. Eisenhower called the latter power "legalized insubordination." The assistant secretaries of defense, on the other hand, profited from the secretary's new power to transfer and consolidate service functions and activities—except "major" operational missions—because they could now issue binding orders in their functional areas.

The secretary of defense could now establish new departmentwide agencies. The new agencies to a large degree replaced a host of interservice boards, abolished since the 1953 reform. The first order of reorganization—or "extended horizontal confederation"—stemmed the competition between strategic programs, an arena of intense interservice interest. The 1958 amendment of the National Security Act created a director of defense research and engineering, whose principal mission was to guide high-technology programs. The incumbent secretary, Thomas S. Gates, also established a new office, the Advanced Research Projects Agency, to assume the lead in research on space-based missile defense and other futuristic projects. As intended, the reforms drove the service departments deeper into the slough of subordination, but the reorganization did not save money, either by dampening service budget requests or bringing greater rigor to weapons procurement and material management.

In the absence of ruthless secretarial action, the reforms did not produce greater consensus because there were too many defense problems and too little money. In 1960 Secretary Gates began to meet with the JCS on a weekly basis to give it more immediate guidance. The greater personal rapport helped dampen disagreements, but the JCS still produced split recommendations, which forced the secretary and the president to make decisions they sometimes would rather have avoided. In statistical terms the chiefs showed great harmony, since they agreed on 99 percent of their recommendations in 1955–1959, but the 1 percent they disagreed upon included every major functional question they faced. Reorganization could not mask the fact that the JCS—with the exception of its Air Force members—did not think the New Look answered the nation's military problems.

The reform of defense decision-making did not, for example, simplify the dilemmas of matching forward, collective defense with the nuclearization of America's armed forces. Nowhere were the problems more perplexing than in NATO. When the Eisenhower administration took office, it inherited the negotiations to rearm West Germany within the existing alliance system. French intransigence upon the issue of a German national military force killed the first formula, the European Defense Community. The negotiations did secure approval for an eventual German army of twelve divisions and 500,000 men. In late 1954 another change in French governments improved the chances for rearming West Germany, and in December 1954 the French National Assembly approved a revised plan that would allow the Germans a national military establishment within the existing NATO system. The Federal Republic of Germany received full control over its internal and external affairs, softening its new status by promising not to arm itself with nuclear weapons unless so ordered by NATO.

In 1955 West Germany began to organize the Bundeswehr. At the politico-strategic level, the Christian Democrat governments of the 1950s, dominated by Konrad Adenauer, wanted to ensure that rearmament did not endanger economic recovery, divide West Germany, or weaken NATO's tie to the American nuclear deterrent. Adenauer had no desire to go beyond a twelve-division army, a position that made the conventional force goals of the Lisbon Agreement even less obtainable. The West Germans also insisted that Bundeswehr divisions occupy positions along the entire border so that no Russian attack could strike only German troops.

West Germany's NATO debut coincided with the New Look's new emphasis on substituting nuclear weapons for conventional ground forces, a policy accepted by NATO in late 1954. Directed by the NATO Council to plan for the early and first use of nuclear weapons against a Soviet invasion, NATO military planners found that the concept of nuclear war fighting carried heavy liabilities. A full-scale NATO war game in 1955 discovered that West Germany could not be saved without being destroyed. During Operation CARTE BLANCHE the war gamers "used" 335 nuclear weapons, 268 of which "landed" on Soviet forces in West

Germany. While the nuclear counter-*blitzkrieg* stopped the Russians, it also caused more than 5 million civilian casualties. Nevertheless, NATO's political leaders adopted a European version of the New Look in 1957 when they approved a military planning document (MC 14/2) that committed NATO to using nuclear weapons to meet any threat. They planned to make the NATO standing force of thirty divisions nuclear-capable. The same principle applied to NATO's tactical aircraft. The NATO Council agreed to stockpile nuclear warheads in Europe (many of the delivery systems were already there), and before the end of the decade SACEUR had probably 7,000 nuclear weapons at his disposal.

The NATO New Look had the advantage of clearly extending American nuclear deterrence to Europe, since the United States would presumably bear the risks of escalation equally with its allies. The lowered level of NATO's conventional forces, however, might invite attack, and they appeared more as "plate glass" and "tripwire" hostage forces than usable fighting units. In fact, the planned use of tactical nuclear weapons enhanced their initial vulnerability, since NATO planners accepted the West German border with East Germany as the principal line of defense despite its geographic liabilities. Such forward defense ensured that the tactical nuclear weapons would land on Soviet forces in East Germany but made it unlikely that NATO's divisions in Germany could fight a prolonged conventional war, which required inspired maneuvering between the inner German border and the Rhine River.

The dilemmas of NATO strategy did not pass unnoticed in the United States and Europe, since a series of crises made it impossible not to examine NATO's military options. In 1956 the East Germans and Hungarians staged abortive revolts against their Soviet occupiers and native Communist governments; in Hungary the fighting threatened to spill over the Austrian border. In 1958 the Russians again challenged the Allies' right to occupy part of Berlin. Two SACEURs, Generals Alfred M. Gruenther and Lauris Norstad, raised the issue of NATO's conventional readiness, which had been further limited by the reduction of the British army and the deployment of French divisions to Algeria. Influential West German politicians questioned the wisdom of relying upon tactical nuclear weapons. In the United States NATO's nuclear strategy came under determined attack from academics like Henry Kissinger and Robert E. Osgood, two gurus of limited war theory, and from Army leaders like Generals James M. Gavin and Maxwell D. Taylor. After Secretary Dulles's death in 1959, the State Department turned restive about massive retaliation and NATO policy. Instead of strengthening the alliance, the adoption of theater nuclear weapons created new political problems.

The difficulty of reconciling strategic nuclear deterrence with forward, collective defense did not ease when the New Look came to Asia. To contain Russia and Communist China, the Eisenhower administration created a network of alliances that would presumably protect America's base system in the western Pacific and strengthen the conventional forces of its Asian allies. The administration quickly concluded bilateral treaties with two natural collaborators: The authoritarian, anti-Communist governments of South Korea (1953) and Taiwan (1955). Both agreements stated that each party recognized "that an armed attack in the Pacific area on either of the Parties . . . would be dangerous to its own peace and safety" and pledged each party to act in common to meet the danger. Rearming Japan proved more difficult. Although the Japanese allowed their national police to become the Self-Defense Force, they would not assume the economic and political burden of providing anything but minimal air, naval, and ground forces of 231,000 men. Even more important, the Japanese government refused to assume any regional military leadership, and before it signed a comprehensive security treaty in 1960, it extracted a promise from the United States not to introduce nuclear weapons into Japan.

The broadened commitment to north Asia carried substantial risks, since both South Korea and Taiwan had no reluctance to host American nuclear forces or to do battle with their Communist neighbors. The wisdom of the treaties with South Korea and Taiwan came under criticism from outside the Eisenhower administration when the Chinese Communists and Nationalists conducted a small war against each other along the Chinese coast. Working from bases on the islands of Quemoy, Matsu, and the Pescadores, the Nationalists in 1953–1954 conducted naval raids against the mainland and infiltrated agents there. The Communists retaliated with threats of invasion and long-range artillery bombardments. While persuading Chiang Kai-shek to abandon his most indefensible islands and to curb his operations, the administration paid for its influence by increasing aid to Chiang and deploying part of the 7th Fleet in the Formosa Strait. It also placed aircraft and artillery with nuclear capability on Taiwan. Another Quemoy-Matsu crisis in 1958 produced a similar commitment. With border incident piling upon border incident along the DMZ, the defense of South Korea did not appear risk-free, even with the presence of American troops and tactical nuclear weapons. As with the Chinese Nationalists, the alliance with South Korea committed the United States to a situation in which either its enemies or its allies could force the political action, including military escalation.

The Eisenhower administration understood the risks in Asia, for it had faced its worst crisis in 1954 when the French military effort in Indochina collapsed. Examining his military options, including a nuclear strike against the Viet Minh army investing Dien Bien Phu, Eisenhower found little taste for massive retaliation among his civilian and military advisers or NATO allies. Although Admiral Radford urged military action, Army Chief of Staff Matthew B. Ridgway feared that only a ground force commitment would halt the Viet Minh. Uncertain that air strikes alone would reverse the French defeat, Eisenhower encouraged the French to accept a negotiated settlement. At Geneva in July 1954, the French and the Vietnamese Communists agreed to the temporary partition of Vietnam and the independence of Laos and Cambodia. With the future of Vietnam still at stake, the administration hurried to repair the non-Communist position in Southeast Asia. While it extended assistance to South Vietnam and conducted covert action against the Communists, the administration patched together the Southeast Asia Treaty Organization (1954). The only new allies were Pakistan and Thailand, for the United States already had treaties with Great Britain, France, the Philippines, New Zealand, and Australia. The organization did not provide the same binding guarantees of collective military action that characterized NATO. A protocol to the treaty in September 1954 extended SEATO's protection to Laos, Cambodia, and South Vietnam, a provision in effect when the Senate approved the treaty (82 to 1) the following February.

The Middle East also received Dulles's pact-making attention. Under American pressure and the promise of increased military assistance, the traditional regimes of Iran, Iraq, and Pakistan joined Turkey and Great Britain in the Baghdad Pact (1955). The principal rationale for the agreement was to deter Soviet military pressure against the unstable, oil-rich Middle East, where British influence was on the wane. The Eisenhower administration thought it could use surrogates, including Israel, to curb Russian influence and Arab nationalism, but it learned the following year that nuclear weapons, alliance politics, and oil did not mix well. When the radical president of Egypt, Gamal Abdel Nasser, seized control of the Suez Canal, the British, French, and Israelis conspired to invade Egypt and retake the canal. Although the Israeli army and air force dealt the Egyptians a crushing defeat in the Sinai, the United States pressured its NATO allies to give up the expedition against the canal, even moving the 6th Fleet into position for military action. Part of Eisenhower's concern came from indistinct noises from Moscow suggesting that the Russians would enter the Middle East cauldron, which raised the specter of a nuclear confrontation.

Dissatisfied with the role of the Baghdad Pact, Eisenhower and Dulles announced a new American commitment in 1957 to assist any Middle Eastern state threatened by aggression from any other state "controlled by international communism." The President received sanction for the "Eisenhower Doctrine" from Congress, which approved his $200 million aid request. Outside the Baghdad Pact nations, only Lebanon and Israel approved the statement. In 1957–1958 the administration found its Middle East version of containment sorely tested. A group of radical army officers destroyed the Iraqi monarchy, and other pan-Arabist radicals with Syrian and Egyptian assistance menaced the Jordanian monarchy and the fragile communal government in Lebanon. The Eisenhower administration saw the Soviets' fine hand in the upheaval, since the Russians had extended military assistance to Egypt and Syria. Although American financial aid and British troops stabilized King Hussein's regime in Jordan, the situation in Lebanon deteriorated into civil war. In order to prevent a coup and arrange a negotiated settlement, Eisenhower occupied Beirut with 15,000 American troops in July 1958. Once again nuclear deterrence had proved largely irrelevant to regional rivalries and American interests. And military assistance alone ($4.3 billion to the Middle East in 1950–1963) did not fully substitute for an American military presence.

The anti-Communist situation in Latin America in the 1950s deteriorated despite American nuclear power. When military dictatorships collapsed in Colombia and Venezuela, the Communists did not immediately profit, but they joined other radicals to keep rural insurrection and terrorism alive. In Cuba the adherents of Fidel Castro and Che Guevara orchestrated their rhetorical and military attacks with an urban guerrilla movement not under their control. The combined internal pressure, coupled with the suspension of American military assistance, sent Fulgencio Batista into exile in January 1959. During the next year Castro turned his revolutionary government toward the Soviet Union, thus galvanizing the Eisenhower administration to impose economic sanctions and to order the CIA to mount an invasion by anti-Castro exiles. Castro's success on America's doorstep made massive retaliation appear bankrupt as a deterrent to Communist subversion in the Western Hemisphere.

Its foreign policy crises did not force the Eisenhower administration to change the New Look, for the president held fast to his de facto ceiling on defense spending. In the face of an economic recession, cascading foreign problems, unbalanced budgets, a restive Congress, uncontrollable increases in domestic spending, and upward pressures upon the defense budget, Eisenhower increased his pressure on the services' priority programs during his second administration. The Navy lost the money for its second nuclear carrier, and its new shipbuilding program met only two-thirds of its estimates. The favored Air Force saved its 137-wing program— the force goals of the 1950s—but received funding only by reducing its manpower. The emphasis on SAC reduced the number of wings in the Tactical Air Command, Air Defense Command, and Military Air Transport Command. The Army and the Marine Corps lost manpower and programs for increased firepower and mobility.

The Eisenhower administration argued that a robust reserve program would meet any likely conventional war contingency and at a more bearable cost, since ten reservists cost roughly the same as one full-time serviceman. Quite properly, the Defense Department focused on the readiness of reserve units and found them undermanned. Although the legislation of 1952 provided a reserve force of 2.5 million, only 700,000 reservists trained with units. The administration proposed a reserve draft and the involuntary assignment of veterans to the National Guard, but Congress instead tried its hand at reserve reform. In the Reserve Forces Act of 1955 Congress raised the reserve ceiling to 2.9 million and liberalized the road into the reserves. Men could enlist directly into the services' reserve components provided they then spent two years on active duty and returned to a reserve unit for three years' training. Others could enlist directly into a unit, spend three to six months on active duty, and then serve out the rest of an eight-year obligation in a unit. The Army extended the requirement for initial active-duty training to the National Guard in 1957. Although the draft had limited influence, the new program worked, for by 1960 the number of drill-pay reservists had climbed to nearly a million.

Depending upon reserves did not give the Army a "New Look," for the Army and the Marine Corps sought greater battlefield mobility and firepower for their reduced numbers of fighting men. The anticipated demands of the nuclear battlefield made dispersion and mobility essential. By modernizing its armored divisions and mounting its infantry in armored personnel carriers, the Army found one solution. Another came from adopting troop-carrying helicopters. Within the Army and Marine Corps aviation establishments, fixed-wing pilots held sway, so the helo pioneers fought against the weight of institutional inertia. Using helos to ferry troops did not cause any great controversy except in the battles for developmental money. The Marine Corps reorganized its infantry battalions for helo transportability after 1956, and the Army had twelve helo battalions by 1960.

The helo advocates also saw the helicopter's potential as a close fire support weapon, especially as a tank killer. In the Marine Corps fixed-wing aviators saw no reason to substitute helos for the close air support planes already available and halted gunship development. In the Army, however, the helo enthusiasts convinced their patrons that the Air Force would not give the transport helos adequate support, and by the mid-1950s the Army's infantry and aviation training centers had created "sky cavalry" helo units. Reassured by a 1956 decision by the office of the secretary of defense that the Army would not develop fixed-wing transports and attack aircraft, the Air Force did not press the doctrinal issue. In 1960 the Army Staff convened a high-level board to review aviation doctrine and organization, and the board reported that the Army should make a major test of the concept of helicopter vertical assaults, complete with gunships. Both the Marine Corps and Army pressed their budget requests for helo development with growing certainty that air-mobile units would be the spearhead of the nation's conventional forces.

The foreign policy crises of the 1950s and the armed services' internal development produced a wave of intellectual interest in the concept of limited war. At first the analysts' concern centered on the use of tactical nuclear weapons, but by the end of the decade the central policy proposals, exemplified by General Maxwell D. Taylor's *The Uncertain Trumpet* (1960) and Robert Osgood's *Limited War* (1957), addressed the problem of conventional combat readiness. In theory the United States could best avoid any level of nuclear confrontation only by improving its ability to employ nonnuclear air-ground combat forces whenever the Communists invaded an allied country. Adopted with escalating enthusiasm by journalists and political pundits, the strategic rage of 1960 became "flexible response."

"Flexible Response"

Safely in the White House, John F. Kennedy argued that he would junk the New Look and bring new rationality and efficiency to American defense policy. Military reform had been a major theme of Kennedy's 1960 presidential campaign against Richard M. Nixon, for he insisted that containment needed more vigorous, innovative application. The new administration adopted the concept of flexible response as the foundation of its defense policy, which meant that the United States would meet Communist military threats with an appropriate level of matching force. Victory would be a return to geopolitical stability without an escalation to nuclear war. Obscured by his personal charm, ironic humor, and intellectual curiosity, Kennedy's character had a strong streak of romantic liberalism that focused his interest on the nonwhite developing nations. His missionary impulse strengthened the administration's belief that nuclear deterrence and the complementary balance of power between NATO and the Warsaw Pact had driven the military competition to different techniques and different places. The most likely challenge would be a "people's war" or rural-based leftist revolution. Such Communist insurgencies would probably occur in Latin America, Southeast Asia, and sub-Saharan Africa. Kennedy did not undervalue NATO, but he thought the great conflicts of the future, stimulated by the growing Russian-Chinese schism, would come outside Europe.

The president's personal and political liabilities also shaped flexible response. Republican attacks upon his inexperience, his inherited wealth, his Catholicism, and his opportunism did not end with the 1960 election. Rather than risk the charge that he was inclined to appease Communism, which he did indeed see in less alarmist terms than Nixon, Kennedy embraced containment with zeal. Kennedy's optimistic assessment of the American economy reinforced his commitment to flexible response. Kennedy's economic advisers believed the nation could safely spend $50 billion for defense without spurring inflation or producing other economic ills. In fact, the administration believed that increased defense spending, matched with a tax cut, would spur a sluggish economy by placing government funds in the one activity where some public consensus existed: national defense. Increased defense spending might also legitimize the "New Frontier" among domestic conservatives.

The Kennedy administration concluded that it could sell accelerated military modernization by bringing more centralization and civilianization to defense decision-making. A Senate investigation of national security decision-making, led by Henry M. Jackson, urged greater curbs on interservice rivalry. A postelection study by another Democratic expert on defense, Senator Stuart Symington, also urged more centralized defense management. Tutored by retired generals James M. Gavin and Maxwell D. Taylor, the president believed the service departments, abetted by the JCS, had become the major barrier to efficient defense program development. The civilians who staffed the national security agencies of the New Frontier shared similar views. Drawn from eastern universities, foundations, banks, and law offices or recruited from western laboratories and the RAND Corporation, the "defense intellectuals" believed they could engineer an organizational revolution within the executive branch.

The Department of Defense became both the target and instrument of reform. Encouraged by his advisers to bring new dynamism to the Pentagon, Kennedy recruited the maverick president of the Ford Motor Company, Robert S. McNamara, to be secretary of defense. A self-made millionaire and moderate on domestic issues, McNamara did not fit the same mold as his New Look predecessors, for he had developed an interest in world affairs uncommon in corporation executives. His team in the office of the secretary of defense (OSD) reflected his high confidence in civilianized, centralized defense decision-making. Roswell Gilpatric, Cyrus Vance, William Bundy, and Paul Nitze represented the tradition of policy activism and internationalism established by their patrons, Dean Acheson and Robert Lovett; Harold Brown, recruited from Lawrence Livermore Laboratory, headed a team of scientist-engineers critical of service research and development; Charles J. Hitch, William W. Kaufmann, and Alain C. Enthoven came from the RAND Corporation, prepared to apply their skills as economic analysts. Drawing upon his experiences as an Army

Air Forces management expert in World War II, honed by fifteen years with Ford, McNamara forged a formidable OSD team, admired by their champions as true "defense intellectuals" and disparaged by their critics as "whiz kids." Forceful, articulate, and persuasive, McNamara quickly became a favorite adviser at the White House and the principal designer of flexible response.

Assured of Kennedy's full support, McNamara applied a range of decision-making reforms. He changed the budget process by demanding that the services adopt the planning-programming-budgeting system (PPBS), newly popularized by eastern business management schools. McNamara demanded that defense budgets be organized by functions like strategic deterrence rather than "inputs" like manpower procurement. With costs estimated over five years rather than one, he developed a Five Year Defense Plan that linked defense spending with missions—strategic forces, general-purpose forces, strategic air and sea mobility forces, and lesser categories that spanned service lines. By recasting the budget process, McNamara made it far easier for his analysts to apply systems analysis, a highly quantified technique of investigating "cost effectiveness," or the predicted increase in military capability for different levels of investment.

Systems analysis allowed Hitch, Brown, Enthoven, and their colleagues to compare (at least on a cost basis) the relative value of weapons programs that performed the same or similar missions. Moreover, the process forced the services to investigate the full financial implications of their programs by stressing systemwide costs (manning, maintenance, modification, basing) over a weapon's full lifetime, which might reach twenty years into the future. Applied with messianic energy by a new office, the assistant secretary of defense (systems analysis), the new technique found many applications. It became a marvelous tool for dismissing service requests and nonquantifiable professional military judgments. It supported the application of "commonality" as an efficiency tool, which justified the creation of new agencies like the Defense Intelligence Agency (1961) and the Defense Supply Agency (1961); the development of a fighter plane like the TFX for both Air Force and Navy use; and the adoption of all-service field uniforms and combat boots. Matching systems analysis with other social science techniques like game theory, OSD could even sortie into the arena of strategic doctrine.

McNamara's "revolution" in the Pentagon gave flexible response a life that outlived Kennedy, for it brought such disarray to the armed forces and Congress that it took another war and a decade of learning and political infighting to devalue its assumptions. The very success of PPBS and systems analysis as defense management techniques—a success dependent on presidential support and congressional confusion—extended the power of its practitioners from the development of military forces to the employ-ment of those forces. In practice, OSD, in collaboration with the NSC staff, challenged the State Department as the primary agency in determin-ing American policy whenever that policy appeared to have military signif-icance. For almost a decade, the most powerful knights of "Camelot" were the civilians and military officers who marched under McNamara's banner.

McNamara focused on improving the nation's strategic nuclear forces, which meant maintaining a survivable second-strike capability. The secre-tary quickly learned the facts of life about nuclear strategy, but he found no easy way to bring either strategic or economic rationality to force planning. Between 1961 and 1966, OSD conducted a series of sophisticated, highly quantified studies of strategic deterrence, including gaming the nuclear wars that might occur should deterrence fail. Presented with service pro-grams on one hand and esoteric calculations on the other, McNamara tried to find a solution to force planning that satisfied his thirst for reason. He found none. At first he thought that the United States should stress its ability to attack Soviet strategic forces and other military targets. As the secretary explained in his Ann Arbor speech of June 1962, a "no cities" doctrine ensured deterrence and provided damage limitation and escala-tion control if war came. Once the secretary examined the implications of his counterforce strategy, he retreated from it. The numbers did not pro-vide economic or strategic reassurance: If the United States planned to retaliate against remaining Soviet forces *after* the Soviets had struck first at U.S. strategic forces, the requirements for delivery vehicles became astro-nomical—and potentially threatening to the U.S.S.R. as an American first-strike force. As McNamara pointed out to the Air Force, "Damn it, if you keep talking about ten thousand missiles, you are talking about preemp-tive attack." If the United States developed such a force, it might frighten the Soviets into beginning the very war both sides sought to avoid.

McNamara moved back toward finite deterrence targeting of the New Look era, a movement that irritated military planners and carried with it the political risk of admitting massive retaliation was not so silly after all. McNamara understood that maintaining a survivable deterrent was a more complicated matter than it had been before the Soviets began to deploy ICBMs. He tried to find an acceptable force structure that would provide "assured destruction" under the worst possible assumptions and include a limited counterforce capability. For planning purposes he directed that American forces be capable of destroying 25 percent of the Soviet popula-tion and 50 percent of Soviet industry; he later admitted that U.S. forces could have destroyed 50 percent of the Russian population and 80 percent of Soviet industry in the late 1960s. But who knew what level of threatened destruction deterred the Russians or whether it influenced them at all?

With such questions unanswered, McNamara accepted a force three times larger in delivery vehicles than the Eisenhower program projected for the 1960s. Nevertheless his program did not meet military requests, which remained wedded to the war-fighting assumptions of the SIOP. By the end of 1963, the McNamara strategic program was largely in place. The ICBM force would increase to around 1,000, a happy medium between the New Look's 600 and the 1,450 to 2,000 missiles the Air Force wanted. The heart of the force would be the solid-fueled Minuteman in two new models. The submarine force would jump from twenty-nine to forty-one boats, carrying 656 missiles. The manned bomber force could be reduced from its high of 1,500 toward a more capable force half as large.

McNamara's analysis of assured destruction requirements, measured in part against predictions of Soviet ICBM programs through the 1960s, reinforced the secretary's conviction that the Russians would someday reach nuclear parity. It was not a conclusion that made force planning easier or that enhanced Kennedy's political future. McNamara redirected strategic force planning by checking the Air Force's bomber program; he canceled both the B-70 supersonic, high-altitude bomber and the "Skybolt" bomber-carried missile. By increasing warhead accuracy, the United States might reduce warhead yield, a development that would allow more warheads to be placed on the future generations of missiles installed in silos and submarines. Shortly after McNamara capped the growth of delivery vehicles (1963–1964), he approved the development of multiple, independently targetable reentry vehicles (MIRVs) as the next hedge against a Soviet first strike. McNamara favored the strategic triad of ICBMs, SLBMs, and bombers, for his studies suggested that such a mixed force defied a disarming first strike and assured the ultimate deterrent of counter-city retaliation. Despite his critics' argument that "assured destruction" was only "massive retaliation" repackaged, the McNamara program, which now included substantial counterforce potential, surged forward to completion by 1967.

McNamara rejected the options of active and passive defense against Soviet missile attack, for the secretary believed that strategy, economics, and public ignorance made defense pointless. Although OSD improved the bomber defense system and supported major improvements in satellite and ground radar surveillance, McNamara beat back service-sponsored antiballistic missile (ABM) programs until Congress and President Lyndon Johnson forced him to accept a minimal commitment to ABM in 1967. McNamara never argued that the Army could not hit an incoming warhead, only that the Russians could overwhelm either a point defense or area defense system with a minimal increase of warhead numbers. McNamara applied similar logic to the protection of urban Americans from the effects of nuclear weapons. In the technical sense the availability of fall-out shelters would no doubt save lives if war came. Such public shelters, however, would cost around $40 billion, the same loose estimate as for the ABM system. McNamara's strategic advisers also feared that civil defense systems might lead the Russians to conclude that the Americans believed they could wage nuclear war and survive. When public hysteria greeted a minimal government shelter program in 1961–1962, McNamara found an additional excuse to rely on assured destruction.

The Kennedy administration also had to face the unpleasant reality that no easy technical solution would eliminate the risk of nuclear war. Kennedy adopted Eisenhower's negotiations for arms control, especially to limit nuclear testing, for the medical effects of radioactivity in the atmosphere had created a public constituency for a test ban. At the same time the United States and Soviet Union shared the conclusion that limiting nuclear testing would impede other nations from going nuclear. In October 1963 the United States, Great Britain, and the Soviet Union agreed to conduct nuclear tests only underground. The signatories of the Limited Test Ban Treaty then extended it to other nations to sign. For the first time in the nuclear age, arms control had become an important element in American national security policy.

The puzzles of nuclear deterrence reinforced Kennedy's commitment to improve the nation's general-purpose forces. At the center of flexible response theory was the assumption that deterring and fighting with non-nuclear forces would reduce the likelihood of nuclear escalation. Accepting these arguments with enthusiasm, McNamara argued that the United States needed a "two and a half war" conventional force capability that would allow it to mount a successful defense of north Asia, Europe, and any insurgency-threatened state within its alliance system. Although the United States did not reach this level of readiness, the administration increased the size of the armed forces by 250,000 men and spent 80 percent of its added defense funds (around $10 billion a year) on conventional forces.

Flexible response came to NATO with mixed results because it represented mixed goals. First, McNamara's experts scrutinized the Soviet armed forces with economic analysis as well as traditional order-of-battle studies and concluded that the real Soviet threat was forty-six divisions, not the force double that size estimated by New Look planners. Conventional defense appeared to be a real option. Under American initiative NATO forces in central Europe increased from twenty-one to twenty-seven divisions and from 3,000 to 3,500 aircraft; weapons modernization continued apace to give the alliance more fighting power. In 1963 NATO's annual exercises included troops flown to Germany from the

United States; the Army then accelerated a plan to preposition weapons, vehicles, and supplies in Europe for the reinforcing troops. The issue of NATO nuclear weapons and the larger question of the reliability of American strategic deterrence, however, brought disarray to the alliance. The flexible response strategy, officially approved in memorandum MC 14/3 by NATO's defense planners in 1967, suggested that the United States might not risk nuclear war for Western Europe. Ironically, at the very time NATO developed both the forces and strategy that might have reduced its dependence on tactical nuclear weapons, another major change in the alliance resurrected the prospect of early nuclear escalation.

Even before the adoption of MC 14/3 the Kennedy administration did all it could to reassure NATO's leaders that flexible response did not mean abandonment, but it sent other conflicting signals. In 1962 the United States canceled an expensive air-launched missile program that would have modernized Britain's strategic bomber force. The United States also held fast to its decision not to assist the French nuclear weapons program. President de Gaulle had domestic reasons for going forward with the *force de frappe,* but his grand design to reduce Anglo-American influence in Europe and to complicate Russian calculations shaped French policy. French nuclear theorists disagreed with McNamara that a French nuclear capability threatened the stability of deterrence. The French insisted instead that their force filled a credibility gap created by flexible response. To reinforce French military independence, de Gaulle announced in 1966 that France would leave NATO's integrated military organization. This decision deprived the alliance of geographic depth for its logistical system and closed French air bases to NATO aircraft. The French partial defection from NATO showed the Soviet Union that the alliance might have internal defects that could be exploited by clever diplomacy, and it also made West Germany the critical continental member of the alliance, binding NATO to Germany's demands for forward defense and the early introduction of nuclear weapons.

The essence of flexible response strategy appeared in McNamara's drive to improve the armed forces' ability to move and fight without nuclear weapons. Although he doubted the wisdom of building nuclear-powered carriers, he allowed the Navy to modernize naval aviation and maintain a twenty-four carrier force. He approved an amphibious force building program that would allow the Marine Corps to deploy two full division-wing teams. The secretary pressed the Army to develop field forces with greater firepower and mobility. Although the Army added two divisions, its major reforms were structural. In one developmental path, the Army reorganized its armored and mechanized infantry divisions to resemble the German Panzer forces of World War II in flexible structure and tactical concepts.

The other developmental path brought Army aviation programs to the highest priority. In 1962 McNamara made two important decisions that opened the air mobility age. He created Strike Command, a joint Army–Air Force organization that joined the Army's most mobile forces (the two airborne divisions) with the Tactical Air Command and Military Airlift Command. The secretary approved major expansions in TAC and MAC, especially the procurement of large strategic transports. He also threw his weight behind an internal Army study of tactical air mobility that recommended the formation of an entire air assault division. This division would not only carry infantrymen into battle, but include "air cavalry" forces of armed helicopters that could attack the enemy independent of ground action. In addition, the Army extended greater helicopter capability to all its divisions. At the same time, it curbed its fixed-wing programs in order to dampen Air Force concern that the Army would soon provide all its own close air support.

McNamara also turned his attention to the New Look reserve structure and did not like what he found. In June 1961 Kennedy met Khrushchev in Vienna for a heated debate on world politics, and the president returned dismayed that he had impressed the Soviets as a weak leader. Khrushchev strengthened this fear in August when he erected a wall to stop refugees from reaching West Berlin and then threatened Allied control of their part of the city. McNamara called 148,000 reservists to active duty, partly to improve readiness, in part as a diplomatic signal. The results were mixed. Air Force (Guard and Reserve) and Navy air and surface units showed reasonable readiness, but Army Reserve and National Guard units showed a shocking lack of training, manpower, equipment, and enthusiasm. After demobilization the following year, McNamara proposed to merge the Army and Air Force Guard and Reserve, which set off a storm in Congress. The secretary settled for a less dramatic approach by giving the Air and Army Guard the principal responsibility for providing combat units and assigning Air Force and Army Reserve units supporting missions. He also provided additional training funds for "selected" units and supported internal reforms that reduced drill-pay reservists from 937,000 to 871,000 but improved unit readiness.

The major test of flexible response came from Cuba, where Castro threatened American domination of the Caribbean basin. The Castro threat, which made Cuba a bastion for exporting revolution, agitated the administration. It also tied Communist subversion into part of a global pattern. In January 1961 Khrushchev stressed in a major speech that the Soviet Union would support "wars of national liberation" and protect the Third World bastions of socialism that such wars produced. Similar sermons from Castro, Che Guevara, and Chinese Defense Minister Lin

Biao convinced Kennedy that the United States did not have an adequate capacity to stop Communist subversion. As he told his closest advisers, the United States would have to become more proficient at counterinsurgency. In April 1961 he demonstrated his own and the nation's ineptness in covert operations by making the decisions that botched the Cuban exile invasion at the Bay of Pigs. Neither a true covert operation nor a conventional invasion, Operation ZAPATA depended on a revolt that never occurred, air cover that proved inadequate, and interagency coordination that failed. After a series of postmortems, the most important directed by JFK's personal military adviser, Maxwell D. Taylor, the administration spurred the CIA, the Agency for International Development, the U.S. Information Agency, and the armed forces to give counterinsurgency the highest priority. Kennedy gave the CI crusade his personal touch by forming the Special Group/Counterinsurgency, dominated by his brother Robert, Taylor, and McGeorge Bundy.

Demonstrating the old proverb that Irishmen always get even, Kennedy approved joint maneuvers in 1962 that tested the contingency plan for an invasion of Cuba. After a purge of the CIA's operations directorate, he unleashed Operation MONGOOSE, a series of schemes to bring Castro down through Cuban exile—CIA collaboration. He also gave his personal attention to the growth and reorientation of the U.S. Army's Special Forces, an elite and neglected force of 2,000 that was supposed to organize sabotage teams in Asia and Eastern Europe in the case of general war. McNamara organized his own OSD task force and linked it with a similar group created in the JCS. Giving the Army the lead in developing CI forces and doctrine, Kennedy and McNamara expanded the Army's military assistance and civil affairs schools and held CI seminars for high-ranking civilian officials and military officers. Special Forces, however, held center stage—green berets and all—for the president ordered it to assist native villagers, rural militias, and foreign ranger forces to combat Communist guerrillas. In November 1961 the first Special Forces teams reached the embattled central highlands of South Vietnam, but the geographic orientation of the government's CI effort remained Latin America.

For both the United States and the Soviet Union, Castro's survival had passed the unconventional stage, for the Russians had started to provide the Cubans with a flood of advisers, ground weapons, aircraft, and air-defense missiles. In the summer of 1962 intelligence reports from Cuba mentioned new missiles, but closer investigation suggested that the installations were for air defense.

In September, however, air reconnaissance officers remained concerned about a pattern of construction that they had identified from limited flights, but not until early October did they receive permission to collect definitive photographs using an advanced model of the U-2, controlled by the CIA. The U-2 flight, conducted October 14, produced convincing evidence that the Russians were building sites for two types of offensive missiles, the medium-range (1,000 miles) SS-4 and the intermediate range (2,200 miles) SS-5. Further analysis suggested that the total missile force might number as many as eighty missiles of both types. At the time the U.S.S.R. had only about thirty ICBMs capable of reaching the United States; eighty MRBNs (the SS-4s) and IRBMs (the SS-5s) did not reverse the strategic advantage of the United States, but they might have dangerous implications for the nation's alliance system if the Russians went unchallenged. Kennedy's political career was no less at stake. The crisis also heartened those politicians and generals who longed to overthrow Castro and give the Russians a bloody nose, even if only symbolically. When presented with the photographic evidence collected and analyzed by the experts of the National Photographic Interpretation Center (NPIC), the administration decided to respond. After weighing the implications of an air strike on the missile complexes, Kennedy decided to force the Russians to withdraw the missiles if he could, but to prepare for a conventional invasion of Cuba and a nuclear war with the Soviet Union if his crisis diplomacy failed. As one participant recalled, "the smell of burning hung in the air."

For one week (October 21–28, 1962), the United States and the Soviet Union flirted with nuclear war, and then they both blinked, to the vast benefit of both nations. After about a week of intensive debate within his administration, President Kennedy accepted an option fashioned largely by his brother and Robert McNamara: a selective naval blockade of Cuba that would prevent further military assistance to the Russian and Cuban armed forces on the island. The president threatened further action if Khrushchev did not bring the missiles home, a point he made in a dramatic national radio and television address on October 22. Although he could not be sure that the Russians had nuclear warheads in Cuba, Kennedy had to proceed as if they did. It was well that he did so, for NPIC found a warhead storage site after the crisis abated, and the Russians later admitted that they had had around twenty warheads in Cuba. The crisis peaked on October 27, the day the SS-4 sites became operational. Early in the day an Air Force U-2, flown by Major Rudolph Anderson, plunged to the earth, hit by a Russian air-defense missile. Without direct authorization, the commander of SAC, General Thomas S. Power, put his force in Defense Condition (DEFCON) 2, a posture that placed his bombers and missiles in the last stages of prewar readiness; Power had the orders transmitted in the clear for the edification of the Russians. Khrushchev also may have had second thoughts about his ability to control his commander in Cuba, General Issa Pliyev, who had shot down the U-2 without prior approval. Although control procedures for handling the missiles and nuclear warheads were more restrictive, General Pliyev may have had some latitude in launching missiles (including nuclear) at an American invasion fleet, already under way for Havana. Khrushchev could not stop an uncompromising message already sent to Washington, but he could send another personal plea, which he did. On October 28 he agreed to withdraw the missiles if the United States would not invade Cuba. Kennedy promptly accepted the offer.

The peaceful resolution of the Cuban Missile Crisis of 1962 appeared to prove the wisdom of flexible response and its accompanying readiness programs. Alerted strategic forces, especially SAC's bombers, posed such a threat to the Soviet Union that a nuclear exchange appeared unlikely. NATO's conventional forces (and its tactical nuclear weapons) seemed to ensure no Soviet response in central Europe. The Navy's carrier battle-groups and antisubmarine task forces held the balance at sea. As Kennedy and Khrushchev exchanged messages that combined threats and concessions, McNamara assembled an invasion force in the Caribbean and at southern ports that rivaled the task forces organized during World War II. In assessing the success of its crisis diplomacy, the Kennedy administration concluded that the combination of political will, strategic nuclear superiority, and conventional military readiness had given Khrushchev no rational alternative but retreat. Flexible response, applied with cautious threats of escalation, had restored America's initiative in the Cold War. This conclusion was further reinforced in April 1965, when President Lyndon Johnson deployed a brigade of Marines and part of the 82d Airborne Division to halt a civil war in the Dominican Republic. Thus far the simultaneous test of flexible response in Southeast Asia had not yet brought any major reassessment of American defense policy.

SEVENTEEN

In Dubious Battle: Vietnam, 1961–1967

On his last day in office, January 19, 1961, when President Eisenhower briefed his successor on affairs in Southeast Asia, the departing president emphasized the situation in Laos and the grave possibility of U.S. intervention there. Not once did Eisenhower mention Vietnam. Yet Vietnam, not Laos, engulfed the presidencies of John F. Kennedy, Lyndon B. Johnson, and Richard M. Nixon. No dramatic event—no musket volleys on Lexington Green, no artillery rounds battering Fort Sumter, no Japanese Zeros shattering a quiet Sunday morning in Hawaii, no Soviet tanks rumbling across the 38th Parallel—announced to the American people that they were at war. Instead the conflict approached stealthily, yet steadily, like a guerrilla setting up an ambush. Suddenly (or so it seemed), a dozen years after the Korean War ended, the U.S. was again engaged in a war on the Asian mainland.

Riddled with ambiguities, uncertainties, and paradoxes, the Vietnam War defied easy generalizations. Pitting North Vietnam and a very substantial number of South Vietnamese against other Southerners, it was both a civil war and an international conflict involving the U.S., China, and the Soviet Union. Moreover, the international situation changed dramatically between 1964 and 1972, as the Chinese-Soviet estrangement became increasingly obvious and U.S. policy moved toward détente with both Communist superpowers. For the Vietnamese the war was unlimited, but for the major powers it remained limited: a situation fraught with

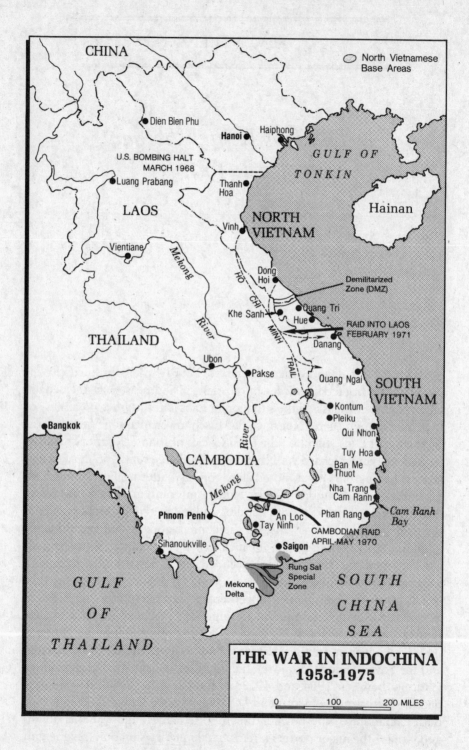

CHINA

Dien Bien Phu

Hanoi Haiphong

GULF OF TONKIN

U.S. BOMBING HALT
MARCH 1968

Luang Prabang

Thanh Hoa

LAOS

Vinh

NORTH VIETNAM

Hainan

Vientiane

Mekong River

Dong Hoi

Demilitarized Zone (DMZ)

Quang Tri

Khe Sanh Hue

THAILAND

RAID INTO LAOS
FEBRUARY 1971

Ubon

Danang

Pakse

Quang Ngai

SOUTH VIETNAM

Bangkok

Kontum
Pleiku

Qui Nhon

Mekong River

CAMBODIA

Tuy Hoa

Ban Me Thuot

Nha Trang
Cam Ranh

Mekong

Phnom Penh

An Loc
Tay Ninh

Phan Rang

Cam Ranh Bay

CAMBODIAN RAID
APRIL-MAY 1970

Sihanoukville

Saigon

Rung Sat Special Zone

SOUTH CHINA SEA

GULF OF THAILAND

Mekong Delta

North Vietnamese Base Areas

**THE WAR IN INDOCHINA
1958-1975**

0   100   200 MILES

intra-allied tensions. Foreign intervention both lengthened the war and increased its ferocity.

The fighting contained conventional and unconventional elements simultaneously, not just in different regions but sometimes in the same province. What was true in one place was often irrelevant in another because the conflict varied depending on where soldiers were stationed, when they served, and the nature of their assignments. Combat action in only ten of South Vietnam's forty-four provinces accounted for half of all American combat deaths, and each of the five northernmost provinces was in that top ten. On the other hand, few Americans died in the Mekong Delta. Combat intensity varied from one year to the next, with 1968 being the most fierce. In round numbers, 15,000 American were killed in action (KIA) from 1964 to 1967, another 15,000 in 1968, and then 15,000 more during the rest of the war. Death fell most heavily on men assigned to maneuver battalions (meaning infantry and light mechanized units), who averaged about fifteen times the KIA rate of all other forces. But at the war's height during 1968–1969, 88 percent of all servicemen were in non-combat occupational specialties.

Vietnam was always about more than the fate of that Southeast Asian country. Three presidents based their decisions as much on domestic political considerations as they did on the war's exigencies. Democrats were especially unwilling to risk being perceived as "soft" on Communism by "losing" more territory and thereby igniting a new McCarthyism. "God Almighty," said Johnson as he contemplated what would happen if Southeast Asia became Communist-dominated, "what they said about us leaving China would just be warming up, compared to what they'd say now." Policymakers also worried about international "credibility." NSC-68 asserted that Communists were "seeking to demonstrate to the free world that force and the will to use it are on the side of the Kremlin, that those who lack it are decadent and doomed." Proving that the U.S. was neither decadent nor doomed required that presidents be tough, that they not back down from a fight. Successive presidents understood the link between "manly" behavior and political legitimacy. The Kennedy administration went out of its way to project a cult of toughness, and Johnson feared that if the Communists overran South Vietnam, political opponents would claim he "was a coward. An unmanly man. A man without a spine." Nixon often insisted that neither he nor his nation would be defeated and humiliated and thus devalue his image of manly courage.

The containment policy, reinforced by a questionable "Munich analogy" and an unproven "domino theory," impelled and then sustained the intervention. One of World War II's foremost "lessons" was that democratic nations must never appease aggressors, as the British supposedly did at Munich; preventing a third world war seemed to require free nations to repel aggression anywhere it reared its ugly head. The domino theory postulated that if the Communists knocked over one nation, then its neighbors would automatically topple into the Communist camp. Containment and its corollaries caused policymakers to ignore the Communist world's diversity. Policymakers also did not understand that anticolonial movements would have roiled Asia even if Communism never existed, and they ignored poignant warnings against involvement in Southeast Asia. For example, in 1949 the JCS asserted that the "widening political consciousness and the rise of militant nationalism among the subject people cannot be reversed." Any effort to do so would be "an anti-historical act likely in the long run to create more problems than it solves and cause more damage than benefit."

Finally, as always, soldiers waged two wars, one against the enemy and the other against the environment. Vietnam had varied terrain and ever-changing (though almost always miserable) weather. In the south the densely populated Mekong Delta was flat and watery, laced with swampy jungles and the Mekong River's tributaries. Near Saigon and stretching northward for fifty miles were rolling hills covered with intermixed jungles and savannah-like grasses. Then came the southern terminus of the Truong Son Mountains, a region called the Central Highlands, a rugged 20,000 square mile plateau covered with tropical forests, bamboo, and elephant grass (which had such razor-sharp edges that soldiers believed anyone who walked through it qualified for a Purple Heart). Semi-nomadic, burn-and-plant ethnic groups called Montagnards inhabited the Highlands. Finally, South Vietnam's northernmost end featured the Truong Son Mountains, a feral region of rain forests, jagged peaks, and surging rivers. From south to north these regions corresponded to what Americans would label IV Corps Tactical Zone (IV CTZ), III CTZ, II CTZ, and I (pronounced "eye") CTZ. South Vietnam had dry and rainy seasons depending on the southwest and northeast monsoons. The best campaigning weather prevailed during the dry season from February through May; major enemy offensives in 1968, 1972, and 1975 all occurred during this window. The dry season was also a boon for the Americans, since it allowed for more air strikes, greater helicopter mobility, and more reliable movement on the roads.

The United States and Revolution in Southeast Asia

President Truman's decision in mid-1950 to intervene in Southeast Asia came against a seemingly perilous backdrop. Mao Zedong's victory in the Chinese civil war appeared to tilt the world balance of power in the Communists' favor, and fears of a Soviet threat to Western Europe fostered an almost desperate need for France to participate in NATO. But events limited France's ability to devote resources to European defense. France had ruled Vietnam, as well as Laos and Cambodia, from the midnineteenth century until the Japanese replaced them as imperial overlords during World War II. Led by Ho Chi Minh, Vietnamese nationalists (called the Viet Minh) fought against the Japanese and proclaimed an independent Democratic Republic of Vietnam (DRV) on the day Japan surrendered. But the Vietnamese desire for independence collided with France's effort to reestablish its colonial empire after World War II, resulting in the First Indochinese War, which began in 1946. Although Ho was prominent in founding the French Communist Party and the Indochinese Communist Party, he was above all else a nationalist who sought a unified, independent Vietnam. Only after democratic nations such as France and the U.S. refused to support the DRV's bid for independence did Ho turn to China and the Soviet Union for support; both extended diplomatic recognition in January 1950.

Initially the Truman administration perceived events in Vietnam as a colonial war in which France was trying to reassert its sovereignty. But because France might undermine the containment policy in Europe if the Americans refused to help it in Indochina, the U.S. supported the war effort even though many officials understood that the vast majority of Vietnamese favored Ho and that his movement contained both Communists and non-Communists. After the Korean War erupted, the U.S. commitment to France intensified, since the Indochinese and Korean battlefields seemed to be essential in stopping Chinese Communism.

After eight years of war, in 1954 France appealed to Eisenhower to save its beleaguered garrison at Dien Bien Phu, but he declined. The U.S. was not eager to undertake another Asian land war so soon after Korea. The JCS presented a foreboding picture of how difficult the task would be, and the British and other allies rebuffed the administration's effort to create a multinational rescue force. The Geneva Conference ratified France's defeat even though it gave the Viet Minh less than a complete victory. In part the Viet Minh were eager to settle the war because war-weariness afflicted their country. And China and the Soviet Union pressured them to accept a compromise because they wanted to lessen great power tensions and deprive the U.S. of an excuse to intervene more directly in Southeast Asia. The Viet Minh agreed to a temporary partition of their country along the 17th Parallel that allowed their military forces to regroup northward, with French units regrouping to the south. (Thousands of southern Viet Minh, however, did not regroup to the North, but instead stayed in the South.) The conference's Final Declaration decreed this demarcation line was *not* a political or territorial boundary, and it promised that Vietnam would be reunified through a nationwide election in 1956, which nearly everyone assumed Ho would win.

Viewing the prospect of Communist domination of Indochina as a disaster, Eisenhower sought to convert Vietnam's southern half into a non-Communist nation. One step toward establishing "South Vietnam" was SEATO, which Eisenhower hoped would deter Communist expansion despite its defects: Some of the region's foremost nations—India, Burma, Indonesia—refused to join, and it only required signatories to *consult,* not necessarily *act,* in case of aggression. Although the Geneva Accords barred Laos, Cambodia, and southern Vietnam from joining alliances, SEATO extended protection to them, providing a diplomatic façade behind which a non-Communist South Vietnam might emerge. Another important step was to nurture a South Vietnamese leader who could become his country's George Washington. Onto the stage stepped Ngo Dinh Diem, who became president of the Republic of Vietnam (South Vietnam) in 1955, after a rigged election in which he received 98.2 percent of the vote.

Diem was a courageous, selfless, and fervent anti-Communist and he knew many influential Americans, including John F. Kennedy, a Catholic senator, and Cardinal Francis Spellman, the nation's leading Catholic spokesman. Like Kennedy and Spellman, Diem was a Catholic, but he ruled a predominantly Buddhist country. Moreover, he had *not* fought either Japan or France, which made his nationalist credentials suspect compared to Ho's. Ideologically, South Vietnam was no match for the Viet Minh, who practically monopolized the nationalist mantle, vowing to rid Vietnam of European imperialists and their clones, and promising a new economic and political order based on redistributing wealth and power. An autocrat, Diem also blocked reforms urged on him by the U.S., such as opening the government to dissenting views.

Eisenhower not only increased financial aid to South Vietnam but also provided military support. The U.S. established a Military Assistance Advisory Group (MAAG). As the French withdrew, MAAG assumed responsibility for equipping and training the Vietnamese National Army, which became the nucleus for the Army of the Republic of Vietnam (ARVN). Violating the Geneva-established limits on foreign troops, the number of American advisers reached 700 by the late 1950s. Encouraged by Eisenhower, Diem refused to participate in the elections scheduled for 1956, which were never held, and imposed a measure of stability on his country, in part through authoritarian methods. Diem believed dictatorial leadership was necessary to prevent his fledgling nation from disintegrating under the stresses of its social, religious, and ethnic factionalism and the Viet Minh's potential threat. While repressing political opponents, Diem's army defeated the Binh Xuyen, Saigon's foremost criminal organization, which maintained its own pseudo-military force. Through military campaigns and CIA-financed bribery, he also vanquished or co-opted the Hoa Hao and Cao Dai, powerful religious sects that fielded their own armies.

Only then did he turn against his most dangerous adversary, those Viet Minh who had not regrouped to the North after Geneva. In 1955 the Communist Party had 60,000 members in the Mekong Delta and the Saigon region, but by the end of 1958 that number was a mere 5,000. However, suppression of the Viet Minh was successful primarily because Ho's Hanoi-based government urged southerners to engage only in *political* organization. Facing severe reconstruction problems after the First Indochina War, Communist leaders hoped to complete the Geneva process peacefully and wanted to avoid provoking the Americans into greater involvement. Suffering severe repression, the southern Viet Minh became restless with the North's passivity, and in 1956–1957 they began fighting back against the South Vietnamese police and military forces. Still, the battle remained unequal and some Communists feared the South's revolutionary flame might be extinguished.

In 1959 Ho Chi Minh and his inner circle sanctioned the use of armed force in pursuit of national liberation and unification, returned a small number of Viet Minh (known as "regroupees") who had regrouped to the north after Geneva, and established Group 559 to shuttle men and equipment along the Ho Chi Minh Trail running from North Vietnam through eastern Laos and northeastern Cambodia. In 1961 the North created the National Liberation Front (NLF), designed to attract all groups in the South but that was Communist-dominated, and organized all southern military units into the People's Liberation Armed Force (PLAF, also called the Viet Cong—which was short for Vietnamese Communist—or, more simply, the VC). To command the VC, North Vietnam established the *Trung Uong Cuc Mien Nam* (Central Office for South Vietnam, or COSVN). General Tran Van Tra commanded COSVN's Regional Military Headquarters, and in late 1963 or early 1964 Senior General Nguyen Chi Thanh, a member of the North's Politboro, became its foremost political officer and its dominant figure until his death in the summer of 1967. Although U.S. political and military leaders thought COSVN was a fixed headquarters with a Pentagon-like bureaucratic structure that could be located and destroyed, in reality it was simply a mobile, forward command post consisting of a few senior officers.

In taking these measures the North's leadership walked a tightrope. While supporting the VC, it did not want to alienate the Soviet Union, which was following a policy of "peaceful coexistence" with the West; or the Chinese, who were still recovering from their civil war and Korea. Many officials also worried that the escalating conflict detracted from rebuilding the war-torn North, and they feared a full-scale war with the U.S.

The Advisory Years in Vietnam

By the time Kennedy assumed the presidency, what had been a "problem" for Eisenhower was becoming a crisis. As the insurgency grew more aggressive, Kennedy intervened more dramatically, waging what the Communists called a "special war"—a U.S. sponsored war, but fought primarily by ARVN without direct large-scale American combat involvement. The number of advisers increased from fewer than 1,000 to 16,000 (some undertook limited combat roles) and ARVN received new weapons, including napalm, helicopters, fixed-wing aircraft, and armored personnel carriers. To oversee military activities in Vietnam, in 1962 the U.S. established Military Assistance Command, Vietnam (MACV), which absorbed MAAG. The Air Force began Operation RANCH HAND, an aerial herbicide-spraying program to deny the VC cover and to kill their crops. The U.S. also nurtured various CIA counterinsurgency initiatives, including helping the Special Forces organize Montagnards into Civilian Irregular Defense Groups, which ultimately numbered 45,000 men who defended South Vietnam's western border in the Highlands.

Equally important, the U.S. supported the Strategic Hamlet Program, a "pacification" plan South Vietnam launched in late 1961. Pacification entailed winning the peasants' "hearts and minds" by separating them from the guerrillas, providing security from VC attacks, and improving living conditions through social, economic, and political reforms. Doing all three tasks well proved a challenge throughout the war. Diem's program compelled peasants to move from scattered villages into hamlets surrounded by moats and barbed wire and, in theory, protected by local defense forces. Once inside a strategic hamlet, occupants supposedly benefited from fair elections, improved medical care, and land reform. But people resented being forced to leave ancestral lands to move into stockades; training and weaponry for local militias were rarely sufficient; promised reforms remained unfulfilled; and many officials were incompetent and corrupt. Still, strategic hamlets created problems for the VC by preventing them from having an overt presence in some hamlets and villages.

The infusion of advisers and new weapons, combined with the success of some strategic hamlets, stopped the hemorrhaging that characterized Diem's war effort from 1960 through mid-1962. Neither combatant foresaw imminent victory. ARVN won a few battles and lost others, most notably at Ap Bac in January 1963, when outnumbered VC fighting with small arms defeated ARVN forces equipped with helicopters and armored personnel carriers. MACV commander General Paul Harkins, exuding overoptimism, proclaimed Ap Bac an ARVN victory. Like his successors, he often failed to assess the battlefield accurately.

Whatever was happening on the battlefield, many U.S. leaders feared Diem would ultimately fail because they believed political and economic reforms were more important than battles. The Army's *Operations Against Irregular Forces* manual maintained that an insurgency was the "outward manifestation" of popular discontent with social and political conditions. An important corollary was that repression alone would not suffice; the only permanent solution was to rectify the underlying conditions that produced the insurgency. From the perspective of many Americans, Diem relied too heavily on repression and too little on reform. True, some officials supported Diem because, if nothing else, he imposed stability on his fractious population. But others wanted an "Americanized" South Vietnamese government, one that conducted free elections, tolerated public dissent, and adopted liberal reforms. However, in 1963 when Buddhists protested against religious restrictions, the regime responded with force, which in turn sparked widespread rioting. In one particularly gruesome incident, Diem's brother Ngo Dinh Nhu, who commanded both ARVN's special forces and the South's secret police, ordered a raid on the Xa Loi pagoda in Saigon that resulted in the death of more than thirty monks.

Convinced that authoritarianism foreclosed success, the Kennedy administration sanctioned a coup, which resulted in Diem's murder in early November 1963. The U.S. hoped new leadership would follow American guidance about democratic reforms and inspire more vigorous efforts on the battlefield and in pacification. Instead, seven more coups wracked the nation during the next year. From 1963 until 1966, Saigon's political machinations virtually paralyzed ARVN, severely hindering the war effort. With increasing support from Hanoi, the VC began making impressive gains. Sensing the demise of America's "special war," in December 1963 North Vietnam's 9th Party Plenum not only stepped up the political struggle but also ordered the insurgency to go on the offensive, hoping to win a swift victory and thereby preempting a protracted war involving the U.S. By 1964 the Communist leadership had returned approximately 44,000 regroupees to the South. In part because of a dwindling supply of regroupees, the first complete unit of northern-born regulars from the People's Army of North Vietnam (PAVN, also known as the North Vietnamese Army or NVA) entered the South in very late 1964. However, the North had refrained from interjecting large numbers of PAVN regulars into the conflict for fear of unduly provoking the Americans. By mid-1966, when approximately 267,500 U.S. military personnel were serving in South

Vietnam, only an estimated 46,300 NVA were south of the Demilitarized Zone (DMZ), which divided North and South Vietnam.

The assassin's bullet that killed Kennedy just three weeks after Diem's death left the new president, Lyndon B. Johnson, to try to salvage the war. Knowing the U.S. had no commitment to fight in Vietnam and hoping to avoid getting "tied down in a Third World War or another Korean action," he initially followed Kennedy's policy of providing money, advice, training, and equipment so the South Vietnamese could fight their own war. By early 1964 this approach was failing, and to avoid imminent defeat Johnson began "Americanizing" the war. In March 1964 he approved National Security Action Memorandum (NSAM) 288, which stated that while the U.S. hoped to maintain a non-Communist South Vietnam without using American combat forces, it was vital to take "every reasonable measure to assure success in South Vietnam." Among those measures was increasing the number of advisers to more than 23,000 and authorizing OPLAN 34A, a covert sabotage program against North Vietnam that utilized intelligence collected by destroyers on the Navy's DESOTO patrols off North Vietnam's coast. Johnson replaced Harkins as MACV commander with General William C. Westmoreland, who had held many of the Army's most visible positions, including command of the 101st Airborne Division and superintendent of West Point. Finally, the administration drafted a resolution saying the country would "use all measures, including the commitment of armed forces" to preserve South Vietnam. Given a suitable pretext, it would introduce the resolution into Congress.

Events in the Gulf of Tonkin provided the pretext. According to administration spokesmen, North Vietnam launched unprovoked assaults in international waters against the destroyer *Maddox* on August 2, and against *Maddox* and another destroyer, *C. Turner Joy,* on August 4. The administration was being deceptive: Johnson knew the first attack was a response to recent OPLAN 34A operations. And he had reason to suspect the second attack never occurred, since the initial reports were confusing and contradictory. In fact, no attack occurred on August 4; jittery sailors had misconstrued radar and sonar readings as torpedoes.

While misleading the American public, the administration threatened North Vietnam, telling Hanoi that it assumed the first attack was a mistake and so did not respond, but the second was "obviously deliberate and planned and ordered in advance," designed either to reveal the U.S. as a paper tiger or provoke it into a wider war. The North, knowing the August 2 attack was a response to sabotage operations and the second attack was fanciful, concluded the U.S. was looking for an excuse to escalate. Aside from Democratic senators Wayne Morse and Earnest Gruening, no members of Congress ferreted out the administration's fabrications. The Gulf of Tonkin Resolution, which permitted the president "to take all necessary measures to repel any armed attack against the forces of the United States and to prevent further aggression," passed the House of Representatives 416–0 and the Senate 88–2 (only Morse and Gruening dissented).

Johnson soon invoked this resolution to justify a larger war, though he was invariably less than candid about the escalatory steps he sanctioned. "Everything that we do in public, whatever we say in public, is just for the public," he told South Vietnam's president. "Together we'll make the important decisions, things that we don't want the public to know."

Bombing the Ho Chi Minh Trail and North Vietnam

Rather than withdraw life support from a dying patient and accept defeat in South Vietnam, Johnson resorted to aggressive life-saving measures because the president believed in the domino theory, wanted to maintain international credibility, fretted about a new McCarthyism, and, being a proud Texan, was not about to back down from a fight. Between late 1964 and early 1968 the U.S. waged a progressively larger, more Americanized war on five fronts: an aerial campaign to interdict the Ho Chi Minh Trail; an air war against North Vietnam; a ground war (primarily against PAVN) with an accompanying air war inside South Vietnam; a naval war; and a pacification campaign against the VC.

The air war against the Ho Chi Minh Trail and another against North Vietnam began almost simultaneously. In December 1964 a joint Air Force-Navy operation, codenamed BARREL ROLL, began attacks in the Laotian panhandle to hinder infiltration of men and supplies. However, after the spring of 1965 aircraft involved in BARREL ROLL supported anti-Communist ground forces in northern Laos, while a new operation, STEEL TIGER, targeted the trail. Beginning in 1968 another new operation, COMMANDO HUNT, superceded STEEL TIGER. Before the war ended the U.S. had dropped 3 million tons of bombs on Laos, which was about twice the tonnage dropped on Germany during World War II.

Meanwhile the air war over North Vietnam began with Operation PIERCE ARROW, a retaliatory strike following the Gulf of Tonkin incident. Two more retaliatory strikes (FLAMING DART and FLAMING DART II) occurred in February 1965, but by then the administration had approved Operation ROLLING THUNDER, a sustained bombing campaign against the North that commenced on March 2, 1965. The codename came from a line in Stephen Crane's novel *The Red Badge of Courage*: "The battle roar settled to a rolling thunder, which was a single, long explosion."

The rationale for bombing the North was to raise South Vietnam's morale, compel Hanoi to abandon the VC, and interdict the flow of men and supplies moving toward South Vietnam. While the rationale was clear, *how* to conduct the bombing generated an intense debate. Most civilian advisers preferred a gradual approach, which could become more intense if North Vietnam persisted in supporting the war. On the other hand, the armed forces preferred to hit the enemy immediately and hard. Harkening back to the bombing campaigns against Germany, the Air Force proposed a 94-target plan to destroy the North's economic centers in just sixteen days. Several assumptions, all of which proved faulty, lay behind the plan. One was that the VC could not survive without the North's substantial support, and another was that North Vietnam's fledgling industrial facilities were a treasured asset.

Johnson chose a gradual squeeze and nursed ROLLING THUNDER through three overlapping phases. Initially, interdiction dominated. Even the JCS, disappointed at Johnson's "slow squeeze" strategy, believed that attacking lines of communication would demonstrate American resolve and diminish the North's support for the VC. But North Vietnam mobilized civilian repair crews to rebuild roads and bridges, built redundancy into the transportation network, and appealed to China and the Soviet Union for more support. When trucks were too few or too vulnerable, the enemy used porters or bicycles designed to carry up to 500 pounds. Moreover, enemy forces in the South needed little external support. The VC grew much of their food, produced medicine from local plants, captured weapons and ammunition from ARVN, and bought supplies on South Vietnam's thriving black market. Those PAVN forces inside South Vietnam were light infantry with no tanks, planes, and heavy artillery requiring a complex logistical system. Total daily requirements for enemy forces in the South totaled 380 tons, of which only thirty-four tons per day came from outside sources. Seven two-and-a-half-ton trucks could fill this need. No amount of bombing could stem the trickle of supplies that needed to reach the South.

In late 1965 the JCS, despite skepticism from other agencies, determined that oil was *essential* to the North's infiltration capability. The next spring Johnson permitted the bombing to shift from interdiction to oil, beginning with attacks on small storage facilities in unpopulated areas. Then in late June bombs struck large POL (petroleum, oil, and lubricants) facilities in Hanoi and Haiphong, which had previously been off limits. The oil campaign seemed a great success: Warplanes destroyed 80 percent of the North's bulk fuel capacity. It made no difference. Never needing much fuel, North Vietnam now received more POL supplies from China and the Soviet Union, and dispersed 55-gallon fuel drums along transportation routes and in small underground storage sites. In the Jason Summer Study, a group of leading scientists examined data the administration provided and concluded that "North Vietnam has basically a subsistence agricultural economy that presents a difficult and unrewarding target system for air attack."

The oil campaign's failure, with the glaring discrepancy between the military's optimistic prestrike predictions and the pessimistic poststrike reality, convinced McNamara to search for a better option that would impair Hanoi's ability to continue supporting the war in the South. He settled upon a proposal recommended by a special study group that called for a network of manned and electronic obstacles stretching from the South China Sea across Vietnam just below the DMZ and continuing into the Laotian panhandle. Carefully positioned technical devices (such as seismic and acoustic sensors), weapons, and manned positions might substantially reduce the flow of men and supplies. Although neither MACV nor the JCS was enthusiastic about the project, in January 1967 President Johnson not only approved it but also assigned it the highest national priority. The so-called McNamara Line ran into difficulties from the start. PAVN operations disrupted construction, Laos rejected the idea of a cross-border barrier, and Westmoreland insisted that it drained manpower that could be better used in search-and-destroy missions. Still, air-delivered seismic intrusion detectors (ADSIDs) helped to pinpoint trucks moving down the Ho Chi Minh Trail, allowing U.S. warplanes to destroy a substantial number of them, and undoubtedly killing a large number of PAVN soldiers as well.

But if McNamara had lost faith in the air war against North Vietnam, the same was not true for the air chiefs. Having only marginally influenced the war by interdiction and attacking oil, they asserted that the North's real Achilles' heel was industry and electric power. Although some advisers warned Johnson that North Vietnam contained no worthy industrial target system, in the fall of 1966 he sanctioned raids on the North's only steel factory, its sole cement plant, and all its thermal power plants, though the *largest* of these only produced the kilowatts necessary for an American town of 25,000. Soon 87 percent of North Vietnam's electric-generating capacity and its few industries were in ruins, but the North compensated with thousands of generators and additional Chinese and Soviet aid. Another Jason Summer Study discovered that the bombing "had no measurable effect on Hanoi's ability to mount and support military operations in the South."

ROLLING THUNDER increasingly resembled Stephen Crane's "single, long explosion" with broader geographic scope, more sorties (the number increased fourfold between 1965 and 1968), more bombs, and expanded target lists. But political, military, and operational constraints prevented it from ever becoming the unrestricted effort the JCS advocated. Political constraints flowed from Johnson's "negative objectives"—that is, things he did not want to happen. While pursuing his positive objective of an independent, non-Communist South Vietnam, the president wanted to avoid alienating NATO allies, undermining his "Great Society" domestic social reform programs by diverting attention and money from them, or, most important, provoking large-scale Chinese or Soviet participation in the war. Paradoxically, to save ARVN the U.S. had to apply force, but to avoid a wider war it had to limit the force it applied. For the Vietnamese, of course, it was always a war without limits.

No one knew what the Chinese or Soviet threshold was for entering the war. Along with economic aid and military equipment, China sent 320,000 troops to North Vietnam between 1965 and 1969, primarily engineering units and antiaircraft troops. North Vietnam received assurances that if the Americans invaded, China would intervene, and the Communists made sure the U.S. knew of these assurances. As for the Soviets, they provided the North everything from medical supplies to jet fighters and by 1969 eclipsed China as Hanoi's primary benefactor. The Kremlin also sent 3,000 "advisers," some of whom manned antiaircraft defenses. And the U.S.S.R. threatened to send "volunteers" to the North.

At one point Johnson asked JCS Chairman Earle Wheeler and MACV Commander Westmoreland at what point the Chinese or Soviets might intervene. "That," responded the latter, "is a good question." Indeed it *was,* and the president could ill afford to ignore it. Because the enemy had two "big brothers that have more weight and people than I have," he hedged the bombing with restraints, which loosened as the war continued but never disappeared. He specified strike days, selected targets, limited the number of sorties, and for most of ROLLING THUNDER forbade attacks within thirty nautical miles of Hanoi and ten miles of Haiphong, and in a twenty-five-mile-wide buffer zone along the Chinese border. Deciding whether to hit a target, said McNamara, required balancing the target's value, the risk of pilot loss, and the possibility of widening the war. Some targets were so insignificant they were not worth the risk of lost planes and airmen; others, political leaders feared, might ignite World War III.

Another political restraint consisted of eight bombing halts, most of them only a few days but with one lasting more than a month. Because North Vietnam insisted it would not negotiate while being bombed, the administration confronted pressure to stop the bombing as a diplomatic signal that the U.S. was willing—even eager—to negotiate. The armed forces predicted—correctly—that the enemy would use these lulls, not to negotiate, but to rebuild defenses, repair damage, and hasten men and material southward.

Three military constraints limited ROLLING THUNDER. Initially, airfield construction was so slow it delayed the buildup. Even as planes arrived, they confronted a munitions shortage because the production of 500- and 750-pound bombs was insufficient until the spring of 1967. A tangled command system also hindered ROLLING THUNDER since, in a violation of the concept of unity of command, no single commander controlled theater air operations. BARREL ROLL and STEEL TIGER remained divided from ROLLING THUNDER, and the air war inside South Vietnam was another separate enterprise. In the skies over North Vietnam, "order" emerged in April 1966 when CINCPAC Admiral Ulysses S. Grant Sharp divided the target area outside South Vietnam into seven "Route Packages." General Westmoreland scheduled strikes in Route Package I, which lay immediately north of the 17th Parallel. The other six were under Sharp's command, with Route Packages II, III, IV, and VI B (including Haiphong) allotted to the Navy, and Route Packages V and VI A (including Hanoi) to the Air Force. No matter where B-52s flew, they remained SAC's responsibility. The most significant military restraint was a bombing doctrine that emphasized destroying an enemy's capability to fight by ruining its vital centers. The air chiefs devised plans to wreck the North's economy by attacking the transportation system, oil, its few factories, and electric power. But with a rudimentary transportation system and tiny industrial base, North Vietnam was not a vulnerable target for a sustained air campaign with urban-industrial targets.

Operational controls such as the weather and enemy defenses also imposed limitations. From May through August the skies were relatively cloud-free. For the rest of the year weather conditions made daylight bombing difficult, and at night planes had to use flares to see a target. Pilots found their targets less than one-third of the time. Among the bomb-carrying planes—F-105 Thunderchiefs (called "Thuds"), F-4 Phantoms, A-4 Skyhawks, and A-6 Intruders—only the Navy's Intruders had an all-weather capability, but usually no more than two squadrons (thirty-two planes) were available. North Vietnam responded by mobilizing repair crews, evacuating the cities, and adjusting work schedules to reduce vulnerability—which was fairly easy, since bombing raids followed predictable routines, and strike packages were big, obvious, and often compromised in advance by enemy spies and signals intelligence. As for active defenses, with Soviet and Chinese assistance, the North built a formidable, layered air-defense system integrating radar, antiaircraft artillery, surface-to-air missiles (SAMs), and MiG fighters.

Before ROLLING THUNDER ended on October 31, 1968, the U.S. had dropped 634,000 tons of bombs (approximately 100,000 tons more than it dropped in the Pacific theater in World War II), doing $600 million in damage and killing 52,000 civilians out of a population of 18 million. Although the enemy claimed it shot down more than 3,000 planes, the U.S.

lost "only" 938 (hundreds of others suffered damage), costing about $6 billion. In warplane losses alone it cost $10 to inflict $1 worth of damage. And between 1965 and 1968 North Vietnam received more than $2 billion in foreign aid, more than compensating for its losses.

In any event President Johnson never believed the U.S. could win the war by bombing the North. Indeed, he often privately expressed ambivalence about the entire war. "I don't think anything is going to be as bad as losing," he told McNamara in January 1965, "and I don't see any way of winning." Nonetheless, he plunged ahead.

Entering the Ground War

Shortly after authorizing ROLLING THUNDER, the president initiated an American ground war inside South Vietnam in addition to an enormous air war. The buildup began when two Marine battalions arrived at Da Nang to guard the air base there; and by June 1, 1965, the ground forces approved for Vietnam numbered 77,250. Painting a bleak picture of ARVN, Westmoreland asked for reinforcements to provide "a substantial and hard-hitting offensive capability on the ground to convince the VC that they cannot win." Johnson asked his military advisers whether the enemy could match an American buildup. The "weight of judgment," Chairman Wheeler responded, was that the enemy could not. The president also consulted the "Wise Men," a bipartisan group of elder statesmen who seconded the military in recommending an expanded war. And McNamara believed the only options were to withdraw and be humiliated, continue the same failed strategy, or expand the effort, with the latter option presenting "the best odds of the best outcome with the most acceptable cost to the United States." Dissenting voices were few, with Under Secretary of State George Ball being a notable exception. He predicted that approving Westmoreland's request would result in "a protracted war involving an open-ended commitment of U.S. forces, mounting U.S. casualties, and no assurance of a satisfactory solution, and a serious danger of escalation [involving the Chinese or Soviets] at the end of the road."

Johnson chose a bigger war. In late July he authorized 50,000 more men immediately, another 50,000 by year's end, and, implicitly, still more troops if Westmoreland needed them. Thus began the gradual increase in American military personnel inside South Vietnam that peaked at 543,400 in early 1969. By ratcheting up the war's scale and intensity, both in the skies over North Vietnam and especially inside South Vietnam, Johnson hoped to find Hanoi's breaking point. When the destruction reached the right intensity, he believed the enemy would negotiate on U.S. terms to avoid greater suffering.

"This is no longer South Vietnam's war," a White House aide wrote in a memo capturing the significance of Johnson's decision. "We are no longer advisers. The stakes are no longer South Vietnam's. We are participants. The stakes are ours—and the West's." The Communists also recognized how crucial Johnson's decision was. In their parlance, it marked the failure of America's "special war." But rather than negotiate, as Hanoi had hoped, the U.S. was escalating to what North Vietnamese strategists labeled a "limited war," sending its own forces to rescue a disintegrating ARVN. The North's gamble that it could defeat Saigon without provoking the U.S. to increase its involvement had failed. America's escalation compelled the Communists to undertake a strategic reevaluation. During centuries of intermittent warfare the Vietnamese had expelled the Chinese, thrice repelled Kublai Khan's Mongols, and then whipped France. Now confronting another powerful adversary, they sought to defeat it through *revolutionary* (or people's) war, which was neither guerrilla warfare nor conventional warfare, though it incorporated features of both. The Vietnamese embraced a "war of interlocking" in which "the regular army, militia, and guerrilla forces combine and fight together."

At the apex of the enemy's military structure was PAVN, a conventionally organized army that grew to eighteen infantry divisions and twenty independent regiments, plus armored and artillery regiments. The VC's Main Forces, organized into battalions, regiments, and even divisions, were akin to PAVN regulars, while their Local Forces consisted of companies that operated at the province level. Beneath the Main and Local forces was the "militia," which incorporated part-time guerrillas; self-defense forces that included older people, women, and youths; and secret self-defense forces that were identical to self-defense forces except they lived in hamlets controlled by South Vietnam. The Viet Cong Infrastructure (VCI) was responsible for gathering intelligence, collecting taxes, recruiting, and conducting sabotage and assassinations. Although the U.S. military considered regular forces distinct from irregulars, Communists perceived them as complementary, like yin and yang, a union of opposites with a synergistic effect that made their combined power greater than either of them alone.

The Vietnamese made no distinction between political and military struggle (*dau tranh*); the relationship between the two struggles was symbiotic, with political *dau tranh* being the anvil and military *dau tranh* the hammer. Their interweaving of political and military *dau tranh* and their willingness to forego tidy strategic formulas fascinated one American general who observed that the VC/NVA conducted "a different kind of war" in each province. One might be relatively peaceful as the enemy stressed political *dau tranh,* while simultaneously conventional warfare convulsed a neighboring province and guerrilla conflict simmered in another. To the Vietnamese no distinction existed between civilians and combatants, so they enlisted not just battle-age men but women, children, and old folks. One study concluded that women commanded 40 percent of all PLAF regiments, while children served as lookouts, built booby traps, and flung grenades.

Ho and his followers understood that a *protracted* war might be necessary: Nurturing political support took time, and a powerful adversary was not quickly defeated. But they reasoned that time was on their side since the U.S. had no compelling national interest to fight in Vietnam, while they did. Their goal was to deflate America's "aggressive will," to win a political and psychological victory that made the U.S. unwilling to continue fighting. Avoid losing long enough and inflict a drip, drip, drip of casualties, and over time the U.S. would accept defeat.

As a result of their strategic debate the Communists decided to match the U.S. escalation, with the objective of bogging their foes down in a protracted struggle and creating a stalemate that sapped American (and South Vietnamese) morale. Hanoi directed much of its effort to convincing the U.S. that its "limited war" had failed. For the U.S. to win it would have to escalate dramatically, possibly igniting a "general war" involving the Chinese or Soviets. When confronted with a choice between "general war" or de-escalation, most enemy strategists presumed America would choose the latter.

While the adversary wrestled with its strategic options, and with reinforcements on the way, Westmoreland formalized a "Concept of Operations" outlining a three-phase victory plan. Initially the U.S. and its allies would halt the losing trend by year's end. During Phase Two, spanning the first half of 1966, they would assume the offensive, destroying enemy units in high-priority areas. Phase Three entailed the enemy's nearly complete destruction by the end of 1967, thus allowing U.S. troops to begin withdrawing. As so often happened, a seemingly good plan did not withstand the test of combat.

Westmoreland's troop buildup went slowly, with one hindrance being logistical support. Problems began in the U.S., where the production base operated at a low level in 1965. As the war geared up, production lagged behind demand, partly because most strategists assumed the war would be over no later than 1967; due to the lead times involved, many manufacturers feared production would peak just as the war wound down. For some specialized items only a single source existed, and often it could not increase production fast enough to meet requirements. Labor strikes in 1967 at key industries further delayed production, and many industries considered consumer goods more profitable than supplying the military.

Critical items such as M-16A1 rifles and M-107 self-propelled gun tubes always remained in short supply.

In Vietnam the U.S. had to build a logistics infrastructure, which eventually included six deep-water ports, seventy-five tactical airfields, twenty-six hospitals, a road network, and several dozen permanent base facilities, from scratch. Despite the activation of the 1st Logistical Command in April 1965 to oversee the effort, requirements often overwhelmed the military's ability to transport, unload, and distribute supplies. Because the government kept the Military Sea Transportation Service small so that private industry could profit during wartime, MSTS employed hundreds of ships from the merchant marine and the National Defense Reserve Fleet. Mobilizing these ships took time, and even when ships were available port facilities in Vietnam were so limited, and lighters and warehouses so few, that at times dozens of ships waited at anchor to unload, accumulating demurrage charges of from $3,000 to $7,000 per day per ship. Crews frequently unloaded supplies in advance of a system to receive them, preventing the establishment of orderly management procedures. In 1965 the Army was automating its supply system, but a lack of computers and skilled technicians meant using a manual system in Vietnam, which the supply volume overwhelmed. Since MACV did not establish a theaterwide standard of living, each commander strove to give his soldiers the highest possible level of comfort; many units overordered everything from ammunition to ice cream. A tsunami of supplies, much of it resulting from duplicate requisitions and thus unneeded, poured over the port facilities. Some items that arrived in 1965 were still in depots in 1968, never having been identified and cataloged and therefore unusable. Worried that rising costs undermined support for the war, Army Chief of Staff Harold K. Johnson implored MACV to control supply expenditures.

A second factor constraining the buildup was manpower mobilization. All the Pentagon's war plans were contingent upon calling up the Reserves and National Guard, whose units included logistical and engineering skills that would have eased, though not eliminated, the logistics imbroglio. But the president refused to authorize mobilization. Doing so during Korea and the 1961 Berlin crisis elicited public outcries and sapped morale. Also, Johnson could mobilize the Reserves only by requesting a congressional resolution or declaring a national emergency. The former might provoke an acrimonious debate and make a commitment to South Vietnam more difficult. As for a national emergency, it permitted only a one-year mobilization; since Westmoreland expected the war to last longer than that, a call-up was of limited utility. Mobilizing was such a dramatic step that it might increase tensions with the Chinese and Soviets. Finally, Westmoreland assured the president he could win the war without mobilization, and the JCS concurred; when McNamara asked the chiefs in late 1966 whether they favored a Reserve call-up, each said no. For the most part the Guard and Reserves remained safe havens from the war for well-connected men, mostly white and college educated.

Johnson's decision not to mobilize meant the U.S. fought with an army of draftees and draft-inspired volunteers—60 percent of "volunteers" enlisted to avoid conscription. In general, the Coast Guard, Navy, and Air Force (the safest services) and, with some exceptions, the Marines, relied on volunteers; the Army was dependent on draftees and draft-inspired enlistees. Drafting men and converting them into soldiers took time; creating specialist units, such as engineering and communications, took even longer. Since far more men reached draft age between Korea and Vietnam than the armed forces needed, the Selective Service System had liberalized deferments and imposed exacting mental and physical standards for service, which ensured a high rejection rate. Average inductions between 1955 and 1964 were 100,000 per year, but they now rose to approximately 300,000 annually, as the armed forces expanded from 2.7 million in 1965 to 3.5 million by mid-1968. Almost 27 million men reached draft age between 1964 and 1973, and 60 percent of them escaped service. Out of the 40 percent who wore a uniform, only about a quarter (or 10 percent of the available male population) went to Vietnam, and of those approximately 20 percent (2 percent of the entire male age cohort) served in combat.

Through "manpower channeling" the draft encouraged young men into activities deemed essential for the nation's health and safety, while still providing manpower for induction. Middle- and upper-class whites regularly received deferments or took active measures to avoid service. As the chairman of a Los Angeles draft attorneys panel put it, "Any kid with money can absolutely stay out of the Army—with 100 percent certainty." They stayed in college; applied for conscientious objector status; filed appeals through lawyers, who were wildly successful because draft boards broke the law with shocking regularity; hired medical specialists who, because of the draft's physical and mental regulations, invariably found a reason for exemption; or traveled to induction centers known for leniency, such as Seattle, where examiners divided men into those with doctor's letters and those without, and exempted everyone with a letter no matter what it said. While draft *evasion* was widespread, draft *resistance* on moral principles was limited.

Despite the endemic evasion, at no time did a manpower shortage arise. Poorly educated, working-class men who lacked the skills and money to attend college or hire lawyers and doctors bore a disproportionate burden. During the five years of most active fighting, for every volunteer killed or wounded, nearly two draftees became casualties. Blacks bore an especially heavy burden. Although African-Americans comprised 11 percent of the population, they represented 20 percent of Army combat deaths from 1961 to 1966. The reasons for this were complex. For many African-Americans the military (aside from the Guard and Reserves) offered an escape from the unemployment that haunted them in civilian society. They often volunteered for elite units, such as airborne, since that conveyed higher status and provided an extra $55 dangerous duty pay per month; and with fewer opportunities outside the military, black men reenlisted at twice the rate as whites. The result was that in 1965 African-Americans comprised 31 percent of combat infantrymen. Beginning in 1967 the armed forces undertook measures to reduce black casualties, but at war's end they still comprised 15.1 percent of Army casualties and 13.7 percent of total casualties.

One program that targeted disadvantaged youth was humane in theory but flawed in execution. Project 100,000 lowered entrance standards for the poor on the assumption that military service was a means to social advancement. The armed forces would rehabilitate America's subterranean underclass by providing education and training in skills transferable to civilian life. From 1966 to 1968 Project 100,000 brought 240,000 men into the military, 41 percent of them black. Few received useful education or training, and a disproportionate number received combat-related assignments; the death rate among Project 100,000 men was twice the overall rate.

Lack of widespread international support was a third factor that, at least to a modest extent, limited the buildup. Johnson instituted a "Many Flags" program to entice other countries to reinforce ARVN and MACV. It turned out to be a "Few Flags" program. Although a political disappointment for the Johnson administration, the failure to attract more international support did not cause universal dismay, since the JCS feared that large allied units would be difficult to maintain and would complicate operations inside South Vietnam. No NATO nation supported the U.S. effort; indeed, Great Britain maintained an embassy in Hanoi throughout the war, and its merchant ships were the North's leading noncommunist traders. On the other hand, four members of SEATO—Australia, New Zealand, Thailand, and the Philippines—and South Korea sent combat formations. Though the number of foreign flags was small, that did not mean the allied contribution was insignificant. Collectively, they represented a substantial reinforcement for U.S. and South Vietnamese forces.

Washington's most stalwart ideological allies were Australia and New Zealand, who were linked to the U.S. through both SEATO and the Australia, New Zealand, United States Security Treaty (ANZUS) of 1951, which was a more binding defense treaty than SEATO. The 1st Battalion, Royal Australian Regiment arrived in the spring of 1965, reinforced by a New

Zealand artillery battery. By 1966 the Aussies had committed three battalions, or the equivalent of a full division, with supporting armor and artillery units. By far the largest allied contingent came from South Korea, ultimately consisting of the ROK Capital Division, the 9th Division, and the ROK Marine Brigade. By the end of 1965, 21,000 South Koreans were in Vietnam; a year later there were 45,000; and two years after that their numbers peaked at 50,000. In return for such a major reinforcement, the Johnson administration increased economic aid to South Korea, paid for reequipping the ROK forces that replaced the ones sent overseas, and defrayed the cost of the Koreans serving in South Vietnam. Thailand not only permitted the U.S. to construct numerous bases on its territory, which were vital in the air war over North Vietnam, but also sent an advisory mission to South Vietnam in 1966, a volunteer regiment (called the "Queen's Cobras") the next year, and the Black Panther Division in 1969. The Thai contribution peaked at about 11,600 troops in 1969–1970. In addition, Thai pilots flew secret combat missions over northern Laos and, again secretly, Thai artillery supported U.S. efforts in Laos. As for the Filipinos, in 1966 they dispatched the Philippines Civic Action Group of three engineer battalions; this force of slightly more than 2,000 served through 1968, was then reduced to about 1,600, and soon represented little more than a token force.

The allied contribution was not without cost. Out of the 372,853 South Koreans who served in Vietnam during the war, 4,687 were KIA and another 8,352 were WIA. Among the 46,852 Australians who deployed to South Vietnam, 494 were KIA and 2,398 were WIA. Although their contingent never reached more than 552, the New Zealanders still had 35 dead and 197 wounded. And 351 Thais died in combat.

As the buildup commenced, Westmoreland formulated his strategy. Believing "it was the basic objective of military operations to seek and destroy the enemy and his military resources," he adopted an attrition strategy employing firepower in "search and destroy" operations to kill and wound NVA regulars and VC Main and Local Forces. U.S. forces primarily conducted these operations far away from South Vietnam's population centers, often in remote border regions. The goal was to reach the "crossover point," when the U.S. inflicted more casualties than the enemy could replace, insuring the VC/NVA's defeat. A brigade commander captured the Army's belief that its technological superiority, mobility, and especially firepower would prevail when he wrote that an officer "spends firepower as if he is a millionaire and husbands his men's lives as if he is a pauper. . . . During search and destroy operations, commanders should look upon infantry as the principal combat reconnaissance force and supporting fire the principal destructive force." In a mirror image of MACV's strategy, Hanoi also embraced attrition. Realizing it could not defeat the

U.S. outright, it sought to inflict a steady stream of casualties—on occasion, even at substantial cost to themselves—in the belief that the mounting losses would fracture American will as it had the French. In sum, while MACV reduced the VC/NVA *physically,* the North Vietnamese focused on destroying the South Vietnamese and Americans *psychologically.*

Not everyone agreed with Westmoreland's approach. The CIA predicted the enemy would avoid major confrontations and thereby preclude a high attrition rate. The VC/NVA could control the war's pace, scope, and intensity by withdrawing into their sanctuaries in Cambodia, Laos, and north of the DMZ if they began suffering unbearable losses. Quickly disillusioned with Westmoreland's pursuit of a military victory, McNamara and other DOD officials favored a more defensive posture that would, over the long haul, frustrate the enemy's strategy. Some military officers, including Admiral Sharp, thought the VC/NVA had such a high tolerance for casualties that they would outlast the U.S. in a war of attrition. And the Marine Corps, especially Lieutenant General Victor H. Krulak, favored a counterinsurgency strategy, based on the belief that population security was crucial. Instead of pursuing the enemy's big units, the III Marine Expeditionary Force of two divisions favored Combined Action Platoons (CAPs), MEDCAP patrols, and Stingray operations. Consisting of a Marine rifle squad linked with a local militia platoon, a CAP provided a village continuous protection; wherever a CAP existed, security improved. MEDCAPs offered villagers immediate medical assistance. Small, long-range strike teams equipped with secure long-range radios were called "Stingrays"; backed by quick-reaction forces, they avoided excessive destruction and casualties, especially among civilians, by calling in air strikes and artillery with terminal guidance. The Corps viewed small-unit warfare not as a supplement to big sweeps but as an alternative to them. Westmoreland despised what he considered the Marines' timidity and pressured them to forget pacification and start killing NVA. Despite its commitment to pacification, the Corps could not avoid fighting a number of big battles along the DMZ. Fought almost exclusively against the NVA, which was concentrated in I Corps in 1966–1968, these slugfests were reminiscent of World War I combat. Nor could the Marines completely compensate for the South Vietnamese government's incompetence or the cruelties inflicted on peasants by wanton firepower.

Despite festering doubts, the first big search and destroy operation began in late 1965, resulting in the Battle of the Ia Drang Valley. During the engagement the 1st Cavalry Division (Airmobile) survived its initial combat test. Going to war on rotor blades rather than legs or wheels, the 1st Cav represented a novel concept, since it depended on helicopters for mobility, fire support, and reinforcements. Dropping out of the air into the enemy's midst, the Cav endured near-catastrophes at Landing Zone (LZ) X-Ray and at LZ Albany. Only firepower from helicopter gunships, warplanes (including the first use of B-52s in a tactical support role), and distant artillery saved the Cav. When the fighting ended the division had 305 KIA and 524 WIA, but its commander claimed victory because, according to U.S. military records, the NVA suffered 3,561 KIA and withdrew from the battlefield. Having out-killed the enemy approximately ten to one, MACV believed Ia Drang had validated the attrition strategy. As American forces expanded, Westmoreland sought to replicate the battle. Beginning in 1966 the U.S. conducted a succession of multibattalion (sometimes even multidivision) operations, each designed to find PAVN or VC units and pulverize them with unprecedented firepower. Soldiers also conducted scores of smaller missions. Repeatedly the return in enemy killed and base areas disrupted was disappointingly small when compared to the tremendous effort expended.

An essential concomitant to the ground operations was an air war, which was as fragmented as ROLLING THUNDER. Headquartered in Saigon, the 7th Air Force controlled Air Force planes based in South Vietnam and Thailand. In I Corps the Marines employed their own helicopters, as well as F-4s, A-4 Skyhawks, and A-1 Skyraiders. Carrier-based Navy planes bombed throughout South Vietnam, while the Army utilized its helicopters to move men and material and provide tactical fire support, and provided airlift capabilities with its turbo-prop and jet transports. Beginning in June 1965, SAC's B-52's conducted huge "Arc Light" strikes against enemy base camps, troop concentrations, and supply lines; the number increased from 1,538 in 1965 to 6,611 two years later. Finally, South Vietnam's Air Force supported ARVN. Unlike ROLLING THUNDER, the president imposed few restrictions on these air wars since neither the Soviets nor Chinese cared if the U.S. bombed its ally's homeland.

Before the war ended approximately 4 million tons of bombs fell on South Vietnam, which was more than four times the tonnage the U.S. dropped on the North. Yet reliable data on the bombing's effectiveness was scarce. Post-strike ground surveillance was rarely adequate; pilot reports were subjective; and dense foliage, foul weather, and the enemy's clever tactics limited visual and photo reconnaissance. Although NVA/VC prisoners often described the terrifying *psychological* impact of Arc Light strikes, the lack of evidence regarding their *physical* effects dismayed 7th Air Force's commander, General William W. Momyer. Without hard data on what the bombing did to the enemy, the number of sorties and tonnage dropped often became less than satisfactory measurements of the air war.

As it turned out, the attrition-firepower strategy was flawed. Having suffered from U.S. firepower at the Battle of the Ia Drang Valley and in several subsequent conventional engagements, the NVA/VC began avoiding large-scale confrontations. One reason why so many operations did a lot of searching, but not much destroying, is that the U.S. had a difficult time actually finding enemy forces. Simply stated, the NVA/VC refused to be found—except when they wanted to be. Approximately three-fourths of all encounters were at the enemy's choice of time, place, and duration, and more than 96 percent were with company-size or smaller units, making it difficult to inflict unbearable attrition. When Americans did encounter the enemy, the result was usually not a pitched battle but a "firefight," a brief, vicious exchange of gunfire at close range, often ignited by an enemy ambush in which the NVA/VC fought on carefully selected terrain and from well-constructed defensive positions. As the 101st Airborne's Major General Olinto Barsanti put it, "Enemy contact in the jungle usually occurs at point blank range, and more often than not the enemy will enjoy the advantages of fortifications, snipers in trees, communication trenches, and minefields to the front and flanks." Enemy positions were so craftily camouflaged that not even the gun flashes were visible. Because the opening fusillade momentarily stunned those still alive in the ambush zone, the grunts' return fire was initially sporadic. When they began fighting back in earnest, they established a defensive perimeter and called for external firepower support.

Several factors reduced the lethality of American firepower. Frequently the Communists incorporated a withdrawal phase into their plans and "retreated" before shells, bombs, and helicopter aerial rocket artillery (ARA) gunships arrived. Even if they did not withdraw, the NVA/VC rarely endured firepower's *concentrated* fury. Fearing friendly fire incidents, artillerymen and pilots did not want shells or bombs to hit close to a friendly unit. Consequently, enemy tactics emphasized "hugging" the Americans and fighting at close quarters. Vast in quantity, firepower often landed well away from U.S.—and close-by enemy—positions. Applying firepower often required a delicate choreography: To avoid hitting each other in midair, ARA, bombs, and shells struck sequentially, not simultaneously. And fire support often came only from ARA and shells. The Army called for air support in only 10 percent of its engagements, primarily because half the ground encounters lasted less than twenty minutes, and many others were too small to warrant outside assistance. Planes that diverted from preplanned missions to meet an emergency arrived over the battlefield in about twenty minutes—just as many firefights ended. If planes "scrambled" from their bases it took twice as long to reach a battle, by which time the enemy was often long gone.

Much firepower was wasted or counterproductive. In 1966 the Army fired only 15 percent of artillery rounds in direct support of troops; the rest went to "harassment and interdiction" (H&I), which meant firing into pre-

targeted areas where the enemy might (or might *not*) be. In 1967 an estimated 350,000 tons of H&I shells killed, at most, one hundred NVA/VC.
Firepower also increased *American* casualties. Shells and bombs sometimes fell short or went long, or hit the wrong target; an especially grim
friendly fire episode occurred in November 1967 near Dak To when an
artillery round fell short and a bomb hit a company command post, collectively killing forty-three men and wounding forty-five. Approximately 2
percent of shells and 5 percent of B-52 bombs were duds. The enemy was
adept at locating duds and converting them into mines and booby traps.
Although not all mines or booby traps came from dud munitions, many
did, and in just the first half of 1967 these devices killed 539 Americans
and wounded 5,532 more.

Finally, indiscriminate firepower was counterproductive because it
killed and maimed South Vietnamese citizens, destroyed their property,
and forced people to flee their farms to avoid shells, bombs, and the chemical defoliants (known as Agents Orange, Blue, White, Purple, Pink, and
Green) that poisoned the landscape. Between 1965 and 1972 more than
400,000 civilians died and at least double that number were wounded; 20
percent of the population became refuges between 1964 and 1969; and so
many fields went untended that Vietnam had to import rice. "Every artillery shell the U.S. fires in South Vietnam might kill a VC," noted one CI
expert, "but surely alienates a Vietnamese peasant."

When the NVA/VC did not want to fight or were hard pressed, they
sought safety in Cambodian or Laotian sanctuaries, slipped across the
DMZ, or hid inside the South. Since the president forbade Westmoreland
from pursuing enemy forces into Cambodia, Laos, or North Vietnam, it
meant the NVA/VC dictated the frequency and intensity of combat and
therefore had substantial control over their attrition rate. As for hiding, an
NVA/VC unit could disperse over a vast area, hiding among lowland hamlets or under the Central Highlands' triple canopy jungle. With minimal
logistical requirements units rarely stayed in one place for more than a few
days, and when on the move they exploited U.S. operational patterns. For
example, infantrymen were reluctant to operate beyond the range of artillery support. Since 105-mm howitzers had a range of no more than 10,000
meters, the enemy drew 10,000-meter circles around U.S. fire bases housing the 105s and stayed outside the circles. Or they moved at night or during foul weather, which grounded reconnaissance planes and helicopters.
And the VC/NVA excelled at military intelligence, in part because American radio communications personnel rarely took adequate security precautions. As one general confessed, "The enemy knew everything there was to
know about us," including when, where, and under what conditions the
U.S. was going to strike, which made it easy to avoid contact. The Commu-

nists were also camouflage experts: Tunnels and bunkers were so well concealed they were invisible from even a few yards away. The most famous example was at Cu Chi, where tunnels allowed the VC to live near—even directly *under*—the 25th Infantry Division's base camp.

One final way the VC/NVA avoided American firepower was to rely on "economy of force" measures, such as snipers, booby traps, mines, and standoff attacks. Snipers killed or wounded a grunt here and there, but booby traps and mines truly haunted soldiers. From January 1967 through September 1968, booby traps and mines accounted for approximately 25 percent of all soldiers and Marines who died. Frequent indirect attacks by mortars and rockets—more than 32,000 of them in 1967 and 1968—added to the fear and frustration. Rarely did these measures cost the enemy more than a few bullets, some explosives, or a dozen or so mortar rounds and rockets. In a typical example, during one month a U.S. company had four men KIA and about thirty WIA from booby traps and mines, yet not one of the grunts saw an enemy soldier or fired a single shot.

U.S. inexperience, which made combat units less effective, aided the VC/NVA in reducing the effects of American firepower. Westmoreland maintained the standard prewar one-year rotation policy (thirteen months for Marines) to spread the burden of service and to sustain morale, but the results were lowered combat proficiency and a higher casualty rate. Units endured renewed inexperience as veterans completed their tours and novices assumed their places. Not only did this exact a steep price in unit cohesion, but the newcomers fought against seasoned enemy soldiers who served for the duration. The failure to capitalize on hard-won experience had mortal consequences: Twice as many grunts died in their first six months as in the second half of their tours. Adding to the inexperience and detracting from combat effectiveness was the six-month tour for battalion commanders. Westmoreland, said an officer, "couldn't have found a better way if he had tried, of guaranteeing that our troops would be led by a bunch of amateurs." While a six-month tour helped train officers for the next war and nourished their careers, it had deadly consequences in the current conflict. According to a DOD report, in those unusual instances when battalion commanders held their position for more than six months, their units "suffered battle deaths 'in sizable skirmishes' at only two-thirds the rate of units under battalion commanders with less than six months' experience." Operations that repeatedly moved units from place to place compounded the inexperience of both grunts and officers. "Every time we were getting familiar with an area, we moved to a new one," lamented a platoon leader. "The enemy always knew the territory. We were strangers wherever we went."

Despite all their efforts the VC/NVA died in large numbers because

U.S. ground and air operations were so continuous and American firepower so awesome. But exactly how many perished? One difficulty in assessing the attrition strategy was the "body count," which became a crucial measure of progress. As with efforts to assess the air war's effectiveness, reliable data regarding enemy deaths was rarely available. Many body counts were fictitious because getting an accurate count under combat conditions was dangerous. When the NVA/VC learned that Americans scoured battlefields looking for corpses, they planted mines and booby traps, posted snipers, and set ambushes. Rather than make an actual count, officers gave estimates, which headquarters rarely questioned unless they seemed too low, in which case negotiations ensued that arbitrarily increased the number. Another factor that inflated the count was including civilian deaths, since many soldiers acted on the slogan that "If it's dead and Vietnamese, it's VC." One of the president's advisers alerted him that MACV's numbers were suspicious because "nobody seemed to know how many innocent bystanders, impressed baggage carriers and others have been included in the VC 'body counts.'" More than 60 percent of the generals who responded to a postwar survey considered the body count a fraud.

Compounding the inflated body counts was the difficulty of knowing how many VC/NVA the U.S. was fighting. In early 1967, when MACV estimated VC strength at 277,150, the CIA's special assistant for Vietnamese affairs believed that number should probably be doubled. Since field reports routinely overestimated enemy dead and MACV underestimated the number of VC, was the attrition strategy really working? Westmoreland was sure it was. In part because MACV arbitrarily removed self-defense forces, secret self-defense forces, and the infrastructure from the enemy order of battle (though it still added the dead from these categories to the body count), he calculated the VC numbered only 224,651 by the end of 1967. So great were enemy losses that Westmoreland believed he had crossed the crossover point; in a speech at the National Press Club he announced Communist hopes were bankrupt and an American victory imminent. Army Chief of Staff Harold Johnson was not so sure. "I only hope that he has not dug a hole for himself with regard to his prognostications," he wrote. "The platform of false prophets is crowded!"

The Naval War and Pacification

Although the ground war was of paramount importance, the 7th Fleet's surface ships also played a major role. Approved in March 1965, Operation MARKET TIME interdicted enemy vessels operating in South Vietnamese waters. The operation was so successful in ruining the North's maritime resupply lines that Hanoi hastened improvements to the Ho Chi

Minh Trail and developed Sihanoukville in ostensibly neutral Cambodia as a transshipment point. A complementary operation, GAME WARDEN, sought to deny enemy access to the Delta's rivers and to the Rung Sat Special Zone covering the Saigon River's mouth. Bombers, fighters, and electronic warfare planes flying from carriers based at Dixie and Yankee Stations flew ROLLING THUNDER missions, interdicted the Ho Chi Minh Trail, and supported ground operations inside South Vietnam. Organized as a task group, gunfire support ships consisted primarily of destroyers and cruisers but briefly included the battleship *New Jersey*; their guns supported ground operations along South Vietnam's 1,200-mile coastline, though after mid-1966 they concentrated on I Corps.

The Riverine Assault Force consisted of four river assault squadrons, each with several armored troop carriers and five armored gunboats (called "monitors" after their Civil War predecessors), and originally operated in the Rung Sat before expanding to the Mekong Delta. In June 1967 this "Brown Water Navy" linked up with the 9th Infantry Division to form the Mobile Riverine Force, which landed and extracted troops in the Delta's swamps and provided close gunfire support. Between 1968 and 1971 the Mobile Riverine Force played a pivotal role in SEALORDS (Southeast Asia Lake, Ocean, and Delta Strategy), which was an inland supplement to MARKET TIME's coastal blockade. The war's largest naval operation, SEALORDS erected a series of infiltration barriers along the South Vietnamese-Cambodian boundary; although it did not completely stop infiltration, it certainly complicated the enemy's efforts.

The fifth war front was the pacification campaign, which confronted many difficulties: Communist military strength in the countryside; jurisdictional disputes among competing American bureaucracies such as MACV and the U.S. Agency for International Development; weak Vietnamese local leadership; and an overemphasis on bestowing material benefits and equating them with progress in winning peasant loyalty. In essence, pacification measures preserved the status quo, though at a higher standard of living. The VC's promise to *redistribute* status and wealth had greater appeal.

Another handicap was that MACV and the JCS preferred destroying the enemy to winning hearts and minds. Summing up the Army's attitude, one general said he wanted to mesh pacification with military operations but that *"military operations would be given first priority in every case."* Considering pacification unduly defensive, Westmoreland gladly left this "other war" to ARVN, supplemented by Territorial Forces consisting of Regional Forces (RF) companies and Popular Forces (PF) platoons. The RF/PF were village- and hamlet-level militias, but they were often poorly armed, trained, and motivated, and they sometimes made arrangements with the VC to avoid violence. The division of labor between Americans and Vietnamese seemed logical because U.S. forces could best take on large VC and NVA units, it minimized the involvement of foreign troops in politically sensitive activities, and indigenous forces understood local conditions and spoke the language. Beset by poor leadership, low morale, and corruption, ARVN often victimized rather than aided peasants. Even when support for the NLF dropped as the violence escalated and the Communists' demands for taxes, labor, and recruits increased, the ebbing enthusiasm did not translate into appreciable gains for Saigon.

Two seemingly positive steps occurred in 1967. One was the establishment of Civilian Operations and Revolutionary Development Support (CORDS), which organized all civilian pacification agencies under *military* command. Heading the organization was Robert Komer, who held the rank of ambassador and the military equivalent of a three-star general, and who reported directly to Westmoreland. CORDS integrated all U.S. programs targeting South Vietnam's social and economic development, and it brought all military and civilian personnel under a single chain of command. The other apparent improvement was the Hamlet Evaluation System (HES), which rated hamlets from "secure" (A, B, and C) to "contested" (D and E) to "Viet Cong–controlled" (V). Although it had the potential to assess intangibles such as peasant loyalty, HES was better at measuring quantitative factors such as security and control. But freedom from a VC attack often masked continuing enemy influence. Many C hamlets were contested, and many D and E hamlets were probably VC-controlled. HES data showed more people coming under South Vietnam's control, but large numbers of them were refugees whose loyalty to the government was suspect. Worse, some data was as fictitious as body counts. During 1967–1968 about 20 percent of villages were never evaluated yet appeared in HES reports as relatively secure. Equally misleading, deferential villagers habitually told authorities only what they thought those officials wanted to hear.

Two and a half years of conflict along five fronts produced two unhappy results. One was a stalemated war at ever-higher levels of violence, notwithstanding Westmoreland's assertion that he had breached the crossover point. The U.S. won most (but by no means all) of the battles, but the war was no closer to an end. An official history of PAVN noted that its soldiers feared U.S. shells and bombs and "the protracted, ferocious nature of the struggle," and that at times morale flagged, but the enemy refused to break. General William E. DePuy, one of Westmoreland's foremost advisers, considered the enemy's capacity to absorb punishment the war's biggest surprise.

The second grim result was rising dissent on the American home front.

EIGHTEEN

The Lost War: Vietnam, 1968–1975

"Time is the crucial element at this stage of our involvement in Vietnam," wrote an administration insider in November 1967. "Can the tortoise of progress in Viet-Nam stay ahead of the hare of dissent at home?"

Antiwar sentiment grew against a backdrop of social instability, a foundering economy, and a rising death toll. Urban race riots so threatened social tranquility that the administration repeatedly had to use the Army and National Guard to restore order. "[M]y God," exclaimed a general who returned to the U.S. in 1969, "they've had a war in Detroit, and Baltimore, and Washington." Refusing to cut domestic programs or raise taxes significantly, the administration paid much of the war's steep price with deficit financing, resulting in inflation, soaring trade deficits, and rocketing interest rates. Even the staunchly anti-Communist *Wall Street Journal* wondered whether "the U.S. is inflicting more injury on the Communists or on itself." Caskets returning from Vietnam increased from an average of 477 per month in 1966 to 816 per month in the first half of 1967, and both military and civilian leaders understood that deaths, not antiwar protests, were sapping public support.

Within weeks after the Gulf of Tonkin Resolution in 1964, Secretary of State Dean Rusk noted that citizens were "already beginning to ask what are we supporting and why." The president had few good answers. To assert that the U.S. was supporting freedom rang hollow. In 1966 a junta headed by Generals Nguyen Cao Ky and Nguyen Van Thieu crushed the

Buddhist Struggle Movement, which demanded free elections and a civilian government, killing and wounding hundreds of civilians. In a rigged election the next year, Thieu became president and Ky vice president; the curtailment of civil liberties became one of their regime's hallmarks.

The disaffection that began as a rivulet in 1964–1965 became a full-sized river by mid-1967. It included both hawks who wanted to crush North Vietnam even if it led to war with China and the Soviet Union, and an amorphous flock of doves who wanted the U.S. out of the war. A comparative few doves engaged in active protests, while a much larger number opposed the war without publicly protesting. Even the protesters were splintered among pacifists, liberals who disliked the war on ethical and practical grounds, and "New Left" radicals who railed against capitalism and racism. Rent by fractious disputes, the antiwar movement lacked cohesive leadership and a national organization, so most protests were small and local. But a few had national significance, such as the Spring [1967] Mobilization to End the War, which attracted hundreds of thousands of people. The administration tried to quash the antiwar movement, often by illegal means. In violation of its charter prohibiting domestic surveillance, the CIA's Operation CHAOS and the FBI's Operation COINTELPRO employed illicit wiretaps and forged documents, framed protesters on drug charges, and incited violence through agents provocateur to subvert antiwar protesters.

Whether they discussed it around kitchen tables or marched in the streets, the war's dovish opponents viewed Vietnam as an anticolonial civil war with no impact on America's vital interests, feared that the war undermined social reforms and domestic stability, or questioned its morality. Those most opposed to the war included older Americans, the undereducated, women, African-Americans, and Jews. The young, the highly educated, males, whites, and Republicans most avidly supported the war. Prowar sentiment was weakest among those over fifty, strongest among those under thirty. College-educated individuals consistently favored the war more than those with a high-school education. Of course, many young, educated males who rhetorically embraced Vietnam evaded the draft. Even under a Democratic president, Republicans predominantly favored the war.

Antiwar sentiment even crept into the administration. Foremost among those who questioned the war was Robert McNamara, the first of three secretaries of defense who began as hawks and morphed into doves. Although maintaining a prowar façade, he privately expressed doubts, warning the president that there might be "a limit beyond which many Americans and much of the world will not permit the United States to go. The picture of the world's greatest superpower killing or seriously injuring 1,000 noncombatants a week, while trying to pound a tiny backward nation into submission on an issue whose merits are hotly disputed, is not a pretty one."

In the fall of 1967 the administration launched a "Success Offensive" to shore up public opinion. Johnson ordered the embassy in Saigon and military leaders to "search urgently for occasions to present sound evidence of progress in Viet Nam." They dutifully responded with a barrage of optimistic data. The "Wise Men" and Westmoreland played prominent roles. An informal, bipartisan group of senior advisers, the Wise Men included such notables as former Secretary of State Dean Acheson, U.S. Ambassador Arthur Goldberg, former ambassadors Henry Cabot Lodge and Douglas Dillon, and retired generals Omar Bradley and Matthew B. Ridgway. After receiving carefully screened briefings, which were not altogether accurate, they concluded the war was going well. Westmoreland returned to the U.S. and expressed exuberant optimism in several highly publicized appearances. The hemorrhaging eased. In July 1967, 10 percent of the population thought the U.S. was losing, 34 percent believed it was winning, and 46 percent considered the war a stalemate (10 percent had no opinion). When 1967 ended the figures were 8 percent, 51 percent, and 33 percent (8 percent still had no opinion). However, in return for increased support, the administration promised a victory soon.

The War Reaches a Climax

Unknown to those conducting the Success Offensive, Hanoi decided to launch an enormous campaign consisting of a deception phase followed by what enemy strategists called a "General Offensive–General Uprising." Because the General Offensive–General Uprising occurred during Tet, the Vietnamese Lunar New Year and Vietnam's most popular holiday, the media and policymakers in the U.S. referred to it as the Tet Offensive.

Designed to lure U.S. troops out of populated areas, the deception phase began in the fall of 1967 with a series of assaults in isolated border areas, which culminated in the siege of the Marines' Khe Sanh combat base near the Laotian border. As two NVA divisions closed in on the base, Westmoreland and President Johnson became fixated on superficial analogies between Khe Sanh and Dien Bien Phu and became determined to avoid France's fate. When the siege's final stage began on January 20, 1968, with a barrage of artillery and rocket fire, it triggered Operation NIAGARA, an aerial campaign in which bombs fell continuously, like water cascading over Niagara Falls. Before the siege ended on March 30, more than 24,000 fighter-bomber and 2,700 B-52 sorties had pulverized the NVA positions. Although MACV estimated that NVA losses were at least 10,000, primarily from the B-52 Arc Light strikes, the official body count was only 1,602. Officially, the Marines had 205 KIA and more than 1,600 WIA. ARVN rangers held Khe Sanh's southwest perimeter and suffered heavy casualties, but the exact number is unknown. In addition, between 1,000 and 1,500 Montagnards died in the fighting.

With U.S. attention riveted on the sanguinary border battles, the VC/NVA took up positions for their General Offensive—General Uprising, which began on January 30–31, 1968, and, for the first time in the war, targeted urban areas. Catching U.S. and ARVN forces by surprise, the initial attacks struck twenty-seven of forty-four provincial capitals, five of six autonomous cities, fifty-eight of 245 district towns, and more than fifty hamlets. Westmoreland was so preoccupied with Khe Sanh that he thought these attacks were a diversion and that the main assault was still coming against the combat base. And MACV's intelligence chief acknowledged that even had he known exactly what the NVA/VC were going to do, "It was so preposterous that I probably would have been unable to sell it to anybody. Why would the enemy give away its major advantage, which was its ability to be elusive and avoid heavy casualties?"

Why indeed? The offensive resulted from a strategic debate as to whether *thoi co* (the opportune moment) had arrived, when a shift from political to military *dau tranh* and from guerrilla to conventional warfare might alter the strategic balance. Those favoring aggressive action prevailed, and pre-Tet propaganda proclaimed a "new era, a real revolutionary period, and an offensive uprising period" in which success was certain. As with Johnson's Success Offensive, the Communists were promising victory, which would come not against the Americans but against the South Vietnamese, who were the Tet Offensive's foremost targets. Realizing they could not knock out the powerful Americans, enemy forces planned to attack only symbolic U.S. targets, such as its Embassy. On the other hand, enemy strategists hoped to crush ARVN in a General Offensive and overthrow the South's government by inciting an urban-based General Uprising. The primary reason for the deception battles was to lure U.S. troops out of the cities, leaving South Vietnamese forces, officials, and their clients isolated and vulnerable.

Communist leaders saw a range of possible outcomes. The worst was that the U.S., with its "limited war" strategy in tatters, would escalate again as it had done in 1965, pouring more troops into Southeast Asia and perhaps invading Laos, Cambodia, or even North Vietnam. The best outcome was an overwhelming victory, one that collapsed South Vietnam and undermined America's "aggressive will." Between the extremes was a third possibility. Although the VC/NVA won important victories, "the enemy might still have many forces supported by big bases and would continue to fight." Nothing in the Communists' planning anticipated that the offensive's most important effect might be on the American home front, both among government officials and the public at large.

The result did not precisely accord with any of Hanoi's expectations. Despite being surprised, U.S. forces reacted with incredible mobility and firepower. In some places ARVN and the Territorial Forces fought tenaciously, and the General Offensive was quickly crushed except in Saigon and Hue, where fighting raged for weeks. Tet ended when the last enemy units were driven out of Hue in late February, leaving behind a ruined city and several mass graves filled with civilian victims of Communist massacres. As for a General Uprising, although the Communists extended their control in *rural* areas and temporarily crippled pacification efforts, they misjudged the *urban* population's revolutionary temper. No urban revolts occurred. Exactly how many casualties the VC/NVA suffered is unknown, but experts estimated more than 30,000 dead or captured, with thousands more wounded. In addition, many VC operatives came out into the open for the first time, which made them vulnerable to retribution. Hanoi admitted it "had somewhat underestimated the capabilities and reactions" of U.S. and South Vietnamese troops and had set its goals too high.

From a tactical military perspective, Tet was a victory for the Americans and South Vietnamese. But war is more than tactics. Despite the "victory," the U.S. had suffered a strategic defeat, much in the same way Sioux victories at the Rosebud and Little Bighorn, or Japan's success at Pearl Harbor, presaged strategic defeat. Juxtaposed against the Success Offensive, Tet had a cataclysmic political and psychological effect in the U.S., vitiating the illusion of progress and convincing many political elites that the war could not be won at an acceptable cost.

Tet impelled the administration to reexamine the war. A potent prelude to the reassessment was the gloomy perspective of Chief of Staff Harold K. Johnson, who told the president the JCS believed "we have taken several hard knocks. The situation can get worse." Although publicly claiming victory on the basis of a huge (inflated) body count and the enemy's inability to hold a single city, Westmoreland privately questioned whether the South Vietnamese could survive another onslaught. After initially telling the president he would merely *welcome* reinforcements, he soon acknowledged that "we face a determined, highly disciplined enemy, fully mobilized to achieve a quick victory." He *needed* more troops. Dismayed by this pessimism, the president dispatched Chairman Wheeler to Saigon for a first-hand investigation, which did nothing to restore optimism. Tet "was a near run thing," he reported, and similar offensives were in the offing because the VC/NVA, despite heavy losses, had "the will and the capability to continue." Wheeler feared further reverses unless the government met Westmoreland's plea for reinforcements: 206,756 men, which would raise the number of troops in South Vietnam to 731,756. Sending them entailed further Americanizing the war, mobilizing 280,000 Reserves, and potentially ruinous expenditures.

Wheeler may not have believed the situation was as dire as he reported because he was, at least partially, using Westmoreland's reinforcement request as a ploy to rebuild the strategic reserve. But President Johnson did not know about the chairman's machinations, and Wheeler's message stunned him, especially since CIA estimates reinforced it. In this crisis atmosphere Johnson asked his new Secretary of Defense, Clark Clifford, to undertake a complete reassessment, undoubtedly expecting hawkish advice. One reason the president appointed Clifford to replace the dovish McNamara was that he was adamantly prowar. It took Clifford little time, however, to join the doves. After receiving a series of briefings the secretary concluded U.S. policy had failed "because it was based on false premises and false promises." No quick solution was imminent; more troops, guns, planes, and ships would simply increase VC/NVA casualties and cause "significantly higher" U.S. deaths, which were already exceeding the Pacific Theater's monthly KIA rate during World War II. Nor could Johnson ignore economic problems. The 206,756 reinforcements would cost $2.5 billion in 1968 and $10 billion the next year—huge expenditures, considering the faltering economy. Topping it off, an international gold crisis portended a global depression.

As the administration pondered Westmoreland's request and Clifford's reassessment, the *New York Times* revealed the purported dire need for reinforcements. The official optimism about a magnificent victory during Tet now seemed as fraudulent as the Success Offensive. Why did Westmoreland need additional forces if he had just slaughtered the VC/NVA? Perhaps seeking advice that accorded with his own instinct to fight on, Johnson assembled the Wise Men, who supported the war during the Success Offensive. One briefing they received confirmed the military's less than realistic grasp of the situation. When General DePuy claimed the enemy had lost 80,000 dead during Tet, one of the Wise Men, U.N. Ambassador Arthur Goldberg, asked what enemy troop strength was when the offensive began. No more than 240,000. What, Goldberg continued, was the ratio between killed and wounded? About three to one. If these calculations were correct, Communist casualties were 80,000 *more* than their estimated strength! With no effective enemy forces left, Goldberg wondered, why were reinforcements necessary? After all their briefings the Wise Men concluded the U.S. could "no longer do the job we set out to do in the time we have left, and we must begin to take steps to disengage."

A dismayed president addressed the nation on March 31. Taking the first steps toward de-escalation and de-Americanization of the war, Johnson announced he was curtailing the bombing over most of North Vietnam and was sending only 13,500 more men, thus capping America's commitment and confirming the Communists' hopes that the U.S. would de-escalate if its "limited war" strategy failed. With the U.S. doing less, the president insisted the South Vietnamese must do more, and the war's burden now began shifting to South Vietnam in a process later called "Vietnamization." Donning the peacemaker's mantle, Johnson offered to open negotiations, although nothing in the speech indicated he had forsaken the goal of a non-Communist South Vietnam. In a dramatic few moments at the end of the speech, Johnson also announced that he would not run for reelection. Shifting to gradual de-escalation and Vietnamization were ways to buy time for the South to become stronger and, perhaps, survive. Hanoi's strategists had been correct: The decisive moment had arrived in early 1968. The U.S. either had to escalate dramatically or begin to disengage, and now Johnson edged toward disengagement.

Tet was only the first in a series of coordinated attacks during the spring and summer. A little more than a month after Johnson's speech, the enemy launched a second offensive, called "mini Tet." Although lacking Tet's intensity, the two weeks between May 5 and May 18 were the war's most costly for the U.S., with 1,168 KIA and 2,479 so badly wounded they required hospitalization (as opposed to 1,120 dead and 1,909 hospitalized during Tet's two worst weeks). In August the NVA/VC conducted a third offensive—"mini-mini Tet." But the U.S. had conducted a number of preemptive actions, and this offensive was only a pale replica of the earlier two. Still, 308 more U.S. soldiers died.

The Tet Offensive was not a precise turning *point* because the war remained mired in a stalemate. However, though it had not collapsed, America's "aggressive will" wavered. Reinforced by the two succeeding offensives, Tet represented a turning *curve* that started the United States down the road to withdrawal and defeat.

Vietnamization

By the time the VC/NVA launched another nationwide offensive in February 1969, they had moved toward a new strategic approach, the U.S. had a new president, and MACV had a new commander. The offensive lasted six weeks, demonstrating that despite horrific losses the previous year the enemy had not disintegrated. Although the VC/NVA sent another 1,740 Americans home in caskets, they suffered severely themselves. By mid-1969 morale among the surviving VC/NVA was plummeting. Between 1969 and 1971 captured documents revealed defeatism, desertions, self-inflicted wounds (even suicides), grave supply shortages, and insufficient recruiting. PAVN's official history admitted: "Some of our cadre and soldiers became pessimistic and exhibited fear of close combat and of remaining in the battle zones." But as a senior U.S. commander remarked, although the enemy "has *really* taken a lot of punishment," the VC/NVA were tough, and they were "*used* to a hell of a problem. He *lives* in an environment where he's got a hell of a problem. . . . He's a pretty determined chap, when you get right down to it."

Whether as a result of heavy losses in four consecutive offensives, declining morale, or a matter of strategic choice (or a combination of all three), the enemy adopted a new approach. COSVN Resolutions 9 and 14, both issued in July 1969, unveiled a protracted war strategy, one in which the VC/NVA would wait for American strength to ebb before trying another major strike. Victory, the Communists now realized, would not come suddenly through a Tet-like offensive, "but in a complicated and tortuous way." Many large units pulled back to base areas in Cambodia and Laos, while those that stayed in the South broke into smaller units and employed sapper (commando) tactics and indirect attacks with mortars and rockets to conserve strength while still inflicting casualties on U.S. forces. As combat intensity declined, political *dau tranh* received heightened emphasis and the enemy attention shifted from urban to rural areas, where the goal was to disrupt a revived pacification effort. Propaganda activities increased and terrorist incidents such as assassinations and abductions rocketed from 7,566 in 1967 to 12,056 in 1970. While this strategic shift was underway, another change occurred: VC casualties were so heavy during 1968 that NVA soldiers began replacing southerners in PLAF units while the VC rebuilt its strength, a task that achieved considerable success by 1972.

The new president was Republican Richard Nixon, who hinted during the 1968 election campaign that he had a plan to end the war quickly. One option was simply to withdraw, blame the war on the Democrats, and extol Republican virtues for extricating America from the mess, even if on less than favorable terms. But, priding himself on toughness and vowing that he would not be the first president to lose a war, Nixon determined to preserve a non-Communist South Vietnam and achieve "peace with honor." However, his administration had no plan; it overestimated U.S. capabilities, underestimated enemy resolve, and had limited options because of burgeoning antiwar sentiment and the South Vietnamese government's failure to gain widespread support.

Soon after the administration assumed office, Henry Kissinger, who was Nixon's special assistant for national security affairs, issued NSSM #1, which ordered a survey of the relevant government agencies to provide a "snapshot" of the situation. Although all the agencies thought South Vietnam's situation was improving, they questioned whether it could survive even a peaceful competition with the NLF, and all agreed that the South's armed forces could not defeat the NVA/VC in the foreseeable future. The enemy could endure the current rate of attrition almost indefinitely and believed it could persist long enough to obtain a favorable negotiated settlement. Beyond these areas of agreement, MACV, CINCPAC, the JCS, and the Saigon embassy were relatively optimistic about South Vietnam's prospects. But false data underlay much of the optimism since MACV suppressed negative analyses from the field. On the other hand, the office of the secretary of defense, the CIA, and elements within the State Department were more pessimistic, believing recent pacification improvements were illusory and that enemy forces were far more numerous than the optimists thought. So far during the war, optimists had been consistently wrong.

With nothing resembling a government-wide consensus on exactly how to proceed, the president envisioned winning the war by isolating the North diplomatically and intimidating Communist leaders with military action. In what was called "linkage," Nixon promised the Soviets arms limitation talks, economic cooperation, and other benefits if they exerted pressure on North Vietnam to accept an "honorable" settlement. Kissinger explained to the Soviets that the U.S. could not accept the South's imminent demise or "a settlement that looked like a military defeat," but that the U.S. "had no objection to gradual evolution." That is, the U.S. considered the South's immediate defeat intolerable but did not object to a "decent interval" between the withdrawal of American troops and South Vietnam's collapse. Moscow, however, was never able to translate its considerable aid to North Vietnam into political influence. Nixon also tried to establish linkage through China, but the Chinese had no desire to help the Americans and exerted no more influence over the North than did the Soviets. Nonetheless, these overtures initiated a reorientation in foreign policy as the U.S. sought a détente with both Communist powers, culminating in presidential visits to Moscow and Beijing in 1972.

Nixon's faith in military power revealed itself in his "madman theory" and Operation DUCK HOOK. The threat of drastic, almost irrational, action underlay the madman theory. "I want the North Vietnamese to believe I've reached the point where I might do *anything* to stop the war," the president told an aide. "We'll just slip the word to them that 'for God's sake, you know Nixon is obsessed about Communists. We can't restrain him when he's angry—and he has his hand on the nuclear button'—and Ho Chi Minh himself will be in Paris in two days begging for peace." To give substance to this theory, Nixon ordered the NSC to plan for savage strikes. Known as DUCK HOOK within the White House (and PRUN-ING KNIFE by the military), the operation would exert maximum political and military shock. The administration alerted North Vietnam that if no substantive progress toward peace occurred by November 1, the U.S. would resort to "measures of great consequence and force."

Events undercut DUCK HOOK and the November 1 deadline. Nixon inadvertently weakened his threats by announcing the first troop withdrawals in June and then enunciating the "Nixon Doctrine" the next month, signaling a decreased military presence in Asia. Henceforth the U.S. would supply equipment and economic aid but would not readily provide troops to Asian nations, who must defend themselves. The JSC did not consider DUCK HOOK feasible because the November 1 deadline coincided with dismal weather over North Vietnam, the aerial refueling capacity to support the proposed blitz was insufficient, and additional aircraft carriers could not arrive in time. Both Secretary of Defense Melvin R. Laird and Secretary of State William P. Rogers feared a dramatic escalation might undercut the war's limited remaining support. The New Mobilization Committee to End the War initiated monthly national moratoriums on October 15, resulting in a huge antiwar protest; the next one, scheduled for November 15, promised to be even bigger. Finally, although they expected the U.S. to unleash its bombers and perhaps even invade, the North Vietnamese refused to buckle.

With linkage a failure and DUCK HOOK shelved, the administration had little choice but to embrace the policy Johnson outlined in his March 31 speech: Buy time to win the war by quelling dissent and reducing casualties, lessen the U.S. commitment, and prod South Vietnam to greater efforts on its own behalf. To achieve these goals Nixon embraced the dual policies of Vietnamization (accompanied by U.S. troop withdrawals) and pacification, occasionally undertook unexpected military actions to keep Hanoi off balance, and worked assiduously to undermine the antiwar movement.

A new MACV commander confronted the daunting task of managing the war's de-Americanization while still trying to preserve a viable South Vietnam. After the Tet Offensive, President Johnson replaced Westmoreland, who became chief of staff, with General Creighton W. Abrams. In certain ways the war remained much the same as under Westmoreland. Some large operations, indistinguishable from those under his predecessor, still occurred, and a heavy reliance on firepower remained standard fare with many units. On the other hand, Abrams adopted a "one war" strategy that reduced the overemphasis on the big-unit war; battles, he stressed, were not that important, since the true measure of success was not the body count but population security. Understanding that the Communists made no distinction among the big-unit war, pacification, and territorial security, that they operated on the proposition that "this is just one, repeat one, war," the MACV commander wanted the U.S. to confront them "simultaneously, in all areas of the conflict." Protecting the population—which would allow pacification to progress—required small patrols and ambushes rather than big units thrashing around in the jungles, limiting firepower in populated areas, building effective South Vietnamese forces, and neutralizing the VCI. Abrams admitted that most of this was "completely *undramatic*. It's just a lot of damn *drudgery*. . . . But that's what we've got to do."

The "one war" approach was partly a matter of choice but was also dictated by changed circumstances. One was the enemy's decreased aggressiveness, which permitted U.S. forces and ARVN to concentrate on population security rather than worrying about major enemy offensives. Another change occurred after the Battle for Dong Ap Bia (called "Hamburger Hill" by troops who fought there). During the ten-day slugfest in mid-May, 1969, three battalions from the 3d Brigade, 101st Airborne Division, and two battalions from ARVN's 1st Division made repeated assaults against entrenched NVA positions. Despite losing 56 KIA and 420 WIA to capture the hill, the U.S. soon abandoned the hard-won position and the NVA returned, reinforcing the public perception that the war was not just futile, but absurd. To prevent future sanguinary battles, the president insisted that MACV make reducing casualties a primary objective. A new mission statement no longer called for the enemy's defeat but instead directed MACV to provide maximum assistance to strengthening ARVN and to reducing infiltration down the Ho Chi Minh Trail. Abrams's emphasis *had to* shift from fighting the war to improving ARVN and to searching out the NVA's logistical system and destroying it.

A third change involved financially induced austerity measures, which limited Arc Light strikes, artillery fire, tactical air support, and fuel consumption. Between 1968 and 1970 the B-52 sortie rate fell from 1,800 to 1,000 per month, and H&I fire was restricted to reduce munitions consumption. Such reductions, said Abrams, were "*entirely* a budgetary motivated thing" that had nothing to do with the tactical situation. Finally, the departure of American troops transformed the war, reducing casualties, saving money, and buying more time by appeasing the antiwar movement. After the first increment of 25,000 men departed in the summer of 1969, the withdrawals became irreversible, especially since Secretary of Defense Laird, initially a hawk, soon joined McNamara and Clifford in the dovecote and pressured the president to continue the drawdown. Not only were the withdrawals faster and larger than Abrams advised, but they were also *unilateral* (North Vietnam rejected mutual withdrawals) and *total,* even though MACV had assumed the U.S. would leave a residual force, as it had done in Korea. Because of the need to undercut antiwar protests and to revive a flagging economy, Nixon felt that bringing the troops home took precedence over the South's survival. While the withdrawals scored political points at home, they reduced Hanoi's incentive to negotiate: Why sign an agreement if the U.S. was disengaging anyway, and withdrawing so quickly that, as Kissinger noted, it placed "a burden of credulity on Vietnamization"?

Negotiating and Fighting

Ideally, America's withdrawal would have marched in lockstep with the peace negotiations, a reduced level of enemy activity, and success in Vietnamization and pacification so that South Vietnam could defend itself. Then even if the Communists refused to negotiate a settlement, a reinvigorated South could confront them with the prospect of perpetual war. Virtually everyone understood that, at best, Vietnamization would be a difficult, long-term process. Kissinger believed it would *never* work, Laird thought it was a farce, and Abrams considered it a "slow surrender," nothing but a fig leaf to cover America's retreat. Unless the NVA returned to North Vietnam, MACV concluded in 1969, "there is little chance that *any* improvement in the Republic of Vietnam's Armed Forces or *any* degree of progress in pacification, no matter how significant, could justify significant reductions in U.S. forces from their present level."

Building an army even in peacetime is difficult. Doing it in wartime compounds the difficulty. ARVN began with systemic problems, foremost among them being leadership. Abrams correctly asserted that ARVN was "not going to be *any* better, no matter *what* we do, no matter what we *give* them in the way of equipment, and no matter *what* we do with them in the way of training, unless they've got the kind of leadership that'll take a hold of it and carry it." But solid, aggressive leadership was scarce because President Thieu, always fearing a coup, selected commanders based on political loyalty, not combat ability. Most of his officers had *not* joined the struggle for independence against France, or if they had, they served *with* the French. Because the commissioning system relied on formal education and few men received secondary schooling, the majority of the population was excluded from becoming officers. Many of the educated, urban elite who did serve as officers had trouble relating to their peasant soldiers, and they engaged in corrupt activities, including using their units to protect criminals, hiring soldiers out as laborers, selling promotions, misusing American supplies, and trading with the enemy. MACV urged the South to commission qualified men from the enlisted ranks and replace incompetent officers, but Thieu rarely took action. As of late 1970 a senior American official rated only *one* South Vietnamese general as "fully competent."

Even if South Vietnam had competent officers, they served in a dysfunctional system. As in the U.S., the draft system contained many exemptions and deferments. Bribery to avoid being conscripted was so widespread that large numbers of men avoided service. Among those who did serve, 65 percent were conscripts pressed into service. Few believed Saigon could defeat the VC/NVA, and desertion was a chronic problem. ARVN lost about one-third of its strength annually through desertion, though this figure is somewhat misleading because many "deserters" joined RF or PF units closer to their homes, and some men left during the planting and harvesting seasons to help out on the farm and then voluntarily returned. Still, desertion was a disruption at best, a serious manpower drain at worst. Soldiers endured poor food and housing, low pay, medical malpractice, and inadequate training, all of which led them to resent their government. Another problem was that the government recruited, trained, and based almost all ARVN units territorially. Specific units occupied permanent installations where their families joined them, which tied those units to those locales. Soldiers stationed in a particular location fought valiantly to defend their families. But if the government ordered those troops outside their region, the unit could disintegrate as men deserted to stay close to their wives, children, and parents. Keeping their families safe trumped national survival.

With U.S. troop departures underway, the effort to expand and improve South Vietnam's military and security forces began. ARVN's expansion was impressive, increasing from 380,000 in 1968 to 416,000 two years later, primarily through tightening deferments, expanding the draft age, and mandating that soldiers serve for the duration. Both the South Vietnamese navy and air force approximately doubled in size between 1968 and 1970. The Territorials also expanded, going from 393,000 in 1968 to 453,000 in 1970. The regular forces and the RF/PF received upgraded equipment, including M-16 rifles and M-79 grenade launchers, and the regulars benefited from infusions of artillery, tanks, helicopters, aircraft, and ships. By 1971 the National Police numbered 114,000, while a newly created People's Self Defense Force (PSDF), which was an unpaid, lightly armed militia that included men, women, elders, and children, *supposedly* contained 4,429,000 members. These disparate forces did not work together easily. "The regular forces look down on the Territorial Forces," noted Abrams, "and the Territorial Forces look down on the Popular Self Defense Forces, and everybody looks down on the police."

Captured documents revealed that Vietnamization worried the VC/NVA, especially the upgrading of the Territorials and the PSDF, both of which provided local security. The crucial question, however, was whether quantitative growth equaled qualitative improvements, and that could not be answered until ARVN and the Territorials faced a test in major combat. As Abrams asked CORDS director William Colby, if ARVN could *not* meet the challenges that lay ahead, "*Then* where are we?" "Then," responded Colby, "we're in a hell of a state."

Vietnamization's concomitant was pacification, which assumed heightened significance, as indicated by a three-month Accelerated Pacification Campaign (APC) that began on November 1, 1968. Since it seemed to be reasonably effective, it continued for three years. Because the VC endured heavy casualties during Tet and the South Vietnamese abandoned hamlets and villages to defend the cities, a vacuum existed in rural areas. Under the APC the government returned to the countryside and the surviving VC apparatus suffered, particularly since MACV shifted much of its military effort to support pacification directly. A combined U.S.–South Vietnamese Phoenix Program targeted the VCI. Although assassinations did occur, many of the targeted individuals died when they fought back rather than surrender, and even more were captured. Others "rallied"—that is, changed sides via a *Chieu Hoi* (Open Arms) program that offered defectors a monetary reward and lenient treatment. For the most part these two programs neutralized low-level operatives. Large numbers of hard-core VCI remained unidentified and thus the infrastructure survived intact. In some places the VC cadre conducted a "Phoenix in reverse," assassinating or abducting more than 50,000 village and hamlet officials and PF leaders between 1969 and 1972. MACV complained about the "continued inability to develop a detailed understanding of the Viet Cong capacity to evade, withdraw, and escape at will" after terrorist incidents or following attacks. Nonetheless, Abrams thought it was "far more significant that we neutralize one thousand of these guerrillas and infrastructure than kill 10,000 North Vietnamese soldiers."

While hunting down the VCI and welcoming defectors, the U.S. and South Vietnam initiated civic action campaigns to enhance the government's image and to improve rural living conditions, which officials assumed would alleviate the insurgency's underlying causes. The U.S. tallied an impressive number of roads, bridges, schools, playgrounds, and dispensaries built or rebuilt, of wells dug, of food distributed, and of health services rendered. Then in 1970 Thieu's administration finally addressed the contentious land reform issue, passing a Land-to-the-Tiller Law that distributed several million acres to hundreds of thousands of tenant farmers. The perception of the government as exclusively the protector of the rich and powerful blurred, as at least some previously landless farmers now had a stake in Theiu's regime.

Very much *wanting* pacification to succeed, many officials discerned progress, and to some extent enemy observers and HES evaluations supported that optimism. "Our side," wrote an NVA colonel, "suffered seriously from the subsequent pacification plans dreamed up by the Americans, such as Operation Phoenix and the Chieu Hoi campaign." A postwar Communist study confessed that South Vietnam's expanding regular and security forces and the new pacification programs "created immeasurable difficulties and complications for our armed forces and civilian population." HES scores indicated that South Vietnam controlled some 90 percent of the countryside by 1972. But many people living in "secure" villages were there only to find shelter from American firepower; ARVN's mistreatment of the population continued; many government officials remained incompetent and corrupt; and HES data was still subjective, falsified, or inflated because of command pressure for positive results. Perhaps most important, physical control did not necessarily equate with heartfelt allegiance.

Perhaps nothing demonstrated pacification's limitations more than the 1971 election, when Thieu's government was unwilling to risk an honest plebiscite. Assisted by the American ambassador and the CIA, Thieu rigged it so that he ran unopposed. The U.S., which wanted at least the appearance of a genuine election, offered a candidate a $3 million bribe to remain in the race. The police threatened to arrest citizens who tried to vote for anyone but Thieu, opposition newspapers were shut down, and province chiefs received orders to do whatever was necessary to ensure victory. "It was a ridiculous election," as Thieu's vice president admitted, "just like a Communist one."

In short, a weakened NLF did not automatically translate into a stronger, more popular South Vietnamese government. Until the South stood alone against its foes, no one knew whether pacification gains were permanent or fragile and reversible.

Fighting for a Decent Interval

To buy time for Vietnamization and pacification, to prevent any large-scale VC/NVA action that might impede America's retreat, and to put pressure on Hanoi to negotiate an "honorable" settlement, the president ordered a number of unexpected actions: The secret bombing of Cambodia, a ground incursion into that country in 1970, a raid into Laos in 1971, and a ferocious aerial response to the enemy's Easter Offensive of 1972.

Both the Communists and the U.S. had routinely violated Cambodian neutrality, the former by maintaining sanctuaries there and the latter by cross-border raiding under a program called DANIEL BOONE (later renamed SALEM HOUSE). When the JCS assured Nixon that the U.S. could destroy COSVN and degrade Communist capabilities throughout III and IV Corps by striking Cambodia, he went further, ordering secret B-52 strikes against enemy positions. He hoped the raids would also send a madman message to Hanoi that this president was not bound by the self-imposed restraints that limited his predecessor. Under what became Operation MENU, the bombing began on March 18, 1969, unknown to the public, Congress, the Secretary of the Air Force, and the Air Force chief of staff. Even the military's normally classified reports contained false data indicating the raids struck targets inside South Vietnam. Despite Nixon's zeal to conceal MENU, a *New York Times* report exposed it a few months after it began.

When the operation ended in late May 1970, the big bombers had flown 3,875 sorties. As was true of most B-52 strikes inside South Vietnam, the damage inside Cambodia was difficult to assess, but the bombing had clearly *not* eliminated COSVN or the sanctuaries. Consequently Nixon sanctioned a ground invasion to finish the job and to reinforce his madman image. In March 1970 the pro-American Cambodian prime minister, General Lon Nol, deposed his country's head of state, Prince Norodom Sihanouk. Favoring vigorous action against the VC/NVA, Nol ordered the Cambodian army to attack them in three border provinces and closed Sihanoukville. This port city had been a major Communist supply point from which food and equipment moved along the Sihanoukville Trail to positions adjacent to IV and III CTZs. Ostensibly with General Nol's consent, in late March the South Vietnamese raided Communist bases in Cambodia's Parrot's Beak region. Responding to these threats, as well as to the MENU bombing, the VC/NVA, and an indigenous Communist Khmer Rouge movement headed by Pol Pot, counterattacked and soon threatened Cambodia's capital of Phnom Penh. Despite opposition from Laird and Rogers, Nixon ordered 50,000 ARVN into the Parrot's Beak and 30,000 U.S. forces into an area called the Fishhook, hoping to relieve pressure on Cambodia's army, destroy the sanctuaries, and capture COSVN.

Crossing the border on April 29–30, the raiders did not find COSVN and in most cases the VC/NVA fled rather than fight, though pitched battles occurred at a base area nicknamed "The City" and at the towns of Krek, Mimot, and Snoul. Despite perennial problems with timid leadership, ineffective artillery fire, and faulty communications, in a few places ARVN fought aggressively, which seemed promising for Vietnamization. The U.S. and South Vietnamese captured an impressive array of food and equipment, though some of the weapons were obsolete. The CIA estimated the Communists could replace their losses in three months. Other agencies believed the losses crippled enemy capabilities for as much as a year. In one sense the sheer size of the supply caches was dismaying: A year of MENU bombing and COMMANDO HUNT operations against the Ho Chi Minh Trail had not prevented the depots from being stuffed to overflowing.

The incursion had three negative effects. First, it converted the Vietnam War into an Indochinese War by engulfing Cambodia in the ground war, ultimately resulting in a holocaust that killed up to 2 million Cambodians after the demonic Pol Pot assumed power. Second, North Vietnam did not capitulate to Nixon's madman gambit by offering concessions but instead hardened its negotiating stance in large part because of the third negative consequence: The operation reenergized antiwar opposition in the U.S., which had become quiescent when it appeared Nixon was liquidating the war through troop withdrawals, Vietnamization, and pacification. As frustration mounted that the president was now widening rather than ending the war, renewed demonstrations erupted, and not just in the streets. Secretary of the Army Stanley Resor explained to MACV that "there were great delegations of people, some of them very substantial people, coming down to call on their congressmen to do something about getting out [of Vietnam] faster."

To MACV's dismay, antiwar sentiment compelled Nixon to limit the U.S. penetration to thirty kilometers and to announce a June 30 deadline for withdrawing U.S. ground forces from Cambodia. Congress went further, passing a bill in late 1970 containing the Cooper-Church Amendment, which prohibited all future U.S. ground (but not air) activity in Cambodia and Laos. In addition, the Senate repealed the Gulf of Tonkin Resolution, though the president continued the war by relying on his authority as commander in chief. Thieu did not feel bound by the limitations imposed on U.S. forces. Although ARVN suffered from poor leadership and insufficient battlefield aggressiveness, it penetrated twice as far as the Americans and operated in Cambodia for the next several years, supported by U.S. artillery, B-52 strikes, and tactical air support.

The Cambodian incursion, claimed the president, was "the most decisive action in terms of damaging the enemy's ability to wage effective warfare that has occurred in this war to date." This was an exaggeration. Abrams thought the operation, at best, caused the enemy "some temporary inconvenience." Another general considered it a disaster that fatally wounded South Vietnam because of the widespread unrest it generated on the American home front. The enemy agreed. As a high-level Communist leader put it, "Nixon paid dearly for our temporary discomfiture by sustaining major political losses."

Closing Sihanoukville and disrupting the VC/NVA's Cambodian sanctuaries reflected Abrams's emphasis on attacking enemy logistics to disrupt Hanoi's plans, to buy time for Vietnamization and pacification, and to prevent a debacle among the dwindling number of U.S. forces remaining in South Vietnam. With Sihanoukville no longer available and MARKET TIME frustrating seaborne supply efforts, the Communists began urgent measures to improve and defend the Ho Chi Minh Trail. More and more trucks provided by Beijing and Moscow moved on a steadily improving road network. Repair facilities proliferated, bomb damage was quickly repaired, a newly constructed pipeline transported fuel, and antiaircraft and SAM batteries shifted southward to protect the indispensable Trail and pipeline.

At the heart of the interdiction effort was COMMANDO HUNT, which began in November 1968 and ended in April 1972. Operation FREEDOM DEAL, a new name for the Cambodian bombing that was now conducted openly, complemented COMMANDO HUNT by attacking the Trail in northeastern Cambodia. Arc light strikes, fighter-bombers, and night-flying AC-130 Spectre gunships struck at reinforcements, trucks, supply caches, and enemy defenses. Converted cargo planes armed with rockets and 20-mm automatic cannons and equipped with a vehicle ignition detector codenamed BLACK CROW, the AC-130s initially killed many truck drivers in their cabs and caused others to abandon their vehicles as soon as they heard them overhead. But a U.S. aeronautics magazine inadvertently alerted the Communists to BLACK CROW, and soon truck drivers were wrapping their ignition systems in aluminum foil to suppress emissions.

In the midst of COMMANDO HUNT Nixon sanctioned another effort to disrupt the Trail and remind Hanoi that he did not play by Johnson's self-imposed rules. While ARVN was still engaged in Cambodia, it invaded Laos on February 8, 1971, in Operation LAM SON 719. The goal was Base Area 604 centered on Tchepone, a key logistics node. Intelligence indicated NVA infantry, armor, artillery, and air defenses were concentrated there, that the jungle-covered area was ill-suited for helicopter warfare, and that Hanoi *knew* about the invasion weeks in advance. Equally problematic, because of the Cooper-Church Amendment, *for the first time* no American troops or advisers would accompany ARVN, though it would receive support from U.S. helicopters, planes, and artillery—and from hard fighting on the Vietnamese side of the border in I Corps. In essence, U.S. forces kicked open the door for ARVN's invasion, resulting in 215 Americans KIA and another 1,100 WIA during the first four months of 1971.

Despite the potential pitfalls, Nixon let the operation continue, thus widening the war a second time by invading a country that had been off limits during the Johnson administration. President Thieu committed 20,000 men to LAM SON 719. Some of his best units participated, including the ARVN 1st Division, the 1st Armored Brigade, three ranger battalions, and most of the elite airborne and marine units from the strategic reserve. At a dreadful cost in men, ordnance, and supplies, the NVA attacked day and night, keeping continuous pressure on ARVN that sent it reeling in retreat. American intelligence estimated the Communists committed approximately 110 tanks to the battle and lost seventy-five of them. Sixteen of the thirty-three NVA maneuver battalions involved in the fighting were complete losses. The South Vietnamese had thus fought tenaciously at times, but not often enough. Pictures showed panic-stricken ARVN soldiers fleeing by hanging on to helicopter skids, and even some of the South's elite units collapsed. The last ARVN troops crossed back into South Vietnam on March 24. They left behind thirty-seven of their sixty-two tanks, ninety-eight of their 162 armored personnel carriers, and many of their dead. "They knew they'd been whipped," observed a Marine general, "and they acted like they had been whipped."

Only American air power and artillery saved ARVN from catastrophe. Though rain and fog often grounded them and enemy defenses were deadly, tactical fighters still dropped 20,000 tons of napalm and bombs, B-52s added 32,000 tons, Hercules transports dropped twenty-five 15,000-pound air-fuel bombs, Air Force gunships patrolled the night skies, and U.S. helicopters flew 160,000 sorties. Tucked along the border were eighteen U.S. Army 155-mm howitzers, sixteen 175-mm guns, and eight 8-inch howitzers. As ARVN's situation in Laos deteriorated, it also suffered defeats at Dambe, Snoul, and Krek in Cambodia, despite U.S. air and artillery support. Although the debacles in Cambodia involved more forces on both sides than LAM SON 719, they received less publicity.

In what one general considered "an Orwellian untruth of boggling proportions," the president did what he had done after the less than successful Cambodian incursion: Proclaimed LAM SON 719 a victory, asserting that it proved "Vietnamization has succeeded." From the start Nixon sought to portray events in Laos in a positive light, telling Kissinger, "I can't emphasize this too strongly; I don't care what happened there, it's a win." In fact, after two years of Vietnamization, ARVN had suffered another setback. This did not necessarily mean the program would *ultimately* fail, but it created profound doubts about its progress and in doing so weakened the U.S. negotiating position. The president understood this, for privately he complained about ARVN's poor performance. LAM SON 719 had two other negative consequences. First, it caused no lasting damage to the enemy's Laotian transportation network. According to a MACV briefing, by early April the NVA were "right back in there again, balls out." Finally, the operation also sparked renewed antiwar demonstrations, sowing concern among Republicans about the president's reelection. On the positive side, it may have delayed an NVA offensive in I Corps, thus buying time for both South Vietnam and the orderly redeployment of American forces.

Despite the Cambodian incursion, COMMANDO HUNT and FREEDOM DEAL, and LAM SON 719, the North met its supply and reinforcement goals. NVA Colonel Bui Tin explained how: "We put so much in at the top of the Trail that enough men and weapons to prolong the war always came out at the bottom." This was a callous approach, costly in men and material. But it worked, as the Easter Offensive revealed.

Beginning on March 30, 1972, North Vietnam's Easter Offensive was a three-pronged campaign, one prong coming across the DMZ aimed at Quang Tri City, another directed from Kontum toward the coast in II Corps, and a third surging across the Cambodian border toward An Loc in III Corps. The assaults revealed Hanoi's decision to reverse the protracted-war, economy-of-force strategy it had followed for the previous few years and to escalate directly to military *dau tranh*'s conventional warfare phase. In a remarkably short time the NVA had transformed itself from a light-infantry force into a Soviet-style mechanized army. In the Easter Offensive it employed 1,200 Soviet-made tanks and a huge artillery array in support of fourteen of its fifteen divisions, most of which had previously remained outside South Vietnam. The rebuilt VC supported the major thrusts with hundreds of small attacks in urban areas and the Mekong Delta. Within a week after the offensive began, Abrams realized the enemy had "committed every *goddamn* thing he owns!"

The offensive's primary architects were the minister of defense, General Vo Nguyen Giap, one of the Viet Minh's founders, who remained the North's foremost strategist for most of the war; and his chief of staff, General Van Tien Dung. They hoped for a knockout punch to defeat Vietnamization, gain a decisive victory in 1972, and force the U.S. to negotiate from a weakened position. Since fewer than 70,000 Americans remained in Vietnam, the NVA concentrated against ARVN, its elite units weakened by LAM SON 719. A crushing success seemed likely. However, enemy strategists realized they might have to settle for less, such as merely improving their position by creating enclaves inside the South and by weakening pacification.

Because MACV intelligence misjudged the offensive's timing, size, and location, the offensive caught ARVN and the Nixon administration by surprise. After all, it seemed foolhardy for the North to attack in 1972, when all the Americans would soon be gone. ARVN quickly neared collapse. Fearing he could not win reelection if South Vietnam fell and that a humiliating defeat might hamper relations with China and the Soviet Union, Nixon responded aggressively. Domestic antiwar sentiment made reintroducing ground troops impossible, so he assembled an aerial armada. The previous summer he had shouted that he did not intend to "go out whimpering"— that he was going to "bomb the livin' bejesus out of 'em" and that he wanted to "level the goddamn country!" Now he had an opportunity to do just that, to infuse life into the madman strategy and DUCK HOOK. The number of B-52s on Guam rose from 47 to 210, the number of F-4s reached 374, and the carriers on Yankee Station tripled from two to six. Unleashing this formidable force, Nixon believed, would shatter the invasion, save Vietnamization and pacification, and compel Hanoi to negotiate a favorable settlement. When B-52s struck Haiphong for the first time during the war on April 16, the administration hoped it sent "a warning that things might get out of hand if the offensive did not stop."

The North did not cave in to the threats. But this time an iron fist lay clenched behind them. Even as air power hammered the NVA in the South, on May 8 the president announced the mining of Haiphong (other major ports and inland waterways were also soon mined), a naval blockade, and Operation LINEBACKER I, which was a sustained bombing campaign against the North. Urging his military advisers to "recommend action which is very *strong, threatening,* and *effective,*" he intended "to stop at nothing to bring the enemy to his knees." By the time LINEBACKER I ended on October 23, 155,548 tons of bombs had fallen on North Vietnam. Yet in his May 8 speech Nixon also issued an "ultimatum" that really spelled out terms for *America's* withdrawal. All the U.S. wanted was the return of its prisoners of war and an internationally supervised ceasefire. Once North Vietnam met these conditions, the U.S. would "stop all acts of force throughout Indochina, and at that time we will proceed with a complete withdrawal of all American forces from Vietnam within four months."

In some ways LINEBACKER I resembled the original ROLLING THUNDER. The new air campaign retained the Route Packages and lacked an overall commander; hit targets in the Chinese buffer zone and inside restrictive zones around Hanoi and Haiphong only with JCS approval; confronted a substantial array of enemy defenses; and experienced disruptions caused by bad weather. LINEBACKER I also differed from ROLLING THUNDER in significant ways that made it comparatively more successful. Nixon's détente with the Soviets and Chinese reduced the chances of igniting World War III, thus allowing him to employ air power in ways Johnson never dared to try—for example, sending B-52s against the enemy heartland. By launching conventional assaults the Communists developed huge logistical requirements; however, the mining, blockade, and bombing damaged their essential resupply efforts by sea and railroads.

New weapons enhanced the bombing, especially "smart bombs," which were laser-guided and electro-optically guided munitions that struck targets with unparalleled accuracy. A few planes now achieved greater results than ROLLING THUNDER's large strike forces.

Most important, LINEBACKER I supported a more limited policy objective than ROLLING THUNDER. As often happened in warfare, the losing side reduced its war aims. Johnson sought an independent, non-Communist South Vietnam; Nixon's objective was an independent South Vietnam that did not collapse immediately after America's withdrawal. Kissinger told the Soviet ambassador that if renewed war broke out after the U.S. withdrawal, "that conflict will no longer be an American affair; it will be an affair of the Vietnamese themselves, because the Americans will have left Vietnam." He relayed a similar message to China, saying all the U.S. wanted was for the South to survive for a "decent interval," which he defined as five years. Nixon contemplated using air power to insure the South's existence until at least 1977, when his second term would end, thus removing any imputation that he lost the war.

With the enemy's conventional forces more vulnerable to aerial destruction than their guerrilla operations had been, and with the NVA experiencing untold difficulty in waging combined-arms warfare for the first time in its history, the Easter Offensive soon sputtered. The NVA, said Abrams, were "losing tanks like he didn't care about having any more, *and* people, *and* artillery, *and* equipment." After suffering such a disaster, the NVA would not soon launch another offensive. Moreover, despite fearsome losses of men and equipment, ARVN survived under a protective airpower umbrella, and LINEBACKER I pummeled the North. Although Nixon's ferocious response shocked Communist leaders and the offensive failed to deliver a knockout punch, the VC/NVA nonetheless attained advantages that pointed toward ultimate success. Counterbalancing the destruction LINEBACKER I did to the North was the destruction in South Vietnam, where combat reduced cities to rubble and created more than a million new refugees. The NVA established control over a belt of strategic terrain running from the DMZ along the Laotian and Cambodian borders to the northern Delta, thus strengthening its grip on the Central Highlands, improving the security of its sanctuaries and the Ho Chi Minh Trail, and gaining essential territory for launching subsequent military actions.

ARVN had barely escaped defeat, as Hanoi, MACV, and many South Vietnamese understood. To the Communists the offensive signaled Vietnamization's failure because the South still could not stand on its own. While praising a few ARVN units that fought well, Abrams and other high-ranking Americans admitted Vietnamization's prospects were precarious, and that only a torrent of bombs averted a catastrophe by compensating for ARVN's feeble fighting spirit. "*Equipment* is not what you need," Abrams emphasized to General Cao Van Vien, chief of the Joint General Staff. "You need men that will *fight*. And you need *officers* that will fight and lead the men." Neither the men nor the officers seemed in the offing anytime soon. As for the South Vietnamese, a soldier recalled the sense of impending doom: "We all believed we had fought heroically in Quang Tri, but that our best was not good enough."

Even though the Easter Offensive accomplished less than enemy strategists ideally sought, it also revealed that Vietnamization and pacification had not yet created a stout-hearted South Vietnamese nationalism that could match the Communists. And time was swiftly running out.

An Army in Distress

Throughout the war American soldiers committed a number of war crimes, the most heinous being the slaughter of civilians at My Lai and the neighboring hamlet of Co Luy on March 16, 1968. Under the command of Lieutenant William L. Calley, the 1st Platoon of Company C, Task Force Barker, 11th Infantry Brigade, Americal Division, massacred approximately 500 women, the elderly, boys and girls, and infants in My Lai. Some of the women were raped and sodomized before being killed in exceptionally inhumane ways. At Co Luy, the 1st Platoon of Company B committed a similar crime, though on a lesser scale, since the grunts murdered "only" ninety-seven civilians. The lone American to act honorably during the day was Warrant Officer Hugh C. Thompson Jr., a reconnaissance helicopter pilot. Seeing the slaughter unfolding, he landed his helicopter to save a group of Vietnamese civilians from soldiers advancing upon them with murderous intent. When he returned to base, Thompson informed his superiors of the massacre. Soon numerous officers knew something had gone terribly wrong at My Lai and Co Luy, but they conspired to cover up the massacre until late 1969, when the war crime finally became public knowledge. As a result, the Army undertook two investigations, one public, the other secret. Headed by Lieutenant General William R. Peers, a formal board of inquiry confirmed the massacre's magnitude and the cover-up. But witnesses lied or had selective memories, and documents had been destroyed. Everyone escaped punishment for the murders and the cover-up except for Calley, who was convicted of killing twenty-two unarmed civilians and sentenced to life imprisonment. In late 1974 Nixon paroled him. "Every unit of brigade size has its My Lai hidden some place," alleged Colonel Oren K. Henderson, an officer charged (but not convicted) in the cover-up. That may not have been an exaggeration. Along with the

Peers investigation, the Army established a secret "Vietnam War Crimes Working Group" that amassed 9,000 pages of evidence implicating Americans in rapes, torture, murder, and massacres. The Working Group, whose records were secret until 1994, substantiated more than 300 cases, while another 500 allegations could not be proven. However, many of the "investigations" were perfunctory. For example, one case that landed on the discard pile contained allegations about a Tiger Force reconnaissance unit from the 1st Battalion, 327th Infantry, 101st Airborne Division that murdered women and children in Quang Ngai Province in 1967. As was finally exposed in 2003, the Tiger Force unit had indeed killed at least 120 civilians. According to the officers who helped compile the records, even the 800 proven and unsubstantiated cases combined represented only a small fraction of the Army's war crimes. The Marines also committed atrocities, most notably in Son Thang where a five-man "killer team" slaughtered sixteen women and children, including a twenty-year-old blind woman and ten boys and girls under the age of thirteen.

To say that wars—all wars—spawn atrocities and to affirm that the vast majority of Americans served faithfully and bravely does not remove the stain that war crimes left on the American record.

As the withdrawal accelerated, the disciplinary problems revealed by atrocities took new directions among units remaining in Vietnam. A hairline crack in the Army's morale and discipline that first appeared in 1969 had become a yawning crevice by 1971. Part of the problem was the unruliness afflicting American society in general, and part of it came from the soldiers' realization that America was quitting the war. "Nobody wants to be the last man in Viet Nam killed," said Lieutenant Frank M. Campagne. Future chief of staff Colin Powell believed soldiers were "no less brave or skilled, but by this time in the war, they lacked inspiration and sense of purpose." At the bottom of the disciplinary abyss lay poor leadership. "These sorry asses would go out of their way to get their ticket punched and show an increased body count," remembered Campagne about professional officers. "They didn't care who or how many guys got 'wasted' doing it, because these sorry asses stayed on the fire base or the rear area way in the back." A "Study on Military Professionalism" ordered by Chief of Staff Westmoreland agreed, revealing that ethical transgressions were pervasive in the officer corps. In pursuit of selfish career goals, senior officers "sacrificed integrity on the altar of personal success." They became preoccupied with "trivial short-term objectives even through dishonest practices" and compelled subordinates "to lie, cheat, and steal to meet the impossible demands of higher officers."

Some rebellious behavior was relatively innocuous. Soldiers sympathized with the antiwar movement, lacked proper haircuts, displayed peace medallions, and penned "UUUU" on their helmets, the code for "We are the Unwilling, led by the Unqualified, to do the Unnecessary, for the Ungrateful." Other problems were more serious. For all the American services stationed throughout the world, the desertion rate jumped from 8.43 men per thousand in 1966 to 33.9 in 1971. The Army-wide desertion rate was especially serious, soaring from 14.9 per thousand to 73.5 per thousand during those five years. Desertions hindered the ability of the armed forces to function effectively, not just in Vietnam but worldwide. In South Vietnam, rear area "fragging" (slang for murder or attempted murder, often with a fragmentation grenade) became common, especially in the Army, which had 126 incidents in 1969, 271 in 1970, and 333 in 1971. (The Marines had between 100 and 150 incidents, while the Air Force and Navy had a mere handful.) These numbers do not include "accidental" killings in the field where, admitted one lieutenant, "I was very frightened, not just of what was in front of me, but what was behind me." Although popular culture portrayed unpopular officers as the primary fragging target, most victims were enlisted men, including NCOs. The perpetrators, their judgment often impaired by drugs or alcohol, were usually lower-ranking enlisted personnel settling personal disputes, not making some grandiose antiwar statement.

Equally disturbing were "combat refusals." While some of these were mutinies—by 1971 the Army occasionally used military police to assault mutinous troops—many were wise decisions by experienced troops who understood the tactical situation better than their superiors. "Nothing against you, Lieutenant," said one grunt to his commanding officer, "but this is just stupid. We move out and the point's [the point man leading the patrol] getting ambushed before the rear squad's even cleared the laager. We've been hit day after day, and we're just not going." During 1970 even the fabled 1st Cavalry Division experienced several dozen combat refusals. In order to avoid a combat refusal, some officers began ordering "search and evade" missions, purposefully sending their men into areas where they would *not* encounter the enemy.

Among the most pernicious disciplinary issues were racial friction and drug abuse, both of which flared in rear areas. Out in the bush, said a black rifleman, "everybody was the same. You can't find no racism in the bush." But in base camps and on ships, racial friction was always simmering, and it sometimes escalated into full-fledged riots with deadly consequences. Among other complaints, a black soldier convicted at a general court-martial was likely to receive a harsher penalty than a white convicted of the same offense, and blacks more commonly received less than honorable discharges. Since drug abuse imperiled everyone on combat operations it, like racial conflict, occurred primarily in the rear. Marijuana was the primary drug of choice until 1970, when cheap, high-grade heroin became the foremost culprit—behind alcohol, which was *the* most serious problem. In the spring of 1970 two servicemen a month died from drug overdoses; by that fall two *per day* were dying. So many soldiers got "high" on drugs and started shooting wildly that some officers believed drugged GIs were a more serious menace than the enemy.

"What the hell is going on?" wondered Abrams. "I've got white shirts all over the place—psychologists, drug counselors, detox specialists, rehab people, social workers, and psychiatrists. Is this a goddamned army or a mental hospital? Officers are afraid to lead their men into battle, and the men won't follow. Jesus Christ! What happened?" The general knew that "it does no good to sit around and piss about the good old days, because they aren't here—if they ever were." He also understood that even though the majority of soldiers continued doing their duty honorably, the disintegration was so severe that he needed "to get this Army home to save it."

Peace Without Honor

Even as the Easter Offensive raged across South Vietnam and LINE-BACKER I inflicted crippling losses on the North, negotiators inched toward a truce. The battering inflicted by American warplanes convinced the Communists they must get the U.S. out of the war as soon as possible. With indications the Congress that assembled in January 1973 would be so dovish that it might legislate an end to the war, Nixon was also anxious to settle. Both sides retreated from long-held positions. The Communists' key concession was to drop their demand for Thieu's ouster and the creation of a coalition government in the South. Nixon's most significant concession—the most significant in the entire negotiating process—was agreeing to allow NVA troops to remain *inside* South Vietnam after previously insisting on mutual troop withdrawals. The president's new position acknowledged reality; as Kissinger stated, "no negotiations would be able to remove [the NVA] if we had not been able to expel them with force of arms." The NVA's presence in the South virtually guaranteed the Communists' ultimate success, even if Thieu remained in power for the time being. The U.S. also failed to insist on a ceasefire that recognized two Vietnams, thereby conceding, as the Geneva Conference had insisted in 1954, that the 17th Parallel was *not* an international boundary.

The U.S. and North Vietnam completed a treaty on October 8, agreeing to sign it by October 31. But the U.S. negotiated its retreat without fully consulting South Vietnam—with good reason, since Nixon capitulated on such crucial issues. "The real basic problem," wrote one of his aides, "boils down to the question of whether Thieu can be sold on it." He could not.

Fearing his government would not survive if the NVA remained in the South, and wanting the 17th Parallel recognized as a boundary between sovereign nations, he insisted the treaty required major changes. In an effort to placate his recalcitrant ally, Nixon assured Thieu "that the United States will react very strongly and rapidly to any violation of the agreement," and warned him that it was essential "your Government does not emerge as the obstacle to peace which American public opinion now universally desires." Thieu was not placated, resulting in a paradoxical situation: Since the U.S. had a deal with its enemy, its ally was *the* obstacle to peace.

Nixon directed Kissinger, who considered Thieu's proposed changes "preposterous," to present them to North Vietnam, but the North's chief negotiator, Le Duc Tho, insisted the U.S. fulfill the October 8 agreement. When negotiations failed to break the deadlock, Nixon tried to get tough, first with his ally and then against his foe. He sent Thieu several messages threatening to move forward with the treaty "at whatever cost." When the South Vietnamese president did not relent, Nixon threatened the North with another aerial barrage. When the Communists rejected any amendments, he ordered Operation LINEBACKER II, which lasted from December 18 until December 29. Like so many operations, it yielded ambiguous results. Relying extensively on B-52s, it rearranged much of LINEBACKER I's rubble, crippled the North's air defenses, and inflicted additional damage, particularly on previously restricted targets in Hanoi and Haiphong. But the U.S. lost fifteen B-52s and thirteen other warplanes, leaving thirty-one crewmen as prisoners of war and another ninety-three missing and presumed dead.* Moreover, the operation provoked outrage. Domestically, impeachment threats hung in the air, and Congress vowed to cut off war funding contingent upon the withdrawal of all U.S. troops and the return of its prisoners. Nixon knew he had to obtain a deal quickly, because the bombing was not politically sustainable. Even though he threatened the North with still more bombing, the outcry was so great "we cannot consider this to be a viable option." Internationally, in contrast to their tepid objections to LINEBACKER I the Soviets and Chinese now reacted angrily, raising fears that détente was at risk.

Nixon used LINEBACKER II to try to influence both North and South Vietnam. Rather than risk a third LINEBACKER, the North returned to the conference table determined to get the U.S. out of the war

---

*During the war the U.S. lost a total of 3,339 fixed-wing aircraft. Of these, 2,430 were combat losses, and 909 were operational losses (primarily accidents). Although the percentages are far from precise, antiaircraft artillery and semiautomatic and automatic small arms fire were responsible for far more combat losses than SAMs or MiGs. In trying to avoid SAMs and MiGs, pilots often descended into AAA or small arms range.

even if it meant accepting a few cosmetic changes to the October 8 agreement. Nixon hoped LINEBACKER II would reassure Thieu that the U.S. would not desert him or allow the enemy to break the agreement with impunity. When Thieu still balked, Nixon insisted he was going to sign an agreement, alone if necessary, in which case "I shall have to explain publicly that your Government obstructs peace." Not wanting an open break with the U.S., Thieu unhappily acquiesced.

On January 23, 1973, all parties—the South, the U.S., the North, and the NLF—signed the Paris Peace Accords, which were only slightly modified from the October 8 document. The agreement called for a ceasefire in place (which left at least 100,000 NVA in the South), complete American withdrawal, and prisoner exchanges, though the North betrayed the VC because the accords excluded them from the prisoner swap. In a protocol kept secret from the public and Congress, Nixon pledged the U.S. to pay at least $3.25 billion in what were essentially reparations. The president insisted he achieved "peace with honor," but even viewed in the *best* light the accords left the South in a precarious position. Former secretary of state Dean Rusk said they were "in effect a surrender"; South Vietnam's Vice President Ky described them as a "Sellout"; and Chief of Naval Operations Elmo Zumwalt asserted that two words that could never describe the outcome of Nixon's policy were "peace" and "honor."

An Indecent Interval

The Paris Peace Accords removed the U.S. from the war and brought its prisoners of war home, but they did not resolve the fundamental issue: Was Vietnam one nation or two? Consequently, as Nixon and Kissinger expected, the Vietnamese civil war continued with barely a pause. Thieu ordered ARVN to reclaim as much territory as possible, and it recovered some areas the NVA had "liberated" during the Easter Offensive. The NVA did not yield terrain without exacting a sanguinary price. ARVN suffered 25,473 KIA in 1973 and another 19,375 in the first eight months of 1974, and was stretched dangerously thin. Initially the South seemed to benefit from Projects ENHANCE and ENHANCE PLUS, two gargantuan efforts to beef up the South's arsenal before the ceasefire went into effect, because the terms limited resupply to one-for-one replacements. The Department of Defense engorged the South's armed forces with equipment, but as Lieutenant General Phillip Davidson observed, the U.S. had provided "airplanes they couldn't fly, ships they couldn't man, and tanks and other equipment they couldn't maintain." By late 1974 many ARVN soldiers were dispirited and desertions were running about 24,000 *per month*.

After the Americans departed, the Communists were more confident than ever of ultimate victory. They moved cautiously, however, for fear of provoking another LINEBACKER and because they needed time to rebuild their own weakened forces. Encouraged by cuts in U.S. aid to South Vietnam, the convulsions in the U.S. caused by Nixon's misdeeds during the Watergate scandal, continued Soviet support, and growing unrest against Thieu's dictatorship, they began driving ARVN from territory South Vietnam acquired in its immediate post-peace land grab, and adopted a two-year plan to unify Vietnam. Limited offensives in late 1974 and into 1975 would create favorable conditions for a climactic "General Offensive—General Uprising" in 1976.

Northern strategists often miscalculated during the war, usually to their regret. This time, however, they miscalculated to their advantage. In mid-December 1974, the NVA in Cambodia attacked Phuoc Long Province northwest of Saigon and captured it in only three weeks. Despite this blatant violation of the Paris Peace Accords, the U.S. did not react with anything more forceful than diplomatic notes. Convinced that Nixon's successor, President Gerald R. Ford, would not intervene militarily, the Communists launched an offensive in the Central Highlands on March 10, 1975, aimed at Ban Me Thout. Within a week the Communists controlled the city and stood poised to bisect the South by advancing to the South China Sea. They would not have to fight very hard to do so. Without any advance notice, Thieu ordered ARVN to abandon the Highlands. Since it had no plans for withdrawing, the retreat degenerated into a rout. When General Van Tien Dung unleashed a second offensive, this one in I Corps, ARVN suffered another debacle despite a few pockets of heroic resistance.

Pleased by these unexpectedly easy successes, Hanoi ordered General Dung to discard the two-year plan and complete the South's destruction in 1975. Substantially rebuilt after the nadir years of 1968–1971, the VC played vital roles in supporting the North's conventional forces. By mid-April the NVA was approaching Saigon, delayed only by a ferocious last stand at the strategic crossroads of Xuan Loc by the 18th ARVN Division against four NVA divisions. On April 29 the Vietnam War's last battle started when NVA rockets blasted Tan Son Nhut air base, which had been MACV's headquarters. The next day the South unconditionally surrendered.

South Vietnam had collapsed after an indecently brief interval. If the war's beginning was ambiguous, its ending was not. The U.S. and the South Vietnam it tried to create had lost, unequivocally.

In succession the VC/NVA defeated America's special war, limited war, and Vietnamization-pacification strategies. By 1975 the U.S. could not afford the cost of propping up Thieu's government; the public no longer had any interest in Vietnam; and America could not continue to ignore its other domestic and worldwide commitments. Throughout its brief history, the South had always been too dependent on the U.S. to stand on its own. William Colby once asserted: "There's no reason why 17 million South Vietnamese can't hold off 18 million North Vietnamese." But there was a reason: The South's population, like America's, was never willing to pay anything close to the steep price the North Vietnamese and VC did in pursuit of what they considered the sacred goals of national unification and independence. In a larger sense, the Communist victory flowed with the tidal wave of decolonization that washed over the globe after World War II.

Approximately 260,000 South Vietnamese military personnel died and many hundreds of thousands more were wounded during the war. Hanoi stated that 1,100,000 VC/NVA were KIA or died of wounds; precisely how many were WIA or missing in action is unknown, but the numbers were substantial. An estimated 500,000 Vietnamese civilians, North and South, lost their lives, and perhaps three times that many were wounded. By comparison, U.S. losses were modest: 47,434 battle deaths, 10,786 nonbattle deaths, and 313,616 WIA, about half of whom required hospitalization.

Not the least of the war's legacies was an array of haunting questions that have no definitive answers: How and why did the U.S. lose the war? Could it have been won at an acceptable cost? If so, how? Was Southeast Asia worth the prolonged ordeal? After all, although South Vietnam, Cambodia, and Laos ended up in the Communist camp and endured decades of postwar misery and privation, no other dominoes toppled—not Thailand, not Malaysia, not the Philippines, not Indonesia.

The Reckoning

The Vietnam War mortgaged America's global containment and forward, collective defense for a decade. European leaders of NATO wondered about the wisdom of a government that squandered lives and resources to fight a determined Asian enemy in an inconsequential corner of the world. And the war's fiscal implications were severe. Between 1965 and 1974 the defense budget rose from $47 billion to $74 billion, but the increase was illusory. Fueled by domestic social spending and war expenditures, inflation reduced the purchasing power of defense dollars by one-third. The decline in defense spending reflected widespread discontent with the conduct of national security affairs, the erosion of support for the war, and a declining faith in the government.

The reduced commitment to defense did not reflect a diminished Soviet threat. During the Vietnam era the Russian armed forces embarked on a modernization program that dwarfed the comparable American effort. Soviet armed forces increased in size and fielded a sophisticated family of ground and air weapons in numbers that made "Flexible Response" less attractive as a NATO strategy. Russia also increased its nuclear warheads, improved their accuracy and warhead weight-to-yield ratios, and adopted solid fuels that decreased launch time, all of which made a disarming first strike a greater technical possibility. Two new missiles, the SS-9 and the SS-11, were especially worrisome, as was the prospect of the Soviets developing MIRVs—multiple, independently targeted reentry vehicles—which might give them superiority over America's forces. Soviet advances in anti-ballistic missile (ABM) defense based on ultra-high-speed missiles and phased-array radars worried SAC's planners, though the U.S. ABM program was actually making better progress. A fleet of nuclear attack submarines, heavily armed surface attack groups, and land-based naval aviation gave the Soviets the capability to contest NATO's control of the Atlantic and Mediterranean. Thus, although the U.S. did not scrap all its modernization programs, the decade of deferral brought an erosion of America's relative superiority. When the Vietnam War ended, U.S. officials spoke in morose terms of "sufficiency" and "rough parity" in nuclear forces, and the situation in conventional forces appeared equally dismaying.

The Nixon administration tried to cap the nuclear arms competition with the Soviet Union with two treaties signed in May 1972, the ABM Treaty and the Interim Agreement on intercontinental nuclear delivery vehicles. After complex negotiations, the U.S. and Russia agreed to curb their ABM programs and set a ceiling on their most threatening offensive programs. The ABM Treaty, which had no time limit, restricted both nations to two ABM sites of no more than 100 missiles, which basically made antimissile defense futile; the U.S. eventually stopped work on its only site. The Interim Agreement, which was to run five years, set limits on the number of missiles each side could deploy as ICBMs and SLBMs. The U.S. held its ICBM force at 1,054 and its SLBM ceiling at 710 mounted in forty-four submarines, while the Soviets set their ICBMs at 1,618 and their SLBM ceiling at 950 in sixty-two subs. U.S. technological advantages offset the Soviets' larger numbers.

The treaties—labeled "SALT I" in diplomatic shorthand—did no more than modify the arms competition, since both sides continued with programs that escaped treaty limitations: Long-range bombers and MIRVs. They eventually tackled the MIRV problem in negotiations that resulted in the Vladivostok Accords (1974), which set a mutual ceiling of 2,400 on all delivery vehicles (including bombers) and of 1,320 MIRVed delivery vehicles, which included bombers armed with cruise missiles. While Vladivostok established equality in the number of offensive systems, it did not address the possibility that Russia's large missiles could bear so many MIRVs that they might constitute a first-strike threat.

Meanwhile, U.S. conventional forces underwent dramatic reductions, from 3.5 million men (1968) to 2.1 million (1975). By 1974 the armed services had 46 percent fewer aviation squadrons, 47 percent fewer ships, and 16 percent fewer divisions than they had a decade earlier. One explanation for the decline was a change in manpower policy. To help defuse the anti-war movement, in 1971 the Nixon administration announced it would end the draft, and in 1973 an All Volunteer Force replaced conscription. But volunteers were scarce, notwithstanding florid rhetoric about the patriotism of American youth. The cost of a volunteer versus a conscript either doubled or tripled, depending on what costs one counted, and the quality of enlistees dropped, whether measured by their possession of high-school diplomas or intelligence testing. Compounding the cost and quality problems, the increased number of black and female recruits created difficulties that resisted easy solutions, and career officers and NCOs left the service in droves. The Department of Defense thought it could compensate for the chaos in the active forces by stressing a "Total Force" policy that improved reserve units, but the draft's end also worked havoc on reserve enlistments. Inflation, soaring costs, mismanagement, and technological risk-taking hampered the modernization of equipment and munitions. To replace each old tank, ship, and aircraft generally cost double the original investment. The solution—not a good one—was to buy fewer units and spend less on operations and maintenance. The accepted efficiency measurements all declined as the armed forces flew less, steamed at sea less, shot fewer munitions less often, and held fewer exercises.

Congress exploited the public disillusionment with Vietnam to assert its influence on national security policy. It not only approved a decline in military spending but also limited executive branch flexibility through a combination of the legislative veto and new laws. The most significant of the latter included a July 1973 law that prohibited direct or indirect combat activities over, on, or even near Laos, Cambodia, and both Vietnams after August 15; the War Powers Act (1973), which required congressional approval of troop deployments abroad in combat situations within sixty days of commitment; and the Budget and Impoundment Control Act (1974), which weakened presidential authority to manage federal spending. Congress also placed legislative limits on future covert operations. Nixon's Watergate scandal emboldened Congress to attack what some of its members characterized as an "imperial presidency" dedicated to supporting "militarism."

In 1975 it seemed almost impossible to conceive of it, but fifteen years later the U.S. would win the Cold War as the Soviet Union collapsed, leaving the United States as the world's sole remaining superpower.

NINETEEN

The Common Defense
and the End of the Cold War,
1976–1993

W hen the American people celebrated the two-hundredth anniversary of their national independence in 1976, they still bore the wounds of the Vietnam War. Alienated from both their political leadership and their armed forces, they charged them with collusion in wasting lives and money against falsely exaggerated threats. Fifteen years later, the nation emerged the acknowledged victor in the strategic part of the Cold War. With the collapse of the Soviet Union in 1989–1991, the United States lost the only direct military threat to its own existence and that of its major allies: The members of NATO, Korea, and Japan. Three successor republics—Russia, Ukraine, and Kazakhstan—still controlled the divided Soviet nuclear force, but they wanted to trade disarmament for economic assistance. The end of the strategic arms confrontation—a kind of nuclear Russian roulette—did not, however, solve the issue of nuclear proliferation by regional powers such as Pakistan and North Korea. Nor did it have any special relevance to the forty-some conflicts—most of them insurgencies or civil wars—that plagued a world whose national borders had been torn asunder by the two world wars and the end of European colonialism. The end of the Cold War did not provide easy answers to the traditional questions of American defense: "How much is enough?" and "Enough for what?"

Borrowing from the ancients, John F. Kennedy once observed that victory had a thousand fathers, but defeat was an orphan. The end of the Cold War represented the efforts of millions of fathers in the United States and its allied nations, but the Constitution and American tradition focus the paternity of international security policy on the presidency. Jimmy Carter, Ronald Reagan, and George H.W. Bush and their advisers all supported the armed forces that contributed to the collapse of the Soviet Union. Congress, especially such key members as Henry Jackson, John Stennis, John Warner, Barry Goldwater, John Tower, and Sam Nunn, shared the victory. But in the end the exhaustion of the Russian people, the patriotic endurance of the national minorities in the Soviet Union, the rebelliousness of the member states of the Warsaw Pact, and the greed and moral poverty of the Communist party brought the Soviet Union down. Although the United States could find some comfort in its role in the demise of Soviet Communism, it could not claim that military strength alone had provided a new measure of national security. Nevertheless, its military renaissance in the 1980s provided a final, unanswerable challenge to the Soviet Union and essential reassurance to its allies that it would bear—the Vietnam War notwithstanding—the major share of the military burden for the defense of Western Europe, the Western Hemisphere, parts of the Middle East, and north Asia.

Talk about a "new world order" produced more unsettling questions about the use of military force than it answered. By 1993, in fact, the United States had not altered its fundamental strategy of nuclear deterrence and collective forward defense, only the level of forces required to sustain the strategy. Although the threat of Soviet intervention in regional conflicts had disappeared, the conflicts themselves had not diminished. The end of mutually canceling American and Soviet intervention indeed may have contributed to regional conflict by removing the threat of foreign action. The emerging threats stemmed from problems that stood outside the East-West confrontation, problems like the fusion of narcotics insurgency and Maoism in Latin America, Black nationalism in Africa, Islamic fundamentalism in the Middle East, and the economic and military resurgence of China and Japan. The approach to the twenty-first century did not look like the road to nuclear Armageddon, but it did not look like a smooth path to global peace either.

Coping with New Challenges

Making an electoral virtue of his foreign-policy innocence, President Jimmy Carter took office in 1977 convinced that he had a historic opportunity to curb the spread of nuclear weapons, prevent the loss of American lives in war, pursue détente with the Soviet Union, reduce defense spending, shift the burden of collective defense to America's allies, and expand the power of moral suasion by applying a "human rights" test to diplomacy. When he left office four years later, Carter had abandoned the policies of the "peace phase" of his presidency. Buffeted by world events and the divided interpretations of those events by his advisers, Carter admitted that the Cold War had not ended and in so doing legitimized Ronald Reagan's candidacy in 1980 and even cast serious doubts upon his own competence.

Carter's management of national-security policy never reached the level of disaster his critics claimed, but it was most notable for its vacillation and moralistic amateurism. The Carter administration, reflecting the personal style of the president, managed to irritate and perplex in equal measure the American people, Congress, America's allies abroad, and the Soviet Union—a sure formula for frustration. To be sure, the Soviet Union showed no willingness to defuse the global competition. Deterred in Europe, the Soviet Union actually pursued a policy of "horizontal escalation" preached by Communist radicals like Lin Biao and Che Guevara. In 1975–1976 the Soviets sponsored a Cuban military force for Angola, divided by civil war and already influenced by Congolese and South African intervention. Two years later the Cubans sent another army to Ethiopia to secure a Communist victory and to wage war with Somalia, an apostate socialist dictatorship. In the Horn of Africa alone the Russians dumped $11 billion worth of arms. The Soviets staged a coup against a Communist regime in Afghanistan in December 1979 and inherited a vicious guerrilla war waged by the Islamic tribes, who had refused to modernize according to the Leninist prescriptions decreed by the politicians in Kabul. Not a part of the pattern of socialist upheaval, the Iranian Revolution of 1979, which brought Islamic fundamentalists to power, added another dimension of complexity to the world scene. So did the Vietnamese invasion of Cambodia the same year, which seemed designed to not only displace the crazed regime of Pol Pot but also supplant Chinese influence with Russian sponsorship of the new, unified Communist Vietnam. The Carter administration proved to be singularly unlucky in the crises it faced, but it also managed to be the author of its own difficulties.

The Carter administration compounded its problems by launching a purge of the American covert operations groups and military Special Forces. Reflecting his Wilsonian assumptions about the innate evil of nations and governments, Carter wanted to reduce his own potential for sin by reducing his capability *to* sin. By depriving the CIA's operations directorate of skilled personnel in the "Halloween Massacre" of 1977 and accepting a reduction of the Army Special Forces, Carter denied himself anything but a conventional military response to the knotty problems of terrorism and hostage rescue. Since the requirement for special operations and counterinsurgency did not go away, the Carter administration, whether by design or inattention, allowed such activities to be subcontracted to other nations, principally Israel and Argentina.

The first Carter defense policy reflected both post-Vietnam public opinion and the noninterventionism of the president, Secretary of State Cyrus Vance, and Vice President Walter F. Mondale rather than the confrontationist bent of National Security Adviser Zbigniew Brzezinski. Secretary of Defense Harold Brown, the most experienced and least ideological of Carter's advisers, coped with both camps and tried to fashion programs that satisfied the divided counsel at the White House. When Carter took office, public opinion polls showed that Americans thought that defense spending was adequate, that the armed forces could perform their missions, and that Russia might have increased its military capability but did not intend to use its military for coercive purposes. The public thought that only nuclear deterrence and the defense of NATO justified military spending. Carter's first two defense budgets reduced Ford's projections for real growth in military spending; when modified by inflation, Carter's proposed spending levels resulted in a slight decline in real authorizations and outlays. The administration managed its economies in a number of ways: Canceling the B-1 bomber program, cutting the Navy's shipbuilding plans, stretching out the costs of expensive programs like MX ICBM and tactical aircraft procurement, slowing the growth of military pay, and reducing operations and maintenance spending.

The administration based its initial strategic arms programs upon the assumptions of mutual assured destruction, for Carter was convinced he could use the SALT II negotiations to accomplish sharp reductions in the levels of nuclear weapons. This optimism was short-lived

In 1977, abandoning the Vladivostok Accords, the Carter administration proposed to the U.S.S.R. that each side make deep cuts in its MIRVed ICBM force. Since most of the Soviet strategic forces were ICBMs, this reduction would have borne most heavily on the U.S.S.R. Not surprisingly, the Soviets sharply rejected the Carter plan. Thereafter the administration returned to more traditional and modest plans to reduce the Russian counterforce first-strike potential. In June 1979, Carter and Brezhnev signed a second set of strategic arms control agreements, the SALT II treaty. Focused upon curbing the growth of warheads on MIRVed ICBMs, the "basic agreement" of seven years' duration established tiered caps on all strategic systems: 2,250 on the total number of missile launchers and heavy bombers; a subceiling of 1,320 on all MIRVed missiles and bombers armed with air-launched cruise missiles; a subceiling of 1,200 on all sea-based or land-based MIRVed missiles; and a final limit of 820 on all MIRVed land-based ICBMs. A three-year protocol put temporary restraints on mobile

ICBM and cruise missile development. SALT II's parameters allowed the United States to complete its existing strategic modernization programs and placed a cap on the Soviets' most menacing program, the deployment of heavy ICBMs with MIRVs in numbers and accuracy that might create a disabling first-strike capability.

The SALT II negotiations proceeded alongside an internal review of American nuclear strategy that produced force structure changes that were controversial but eventually strengthened the American negotiating position. Barely in office, Carter ordered a study that produced Presidential Review Memorandum 10 (June 1977), which then took on another half-life in studies of targeting and strategy that ended with the president's endorsement of Presidential Directive 59 two years later. PD 59 found America's strategic forces adequate but ripe for improvement. The concept of a countervalue, minimal deterrent position seemed less acceptable, since the Soviets might soon put at risk the American ICBM force and all land-based command and control installations. Carter wanted more emphasis on a "countervailing strategy" that would allow the United States to fight a nuclear war at various levels of intensity with greater flexibility in adding and omitting targets from the SIOP. Eventually, SIOP 6, the actual nuclear war plan, contained major, selective, limited, and regional targeting options; from 4,100 targets in 1960 the possible target list climbed to over 50,000. The nuclear planners (hardly a unified community) tended to believe that such a robust posture would strengthen deterrence in a crisis and encourage the Soviets to negotiate. Others thought force improvements served less peaceful purposes. In any event, PD 59 suggested that the United States desperately needed more deliverable warheads: MIRVs on ICBMs, MIRVs on SLBMs, cruise missiles launched from air, sea, and ground platforms, and bomber-carried short-range attack missiles and bombs.

The burden of the counterforce role fell upon the Air Force's MX ICBM, a 95-ton missile capable of carrying ten MIRVed warheads. ICBM vulnerability and SALT II dictated that the Air Force design a mobile system whose numbers could be verified by the Soviets but whose location could not be determined for targeting. The result was a plan to shuttle 200 MXs among 4,600 different launching positions built on public lands in the western United States. Technically the solution had merit, but its cost and political liabilities made it vulnerable. In the meantime, the Navy pressed ahead with the *Ohio*-class submarine capable of firing twenty-four MIRVed Trident missiles, while the Air Force worked on an air-launched cruise missile for its aging B-52 bomber force. Neither of the latter programs, however, promised to enlarge counterforce capability until late in the 1990s.

The Carter administration also embraced its predecessors' emphasis on NATO, but its own internal confusions and the influences of recession, inflation, and budget deficits restricted its initiatives. Carter's first efforts at alliance leadership produced a significant victory, for in 1978 the NATO leaders pledged their nations to a Long Term Defense Program that would increase each ally's real defense spending by 3 percent a year. For the United States the emphasis upon NATO drove conventional force modernization and provided some advantage to Army programs like the M-1 tank, the Bradley infantry fighting vehicle, a new family of mechanized air-defense vehicles, new attack and transport helicopters, and advanced artillery and rocket systems capable of using precision-guided munitions. The administration also showed considerable energy in pursuing integrated interallied efforts for the interoperability, standardization, and rationalization of NATO's forces and defense investments, but it accepted a concept of NATO defense that assumed a European war would last no longer than thirty days. Therefore it emphasized stockpiling munitions and equipment for only the six active Army divisions that it thought might fight in Europe in a crisis.

The Soviet deployment of a new mobile, MIRVed theater nuclear missile, the SS-20, forced the alliance to assess its own nuclear posture in Europe. The Carter administration's first sortie into tactical and theater nuclear matters did not go well. In 1978 the administration approved the final development and deployment of a reduced-blast, enhanced-radiation warhead for American artillery. The "neutron bomb," which was designed to cripple Russian tank formations while limiting blast-caused civilian casualties in West Germany, produced a political controversy that convinced Carter to defer the program just as the Allies accepted it. Embarrassed by its mishandling of the neutron bomb affair, the administration responded enthusiastically to the suggestion of West Germany's Helmut Schmidt that NATO meet the challenge of the SS-20 by deploying its own new theater nuclear weapons. After complicated negotiations, the alliance in December 1979 agreed to a "two-track" policy to pursue a European nuclear-weapons pact with Russia while deploying two new mobile theater nuclear weapons, the Pershing II intermediate-range ballistic missile and the ground-launched cruise missile (GLCM). The 108 Pershing IIs would go into positions in West Germany, while the 464 GLCMs would be emplaced in Italy, Great Britain, the Netherlands, and Belgium. The two-track decision concerned the Russians; it also provided a new sense of purpose and alarm within the European peace movement, an alliance of people frightened of a nuclear Europe, religious pacifists, antinuclear romantics, and anti-American appeasers. Although the peace movement did not force abandonment of the plan, it did nothing to encourage the Soviets to negotiate a regional arms control agreement.

Carter's conversion in 1979 to a more ambitious defense policy stemmed from developments outside Europe. Initially Carter believed that his policy of regional accommodation, human rights advocacy, and military restraint had improved America's relations with the developing world. In the Western Hemisphere the administration signed a treaty with Panama that promised to end American domination of the Canal Zone and the canal itself by the end of the century, allowed the *Sandinista* rebels to topple the Somoza regime in Nicaragua, and applied sanctions against the authoritarian regimes of Brazil and Argentina. Finding the regime of South Korean President Park Chung-hee politically distasteful, the administration began to withdraw the one American division in South Korea. It ended the thirty-year-old U.S. alliance with Taiwan and formally recognized the People's Republic of China. In Africa it sympathized with a negotiated settlement that brought black rule to Zimbabwe (formerly Southern Rhodesia) and pressured South Africa to end its support for a white regime in South-West Africa (now Namibia). Along the southern rim of Eurasia the administration either did not act or moved with indecision and tardiness. Smarting from sanctions against its nuclear program, Pakistan flatly rejected offers of conventional military assistance. A revolution in Iran moved toward Islamic extremism in 1979 when the Carter administration first withdrew its support from the Shah and then failed to find a moderate alternative to the Ayatollah Khomeini. The seizure of American embassy personnel in Tehran and the abortive attempt to rescue them in April 1980 only dramatized the apparent American impotence.

In response to these setbacks the Carter administration first asserted that it would continue its minimalist defense policy and noninterventionism, but as early as 1978 the president began to make statements implying that his benign view of the world might be flawed. He first slowed and then canceled the troop withdrawal from Korea after both Japan and China questioned the wisdom of the plan. He then committed American troops to police the Sinai peninsula when the Camp David Accords of 1978 brought a separate peace between Egypt and Israel; to support the continuation of the peace process, Carter approved massive military and economic aid programs to both nations as well as tacit American military support. The administration, appalled by the Iranian takeover of the U.S. embassy in Tehran (November 1979) and the Russian intervention in Afghanistan (December 1979), announced that it now viewed the Russians as perfidious betrayers of détente. In fact, the administration was overtaken by public opinion, which had shifted to a more hostile view of Soviet intentions and a more positive view of increased defense spending. At the end of 1979 Carter finally submitted budget requests that represented real increases in military spending. Most of the increases were targeted at a specific problem, the increased American commitment to the Persian Gulf region.

In its last year in office, the Carter administration initiated a crash program to improve its search for two Middle Eastern goals: An end to the Israeli-Arab wars and a remedy for Iran's collapse as the policeman of the Persian Gulf. Both goals had a common theme: To prevent an increase of Russian influence in the region. As the "Carter Doctrine" announced in January 1980, the United States would not accept Soviet-supported revolutionary change in the Middle East, especially in the Persian Gulf. Arms assistance to Israel, Egypt, and Saudi Arabia increased, but the administration did not depend upon surrogates alone. Instead it announced the creation of a new headquarters, the Rapid Deployment Joint Task Force (RDJTF), which had authority to call upon more than 200,000 troops from all the services for Persian Gulf contingencies. Obtaining rights to the Diego Garcia atoll in the Indian Ocean, it developed the base into a major air installation and anchorage for seventeen preloaded merchant ships designed to support the initial commitment of RDJTF units. In addition, the administration sought additional base access in Egypt, Kenya, Somalia, and Oman. Equally symbolic of its new attitude toward the Soviet Union and its late response to public opinion, the administration withdrew the SALT II treaty from Senate consideration, but it pledged to respect the treaty's limitations as long as the Russians did too. Nevertheless, the eleventh-hour return of the Carter presidency to traditional pre-Vietnam defense concerns did not save it from a stunning rejection by the voters in November 1980.

The Reagan Rearmament

Although he had served in the Army Air Forces of World War II, for which he made training films, Ronald Reagan, former governor of California and the darling of Republican conservatives, had no special insight into America's defense problems. Instead, he had a deep intuition that the world respected military force and that the American people wanted an assertive foreign policy. His sweeping electoral victory over an incumbent Democratic president gave him—at least as he saw it—a mandate to rearm the armed forces. He entrusted this task to Secretary of Defense Caspar Weinberger, a World War II veteran from the staff of Douglas MacArthur and an experienced government manager from service in Washington and Sacramento. Weinberger became the Pentagon's chief cheerleader, a foreign-policy activist who rivaled Reagan's two secretaries of state, and a dogged foe of any congressional attempt to challenge the administration's defense budgets. His principal allies (although not always consensual ones) for defense spending were Secretary of the Navy John Lehman and Assistant Secretary of Defense (International Security Policy) Richard Perle. Weinberger's influence grew in part because he faced no dominating national security adviser in the White House, where Reagan used five men of modest talents and political skill until he appointed his sixth, General Colin L. Powell.

The Reagan administration based its defense planning on the most demanding criterion: Preparedness for a sustained nuclear or nonnuclear war with the Soviet Union and its allies. Since the Russians could exercise military power on a global scale, the United States must be prepared to be equally capable, with a special emphasis on naval and air forces. At a minimum, as Weinberger stated, the United States had to defend its interests in Europe, the Middle East and South Asia, and north Asia, and ". . . our long-range aim is to be capable of defending all theaters simultaneously." As stated in National Security Decision Document (NSDD) 238 (1981), the United States needed far more military capability outside of the NATO central front. As refined in NSDD 32 (1981), the strategic approach included greater reliance on Allied participation and military assistance, more conventional-force investments and forward deployments, and the addition of Latin America as a crisis region. The president also called for active support of anti-Communist insurgencies wherever they could be found. For example, the "Reagan Doctrine" declared support for the anti-*Sandinista* guerrillas *(contras)* waging war in and around Nicaragua; for the Afghan *mujahideen* tribesmen then killing Russians and Afghan Communist troops; and for four other insurgencies. Reagan had nothing less in mind than a fusion of Ike's rollback and New Look with JFK's flexible response.

Reagan understood that his strategic grand design required grand budgets. Communicating his proposals with a relaxed, jocular militancy that soothed his constituents and frightened the rest of the world, the president proposed and Congress accepted—without major alteration—six years (fiscal years 1980–1985) of increased defense spending, the longest sustained peacetime investment in the armed forces in the twentieth century. The annual increases averaged 7.8 percent. The authorizations in this honeymoon represented a 56 percent increase over Carter's last defense budget, itself an increase over the previous year. Although computations of defense spending are often exercises in creative accounting, the Reagan administration probably spent about $2.4 trillion on the armed forces, of which an estimated $536 billion represented its own increases over the previously projected or estimated budget trends of the decade. Its largest single-year budget (1985) was $296 billion.* In investment terms, the larg-

* Fiscal year 1986 was higher in current dollars but less in inflation-adjusted dollars.

est increases went into force modernization, improved readiness through maintenance and training, and increased military pay and allowances. The structure and personnel levels of the armed forces changed little. Most of the seventy-four ships added to the fleet by 1987 came from keels laid under earlier authorizations, but John Lehman launched them with claims that they were the first addition to *his* 600-ship navy. Not until 1986 did Congress force a cut in Reagan's string of growth budgets, and even then the outlays of previous defense budgets keep annual defense spending close to $300 billion a year.

The Reagan administration placed the military competition with the Soviet Union at the center of its strategic vision and as the rationale for its defense buildup. The administration benefited by signs of the impending fall of the Soviet Union, forecast by a succession crisis when Leonid Brezhnev died in November 1982. Two more Soviet presidents died in office before Mikhail Gorbachev took power in March 1985. Another sign of the times was the declaration of a martial-law government under General Wojciech Jaruzelski in rebellious Poland in December 1981. Under the "Brezhnev Doctrine" the Red Army itself should have cowed the Poles, but Moscow, stunned by protests from the United States, Western Europe, and Pope John Paul II, stayed its hand. The lesson did not go unnoticed throughout the Warsaw Pact. Nevertheless, on the surface the Soviet Union, whose own defense budget appeared to be growing each year, had not surrendered its momentum in the arms-modernization competition. The Reagan administration believed that only military strength and the will to use it would prove the crucial instruments of global and regional efforts to stop Soviet expansionism. To stabilize strategic deterrence—its short-term goal—the administration accelerated the SSBN and cruise missile programs and revived the B-1 bomber. The MX ICBM was a knottier problem. The new administration wanted the new missile, but the Carter basing plan was strongly opposed by Reagan's political allies. Advised by a presidential commission, Reagan eventually decided to deploy 100 MX ICBMs in existing fixed silos, thereby acknowledging congressional dismay at all the mobile basing schemes being investigated by the Air Force. Reagan's cautious approach to arms control negotiations with the Soviets suggested that the anti-Communist hardliners in the Defense Department had control of strategic policy; yet the administration also extended the commitment to live within the SALT II restrictions.

The issue of strategic defense proved to be the linkage between accelerated nuclear deterrent programs and continued arms control agreements with the Soviet Union. Reagan himself found the idea of protecting American cities emotionally appealing and politically congenial, but his advisers thought in more limited terms, using strategic defense either as a SALT bargaining chip or as a more limited point defense system for American missile, submarine, and bomber bases. Although the ABM Treaty seemed to outlaw strategic defense in the name of mutual assured destruction, Reagan ordered the Joint Chiefs to give the matter more attention. He embraced a phrase from a JCS briefing: "Wouldn't it be better to protect the American people than avenge them?" In a major speech in March 1983 he announced his "Strategic Defense Initiative," or SDI, a major program for defense against Soviet ballistic missiles. Reflecting a popular movie of the time, the program became "Star Wars," even though its space-based elements were far from intergalactic. Nevertheless, the Pentagon established a Strategic Defense Initiative Office with its own budget, tripled to $3.1 billion by 1986, and authority over the separate ABM military programs then in existence. These programs investigated the application of nuclear, laser, and kinetic energy systems against missiles as well as the requirements for acquiring targets in the various stages of missile flight.

Although it gave the rhetorical "back of the hand" to its domestic critics, who favored a nuclear freeze, the Reagan administration continued strategic weapons negotiations with the Russians and labeled its own program the Strategic Arms *Reduction* Talks (START). Its first proposals clearly showed just who would be reducing—the Soviet Union. A "deep cuts" initiative in 1982 proposed that each side settle for 850 ICBMs and SLBMs limited to 5,000 warheads, a formula that would have eliminated 3,670 Russian ICBM warheads but not one American warhead. The Russians wanted something in return, of course, and that "something" was a limitation on cruise missiles and SDI. The United States then focused on another program, Soviet vehicle and rail-based mobile missiles. The Russians argued that American SLBMs in the *Ohio*-class submarine and D-5 missile programs would soon give the United States an invulnerable first-strike option, an overoptimistic estimate. Despite the jockeying, Reagan and Gorbachev brought some temporary hope when they agreed at a summit meeting in Iceland (October 1986) to a formula cap of 1,600 strategic nuclear delivery systems of all kinds and a ceiling of 6,000 warheads. The negotiating then focused on SDI, on which the administration held fast. Gorbachev rejected any arms control agreement that excluded SDI, and the talks collapsed. As a result, strategic nuclear programs remained a political issue that Reagan could not ignore.

Enjoying unusual rapport with his counterparts in Great Britain, France, and West Germany, the president pressed his NATO allies toward greater defense spending of their own and the completion of the GLCM-Pershing II deployment program. He especially endeared himself to British Prime Minister Margaret Thatcher by overruling Secretary of State Alexander Haig in the Falkland Islands crisis of 1982. Risking alienating the Latin American conservatives, Reagan ordered the American military to provide intelligence and logistics support to the British joint task force that recaptured the islands from Argentina. A newly assertive and rearmed U.S. Army and Air Force pushed their European counterparts toward a concept of high-technology deep battle in which all elements of the Warsaw Pact would be attacked simultaneously. NATO accepted "AirLand Battle" doctrine in 1985, impressed with the revival of America's NATO forces and the implied relief from their own expensive modernization programs. The Europeans also nudged the administration forward on theater nuclear force negotiations and a conventional forces treaty.

The theater or intermediate nuclear weapons negotiations began in November 1981 and ended with a treaty in December 1987 after a predictable series of stops and starts. As in other negotiations with the Soviet Union, the American team, in this case led by the expert and venerable Paul H. Nitze, had to cope with double-dealing in Washington and second-guessing in NATO. The Russians waited for their opponents to self-destruct in the diplomatic sense and sign a treaty that would give the U.S.S.R. advantages it could not win in an arms competition. Reagan, however, placed the Soviets on the immediate defensive by suggesting the total abolition of all intermediate-range nuclear weapons deployed by both the Americans and Russians in Europe. Such a proposal, however, excluded British and French forces—as well as nonmissile-delivery systems—and was vague on how much of the U.S.S.R. actually lay within Europe. The Russians recoiled and fought a delaying action for four years in the hope that the European peace movement would force cancellation of the GLCM and Pershing II deployment program. But the NATO governments persisted and deployed the American systems, and a new Soviet leader, Mikhail Gorbachev, accepted the political-strategic reality that he could not disarm France and Great Britain. Although Nitze himself fell victim to bureaucratic machinations, the ultimate treaty reflected his recommendation to ban all American and Russian short- and medium-range ballistic missiles in Europe. Even more impressive was a provision for on-site inspection of the missiles' destruction in both the Soviet Union and the United States.

Outside the central strategic relationship with NATO and the Soviet Union, the Reagan administration proved as aggressive as its rhetoric. In Latin America and the Middle East it joined in battle with an assortment of revolutionaries, Soviet-sponsored governments, Iranian Islamic fundamentalists, Filipino rebels, Arab nationalists, terrorists, Lebanese sectarian militias, and African socialist governments. In action the Reagan Doctrine proved a mixed blessing and left a mess for subsequent administrations to clean up. In the broadest sense the war on Communist revolution produced greater relative success in Latin America, the least benefit in the Middle East. In Central America the administration inherited one insurgency in El Salvador and created another in Nicaragua, defining its enemy in both cases as vicious revolutionaries under the spell of Cuba and the Soviet Union. The *Sandinista* government in Managua, Nicaragua, solidified its power in 1980 and 1981 with hard-core *commandantes,* most noticeably Daniel Ortega. Nicaraguan resisters fled into Honduras and Costa Rica and looked for aid from the military regimes in Panama and Honduras. The Reagan administration charged to their assistance, either with direct aid and action through the Central Intelligence Agency or via intermediate nations like Panama, Honduras, Argentina, and Israel. At the same time American civilian and military advisers assisted the Salvadoran government, under siege since 1979 from the *Frente Marti Liberacion Nacional* (FMLN). Newly established American bases in Honduras supported both wars, and the U.S. Army held maneuvers along the Nicaraguan border to intimidate the *commandantes.*

The American military action in the Middle East did not fall neatly within the Cold War politics of the Western Hemisphere and proved extremely frustrating. Two major regional traumas fused the issues of the security of Israel and the menace of Islamic fundamentalism. Few could match the zeal of the Iranian Shi'a revolutionaries, who were dedicated to overthrowing the Syrian and Jordanian governments by subversion even while they fought off the even more-hated Sunni Iraqi armies directed by Saddam Hussein, the most vicious tyrant in a dangerous region. The war between Iran and Iraq was one reality, and the Iranian sponsorship of terrorist organizations a piece of that war. The other flashpoint was the civil war in Lebanon, which had begun again in 1975; as the Christians, Sunni Arabs, and Druze hill tribes weakened each other, they created a power vacuum for the Palestinian guerrilla movement and Iran-backed terrorists and gangs (known as Hezbollah or "Party of God") to set up business in Lebanon. Syrian forces shifted west into Lebanon to guard the Beka'a Valley and the Palestinians. In the spring of 1982 the Israeli Defense Force drove into Lebanon against the Palestinians and waged a lightning campaign all the way to Beirut. As part of an international agreement, the United States sent a Marine expeditionary unit (about 2,000 officers and men) to police a ceasefire and expulsion agreement that sent the surviving Palestinians into exile in September 1982.

In less than a month, however, the Marines returned to back American efforts to prevent the collapse of the Lebanese government and army, dominated by the Christians, after terrorists assassinated President Bashir Gemayel. Rival factions correctly determined that the Americans, who could fire only to protect themselves, had actually chosen sides. Druze and Shi'a militia units put the Marines stationed at the Beirut international airport under sporadic fire, which took Marine lives. In August and September 1983 the situation deteriorated rapidly with the withdrawal of the last Israeli forces around Beirut. Swayed by the influence of presidential envoy Robert C. McFarlane, the local American commanders (no one was in complete charge) agreed to discourage the Druze and Shi'as with Lebanese artillery and U.S. Navy shellfire. In the early morning of October 23, 1983, a truck-carried bomb exploded underneath the airport office building holding the Marine ground-force headquarters; in the blast and collapse 241 men died, 239 of them Americans and 220 of them Marines. The disaster caused a crisis within the Reagan administration that eventually led to withdrawal in February 1984.

The battle, however, continued in Lebanon and elsewhere, for the Reagan administration turned to airpower to awe its enemies. The first incident occurred in August 1981, when Navy jets shot down two Libyan interceptors over the Gulf of Sidra, the result of an American initiative to challenge Muammar Gaddafi's definition of "national" waters and airspace. The second air foray found Navy jets in action against Palestinian terrorists (murderers of a handicapped American Jewish tourist) who had boarded an Egyptian chartered airliner bound for Tunisia. On October 10–11, 1985, Navy F-14s, supported by an Air Force armada of intelligence and refueling aircraft, forced the airliner down on Sicily, and the terrorists passed into the hands of Italian judicial officials.

The terrorist war in the Middle East, however, escalated as various Palestinian and Iranian factions (with European allies) vied for fame and fortune with bombs and guns. Terrorist attacks and hijacking incidents doubled in 1983–1985 and produced 2,000 casualties, half of them Americans. In NSDD 138 (April 1984), the president approved a military and clandestine war on terrorists. In January 1986, convinced that Gaddafi was the most prominent and certainly most vocal of the terrorist sponsors, Reagan ordered increased air operations along the Libyan coast. In April the Navy easily defeated a forlorn attack by Libyan gunboats on a carrier task force, but the terrorists struck back by destroying an airliner bound for Athens and bombing a disco in West Berlin, killing and wounding American soldiers and their friends. Intercepted communications clearly linked the terrorists to Gaddafi, so Reagan ordered a massive air strike by Air Force F-111F bombers and Navy carrier aircraft on high-value political and military targets in Tripoli and Benghazi on either end of the Gulf of Sidra. With the loss of one aircrew (two men), the strike force devastated its Libyan targets, mostly military bases, and caused around 200 casualties. The administration believed it had dampened Gaddafi's enthusiasm for terrorism and demonstrated that it would not allow the Beirut fiasco to weaken its will.

But this inconclusive use of military force in the Middle East led to cascading complications, some of which contributed to the Reagan administration's disarray in its second term, but the president could claim at least one unambiguous triumph: the liberation of Grenada in October 1983. An impoverished island jewel of the Lesser Antilles, Grenada had traded British colonial status first for autocracy, then revolutionary socialism under a local demagogue, Maurice Bishop. Unhappy with his personalist rule, his associates slaughtered Bishop and his revolutionary court on October 19 with the tacit approval of their East European and Cuban political and military advisers. Encouraged by the Organization of Eastern Caribbean States and the resident Crown governor-general, the Reagan administration ordered a joint amphibious and airborne assault on the island on October 25. Although the United States eventually put 6,000 servicemen on the island, the burden of the six-day campaign, which cost the lives of nineteen Americans and about seventy Cubans and Grenadian soldiers, fell upon five battalions of Marines, rangers, and paratroopers. The Americans fought with scanty intelligence, rules of engagement that inhibited the use of artillery and air support, and helter-skelter planning and interservice coordination. Part of the difficulty was the speed with which the operation developed; another was the high priority placed upon the rescue of several hundred American students attending a medical college on the island. Although the Grenadians rejoiced in their rescue from a police state, the armed forces endured much post hoc criticism of their special operations performance, their communications, and their joint cooperation. The Defense Department's rough treatment of the media during the affair did not help. No one, however, could fault the ardor and technical skill of the American servicemen in Grenada, for they had performed admirably in a tactical situation of unusual confusion and uncertainty.

The Enemy of My Enemy

As quickly as the national consensus had emerged in the late 1970s for a more militant foreign policy and greater defense spending, the Reagan rearmament stalled in 1986–1987 and tailed off through the presidential election of 1988. Defense authorizations no longer showed real growth but declined by an average of 3 percent a year after 1985. Cash from prior authorization years, however, kept defense outlays around the $290 billion level. Public opinion polls showed that the public now thought that defense spending was too high or about right, not too low. Several domestic political developments combined to force Congress to quit accepting the administration's projected expenditures on defense. The most ominous problem was the national debt, which doubled between 1980 and

1986, and debt service payments, which tripled in the same period. Even though the administration and Congress cooperated in cutting domestic spending 21 percent, neither had any taste for reducing the retirement and health-entitlement programs that touched the entire electorate or for cutting obvious or hidden subsidies to powerful economic lobbies. In 1985 Congress passed the Balanced Budget and Emergency Deficit Control Act, which required a plan to reduce the growing annual deficits or forced mandatory budget cuts. Since the defense budget represented the single largest budget item that could be easily cut, military spending became an obvious target.

These pruning instincts received timely encouragement by a series of revelations in 1981–1986 that the Pentagon and its defense contractors had reached new heights of waste, fraud, and abuse in the procurement process. Defense inspectors, military officers, and media muckrakers discovered toilet seats, coffee pots, and hammers priced at many times their commercial value. Part of the problem was Defense Department accounting, which required that overhead or indirect costs be apportioned to every purchased item, hence creating $430 hammers. Another difficulty was that the military wanted toilet seats and coffee pots that could sustain the stresses of military operational use, no doubt exceeding some reasonable requirements. The major problem, however, was that defense contractors, especially aircraft manufacturers and shipbuilders, wanted to protect themselves from future hard times both by making large profits and by funding plant modernization. As subsequent investigation showed, several prominent defense contractors had crossed the line into illegal profiteering, but Defense management practices had been so regulation-bound and ineffective that the department shared the blame.

The tides of influence in Washington shifted away from the hawks. In the 1986 elections the Republicans lost control of the Senate and thus much of their leverage on behalf of Reagan's defense program. Internal reforms in congressional procedures tended to work to the benefit of those senators and representatives who wanted a pause in defense spending; rules, deaths, and retirements in the Budget and Armed Services Committees put doubters in power. Moreover, the coldest Cold Warriors around the president began to disappear; by 1987 Weinberger, Lehman, and Perle had left government, and William J. Casey, a true Machiavellian director of the CIA, had died. Congress once again exercised its powers to shape defense policy; for example, it forced the Department of Defense to establish an assistant secretary's office to supervise special operations and low-intensity conflict policies and established a Special Operations Command (headed by an Army general) to pull together separate service activities. Within the executive branch, subtle shifts of power occurred. At the White House, James A. Baker III, a friend of Vice President George Bush, replaced Donald Regan as chief of staff and formed an alliance with Secretary of State George Shultz, whose job he then assumed in the next administration. The White House–State Department alliance reduced the influence of the Department of Defense, headed after 1987 by Frank Carlucci, an able Washington operative but no political giant. The National Security Council staff under Rear Admiral John Poindexter stumbled toward self-destruction.

The erosion of the White House's mastery of international security politics at home and abroad stemmed in part from Reagan's willingness to give his subordinates wide latitude and de facto powers that either skirted the fine line of illegality or crossed it in defiance of congressional injunctions. One limitation was self-imposed: A promise not to trade with terrorists for the lives of hostages or other victims. Yet the administration did exactly that, though too late to save the lives of its CIA station chief in Lebanon or, later, a Marine lieutenant colonel working with the United Nations supervisory team. In 1984 or 1985 the Reagan administration opened secret negotiations with Iranians who claimed to have influence with the Hezbollah terrorists who held nine Westerners (five Americans) kidnapped in Beirut and its environs. These Byzantine contacts opened a conduit of arms sales to the Iranian armed forces, starved for antiair and antitank weapons and spare parts in their war with Iraq. The arms sales, however, did not proceed directly but through a series of middlemen, some with links to Israel, whose interest in aiding Iran could be measured by Iran's enemies, Iraq and Syria. Whatever weapons that left Israeli stocks could then be replaced from the United States. Impoverished Egypt could provide Iran with Russian weapons from its dated military inventory with Saudi Arabia as the banker; some of these weapons went to Iran, many more to Afghanistan. Although this bit of ordnance legerdemain might have been only unwise and disingenuous, a further complication ran against a direct congressional prohibition: That of arms transfers to the Nicaraguan *contras*. Managed by Marine Lieutenant Colonel Oliver North, an NSC staffer in the confidence of Bill Casey, profits from arms sales to Iran then flowed to the *contras*—with some large rake-offs by more middlemen, Americans and others. First exposed by the Iranians in 1987, the Iran-*contra* affair did not produce much law enforcement, but it did put the administration on the defensive.

Unlike the Carter administration, the Reagan administration did not fall prey to its fears and gaffes, largely because it could see progress in several important commitments in 1986–1988. Relations with the Soviet Union showed the most improvement, largely because the seeds of self-destruction had taken root in the Russian empire. By 1988 the Russians had largely conceded defeat in the Third World and along the rim of the "evil empire." Gorbachev announced that Russian troops would withdraw from Afghanistan; the Cubans started home from Angola, Ethiopia, and Namibia. Civil unrest in late 1989 shaped nationalist politics in the Baltic states of Latvia, Lithuania, and Estonia, as well as in Poland, Hungary, East Germany, and Czechoslovakia, which overthrew their Communist regimes. The Romanian Communist regime then collapsed in bloody counterrevolution, and no Russian troops rushed to save that government or any other. Outside the Soviet orbit separatism began to divide Yugoslavia into warring republics of mixed ethnic and religious allegiances. Police states of greater or lesser viciousness faded away in the Philippines, South Korea, Haiti, Chile, and South Africa. After some dissembling the Soviets announced a unilateral reduction of their Warsaw Pact forces and took greater interest in the conventional arms reduction talks for NATO and the Warsaw Pact; the Russians seemed prepared to trade off their own divisions for NATO reductions on a surprising 5:1 ratio. Despite ups and downs, the war against the FMLN in El Salvador showed some hope, especially after the election in 1984 of a legitimate civilian president, Jose Napoleon Duarte. In Nicaragua anti-*Sandinista* sentiment rose, some attracted to *contra* guerrilla warfare, more dismayed by the *commandantes'* wretched economic management.

The Middle East situation proved the most intractable in the waning days of the Reagan administration, but the president did not shy from additional military action. The Israeli connection worsened since hardliners refused to negotiate with any Palestinian group, domestic or in exile, and a program of settlement (spurred by Jewish immigrants from Russia) marched into the "occupied territories" west of the Jordan River. The Palestinians, however, struck back with the *intifada,* a civil insurgency that confounded the Israeli police and army. Syria, however, limited its own intervention to exercising influence in Lebanon, where the Muslims slowly grasped power. The United States tried to keep the situation stable with accelerating economic and military assistance to Israel and even greater commitments to Egypt. It also supported UN resolutions demanding that Israel not annex territory it had held since 1967 and that it negotiate some peaceful solution to the Palestinian problem.

Diplomatic crises with Israel and angry bouts with terrorists and their patrons did not exhaust American travails in the Middle East. The Iran-Iraq war only enmeshed the Reagan administration in deeper commitments in the region, especially with Kuwait and Saudi Arabia. To the degree that the United States had a favorite in the Iran-Iraq conflict, it was Iraq, which received Western military assistance while Iran did not (officially). But Iraq hardly looked like a constant friend. Its armed forces and those of Iran attacked oil tankers and other neutral ships in the Persian Gulf as early as 1981, and by 1987 those attacks, the majority by Iraqi warplanes, totaled 451. The attacks menaced oil shipments to the West and Japan from Saudi Arabia and Kuwait. From a long-term perspective, Saudi Arabia appeared to be the logical (and wealthiest) successor in the pro-Western regional role that Iran had played until 1979. For the Saudis, money talked, and Americans generally liked the message. First, the Saudis had some leverage over Egypt, Syria, and Jordan and through them on the Palestinians, and Saudi diplomacy and money supported negotiations and moderation. Next, the Saudis provided money and military assistance to the Afghan rebels; with the bombing death of Pakistani President Zia ul-Haq in 1988, probably at the hands of dissident Pakistanis, the United States needed additional influence from a Muslim ally to keep Pakistan secure as a base of operations against the Russians in Afghanistan. Moreover, the Saudis could and would spend money—some $22 billion between 1981 and 1990—on American arms. In addition, the Saudis allowed the United States to spend the profits from arms sales on base construction in Saudi Arabia. By 1990 Saudi Arabia had the base capacity for an air force five times larger than its own. Project PEACE SHIELD (1985) gave it an air control and defense system that rivaled those of NATO. Its modern port facilities could handle shipping well above commercial needs. To keep the alliance with Saudi Arabia and Kuwait secure, the United States government believed it could not let the 1985 surge in incidents in the Persian Gulf go unanswered.

Early in 1987 the United States Navy, soon joined by special-operations air-ground units from the Army and Marine Corps, moved into the Persian Gulf in combat strength. Rather than its small normal patrol force, the Navy's task forces in the Gulf and the Arabian Sea increased to thirty warships, among them carriers and battleships. The mission was to ensure free passage for Kuwaiti tankers, some of which were switched to American registry. The Navy launched retaliatory attacks on Iranian ground-based missile sites, missile gunboats, and minelayers. In 1988 it easily destroyed much of the Iranian gunboat navy and extended its attacks to nautical guerrilla bases on Iranian oil platforms in the Gulf. An omen for the future, the worst loss came from an Iraqi aircraft that fired two Exocet missiles into the frigate *Stark,* killing thirty-seven and wounding twenty-one American sailors. The most annoying effort the Iranians could mount was seeding the Gulf with floating mines, which took their toll on the tankers and one Navy frigate. The Navy admitted that its mine-clearing capabilities had limitations, a traditional lament that had not been acted on since World War II. The Navy also discomfited the administration when an advanced-technology air-defense cruiser, *Vincennes,* accidentally shot down an Iranian airliner, killing all 290 passengers. Frustrated in its ground war and concerned about the American intervention, the Iranian government accepted a UN-negotiated ceasefire in July 1988. Palestinian radicals with Iranian assistance, however, extracted their warped idea of revenge, blowing up Pan American Flight 103 over Scotland in December 1988. The violence in the Middle East had not ended; even the death of the charismatic Ayatollah Khomeini the following year did not end the fear that Iran would overthrow its Arab foes in the cause of a purified form of Islam.

Although the Reagan administration had barely dodged some real and political bullets foreign and domestic, the president had reason to believe that he would depart office leaving the American military "standing tall" and in the hands of his former vice president, George H.W. Bush, an easy winner in the presidential election of 1988 over a liberal Democrat, Michael Dukakis. The central strategic relationship with the Soviet Union showed several signs of improvement. The INF treaty, ratified by Congress in 1988, had created a favorable momentum for more START negotiations and NATO-Warsaw Pact conventional-forces reductions discussions. Symbolizing the new spirit of détente, American and Russian defense and military officials began visiting each other's military forces.

Real defense spending had fallen off by 10 percent in 1986–1989, but from levels so high that the services and defense industries had thus felt only slight pain. In 1988 the administration finally admitted it had a problem and actually submitted a "no real growth" budget, with much of the savings to come from reducing commitments to strategic weapons and shipbuilding. The MX missile program came to a halt with fifty, not two hundred, missiles and not a mobile one among them; the complementary program for a smaller, mobile missile—"Midgetman"—still existed, but only in the talking stage. The B-1 bomber program halted just short of 100 aircraft, overtaken in Air Force enthusiasm by the B-2, a flying wing with radar-deflecting or "stealth" characteristics. The Air Force, more or less in secret, already had a stealth attack aircraft, the F-117A.

For all the ominous predictions about a major collapse in the political support for defense spending and high-tech weapons, the armed forces had every reason to view the future with modest optimism. Uniformed personnel strength stood stable at 2.1 million, and the officer corps, career enlisted force, and first-termers all looked outstanding by every measure of skill, commitment, and trainability. All the services had virtually rearmed themselves in the 1980s, even though they all had much-coveted weapons, aircraft, and vehicles still in the development stage. Serious training and crisis deployments had given the military valuable experience. A much heralded congressional initiative, the Goldwater-Nichols Defense Reorganization Act (1986), demanded that the services educate their officers and train their forces for more effective joint operations.

In January 1989 Ronald Reagan snapped off one of his best Hollywood salutes and rode off into the sunset—aboard a Marine helicopter and Air Force One—to retirement in California. The armed forces had given him one last present: two Libyan MiGs shot down on January 4 over the Gulf of Sidra. To the degree that enhanced military capability had relevance to American foreign policy and an unsteady pattern of international relations, Reagan had certainly left the defense establishment more capable than he had found it. Unfairly portrayed by his critics as a pliable Washington functionary whose ambition consistently outstripped his performance, George Bush, a former Navy pilot who had seen real Japanese bullets in World War II, assumed the role of commander in chief and immediately plunged into a maelstrom of crises. The results could only have bedazzled the most imaginative writer of Washington political novels or the high-tech "shoot-'em-ups" that had become so fashionable in the 1980s.

The Bush Administration Confronts Regional Crises

Like deer frozen in the headlights of an oncoming car, the Bush administration, much of Congress, and the American armed forces found themselves barely able to respond to the rush of events that marked the end of the Cold War in 1989–1991. The administration's policy immobility had nothing to do with its human talent. The president himself, who continued to dodge charges that he was a collaborator in the Iran-*contra* affair, had been an important participant in national security affairs for almost twenty years. Secretary of State James Baker had eight years of hard service in the Reagan administration. And although Secretary of Defense Richard Cheney had no special experience in defense matters and had dodged military service in the Vietnam era, he proved a quick learner, an aggressive advocate for the military, and a political realist, a quality he had learned as the chief of staff of Gerald Ford's White House organization. The national security adviser, retired Air Force Lieutenant General Brent Scowcroft, had served Ford in the same role. Admiral William Crowe, a cerebral submariner with a Princeton Ph.D., served out his term as chairman of the Joint Chiefs of Staff, then turned the empowered position over to General Colin Powell, who became the first Army ROTC graduate, youngest, and first African-American to hold the post. More relevant, Powell had ample Washington experience in the White House and on Caspar Weinberger's staff, as well as a respectable record as a field soldier in Vietnam and Europe. The political appointees on the National Security Council staff, in the State and Defense Departments, the CIA, and other organizations with national security responsibilities were also strong on experience and public-service commitment. Their intellectual preparation and political savvy, however, would be sorely tested in the next four years.

The collapse of the Soviet Union and the Warsaw Pact came in a rush, with the first erosion of Soviet power most dramatic in the Baltic republics, Poland, East Germany, Hungary, Romania, and Czechoslovakia. Leading the revolt, in late 1989 the East Germans destroyed their Communist leadership and security organizations in a mass revolt that bullets could not stop. The Berlin Wall and the fence that marked the "Iron Curtain" came down, and in November 1990 the Warsaw Pact dissolved as a military alliance amid cries of "Russians Go Home!" NATO scrambled from its fortieth-anniversary celebration in 1989 to participating in the negotiations the following year that produced a unified Germany in September 1990, which became a member of the alliance. The Bundeswehr painted Iron Crosses on Russian-made combat vehicles and moved to the Polish border, which the Germans pledged to respect. Gorbachev, with American encouragement, struggled to survive. He pledged political liberalism and capitalism at home and presided over the official dissolution of the Communist Party of the Soviet Union in early 1990. He signed a conventional-forces agreement in November 1990, and a START agreement in July 1991. In August 1991 a cabal of Russian party and military leaders staged an unsuccessful coup that folded (despite the fact that Gorbachev was held captive) because the Russian army and security services would not fire upon the thousands of enraged comrades who rallied to Boris Yeltsin, newly elected president of the semi-autonomous Russian republic. The anger of 1917 had returned to Russia, but this time the Bolsheviks were not the beneficiaries. By the end of 1991 the Soviet Union had passed into the dustbin of history, replaced by a commonwealth of independent states whose loose unity was soon more honored in the breach than in the observance. The rest of the world watched with wonder.

The Bush administration, hectored by the Democratic majority in Congress and nudged by its NATO allies, began to review the uncertain international security environment in 1989. The following year it admitted that its defense plans, which projected a return to real growth budgets, had been overtaken by events. In 1990 Congress ordered a 13 percent reduction of defense spending over the next five years. Bush then proposed a modest and phased reduction of the armed forces that might cut active operational units, especially those assigned a NATO role. The administration accepted a postponement of varied NATO nuclear and conventional modernization plans and a reduction of allied defense spending on the order of 4.7 percent a year, pleading that murky developments outside Europe precluded unilateral disarmament, already underway in the remnants of the Soviet Union. Under the guidance of General Powell, the Joint Chiefs of Staff drew up an array of plans to cut spending and reduce the force structure as much as one-third, the most dramatic adjustment since the beginning of the Cold War. The individual services found these reductions unimaginable, since the most dramatic effect of such cuts would be the end of quality recruitment and the draconian release of career officers and noncommissioned officers in order to produce a force as small as 1.8 million.

Ever skeptical that the rash of democratization and demilitarization would usher in a "new age" military, the armed services did not have to wait long for new missions. Continued chaos in Lebanon and an abortive popular revolt in China in 1989 did not produce U.S. military intervention, to no one's dismay except the Lebanese and the Chinese reformers. In the Philippines, Corazon Aquino survived with American military assistance both the insurgency of the Communist New People's Army and rebellion in her own armed forces, but she lost the popular mandate to former general Fidel Ramos. Nationalism, Filipino greed, and a volcanic eruption in 1991 drove the Americans from their Subic Bay naval base and Clark air base, but this retreat from empire had little meaning in the grand rearrangement of American forward deployments. With existing bases in Korea, Japan, and Guam, the military could still maintain an adequate presence in the western Pacific.

The Central American War (1979–1992) had provided the Reagan interventionists with their greatest victory at a bearable cost in American lives: Fewer than 100 in over a decade. The central strategic challenge was to isolate the Salvadoran insurgents from external aid from Nicaragua, Mexico, and Cuba, the latter a conduit for Soviet arms and American weapons shipped from Vietnam. Using bases in the Canal Zone and a new base structure in Honduras, U.S. air and naval forces basically blockaded Nicaragua, which had no land border with El Salvador. Honduras provided a sanctuary for U.S.-sponsored counterinsurgency forces. The permanent U.S. military presence, Joint Task Force Bravo, never numbered above 6,000, but U.S. Southern Command rotated "exercise forces" of up to 10,000 in and out of Honduras, which reduced Nicaraguan overland supplies to the FMLN and protected the counterinsurgents.

Without the expansion and concurrent reform of the Salvadoran armed forces, the interdiction of supplies to the FMLN from abroad could not alone defeat the insurgency. Members of Congress, outraged by human rights abuses (real enough) by the Salvadoran army and police, curbed some funding and restricted the members of Military Group El Salvador to fifty-five. The U.S. Army-Marine training mission sent teams to six different regional commands, enough to retrain six different battalions. The key to success in improving the Salvadoran security forces rested on the use of Honduras to train Salvadoran battalions, which fell into the hands of 180 trainers with $8 million per battalion to execute an eight-week program. The same training teams, built around Special Forces soldiers who spoke Spanish, trained the Nicaraguan *contras,* a coalition of expatriates and oppressed Miskito Indians, who then mounted operations against the *Sandinistas*. Big dollars also work wonders in small countries. Financed by the U.S., the Salvadoran armed forces increased from 11,000 to 56,000—and cut rural atrocities and corruption. Military and economic aid to Central America was $3.7 million in 1979 but increased to $200 million a year by 1985. Aid to Honduras and El Salvador between 1980 and 1990 topped $1 billion.

The Central American War never excited widespread domestic opposition because of regional disinterest and the lack of American military deaths, fewer than fifty in a decade from all causes. Polling in 1982 showed that Americans disapproved of intervention, but they did not know who the United States supported. Over time and at the cost of 75,000 deaths, the FMLN shrank to below 5,000 guerrillas, although it could make spectacular raids. Rightist "death squads" with ties to the Salvadoran security forces and the ARENA political party of ex-Colonel Roberto D'Aubuisson confused the effort to pacify the countryside by massacring suspected guerrillas or moderate reformers, including Catholic Church leaders. Under American pressure an elected, reformist government gradually purged the military. The first break came in Nicaragua. With 25,000 deaths and eroding power in the rural areas, the Daniel Ortega regime agreed to supervised elections in 1990 if the United States would stop backing the 12,000 armed *contras*. To his surprise, Ortega lost the election to a political widow, Violeta Chammoro, a woman of impeccable nationalist-reformist credentials. After two years of negotiations, the FMLN, stripped of foreign aid, agreed to disarm (slowly) and enter the Salvadoran electoral system. In 1992 the war faded away, and the Central American states began to demobilize.

Manuel Noriega of Panama and Saddam Hussein of Iraq made the case that the United States still required combat-ready armed forces of wide capabilities. After the death of his patron, General-President Omar Torrijos, in an air crash in 1981, General Noriega, chief of intelligence of the Panamanian defense forces and an addict of money, sex, and voodoo, used his management of violence and graft in the security establishment to create a de facto dictatorship behind a facade of constitutionalism. While maintaining a relationship with the American intelligence establishment through his usefulness in the anti-Communist crusade in Central America, Noriega also developed ties with Fidel Castro and Latin American drug-dealers, who found Panama a useful entrepôt for arms, money, and drugs. Ignoring a free election in May 1989 that had defeated his candidate, abusing Americans in Panama, and winking at the police murder of a Marine officer, Noriega challenged the United States to do anything and even declared war. Outraged, President Bush in December 1989 ordered the execution of Operation JUST CAUSE, the largest military posse in recent memory, which was organized to serve a Florida indictment against Noriega for drug-dealing. Launching a major joint operation from bases in the Canal Zone and the United States, 26,000 American troops ruined the Panamanian defense forces in an eight-day (December 20–28, 1989) campaign and cornered Noriega in the residence of the Papal Nuncio, where he surrendered. JUST CAUSE showed that the armed forces could do a Grenada-type operation with much greater deftness. The real victims of the battles in Panama City and Colon were Panamanian civilians, caught in gunfights and fires and victimized by the gangs of thugs and released prisoners that Noriega called "dignity battalions." Losses for the Panamanian military ran to 314, with civilian deaths calculated between 200 and 300. American losses were 23 killed and 322 wounded. The level of physical destruction, designed and accidental, caused a postinvasion crisis, and there is little question that arrangements for public security and civilian affairs operations could have used more attention. Nevertheless, JUST CAUSE could be reckoned a success.

Operation DESERT STORM: The Road Not Taken

On August 2, 1990, the very day when President Bush announced a plan to focus defense planning on regional conflicts, the Iraqi mechanized divisions of Saddam Hussein plunged across the border of Kuwait and in six days eliminated conventional military resistance against an outnumbered and uneven Kuwaiti defense force. On August 8, with his crack Republican Guard divisions closing on the border of Saudi Arabia, the Iraqi dictator declared the "lost province" of Kuwait annexed to Iraq. Saddam Hussein condemned the Kuwaiti ruling family, the al-Sabahs, for mistreating foreign workers and supporting Iraqi dissidents; however, for Saddam the invasion represented primarily a financial coup de main that would place Kuwaiti oil in Iraqi hands. It was a desperate attempt to increase the oil revenues that he needed to pay his war debts, rebuild his army and air force, pacify his core Sunni Muslim supporters, pursue his grandiose plans to build nuclear and chemical strategic weapons, and replace the now-lost largesse from the Soviet Union and the anti-Iranian Western nations. The Iraqi conquest of Kuwait also put Saudi Arabia at risk; the loss of the Saudi kingdom would have created a global oil crisis and destroyed for the second time in a decade the American effort to develop a *rich* Islamic partner in the Middle East. (Egypt met the religious test but not the prosperity standards.) An unchallenged Iraqi victory there would have increased the danger to Israel and to every established Arab regime in the region. Despite the gnawing suspicion that American diplomacy had appeased rather than warned Saddam Hussein, the Bush administration quickly rallied, and on August 5 the president declared that he would wage war if necessary to restore Kuwait's independence.

The American-led coalition of twenty-four nations that won the Gulf War by March 1991 did not spring to arms automatically or easily, and to a large degree the Bush administration earned the dramatic military victory in the face of considerable political odds. The first challenge was to persuade the Saudi ruling family, led by King Fahd ibn Abdul-Aziz, to permit American troops to come by the thousands and inundate a highly structured, traditional Muslim society with young Westerners, including female service personnel. After some debate the ruling elders of the House of Saud admitted that the Iraqi army posed the greater danger and pledged their full cooperation to Bush's envoy, Secretary of Defense Dick Cheney, on August 7, 1990. A key American ally in the negotiations was Prince Bandar ibn Sultan, the ambassador to Washington. The first diplomatic victory forced more frenetic international activity to isolate Iraq and muster overwhelming power to protect Saudi Arabia and, eventually, persuade Saddam Hussein to bring his army home. The United States used the United Nations as a major forum for coalition diplomacy, and between August and November 1990 the United Nations called for several kinds of sanctions to free Kuwait. Ultimately, the UN Security Council authorized the use of force to defeat Iraq if it did not withdraw from Kuwait by January 15, 1991.

Using the United Nations to give the rescue mission international legitimacy did not solve all the difficulties that faced Secretary of State Jim Baker. One major task was to prevent the Soviet Union, staggering but still potent, from providing any military assistance to Iraq or attempting to mediate a separate peace settlement. Although the Russians played coy, Gorbachev again bowed to reality and stepped to the sidelines in January 1991. In addition, Baker had to tolerate all sorts of instant peacemakers, foreign and domestic, whose futile exertions were cleverly encouraged by Iraqi Foreign Minister Tariq Aziz.

Iraq entered the confrontation with several frightening trump cards. It held over 2 million foreign nationals hostage, about 8,000 of whom came from the United States, other NATO nations, and Japan. Iraq also had a chemical and bacteriological warfare capability, and Western intelligence knew that its nuclear weapons program had advanced to a dangerous stage. These "weapons of mass destruction" made the potential targets determined to eliminate them. The United States, however, did not want one of these target nations, Israel, to join the coalition since its commitment would give Saddam more credibility when he called for holy war and radical rebellion by the Arab masses against "pro-Israeli" Arab governments. King Hussein of Jordan, in fact, tilted toward Iraq, and President Hosni Mubarak of Egypt waffled, for both faced real internal threats. It became essential to keep Israel out of the war; otherwise, Baker feared, his Muslim partners would leave the Western coalition.

In addition to ensuring that some nations would not participate, American diplomacy recruited a true international force—and not one bought with American dollars. Twenty-three other nations contributed air and ground forces of some kind, ranging from full divisions to medical and chemical warfare teams. Twenty-three navies participated in operations in the Middle East and Mediterranean as well as eleven different air forces and twenty-two different armies. Turkey made a major contribution outside the Kuwaiti Theater of Operations (KTO) by massing its forces on Iraq's northern border to produce a second front, and it opened its air bases to U.S. Air Force units. The military units from NATO countries fit easily into a system of coalition command, but to recognize Saudi participation and Arab sensitivities, the ground units of the Gulf Cooperation Council (Saudi Arabia, Kuwait, Qatar, the United Arab Emirates, and Oman) remained under the command of Saudi Lieutenant General Khalid ibn Sultan rather than the formal coalition theater commander, General H. Norman Schwarzkopf, U.S. Army and commanding general of U.S. Central Command (CENTCOM), the successor of the RDJTF. Outside of General Khalid's command, the largest Allied contingents were a British armored division and a French light armored division. Showing many flags along the "line drawn in the sand" did not exhaust American diplomatic goals; unlike the purchased Allied participation in Korea and Vietnam, the United States wanted some help—a great deal of help—with the direct costs of the war, estimated later at $100 billion from the treasury of the United States. The "United Fund" for the alliance reached $54 billion pledged and paid after the war's end; outside of the Gulf Cooperation Council the largest donors were Japan, Germany, and Korea. Other nations provided base rights, services in kind, relief funds, and subventions to the cause.

The Bush administration's successful diplomacy helped provide domestic political legitimacy to the intervention. The tides of support and reservation ebbed and flowed through Congress, the national media, and the public; approval of Bush's early actions slipped away as August cooled into October, for serious questions arose about the nature, scope, and duration of the commitment. In November 1990 one national poll found that the public could muster a majority for only one reason to attack

Iraq: To destroy its nuclear weapons. Only about one-third favored restoring the Kuwaiti government or protecting Middle East oil. Foreign policy gurus of both political parties clucked over the dangers of an extended ground war, the Iraqi use of nuclear or chemical weapons, and the danger of alienating the Arab world forever. Not until January 12, 1991, did Congress vote its support for the war, 52–47 in the Senate and 250–183 in the House. Another concern was the fate of the Western hostages, but Saddam Hussein, in one of several major miscalculations, released them in December. Calls for peaceful negotiations came from virtually every European capital, influenced by Iraqi threats of terrorism and Saddam's demand for a final Palestinian solution. Whipsawed between his instinct to lead a crusade against Saddam Hussein and his craving for public approval, George Bush himself swayed in the breeze, but he had already set in motion a military juggernaut that he feared he would have to use to free Kuwait, if only in order to restore world confidence in America's will to use force.

Dubbed Operation DESERT SHIELD, Central Command hastily patched together a rump version of a Middle East contingency plan (1002–90), and on August 7 the first F-15s landed in Saudi Arabia, followed by transports bearing the ready brigade of the U.S. 82d Division (Airborne). Their mission was simple: deter or stop an Iraqi invasion of Saudi Arabia. Only eight weeks later would Schwarzkopf's subordinate commanders feel certain they could accomplish this task. When the DESERT SHIELD deployment began, General Powell and the Joint Chiefs believed they would need four months to get an adequate force of 250,000 into the KTO and its relevant waters. Moving troops stretched Transportation Command's air fleet beyond capacity, and civilian charter carriers had to fill the breach. Before the war ended aircraft had moved almost 500,000 troops and almost 600,000 tons of supplies to the Gulf.

But the logistical foundation of a high-technology foreign war, especially one using mechanized and airmobile ground forces, must move by sea. Fewer than 3,000 troops (mostly drivers) came by sea, but ships brought 3.4 million tons of supplies and equipment and 6.1 million tons of fuel. Unlike similar buildups in World War II, Korea, and Vietnam, adequate port facilities awaited the vessels; unlike World War II, no lurking submarines took their toll. Even with a decade of preparation, the logistical basis for a major air war, especially the stockpiling of fuel and ordnance, required mighty labors. Improvisation and extemporized organization—including vast contracting to Middle Eastern businesses—became the order of the day and transformed the Saudi kingdom into a military bazaar. In the meantime Schwarzkopf's principal forces fell into place—or, rather, drove out into the desert: the Army's 82d Division (Airborne), 101st Division (Air Assault), and 24th Infantry Division (Mechanized); and the I Marine Expeditionary Force, an integrated air-ground team of one mechanized division and one tactical aircraft wing of fighter-bombers and helicopters. Air Forces Central Command under Lieutenant General Charles Horner, a joint and combined air component based on land and abroad carriers, had 600 Air Force combat aircraft of eight types and the Navy three (soon four) carrier groups available. Total allied air strength in the theater in September 1990 was over 1,200 planes.

As the diplomats pulled and the logisticians hauled, the Bush administration looked into the future in October–November 1990 and saw no easy light at the end of the sandstorm. A dictator with no significant internal opposition (at least no one who could kill him before he killed them), Saddam Hussein believed time was on his side. His own forces redeployed to defend Kuwait, regular army divisions were sent to the Saudi border to hunker down in elaborate sand fortifications and barriers, the crack mechanized Republican Guard divisions deployed as a mobile reserve west and north of Kuwait City. Estimates of Iraqi divisions in the KTO ran as high as thirty-six divisions, with 400,000–450,000 troops and 4,000 tanks. (Although electronics intelligence and photo reconnaissance could provide order-of-battle information, it could not gauge morale, training readiness, or the actual numbers of effectives, only "bean counts" of equipment and unit identifications.) From a coalition perspective, the Iraqis looked formidable, especially if they used their estimated 3,000 artillery pieces to spray the front with poison gas. Economic sanctions against Iraq took their bite in September; oil no longer left Iraq and few goods (including food) came in by air or sea. The economic embargo became a naval blockade. The coalition navies patrolled the Persian Gulf and the Red Sea, especially the latter, since Iraq tried to slip supplies through Aqaba, the historic port of timorous Jordan. The navies challenged 7,500 merchant ships, conducted 964 boardings, fired 11 warning shots, and forced 51 ships to divert, with 90 percent of the incidents in the Red Sea. The economic war had, however, no appreciable impact on Saddam Hussein's will or his army's capability.

In early October the president asked whether the Joint Chiefs or the Central Command had an offensive plan for the liberation of Kuwait. The answer was "not quite," although Cheney, Powell, and Schwarzkopf had discussed the option. They assumed that any offensive campaign would involve a massive air action, surpassing the scale of LINEBACKER operations in Vietnam in 1972; they also thought some ground campaign would be necessary but paled at the possible casualties. In fact, no senior military officer showed much enthusiasm for a ground attack. Nevertheless, Central Command tried its hand at some preliminary plans utilizing the force that would be on the ground in December and produced concepts that looked more like the Battle of the Somme than Patton's drive across France in 1944. The problem was clearly the numbers and structure of the existing forces, so light and amphibious that any ground campaign would have to hug the coast. No matter how the joint planners struggled in Washington or Saudi Arabia, they could not produce an option of quick victory and light casualties unless the United States doubled its forces in the KTO. On November 8 Bush announced he would increase the American forces in order to create an offensive capability. The Joint Chiefs knew the numbers: Two heavy divisions and an armored cavalry regiment of the U.S. VII Corps would leave Germany for Saudi Arabia and draw into its structure two more heavy divisions from the United States, the 1st Infantry Division (Mechanized) and the 1st Cavalry Division (Armored). The Marine Corps would add another division to the I MEF and place a second amphibious brigade in the Gulf. The Navy would roughly double its ships in the area, and the Air Force would increase its operational squadrons by about one-third. The allies would also enlarge their committed forces.

The expanded size of DESERT SHIELD forced Bush to face a serious popular test of his commitment: the mobilization of military reservists for extended active duty that might last as long as two years. The first call in August brought 40,000 reservists to active duty; three more calls from November until January brought the number of activated reservists to 227,800, and an additional 10,000 volunteered for active duty. Though facing income losses and job insecurity, the reservists rallied to the colors, and 46 percent of them eventually served in the KTO. Moreover, the mobilization of reservists from all the services dramatized both the enduring strengths and weaknesses of the Total Force program. Three Army National Guard armor and infantry brigades could not meet deployment standards without additional intensive training and never reached the Gulf. Almost half of Army active-duty and reserve medical personnel could not meet deployment standards, and about one-fifth of all reservists proved unfit by training, physical condition, employment, or dependency. The active force faced a major problem of the "new age" military: About 25,000 service personnel could not deploy unless they made arrangements for others to care for their children. On the plus side, reservists of all the services and levels of military experience, from Vietnam veterans to high-school youths, fell in and soldiered alongside their active counterparts. Reserves provided the muscle of the logistics organization. Air Force reserve personnel became indistinguishable from their regular counterparts, and Army National Guard artillery and engineer battalions served with distinction in combat. as did the Marine reserve battalions augmenting the I MEF. On balance, the Total Force program worked at both the political and operational levels.

As DESERT SHIELD Phase II flooded Saudi Arabia with additional forces, military planners in Washington and Riyadh created the broad concepts for an offensive war against Iraq, working under the political guidance of Cheney and the strategic vision of General Powell, Air Force Chiefs of Staff Michael Dugan and Merrill McPeak, General Schwarzkopf, and General Horner. Representatives from the Navy and Marine Corps provided their expertise on Schwarzkopf's and Horner's staffs, but the naval services were not satisfied that real "jointness" characterized the planning. In any event, the planners all assumed that an offensive campaign characterized by speed of decision and tolerable casualties required an enormous air offensive. Although relatively untested by Iran, Iraq's air-defense system looked formidable: A Soviet-style, highly integrated system of 1,000 aircraft (protected in concrete bunkers), 7,000 antiaircraft guns, and 10,000 antiaircraft missiles, all linked with redundant radar systems and communications nets. Clearly, this system would have to be defeated, but it could not have high priority alone. The Iraqis also had an estimated 600 Scud missiles, mobile and fixed, capable of hitting targets as far away as Tel Aviv and Riyadh; these missiles could carry chemical and biological weapons as well as high explosives. The air planners also planned to strike Iraq's fixed political and military headquarters, its arms factories (including suspected nuclear weapons facilities), its military bases, and its communications-electrical power systems. The planners envisioned a thirty-day campaign that would start with a "strategic" air war on Iraq proper, then shift to the Iraqi forces in Kuwait. If a ground campaign proved necessary, air attrition would pave the way.

With their memories of the frustrations of the Vietnam War, the air offensive planners envisioned a bold strike, of an intensity dictated only by the plans, the weather, the air forces capability, and the enemy, not by the media or by political irresolution. One way to ensure this operational freedom, which would exploit tactical and technological surprise, was to destroy the targets (some 400 sets in the air war plan) with a minimum loss of civilian lives. This requirement meant that Iraq's air-defense system had to be overwhelmed, so that the coalition bombers could use their new-generation precision-guided munitions without annoyance. Untested in real war since 1975 but trained and exercised throughout the 1980s, the massed air forces (2,600 aircraft, 1,900 of them American) had resources not fully appreciated by their own users, let alone the Iraqis. The aircraft and munitions themselves had been electronically mated with their targets with new precision, based on terminal guidance systems that gave precise thermal or visual aim points. The strike aircraft could find their targets under the direction of airborne air control (AWACS) and airborne ground target acquisition (JSTARS) systems, and they could be assisted by a fleet of aerial refuelers and electronic war aircraft. Teams of aircraft were prepared to hunt out and destroy all air-defense radar systems, assisted by Air Force and Army special operations helicopters. The major new capability was the F-117A Stealth attack bomber, whose radar-defeating characteristics made it invisible at night. To its own air capability the U.S. Navy added the Tomahawk cruise missile, also capable of precision attacks and terrain-following navigation right to the sites of Iraqi guns.

Under General Schwarzkopf's direct prodding, ground war planning produced a scheme of maneuver for the liberation of Kuwait and the ruination of the Iraqi armies deployed south of the Euphrates River. The key to the plan appeared obvious. Most of the main effort would come through Iraq itself. A fast envelopment by the armored VII Corps would sweep into the area between the Iraqi city of Basra and Kuwait from the desert and oil fields to the west. The VII Corps would deploy one armored cavalry regiment, one mechanized infantry division that would breach the border defenses, and four armored divisions (one British). To protect the VII Corps' western flank, the U.S. XVIII Airborne Corps would conduct air-mobile and mechanized operations all the way to the Euphrates River, where it would interdict the highway-and-bridge complex that led to Baghdad. This corps was composed of the French 6th Light Armored Division, the 101st Air Assault Division, the 82nd Airborne Division, the 24th Infantry Division (Mechanized), and a second armored cavalry regiment. To fix the forward-deployed regular divisions of the Iraqi army, which would let VII Corps destroy the Republican Guard unmolested, two offensives would cross the Kuwaiti border and drive directly for the capital. The first was an all-Arab corps directed by General Khalid, the second (and nearest to the coast) the I MEF of two divisions (plus an Army armored brigade) and aircraft wing. Two Marine amphibious brigades remained at sea to provide at least a diversion, perhaps a seaborne assault. In place without refinements in November, Schwarzkopf's plan required tactical surprise, plenty of air support, and logistical labors worthy of Hercules.

Schwarzkopf and his subordinates prudently remained cautious about the prospects of the ground campaign, stressing the formidable nature of the Iraqi defenses in Kuwait. In fact, they remained concerned about gas attacks, but their private appreciation of the Iraqi army changed with accumulated intelligence evidence collected by technical means and human sources. Such terms as "veteran" shifted to "war-weary" and "crack" to "ill-trained." About two weeks into the air war, three Iraqi mechanized brigades attacked screening Marine and Arab reconnaissance forces at Khafji. All three spoiling attacks collapsed in flaming destruction under Allied ground and air counterattacks; Iraqi performance and POW interviews painted a picture of an Iraqi army fading under air bombardment and the prospect of an Allied offensive. On the other hand, Schwarzkopf worried about the uncertain levels of air destruction being meted out to the Republican Guard and the possibility that the Iraqis would curl back into Basra and Kuwait City and conduct a protracted urban defense, some sort of Arab Stalingrad in which his armored forces would be checkmated and his infantry exposed to heavy casualties.

When the last flurry of peacemaking faded, President Bush ordered the implementation of DESERT STORM on January 15, which brought the beginning of air operations two days later. The ground offensive started on February 24, and the war ended with a coalition victory and ceasefire on February 28. The Kuwaitis regained their ruined country under a blanket of black smoke, the product of hundreds of flaming oil wells sabotaged by the fleeing Iraqis. Some American troopers washed their Bradley fighting vehicles with the water of the Euphrates, and all looked in wonder at fields of destroyed and abandoned Iraqi tanks and mechanized vehicles. Variously predicted at between 1,000 and 5,000, American deaths were so light that they became individual tragedies, not organizational traumas. The Air Force lost 20 dead in battle, 6 in other deaths in prewar training and in thirty-nine days of fighting. The Army and the Marine Corps suffered 122 battle deaths (35 to friendly fire) and 131 noncombat fatalities. The Navy lost 6 sailors in action, 8 to other causes. And 15 American servicewomen died in the war, twice the number killed in seven years in Vietnam. The Allied forces of 254,000 suffered 92 combat deaths and 318 wounded. The damage to the Iraqi armed forces in terms of effectiveness was decisive. Only one-quarter to one-third of its ground, air, and naval forces survived the war, but this force proved adequate to keep Saddam Hussein in power in the face of Kurdish and Shi'a rebellions in 1991. Despite disturbing television pictures of charred vehicles, Iraqi casualties did not represent a slaughter of the innocents. Saddam's government gave one estimate of around 20,000 dead, of whom 1,000 were civilians. Careful counting placed Iraqi losses at around 10,000 military dead and perhaps 2,000 civilians, 300 of them killed by a single bomb in a command-and-control bunker. The coalition forces accepted the surrender of perhaps 86,000 Iraqi soldiers, which proved to be almost half of the effectives in the KTO in February 1991. The survivors had retreated or deserted, not perished in the "mother of all battles."

Although the air campaign did not fulfill all its expectations, it ruined the organizational and technical foundations of Iraqi strategic military power, for the bombing of Iraq's air-defense system and military infrastructure came close to meeting General Horner's objectives. The Iraqi air force perished in the air (42 planes and helicopters), burned on the ground

(81), or fled to Iran (137); the rest sat out the war in their bunkers. Varied attacks by night and day at different altitudes and different directions by B-52s, F-117As, F -111Fs, strike versions of the F-15 and F-16, and Navy and Marine A-6s and F/A-18s gave the Iraqi air defenses unsolvable dilemmas, compounded by the secret use of pilotless drone decoys and Tomahawk cruise missiles. Coalition aircraft flew more than 116,000 sorties, 41,000 of which dropped ordnance, at a cost of only 52 fixed-wing aircraft from combat (37) and operational mishaps (15). Of the actual strike sorties, 23,000 fell on the Iraqi army in the KTO; the remaining 18,000 hit targets in Iraq that might be called "strategic." The combination of high pilot experience, sophisticated planning, electronic warfare, advanced technology aircraft, state-of-the-art avionics, and precision-guided munitions gave tactical air warfare a new dimension of effectiveness.

The air war did not proceed as planned or with predictable results, and the distractions annoyed Schwarzkopf. CENTCOM wanted more sorties flown against the Iraqi army in the KTO, not against hard targets around Baghdad that had little bearing on the ground war to come. The Iraqis posed a strategic challenge by launching almost 400 SS-1 Scud B ground-launched ballistic missiles at targets in Kuwait, Saudi Arabia, Bahrain, and Israel, January 15–17, 1991. An advanced missile developed by the Soviets on the technology of the German V-2, the Scud B had a range of 400 miles, traveled at hypersonic (Mach 2) speed, and carried a one-ton explosive warhead. It could also carry chemical weapons, as it had against the Iranians (50,000–100,000 estimated casualties from all kinds of chemical weapons), and Iraqi "weapons of mass destruction" fell to the control of General Ali Hassan al-Majid, notorious comrade of Saddam Hussein and known as "Chemical Ali," the scourge of Iranians, Kurds, and dissident Shi'a. The Iraqi Scud B was mobile, on a truck-like transporter-erector-launcher (TEL), but it still took at least thirty minutes or more to take on its liquid fuel. Nevertheless, the Scud B attacks threatened to draw Israel into the war and unnerve the Arab allies, both potential calamities for the coalition. Air defense suddenly took priority over the air offensive and continued throughout the war.

The defense against the Scuds fell to a U.S. Army brigade armed with the MIM-104 (GE) Patriot, a ground-launched air-defense missile first deployed in 1985 and thus untested in combat. The Patriot, also supersonic, could reach targets 100 miles away and as high as 74,000 feet. Guided by radar, it carried a high-explosive fragmentation warhead designed to kill Soviet aircraft and tactical missiles. Because it flew at twice the speed of the Patriot's intended targets, Scud B (or al-Hussein) presented problems for Patriot's computer software, guidance systems, and warhead. The Scud's flight speed made a late intercept explosion an uncertain method of destruction. The Patriot's pattern of deployment also focused on critical military facilities in Saudi Arabia and other Gulf allies.

In the first week of the Gulf War the Iraqis fired eighty-eight Scud Bs at targets in Israel (42), Saudi Arabia (43), and Bahrain (3). Twelve Scuds fell on Israel before a Patriot battalion deployed there in the emergency. Patriot radars identified and tracked the other seventy-six Scuds and calculated their flights to the likely targets. Forty-seven Scuds seemed bound for critical targets, and Patriots streaked off for the intercept, forty-five of which may have been successful. Nevertheless, forty-two people died from Scud attacks, six in Israel. Twenty-eight Army personnel died and ninety-eight fell wounded in one Scud explosion in a warehouse billet-workplace in Dhahran, Saudi Arabia, on February 25. In this one (and dramatic) incident, the Patriot's target acquisition software had eroded from extended use, an unanticipated effect. This episode enhanced the impression that the Patriot could not be judged a leak-proof defensive weapon. The growing analysis showed that of the 158 Patriots launched, the "hits" had not necessarily destroyed the Scuds. Half the Scuds had destroyed themselves within flight because of poor engineering. While the Army overcame the Patriot's warhead and software problems, CENTCOM used fifty tactical aircraft and U.S. and British special forces to conduct the "Great Scud Hunt" in Iraq's desert wastelands. In the desert the spotter teams searched for Scud TELs, and the allied air forces sent 2,400 sorties against potential sites with limited success, but the strikes kept the TELs on the run or hidden in caves. General Schwarzkopf understood why General Horner had to divert strikes from Iraqi armor and artillery, but he did not like the distraction. Fixing the Patriot became a postwar priority.

Another air war problem was the question of targeting and civilian casualties. Although Washington did not alter the air plans much, it did intervene to stop missions in the Baghdad area for fear of bad publicity (from the American media inside Iraq) about civilian bombing deaths. Although the armed forces had developed criteria they believed met moral and legal tests of "innocence" for civilians, military commanders could not always persuade civilian leaders that Iraqi politicians, police, technocrats, and weapons engineers had forfeited noncombatant status. When in doubt, the air planners lost political and psychological targets. The war ended, however, before the problem reached Vietnam-era levels of dissent.

With confidence born of hard training and immense fire support, Schwarzkopf's four-corps army (with two corps designated as U.S. 3rd Army) rolled into action in the early hours of February 24 and halted in victory 100 hours later. On paper the Iraqi army facing them numbered fifty-one divisions (eight of them Republican Guard), but only seventeen of them were truly mobile. The rest were committed to the belt of defenses between the border and Kuwait City and across the mouth and eastern edge of the Wadi al-Batin, a broad depression that the Iraqis believed the Americans would use for a short envelopment just north of Kuwait City. Seven divisions guarded the coast from the embarked Marines. Intelligence analysts now suspected that the Iraqi divisions totaled much less than their nominal strength of between 400,000 and 500,000, and that their equipment had been hard hit by Allied air attacks and a lack of maintenance; nevertheless, the defensive barriers, surviving artillery, and a decently handled force of 200,000–250,000 Iraqis could still inflict worrisome casualties, especially with chemicals. The Allies did not enjoy numerical superiority.

The first attacks, however, dramatized American military prowess, as most of the breaching operations progressed ahead of schedule with few casualties. Suppressing artillery fire and engineering vehicles allowed the troops to destroy the ditches, fortifications, walls, and tank traps; mines proved, as always, the real problem. Since I MEF and the 1st Infantry Division had both started the mobile phase of the operation—accompanied by the western sweep of XVIII Corps—Schwarzkopf ordered VII Corps and the Arab divisions to start the envelopment eighteen hours ahead of schedule. Despite some serious but small battles with elements of four Republican Guard divisions, the coalition armies swept forward amid cold, rain, oil smoke, and inhospitable terrain. Close air-support aircraft, mainly Air Force A-10s, Marine AV-8s, and Army helicopters, cleared the way, but much of the margin of victory came from Allied heavy artillery and mobile rocket batteries. The U.S. VII Corps, however, did not close the trap on the Republican Guard, being slowed by tank refueling (every three hours), fear of friendly-fire casualties (e.g., seventeen of twenty destroyed Bradleys), and an inordinate concern for an orderly advance. What should have been a speedy pursuit remained a careful attack. When the shooting stopped Saddam Hussein had salvaged enough of his army—most of four Republican Guard divisions and the refuse of the regular forces—to remain in power.

Some Americans, military and civilian, soon wondered if the Bush administration had not started its celebration too soon. Although Iraq accepted the draconian terms of disarmament, reparations, and compensation imposed by UN Resolutions 687 and 688 (April 1991), Saddam Hussein blocked international inspection of his remaining facilities (especially those with nuclear and chemical-weapons potential) and searched for ways to escape the still-binding economic sanctions while he rebuilt his security forces, at least for suppressing internal rebellion. During the war the American public would have supported a campaign to remove Saddam Hussein from power, but a wider war and a partitioned Iraq did not appeal to the European and Arab Allies. One consideration was that a destroyed Iraq could play no future role in containing Iran. Such realpolitik also exposed thousands of Kurds and Shi'as in Iraq to death and exile. The best the Allies would do was to provide them with relief, and Operation PROVIDE COMFORT in 1991 protected and fed nearly 60,000 Kurds. Iran welcomed Shi'a refugees.

The Persian Gulf War demonstrated that the United States armed forces could fight and win one type of conventional war far from its own shores—as long as the enemy chose to fight like a Soviet surrogate and allowed itself to be isolated from meaningful external aid. In a strategic sense, the war showed that Russia could not help its protégés, even those close to its own borders. One analyst remarked that the war proved that the United States could win where there were no trees. In an operational sense the Americans showed that they had the skill, leadership, training, equipment and doctrine to prevail—if allowed to execute their own plans within predetermined strategic goals. George Bush asserted that the Gulf War showed that America had put the ghost of Vietnam behind it. Two years later the more general judgment was that the United States should put the ghost of the Gulf War behind it too.

TWENTY

World Disorder New and Old, 1993–2001

The afterglow of the Gulf War victory carried the armed forces through the end of the Reagan-Bush years, 1991–1993. The era closed with decreased defense spending and low-risk military interventions. The collapse of the Soviet Union, brought on by its own internal contradictions as well as NATO vigilance, cast an aura of success around the Republicans' management of national security. The administrations' fumbles appeared to be small stumbles on the road to Cold War victory. For the public, American defense had three issues. Did we win? How much did it cost? How many people died? The lives lost meant only American military personnel. Even with the surge of defense spending in the first Reagan term, the cost of defense remained in the 6 percent range of Gross Domestic Product. Even with the spike in defense spending for the Gulf War, an additional $50 billion, defense spending declined during George H.W. Bush's presidency. In the election campaign of 1992, all the presidential candidates promised a "peace dividend" that could be justified by the reduced Soviet nuclear threat. A drawdown of NATO forces became possible because the Red Army had left Eastern Europe. Relative peace prevailed in the Middle East and South Asia, tied to the Russian defeat in Afghanistan, an acceptable Israeli level of security, and the exhaustion of Iraq and Iran. President Bush pledged a 30 percent cut in defense budgets over the next five years if reelected, drawing defense spending down to nearly $250 billion. His rival, Governor William J. Clinton of Arkansas, said he could do even better by squeezing an additional $60 billion out of the defense budget over the same period.

American military relations abroad and industrial health at home put finite limits on slashing defense procurement. By 1990 the United States had replaced the Soviet Union as the principal arms merchant in the world. Measured in dollars, Middle Eastern nations were the best customers. At an all-time peak of $20 billion in 1990, foreign arms sales climbed to $32 billion in 1992. The purchasers were Israel, Egypt, Saudi Arabia, and Kuwait. Lesser sums might provide greater leverage in poorer countries, at least in theory, but foreign investment in aircraft, ships, electronics, and missiles reduced unit costs for the Pentagon, a real incentive for salesmanship.

Military intervention in the Reagan-Bush years placed American troops in harm's way throughout the world, but at a limited cost in military deaths. Between 1981 and 1993, including operations in Lebanon, Grenada, Libya, El Salvador, Saudi Arabia, Kuwait, Iraq, and Panama, American KIAs numbered only 555. To put this number in perspective, the armed forces lost an average of 1,200 lives a year in training accidents and lost an average of around 300 members to suicide a year during this twelve-year period. In addition to military operations that produced combat deaths, American service personnel were at risk in peacekeeping missions in Honduras, Chad, Bolivia, Colombia, the Philippines, Liberia, Sierra Leone, Zaire, and Somalia. Despite Reagan's preference for unilateralism and Bush's tempered multilateralism, the United States sent money, observers, and logistical support to twelve United Nations peacekeeping missions, between 1988 and 1992, seven of which remained active in 1993. Despite its unhappiness with State Department humanitarianism and the UN's assessment plan, Congress still paid one-third of the UN's annual peacekeeping bill of nearly $2.5 billion. The armed services sent humanitarian missions to cope with floods in Bangladesh and volcanic eruptions in the Philippines and Italy. After the Gulf War, the armed forces looked more like an armed Peace Corps mission than the world's unchallenged military power.

Part of the illusion of a "new world order" envisioned by President Bush depended on treaty negotiations to reduce the nuclear arsenals of the United States and the Russian Federation (the core member of the Commonwealth of Independent States) as the heir of the U.S.S.R. The negotiators also sought a reduction of the NATO and Russian-Warsaw Pact forces in central Europe. The new Strategic Arms Reduction Treaty (1992) sought levels of delivery vehicles and warheads from 30 to 60 percent lower than the 1980s levels. The ultimate goal was for the U.S. and Russia to maintain an ICBM force of around 500–600 and a submarine force armed with 1,750 missiles. The Russians agreed to cut their ICBM force in half and their SLBM force by a third. Such phased reductions would eventually cut Russian warhead numbers from 9,500 to 3,000–3,500, the same number of American warheads. Both sides agreed to closer control and better survivability in order to foreclose first strikes. The treaty arranged for American technicians to help dismantle and account for Russian missiles; the first on-site inspectors reported appalling security lapses and dangerous design flaws in Russian ICBMs. The treaty disarmed the new states of Belarus, Ukraine, and Kazakhstan, which gave up ICBMs with 3,100 warheads and thus moved off the U.S. target list.

The United States also abrogated the ABM Treaty (1972) that limited antimissile missile development. The treaty had already been modified with imagination to justify "Star Wars" (a hypothetical missile defense system). In June 1992, the State Department announced that the U.S. would no longer deny itself ABM missiles and their acquisition and tracking systems. The projected ABM system would be deployed against rogue nuclear states. The Missile Defense Act of 1991 trumpeted a new mission, to provide "global protection against limited strikes." The concern for ABM defense actually reflected the failure of the United States and its UN allies to curb nuclear proliferation, a concern heightened by fear of the leakage of Russian expertise and technology to the Muslim world. The advances in ABM technology made a modest system to counter a limited threat appear feasible and affordable.

The Soviet Union's disintegration allowed the United States and its NATO allies to complete the Conventional Armed Forces in Europe Treaty (1990), based on the correct assumption that the Warsaw Pact was no more. East German soldiers entered the Bundeswehr or faced the trauma of working. Six Eastern European nations cut their major weapons inventory from 20 to 50 percent. Seven spin-off U.S.S.R. republics made more modest cuts; Georgia radically increased its forces, an omen of civil wars to come. The core Russian republic (Moscow) lost 50,000 aircraft, artillery pieces, and mechanized vehicles to the separatist republics but retained 5,150 aircraft, 13,000 tanks, 13,175 artillery pieces, and 20,000 armored combat vehicles, more than adequate to fight its rebels and neighbors but not a streamlined NATO, which had reduced its inventory of 81,000 major systems to 76,000, not exactly unilateral disarmament.

The faith that the Cold War had ended in victory encouraged the assumption that the nation's security problems had faded to minor nuisances. President Bush even sent veterans a fancy letter that thanked them for their Cold War service, a nice touch in a reelection campaign. The best concept cautionary planners could argue was that the armed forces should retain the capability to fight another Gulf War with enough force structure for peacekeeping missions and minor counterinsurgency expeditions.

General Colin Powell, JCS chairman, and Congressman Les Aspin, chair of the House Armed Services Committee, argued for a base force of 1.6 million but accepted an active duty force of 1.4 million, or 600,000 fewer active duty personnel than the troop strength at the climax of the Gulf War. The Pentagon created programs to force senior officers and NCOs to retire, reduce the million-person civilian defense force by one-third, and inflict job losses of 300,000–400,000 on the defense industry. Congress even relinquished the power (rich in patronage) over military installations to a Base Reduction and Alignment Commission (1988), a sure sign of reduced interest in defense spending.

The services, faced with strength cuts, planned to be smaller, but to be more mobile and armed with precision-guided weapons employed by highly skilled long-term professionals. For example, the average age of military personnel inched up from twenty-six toward thirty, with accompanying changes in rank structure and benefits for scarce technicians and expert field operators. Instead of a future 600-ship Navy, the 1980s plan, the Navy sought 200–230 surface craft and 120 submarines by 2000. The Air Force closed down Strategic Air Command and assigned nuclear capable units to a joint service Strategic Command (1992) that also controlled the Navy's ballistic missile submarines, reduced to fourteen, with four others converted to launch cruise missiles. The Army would stand down four divisions (sixteen to twelve) and eliminate one corps from its Germany-based NATO force. The Marine Corps by law would field three divisions and three aircraft wings but would reduce each by the equivalent of three infantry regiments (around 10,000) and supporting forces and stabilize at around 175,000 or almost 40,000 below wartime manning levels. All the services hoped that better training, less personnel turnover, and new weapons would offset numbers. One sign of the times was that the joint Transportation Command, a budgeting stepchild, received more money to buy large transport aircraft (the C-5 and C-17) and build squadrons of preloaded and predeployed logistical ships for all the services, not just the Marine Corps.

International statesmen—and not just allies—watched the United States reduce its forces with concern. The secretary-general of the UN, Boutros Boutros-Ghali, looked into the future in his *Agenda for Peace* (1992) and predicted the rise of rogue and failed states that would require UN action, especially if nuclear proliferation increased. The United States was the only UN member with a full-service global military capability. His successor, Kofi Annan, preached preemptive military intervention to resolve the growing number of civil wars, insurgencies, and communal conflicts, like the Tamil-Sinhalese war in Sri Lanka or the drug cartel wars that had ravaged Colombia. The thrust of these arguments raised strategic questions about post–Cold War use of force. What of genocide in the Sudan? Piracy off the Horn of Africa? What could be done about the civil war in Yugoslavia? What of the alliance of Persian fanatics and Arab terrorist organizations like Hezbollah, firmly rooted in Lebanon and Syria? And what was one to make of an expatriate Saudi millionaire engineer who in 1989 declared war on the United States as part of a *jihad* against Israel? Who was Osama bin Laden?

The Clinton Administration: Avoiding War and Inviting Future Conflict, 1993–2001

The disintegration of the Soviet Union set off a surge of strategic reassessment in Washington as the new Clinton administration and Congress faced a world without a plausible enemy. For planners who needed an enemy to shape contingency planning, the People's Republic of China became the villain-of-choice. Although it had modernized its armed forces and developed its strategic nuclear force (about 200 missiles, aimed presumably at Russia, Taiwan, and Japan), China never became a convincing threat because of U.S.-PRC economic interdependence. In truth, regional threats like Iran and North Korea fit the strategy of nuclear deterrence and forward, collective defense. This strategy, however, presented many options. Clinton endorsed a DOD report, "A National Security Strategy of Enlargement and Engagement," in 1996, followed by "A National Security for a New Century" in 1997. Both paid lip service to military leverage in diplomacy with a stress on economic well-being and promoting democracy abroad. In the mandated *Quadrennial Defense Review* (1997), the strategic gurus in DOD began to stress "post-modern warfare" and "asymmetric warfare," which encouraged more uncertainty, an invitation to solving strategic dilemmas by reorganization. A study by a congressional panel, the Commission on Roles and Missions of the Armed Forces (1995–1996), argued that theater and functional field commanders needed more power and resources, allocated directly by Congress or by a stronger JCS. The commission, loaded with experts, identified the threat of weapons of mass destruction (WMD) proliferation, information warfare, peace operations, and "operations other than war" as the missions of the future.

The Pentagon struggled to bring more definition to strategic thinking in the post–Cold War era. The JCS offered its analysis in "Joint Vision 2010" (1995) and "Joint Vision 2020" (2000). The JCS conceded that nonstate threats required more attention and that rogue state interest in WMD justified serious concern. The Chiefs urged more investment in missile defense and space-based information acquisition systems accompanied by modest force integration. Secretary of Defense William S. Cohen (1997–2001) admitted in his annual report of 1999 that a capabilities-based strategy appealed to him but could cost an additional $112 billion over the next six years. Readiness training and technological exploitation could make the budget unacceptable in Congress, which he knew well as a former U.S. Senator. Congress again tackled the "how much and for what" question with a blue-ribbon U.S. Commission on National Security/21st Century. The commission's reports (1999–2001) identified the force priorities: nuclear offensive and defensive forces for deterrence, better homeland defense against all WMD, conventional forces for major regional wars, and more rapidly deployable expeditionary forces for humanitarian and peacekeeping missions. The basic thrust, however, was that the U.S. should avoid diplomatic commitments that increased the chances of war. Within an administration focused on domestic reform, there were few experts in international security affairs since twelve years of Republican executive branch domination had blocked a new generation of Democratic realpolitik foreign policy activists.

Of all the policy issues for which Bill Clinton could claim real expertise, national defense was not one of them. A child of the rebellious 1960s and a passionate liberal-intellectual who viewed defense spending as a barrier to domestic reform, Clinton surrounded himself with staffers unmoved by the Pentagon's concerns. Clinton's agenda focused on economic growth and underclass empowerment. As a student at Georgetown University, a Rhodes Scholar at Oxford University, and a law student at Yale, Clinton fancied the life of classrooms and coffeehouses and shrank from the prospect of military service in the 1960s. To avoid conscription, he joined Army ROTC at Arkansas where he planned to attend law school, gambling that the Vietnam War would end before he was commissioned. Winning this wager with fate, Clinton sought extended educational deferments until the Army did not want him. Since many other college students of his generation had dodged Vietnam service, Clinton's suspended patriotism did not bar him from Arkansas politics. In 1992 he astounded the experts by upsetting an incumbent president who had just won a war. The election issues, however, were domestic and stressed Republican disdain for economic growth, urban renewal, and social reform.

Like Jack Kennedy, with whom he shared some common instincts, Bill Clinton's first-year performance as commander in chief impressed no one except his liberal, antimilitary White House staffers. He appointed relative unknowns, Anthony Lake and Samuel "Sandy" Berger, as national security advisers. Moreover, Clinton faced Colin Powell, the charismatic-celebrity JCS chairman, and a Congress full of defense experts like Senators Sam Nunn, John Warner, and William S. Cohen and Congressmen

Sonny Montgomery, Ike Skelton, Leon Panetta, and Les Aspin. Clinton thought he could improve his toxic relationship with his admirals and generals by appointing Aspin as secretary of defense. A policy "wonk" like the president and equally talkative, Aspin lasted less than a year. In December 1993, Dr. William J. Perry, an engineer-manager and protégé of the revered Harold Brown, moved up from deputy secretary to replace Aspin. During Clinton's second term, Perry, suffering from crisis burnout, left office voluntarily. Clinton replaced him with Senator Cohen. In the meantime, Powell retired and became a Republican. No other chairman or service chief ever approached his influence. Clinton's military detractors came from the Republican Party and from the unified and specified field commanders (the CINCs), especially General Wesley K. Clark, U.S. Army and SACEUR. A master of the quick study, Clinton learned the issues and made himself more sympathetic to the JCS, and he let Perry and Cohen manage the armed forces. In any event, Clinton also felt more comfortable as diplomat in chief, served by a State Department staffed with veterans of the Carter administration, many of them disciples of the noninterventionist former secretary, Cyrus Vance.

Once in office, Secretaries Aspin and Perry favored a capabilities-based strategy that could meet varied contingencies, but they tightened the definition to mean fighting two regional wars simultaneously, presumably with Iraq or Iran in the Middle East or North Korea. Few military planners regarded this view as realistic. The administration, in fact, continued to reduce the size of the armed forces until they reached 1.36 million in 2000. The defense budget declined to $267.2 billion but reversed course to $318 billion as the economy improved and the federal budget actually showed a surplus. Nuclear force modernization, spending on quality personnel, and investment in electronic improvements of weapons systems took priority over maintaining more people and units. "Star Wars" came to earth with the widespread development of night-vision devices, reconnaissance and armed pilotless aircraft, air and artillery ordnance with radar and terminal guidance, satellite communications and ground positioning systems (GPS), and advanced armor for people and vehicles. By 2000 the American infantryman had begun to look like his futuristic comrades in the movie *Starship Troopers*. Vietnam War GIs looked as anachronistic as their grandfathers in the movie *Saving Private Ryan*. All the "gee whiz" technology did not translate into strategic aggressiveness. International approval and the fear of public reaction to service deaths had a determinative influence on American interventionism or intervention avoidance.

The Issue of Intervention

In seven cases, Clinton shied from using decisive military force to shape commitments he inherited or initiated. In geographic terms, these examples of the Clinton way-of-nonwar occurred in Somalia, Rwanda, Haiti, Kosovo, Iraq, Bosnia, and Afghanistan. The bounded use of military force seemed like a good idea at the time—at least in public acceptance—but the unhappy consequences in two cases (Iraq and Afghanistan) left much more to be resolved later at greater cost. The Clinton administration certainly avoided military deaths. During Clinton's eight years as commander in chief, the U.S. armed forces lost only eighty men and women killed by enemy action; thirty-seven of them died in two terrorist attacks on military support bases in "friendly" countries, Saudi Arabia and Yemen. At least the armed forces could report that they had cut accidental training deaths in half and murder-suicides by a third from the averages of the 1980s. Such numbers also suggested a reduction in stressful training and reduced deployments as well as more supervision and counseling. The mission of the day was force protection.

The interventions in Somalia and Haiti demonstrated the limitations of humanitarian action. While it would be comforting to believe that the Clinton administration wanted to save lives regardless of race, creed, and nationality, avoiding American deaths had the highest priority. Clinton inherited George Bush's commitment of December 1992 to Operation RESTORE HOPE, a UN humanitarian relief effort to feed Somalis displaced by wars with the Ethiopians, Eritreans, and other Somalis as well as a drought. Fifteen Somali clans and factional armies vied with each other to steal UN relief supplies of food and medicine and to intimidate the thousands of unarmed relief workers. As the last vestiges of government disappeared throughout Somalia in November 1991, the United Nations arbitrators left the capital of Mogadishu and tried to organize a humanitarian relief effort that had military protection and could function throughout all of Somalia. Since the United States was already part of the relief effort run by air from Kenya, the Bush administration agreed to lead Operation RESTORE HOPE, authorized by the UN Security Council in December 1992. Somalia would be regarded as a failed state without a legitimate government, so the UN would provide political guidance through Secretary-General Boutros Boutros-Ghali, who accepted Lieutenant General Robert B. Johnson, USMC, as commander of the United Task Force Somalia (UNITAF) organized under the United Nations Somalia Mission (UNOSOM). Answering the UN call for troops, twenty-three nations sent military units to Somalia (seventeen sent ground combat units) for UNOSOM I (December 1992–May 1993) or UNOSOM II

(May 1993–March 1994). At peak strength UNITAF numbered 38,000, about one-third American, with thousands more troops afloat or in Middle East support bases and operated under American command. An estimated 50,000 Americans eventually served in Somalia.

Given its bias toward international humanitarianism, Clinton's State Department embraced Operation RESTORE HOPE, even though the Pentagon had reservations about the mission and troop levels. President Bush had announced that the United States might send as many as 28,000 troops to make Security Council Resolution 794 work and "to establish a secure environment for humanitarian relief operations in Somalia as soon as possible." The intervention should not favor any Somali political faction. In fact, the Somali warlords had no stomach to fight the Marine air-ground amphibious brigade that led 23,000 peacekeepers into Somalia in December 1992. The heart of the long-term stabilizing UNITAF would be Special Forces, a U.S. Army brigade, and a UNITAF service support command, totaling only 5,500 officers and men. The 10th Mountain Division brigade would provide the UNITAF with a quick reaction force should the Somalis attack UNOSOM. Although not free of sporadic fighting, the occupation of Somalia went smoothly enough because the two most powerful clan coalitions, the Hawiye/Habar Gidr of Mohamed Farrah Aideed and the Hawiye/Abgal of Ali Mahdi Mohamed, wanted to see how and when to turn UNITAF's presence to their rival purposes.

With humanitarian relief operations progressing well enough, the United Nations sent negotiators to Somalia to join Ambassador Robert Oakley, the U.S. special representative to UNOSOM, in persuading the warlords to disband their private armies, to stop stealing UN relief supplies, and to form a government. The Somali warlords did not care that the UN International Emergency Children's Fund was the leading relief agency or that children and the elderly made up most of the 400,000 Somali dead. They took from the poor and gave to themselves or sold to others for guns and drugs. UNITAF had done some modest gun collecting (mostly junk), while the Somalis had brought in AK-47s, light machine guns, heavy machine guns mounted on light trucks, and RPG light missiles, many of the weapons Soviet-surplus from Afghanistan and Ethiopia. Nevertheless, Boutros-Ghali, prodded by the United States, decided to declare victory in May 1993 and to enter a nation-building phase with UNITAF protection, labeled UNOSOM II and UN directed. Many of the humanitarian relief agencies joined the victory parade and turned over their operations to UN agencies, undermanned and unprotected. When General Johnson returned to Washington, Clinton joined the chorus of success, bought at the cost of eighteen dead (ten in accidents) and twenty-four wounded.

In less than a year (June 1993–March 1994), the Somali warlords commanded by Mohamed Farrah Aideed fought the Battle of Mogadishu and drove UNOSOM II out of Somalia. In a sense, it was Beirut all over again. The new UNOSOM II force shrank as its mission expanded to include breaking up the warlord militias. A retired American admiral, Jonathan T. Howe, became the UN political official in Somalia, and a U.S. Army general became the deputy UNITAF commander. The American force, however, shrank to a battalion task force from the 10th Mountain Division and a Special Forces group, which would be the quick reaction force for the polyglot army of light infantry battalions from twenty countries, the largest force 4,000 Pakistanis. Aideed concluded that UNOSOM II might support his enemies and confiscate his weapons caches if he did not turn his restless Mogadishu bands loose in an urban guerrilla campaign against the UN forces. In early June, Aideed's forces ("the Somali National Army" or SNA) attacked two Pakistani companies and other scattered units, killing twenty-four and wounding fifty-six. On June 6 the UN Security Council declared war on the SNA. With a heavy emphasis on using armed helicopters and AC-130 aircraft gunships, UNOSOM II forces could inflict casualties, but they could not convert deaths to victory. Much of Mogadishu rallied to Aideed to fight the foreigners. Instead of reinforcing UNOSOM II with U.S. Army tanks and Bradley mechanized fighting vehicles, Secretary Aspin persuaded Clinton to send a separate Quick Reaction Force (QRF), Task Force Ranger, to Mogadishu outside of UNITAF control. This elite force included a Ranger battalion, the operators of Delta Force, and helicopters from the 160th Special Operations Aviation Regiment ("Nightstalkers"). TF Ranger brought with it the most advanced night operations and target acquisition technology the Army had.

Using intelligence information collected by the UNOSOM II forces, including Somali agents, TF Ranger targeted Aideed and his senior commanders, who had already survived one major Quick Reaction Force (QRF) raid in September. The SNA fired RPGs at U.S. helicopters and led Somali mobs into the fray against the UN infantry. On October 3–4, 1993, TF Ranger and a Delta detachment raided a meeting of SNA leaders and completed the captures as planned. Before the raiding force and its rescuers escaped the SNA part of Mogadishu, however, TF Ranger had lost two UH-60 Blackhawks, three of six pilots and crew, two senior Delta sergeants, and eleven Rangers dead and fifty-seven wounded.* The raiders killed 300–500 Somalis. Covered in bloody detail by foreign TV crews, the battle felt like a defeat and ended the Aideed hunt as the Clinton administration lost

---

* Before the fighting faded away two days later, three more GIs died and thirty-four were wounded.

heart for Somali nation-building. In part for their role in the operation, Aspin resigned and Admiral Howe came home. A Marine task force covered the UNOSOM II withdrawal, justified by a temporary ceasefire. Watching the action on TV, Osama bin Laden marveled at American timidity.

The Haitian intervention (1994–1995), or Operation RESTORE DEMOCRACY, put an expeditionary force in that impoverished, chaotic African-Caribbean country, a model failed state. Legitimized by the Organization of American States and the UN, the United States chose to place Father Jean-Bertrand Aristide in the Haitian presidency, an office to which he had been elected under outside supervision. A junta of kleptomaniac army officers and street gangs pretending to be police had kept Aristide from office and attacked the demonstrations by his faithful. The gutters of Port-au-Prince ran with blood. Human rights and civil rights leaders in the United States demanded intervention. Ships of Atlantic Command had been blockading Haiti since October 1993, but without political effect. Almost a year later, after former president Jimmy Carter had convinced the Haitian generals that the U.S. Army would crush them, Clinton committed 20,000 American troops (about half Army, half Marine) to a UN multinational force dedicated to putting and keeping the Aristide government in place. The intervention started on a sour note. A Haitian mob chanting "Somalia! Somalia!" prevented one U.S. Navy ship from landing a military relief and security team. After six months of policing, the UN forces departed. Between September 1995 and March 1996, 2,800 American troops returned to support the UN mission in Haiti that conducted civic aid programs and supervised elections. All the help did not prevent Father Aristide from being a tyrant, but it improved Clinton's image.

The major interventionist challenge, however, for the Clinton administration became the dissolution of Yugoslavia. A tarpit of communal rivalries since the Turkish expansion into the Balkans in the fifteenth century, modern Yugoslavia had been a patchwork kingdom created after World War I, built on the wreckage of the Austro-Hungarian and Ottoman empires. It remained unified as a dreary Communist state after World War II, ruled by Marshal Tito, who was born Josef Broz. When one stripped away the glue of the Tito government and the Yugoslavian Communist Party, united in their hatred of Russia, Yugoslavia was an artificial state. Ethnicity was not an issue, since the Balkan peoples were predominantly southern Slavs. Most of them spoke Serbo-Croatian, a Slavic language. Culture, religion, and history had divided them into warring communities, exacerbated by the civil war that went on during the Italian-German occupation, 1940–1945. In the north, Slovenia and Croatia preserved their Catholic faith and European orientation from their roots in the Austro-Hungarian Empire. Serbia had been a hotbed of anti-Austrian separatism for centuries. Serbs regarded

Source: U.S. Army Center of Military History, *Bosnia-Herzegovina: The U.S. Army's Role in Peace Enforcement Operations, 1995–2004*

the Muslims and Croats as equal enemies. The Serbs saw themselves as the champions of Slavic culture and the Serbian Orthodox Church, as well as the only true patriots who had fought the Turks and the Germans. The capital of Yugoslavia was Serbian Belgrade, and Serbs dominated the Yugoslavian Communist Party and national armed forces. The dominant political figure after Tito's death was the Serbian-Yugoslavian president, Slobodan Milosevic, a bitter rival of Franjo Tudjman, the Croatian political boss and former general.

The dark and bloody ground of Yugoslavia was and remained Bosnia-Herzegovina (capital, Sarajevo), where Serbs, Croats, and Muslims had lived in uneasy peace. Bosnia had been an economic gate to Italy and the Muslim world. It had been a patron of the Serbian province of Kosovo, which borders on Muslim Albania. The majority of Kosovars are Albanian Muslims and keenly aware of the history of war and massacre that poisoned their relations with the Serbs. The southeastern corner of Yugoslavia was the Macedonian province (now a republic) and a Greek Orthodox region tied to the Macedonian people of northern Greece and unfriendly to Muslims and Serbs alike. All of the provinces of Yugoslavia had or could find enough weapons to wage war for decades. The Yugoslav national army had inherited German weapons from World War II and Soviet weapons from its brief alliance with the U.S.S.R. The dissolution of the Warsaw Pact armies and open borders meant Croatia and Serbia could draw weapons from all of Eastern Europe and Russia. The Muslims could import arms (with Arab money) from the sea and through Albania. Fifty years of conscription provided thousands of officers and men for a bloody civil war.

The Yugoslavian civil war did not start with Slovenia's secession (1991). Quick recognition of Slovenia's independence by its European neighbors, however, prompted Tudjman to announce that Croatia would no longer take orders or pay taxes to Belgrade. The Croatian army began to drive the Serbs, 20 percent of Croatia's population, from their towns and to extend Croatia's frontiers to the Adriatic. The Croats also resurrected the symbols of the pro-Nazi Croatian militias, known for massacring Serbs in World War II. Although the Croats had no love for Muslims, they had been and would be their allies in a war against Serbia. The earliest campaigns put the Croatian forces on territory claimed by the neighboring semi-autonomous province of Bosnia-Herzegovina, where Tudjman's forces armed Croats and Muslims alike. The Croats claimed they were only waging a preventive war against the Serbs since Milosevic had already in 1989 opened a campaign of repression against the Muslim-Albanian majority in Serbia's rebellious province of Kosovo. Claiming to be victims of Croatian aggression, the Yugoslavian-Serbian army struck back at the Croats and Muslims and forced Tudjman to agree to a ceasefire in January 1992. The Muslim Bosnians, convinced of Croatia's support, declared Bosnia-Herzegovina an independent nation, which immediately set off a Serbian invasion that occupied 70 percent of Bosnia by year's end. The Croats proved reluctant allies, guarding their conquests outside of Bosnia. With Milosevic's full support, the Bosnian Serbs declared themselves a new republic (under President Radovan Karadzic) with its own army, commanded by Ratko Mladic, a career officer-warlord of murderous instincts. By the end of 1992, the center of "the former Yugoslavia" had been plunged into cycles of conventional battles between Bosnian and Serbian armies, which the Serbs won; warfare between sectarian militias spawned urban sieges and massacres of Bosnian male "POWs." The Serbs raped women and abused children and the elderly. The basic Serbian goal was "ethnic cleansing," which meant driving Croats and Bosnians from territory that would become Greater Serbia. The Serbs drove 750,000 Bosnians from their homes and into the inept hands of the Bosnian government, led by a Muslim, Alija Izetbegovic. The war in Bosnia became the central front of

Yugoslavian state suicide and provided plenty of gruesome coverage for CNN, the BBC, and other international media networks.

Stirred by the international humanitarian outcry about Balkan atrocities, the North Atlantic Treaty Organization, led by Great Britain and France, edged toward intervention in 1992. At their annual meeting in June, the NATO foreign ministers called upon the alliance to plan for peacekeeping operations by a UN Protective Force (UNPROFOR). The Bush administration declared the United States a nonplayer in a European problem. Candidate Clinton criticized Bush's insensitivity to Bosnia's victims. Bush responded by authorizing relief supplies to be flown into Bosnia. In July 1992, under UN Security Council authority, NATO declared a total arms embargo and economic sanctions on Serbia. The enforcement of the naval blockade tightened, and NATO declared Bosnian air space a "no-fly zone" for all belligerent aircraft. Despite peace plans and limited negotiations, the war went on. In December the NATO foreign ministers agreed that NATO should, under UN authority, place coalition forces on the ground in Bosnia to interpose themselves between the warring armies while UN negotiators tried to make local ceasefires and set up safe refugee camps for the more than 350,000 homeless Bosnians still in the battle zone. In effect, NATO entered the war as allies of the Croats and Bosnian Muslims. In fact, Austria and West Germany had done little to curb the flow of weapons and money from their citizens (and churches) to the Croats, the supporters of the Bosnians from afar.

As the Bosnian Serbs showed no willingness to stop their march of ethnic cleansing, the UN committed a ground UNPROFOR to Bosnia's beleaguered cities and refugee centers in April 1992, but did so under rules of engagement that posed little threat to Mladic's army. This peace enforcement operation expanded the UN-NATO observer-support presence in Sarajevo and included infantry battalions from NATO and other European nations. The most demanding mission was protecting relief convoys and refugee camps—and moving Bosnians away from Serbian artillery and thus aiding the ethnic cleansers. UNPROFOR had limited troops (around 10,000 of the required 34,000) and UN-determined rules of engagement that made even self-defense problematic. The Serbs rejected a UN plan for Bosnian partition and a ceasefire because Karadzic and Milosevic smelled victory. The tepid UN-NATO response, affected in part by America's limited involvement, told them they had time on their side.

The Clinton administration inherited a limited air and naval commitment to UNPROFOR it did not want to expand. American reluctance was linked to an unrealistic desire for Yugoslavia to remain whole and doubts about the political restraints on the ground UNPROFOR. Clinton, however, conceded the State Department's argument that the U.S. needed more military-based leverage on Balkan peacemaking, so the president ordered the use of USAF transports to fly relief supplies to the Bosnians (February 1993). He then agreed to join the NATO air forces to enforce the no-fly zone more aggressively. As the Bosnian Serbs pressed northward, the Bosnians rallied with reinforcements from the Muslim world, many of them veterans of the war against the Russians in Afghanistan and the civil wars going on between the Russians and Muslim ethnic minorities. Evidence of Bosnian Serb massacres mounted, and NATO authorized air strikes on Serb armor and artillery positions. On April 12, 1994, USAF aircraft launched their first strikes on Serb ground targets. Still the Bosnian Serbs marched north, emptying villages along the way. Frustrated, Clinton actually withdrew American aircraft from UNPROFOR at the end of 1994. The most he would do was send a U.S. Army mechanized infantry battalion to the Republic of Macedonia, a symbolic gesture at best. The UNPROFOR troops at risk came from France, Great Britain, Canada, Turkey, Russia, the Netherlands, and Scandinavia.

The war in Bosnia reached its climax in 1995 and ended in negotiations (the Dayton Peace Accords) that partitioned Bosnia and allowed the Serbs and Croats to hold the territorial gains they had made against each other and the Bosnians. The United States finally played an influential role through Ambassador Richard C. Holbrooke, a diplomat who could threaten almost anyone credibly. The real catalyst for peace was Bosnian Serb atrocities and the vengeful NATO response. In the summer of 1995, the Serbs had placed the "safe" cities under siege with artillery and marauding infantry. The protected cities of Gorazde, Sarajevo, and Srebrenica shuddered under sporadic bombardment. The Bosnians captured Srebrenica in July 1995, unchallenged by the resident Dutch battalion, which had thirty of its men held as hostages. In the chaos, the Serbs slaughtered 7,000 male Bosnians. As the enormity of this atrocity reached the world, NATO authorized heavy air strikes and limited ground attacks that stopped Mladic's army at the gates of Sarajevo, Gorazde, Bihac, and Tuzla. The Bosnian Serb aggression sparked new determination to stop the war by force. The UN War Crimes Tribunal indicted Karadzic and Mladic for genocide and crimes against humanity; the North Atlantic Council basically declared war on the Bosnian Serbs; and the U.S. Congress lifted the ban on arming the Bosnians.

The NATO decision to mount a limited offensive against the Bosnian Serbs brought the United States into the war and produced war-ending results. Clinton finally conceded that Secretary of State Warren Christopher, Holbrooke, and General Clark were right in asserting that only American military power could stop the Serbs. With USAF and USN fighter-bombers in the lead, the air forces of UNPROFOR began offensive strikes in Operation DELIBERATE FORCE on August 1, 1995. The air attacks, constrained by weather and intelligence limitations, did not produce much Serbian reaction except the withdrawal and protection of Mladic's heavy artillery. The Bosnian government, however, agreed to a ceasefire and more negotiations. DELIBERATE FORCE reached a new level of destructiveness in seventeen days (August 29–September 14, 1995) of intense operations. During the period, U.S. aircraft from all the services, including Army helicopters, provided two-thirds of the ground attack sorties (2,470) on Serbian forces. American aircraft flew one-third of the support missions (1,065), which included refueling, comm-electronic support, target acquisition and bomb damage assessment, and search and rescue missions. The U.S. Air Force ran the campaign. By September 14, the air commander reported that DELIBERATE FORCE had destroyed 70 percent of its target list, especially the Serb's air-defense system. UN ground troops had advanced and ensured that the Bosnian Serbs fell back from their city sieges. The air offensive alone, however, did not turn the war against the Serbs since the retrained Croatian army also launched a counteroffensive that drove the Serbs out of the Krajina region of Croatia, held by the Serbs since 1991, and advanced into Serbian lands in Bosnia. The American-led air campaign, run more efficiently than the Gulf War air offensive, certainly hurt the Bosnian Serb army, but the Croatian ground offensive was at least as important in bringing the Bosnian war to an end. The Croatian army now matched the Serbs, thanks to an American contractor who provided an advisory mission of hundreds of veterans and technical experts.

The Bosnian Serbs and their sponsors in Belgrade needed a truce and recovery time, hoping that a ceasefire would lead to NATO disarray. Economic sanctions had hurt Serbia; support from the Slavic world had plunged with the turmoil in the former U.S.S.R. President Milosevic convinced Karadzic that time was on their side and that a peace now would preserve the Serb conquests in Bosnia. After many false starts, Holbrooke, an imperious negotiator, managed to coerce Serbia, Croatia, and Bosnia to sign the Dayton Peace Accords (November 1995), which pledged the signatories to stop fighting; to respect the legitimacy of an independent Bosnia-Herzegovina government that would control 51 percent of Bosnia; to disarm; to prosecute war criminals; to rescue the refugees; and to respect human rights. The UN would pass political responsibility for the settlement to NATO, which would replace the UNPROFOR with a multinational Implementation Force (IFOR) commanded by an American general. In December 1995, President Clinton announced that the U.S. would send 20,000 troops from a reinforced armored division to Bosnia-Herzegovina, 5,000 more to the Balkan war zone (primarily Croatia), and 7,000 more troops to bases in Europe that would support IFOR. The actual U.S. IFOR contribution numbered 17,000 in a 60,000-man international army, with units from all NATO members and eighteen other countries, predominantly Slavic or Arab supporters of the Serbs and Muslims. The dominant local force was now the Croatian army, which in effect made Bosnia-Herzegovina a Croatian protectorate except for the Republika Sprska, the Bosnia Serb "country" attached to the Federal Republic of Yugoslavia (Serbia and Montenegro). The peace worked—at least superficially—so that in 1996 the IFOR became a longer term Stabilization Force (SFOR) of 30,000, of whom 10,000 were Americans. In 1998 the U.S. Army still remained in Bosnia because the Balkan wars had not yet ended.

In Belgrade, the Serbian regime of Slobodan Milosevic still insisted that it was the legitimate government of all Yugoslavia. Serbia still included Kosovo province, a hotbed of Muslim separatism encouraged by Albania. By 1999 the Kosovars had mounted a resistance movement that included rallies, protest marches, political organization, passive resistance, and small-scale guerrilla raids by the Kosovar Liberation Army (KLA) on the Yugoslavian (Serbian) security forces. The Serbian army and police responded with a vengeance and opened a new campaign of arrests, reprisals, depopulation, and killing. Kosovar refugees flooded the borders of Albania, Macedonia, and Bosnia. In March 1999, the United States joined its NATO allies in a war designed to stop Serbian counterinsurgency operations in Kosovo and to save the Muslim civilian population from more ethnic cleansing. With political wishful thinking in flower in Washington and European capitals, the NATO strategy, to General Clark's dismay, centered on bombing the Serbian ground forces in Kosovo, often embedded in the Kosovar cities and towns and thus shielded by the civilians whom NATO was attempting to save. Although the U.S. Army deployed air-defense units, artillery, and helicopters as well as infantry and special forces to the borders of Kosovo, the Clinton administration, including the JCS, shared NATO's reluctance to confront the Serbian army. The aerial rules of engagement, designed to spare civilians as well as pilots, made it unlikely that the Serbs in Kosovo would feel enough pain to abandon the province. Muslim nations demanded action to save the Kosovars. The UN again turned to a reluctant NATO to handle Serbia, which ignored cease-fire initiatives. In October 1998, NATO had approved an air campaign against "Yugoslavia," but NATO again stalled when Milosevic agreed to negotiate and ordered token reductions of his forces in Kosovo. The war continued, however, and Milosevic danced toward and away from a peace agreement until NATO (with U.S. concurrence) ordered a new air campaign to begin in March 1999. General Clark as SACEUR would execute the plan, but he did not think it would work and requested U.S. Army units for a ground war. Secretary Cohen and the JCS balked, the White House temporized, and the Senate approved only an air campaign by a vote of 58–41. Russia tried to block action in the UN.

In an air campaign (March 24–June 10, 1999) against targets in Kosovo and Serbia proper, a NATO coalition air force tried to duplicate DELIBERATE FORCE, with limited success. The first phase against Serbian forces in Kosovo did little to stop the killing, as the Serbs and KLA grappled among 800,000 terrified Kosovars who had taken flight. The target set shifted to sites inside the rest of Serbia, including Belgrade. Milosevic talked, but still he did not say he would withdraw all of his troops from Kosovo and accept an international military and relief force in the province. He counted on NATO-U.S. disarray on the issue of a ground intervention, fed by bombing errors. NATO air strikes hit the Chinese embassy in Belgrade by accident, bombed a truck convoy of Kosovar refugees, and killed twenty civilians on a Serbian passenger train. Facing a hostile House of Representatives, which would endorse neither the air campaign nor the use of helicopters, Clinton rejected a British proposal for a ground offensive. NATO had put 25,000 ground forces in Albania and Macedonia, but the U.S. sent only a helicopter gunship battalion to Albania as a token force. The Europeans, however, with Britain and Germany leading, increased the pressure on Milosevic until the Serbs agreed to terms on June 9. NATO and Russian forces flooded into Kosovo as a 48,000-man Kosovo Force (KFOR) that included 8,500 American soldiers and airmen. The Europeans stopped the wars of Yugoslavian dissolution and sent Milosevic and his henchmen to the International Criminal Tribunal for trial for genocide and other crimes against humanity. Casualty-avoidance had postponed this strategic necessity by a decade at the cost of thousands of European lives, and the United States had been among the appeasers.

Air-power enthusiasts found much comfort in the statistics of the Bosnian and Serbia-Kosovo air campaign combined. In seventy-eight flying days, U.S. military aircraft had flown about 38,000 sorties, or 60 percent of all NATO sorties. More than one-third of the sorties had targeted ground targets, which had been pounded with 31,000 pieces of ordnance, 8,000 of which were precision-guided. American aircraft had dropped 80 percent of the PGMs. In all, the American air forces lost two aircraft, compared to thirty-eight in the Gulf War. The technical means of finding targets on the ground grew at an astounding pace; satellites and the JSTARS aircraft could find ground targets with radar, photography, electronic tracking, and thermal searches and provide floods of data that could be processed only by high-speed computers and experienced targeteers. Techno-rapture affected all the services, and Washington believed that it could create strategic influence with precision-guided nonnuclear missiles fired from twenty thousand feet. Perhaps the New Age assumption of safe "push button" warfare had finally arrived.

The Threat of Islamic Terrorists, 1993–2001

The issue of regime change in Afghanistan and Iraq by military force also confronted the Clinton administration and produced an even more limited response than the Balkan interventions. After Soviet forces left Afghanistan in 1989, the pro-Communist regime of Mohammed Najibullah did not survive a new civil war mounted against it by a coalition of anti-Soviet Afghan warlords and *jihadis* (holy warriors). Najibullah surrendered his government in 1992 to Burhanuddin Rabbani, who represented a loose warlord grouping known in the West as the Northern Alliance. A rival coalition challenged the new government. Its common feature was its roots in the majority Pashtun peoples who dominated the southern and more populated half of Afghanistan. The Pashtun coalition also enjoyed the support of Pakistan, which had given refuge to 3 million Afghan refugees and supplied the anti-Soviet guerrillas. Pakistani strategic preferences, shaped by its ubiquitous Inter-Services Intelligence Directorate (ISI), saw the Pashtuns as allies against an encircling India and Iran. ISI backed Gulbuddin Hekmatyar, the leading Pashtun-Sunni warlord, but shifted its support in 1992–1996 to a mystical, Islamic fundamentalist movement among the Pashtuns known as Taliban or "students of Islamic knowledge" in Arabic.

Rallied by a fanatical *mullah* (religious authority) named Mohammed Omar and reinforced by young men indoctrinated in Pakistani *madrassas* (Islamic study centers) and trained in ISI paramilitary camps, the Taliban had fought the Soviets, Afghan Communists, and the Northern Alliance with increasing viciousness and success until it captured Kabul in 1996. The Taliban controlled all but the northernmost Afghan provinces and a small part of the Pakistan border. It imposed a ruthless theocratic regime based on the *mullah's* interpretation of the social codes and religious practices they found in the Koran and *sharia* (holy law) drawn from it. In Western eyes the Taliban rejected centuries of hard-earned personal rights, women's liberation, and humane laws. Its religious policies, however, attracted external financial support from Saudi Arabia and other oil-rich Gulf States because the Taliban appeared to be an Arab and Sunni challenger to Shi'a Iran, the Great Enemy.

The Taliban continued to enjoy the hospitable sanctuaries and arms aid permitted by Pakistan, ruled after 1999 by General Pervez Musharraf, who had to manage the ISI and maintain the U.S.-Pakistan alliance. The

Taliban did indeed need outside help. Its mindless excesses encouraged resistance and international condemnation. Moreover, its rivals remained in control of the north and rallied on the principle that "the enemy of my enemy is my friend," at least for now. Some 60 percent of Afghans were not Pashtun. They were Hazaras with Persian roots, Turkomens, Tajiks, and Uzbeks with ties to Iran and the former Soviet Islamic republics of Turkmenistan, Tajikistan, and Uzbekistan. The Northern Alliance had its own heroes of the war against the Soviets. The best known was a Tajik, Ahmad Shah Massoud, the Taliban's Enemy Number One. Since 25 percent of Afghans were Tajiks and Massoud had proven a skilled, resourceful, and dogged leader of the Northern Alliance, he clearly became the center of the anti-Taliban resistance. His sincere patriotism and sympathy for Western humanitarianism also masked the Northern Alliance warlords' lust for revenge, personal power, looting, and control of smuggling and the opium trade, for growing opium poppies was the heart of Afghan farming.

Although the State Department and CIA area specialists warned about the Taliban's potential for mischief, the Clinton administration could see no obvious way to subvert the Taliban except by backing the Northern Alliance, which it chose not to do. That the Taliban could be condemned for human rights violations through the UN was easy enough. The difficulty was that a war on the Taliban required political will General Musharraf did not have. The central concern of U.S.-Pakistani relations remained the security of Pakistan's nuclear weapons and preventing another war with India. These goals required a stable, cooperative Pakistani government, a position that deterred the United States from direct assault on the Taliban.

Instead of worrying about the Taliban-Pakistani alliance, the administration focused on the consequences of the Gulf War and the central fact that a dangerous Saddam Hussein remained in power. Certainly the Iraqi dictator intended to stay in power until he transferred the family-clan tyranny to his sons, Qusay and Uday, murderous megalomaniacs like their father. The central instruments of control were the Baath Party, the security police, and a private army, the Republican Guard. Having lost a conventional war to the United States, Saddam Hussein formed two population-based regional paramilitary forces for local guerrilla-type resistance, the al Quds army and the Saddam Fedayeen (Saddam's Faithful Warriors), which cowed any insurgency. Within these sacrificial armed mobs, the Republican Guard would defend Baghdad. The other part of Saddam Hussein's desperate strategy would be the deterrent value and shocking use of chemical, nuclear, and biological materials mounted on missiles or spread by aircraft and other means. Although Iraq faced serious economic sanctions, including a ban on legal oil exports, Saddam intended to develop the impression that he had or would develop WMD capabilities prohibited by the terms of his 1991 surrender. He gambled that the U.S., the UN, and his regional foes would weaken in their resolve to enforce the arms ban and economic embargo, since they had not stopped him from crushing the Kurdish and Shi'a revolts of 1991.

The anti-Saddam coalition, especially the United States, intended to enforce the WMD ban through two groups of technical inspection teams formed by the United Nations and the International Atomic Energy Agency (IAEA). For nine years these teams struggled to identify, assess, and destroy the WMD and industrial facilities that could make nuclear, chemical, and biological warheads and the missiles and shells that carried them. Iraq cooperated only when threatened by force or when it became convinced that it would get some relief from its economic decline. The inspectors found that Iraq had WMD capabilities and had allowed their destruction, but Iraq had also made real and desperate efforts to obtain new WMD and to conceal others. In order to threaten Israel, Iran, and Saudi Arabia, the Iraqis tried to create the illusion of a vast WMD capability. Within this massive hoax Saddam Hussein never quit looking for ways to avoid the WMD ban and create a new WMD force. Exasperated by Saddam's duplicity, Secretary of State Madeleine Albright announced that the U.S. would not accept an Iraqi pledge of disarmament unless Saddam surrendered power and a new regime allowed extended, comprehensive inspections inside Iraq. Congress approved of more pressure to remove Saddam Hussein in 1998. The prospect of regime change threw the UN Security Council into disarray. Saddam Hussein intended to leverage the WMD threat into safety from coercion. His fantasies killed him, his sons, and tens of thousands of others.

Only after the Iraq invasion of 2003 did the true nature of Iraq's WMD program become clearer. The IAEA inspectors, who specialized in nuclear materials, concluded that Iraq had probably destroyed or converted its ability to make nuclear warheads, but that it had the technicians and latent facilities to go nuclear again, although it would have taken five to ten years to do so. The threat was real but not immediate. The United Nations Special Commission (UNSCOM), investigators of all WMD programs, found compelling physical evidence, verifying a defector's report in 1995, that Iraq had retained a limited chemical and biological weapons capability, banned by the 1991 terms. In order to make an agreement to sell oil for medicine and food, the Iraqis became more cooperative about inspections of fixed sites, but they also mounted technical equipment on trucks so that these production assets could be moved away from prying eyes. Iraq was also evasive on the issue of surviving missiles and warheads. When the inspectors left Iraq in late 1998, they believed that Iraq did not have nuclear weapons or the capability to make them soon. The status of chemical and biological weapons remained more uncertain, and 2003 inspections by the UN Monitoring, Verification, and Inspection Commission (UNMOVIC) found evidence of these types of WMD and missiles to carry WMD warheads.

The United States regarded Iraq's disregard for the WMD ban as serious business. It provided experts to the UNSCOM and IAEA teams. It maintained electronic monitoring systems that recorded events from underground to the ionosphere. It maintained its own intelligence sources within Iraq and exchanged information with British intelligence agencies. It built relations with the Kurds, the Shi'a Arab opposition, and Sunni expatriates like Ahmed Chalabi, who ran an exile movement. Sources within the regime provided Chalabi with information that suggested a robust WMD program. The program had an ardent director: Ali Hasan al-Majid al-Tikriti, or "Chemical Ali," the mass murderer of Kurds and Iranians with poison gases. Saddam Hussein made Chemical Ali the master magician to mislead the IAEA and UNSCOM inspectors. Saddam enhanced his evil image by allowing his intelligence service to attempt to blow up George H.W. Bush during a victory tour to Kuwait in April 1993. Saddam Hussein calculated that he could provoke the United States into enough reaction that it would split the UN coalition and brand the U.S. as too pro-Israel to make it a firm ally of Saudi Arabia and the Gulf emirates.

The Clinton administration did indeed conclude that Saddam Hussein needed a lesson in cooperation, and it ordered up its favorite weapon, limited air strikes. After the Bush assassination attempt in June 1993, Clinton authorized the destruction of the headquarters of the Iraqi intelligence and police service; twenty-three Navy cruise missiles fired from warships in the Persian Gulf leveled the building at night to avoid civilian casualties. Under more permissive rules of engagement, a U.S. aircraft returned fire on several Iraqi antiaircraft missile batteries. In regional politics, however, the administration still worried about Iran as a military threat, pointed in that direction by its Arab allies. Plagued by many distractions at home and abroad, the administration fell back in line with the Saddam-containers. By 1998, however, terrorist attacks and Iraqi lack of interest in proving its WMD innocence convinced Clinton to execute another aerial punitive expedition on Baghdad. In December 1998, U.S. and British aircraft conducted Operation DESERT FOX, a four-day campaign that sent 650 sorties and 415 cruise missiles at Iraqi headquarters, the air-defense system, weapons storage sites, suspected WMD installations, and military barracks. Persuaded that Iraq would remain disarmed and Saddam chastised, the administration turned to the Kosovo crisis and another new threat, a terrorist bombing campaign against American targets.

Behind the passing storms of civil wars in the Gulf, Bosnia, Kosovo, and Somalia, came the rising thunder of international, nonstate terrorism. Unlike the European terrorists of the 1980s, murderous romantics left behind by the popular protests of the 1960s and 1970s, the new Arab terrorists had learned their business in the Palestinian uprising, the *intifada*, in Israel. Others, most notably the Abu Nidal group and Hezbollah, took the war on tourists and commuters on to aircraft and cruise ships. Other targets included officials, military advisers, and public figures. The rise of Arab terrorism represented the wisdom of the defeats in 1973 and 1982 at the hands of the Israeli armed forces and the American victory in the Gulf War. The most prominent American victims were members of the diplomatic service, armed forces, CIA, and other travelers abroad. Except for shocking TV coverage, this war did not engage the American public.

The Clinton administration understood the menace of international terrorism because the Reagan and Bush governments knew the numbers and had passed on the challenge. Between 1968 and October 1980, terrorists made more than 7,000 attacks, 2,700 of which involved Americans, 173 of whom died and 970 of whom were wounded. In 1981 Congress appropriated $40 million to turn diplomatic centers into fortresses. By 1984 the State Department had created a counterterrorism office led by veteran diplomats like Robert B. Oakley and L. Paul Bremer III. The State Department took the initiative in forming a high-level counterterrorism interdepartmental group to coordinate planning to protect Americans abroad and to watch for incoming terrorists. The first assumption was that terrorists could not function without government support. Incidents in the 1980s did reveal the fine hand of Libya, Syria, and Iran, which supported Hezbollah and other Muslim groups that focused on the destruction of Israel and the forced departure of its partner, the United States, from the Middle East. Pro-American regimes in Egypt, Jordan, Kuwait, and Saudi Arabia also faced a rise of Islamic radicalism. Among the more shadowy groups that joined the government's watch-list was something called al-Qaeda, or "the base," which appeared to be organizing in Egypt, Yemen, the Sudan, and Pakistan.

Like other Arab fundamentalists driven from their conservative homelands, Osama bin Laden, a Saudi exile living in Yemen and probably only twenty years old in 1978, found a home in the war against the Soviets in Afghanistan. Wealthy from a family construction business, university-educated as an engineer, neither an Islamic scholar nor a soldier, Osama bin Laden advanced within the Pakistan-based *mujahideen* support system as a patron of the training camps and *madrassas* that indoctrinated young Muslims for the *jihad*. His politics found ideological focus in the Egyptian reactionary radicalism of the Muslim Brotherhood, foes of Egypt's military regimes of Anwar Sadat and Hosni Mubarak, reviled allies of Israel and the United States. Bin Laden's mentors were a Palestinian intellectual, Abdullah Assam, and an Egyptian doctor turned radical Islamicist, Ayman al-Zawahiri. As a leader of the Afghan Arabs, bin Laden drew volunteers to Pakistan to fight the Soviets and developed contacts with *jihadis* from the United States to the Philippines and throughout the Arab world. He understood electronic communications and banking. At six feet five inches, he also had presence, enhanced by his aesthetic thinness, proper beard, and accompanying glower. He had brains, a cause, and a store of hatreds that made him a formidable foe. He was delighted to be the cheerleader, planner, and banker for any terrorists who would target the United States, the true Satan. He and Zawahiri called their network al-Qaeda, "the base" for war on the Zionists and Arab reactionary regimes. After Azzam died in a mysterious bombing, bin Laden left Pakistan for the Sudan, where he could create a base separate from the Pakistani-Afghan battleground. Until proscribed by Saudi Arabia in 1994, he had access to Islamicists without much interference. He was especially impressed when an expatriate Muslim *mullah* and a Saudi financier managed to plan and organize a car-bomb attack on the parking garage of New York City's World Trade Center towers in February 1993. The explosion killed six and hurt a thousand passersby, but the building did not collapse. The subsequent investigation and trial of the Arab-American cell connected the attack to al-Qaeda. Along with the Gulf War, this event convinced bin Laden to move his *jihad* to the Sudan, a friendly host and far from American influence.

Terrorist groups could adopt al-Qaeda just as it embraced them. Attacks on Americans in Somalia, Aden, and Saudi Arabia occurred between 1992 and 1995 and drew al-Qaeda's endorsement. In June 1996, a truck bomb and suicide bomber blew up a wing of the Khobar Towers, a U.S. Air Force billet in Dharan, killing nineteen and wounding 372 service personnel, but the sponsor was a radical Saudi group funded by Iran through Hezbollah. Osama bin Laden endorsed the attacks and planned more with direct al-Qaeda participation, designed by his operational terrorist planner, Mohammed Atef, an Egyptian. Although he had made threats against Americans since 1995, bin Laden and four other "directors" of al-Qaeda issued a *fatwa* that called for a *jihad* against "the crusader-Zionist alliance" and its Arab collaborators on February 28, 1998. To accent the commitment, al-Qaeda cells in Kenya and Tanzania attacked the U.S. embassies in Nairobi and Dar es Salaam on August 7, 1998, and killed twelve Americans and 212 Africans while wounding hundreds more. The next dramatic attack came two years later, when boat-bombers blew a hole in the hull of the USS *Cole,* a USN destroyer docked in the harbor of Aden, Yemen. The attack killed seventeen sailors and wounded forty. Osama bin Laden himself had helped with the detailed planning.

The security agencies of the federal government identified Osama bin Laden as a special threat in 1998 and had targeted terrorists in general as a high-priority security issue in Presidential Decision Directive 39 (June 1995). The enormity of stopping terrorists and their bombs from entering any nation (the worst-case event) confounded the best organized, best informed, most alert nations, which the United States was not. Consider the 4,000-mile border with Canada, a cooperative nation. In 2000 alone, the Canada-to-U.S. crossings numbered 489 million travelers, 127 million cars, 11.7 million maritime containers, 11.5 million truck trips, 2.2 million railroad car-crossings, 829,000 airline trips, and 211,000 maritime voyages. The "system" relied on voluntary, peaceful, rapid, and preregistered notification and inspection for economic efficiency, but not security. The best screening could pick up nuclear material, but not other explosives without inspection. Border protection also required close cooperation among the CIA, FBI, Customs Service, State Department, the Immigration and Naturalization Service, Treasury Department, U.S. Coast Guard, Federal Aviation Administration, and Border Patrol as well as state and local authorities. Effective counterterrorism operations—preventing attacks— also required unusual international cooperation and shared national alarm, which the United States, compared with Great Britain and Germany, did not have. The most shocking event of the 1990s inside the United States was the destruction of the Oklahoma City federal building (April 1995) by deranged Americans. Most of the research and planning until 2001 ended at the point where action by law enforcement had to occur. For example, the U.S. Treasury and State Departments knew how terrorists could move and conceal money transfers by electronic means, and the United Nations had prepared a convention signed by forty-one nations (of 189 members) on combating terrorist financing. Only six nations had ratified the treaty by September 2001.

The Clinton administration in 1998 took one major step by moving the midlevel counterterrorism group under the direct control of the National Security Council, which placed its director, Richard Clarke, in close access to the president and the national security adviser. Counterterrorism programs still faced an organizational divide; terrorism abroad was a State Department, CIA, and military concern, but in the U.S., the FBI and Justice Department had the mission. As early as 1996, the Central Intelligence Agency took Osama bin Laden seriously enough to form a bin Laden unit (BLU) within its Counterterrorism Center. The BLU developed a clear picture of Osama bin Laden's key role in al-Qaeda and tracked him when bin Laden moved back to Afghanistan in 1996 to aid the Taliban and to embed his headquarters in those parts of Afghanistan and Pakistan where the Taliban and ISI could protect him and deter American overt or covert action.

All the plans foundered on the rocks of limited intelligence, uncertain international cooperation, operational complexity like the requirement that bin Laden be taken alive, and U.S. military skepticism. The CIA director, George Tenet, saw more risks than he considered bearable. NSC adviser Sandy Berger and Tenet reviewed the plans and doubted their success. Proposals to subcontract bin Laden's capture to the Saudis, the Taliban, and the Pakistanis went nowhere. The Nairobi-Dar es Salaam bombings made a direct attack on bin Laden, including his death, more acceptable. The retaliation Clinton approved, however, was the usual token indirect attack on places, in this case an al-Qaeda camp complex in Afghanistan and possible WMD sites (chemicals) in the Sudan. On August 20, 1998, Navy ships in the Arabian Sea fired a barrage of Tomahawk cruise missiles at these targets, destroying them and killing perhaps twenty to thirty relative innocents. Following good evasion procedures, the al-Qaeda leadership had departed for some other site and kept moving throughout Afghanistan, while Osama bin Laden used electronic means to order more attacks, thus allowing the National Security Agency to track his movements. The CIA and now the Defense Department kept planning, but none of the plans persuaded the senior responsible officials to strike or enlisted foreign allies. The planning did, however, link the future of the Taliban to the destruction of al-Qaeda, a sound analysis but one fraught with greater international complications, such as relations with Pakistan and Saudi Arabia. The CIA looked to the Northern Alliance as a potential source of operatives who could get inside al-Qaeda and kill bin Laden, an act Clinton approved in December 1998. In the meantime, the staff of Central Command, headed by Marine General Anthony Zinni, planned several variants of a heliborne special operations raid, but it could not station helicopters and special operations aircraft close enough to al-Qaeda's base network in southern Afghanistan without using Pakistani bases. More missile strikes seemed unrealistic since Osama bin Laden moved often; and when he stopped, it was in heavily populated cities like Kandahar. Still a low-success option, the CIA at least established an operational base in Uzbekistan and convinced Special Operations Command and Central Command to think about contacts with the Northern Alliance, especially Ahmad Shah Massoud, who wanted to fight the Taliban but regarded the plans to kill or capture bin Laden as fanciful. The contingency planning continued, a worthwhile educational exercise, but bin Laden as a man and al-Qaeda as a terrorist confederation remained at large and harder to track since an American newspaper revealed that intelligence agencies could trace his cell-phone calls.

In the fall of 2000, the United States had survived a confusing presidential election campaign that placed the governor of Texas, George W. Bush, the son of the former president, in the White House. The Electoral College system and a series of judicial decisions on the outcome of Florida's vote-counting ensured Bush's tainted victory. The president-elect, a reformed drinker and born-again Christian, brought little international experience to his new office. From college at Yale and Harvard Business School through his experience as an Air National Guard pilot-lieutenant through his undistinguished business and sports ventures, Bush had not absorbed his father's international experience and Washington bureaucratic skills. When he made Donald Rumsfeld secretary of defense and Colin Powell secretary of state, he probably thought he had solved that problem. His national security adviser, Dr. Condoleezza Rice, had more university time than Washington experience, and her expertise was Russian security issues. The emerging center of power in Washington became Vice President Dick Cheney, the former White House chief of staff and secretary of defense. Cheney ensured that his loyalists, who shared his urge to finish off Saddam Hussein, filled key positions in the White House, at the State Department, and in the Pentagon. In January 2001, National Security Adviser Sandy Berger counseled the Bush team on the terrorist threat with an emphasis on Osama bin Laden and al-Qaeda. Although the FBI and other police agencies had foiled some inept attempts to make the Millennium a terrorist event, the FBI believed that Arab terrorists had created operational units within the United States. The available evidence suggested terrorist planning for some sort of direct attack within the United States. Berger, supported by Richard Clarke, made one point repeatedly: The United States was at war with a new and more deadly breed of Arab terrorists who would stop at nothing to attack the American homeland and thus force the United States out of the Muslim world. The Clinton administration had done little to impress Arab and Iranian terrorists with its retaliatory will. No one knew where al-Qaeda would strike next, but strike it would.

TWENTY-ONE

Wars in Afghanistan and Iraq, 2001–2011

During the presidential election campaign of 2004, a favorite bumper sticker flaunted by unhappy voters read "Bush! Four more wars!" This characterization was unfair since the George W. Bush administration had initiated only two wars—with Afghanistan and Iraq—and they were only dramatic escalations of unfinished conflicts the new president had inherited from his father and Bill Clinton. These wars of choice, however, took on a dramatic new character after al-Qaeda's aerial suicide attack on targets in New York City and Washington, D.C., on September 11, 2001. Three hijacked airliners crashed into the World Trade Center towers and the Pentagon and killed almost three thousand Americans and citizens of seventy other countries in one morning. Passengers of a fourth hijacked airliner bound for the White House or Capitol building fought back and frightened the terrorists into plunging into a Pennsylvania field. The assault, known as "9/11," not only surprised and shocked the American public, but it gave the Bush administration a defense focus it did not have and plunged the United States into what President George W. Bush called "the Global War on Terrorism."

Largely untouched by his father's experience in national security affairs in the twenty years before his election, Bush became commander in chief without much vision about defense. He did complain about Clinton's defense policy, which meant the reduction of the armed forces. Clinton had also made too many commitments to misguided UN-sponsored peacekeeping operations. The Republican candidate who spoke about defense was Dick Cheney, whose four years as Secretary of Defense had hardened his prejudices more than they had sharpened his analytic sophistication. He trusted no nation that had ever been Communist, and he loathed the appeasement of any Arab leader but the oil sheikhs. Since the Gulf War, he had concluded that Saddam Hussein was a greater threat than Shi'a Iran, an avowed enemy of the U.S. since 1979. George W. Bush held similar views. Both shared a common interest in a superior nuclear force, an aggressive attack on "Weapons of Mass Destruction" (WMD) proliferation, and punishing terrorists, the instruments of rogue states.

The new secretary of defense, Donald H. Rumsfeld, age sixty-nine, had similar ideas about defense policy and some very fixed ideas on how to run the Pentagon. Opinionated, pugnacious, an intellectual sponge of data he liked, Rumsfeld saw himself as a great corporate manager, based on twenty-five years as the CEO of a pharmaceutical company in his native Chicago. NutraSweet had made him wealthy and confident that he did not have to court any support for his initiatives, especially that of Congress. At heart he remained captive of the enthusiasms that had first drawn him to politics. Serving as a naval aviator after a university experience noted for his prowess as a wrestler, Rumsfeld went to Washington in 1957 and did not leave for twenty years. His résumé swelled with jobs of increasing power and influence: Congressional aide; congressman; director of the Office of Economic Opportunity; White House counselor; NATO ambassador; White House chief of staff for Gerald Ford. In 1975, Rumsfeld served as secretary of defense for fourteen months, during which time he pressed for more modern nuclear forces and less arms control. During these years, he became close to Dick Cheney. He showed great interest in technological innovation and driving senior officers, including the JCS, to teeth-clenching obedience by challenging their judgment on major weapons programs and strategy.

Rumsfeld maintained ties to the Defense Department as a consultant during the Reagan administration. He became chair of a congressional study of ballistic missile defense and related nuclear issues. He made no friends at the Pentagon by his imperious methods of information control and contempt for service technological conservatism. His experience as a Pentagon gadfly converted him to the latest intellectual rages inside the Beltway: Fourth Generation warfare, "net-centric" warfare, asymmetrical warfare, the "Revolution in Military Affairs," and the "transformation" of the armed forces, which, to the degree it had definition, meant high-risk investment in target-acquisition technology and precision-guided munitions (PGMs) that destroyed from afar. He regarded anyone who did not embrace these ideas as disloyal and incompetent. As secretary of defense, he readily accepted Cheney disciples as influential appointees: Deputy

Secretary Paul Wolfowitz, Undersecretary for Policy Douglas Feith, and Undersecretary for Intelligence Stephen Cambone.

As secretary of defense in early 2001, Rumsfeld made clear that he did not intend to share his role as the president's defense adviser with the chairman of the JCS. Bypassing the serving CNO for being too independent, Rumsfeld appointed General Richard B. Myers, USAF, then Vice CJCS, to succeed General Henry H. Shelton, USA, as CJCS. Myers's experience in air warfare and space operations made him an appealing choice, but others suspected that the new CJCS would not challenge Rumsfeld's crusade to make the Pentagon a model of innovation, whether or not the senior officers cooperated. The secretary proved his point by creating two new offices, one for "force transformation" and the other for "special plans," to avoid the normal JCS and OSD processes. Rumsfeld proved that personal power outranked innovation by embarrassing a reformist Army Chief of Staff, General Eric Shinseki. A Hawaiian *nisei* who had lost part of a foot in Vietnam, Shinseki wanted to turn the Cold War or "legacy" Army into a more mobile, light, high-tech force that could put a brigade anywhere in the world in ninety-six hours and to follow with five divisions in a month. High-technology target acquisition and focused, devastating firepower would make this army unchallengeable. For example, the quick-reaction army would have no vehicle heavier than twenty tons. (The M-1 tank weighs seventy tons.) Shinseki's vision challenged Rumsfeld's proprietary grip on "transformation." Rumsfeld opened an attack on Shinseki that eroded his authority. When Shinseki testified to Congress about Rumsfeld's alteration of Iraq war plans, his replacement had already been named—more than a year in advance. Defense intellectuals thought Rumsfeld wanted to use the war in Afghanistan and a potential war in Iraq as laboratories for innovation without military opposition. Rumsfeld and Cheney had also convinced the president that an immediate increase of fiscal year 2002 defense spending by $43 billion was essential, despite a tax cut of $1.5 trillion for the years ahead. What was transformed was the national debt, which soared.

In its first ten months in office, the Bush administration managed the military commitments it inherited without a crisis. In almost every case, it reduced the commitments by agreement and because circumstances allowed withdrawal. Reporting to Congress "consistent with the War Powers Resolution," Bush described a drawdown in East Timor in the UN mission to twelve Americans and a force reduction in the Balkans. The only bad news came from the Middle East. Operation DESERT FOX had hurt Iraq's military infrastructure but improved its image of undeserving victim. The economic sanctions had unraveled with European and Asian countries seeking new business. Although Iraq could make legal oil deals for food and medicine, millions of illegal barrels of Iraqi oil kept pouring out through Syria, Iran, Turkey, and Jordan. When the United States and Great Britain sought more enforceable trade restrictions in the UN, France, Russia, and Egypt opposed the plan. The UN WMD inspectors did not think they would return to their weapons hunt, with or without American and British technicians, whom the Iraqis branded as spies and coup plotters. It even looked as if those great enemies, Iraq and Iran, might be collaborating in nuclear programs. American members of the UNSCOM and the IAEA inspection teams expressed concern about Iraq's potential WMD threat, positions echoed by knowledgeable Clinton-era CIA officials and former diplomats. Whatever his motives, Saddam Hussein had made himself look like a threat.

The problem of Saddam Hussein made it difficult for the Bush administration to see other issues clearly. The influence of Iraq confrontationists, called neoconservatives or "neocons" by their critics, throughout the executive branch made it difficult for dissenting views to reach the White House. Vice President Cheney had rallied his disciples from the Nixon-Reagan years. In addition to Wolfowitz, Feith, and Cambone, whom he placed near Rumsfeld, Cheney found leverage positions for Richard Perle, James Woolsey, Kenneth Adelman, John Bolton, Elliott Abrams, and others. Because of her personal rapport with the president Condoleezza Rice did not slow the neocon crusade to remove Saddam Hussein as approved by Congress in the Iraqi Liberation Act (1998). Richard Clarke and CIA director George Tenant found that their warnings about al-Qaeda turned into discussions of state-sponsored terrorism, rogue nuclear programs, and Israeli security—not the rise of Islamic fundamentalism in nonstate terrorist forms. Within the Defense Department, such discussions focused on developing antiballistic missiles of great accuracy and strategic mobility that would defend the U.S. and its allies from terrorist or rogue-nation missile attacks.

In the meantime, al-Qaeda patiently planned for a sensational attack on American civilians at work in New York City and Washington. The failure of the 1993 World Trade Center bombing reached obsessive levels for Osama bin Laden and his closet operational deputy, Mohammed Atef. They turned to Khalid Sheikh Mohammed, the Kuwaiti planner of the 1993 operation. Unlike most al-Qaeda leaders, Khalid had lived in the United States for years as an engineering student in the 1980s, spoke American English well, and came to loathe the United States. In 1987 he went to Pakistan for the final stages of the Soviet-Afghan war and became a committed *jihadi*. He helped fund the 1993 bombers and thus became identified by the FBI and CIA as a threat. He roamed the Middle East and Asia until he settled in Afghanistan in 1996 as a confidante to bin Ladin and Atef. For the next five years, Khalid thought about aerial attacks on the United States, and by early 1999 he had al-Qaeda's blessing, money, and foreign contacts. His key associates were an Indonesian and a Saudi who had been involved in bombings in Yemen, Kenya, and Tanzania. By the end of the year, Khalid, bin Laden, and Atef concluded that of all the options, hijacking airliners and sending them on suicide attacks on the World Trade Center, the Pentagon, the White House, and the Capitol building would be just the thing to panic the United States. According to Khalid Sheikh Mohammed's later testimony, the only consensus target was the Capitol building.

Over the next two years, Khalid and his planning team screened and trained recruits for the suicide mission. They needed men who could fly an airliner, function in the United States without suspicion, foil the bans on weapons on aircraft, and welcome death as heroes of Islam. The first four recruits were Saudis. The next four (all former residents of Hamburg, Germany, where they learned English) came from Egypt, the United Arab Emirates, Lebanon, and Yemen. Of this group, the leader became Mohammed Atta, an Egyptian with a university degree in urban planning and architectural engineering. Behind the planners stood bin Laden, who raised at least $30 million a year from Islamic donors throughout the world. (The 9/11 operation cost al-Qaeda only an estimated $500,000.) In May 2000, the "planes operation" team, nineteen members in all, began to enter the United States with legal or counterfeit visas. The operation struggled as the first team members could not speak enough English to take flying lessons. The "Hamburg Four" entered the U.S. from Europe and provided three of the four pilots. The fourth pilot was a Saudi who had lived in the United States and learned to fly because he wanted to be a commercial pilot. The four pilots, who never met as a group, wandered around the U.S. to fly at different places; some left the country and returned. They examined airline schedules, flew on recon missions, and awaited the thirteen terrorists who would seize control of the four airliners. Twelve of the hit team were Saudis; the thirteenth was a UAE citizen. They were all dependable *jihadis*, chosen by bin Laden and Khalid on the recommendation of *mullahs* and trainers. Each team would have a pilot and four crew-passenger attackers. Their weapons were box-cutters. They checked the plans with Ramzi Binalshibh, bin Laden's personal representative and banker, who met the attackers outside the United States. He met most often with Mohammed Atta. Atta confirmed that they would hijack Boeing aircraft (easier to fly than foreign aircraft) fueled for long flights, yet close to New York and Washington. The preparations had moments of compromise. On August 16, federal agents arrested Zacarias Moussaoui, who was taking flight-training lessons in Oklahoma because one of the pilots seemed ready to back out. Unfortunately, Moussaoui knew nothing about the attack plans. At this point, the major critic of the al-Qaeda spectacular was the Taliban. Mullah Omar believed the United States would connect al-Qaeda and Osama bin Laden with the attack and retaliate against al-Qaeda's mountain fortresses in Afghanistan. He thought Israel was a better target. To placate Omar, bin Laden pledged support for a Taliban offensive against the Northern Alliance. He would assassinate Ahmad Shah Massoud, the leading Alliance general. As promised, two al-Qaeda agents, disguised as foreign journalists, killed Massoud with a camera bomb on September 9, as the four hijacking teams went to their rendezvous at Dulles, Newark, and Boston airports.

On the morning of September 11, 2001, three of the four hijacked airliners destroyed both towers of the World Trade Center and part of a wing of the Pentagon. Against a backdrop of explosions, flames, building collapses, and incredible examples of heroism and self-sacrifice, all captured on television, the American people found themselves at war. But with whom?

The Response to 9/11: Operation ENDURING FREEDOM, Afghanistan, 2001–2002

Before all the fires were extinguished and all the remains recovered, the Bush administration with public support announced its international mission: to lead all willing nations in a "war against terrorists of global reach . . . a global enterprise of uncertain duration." Defense of the American people against violent enemies was an incontrovertible responsibility of the federal government. In his cover letter to a new study, "The National Security Strategy of the United States of America," written a week after 9/11, George W. Bush warned the American people that the traditional enemies of freedom, the totalitarian-militaristic states of the twentieth century, had given way to nonstate terrorists who wanted to destroy freedom everywhere and replace it with new forms of fear. Bush's words on the nature of liberty would have pleased Thomas Jefferson and Woodrow Wilson. His broad hints on how to protect the United States might have come from Andrew Jackson or Theodore Roosevelt. The United States faced a point in history, "the crossroads of radicalism and technology," that allowed no hesitation in the face of threats. "[T]he only path to peace and security," said Bush, "is the path of action." The president believed that he would have to strike al-Qaeda hard, then wage preemptive war on other terrorists. Seeking a crusader to kill, Osama bin Laden had created one in Washington and set off "the Global War on Terrorism."

The first order of business for the administration was to reorganize the executive branch to prevent other 9/11 attacks with WMD (including fuel-loaded airliners) on targets inside the United States. The truck-bomb explosions al-Qaeda had mounted abroad now seemed mere murderous annoyances when backlighted by the collapsing towers of the World Trade Center and a blackened wing of the Pentagon. Congress passed the Patriot Act (October 26, 2001), which gave Bush wide authority to reorganize the government search for terrorists. The divide between the FBI, the National Security Agency (NSA), and CIA had to be closed to share the records of thousands of phone calls, sightings, tips, purchases, financial transactions, and personal contacts that would eventually allow the identification of terrorists and divine their purposes. The post–9/11 inquiries revealed enough damning evidence to suggest that with more time the FBI and CIA would have discovered "the plane project." Two of the pilots and one attacker, for example, had appeared on a special watch list, and their al-Qaeda contacts were being tracked. No one, not even the alarmed experts of the CIA's Counterintelligence Center of the NSC's Counterterrorism Security Group, had a clear vision of the 9/11 operation. Evidence and instinct, however, persuaded the CIA to put threats by Osama bin Laden and al-Qaeda in forty different President's Daily Brief intelligence analyses between January 20 and September 11, 2001. There was not enough evidence, however, to put federal agencies on high alert.

Whatever its growing pains and organizational flaws, the Office of Homeland Security (2001–2003) evolved into a full-fledged executive department and pulled together all the federal agencies that processed the flow of people and things across America's borders. Air travelers came to know the agents of the Transportation Security Agency. The integration of FBI and CIA information with Homeland Security traveler identification and tracking closed many of the "black holes" in tracing suspected terrorists. All these changes, useful and necessary, were like civil defense for nuclear attacks. They might deter attacks, and they limited the effects of damage, but they did not eliminate the terrorists. Nothing short of elimination would now satisfy the president and his White House–Pentagon posse of neoconservatives.

President George W. Bush told the nation on the evening of September 11 that he would use all his military, intelligence, and police capabilities to run the 9/11 killers down and "bring them to justice . . . and those who harbor them." As Clarke and Tenant suspected, their analysis and that of foreign intelligence agencies pointed to Osama bin Laden as the source of "the plane project." He had orchestrated the attack from Afghanistan as a guest of the Taliban. NATO agreed that the United States had suffered a foreign attack under Article Five of the NATO treaty and thus deserved the help of all NATO countries; this September 12 call to arms became more focused on October 2 when NATO made al-Qaeda the official enemy. Bush also received a congressional blessing for a retaliatory war. Without knowing exactly what Bush had in mind except action *now,* the Senate (98–0) and the House (420–1) gave the president the authority to hunt down the 9/11 killers in unlimited language reminiscent of the Gulf of Tonkin Resolution (1964). In a televised speech to the nation on September 20, Bush identified Osama bin Laden and al-Qaeda as the enemy, with the Taliban as an accomplice. He told his audience of the government's actions to freeze terrorist funds, stop their travels, find their bases in foreign countries, and cut them off from foreign sponsors. He had also pressured Pakistan to break off relations with the Afghanistan government of Mullah Omar.

Even as the president spoke, the first wave of American forces prepared for an expedition to Afghanistan. Three carrier battle groups and two Marine amphibious battalions assembled in the Arabian Sea. On September 30 a fourth carrier sailed from Japan with U.S. Army Special Forces, Navy SEALS, Air Force special operations forces and helicopters, and part of the 160th Special Operations Aviation Regiment (SOAR) helicopter force embarked. Another group of 1,000 was bound by plane for the Karshi Kandabad (K2) base in Uzbekistan. The advance party of Joint Special Operations Task Force Dagger from the 5th Special Forces Group had arrived there by aircraft by October 1. The CIA already had agents in northern Afghanistan planning operations with the Uzbek warlord Abdul Rashid Dostum and the Northern Alliance Tajik generals to the east who had succeeded the murdered General Massoud. In their first trips into Afghanistan, the CIA operators had two weapons: A fleet of assorted drones for target acquisition and backpacks stuffed with thousands of dollars. They also knew the Northern Alliance leaders and spoke Pashto and Dari, the Afghan common languages. They arranged the first air strikes at night (October 7) and during daylight (October 15) and maintained contact with British SAS teams already in central Afghanistan. Appropriately for a "transformed" force, the first combat loss was a reconnaissance drone. Assured that K2 would be defended by a 10th Mountain Division battalion deployed from Fort Drum, New York, teams from the 5th SFG entered Afghanistan by helicopter on October 19 to start the decisive campaign.

In five months (October 2001–March 2002), Operation ENDURING FREEDOM displaced the Taliban government in Afghanistan and drove al-Qaeda to new sanctuaries in Pakistan and throughout the Middle East. The elusive but talkative Osama bin Laden remained on the run in the mountains between Afghanistan and Pakistan, chiding the Americans on Arab TV for not catching him. For a quick victory with few American deaths (twelve in combat, eighteen in accidents), Operation ENDURING FREE-

Source: U.S. Army Center of Military History, *Bosnia-Herzegovina: The U.S. Army's Role in Peace Enforcement Operations, 1995–2004*

DOM seemed to validate the American military "transformation." The marriage of elite, high-tech ground forces, connected by satellite communications with the Air Force JSTARS command-targeting aircraft and the Global Hawk and Predator drones, could bring devastating air strikes, pinpointed by GPS devices, upon the Afghan armies. The campaign provided an illusion of easy victory in Washington and a taste for more victories.

As TF Dagger prepared for war, the CIA sought a viable Pashtun leader to organize a coalition to lead the southern campaign against the Taliban. The first choice was Abdul Haq, a hero of the anti-Soviet resistance. When Abdul Haq entered Afghanistan with a small band of followers, someone betrayed him to the Taliban, who hanged him publicly on October 26. A last-minute CIA effort to save Haq with a Predator drone attack failed. The CIA looked in vain for a replacement until Hamid Karzai, a former diplomat in exile in Pakistan, agreed to start a Southern Alliance. Assessing the future, Karzai mused that Afghanistan was a luckless country.

As extemporized by COMCENTCOM, General Tommy Franks, U.S. Army, an acerbic Texan artilleryman who pandered to superiors and ter-

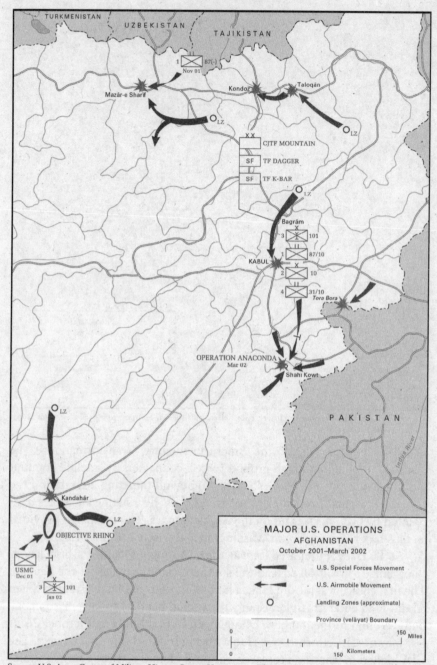

TURKMENISTAN

UZBEKISTAN

TAJIKISTAN

1 | 87(-) | Nov 01

Mazār-e Sharīf

Kondoz

Taloqān

LZ

LZ

XX CJTF MOUNTAIN

SF TF DAGGER

SF TF K-BAR

LZ

Bagrām

3 | 101

1 | 87/10

KABUL

2 | 10

4 | 31/10

Tora Bora

OPERATION ANACONDA
Mar 02

Shahi Kowt

PAKISTAN

Indus River

LZ

Kandahār

LZ

OBJECTIVE RHINO

USMC
Dec 01

3 | 101
Jan 02

MAJOR U.S. OPERATIONS
AFGHANISTAN
October 2001–March 2002

U.S. Special Forces Movement

U.S. Airmobile Movement

Landing Zones (approximate)

Province (velāyat) Boundary

0   150 Miles

0   Kilometers
          150

Source: U.S. Army Center of Military History, *Bosnia-Herzegovina: The U.S. Army's Role in Peace Enforcement Operations, 1995–2004*

rified subordinates, ENDURING FREEDOM went through two phases. From mid-October until early December, TF Dagger, commanded by Colonel John Mulholland, joined Northern Alliance forces armed with Soviet weapons and mounted on horses and any truck that could run. Together they captured a northern tier of key cities (Mazar-e-Sharif, Taloqan, and Konduz) in a series of long marches and brief battles. The basic operational approach was to use Northern Alliance irregulars (Hazaras, Uzbeks, and Tajiks) to force Taliban units to concentrate, only to be savaged by American air strikes. By the end of November high-altitude B-52s, B-1s, and B-2s had dropped 80 percent of the bomb tonnage, unseen and unheard by their victims. The Special Forces advance teams and Air Force strike controllers pressed the attacks by their Afghan allies. In one battle General Dostum ordered his SF team out of the front lines. He feared, he said, that if one of them should die, all of the Americans would go home. In the meantime, the air strikes encouraged major Taliban defections in the north.

The first territorial objective of ENDURING FREEDOM, the city of Mazar-e-Sharif, demonstrated, in Pentagon-speak, the efficacy of the new operational paradigm, proved by the metrics. Translation: It worked. As it closed on Mazar-e-Sharif with Dostum's Northern Alliance army, TF Dagger sent another group for Bagram air base, eighty miles north of Kabul, while a third group marched east toward the Taliban stronghold at Konduz. The simultaneous sieges of Mazar-e-Sharif and Bagram produced dramatic results. Despite an infusion of al-Qaeda regulars and the Taliban's use of Soviet rockets and artillery, air strikes destroyed hundreds of entrenched Taliban until the survivors surrendered or fled. On November 10 Dostum's army entered a jubilant Mazar-e-Sharif; two days later an Uzbek-Tajik army and their bearded SF advisers entered Kabul. While Bagram rapidly transformed into a forward base, a battalion of the 75th Infantry (the Ranger Regiment) and a detachment of Task Force Delta raided Taliban headquarters south of Kandahar, searching in vain for Mullah Omar and al-Qaeda leaders. There was one score. On November 16 an armed Predator drone killed Mohammed Atef with a missile fired into a fleeing truck. The Northern Alliance offensives stalled when the prisoners in Mazar-e-Sharif rebelled and set off a five-day battle (November 24–29) that ended in the aerial slaughter of the rebels. Nevertheless, the Northern Alliance army had already captured Konduz on November 21 despite some heavy fighting with al-Qaeda regulars.

Operation ENDURING FREEDOM had endured and freed about half of Afghanistan and the city of Kabul. It had broken part of the Taliban army and outfought the al-Qaeda *mujahideen*, but the Pashtun provinces of the south and the regional stronghold of Kandahar remained unoccupied. CIA agents had helped organize two small (less than 200) anti-

Taliban Pashtun forces called the Southern Alliance, but Taliban units had attacked and isolated them. The best of al-Qaeda's fighters, protecting Osama bin Laden and Ayman al-Zawahiri, faded back into the eastern mountain ranges on the Pakistani border, where they could occupy caves, tunnels, bunkers, weapons pits, and concrete-reinforced shelters that had foiled Soviet air and ground attacks. TF Dagger and the Afghans bypassed the al-Qaeda sanctuaries (about which they knew much) in order to rescue the Southern Alliance guerrillas and capture Kandahar. One key mission was to save a small band of Southern Alliance fighters led by Hamid Karzai, whose major appeal was his status as an authentic anti-Taliban Pashtun and fluent English speaker. The best news was that a brigade of the U.S. 101st Airborne Division (Air Assault) would soon arrive, and more Special Forces had already reached Bagram, but the urgency of operations into Pashtunland meant that TF Dagger and its shrinking Afghan force would have to take Kandahar. Meanwhile, Task Force 58 created a base, Camp Rhino, southwest of Khandahar on November 24, where it was joined by more Navy SEALS, Navy Seabees, and Army and Australian Special Forces. The Marine mission was to pressure the Taliban and to prevent them from freely moving about the country.

The battle for Kandahar produced some tense moments, since the Southern Alliance Pashtuns did not rally in adequate numbers or possess the skills to fight the best warriors of the Taliban and al-Qaeda. While they had no love for "Afghan Arabs" or the most fanatical Taliban, many southern Afghans preferred cautious and armed neutrality. Nevertheless, two American Special Forces teams infiltrated into the region and organized the Southern Alliance into two groups to assault the city. Accompanied by a Special Forces team to coordinate movements and air strikes, Karzai's small group attacked toward Khandahar from the north, while another anti-Taliban group, headed by Gul Sherzai, assaulted from the south. Undermanned, TF Dagger and their Afghan allies faced not only hardcore al-Qaeda and Taliban *mujahideen* but thousands of new *jihadis* who joined the war from Pakistan. On December 5, a misdirected air strike killed three Americans and wounded eight. Among the six dead and forty wounded Afghans was Hamid Karzai, named the next head of the Afghan government by an exile council in Bonn, Germany. The siege of Kandahar dragged on until December 7, when Taliban troops finally agreed to a surrender and an amnesty proposal, which they used to buy time, then broke out and escaped by the hundreds. The Marines captured Khandahar airport on December 13. In the meantime, another American-Afghan force had taken up the chase of bin Laden.

Even as parts of TF Dagger headed for Kandahar and finished off Konduz, CENTCOM focused on the bin Laden mission while at the same time increasing the American ground units inside Afghanistan. The units that streamed in to manage Bagram and two other airbases were not shooters but, rather, engineers, technicians, communicators, staffs, MPs, and electronic and ordnance specialists. With battles waging around them, four Army and two Marine battalions guarded the bases. Then allies began to arrive: a Royal Marine commando battalion and one Canadian infantry battalion. The separate CENTCOM Special Operations Command swelled with SEALS, Australian SAS, and more Special Forces teams. To sort out ENDURING FREEDOM, General Franks asked for help and received the Third Army headquarters (Lieutenant General Paul T. Mikolashek, USA) for deployment to Kuwait. He then named Mikolashek a Combined Forces Land Component Commander (CFLCC) but not commander of Special Operations Forces (SOF) or the air component. The former group, TF Bowie, included a small army of electronic intelligence experts and analysts. Just controlling Bagram alone proved too complex, so CENTCOM formed another center of decision, CFLCC (Forward), at K2 under Major General F.L. "Buster" Hagenbeck, commander of the 10th Mountain Division. None of this reorganization put more dependable troops in the field, in part because TF Dagger did not want them.

Amid all the sound and fury from Konduz to Kandahar, Afghan sources and special operations analysts concluded that Osama bin Laden and his entourage had gone to ground in the Tora Bora region of the White Mountains, some forty-five miles southwest of a former Taliban stronghold, Jalalabad. American air strikes began against an estimated 1,000 al-Qaeda regulars on November 28. Even with plenty of Special Forces/USAF fire controllers, the only unit General Franks would commit to assault Tora Bora was an indifferent Afghan force of 800 under a local warlord. For two weeks the SF spotters and all the target identifiers the USAF could find directed aerial ordnance onto Tora Bora's defense complex. The Air Force used all its ordnance, from a one-ton precision-guided penetrator to a seven-ton BLU 82 air-fuel exploder that burned and smothered anyone within a hundred yards of the burst. Yet every reluctant Southern Alliance advance halted in the face of deadly mortar and machine-gun fire. Ground taken during the day changed hands at night. When resistance faded away by December 16, the SF-Afghan investigators estimated that they had killed perhaps 200–300 diehard fighters who had covered the escape of al-Qaeda's leaders and 700–800 elite *jihadis* into Pakistan. Osama bin Laden had indeed been in the Tora Bora complex, and he boasted about his escape to his global admirers. No one had a better chance to kill or capture him for a decade. Critics wondered whether a Ranger battalion or airmobile battalion might have made a difference in the assault or blocking escape routes, a proposal vetoed by Franks.

Even as Alliance forces and their SOF advisers chased remnants of the Taliban and the operations in Tora Bora withered away, the American forces and their NATO allies shifted to Phase IV operations, meaning humanitarian relief and UN-NATO peacekeeping. The Americans maintained their force autonomy, but NATO contingents fell under British command as the International Security Assistance Force (ISAF), which by March 2002 numbered 4,900 troops (one-third British) from eighteen nations. The numbers and nationalities made coalition cooperation a nightmare. Different rules-of-engagement did not help. Intertribal warfare now poisoned peacekeeping; USAF jets destroyed a convoy of Afghan elders (sixty-five dead) when a warlord said they were Taliban. They were not. One could sense victory but not peace. The senior Air Force officers counted sorties flown (17,000) and ordnance dropped (6,500 strike missions, 17,500 weapons used). The Navy's carrier air had flown the most missions, but the Air Force had dropped the most bombs and rockets, and PGMs had been 65 percent of the total. These were statistics that Donald Rumsfeld loved to describe at press conferences. The humanitarian relief workers counted tons of food delivered and Afghans inoculated. The U.S. Army counted bridges and roads repaired. There were other, more worrisome statistics: Afghans killed by accident and prisoners misidentified and unscreened for too long.

The toxic mixture of intelligence interrogations and the criminal prosecutions of terrorists drove the Bush administration from its self-defined moral high ground in its handling of captured suspected terrorists. During the Afghanistan campaign, U.S. forces captured 5,000 Taliban and al-Qaeda fighters. Most Afghans stayed in Afghanistan for screening. Non-Afghan fighters, representing thirty or more different countries, presented a special problem. Had they been treated as prisoners of war under the Geneva Convention, they would have enjoyed legal protections assumed by the Detaining Power and would eventually have had to be returned to their native lands for disposition. Some native lands would have tried them for criminal acts; Australia actually did convict one returnee. Other countries did not want them or wanted them immediately for execution. Some countries wanted them back in order to release them and let them return to the war. That too happened. Moreover, a POW enjoys protection (enforced by International Red Cross inspectors) against extended interrogations that apply various forms of coercion (sleep and food deprivation) and torture. Yet American and foreign intelligence officers wanted to use coercive methods against al-Qaeda captives like Khalid Sheikh Mohammed (the 9/11 planner) in order to roll up al-Qaeda's complex international network.

After some imaginative legal interpretations by Attorney General John Ashcroft and White House Counsel Alberto Gonzales, the Bush administration announced that its captives were neither POWs nor criminals under American law since they were (with one exception) not American citizens and had not been captured on American soil. They did not belong to a national army. They were "detainees." To make sure the detainees did not go to American soil, where they might fall under all kinds of legal protections, the administration established a prison camp at the Guantanamo Bay naval base in Cuba (GTMO), occupied under an expired lease agreement signed in 1903. At first a primitive tent camp, the GTMO facility evolved in 2002 into a camp that met IRC standards. Behind the scenes, however, CIA and military interrogators used coercive interrogation measures (approved in Washington) until news of these interrogations leaked in the wake of the Abu Ghraib scandal. What emerged from the exposure of illegal practices at Abu Ghraib in Iraq and GTMO was the news that torture, including "waterboarding" or the use of threatened drowning, was also a common practice at secret interrogation centers run by the CIA in foreign countries. The "rendition" issue further eroded public support for the Global War on Terrorism.

The Bush administration tried to salvage something from the GTMO fiasco by claiming that it had extracted time-urgent information that foiled terrorist attacks, a claim challenged by FBI, NCIS, and Army CID agents at Guantanamo. Since only a handful of detainees had such information and its usefulness quickly vanished, this argument impressed only true believers, led by Vice President Cheney. As the screening continued, the number of detainees shrank. Of the 780 "persons of interest" sent to GTMO, 415 had been repatriated to some other nation by 2007, and eighty more were scheduled for release. When the first detainee conviction for terrorist crimes by a military tribunal reached the Supreme Court—after lower courts ruled that U.S. military tribunals fell under Supreme Court jurisdiction, as they had after World War II—the Court in June 2006 ruled that the detainees ("enemy" or "non-enemy") were combatants and could be tried for war crimes only by an international tribunal. Hounded by the Justice Department, Congress in October 2006 passed the Military Commission Act, which allowed the armed forces to try terrorists under international law but with extensive restrictions against the abuse of individual rights. Military lawyers determined they had twenty-four triable suspects, but two more cases were dismissed, and the prosecutions ended for awhile.

Amid all the Phase IV activities, Osama bin Laden and his al-Qaeda elite remained at large somewhere in the mountains. If his hideaway was in Afghanistan, he could be attacked. The Special Forces of TF Dagger and a second special operations group built on the 3rd Special Forces Group, SEALS, and Commonwealth special forces (TF K-Bar) prowled the mountains with the Afghanis. They concluded that al-Qaeda had reestablished itself in a mountain complex (8,000 to 12,000 feet) south of Tora Bora in an area known as the Gardiz-Shah-e-Kot valley region. The number of al-Qaeda fighters in the region might run as high as 1,000. Whether or not Osama bin Laden and his headquarters had chosen this refuge was uncertain, but it was certainly the largest surviving al-Qaeda base in Afghanistan. In March 2002, American tactical forces launched Operation ANACONDA, a maximum effort most notable for the mismatch between the available troops and the demanding missions. Commanded by General Hagenbeck of the 10th Mountain Division, the core forces of TF Mountain were about 1,200 Afghans in four small battalions with Special Forces advisers, a group of 800 semi-autonomous Special Forces soldiers and SEALs, and a three-battalion U.S. Army light infantry brigade. Transport and gunship helicopters came from the 101st Aviation Regiment. The scarcity and character of the ground forces dictated a phased hammer-and-anvil operation in which air strikes would do most of the killing. The largest Afghan force would travel overland from the northeast and attack an enemy complex nestled against Tif Ghal Gar Mountain, which separated the lower and upper Shah-e-Kot valleys. The passes that linked the valleys would be blocked by three other Afghan units. The three U.S. Army battalions and Special Forces units would fly by helicopter to critical terrain where they could direct air strikes and fight any enemy units trying to move between the two valleys. The enemy would be formidable, armed with Soviet artillery, RPGs, machine guns, and small arms. The GIs had no artillery support and had inadequate contact with USAF strike aircraft. The mission itself was appropriate: to eliminate the most menacing Taliban groups still in Afghanistan. There was also a competing mission: Get the al-Qaeda leaders.

The mythical "Mr. Murphy" who uses his powers to frustrate human activities reigned supreme in ANACONDA. The eighteen-day struggle left TF Mountain in control of the battlefield with a tactical victory, March 1–19, 2002. General Franks called ANACONDA a great victory, although the local commanders knew it was more limited. The battle started badly when poor roads, an errant USAF air attack, and enemy mortar and machine-gun fire stopped the main Afghan assault force on the first day. The first American troop insertions came under immediate and accurate mortar and machine-gun fire and had to fight to hold their small mountain enclaves. Apache helicopters and bomber strikes prevented disaster, but logistical flights and medevacs became perilous, and succeeding troop lifts did not occur. More *jihadis* joined the battle, coiling in around the hilltop positions. Then night came, and the enemy withdrew to eat, drink, and sing about their own heroism around their fires. In the meantime, TF Mountain regrouped, concentrated its American units, and changed the plans so that the GIs would sweep the mountains and valleys with Special Forces calling air strikes from one craggy peak to another, moving by helicopter. The Special Forces still had a competing mission: to find and kill al-Qaeda's leaders in the same zone as the U.S. infantry brigade.

"Murphy's Law" intervened on D+2 when ground fire and thin air brought down one SF helo, and in the rescue operation under fire, a SEAL was left behind. More rescue operations tied up much of TF Mountain's fire support, gave *jihadis* a focus of attack, and eventually cost the lives of seven servicemen and resulted in wounds for seven more. Sharp peaks, thin air, and RPGs created a small Mogadishu II. Not until March 6 did ANACONDA take sound tactical form, and by then the enemy survivors were over the hills and far away. The operation became much searching and little destroying, but at least the Shah-e-Kot region had been occupied and turned over to Afghan forces. TF Mountain and its air supporters estimated enemy losses at 700; subsequent analysis put the dead at far fewer. The stubborn, skilled enemy resistance made intelligence analysts believe that the area sheltered Osama bin Laden, but it did not. Instead, the Shah-e-Kot valley had been a rallying point for a defense force of dedicated Taliban, al-Qaeda Arabs, and expatriate Uzbek rebels, all eager to kill infidels.

Operation ANACONDA closed the liberation phase of ENDURING FREEDOM and opened the stabilization phase of the UN-NATO-United States intervention in Afghanistan. Hamid Karzai soon became the president of the new Afghanistan; but, protected by foreign soldiers, he was more warlord than the next George Washington. Except for the regional experts who knew better, the Pentagon thought the latest war for Afghanistan had ended.

The remnants of al-Qaeda and the inner elite of the Taliban had crossed the indistinct border into official Pakistan, in reality the Federally Administered Tribal Areas (FATA), a ten-thousand-square-mile borderlands and the home of four million Pashtun Afghans. The Pakistani government followed a "live and let live" policy with the Afghans, who had fled the Soviets and then fought them from the FATA sanctuaries. The Pakistani army, particularly the ISI, maintained good relations with the Afghans, especially a private army led by Jalaluddin Haqqani, a Taliban Pashtun warlord who hated Karzai and the Americans. Any attacks into the FATA by drones or Special Forces could cause a crisis with Pakistan.

Following Operation ANACONDA, CENTCOM refined the American command structure and operational concepts for stabilizing Afghanistan. In May 2002, General Franks established Combined Joint Task Force 180, formed around the 18th Airborne Corps and commanded by Lieutenant General Dan McNeil. Special Forces teams began to organize the first battalions of a nascent Afghan army at roughly the same time. This mission was eventually transferred to CJTF 180 headed by the 10th Mountain Division. Mirroring the Bush administration's reluctance to engage in nation-building or peacekeeping, a "light footprint" became the basis for American commitment. Troop levels were kept low and oriented primarily toward combat and special operations. The light footprint allowed combat forces to raid and clear objectives, but not hold any ground for significant periods. Insufficient American forces and inadequate Afghan military and police forces enabled the Taliban and al-Qaeda to infiltrate back into Afghanistan from sanctuaries in Pakistan in succeeding years.

Operation IRAQI FREEDOM, 2001–2003

For President George W. Bush, tutored by Vice President Cheney and the bellicose neoconservatives, there could be no "global war on terrorism" without a preventive war with Iraq. Had the administration wanted to select one nation to attack as a sponsor of state-supported terrorism, the CIA and State Department could have provided a long list of candidates. The list would have included Iran, Cuba, Syria, Libya, Sudan, and North Korea. The United States in 2001 did not face an immediate threat from any of these states, especially the worst case threat of weapons of mass destruction transferred to terrorists. Iraq was no different. Its sin was that it was governed by a despicable tyrant, Saddam Hussein, whose sadism toward his own people rivaled that of Josef Stalin. Saddam Hussein had ordered the execution of thousands, including two sons-in-law, for treachery and disloyalty. His sons Uday and Qusay inherited their father's taste for torture and debasement. His inner circle of ministers, advisers, and generals shared his megalomania or kept their places through sycophancy of the highest order. The regime had a well-earned reputation for duplicity, evasion, corruption, and contempt for international norms. It had killed Iranians, Kurds, and Shi'a Arabs with poison gas. It had launched missiles at Israel and Saudi Arabia. On top of all of these offenses, Saddam Hussein had targeted the Bush family for attack and had ridiculed the president's father as a weak, ineffectual leader and a tool of international Jewry.

Taking his own counsel, which he admitted rested on his religious convictions and intuition, George W. Bush decided after becoming president that he would rid the world of Saddam Hussein, which already had congressional sanction in 1998. Bush made several public statements about his mission to remove "evil" tyrants and destroy governments that sponsored terrorists. Bush's instincts took more stimulus from Cheney, Rumsfeld, and the neoconservatives in the national security system. Even before 9/11 the White House had investigated what a global war on terrorism might entail. For a president impatient with the complexities of foreign policy, the national security analyses provided little comfort. No other government (not even Israel's) had much stomach for redefining the continuing struggle against terrorism as a war upon a particular state, including Iraq. Even after the shock of 9/11 and the start of Operation ENDURING FREEDOM, the Bush administration found little international interest in making Iraq Target Number One for international action. Instead, the consensus, communicated by the State Department and CIA, was that Saddam Hussein's days were numbered and that his ability to attack his neighbors had been largely, if not completely, destroyed. Saddam was "contained." The president did not accept these reassurances.

From the summer of 2001 until the start of Operation IRAQI FREEDOM on March 19, 2003, the Bush administration did not debate about getting rid of Saddam Hussein but on how to justify a preventive war if needed. Its argument was that Saddam Hussein's regime should be destroyed before it used WMD to destroy others. To win congressional acquiescence, which he needed, and to receive UN sanction, which he did not really want, Bush had to persuade the public that Iraq was a charter member of "the axis of evil" of state-supported terrorism that he intended to destroy. In meetings on September 17–20, 2001, Bush defined military invasion as the only sure instrument to remove Saddam Hussein, since all other forms of coercion had failed. The president also continued to ask intelligence officers about connections between Iraq and al-Qaeda. There were none of any consequence. Encouraged by Rumsfeld and Cheney, Bush began to doubt that the State Department and the CIA knew much about Iraq, even though three other agencies (the Defense Intelligence Agency, the National Reconnaissance Office, and the National Security Agency) reported to George Tenant in his dual role as Director of Central Intelligence. Bush allowed Rumsfeld to create an Office of Special Plans, the mission of which was to review all intelligence agency reports, which was really Tenant's responsibility or that of the NSC staff. Condoleezza Rice, however, did not challenge Rumsfeld's ploy, probably because she knew Bush and Cheney saw its utility in manipulating the case against Iraq. It was useful to make Bush look as if he were weighing all sorts of anti-Saddam options, which he was not. The administration also wanted to ensure that the UN and IAEA inspectors did not reduce the level of threat Iraq posed with WMD, since the seizure and destruction of WMD was the only issue that could rally skeptics and supporters.

The administration went to extraordinary lengths to ensure that the UN and any other source of expertise and legitimacy did not weaken the WMD case against Iraq. It reinterpreted UNSCOM and IAEA reports to produce positive (not tentative) evidence of renewed Iraqi nuclear programs. It encouraged journalists and public figures to study its analyses and to learn that European nations also had alarmist views. It deliberately leaked classified analysis conducted by Cheney loyalists in the Pentagon, as well as a pessimistic CIA study of Iraqi WMD, completed in October 2002. It accepted specious evidence of Iraqi international efforts to create nuclear weapons. The Office of Special Plans became an enthusiastic patron of the exiled Iraqi National Congress, whose leader, Ahmed Chalabi, had not lived in Iraq for forty years but who claimed to have incontrovertible evidence of Iraqi WMD from agents and defectors. The INC certainly saw itself as the heir apparent for the next Iraqi government. Powell and Rice had reservations about the WMD cover story, but neither, for reasons personal and political, went public with their doubts.

Secretary of Defense Rumsfeld had no doubts that there would be a war, and he wanted it to demonstrate the importance of "transformation" in the American way of war. The first CENTCOM contingency plan he examined in late 2001 looked like DESERT STORM II. He did not like it. Neither did the CENTCOM commander, General Tommy Franks, who found himself caught between cautious planners and an incautious boss. In fact, the proposed expeditionary force was half the size of its 1990–1991 predecessor. So too was the Iraqi army—and its equipment status was even worse than it had been in the Gulf War. The new CENTCOM force would have been 380,000, although Franks thought perhaps 275,000 could produce the "shock and awe" Rumsfeld favored. The optimism about the weakness of the Iraqi armed forces was well founded. Years of undercover persuasion convinced the CIA and JCS that the Iraqi regular army and even most of the regular Republican Guard would not fight and could be purchased with money, amnesty, and future employment. Rumsfeld believed that the force envisioned in Op Plan 1003V was still too large and would take too long to deploy to Kuwait and Saudi Arabia. It would require too much logistical support and be much too expensive. Rumsfeld and Franks shared one romantic assumption: that this allied force (including a British division) would crush the Iraqi army and Republican Guard, then turn around and go home, cheered by the Iraqis whom the allies had liberated. As for the air campaign, it would begin with the ground war, not with a prolonged and preparatory "strategic" phase. The most revealing part of the planning was the absence of troops for rear-area security, for the extended support of an occupation force, for civil affairs and policing, for emergency engineering and public health missions, and for restoring some sort of Iraqi government, collectively known at the Pentagon as Phase IV operations. The only serious attention to follow-on troops was the formation of teams to find WMD, a force of over 600 formed in early 2003. Rumsfeld rejected the State Department plan for nation-building. His response was to create an Office of Reconstruction and Humanitarian

Assistance, headed by retired Lieutenant General Jay Garner, USA, who had directed similar missions after the Gulf War. Rumsfeld's lack of concern for Phase IV operations shocked anyone who understood the anarchy that would follow a tyrant's fall.

For all its crusading self-confidence, the Bush administration saw the advantage of winning allies to its cause. Prime Minister Tony Blair's government became its primary prospective ally. Great Britain offered small but competent armed forces; its diplomats and intelligence officers had skill and experience in dealing with the Arab world. The British connection ensured leverage in NATO and the UN. Even American skeptics valued Blair's potential influence on Bush in slowing the rush to war. The charming PM did not disappoint. Over much of 2002, Blair and his diplomats negotiated the preconditions for Great Britain's participation and identified the flaws in the American planning. To the degree that the administration could recruit allies and international cooperation—essential to winning over or neutralizing the elite U.S. foreign policy establishment and media—it owed a debt to Great Britain. The British argued that the WMD issue had to be central to the justification for war, and Iraq had to be seen as a clear and present danger. Regime change was a means to that end, not an end in itself. What kind of regime would replace Saddam Hussein? The official "Cabinet Paper on Iraq" (July 2002) reported little American planning for postwar Iraq. The British thought that the UN-IAEA inspectors needed one more trip to Iraq if Saddam Hussein would permit it. If he did not, then he had clearly violated nine UN Security Council resolutions on WMD disarmament. The last British concern was that the Bush government would never find an Iraqi–al-Qaeda connection because none existed.

As the Bush administration prepared for war, Saddam Hussein retreated further and further into his own fantasy world. He believed that the United States would not attack because Americans lacked the will to take casualties. His forces could and would kill so many Americans that any Desert Storm II offensive would stall well short of Baghdad. He allowed no one in his inner circle to question his delusions. He also believed that France and Russia, his allies, would deter the United States from displacing him because that was in their economic interests. He planned to save his oil wells and air forces for another postwar rebirth. The WMD threat may have been real to Saddam Hussein and other true believers like his sons, but the missiles, warheads, and deadly chemicals were scattered, hidden, forgotten, decaying, and never existed, although few Iraqis outside of Chemical Ali's circle knew it. The Iraqi high command was so stacked with loyalists that the generals could easily assume someone else's part of the armed forces had real capability. Information-sharing was an invitation to disgrace and death. The Iraqi Military Industrial Commission filed reports that suggested a WMD program existed, for that ensured its flow of money.

Iraqi defense planning reflected fear of a military coup as well as a popular revolt. Iraqi ground troops deployed in two broad rings around Baghdad but concentrated to the north and south of the capital. The weak regular army divisions clustered around Mosul to the north (nine divisions) and Basra in the south (six divisions). The inner circle put two Republican Guard divisions in the north, none in the south. The inner ring around metropolitan Baghdad held four Republican Guard divisions, one Guard brigade, and one regular brigade. The one Special Republican Guard division defended the offices and palaces of downtown Baghdad. The new paramilitary militias had special areas to defend under the most loyal Baath Party officials. Any commander who lost an engagement risked immediate execution. The towns and cities in the Tigris-Euphrates valley bulged with infantry weapons and ammunition, issued by Baath officials so the loyal Sunni militia could crush Kurds, Shi'a, dissident Sunnis, and foreign invaders. The roads to Baghdad ran through these towns and over their bridges.

In the autumn of 2002 a war with Iraq looked certain despite reservations within the Bush administration and Congress. In October the White House asked for a use of force resolution that would allow Bush to use the armed forces as he judged best to meet "the continuing threat" posed by Iraq. The Senate vote was 77–21 in favor of the resolution, while in the House the affirmative vote was 296–139. Neither vote represented the same ringing endorsement of the previous year for the war in Afghanistan. In December the administration released a special White House study, "National Strategy to Combat Weapons of Mass Destruction," which argued that a war against WMD would be a high priority (perhaps the highest) for American defense planning. There was a distinct emphasis on the concept that an immediate threat demanded immediate action. With some dismay, however, the administration had to live with a UN initiative to return to Iraq for more WMD inspections. In September 2002, after Bush's UN speech on enforcing the UN resolutions on disarming Iraq, Saddam Hussein accepted a new UNMOVIC-IAEA inspection group. The inspectors returned to Iraq on November 27, 2002, and left one day before the war started on March 19, 2003. The nuclear investigators of IAEA made 237 visits to 148 sites, including 231 new ones, and found no evidence of a nuclear weapons program. The UNMOVIC teams conducted 731 inspections and found evidence of chemical and biological warfare preparation and missile activity, but most (if not all) had been wrecked by DESERT FOX and not reactivated. The inspectors could have found an Iraq barren of all WMD capability, but by 2003 only Saddam

Hussein's abject surrender could have stopped a war. Inside his cocoon of delusion, Saddam Hussein, the Lion of Tikrit, awaited an American attack he would defeat as he had the attack in 1991.

For General Franks and CENTCOM, Operation IRAQI FREEDOM (OIF) had become only a matter of timing. Plans for the ground offensive, named COBRA II for its 1944 Normandy predecessor, called for a combined, simultaneous air-ground attack that would halt only with the capture of Baghdad and the fall of the Iraqi government. The principal operational challenge was the defeat of the Republican Guard. Iraq was divided into three operational zones. For the north and south, speed was of the essence in order to save the Kurds and Shi'a from slaughter and to prevent the Iraqis from destroying their oil fields, the golden goose for financing reconstruction. The northern area would be assaulted from three directions: the 4th Infantry Division (Mechanized) under Major General Raymond T. Odierno from Turkey, a Special Forces task force with the Kurdish partisans (the *pesh merga*) from the northeast, and the 101st Air Assault Division (Major General David Petraeus, USA) by helicopter from the southwestern desert. The southern region was the objective of the British 1st Armored Division (Major General Robin Brims) and focused on Basra and its nearby oil fields. If necessary, this force could be reinforced from the I Marine Expeditionary Force (Lieutenant General James T. Conway, USMC). The capture of Baghdad became the mission of the U.S. Army V Corps (Lieutenant General William L. Wallace, USA), the principal arm of the Combined Forces Land Component Command (Lieutenant General David D. McKiernan, USA). The other major part of the Baghdad offensive was the I MEF's 1st Marine Division (Major General James Mattis, USMC). The I MEF's air task force from the 1st and 3rd Marine Aircraft Wings flew fixed-wing missions as part of the Combined Forces Air Component Command (CFACC), but its helicopters stayed under direct Marine control. An additional Marine brigade remained afloat in reserve. The last element would be a Special Forces task force, rich in electronics, that would scour the desert between Jordan and Baghdad for WMD sites and pretend to be a mechanized force driving toward the capital from the west, a contingency the Russians emphasized in advising the Iraqis. Even with the development of Kuwait as a base area since 1991, the OIF forces needed six months to assemble in the Gulf region.

The massing of the U.S.-British expeditionary force concerned its senior commanders. As the planners studied the requirements of desert and urban warfare for a mobile, mechanized American army and calculated the logistical and security problems of supporting this force from Kuwaiti bases hundreds of miles away, the generals doubted that they had enough of the right troops. The problems ran back to Rumsfeld and his neocon disciples, whose basic assumption was that the Iraqis would not fight to save Saddam Hussein. They overlooked the Iraqis' history of fighting any foreign invader, however hopelessly. As General Franks's protests weakened in the face of Secretary Rumsfeld's hectoring, the COBRA II troop list shrank. Bush had set an arbitrary limit of 200,000 for the force, and Rumsfeld made even deeper cuts. Had the Army had its way, it would have added the 1st Cavalry Division or the 1st Armored Division or both to the CFLCC. It managed to get two armored cavalry regiments and the 82nd Airborne Division added, but as late arrivals. When Turkey objected to allowing the 4th Infantry Division to launch an offensive from its territory, the division diverted to Iraq, but not in time for the invasion. The commanders felt further shocks when, despite the awesome logistical effort in Kuwait, Rumsfeld limited the number of service support units sent to the theater and cut back the reserve mobilization. For example, planners estimated that CFLCC might have to handle over 100,000 enemy prisoners of war (EPW), but V Corps controlled only one small MP brigade until it received a patchwork National Guard MP brigade that was supposed to provide traffic and police services in Kuwait. The troop shortages did not seem fatal to the COBRA II drive to Baghdad, but the planners worried about the pacification of all Iraq and Phase IV operations. CENTCOM war games until 2003 predicted the need for 300,000 troops. On March 19, CFLCC went to war with 122,000 U.S. soldiers and Marines and 21,000 members of the British armed forces.

In terms of its broad strategic mission, destroying the organized Iraqi armed forces and any WMD in their possession and displacing the Saddam Hussein dictatorship, Operation IRAQI FREEDOM fulfilled its champions' most optimistic expectations. Victory, officially announced by President Bush on the flight deck of the carrier USS *Abraham Lincoln* on May 1, 2003, meant the end of "major combat operations." "Mission Accomplished!" the banner above Bush trumpeted. The president admitted that Iraq still presented reconstruction problems, the understatement of the decade. From the first air strikes on March 19 to the disappearance of the Special Republican Guard in Baghdad, the CFLCC with awesome air support ruined the Iraqi national, uniformed armed forces. Driving M-1A2 tanks, Bradley tracked fighting vehicles, and armed HUMVEES (a super Jeep), the 3rd Infantry Division broke over the border sand berm on March 20 and refueled its tanks in downtown Baghdad on April 7.

No contingency plan ever works exactly as planned, but COBRA II came close. The war started a day early because Bush approved a decapitating air strike on a Baath compound called Dora Farms. Intelligence analysts put the Hussein family there for a meeting, and the president could

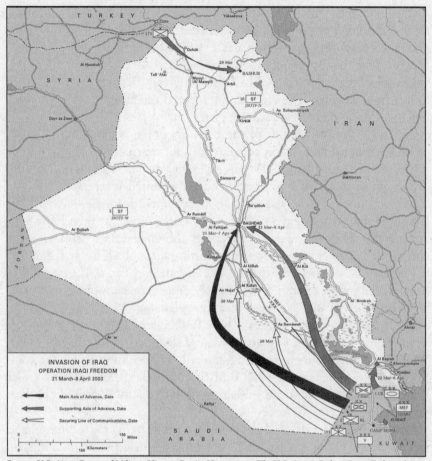

INVASION OF IRAQ
OPERATION IRAQI FREEDOM
21 March–9 April 2003

Source: U.S. Army Center of Military History, *Bosnia-Herzegovina: The U.S. Army's Role in Peace Enforcement Operations, 1995–2004*

not resist ordering two USAF F-117A stealth fighter-bombers to destroy Dora Farms with precision-guided penetrating bombs, followed by a barrage of cruise missiles. People died, but not the Hussein males. Hours before the president told the world that the United States would lead a coalition force into Iraq, Special Operations Forces were on the ground on their missions, and the skies filled with aircraft and drones looking for targets and ruining any Iraq air-defense radars with electronic jamming. Assured of friendly skies, the CFACC aircraft went for the targets throughout Iraq ahead of the ground forces.

Remembering the confusions of the "scud hunt" of 1991, Central Command deployed more than twenty batteries of the improved Patriot air defense missile from four Air Defense Artillery brigades to Kuwait, Saudi Arabia, Jordan, Qatar, and Israel. If the Iraqi nuclear threat was exaggerated, CENTCOM had to assume that its forces might face tactical ballistic missiles with high explosive, chemical, and biological warheads. It was a sound precaution. Between March 20 and April 3, the Iraqis launched seventeen missiles at CENTCOM bases in Kuwait and Saudi Arabia. One missile fell to a Patriot of the 43rd Air Defense Artillery Brigade only three miles from CFLCC headquarters. Patriots destroyed eight other Iraqi missiles. The eight unintercepted missiles, carefully tracked, fell apart or landed without causing harm.

Among the many skills of the U.S. Air Force is its ability to amass statistics that measure effort accurately, if not destruction. The air war of Operation IRAQI FREEDOM was no exception, and there is little doubt, by Iraqi testimony, that air attacks seriously limited Iraqi movement and destroyed units. There was virtually no effective Iraqi air defense. The Iraqis fired antiaircraft gun batteries 1,224 times and launched 1,660 anti-air missiles. They downed six helicopters and one aircraft. Thirteen more aircraft fell to operational accidents. Sorting through all the statistics, the CFACC counters decided their 1,800 aircraft had flown 41,000 combat sorties. Half of the aircraft came from the Air Force, about half from naval aviation. The British, Canadian, and Australian air forces contributed 138 aircraft that flew 3,000 sorties. The CFACC flew 25,000 sorties against enemy targets (moving or stationary) and dropped almost 30,000 munitions, two-thirds of them precision-guided. The coalition air forces, commanded by Lieutenant General. T. Michael Moseley, USAF, made it easier to win with fewer American casualties—and to justify Rumsfeld's passion for limiting the ground forces.

A bold plan, COBRA II depended on the surrender, dissolution, and poor fighting of the regular Iraqi armed forces, including the Republican Guard. With rapid maneuver and focused, massive air and artillery strikes, the ground forces could defeat any intact Iraqi units in detail. When the Turkish government prohibited the 4th Infantry Division attack, the division went by sea to Kuwait. The 173rd Airborne Brigade stationed in Italy assumed the Kurdistan mission. The plan worked. In five days, with negligible losses, CFLCC crossed almost three hundred miles of Iraq and prepared for the final offensive on Baghdad. Iraqi resistance proved haphazard, ill organized, and more of a nuisance than an operational challenge.

Two days into COBRA II, the leading Army and Marine armored and mechanized task forces, however, faced a type of resistance they did not anticipate: ambushes and sudden assaults by non-uniformed Iraqis fighting from homes and shielded by helpless civilians. Vans, pickup trucks, and cars carrying men armed with RPGs, demolitions, and automatic weapons appeared from nowhere on suicide missions. The Saddam *Fedayeen* had joined the battle, however futile. They had been reinforced by 35,000 convicts released from Iraq's prisons and armed by Baath leaders. Engagements spread all along the highways used by American columns and choked with service vehicles in the hundreds; bridges and crossroads became likely battlegrounds. Mosques served as ambush sites. One Bradley team killed at least 500 Iraqis in one brief fight on March 23. The march to Baghdad became memorable for obscure towns where the *Fedayeen* mounted last stands: as Samawah, an Najaf, an Nasiriyah, Karbala, al Hillah, al Amarah, and al Kut. Closer to Baghdad, Republican Guard units joined the fray. The race to Baghdad also ran into the Mother of All Sandstorms (March 25–27), which halted the lead elements of the 3rd Infantry Division and 1st Marine Division, advancing abreast into the Tigris-Euphrates Valley. The Republican Guard also sent a cautionary message when one brigade stopped a major attack by the Apache helicopter gunships of the 11th Army Helicopter Regiment; twenty-nine of thirty Apaches were so damaged by ground fire that the attacking battalion was out of the war for a week.

The logistical challenges that faced the COBRA II forces demanded a heroic transportation effort. The CFLCC consumed 54 million gallons of gas and oil, consumption greater than the Allies for all of World War I. The march to Baghdad required 5,000 tons of munitions and 1.7 million gallons of water. Sand and wind damaged vehicles and electronics. So did *Fedayeen* attacks, which plagued the convoys well behind the 3d Infantry Division's leading brigade. General McKiernan had to assign units of the 82d Airborne and 101st Air Assault Divisions and the 2d Armored Cavalry Regiment to protect his supply lines. Moreover, as the Army and Marine columns entered the Baghdad area, they left the desert and entered a land of canals, marshes, tributaries of the Tigris and Euphrates Rivers, and sprawling villages that made the Americans even more roadbound and dependent on scarce engineer and vehicle service units. Only motorcraft and bridging companies could ensure passage over water obstacles. Much to Franks's and Rumsfeld's dismay, McKiernan ordered a pause to ensure one unbroken attack on Baghdad from five directions. In the meantime, the British had the Basra area in hand, and Joint Special Operations Task Force North (the 10th Special Forces Group and Kurdish *pesh merga*) had watched the Iraqi regular army fade away or surrender and then destroyed those isolated Republican Guard units that stood and fought. The 173d Airborne Brigade arrived to secure the victory.

The final attack on Baghdad on March 30 began with limited-objective attacks all along the city's outer limits in order to eliminate a few Republican Guard units and secure bases for raids ("thunder runs") into the central city. On April 3 the 3rd Infantry Division took Baghdad airport, news Saddam Hussein denied as false reporting. Three Republican Guard brigades defended the airport, but they proved no match for one American armored brigade and Air Force fighter-bombers. On April 6 the tank-infantry task forces massed astride the freeways leading to downtown Baghdad. Three days later an Army column met a Marine column in massive al Firdos Square in the city center. There was no Iraqi official to make a formal surrender agreement. The GIs and Marines watched hysterical mobs and clever gangs enter government buildings and leave with all the loot they could carry. The Iraqis did not know that the White House and Rumsfeld's warriors expected a grateful victory parade.

The Pacification of Iraq, 2003–2011

The non-Arab world thrilled as it watched a mob and a U.S. tank recovery vehicle pull down the statue of Saddam Hussein onto the pavement of al-Firdos Square. The remnants of Saddam Hussein's government and security forces faded into the general population and headed for countryside hideouts. Although there was no plan to resist the Americans with urban guerrilla warfare, all the ingredients for a protracted unconventional war against the hated foreign invaders already existed. Muhammad Yunis al-Ahmed, chief of security for the Baath Party, had the best claim as father of the insurgency. Escaping Baghdad with Saddam Hussein, Yunis left his boss at a safe house near Tikrit and drove into Syria, where he collected money and began to recruit partisans. His goal was to turn the Sunnis into active resistors, not passive victims.

Like the dissolution of Yugoslavia, the end of the Saddam Hussein dictatorship unleashed communal hatreds that reached back centuries. Saddam Hussein had created a Sunni secular tyranny in which power had become concentrated in the hands of the al-Tikriti clan and its allies. Other Sunnis could survive only if they served the government, its captive industries, and the Baath Party. Much of the Sunni professional and commercial class had gone into exile during and after the Iran-Iraq and Gulf wars. The regime had little use for Islamic fundamentalists, even Sunnis. The regime had also stripped power from the traditional clan sheikhs. The Shi'a, the most numerous Iraqi group and known derisively as "marsh Arabs," were tolerated only because they provided an underclass for the oil industry, urban service industries, construction, and anything that required cheap labor. The Kurds of northern Iraq were Muslims but not Arabs. They had been loyal supporters of the Ottoman Empire and allies of anyone who held the Sunnis in check, like the Hashemite kings who ruled Iraq after World War I with British support. Mix in personal megalomania, family feuds, and economic privileges (including office-holding) and the social chemistry was as explosive as a roadside bomb. American Arabists in the

CIA and State Department knew all these tensions and made dire predictions. The White House and Pentagon did not respect this informed pessimism and brought peace to Iraq as if it were World War II Austria.

The CFLCC may have moved into Phase IV stability operations but many Iraqis had not stopped fighting just because Saddam Hussein and his army had disappeared. The country was awash with weapons, and many of them were in the hands of Sunni resistors. For the moment, the Kurds and Shi'a, truly liberated this time, helped root out Baathist officials and secret police. Ominously, varied Shi'a groups formed community militia forces, well armed and commanded by army veterans from the war with Iran. The Shi'a also drew support from their Persian co-religionists, who assumed that a Shi'a-dominated Iraq would become a *de facto* ally. The Kurds already had an army, and they used it to evict any leftover soldiers and officials from the Saddam Hussein regime. The Kurds, internally divided into two factions, would remain part of Iraq instead of creating a real Kurdistan, provided they got the lion's share of the profits of the northern oil fields. The Kurds were the only Iraqis the Americans could really trust. The Sunni insurgents, however, were thick near Mosul in Kurdistan.

In Washington, Bush and Rumsfeld did not realize the enormity of the challenges faced by their Iraqi expeditionary force. Since they didn't regard Iraqi deaths, purposeful or accidental, as a problem, they were comforted by the low U.S. casualties as of May 31, 2003: 214 deaths from enemy action in Iraq and Afghanistan. British deaths for all of 2003 were fifty-three; for other allies, forty-one. There was still fighting in Iraq, especially around Baghdad. The shooters were occasional warriors, just like the looters, said Rumsfeld. They were just too overcome with freedom. The looting, in fact, had destroyed the Iraqi bureaucratic infrastructure and much of its industrial potential—while American troops watched. The general feeling in American units was that the war was over. There were two bits of unfinished business. One was finding Saddam Hussein, his sons, and his most criminal associates and bringing them to justice. The other mission was to find all the WMD caches that the Iraqis surely had. The CIA, Iraqi agents, Delta Force, Special Forces, the 101st Airborne, and the 4th Infantry Division ran the Hussein family to ground. The sons died in a firefight in July 2003, and the father climbed out of a hide-hole in Tikrit in December. Convicted by Iraqis for crimes beyond counting, Saddam Hussein dangled from a rope in December 2006.

Other searchers roamed throughout Iraq searching for WMD. The Pentagon sent out a task force of 1,200 WMD engineers and scientists, led by UNSCOM veteran David Kay. This Iraq Survey Group continued the searches of the extemporized 75th Exploitation Task Force (XTF). The mission of the 75th XTF was to seize known WMD sites, search for

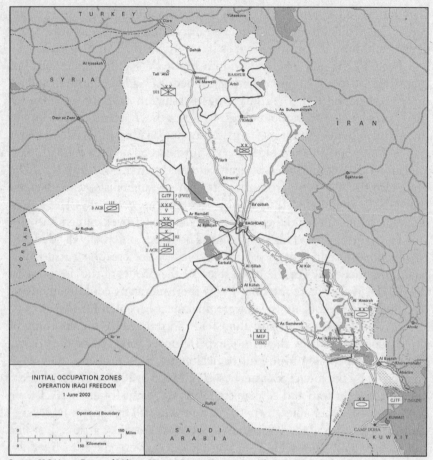

INITIAL OCCUPATION ZONES
OPERATION IRAQI FREEDOM
1 June 2003

——— Operational Boundary

Source: U.S. Army Center of Military History, *Bosnia-Herzegovina: The U.S. Army's Role in Peace Enforcement Operations, 1995–2004*

unknown sites, and then conduct tests for evidence of nuclear, chemical, and biological weapons or the research and manufacturing facilities necessary to make them. Since the Iraqis had launched twenty forbidden ballistic missiles at CFLCC targets during the 2003 war, the 75th XTF units had the highest priority and often appeared among the attacking advance forces. Special Forces actually raided and captured an uninspected research facility in northern Iraq. As the sand settled in the spring of 2003, UN inspectors also returned to Iraq for more inspections and consultation with the Iraqi Survey Group. Both WMD groups found Iraq in violation of the UN resolutions on aiding inspections, reporting WMD destruction, accounting for WMD, halting all missile and WMD development, and renouncing any future interest in WMD. An IAEA assessment of June 16–19, 2003, found that Iraq had 1.8 tons of uranium "yellowcake," which was too little from which to extract even enough enriched uranium for research, let alone weapons.

The spinmasters in Washington moved into high gear to discredit Bush's critics and to reinterpret the pre-2003 evidence to show that the administration had been misled, not duplicitous. The momentary embarrassment of the neocons did not translate into more sensible management of Iraqi affairs by the State Department. Instead, Secretary Rumsfeld scrapped the Office of Reconstruction and Humanitarian Assistance, unappreciated and underfunded, and replaced it with the Coalition Provisional Authority (CPA), essentially an occupation government headed by Ambassador L. Paul "Jerry" Bremer III, who had headed the State Department's counterterrorism office twenty years earlier but was not an Arabist. Without blinking, he executed Rumsfeld's most influential directive: Dissolve the Iraqi government, the top four levels of Baath Party leadership, and all military forces. The order was simply stupid. All three pillars of Saddam Hussein's government had dissolved themselves. The Bremer interdict made it more difficult to screen past Iraqi officeholders for political crimes and, if cleared, hire them for a new government. The key to most successful occupations and counterinsurgency campaigns is to find work for rebels and potential rebels, even at larcenous rates. No matter how expensive, an amnesty-employment program saves time, money, and lives.

A strange mix of true reformers, opportunists, Bush loyalists, and marginal Washington bureaucrats, the CPA presided over a chain of security disasters that in three years brought the rebirth of Iraq to the brink of disaster. Civilians in the CPA, protected by the security of the "Green Zone," a seven-square-mile piece of America inside Baghdad, did little to help the U.S. Army and U.S. Marine Corps deal with an Iraqi effort to force a Somalia-like retreat on a grander scale. The direct attacks on American bases, convoys, and patrols mounted in the summer of 2003. The tactics of urban warfare all produced casualties: sniping, small ambushes, truck bombs, and the ubiquitous improvised explosive devices (IEDs) that killed and maimed with horrific anonymity. The annual death toll of American men and women remained high for four years: 849 (2004), 846 (2005), 822 (2006), and 904 (2007). A series of incidents simply enflamed the anti-American resistance. One was a chain of violent events staged by the Sunnis that turned Baghdad's Shi'a against the occupation. Another was the bombing of UN headquarters in Baghdad that killed the head of mission, Sergio Vieira de Mello, a dedicated humanitarian. On August 29, 2003, two car bombs killed 124 Shi'a worshippers, including a prominent, moderate *ayatollah*. The bomb also wounded 140 other Shi'a as they left the Najaf mosque. Bremer reported the bad news: If the United

States wanted Iraq to be peaceful, stable, and prosperous, it would take years of nation-building and hundreds of millions of U.S. dollars. Bush did not welcome this report. The new CENTCOM commander, General John Abizaid, an officer of Lebanese descent who spoke Arabic, agreed with Bremer's assessment.

A comparison of indicators for November 2003 and November 2005, compiled by *The New York Times*, demonstrates the escalating violence in Iraq.

	NOVEMBER 2003	NOVEMBER 2005
U.S. Troop Deaths	82	96
U.S. Deaths, IEDs	20	40
Iraqi Deaths, Security Forces	65	176
Iraqi Deaths, Civilian	125	600
Deaths, Multiple, IEDs	6	41
Iraqi Security Forces	95,000	212,000
U.S. Troops	123,000	160,000
Foreign Troops	24,000	23,000
Insurgents	5,000	18,000
Iraqis who favor U.S. withdrawal soon	30%	80%

Despite the increase in security forces numbers and promising economic indicators, the war had swung to the insurgents. In the following year, 2006, Iraqi deaths numbered 16,273 by morgue count. Another Iraqi count put the dead at 60,000.

The American military response to the insurgency, once its nature was clear in the autumn of 2003, was to take the offensive in Baghdad and against cities to the north in the "Sunni Triangle," a wedge of land between the Tigris and Euphrates, principally al-Anbar province. The western towns of Ramadi and Fallujah became centers of insurgency and destinations for foreign *mujahideen*, many recruited by al-Qaeda, who wanted to join the *jihad*. CIA and military intelligence officers identified Abu Musab al-Zarqawi, a fanatical Jordanian Islamicist, as the head of al-Qaeda Iraq. Despite Rumsfeld's fantasizing about al-Qaeda, the Sunni forces in the Triangle were principally Iraqi Baathists, members of Saddam's army and police, tribal warriors, and unemployed youths who could earn American dollars as urban guerrillas and bombers. The money came from Syria, Iran, al-Qaeda, and much of the Muslim world. In 2004 the war developed a southern front that ran from the Shi'a slums of Baghdad (Sadr City) to

Basra. The additional enemy was a Shi'a militia, the Jaish al-Mahdi (JAM). A council of clerics and Muqtada al-Sadr, son of a sainted imam killed by Saddam Hussein, directed these forces. The Shi'a militia units had formed to protect their own communities, but they were perfectly willing to kill infidels and Sunnis if ordered to do so.

A series of events between 2003 and 2004 fueled the insurgency and spread it throughout Iraq. One was the Abu Ghraib prison scandal. The prison population of 6,000–7,000 were detainees being held for ninety days or more for screening and interrogation. An MP's private photographs revealed that the jailers had humiliated some prisoners with unclean acts with sexual and excretory implications. Several investigations discovered unauthorized coercion by intelligence personnel, even torture, to extract information and confessions. The Abu Ghraib scandal infuriated Muslims, Europeans, and the American antiwar movement.

Another gaffe was the First Battle of Fallujah, a Marine attack ordered from Washington to avenge the death of four contractors. In April 2004, a task force from the 1st Marine Division fought a door-to-door battle with veteran Sunni partisans until Washington ordered the operation ended— but before the city had been cleared. The units of the new Iraqi army and national police faded from the battle. American casualties (twenty-nine dead) seemed prohibitive to Bremer and even worse to Bush and Rumsfeld, who gave bold speeches but recoiled from the casualties. In addition, the Shi'a militias cowed the international units in the south and thus menaced the roads to the Kuwait logistical centers. In April 2004, the Provisional Iraqi Government, a fig-leaf council to replace the CPA, ordered one of Muqtada al-Sadr's lieutenants arrested and the Shi'a revolt crushed. Fighting broke out again in Karbala, al Kut, an Nasiriyah, and many other towns, but the final battle took place in the holy city of Najaf in August. A task force of one Marine reinforced battalion and two Army cavalry squadrons methodically retook the city until the remaining Shi'a militiamen, sheltered in the Imam Ali mosque, surrendered. In twenty-four days of combat, the Americans lost eight dead and ninety wounded; the Iraqis, an estimated 1,000–2,000. The Americans could win battles and kill Iraqis, but the war continued with no end in sight. Insurgent attacks averaged 500 a month in June 2003, then climbed to almost 3,000 attacks by January 2005. Two-thirds of the attacks came against the foreign troops; the rest were divided almost evenly between Iraqi soldiers and civilians. By the end of 2004, the United States armed forces had lost 1,100 dead in Iraq in combat, losses the nation had not experienced since 1969 in Vietnam. The numbers of service personnel wounded in action—many permanently maimed by IEDs—ran at seven or eight times the deaths.

In order to maintain a force for Operation IRAQI FREEDOM, the

Defense Department had to mobilize National Guard and Organized Reserve Units—primarily Army and Marine Corps ground troops—for service in the war zone. The process began in 2003 for the invasion, but unlike the DESERT STORM mobilization, the activations continued. Only unit rotation could keep the Iraq "boots on the ground" troop levels at 150,000. Activated Guard and reserve units in 2004–2005 provided almost 40 percent of Army personnel and 15 percent of the Marines. Air Force and Navy reservists served in smaller proportions of the total force and often outside Iraq proper. The composition of III Corps, the U.S. Army combatant command in Iraq, 2004–2005, reflected the reserve's contribution to the war. The corps troops included four National Guard battalions. The 1st Infantry Division included thirteen National Guard battalions. The 1st Cavalry Division included two National Guard brigades (nine battalions) and a Marine Reserve infantry battalion. Two National Guard brigades contributed eight battalions to the theater base security forces. Of the sixty-one maneuver battalions in the III Corps, twenty were Guardsmen or reservists from nine different states. The snipers and IEDs did not discriminate, so reservists died too. Between 2003 and 2009, 488 Army Guardsmen, two Air Guard members, and 319 Ready Reserve members of all the services died, about one-fifth of all military deaths in Iraq.

With all of Iraq a war zone, the Bush administration reluctantly concluded that its critics, a growing chorus of informed dissent from all sides of the political spectrum, had been right in 2004. Iraq was a mess, in part because of the American failure to execute an intelligent, well-funded temporary occupation under clear international sanction. Even Ambassador Bremer admitted that his CPA was an "ineffective occupier." George W. Bush now sought wiser counsel among his father's inner circle. Once past his reelection in November 2004, the president steeled himself for the creation of a realistic political-military strategy for Iraq. Part of his challenge was reshaping his own administration. When Colin Powell resigned in frustration as secretary of state, Bush appointed a far wiser and more aggressive Condoleezza Rice to his post and made her able deputy Stephen Hadley his national security adviser. Backed by the CIA and State Department professionals, the Rice-Hadley team became a more effective counterweight to the Cheney-Rumsfeld neoconservatives. White House Chief of Staff Andrew Card also helped Bush deal with the war's realities. The president even listened to advice from former Secretary of State Henry Kissinger and listened less to Vice President Cheney.

The military command in Iraq underwent two important changes when General George W. Casey Jr., Army vice-chief of staff, became the field commander in Iraq and Lieutenant General David H. Petraeus became chief adviser to the new Iraqi armed forces. Although they differed on the war's wisdom and future course, the two generals did agree that a campaign demanded protecting the Iraqi people from many enemies. The essential security mission should be transferred to armed Iraqis. Casey thought in terms of an Iraqi national army and police. Petraeus was not sure that this notional force would be large enough and good enough or be formed soon enough for the mission, especially when he saw Sunni and Shi'a radicals infiltrating these forces. The Sunni and Shi'a militias regarded the Iraqi armed forces and police as inept and vulnerable and made them principal targets for attack. In the first two weeks of January 2005, the distribution of violent deaths showed a persistent pattern: ninety dead in the Iraqi army and police, sixty-nine Iraqi civilians, and twenty-five American service personnel. No members of the other international forces died in combat, although eight died in accidents. George Casey knew the statistics. In order to fight an extended counterinsurgency campaign with limited American participation, he would have to enlarge and improve the Iraqi security forces and bring down American casualties. General Abizaid wanted American patrols off the streets and into well-defended operating bases.

To turn the war over to the Iraqis required a government. Bremer's first expedient, the Iraqi Governing Council, was not successful because it gave the Chalabi group and other exiles too much license for revenge. The Kurds were cooperative but feared by the Iraqi Arabs. After much negotiation throughout 2004, the CPA and the U.S. Embassy organized three major elections to create a representative Iraqi government. The American forces regarded the elections as a necessary political act of indeterminate effect. As one bit of GI graffiti put it: "We came, we saw, we conquered, we wasted a year, but now we've made the fuckers vote!" Not everyone voted. The Sunni politicians boycotted the election for a national constitutional assembly, boycotted the referendum on the new constitution, and then largely boycotted the election to form a new parliamentary government, which would elect a prime minister and approve his cabinet. The three major Shi'a factions claimed 140 out of 275 seats. A Kurdish coalition elected seventy-five members. The Shi'a-Kurd majority then divided the cabinet with a moderate Shi'a civilian, Kamil Mohammed Hasan Nouri al-Maliki, as prime minister. Condemned to death by Saddam Hussein for conspiracy, Nouri al-Maliki in exile had become head of the Islamic Dawa Party. However promising some of the developments of 2005, peace was not at hand. During the year 897 American service personnel died, down slightly from 2004.

The central operational objective was still to pacify the Sunni Triangle, which began with the Second Battle of Fallujah in November 2004. After a careful logistical buildup and repeated warnings for civilians to leave or seek shelter, a task force of 8,000 Marines and soldiers and 2,000 Iraqis took ten days to kill 1,000–2,000 very tough Sunni partisans, reinforced by the *mujahideen* of al-Qaeda Iraq. Senior officers likened the house-to-house fighting to the battle for Hue city in 1968. The fight was truly a joint operation, since the Air Force provided precise close air support and the U.S. Navy committed medical service personnel, engineers, and aviation controllers. Tanks and artillery pounded insurgent strongholds; by one Marine estimate 2,000 buildings were destroyed, 10,000 damaged. The battle cost the Americans fifty-four dead and 425 wounded, many by rocket ambushes and booby traps. For General Casey, the battle proved that the insurgents could not hold city enclaves. For General Petraeus, the battle showed that the Iraqi national army and police still shunned combat. And the war went on, with Marine forces fighting to the top of the Sunni Triangle at Ramadi and beyond, past Haditha Dam and along the Euphrates to the Syrian border. The 2nd Marine Division sent mechanized task forces to chase after Iraqi and *mujahideen* fighters who had escaped Fallujah before its siege ended and tried to roll up the network of caches and strongholds the insurgents used to bring weapons and other Arab fighters into al-Anbar province. The campaign exacted a price. Company L, 3rd Battalion, 25th Marines, a reserve unit from central Ohio, lost ten Marines killed in an amphibian tractor explosion in August 2005. The same company had lost six Marines in a firefight and amtrac explosion in May. The company's losses were the highest of any Marine reserve unit in the war.

Elsewhere American forces found death but not many insurgents. The biggest killers were IEDs set off by electronic remote-control devices like radios and mobile phones. By 2006 hidden bombs were exploding somewhere in Iraq about once every fifteen minutes. Electronic warfare specialists deployed jammers that confounded remote detonations. Eventually they forced the bombers to return to using wire-detonating systems, in theory easier to detect by sight. Bombs were especially deadly in Baghdad, with its traffic jams, mass population, and millions of hiding sites. The bombers had decades of experience upon which to draw. They primarily used the bountiful supply of unexploded bombs and shells. All the services contributed to Task Force Troy, a force of thousands of explosive ordnance detection and disposal experts to combat the IED threat. The only way to stop bombers was to track them down and kill them; special sniper units eventually became skilled enough to kill about fifty emplacers a week by 2007. In the meantime, military vehicles in Iraq became more armored or designed to survive bomb blasts. Bombs declined as troop-killers, but Iraqi civilians continued to be the victims of IED explosions.

With virtually all indicators of economic improvement and public security now plunging in 2005 and 2006, the Sunni insurgents broadened the war by attacking the Shi'a population and the government they supported. It was not a new war, but it was more desperate and deadly. It was fed by two extremist groups, al-Qaeda Iraq and al-Qaeda Mesopotamia, an offshoot group that rejected al-Zarqawi's leadership. In February 2006, agents for al-Qaeda Mesopotamia (AQM) blew up the al-Askari mosque in Samarra, a holy Shi'a shrine, and followed with attacks by car bombs and suicide bombers throughout Baghdad. Violence between Iraqis soared to new levels of horror, with bombings and mass murders averaging 1,500–1,800 deaths a month. Sunni civilians took the brunt of the Shi'a revenge campaign, mounted by Muqtada al-Sadr's JAM private army of 50,000. Members of the Badr Brigade, the military arm of the Shi'a Supreme Council for the Islamic Revolution in Iraq, supported JAM from their positions in the ministries of the interior and transportation. JAM routinely captured as many as sixty Sunni men a night, tortured them, murdered them, and dumped them back in their neighborhoods. The Shi'a had adopted sectarian cleansing for Baghdad. Sunni families fled whole neighborhoods to escape the 2006 bloodbath, the greatest cause of the 35,000 Iraqis deaths that year. Many of the refugees headed for al-Anbar province or another country. The Shi'a vendetta, which killed Americans too, became so mindless that Muqtada al-Sadr actually tried to curb the excesses of his militia. Shi'a politics became even more chaotic in Basra when JAM, the Badr Brigade, a local warlord, and criminal gangs fought each other over the profits of the oil business. With parliament and the important ministries under their control, the collective Shi'a leadership sought to check the vendetta, but only if someone else did the dirty work of pacification the army and police would not.

The local Sunni sheikhs and some public officials in al-Anbar province looked for help to stop the flood of refugees, the advancing Shi'a, and the suicidal foreigners of al-Qaeda who, like mercenaries of old, decided they liked living among the cowed Sunnis. The al-Anbar Sunnis, however, now wanted American help, not American lives, and started negotiations with Marine and Army commanders and civil affairs officers for arms for their own Salvation Council militia, eventually called the Sons of Iraq. They did not get weapons, but were welcomed into the police and army. They were heartened by the death by bombing of the head of AQI, Abu Musab al-Zarqawi, in June 2006. Despite reservations by General Casey and Prime Minister Nouri al-Maliki, the police soon bulged with Sunni ex-soldiers and ex-partisans. The Americans embraced the Sunni Awakening and helped the new allies kill or drive away the two al-Qaeda factions. Casey, however, tried to keep his troops out of the way and urged the Pentagon to reduce his force, concentrated in large, defended bases around Baghdad but inevitably caught in the crossfires and still taking casualties.

The Sunni Awakening caught Washington by surprise, but it helped push Bush toward a new, high-risk strategy for Iraq. Formally called the Baghdad Security Plan or *Fardh al-Aanoon* ("imposing the law"), the plan reflected Bush and Nouri al-Maliki's desperation. The idea of "the Surge" had many fathers. One group of advocates rallied around General John M. Keane, a retired Army vice-chief of wide respect, who had examined the Iraq morass under the sponsorship of Rice and Hadley. Bush made Keane's advocacy easier by forcing Rumsfeld to resign (December 2006) and replacing him with Robert M. Gates, a pragmatist of long Washington service. Keane rallied retired Army and Marine generals steeped in population-centric counterinsurgency. He had no trouble recruiting David Petraeus, who had returned home from his second Iraq tour as a media favorite and a very persuasive champion of counterinsurgency. Lieutenant General Raymond Odierno, USA, whose 4th Infantry Division had been a heavy-handed occupier in 2003–2004, believed in the Surge and directed it for Petraeus as commander of Multi-National Force-Iraq.

Other powerful military and political voices in Washington sought to convince Bush to change strategy. The elite press, fed with leaks of the plan, endorsed the Surge. Bush could also read the report of the Iraq Study Group, a bipartisan group of Washington's most canny and respected leaders under the chairmanship of former Secretary of State James A. Baker III and retired Congressman Lee H. Hamilton, a lifelong internationalist. At the heart of its recommendations was the suggestion that the United States might have to increase its troop strength in Iraq in the short term in order to come home with victory in the long term. The American forces would have to join and train the Iraqi forces and interpose themselves between all the warring parties until the rebels came to terms with the Nouri al-Maliki government. Many of the concepts came from the commission's military advisory panel, which included John Keane.

The basic outline of the Baghdad Security Plan announced in January 2007 was simple enough. American troops would emerge in numbers and combat-ready from their bases and, with the Iraqi army and police, crush any armed forces that opposed the Iraqi government and killed Iraqi civilians. This force would be reinforced by as many as 32,500 combat troops from the United States. The Surge might last a year or more, which meant American troop strength in Iraq would return to 160,000. Where local Baghdad communities defended themselves against al-Qaeda and Iraqi terrorists, they would be protected from seventy security posts around the city. The immediate objective was to crush AQM and JAM and stop the Shi'a pogrom. There were unstated consequences to the plan. The neighborhoods depopulated by JAM would not be restored to the Sunnis. And American soldiers and Marines were going to die in higher numbers, but at least they would not die as passive IED victims.

The battle for Baghdad and four neighboring provinces tested the efficacy of the Baghdad Plan, and the results showed some progress by the end of 2007. The casualty count was clear enough. The U.S.-Iraqi-Coalition forces lost at least 2,592 lives. The American deaths for 2007 (904) were the worst of the war. It was the last year that any other international force lost troops since "the coalition of the willing" had wilted. Six months into the campaign, some of the vital indicators of improving security and social conditions worsened and continued to look dismal into 2010. One critical sign of success, however, was the declining American death toll, which fell off sharply in 2008. Iraqi civilian deaths in 2008 fell to one-quarter of the deaths in 2006 and 2007. The Iraqi security forces almost doubled in two years (2006–2008), and their service deaths dropped by half. By 2010 the American forces left in Iraq numbered only 50,000.

Several factors explain the success of the Baghdad Security Plan. Its primary objective was to break JAM opposition to any government, and the U.S.-Iraqi army did this quickly and efficiently, at least by earlier standards. Implicated in JAM's terrorism, Muqtada al-Sadr went into exile, which brought great relief to the senior Shi'a *ayatollahs* and politicians. The Badr army put on national uniforms or went home. The Kurds enjoyed legal regional autonomy, defended by the *pesh merga*. Despite the Iraqi government's inefficiency and corruption, the nation's economic woes after forty years of war and dictatorship were predictable and reversible. The United States would not press Nouri al-Maliki too hard on corruption (an estimated $4 billion a year), but it would not tolerate abuse of the Sunnis, who had helped drive out al-Qaeda and break up JAM. American commanders supported the 100,000 Sons of Iraq, a neighborhood security force. Sectarian violence would not disappear overnight, and Americans still died but not so many: 314 (2008), 149 (2009), and 60 (2010). The Iraq war, finally, was fading away.

The consequences of IRAQI FREEDOM cannot in 2012 be assessed with certainty. Whether or not it was worth the cost cannot yet be determined and depends on the course of history for Iran, Syria, Saudi Arabia, Kuwait, Jordan, Turkey, and Israel. Dictators seem to have a one-generation half-life, as the fall of the Shah of Iran, Saddam Hussein, Hosni Mubarak, and Muammar Gaddafi suggest. Yet WMD and a three-generation succession have survived in North Korea. Saddam Hussein was a weak regional threat in 2003; he might have been a larger threat in 2013 had he survived in power. The expert consensus is that his regime was bound for ruin, but tyrants have fooled experts before. The tragedy of Iraq is not the 2003 war but the eight years of violence that followed the American invasion. The accumulated cost of the war is sobering: 4,488 Americans dead, 32,223 wounded, and an added defense cost of $806 billion. For the Iraqis, the estimated death toll is a staggering 120,000. The important consequences cannot be quantified. They are held in the minds of a generation of Arab nationalist leaders and the Iranians.

The war probably did little to make terrorism in the Arab world a greater or lesser threat than it had been before 2001. A 2010 compilation of Arab terrorist groups by European experts identified by name eighty terrorist groups. Of the eighty groups, fifty existed before 2001 with roots in the anticolonial, anti-Israel struggle. Of the thirty identified as formed after 2001, only eight could be identified as part of the al-Qaeda network. No doubt there have been some rearrangements after the "Arab Spring" of 2011. Nevertheless, safe havens for al-Qaeda are less hospitable. Afghanistan, Yemen, Saudi Arabia, Jordan, and Pakistan have quit ignoring or supporting al-Qaeda; and Syria and Iraq have reopened diplomatic relations, which makes it more difficult for the fugitive Baathists to be allies to al-Qaeda. Given Ayman al-Zawahri's Egyptian roots and the chaos in Cairo, Egypt may be the next al-Qaeda homeland.

The Iraq war may have convinced Middle Eastern leaders that the United States is a better ally than an enemy in military affairs. In truth, the Iraq war probably did nothing to solve the problems of the Arab world, which is to find some accommodation between fundamental Islam as mutated by nationalism and the challenges of twenty-first-century economic modernization and global interdependence. Will the Iraq war simply reinforce the Arab perception that Israel dictates American regional policies? If the Iraq war is a tragedy from the perspective of American national security policy, it is because it had so little to do with the global war on terrorism. It may not increase the chances of Israel's survival, and it is probably irrelevant to the course of the Iranian Revolution. Iran may be the ultimate strategic winner in the war, since Iraq will no longer be a threat.

The Obama Administration and the War in Afghanistan, 2009–2012

The destruction of Saddam Hussein's Iraq diverted attention from the pursuit and punishment of al-Qaeda's leaders. The war, in fact, made Osama bin Laden look clever and undefeated. The counterterrorism community in Washington and in the field had kept its eyes open and saw the geographic spread and increased incidence of terror in the decade after 9/11 and the first Afghanistan campaign. Despite its fragmentation and flight in 2001–2002, al-Qaeda had found safe havens in southeastern Afghanistan and the ill-policed tribal border areas of the FATA and the two Waziristan provinces. The Pashtun Taliban had also retained its internal order through the Mullah Omar, also in hiding. By 2003 the Taliban had returned to southern Afghanistan.

Without much prompting from Osama bin Laden, Islamic terrorists followed 9/11 and the Afghan war with increased attacks across the globe. In the next decade, *jihadis* carried out deadly bomb attacks in Great Britain, Indonesia, Morocco, Saudi Arabia, the Netherlands, the Philippines, Turkey, Spain, Jordan, Pakistan, Egypt, Algeria, Yemen, Kenya, and India. This list is not complete. Unlike Europe, where Muslim populations are proportionately large, poor, unemployed, and unassimilated, America's 2.4 million Muslims are fragmented by race, geography, cultural origin, and levels of income, not to mention varieties of Islam. A Somali woman operating an airport snack bar in Columbus, Ohio, has little in common with a male Iranian millionaire in Houston, Texas. Working within personal rights laws more restrictive than in Europe for those combating terrorism, American police still had fewer problems identifying and arresting terrorists. The fact that there has been no repetition of 9/11 dulled American public awareness of the real global war on terrorism being waged elsewhere by other nations and American counterterrorism teams. Some nations blame the United States for giving Islamicists a cause for holy war. In addition to its ties to Israel, America's de facto alliance with Saudi Arabia irritates other nations because the House of Saud listens closely to its own radical-conservative Wahhabi clerics. Some Saudis export people and resources to Muslim extremists outside of Saudi Arabia, although the House of Saud crushes dissenters at home. Pakistan's toleration of the Taliban makes it a feeble ally or incomplete enemy. Another exporter of terrorism, Iran, has been run by an anti-American regime since 1979. Muslim extremists have plagued Indonesia and the Philippines. The 9/11 tragedy brought a spike in international sympathy for the United States that rapidly waned with the invasion of Iraq.

Terrorism remains a global problem. By a rough accounting, the victims of terrorist bombings in Europe and the Muslim world (and *not* counting Iraq and Afghanistan, 2001–2011) now exceeds the number of deaths of 9/11 and the American military deaths in Iraq and Afghanistan. One of the worst offenders is Lashkar-e-Taiba (Army of the Pure), a Pakistani terrorist group with links to Pakistan's Interservices Intelligence (ISI) agency. The attacks by Lashkar-e-Taiba (LeT) on the Indians illustrates the deadliness and persistence of just one Muslim terrorist group. LeT detonated thirteen bombs in Mumbai on March 12, 1993, killing 257 people and wounding 700. Eight years later, LeT renewed its attacks on India by assaulting the Parliament building in New Delhi, killing twelve. In August 2003, two bombs in Mumbai killed 44 and wounded 150. On July 11, 2006, the same terrorist group set off seven bombs in an eleven-minute period in the Mumbai commuter train system. The bombs killed 209 and wounded 700 riders. LeT suicide bombers on November 26–29, 2008, attacked ten crowded targets in Mumbai, killing 164 people and wounding 308 bystanders. The world watched the historic Taj Mahal Palace and Tower hotel burn while Indian special police battled with the bombers. Lashkar-e-Taiba is only one of forty-six such groups operating in India.

The fate of post-liberation Afghanistan demonstrated how inattentive the Bush administration was after 2002. Afghanistan had a proven anti-Taliban president, Hamid Karzai, who was momentarily acceptable to the Northern Alliance warlords. Under UN and NATO approval, an International Security Assistance Force (ISAF) of 30,000 patrolled the major cities. In 2004 ISAF and the Karzai government spent $4 billion in U.S. aid money to organize a new Afghan National Army (ANA) and police force. This force struggled to reach a goal of 150,000 in 2008. At the end of 2009, the ANA had only 94,000 soldiers for an area and population larger than Iraq. The Afghan army and police (the Afghan National Security Forces or ANSF) faced serious problems. First, the private armies of the Northern Alliance in the non-Pashtun provinces had no intention of disarming or serving in the ANSF outside their Hazara, Turkoman, Uzbek, and Tajik homelands. Second, in the Pashtun provinces, about half of Afghanistan, the ANSF faced a resurgent Taliban. By 2006 the Taliban had established shadow governments and guerrilla units among most of the Pakistani border and southern provinces. The Karzai government followed traditional practices of appointing personal and tribal loyalists to the ANSF and administrative posts and paid them with half of the aid dollars. Often with no special ties to the people they were supposed to govern and protect, ANSF commanders concentrated on extortion and corruption and not confronting the Taliban. Between 2002 and 2007, terrorist attacks on government and ANSF targets jumped tenfold.

The ISAF units followed rules of engagement that allowed them to fight only in self-defense or as part of an ANSF operation as foreign advisers. The mission was to protect the twenty-six Provincial Reconstruction Teams, the nation-builders. When Taliban units attacked ISAF units, the incidents seemed designed to tempt the foreigners to overreact and alienate the Afghan villagers. Moreover, while forty-three nations sent troops to Afghanistan, only ten nations (other than the United States) sent units of battalion strength or larger, the minimum force for pacification operations. Spain, Italy, and Germany put almost 10,000 troops in the northern and western provinces already policed by the Northern Alliance, and France put its 3,000 crack troops inside Kabul as a palace guard. American units tried to guard the Pakistani border provinces, while the British, Canadians, and the Dutch occupied the heart of Talibanland in the south. In 2007, ISAF numbered 37,000. In ISAF only the British, Dutch, and Canadians in southern Helmand Province attempted limited attacks on Taliban strongholds.

The battle for Musa Qala, Helmand Province, 2006–2007, was typical of ISAF operations and frustrations in pacifying the Pashtun provinces. In October 2006 a British brigade occupied the town and region and established a progovernment *shura* (town council), but in February 2007 the Taliban returned, executed the local leaders, and prevented a brigade of the Afghan army and police from restoring any permanent control. The Taliban initiated the attacks, broken only by NATO air strikes. In October 2007 a different British brigade of 1,200 from four understrength battalions surrounded Musa Qala and cautiously squeezed the Taliban back into Musa Qala town while under long-range mortar and machine-gun fire. The key to success was the defection of a local warlord of Taliban persuasion and his 400-man clan army. To exploit this event, a U.S. airborne battalion assaulted Musa Qala in helicopters on December 7 and took the town after a six-hour battle, losing one dead and six wounded. The British brigade then defeated a Taliban counterattack. President Karzai appointed as governor the Taliban general who had defected and gave him an ANA brigade to hold the region and supervise a campaign to stop growing opium poppies.

The Musa Qala district was still a battleground when the 2d Battalion, 4th Marines escorted an ANSF company back into the region in 2009–2010. In ten years 812 ISAF and ANSF soldiers had died in Musa Qala from snipers, ambushes, rocket and mortar attacks, and IEDs. The villagers were hostile or uncooperative. Whole villages had been abandoned. The jackals howled at night while raiders on motorcycles raced toward ISAF outposts to attack them, then disappeared into the dry hills. Pashtun translators, working for $865 a month and a U.S. visa, seldom located Taliban hideouts. The Uzbeks and Tajiks in the ANSF were no more at home than the Marines. In 2010 the number of ISAF troops in Helmand province reached 25,000. The pattern of ISAF casualties demonstrates two phenomena: the growing Taliban threat and the ISAF shift to more aggressive offensive operations. In 2004 ISAF military fatalities numbered 60(52 Americans), then jumped to 295 (155 Americans) in 2008. When ISAF doubled in strength in 2009 to 71,000, the result of an American surge of over 30,000 troops, fatalities doubled to 521 (317 Americans), climbed to 711 in 2010, then fell back to 446 in 2011 as the counterinsurgency campaign had some successes and ISAF passed more missions to the Afghanis. By the end of 2011 American deaths had reached 1,777 and the allies 950 (382 British). The "boots on the ground" strength of American troops in Afghanistan in 2010–2011 reached 90,000.

Much of the continuing violence in Afghanistan is hidden by the use of civilian contractors, who numbered 113,491 by 2012. Twenty-two percent are American citizens, the others from Afghanistan and all over Europe and Asia. The contractors are attractive targets for raiders that kill and plunder. The largest employer, L-3 Communications, has already lost 370 dead and 1,789 wounded. The next favorite target is the ISAF caterer, the Supreme Group, which has suffered 240 dead. Of the foreigners in Afghanistan only the American and British armed forces have lost more members than the contractors.

Although the Bush administration recognized the growing Taliban menace, it passed this political snowdrift on to a new president in 2009. Barack Obama knew something about the Iraq and Afghanistan wars, which he experienced as a U.S. senator. He decided to be cautious and inquisitive before enlarging the American commitment to Afghanistan. One issue was the legitimacy and effectiveness of Hamid Karzai, reelected in 2009 in balloting reeking with fraud. Linked to the Karzai regime were international charges of corruption and opium trading. Karzai argued with some justification that the Taliban would be worse than he was and that his enemy was not just the Taliban but the Islamicists in ISI and the Pakistani army, who wanted him replaced. Karzai did not care what the American domestic media and liberal politicians thought of him as long as they did not treat him like Saddam Hussein or the late Shah of Iran. Obama did not regard Karzai as an indispensable president, but he did not encourage the State Department or the CIA to look for alternatives. Instead he followed a late-stage Bush policy of putting more pressure on Pakistan. The United States had pressed Pakistan to form a civilian government, which it had in 2008 with the election of Asif Ali Zardari, but he had none of the public respect extended to General Musharraf or Zardari's assassinated wife, the iconic Benazir Bhutto. Almost doubling U.S. foreign aid to Pakistan ($2 billion in 2008, $3.6 billion in 2010) helped buy better Pakistani cooperation against some terrorists. This cooperation focused on al-Qaeda's "foreigners" and the part of the Taliban not sponsored by Pakistani Islamicists. The Obama administration decided to risk relations with Pakistan by mounting Predator drone missions and Special Operations Forces raids into Pakistan without prior warning. At least that is the cover story. In 2008 Predator strikes into Pakistan numbered ten, in 2010 forty-five. The raids into Pakistan scored their greatest success on May 2, 2011, when SEAL Team Six on Army special operations helicopters raided a fortified compound near Abbottabad, Pakistan, and killed Osama bin Laden when he resisted capture. After a number of identification tests, bin Laden was buried at sea. His cause most certainly survived, though weakened by his death and a decade's worth of intelligence material brought out by SEAL Team Six. The death of bin Laden did nothing to end the Taliban's bid to surround Kabul with captive rural provinces.

The Obama administration had already approved another "Surge" in December 2009 and watched 15,000 soldiers and Marines attack the Taliban heartland around Kandahar. To manage the campaign, the president sent General Stanley A. McChrystal, USA, the jedi knight of counter-terrorism who had commanded the joint special operations units in Iraq for seven years. He replaced a harried General McKiernan, perceived as too "traditional" by the White House. Although Obama later relieved McChrystal for some published critical remarks about the Afghan and American governments, the Petraeus-McChrystal population-centric pacification campaign went on without check in 2011. In the meantime, the administration quit hectoring Karzai in public and focused on long-term economic and infrastructure development. As the ANSF slowly assumed more combat missions, American deaths (all causes) dropped below ten a week, the point at which the war became truly forgotten again except by the Afghans and the 140,000 officers and men of the ISAF who still make their appointed rounds in search of the Taliban.

The shift of emphasis in the 2009–2010 campaign plan for Afghanistan was its stress on partnership with the Afghans and the avoidance of civilian casualties, key principles of counterinsurgency. Leader decapitation and band destruction remained important but as a handmaiden to population control. The emphasis on air strikes in 2007–2009 had raised civilian casualties and public ire. President Karzai went to the UN in 2008 and complained about the incidence of civilian casualties caused by ISAF-controlled air strikes. The head of the UN assistance mission in Afghanistan supported Karzai. At whatever risk, ISAF patrols could no longer rely only on drones and fighter-bombers to clear villages. They would also have to depend more on their Afghan allies, also perilous. In February 2010, ISAF and Afghan army and special police began Operation MOSHTARAK, the ultimate "clear and hold" campaign to break the Taliban grip on Helmand province. With 15,000 troops, about half ISAF and half Afghani, the objective of MOSHTARAK ("together") was control of the city of Marja and its poppy-growing region.

The novel aspects of MOSHTARAK were the level of Afghan combat participation, the patience of the advance, and the commitment of "holding" forces of administrators, public works personnel, police, and economic nation-builders. The slowness of MOSHTARAK reflected two determining factors: avoiding civilian casualties (only twenty-eight killed in five months) and the Taliban use of mines and IEDs as its main defense. Four Marine and one Army battalions and three British and one Canadian battalions provided the ISAF advance combat units and suffered forty-eight KIAs while killing perhaps two hundred and fifty to three hundred Taliban fighters. The key operational concept was to iso-

late the Marja region with helicopter-borne blocking forces in eleven different locations and spread "clearing" forces from these enclaves into
the farming villages around Marja. The Taliban defenders numbered no
more than 500, half of whom died in house-to-house battles. Marja fell
after two weeks of some intense but small-scale engagements. The battle
for Marja, however, did not end, since snipers and bombers plagued the
ISAF and Afghan occupiers for the rest of the year. Whether Afghan
security forces could reduce the opium trade and hold the Taliban at bay
without ISAF remained questionable.

A war against the Taliban and al-Qaeda in Afghanistan required a
war in Pakistan and a war by the Pakistani army against terrorists it had
once sponsored—and still did. Partisans like the al-Haqqani network had
become part of Pakistan's war of subversion against India in Kashmir
and along its border. The United States has spent $20 billion on Paki-
stan and bought selective cooperation. The Pakistanis gave up Khalid
Sheikh Mohammed of 9/11 infamy, but cannot find Mullah Omar. The
al-Haqqani terrorists conducted bomb attacks on the U.S. and Indian
embassies in Kabul in 2011. Pakistani politicians and generals may cooperate with American agents in secret, but they also encourage public anti-
Americanism, including violence. To avoid Pakistani interference, the
United States now ships 60 to 70 percent of its supplies to Afghanistan
through two rail-and-truck routes that begin in Latvia and Turkey and
end in the Muslim republics above Afghanistan.

Since the Pakistani government would not accept joint operations into
the FATA, the Americans turned to armed drones as their striking weapon.
Operating in a crowded sky of target-acquisition and surveillance drones,
Predators and MQ-9 Reapers stalk their victims. Since 2007, the drone
strikes by Pakistani count have killed 964 people, 793 of them Pakistanis.
Another analysis sees the strikes in a mounting tempo, 53 in 2009 and 118
in 2010 with at least 100 more in 2011. To put these statistics in perspective, the Pakistanis claim that 25,000 people have died inside their borders
since 2003. The CIA-managed drone campaign continues outside Afghanistan and Pakistan. In 2011, in two different attacks in Yemen, drones
killed three terrorists of Arab descent who also happened to be U.S. citizens, which raises some challenging legal questions.

The global war on terrorism has extracted a high price in lives and
treasure. It also coincided with a decade of growing economic hardship
for many Americans. The war seemed to contribute to the country's economic woes by distorting American foreign policy. The defense budget
in George W. Bush's years doubled from $304 billion (2001) to $616
billion (2008). The national debt climbed from 32.5 percent of Gross
Domestic Product (2001) to 53.5 percent of GDP (2009). Indebtedness

to the People's Republic of China climbed from $78 billion (2001) to $1.1 trillion (2011). One analysis estimates that the global war on terrorism has cost $1.65 trillion. Another $800 billion in expenses may be paid in the years ahead. Adding the costs of homeland security ($589 billion), the United States will spend $3.8 trillion on war and counterterrorism, or $6.6 million for every dollar al-Qaeda spent to send four planes on a suicide mission. Americans would have rejected any administration that did not pursue Osama bin Laden, but the strategy of the hunt remains debatable.

For the Common Defense in the Twenty-first Century

As mandated by Congress, the Department of Defense submitted its 2010 *Quadrennial Defense Review* on the assumption that the war in Iraq would end for U.S. combat units by 2012, as President Obama had promised. With the usual confusion of ends and means, the report stressed that the armed forces would try to deter wars and "prevail" in "today's wars," which would require the capabilities to "defeat adversaries and succeed in a wide range of contingencies." The key mission was to defend the United States and "support civil authorities at home." The armed forces should prepare to operate against the "aggression by state adversaries" and "new trans-national terrorist threats." They should be prepared for "counterinsurgency, stability, and counterterrorism operations." The forces must be ready to meet multiple threats in "overlapping timeframes," meaning at the same time, so the force had to be made flexible and invest in "key enablers." The term "transform" did not appear in the executive summary. The new mantra was to "rebalance" the force and "reform" how the Department of Defense did business.

As required by law, the QDR had to provide estimated costs. Defense spending would peak in fiscal year 2011 at $708 billion, drop to $616 billion in 2012, then slowly grow to $666 billion in 2015 at a real growth rate of only 1 percent. The defense budget would be 4.7 percent of gross domestic product—historically a bearable national expense. Continuing the operations in Iraq and Afghanistan (Overseas Contingency Operations) would require a minimum of $132 billion for 2011.

As Secretary of Defense Robert Gates knew, the budget, normally cut 2–4 percent by Congress, would be a dead document unless the armed forces reduced their personnel. The Army and Marine Corps would have to manage with 60,000 and 20,000 fewer troops, respectively. A more novel part of the QDR was the promise to stop or delay several aircraft and warship programs, so the Air Force and Navy would have to make sacrifices too. The transition to a high-technology force, however, would not stop since information, target acquisition, and precision-guidance for munitions would increase for all the services. Anything that would counter IEDs and WMDs would receive developmental priority. Drones and robots would become commonplace above and on the battlefield. Headed for the junkyard would be HUMVEES, replaced by Mine Resistant Ambush Protected (MRAP) armored vehicles. The digitization of warfare would become the province of a new Cyber Command.

In 2011, as part of a toxic negotiation on reducing the national debt, the Obama administration and Congress agreed to cut the defense budget by $400 billion over the decade ahead. If executed, this plan will reduce personnel costs by cutting the defense military and civilian force by 100,000 or more, but the cuts still cannot be made without 20–30 percent reduction in other categories of defense spending, like weapons modernization. Yet dramatic reductions in military personnel justify drastic investments in robotics and unpiloted vehicles, important but not decisive elements in the future force. The U.S. armed forces may not prevail in whatever conflicts lie ahead unless the American people insist that their political leaders make security decisions on the basis of expert advice from their civilian and military professionals and not make decisions based primarily on their impact on domestic politics. Only then will the United States have a common defense.

Appendix A

Participation and Losses, Major Wars, 1775–2011

	SERVED	BATTLE DEATHS	OTHER DEATHS	WOUNDED
Revolutionary War[1], 1775–1783	200,000+ est.	6,900 est.	18,500 est.	8,500 est.
War of 1812[2], 1812–1815	286,730	2,261	17,500 est.	4,500 est.
Mexican War 1846–1848	115,906	1,733	13,000 est.	4,152
Civil War[3], 1861–1865:				
Union	2,000,000+ est.	112,000 est.	250,500 est.	277,500 est.
Confederacy	750,000 est.	94,000 est.	167,000 est.	194,000 est.
War with Spain, 1898	306,760	385	3,000 est.	1,662
Philippine-American War, 1899–1902	126,468	1,004	3,161	2,911
World War I, 1917–1918	4,734,991	53,402	63,114	204,002
World War II, 1941–1945	16,112,566	291,557	113,842	671,846

1 For the Revolutionary War we have used the statistics collected and analyzed by the Howard H. Peckham group, William L. Clements Library, University of Michigan, 1974.

2 The statistics for the War of 1812 are those provided by Donald R. Hickey, *The War of 1812* (University of Chicago Press, 1989).

3 Statistics for the Civil War (especially for the Confederacy) are elusive, but we have used those provided by E. B. Long, *The Civil War Day by Day* (Doubleday, 1971). However, the author of an in-depth study using pre- and postwar census records has argued for raising the war's final death toll from 620,000 to 750,000. See J. David Hacker, "A Census-Based Count of the Civil War Dead" *Civil War History* 57 (December 2011): 307–348.

	Served	Battle Deaths	Other Deaths	Wounded
Korean War[4], 1950–1953	5,720,000	33,741	2,835	103,284
Vietnam War[5], 1964–1975	8,744,000	47,434	10,786	153,303
Gulf War, 1990–1991	2,225,000	147	235	467
War in Afghanistan[6], 2001–	320,000 est.	1,488	386	15,282
War in Iraq[7], 2003–2011	930,000 est.	3,526	962	32,229

4 At one time the Department of Defense listed 20,617 "other deaths" for the Korean War, an implausible figure when compared to the 33,741 battle deaths for Korea and the nearly 11,000 "other deaths" for the Vietnam War. The Air Force, Marine Corps, and Navy are certain that they had 813 "other deaths," but the Army, which listed 9,429 deaths of this sort at one time, has simply now announced that its "other deaths" are not available. Further research has led us to the number 2,835 for "Other Deaths." The number for "Served" includes personnel deployed worldwide during the conflict.
5 · Defense Manpower Data Center, http://siadapp.dmdc.osd.mil/personnel/CASUALITY/vietnam.pdf. Of the total wounded, only about half required hospitalization.
6 Statistics for wars in Iraq and Afghanistan as of January 25, 2012, from Defense Manpower Data Center, http://www.defense.gov/news/casualty.pdf. The figures for Afghanistan include casualties in fourteen regional countries and Cuba (Guantanamo Bay).
7 Casualties for the Iraq War include deaths in other regional countries, the Persian Gulf, Arabian Sea, Gulf of Aden, Gulf of Oman, and the Red Sea. "Served" means fulltime, global, not just war zone. Because of multiple tours, short deployments, and assignments to Central Command that did not include physically serving in Iraq or Afghanistan, the number of service personnel who "served" in the two wars may run as high as 1.3 million to 1.9 million.

Appendix B

The Armed Forces and National Expansion

	Population Continental U.S. (Millions)	War Department		Navy Department		
		Spending (Million Dollars)	Strength U.S. Army	Spending (Million Dollars)	Strength U.S. Navy	Strength USMC
1790	3.9	.632 (1789–91)	1,000+ est.	.570	Unknown	
1800	5.3	2.5	4,000+ est.	3.4	5,400	525
1810	7.2	2.2	5,956	1.6	5,149	449
1820	9.6	2.6	10,554	4.3	3,988	571
1830	12.8	4.7	6,122	3.2	4,929	891
1840	17.0	7.0	12,330	6.1	8,017	1,269
1850	23.0	9.4	10,929	7.9	8,794	1,101
1860	31.0	16.4	16,215	11.5	9,942	1,801
1870	39.8	57.6	37,240	21.7	10,562	2,546
1880	50.0	38.1	26,594	13.5	9,361	1,939
1890	62.9	44.5	27,373	22.0	9,246	2,047
1900	75.0	134.0	101,713	55.0	18,796	5,414
1910	91.0	189.0	81,251	123.0	48,533	9,560
1920	105.0	1,600.0	204,292	736.0	121,845	17,165
1930	122.0	464.0	139,378	374.0	96,890	19,380
1940	131.0	907.0	269,023	891.0	160,997	28,345

Source: Statistical History of the United States, dated volumes. Social Science Research Council, rev. ed., (1965). U.S. Bureau of the Census, Historical Statistics of the United States of America, 1789–1945 (Government Printing Office, 1949).

Appendix C

The Armed Forces of the Cold War and After

	DEFENSE SPENDING (BILLION DOLLARS)	STRENGTH* U.S. ARMY	STRENGTH* U.S. AIR FORCE	STRENGTH* U.S.NAVY	STRENGTH* USMC
1945	80.9	8,200,000	—	3,300,000	475,000
1950	16.5	593,000	411,000	382,000	74,000
1955	32.9	1,100,000	960,000	661,000	205,000
1960	44.3	873,000	815,000	617,000	171,000
1965	50.6	963,000	825,000	670,000	190,000
1970	75.3	1,300,000	791,000	691,000	260,000
1975	86.0	784,000	613,000	535,000	196,000
1980	143.0	777,000	558,000	527,000	188,000
1985	294.0	781,000	602,000	571,000	198,000
1990	301.0	761,000	531,000	578,000	198,000
1995	252.6	509,000	401,000	435,000	175,000
2000	260.8	477,000	353,000	371,000	172,000
2005	401.7	489,000	352,000	359,000	179,000
2010	533.8	565,000	335,000	327,000	202,000

*Rounded to the thousands.

Source: Bureau of the Census, *Statistical Abstract of the United States, 1992* (Government Printing Office, 1992), 334–342; Office of the Assistant Secretary of Defense (Public Affairs), www.defense.gov/Releases. (1990–2011).

Appendix D

U.S. Troops Stationed Abroad*

	1995*	2000*	2005*	2010*
Europe	110,359	113,140	98,765	79,687
Former U.S.S.R.	87	152	132	162
Latin America	15,730	1,686	2,043	1,947
North Africa, Near East & South Asia	4,733	13,113	3,836	3,286
Iraq and Kuwait	—	—	207,000	85,600
Afghanistan	—	—	20,400	103,700
Pakistan	28	22	146	146
East Asia & Pacific	76,065	76,863	65,646	36,016
Sub-Saharan Africa	696	325	1,576	1,731
Afloat	53,456	115,848	128,398	101,648

*As of last day of year.

Source: Congressional Research Service and Washington Headquarters Service (Information Operations and Reports, Department of Defense).

Appendix E

American Military and Diplomatic Deaths, Terrorist and Military Actions, 1980–2000

	Battle Deaths	Other Deaths	Wounded
Iran Rescue Raid, 1980	0	8	5
Beirut, Lebanon, 1982–1984	263	9	169
Grenada, 1983	18	1	119
Panama, 1989	22	1	324
Mogadishu, Somalia, 1992–1994	29	14	175
Haiti, 1994–1996	0	4	3
Khobar Towers, Saudi Arabia, (Terrorist Attack) 1996	19	0	372
Kenya Tanzania, (Embassy Bombings) 1998	52*	0	12
USS Cole, Yemen, (Terrorist Attack) 2000	17	0	39

*Includes all U.S. and foreign civilian and military embassy personnel.

Sources: Department of Defense, "Military Casualty Information," http://siadapp.dmdc .osd.mil/personnel/CASUALTY/castop.htm; Center for Defense Information, Military Almanac: 2001–2002, http://www.scribd.com/1Anonymouspatriotusa/d/12928711-Military-Almanac-20012002; Department of State, "Bombings of the US Embassies in Nairobi, Kenya and Dar es Salaam, Tanzania on August 7, 1998," http://www.state.gov/ www/regions/africa/board_victims.html.

Index

About the Authors

Allan R. Millett is a University Research Professor, Ambrose Professor of History, and the Director of the Eisenhower Center for American Studies at The University of New Orleans. He is also the senior military adviser to the National World War II Museum. Millett is the Raymond E. Mason, Jr. Professor Emeritus of History at The Ohio State University.

Peter Maslowski is Professor of History (Emeritus) at the University of Nebraska, Lincoln.

William B. Feis is Professor of History at Buena Vista University in Storm Lake, Iowa.